A LITERARY
HISTORY OF ROME
IN THE SILVER AGE

From Tiberius to Hadrian

LITTERARVM VETERVM
STVDIOSIS AMATORIBVS
HAS QVALESCVMQVE SVNT LVCVBRATIONES
DE AETATE ARGENTEA EXARATAS
LIBENTISSIMO ANIMO
IOANNES WIGHT DUFF
D.D.D.
ID. IVL. MCMXXVII

PREFACE TO SECOND EDITION

IN preparing this edition of my father's work on the Silver Age of Latin literature I have made a somewhat greater number of alterations and additions than I did in the 1953 edition of his earlier volume on Roman literary history up to A.D. 14. The bibliographies to each author, which in the first edition were given in footnotes, are now at the end of the book embodied in a comprehensive bibliography which I have endeavoured to bring up to date. On many specific points, however, modern authorities were cited by my father in notes which are still pertinent and which reappear in these pages, some of them with amplification based on the scholarship of the last thirty years.

Much help has come from Mr. A. Hudson-Williams and Mr. L. N. Wild, two of my Aberystwyth colleagues. Professor G. B. A. Fletcher of King's College Newcastle in the University of Durham is a never-failing help in trouble. He has saved the book from many inaccuracies, improved my bibliography, and patiently listened to and grappled with my perplexities. Messrs. Ernest Benn have been very forbearing with my many delays. I am grateful to the printer's reader for his vigilance, and especially to Mr. Geoffrey Hunt, who *restituit rem* by undertaking at very short notice to read the proofs. His keen eye, orderly thoroughness and classical scholarship have been invaluable. Furthermore, he has compiled a new index, introducing sub-headings in the longer entries.

In 1927 the 'Silver Age' (to use the abbreviated title) came out accompanied by a reprint of the earlier volume. Now the second edition appears accompanied by a reprint (with corrections and additions) of the 1953 edition of the earlier volume.

A.M.D.

University College of Wales
Aberystwyth, 1959

vii

PREFACE TO FIRST EDITION

THE favourable reception accorded in several countries to my work on *A Literary History of Rome from the Origins to the Close of the Golden Age*, of which the first edition appeared in 1909, suggested the idea of continuing on similar principles the study of Latin literature into the first and second centuries, during which the Roman empire at its zenith in power and efficiency rendered its greatest services to human civilisation. The project was dropped throughout the period of the Great War, when, even if publication had been feasible, duties on a local Brigade Committee and for a time as Acting Principal of my College effectually removed me from the atmosphere of literary criticism. Even after my publisher, Mr. Fisher Unwin, was good enough to revive the design, progress was extraordinarily slow, owing to the increasing demands made upon time by the recurrent problems of a modern university.

As in the former volume, emphasis has here been laid on the national character imprinted upon Latin literature despite all borrowings from Greek models; and attention has been carefully devoted to the evidence for the facts of an author's life in an endeavour to recreate the environment amidst which he wrote. Nor have material sources, whether Greek or Latin, been overlooked: indispensable though some account of these must be for a true conception of a writer as at once inheritor and progenitor, it is surprising to note how little in this country scholarship has concerned itself with the origin of encyclopædic learning like that of the elder Pliny. The arrangement adopted is different from that in Professor Summers's skilful handling of a slightly shorter period in his *Silver Age of Latin Literature* under headings of various kinds of literature rather than on chronological lines. In the present work, where historical background and literary evolution are alike regarded as of vital importance, the treatment has been not according to *genre* but mainly in the order of time. While the limits set for full discussion of authors are A.D. 14–A.D. 138, these dates are not rigidly observed respecting relevant topics, such as the survival of an author's influence till modern times or the continuance of the Roman educational system; and an epilogue is added to give a brief conspectus of the literature which followed the Silver Age.

An attempt has been made to secure acquaintance with a reasonable proportion of the vast number of treatises and pamphlets written in

Latin and in several modern languages upon matters related to the authors of the period. The obligations incurred to such works may be gauged from references in the footnotes. But it is obvious that no amount of reading in books upon books, however valuable in substance, can avail to produce either a vital chronicle of any age or serviceable estimates of its writers, without first-hand study of the writers themselves and independent appreciation of their significance. I hope, therefore, for success in conveying to readers, by summary, by quotation, and by criticism, something of the impression made on myself during adventures among the literary products of the Silver Age. The illustrative translations from Latin into prose or verse are my own, and have been for the most part composed specially for this volume. Thanks are due to the Delegates of the Oxford University Press for permission to use a few verse renderings which I made for my book on *The Writers of Rome*. The general reader, whose Latin has perhaps grown rusty, may welcome these translations as supplementing the historical and critical portions, while he will doubtless realise that it is optional to consult or not to consult the footnotes.

The bibliographical notes,[1] it should be explained, are intended, not to be exhaustive, but to give by mention of selected editions some clue to the history of the printed text of an author and to include representative modern studies of his literary significance.

I wish to acknowledge kind assistance rendered by Mr. Basil Anderton, M.A., Public Librarian, Newcastle-upon-Tyne, and by Miss Constance Shipley, M.A., Lecturer in Classics at Armstrong College, in reading and criticising some of the chapters of this book. My son, Mr. Arnold M. Duff, M.A., B.Litt. (Oxon.), Assistant Lecturer in Greek in the University of Aberdeen, has also perused several chapters and made useful suggestions, while my wife copied for the press either by hand or by typewriter almost the whole manuscript. Both have helped greatly in the checking of proofs and in the verification of references. To Professor Hermann Dessau of Berlin I owe several references to inscriptions which he sent me some years ago to amplify those in my article on 'Roman Education' in *The Encyclopædia of Religion and Ethics*. In the choice of a frontispiece,[2] intended to illustrate the art of the period, I had the great benefit of advice from Mrs. Arthur Strong, Litt.D., LL.D., formerly Assistant Director of the British School at Rome, in whose penetrating discernment of the true ethos of Roman sculpture I have found much to reinforce my argument that within the analogous domain of literature the Romans knew not only how to borrow from Greece but also how independently to create the beautiful.

---

[1] Except on certain specific points, these notes are, in the second edition, embodied in the Bibliography. *Editor*.
[2] Omitted from this edition.

It is a satisfaction to observe among scholars a growing insistence upon the independent vitality of Roman literature and a growing disinclination to regard it as a pale second-hand reflection of the splendour of Greek literature. My friend, the late Dr. Warde Fowler, appended to his Presidential Address on 'The Imagination of the Romans,' read at the Newcastle-upon-Tyne meeting of the central Classical Association of England and Wales in 1920, a note to the effect that he was in agreement with the contentions advocated on the subject in my *Literary History of Rome*; and only last year a German Professor, Herr Günther Jachmann, chose as the theme of an inaugural lecture at Cologne 'Die Originalität der römischen Literatur.' The value of Roman literature cannot be grasped without recognition of the extent to which Roman authors found fresh stimulus in surroundings widened far beyond those assigned by historical circumstance to the brilliant intellects of Greece.

                                                          J.W.D.

Newcastle-upon-Tyne
July 1927

CONTENTS*

---

* More detailed analyses are given in the body of the book at the beginning of each chapter.

PART III

LITERATURE OF THE FLAVIAN PERIOD
A.D. 69–96

Introduction

Chapter I

PROLOGUE

'Silver' and 'Gold' in Roman literature – The period from Tiberius to Hadrian (A.D. 14–138) – Historical aspects – Cosmopolitan Rome – Tangible remains – Emperors in relation to literature – Risks in writing – Fresh individual forces in Silver literature – The conventional in education – Declaiming and reciting – Epigrammatic point and decorative tinsel – Corrective factors in real life – Serious thought – Stoicism – The Stoic opposition – Influence of Stoic doctrine – Influence of the provinces – Variety in 'Silver' themes and style – Changing features in the language – Concentration on the terse, the surprising, and the poetic – Grammar and vocabulary – A few summary reflections.

IN the literary history of Rome one of the most brilliant and attractive epochs is that part of the first and second centuries of the Christian era which critics have usually distinguished with the epithet of 'Silver.' The Silver Age of Roman Literature is regarded in the present work as that immediately following the great times of Augustan poetry and prose. What has been traditionally reckoned the Golden Age coincided with the productive careers of Cicero and then Livy in prose, and lasted from Lucretius to Ovid in verse. While, soon after it began, Catullus wrote his anti-Caesarian lampoons, it reached its fullest glory when Virgil and Horace by their works threw lustre around the emergence of the imperial family – *ecce Dionaei processit Caesaris astrum*, in the language of the *Eclogues*. Politically, therefore, the Golden Age saw the final overthrow of the old senatorial republic and the inauguration of state-control by a single ruler for Rome and the Roman dominions. Such public oratory as Cicero's, which adorned the earlier phases of the age amidst the unfettered interplay of republican politics, had become an impossible anachronism before its close, when Augustus concentrated in his person all the significant powers of the ancient magistracies – *munia senatus magistratuum legum in se trahere* is the remark of Tacitus. In time, then, the Golden Age may be dated from 70 B.C. to A.D. 14, a stretch of eighty-four years.

The Silver Age is a longer period, even when restricted, as some prefer, to the years between A.D. 14 and 117, that is from the beginning of Tiberius's reign to the end of Trajan's. Here it has been extended to include the reign of Hadrian, A.D. 117–138, after which Latin literature is marked partly by sterility, partly by an artificial archaising movement, partly by the entirely different train of thought expressed in Christian apologetics. Historically, this period of a century and a quarter coincides with the reigns of all but the first two of Suetonius's twelve Caesars, and, in addition, the reigns of Nerva, Trajan and Hadrian, thirteen emperors altogether. If in the preceding age the Empire was still young and so far, under Augustus, only partially tested, now during these succeeding generations, in spite of the enormities of individual emperors and in spite of the ghastly interval of bloodshed among successive candidates for the purple after Nero's suicide, the hold of the system upon the world was firmly established, and its organisation perfected, on the whole, for the benefit of mankind. With the *Pax Romana* came greater safety for life and limb both in Italy and in the provinces; governors abroad were more under the central control; roads were improved to meet the requirements of the imperial post-service for despatches; the water-supply of Rome and other cities was diligently cared for; new harbours were constructed; industry and trade increased, at any rate up to the point at which the policy of the bread-dole effected moral ruin for the population and in the end financial ruin for a state in which the value of free agriculture and free capital was misunderstood. *Nihil est ab omni parte beatum;* and so, upon examination, it is plain that amidst the material well-being and felicities of the second century, even in the prosperous Antonine age with which Gibbon began his history of *The Decline and Fall*, there lurked elements of disintegration which would lead to the troubles of the third century.[1]

During the first century events had revealed the state-secret not only that emperors might be made by other electors than the Senate, but that they might be made even elsewhere than in Rome. The tendency, in fact, was towards a military monarchy, as the careers of Galba, Otho, Vitellius and Vespasian showed. When one considers, it seems well-nigh inevitable that an emperor's absolute power abroad should ultimately expand his theoretically limited power in Italy and Rome towards absolutism. Between Augustus as first citizen at the opening of the century and Domitian claiming to be 'Lord and God' towards its end, vast changes had intervened. The diarchy which Augustus was careful to respect had in time gone far on its way to monarchy; for the senate not infrequently acted under imperial coercion. More and more, too, it grew evident that the basis of the ruler's power was the army – a

[1] W. E. Heitland's contentions in *The Roman Fate*, Camb. 1922, and *Iterum*, Camb. 1925, seem, however, unduly to emphasise the want of power in the central government to remedy weaknesses throughout the empire. His views regarding the stagnation resultant upon 'the inability of the passive parts to vitalise the whole' are not wholly applicable to the first two centuries from Augustus: see H. M. Last, *J.R.S.* XV (1925) Pt. I.

conception abhorrent to Romans of the constitutional republic. In this connexion it is significant that the title *imperator* became commoner than *princeps* about Trajan's time. Moreover, the worship of emperors (or their *genii*) during their lifetime, and the deification of certain emperors after death, outwardly exalted their office. It is, however, difficult to see how the notion of *apotheosis* could seriously survive among thinking readers of Seneca's satire on the dead emperor Claudius; and it is a strange contradiction inherent in circumstances that, while the sacrifice in honour of a Caesar as the public test of loyalty involved the martyr-dom of many Christians, yet the Caesar-worship from which their faith revolted did actually by its attainment of official universality prepare the way for the ultimate predominance of the Christian religion.

The crucial problem for the empire was, as Augustus foresaw, one of consolidation rather than aggrandisement; and the only notable de-partures from this policy during the whole period were connected with the annexations in Britain begun by Claudius and those in Dacia and the East carried out by Trajan. Trajan's Oriental conquests in the first quarter of the second century, though soon abandoned by his successor, brought the Roman Empire to its widest extent, and marked the ex-tremity of contrast between the primitive pastoral settlement near the Tiber and the capital of world-wide dominions into which it had evolved. Rome had in the first century become more cosmopolitan than ever – a phenomenon sufficient to illustrate in the eyes of a Seneca the essential brotherhood of mankind, but in the eyes of a Juvenal the objectionable ubiquity of the alien interloper. It has been argued that, early in the second century, when Juvenal and Tacitus wrote, 'a very small percentage of the free plebeians on the streets of Rome could prove unmixed Italian descent.'[1] Here at once we meet a feature of importance for literature. Rome possessed a wonderful power of romanising the foreigner; but there was sure to be a reaction on her own life and thought. This large cosmopolitan and international element in the capital contributed towards a widening of their horizon for literary men, and to it the human note unquestionably observable in the Silver Age owed a great deal.

The whole period has been made very real to us by writers within recent times who have investigated its political, constitutional, social, religious and artistic history.[2] Modern inquiry has combined with ancient documents to recreate the historical background requisite for appreciation of the literature, in such a way that few epochs of the past are so intimately known. In some degree this clear view is due to the

[1] T. Frank, 'Race Mixture in Rom. Emp.,' *Amer. Hist. Rev.* July 1916, pp. 689–708. Frank thought that in the city of Rome 'perhaps 90 per cent had Oriental blood in their veins.' This Orientalisation was due partly to the immi-gration of free *peregrini*, but more to the importation of slaves many of whom were manumitted and so joined the citizen body.
[2] See Bibliog. *re* p. 5.

strikingly human note, the living interest in man and his concerns, which is characteristic of the ablest writers in the Silver Age. Much of its history and many of its personages have been made to live for us by Tacitus and Suetonius; its society by Petronius's novel, the miscellaneous poems of Statius, the younger Pliny's letters, Martial's epigrams and Juvenal's satires; its science by the elder Pliny; its rhetoric by the elder Seneca and Quintilian; its practical ethics by Seneca the younger. Inscriptions and coins tell their tale; the Colosseum remains the most imposing monument to the Flavian dynasty; Pompeii puts before us the dwellings, decorations and the very street-paving of the time; and Hadrian is brought nearer through his magnificent villa, a veritable *urbis opus*, close under Tivoli, his gateway at Athens, his wall in Britain, and his mausoleum familiar now as the Castel Sant' Angelo at Rome.

Before passing from the historical aspects of the age, one may observe how the emperors comported themselves in relation to literature.[1] They were well-educated men, and several of them showed literary talent. Tiberius in early life cultivated the acquaintance of M. Valerius Messalla Corvinus, the friend of Horace and Tibullus, and modelled his oratorical style on Messalla's. It was said that he imitated the pathetic love-stories of Parthenius of Nicaea, who taught Virgil Greek. Tiberius's successor Caligula was no author, but he had a turn for shrewd criticism, discernible in his sharp remark about Seneca's style as 'sand without lime';[2] and he recognised classic greatness in literature well enough to be insanely jealous of it. The next two emperors, Claudius and Nero, displayed ability as writers, the one in prose, the other in verse. If we then turn to the Flavian emperors, we find that, although none of the three felt so enthusiastic for literature as either Claudius or Nero had done, yet they all extended a certain limited patronage to authors. Vespasian, *bourgeois* man of business though he might be, was not unskilled in Greek eloquence, and composed memoirs. Titus, we know, wrote a poem on a comet; while his brother Domitian was devoted to poetry in youth, and later fostered poetic rivalry by the Capitoline and Alban contests. That competition, when the right circumstances cooperate, can give health to literature is evident from the lasting greatness of Athenian drama: unfortunately, the spirit of Domitian's reign was such as mainly to favour mediocrity or truckling in its poets. Trajan, without profound culture himself and no very active patron of letters, at least maintained friendly relations with such authors as the younger Pliny and the Greek Dio Chrysostom. His successor Hadrian, versatile and Hellenic in taste, dabbled in Latin poetry; but, to judge from the surviving fragments, never so successfully as at the last, when in half a dozen lines he composed his death-bed adieu to his soul.

[1] For fuller treatment see Butler, *Post-Aug. P.*, pp. 1–6, 166–170; H. Bardon, *Les empereurs et les lettres latines*, Paris 1940.　　　　[2] Suet. *Cal.* liii.

Even such a cursory glance at rulers of the time indicates that the drawback for literature consisted not in their particular unfitness to play the literary patron but in a generally untoward environment. Artistic creation of the very freest and highest order was little likely to thrive in the atmosphere of the first century. The risk of danger always lay hidden in the unfathomable temperament of an emperor; and in the very essence of the new *régime* there wrought elements inimical to the safe production of literary work. The outspoken oratory of the past was inacceptable; history was capable of giving offence in high quarters; even drama could be frowned upon for a line misconstrued as a political allusion. At a time when Phaedrus's beast-fables were denounced as libellous insults, it is not surprising that histories of human affairs should be adjudged to the flames. The prospects for literary men must often have appeared dark during the sway of the Julio-Claudian dynasty in situations such as were created by the espionage which Tiberius permitted in his later days, by the incalculable caprice of Caligula, the uncertainties of policy under the wives and freedmen of Claudius, and the egotistic vanity of Nero. The wonder is not that we have so small a yield from times so difficult, but that we have so much that has proved worth preserving. Fortunately, writers took risks. Under Nero, Petronius was safe, up to a point, in writing a novel of low adventure, and Seneca was safe, again up to a point, in writing essays on high moral principles, though even these might be interpreted as implied reproofs. Lucan, on the other hand, was clearly on the thinnest ice in writing an epic about Pompey's heroism in his warfare against Julius Caesar. This was doubly dangerous; because while the poem might very well be regarded as anti-imperial, it might also stir the jealousy of a poet-emperor. Later, under the Flavians, no one could be sure when the court might grow too suspicious to tolerate philosophers any longer in Rome, as happened in A.D. 71 and 89. Deep intellectual speculation has always been liable to enmity as unsettling: and so many members of noble houses had in troublous times found consolation in Stoicism that its teaching particularly tended to be associated with opposition to the imperial system. Apart from this aspect, it may be noted in passing how Stoic thought shows itself in such poets as Persius, Lucan and Juvenal, and in such prose writers as Seneca, the elder Pliny and Tacitus. The period of terror during the later part of Domitian's reign, fifteen years of 'silence' as Tacitus viewed it, pressed most severely upon history. But it was not impossible to write securely, if an author chose remote epic themes as Statius did, or composed scores of occasional epigrams as Martial did. Indeed, there never was a time when dilettanti recited more energetically their latest productions before a select circle of friends. After Domitian's death, history and oratory recovered a modicum at least of their old freedom. Nerva's principate was too brief to affect literature deeply, though it brought that welcome release from tyranny which bore fullest fruit in the historical labours of Tacitus under Trajan. This fresh impulse, however, seemed almost spent by the reign of Hadrian; for Suetonius and Florus were artistically but poor successors to Tacitus. Under Hadrian a revival of interest in Hellenism and the prominence of authors writing in Greek combined with the emperor's example to act as positive setbacks to the fashion of writing in Latin.

In its literary aspects the whole age makes a fascinating study. Its appropriate epithet of 'Silver' concedes the classic superiority of the Golden Age (*aurea prima sata est aetas . . . subiit argentea proles*); but silver, viewed as metal or as literature, retains a value of its own, and the metaphorical title, whether it calls to mind a glittering style or a literary convention already somewhat silvered with time, is both picturesque and instructive. No apology is needed for a survey of literary works created during the greatest period of the Roman Empire. Parallel with its administrative triumphs and its permanent services to civilisation, we discover, in an adventure among its masterpieces, artistic production of high quality, thought commensurate with the achievement of the times, and engrossing portrayal of life. Convention has been alluded to, and we may trace much of it at work among authors; yet it is only fair to point out that the Silver Age had its unique geniuses. Nowhere else is a Tacitus or a Juvenal to be found, each uttering an individual note, and each among the greatest names in the domains of historical prose and poetic satire respectively. Phaedrus in fable, Petronius in the novel, Martial in epigram, Pliny in letter-writing were all fresh forces; nor is there any Seneca elsewhere in Latin, whether we like his style or not. Even the massive proportions of some works composed during this age are impressive though sometimes forbidding – it is so much easier, and commoner, to criticise than to read the thirty-seven books of Pliny's *Natural History* or the seventeen of Silius's epic. Before the incessant industry of the elder Pliny, less hard-working generations might, like his nephew, stand abashed. But such phenomenal diligence is not necessarily attractive; and probably what most draws readers to the Silver Age is that human note already mentioned which, in the midst of widespread artificiality elsewhere, makes many of the authors interesting to all periods. No one can take up Petronius, Juvenal, Martial or Tacitus without feeling that real life and real things are being described and without feeling absorbed by that reality.

The chief formative factors of this complex literature may be rapidly passed under review. Foremost of all the influences at work was the contemporary education in letters and rhetoric.[1] While the general training in letters opened up the treasures of Greek and Latin literature as sources of inspiration for prospective writers, the special training in the principles and practice of speaking profoundly affected style. The predominant study of poets in the rhetorical academies tended to

[1] This is more fully discussed in the following chapter.

obliterate the true demarcation between prose and poetry, leaving upon prose the indelible poetic tint which is characteristic of the Silver Age. The imitation of Virgil, traceable in Lucan, well-marked in Valerius Flaccus, and still more so in Silius and Statius, was by no means confined to these epic writers; it spread to occasional verse, epigram and satire; and it invaded prose, so that the style of Tacitus must be viewed in relation to Virgilian influence. Nor was this only a matter of poetic colour: the bones, as it were, of the language were affected in the altered grammar and syntax which have presently to be discussed and illustrated.

Manner of expression came to be deeply modified by the systematic instruction in rhetoric and by the declamatory exercises (especially the *controuersiae* and *suasoriae*) composed by the student practising the use of figures of speech, exclamations, apostrophes, interrogations, and innumerable other artifices, which he had been taught by a rhetor to consider effective for the purposes of argument or display. The declamation wore more than one aspect. A serious ingredient in the educational system, it was an exercise to be regularly practised by learners as a training in argument; and, whatever its futility under some instructors, sensible authorities like Quintilian had in view the solid kind of argument useful in a law-court.[1] It combined certain of the functions of a modern essay with those of a debating society. It had even a romantic side; for not a few of its themes anticipated elements in medieval tales and modern novels. But it was open to attack from the first. The Romans indeed showed their common sense in calling the exercise *declamatio* – something of loud-voiced overstatement was implied in that half-derogatory term. Being a pillar of the educational fabric it was, like most things in education, pretty sure to be criticised. However much pleasure it might give an admiring parent to hear his son exhibit his eloquence on speech day, this supreme test of the school career and reputed passport to success in life was subjected to incisive attacks, examples of which may be read in Petronius and Tacitus. No one could deny the readiness attainable by such practice in the rhetorical academy, any more than one could fairly overlook the metaphysical importance of some at least of the themes with which medieval Scholasticism was concerned; but in the one case, as in the other, a ceaseless immersion in verbiage caused stagnation of thought. Obscurantist professors of what was in itself an excellent art checked the progress of eloquence and robbed it eventually of life. Yet for generations it defied detraction, and, in spite of defects, produced a long line of capable speakers. Unduly elaborated subtlety was at the worst wearisome: it was not destructive like the shameless perversion of the art practised by professional informers (*delatores*), who saw in the share of confiscated goods allowed to them

---

[1] IV. ii. 29: 'declamatio forensium actionum meditatio' (μελετή). F. H. Colson, *C.R.* 1922, pp. 116–117, suggests that *declamatio*, 'loud shouting,' may originally have been a translation of κατήχησις, 'dinning into the ears.'

B*

by the Government a handsome reward for misapplying rhetoric towards compassing convictions on charges of treason.

Two sets of circumstances reinforced this rhetorical influence; one, the not uncommon habit of continuing exercise in declamations, either privately or under a master, long after college days; the other, an author's custom, derived from Augustan times or earlier, of holding *recitationes* of his compositions in prose or verse before an invited gathering of friends, partly to elicit criticism, partly to advertise a forthcoming work, and also very largely to impress the audience. Under this last aim lay many pitfalls. Literature designed for a kind of parade tended to repeat the qualities of the academic show-piece. The ideal coveted was the production of telling effects. Hence ingenuity was expected in narrative, description and argument, with the result that a wide entrance stood open for the precious and far-fetched. A discourse, an oration, or a poem had to exhibit its author's ability in elaborating academic commonplaces into surprisingly terse epigrams or *sententiae*; it had to wear the variegated adornments of rhetoric so that the style often became outrageously rococo in taste. Of the worst excesses of the Silver Age one feels as did Alceste in *Le Misanthrope*, when he expressed his disdain for Oronte's sonnet:

> 'Ce n'est que jeu de mots, qu' affectation pure,
> Et ce n'est point ainsi que parle la nature.'

Artificiality driven to such extremes meant a divorce from plain common sense; for natural feeling met its death in the exuberant riot of epigram, word-play, antithesis, apostrophes and other devices. Similarly, when presenting a hypothetical case in a *controuersia* or *suasoria*, the speaker's temptation was to cast about for novel arguments; and the quest after something novel was apt to lead far away from reality into unnatural extravagances of perverted ingenuity. Both defence and attack in the *controuersiae* reported by the elder Seneca give, we shall find, many examples of those incredibly smart inventions. Rhetorical gymnastics of this sort, while they had the merit of ensuring a high degree of readiness and finish in speech and in style as a whole, yet fostered in some speakers and authors an empty glibness from which no great literature could grow. The contemporary complaints about the decadence of oratory are significant. Despite all the attention lavished upon it, eloquence deteriorated. Over-cultivation would contribute to a measure of staleness, and political conditions had taken the heart out of the old type; but, beyond all that, the rhetoric of the schools was too remote from truth to produce good style.

It was well for literature, therefore, that actual life counteracted the cramping effects of rhetorical training. Many a promising academic speaker got his first salutary awakening when he had to plead a real case in a law-court. Furthermore, contact with the multiplicity of life

in Rome, and with the various peoples included in the Empire, was
certain to stimulate and deepen an interest in man as such. It would be
a profound mistake to overlook the complex nature of the Silver literature, or to imagine that we could sum up its qualities as if they were
solely those of clever rhetoric, or to forget the realists of the time –
Petronius, Juvenal, Martial. Of these three, while Petronius proves that
he could compose in the conventional vein when he liked, it is Juvenal
who makes the most interesting blend, because he can be at once declamatory and realistic. If the worst manner of the declamations reappears in some of the rant which disfigures Seneca's tragedies, Juvenal
on the other hand is not mastered by but master of the declamatory
element. This simply indicates that rhetorical artifice could be turned
to different purposes by different hands: while it was used with mechanical precision by Valerius Maximus and with oppressive ingenuity by
Lucan, it attained a miraculous brilliance under the pen of Tacitus.
One feels with relief that Tacitus avoids Lucan's besetting sin of over-
doing the epigrammatic; for no Latin author is so absorbingly possessed
by the passion for point as Lucan. Like Ovid in his quest after cleverness, Lucan casts about among several ways of saying the same thing,
serves up obscure subtleties, and inserts digressions favourable to erudite
description. As in his fellow epic-writers Valerius, Statius, Silius, this
love of description again and again beguiles the author into subordinating
the artistic unity of the whole to the elaboration of separate passages.

It has been pointed out that, alongside of this prevalence of the
academic, there was the corrective element of genuine interest in man
to give permanent value to much of the Silver literature. While direct
observation of life was the best antidote to unreal rhetoric, there were
other factors which made for serious thought in preference to merely
smart expression. One, already mentioned, was the Stoic philosophy,
which offered to its followers an ordered view of the world as well as
guidance in matters of conduct, especially at a crisis in life. Now grown
more practical and therefore more Roman, since it had abandoned its
extremest paradoxes, neo-Stoicism counted among the influences which
encouraged a fellow-feeling amongst mankind. Between Stoicism and
Cynicism, which the earlier Stoics had admitted to be a short cut to
virtue,[1] there was much in common. In agreement broadly, although not
in detail, concerning virtue, reason (*logos*), cosmopolitanism and freedom of will, both disciplines reckoned numerous adherents in the early
empire. They now definitely overshadowed the neo-Pythagoreans and
neo-Sceptics. Other schools also had lost ground. The prestige of Epicureanism was waning, while pure Platonism and pure Aristotelianism
failed to attract the Roman mind. But Stoicism contained elements more
commendably intelligible. Above all things, it emphasised conduct: it
was an applied science of life, offering for troublesome enigmas a

[1] Diog. Laert. VII. 121: εἶναι γὰρ τὸν κυνισμὸν σύντομον ἐπ' ἀρετὴν ὁδόν.

solution which, even if not finally satisfying, claimed a true accord with nature, and in the experience of many was found workable. With less demand upon intellectual subtlety than Platonism, practical Stoicism more adequately suited the Roman temperament as a preparation for facing the things that may happen.[1] For many thinking Romans it must have been a consolation to realise that, though they might feel repelled from activity in the political sphere controlled by a Caesar, they yet remained citizens of a cosmopolis – a world-state, wherein they were fellow-citizens with God, participators in the divine essence and free by reason of a freedom divinely conferred. 'God is near you,' writes Seneca, 'with you, within you. This I say, Lucilius: a holy spirit abides within us, watcher of our deeds good or evil, and guardian over us.'[2] In the spiritual realm, then, the Stoic was an intellectual aristocrat, conscious of an eternally virtuous power which enabled him to disdain misfortune and defy a Nero or a Domitian. Nor was this position the outcome of tumid rhetoric or ingenious theorising: it was put to the proof: it was a faith in which men died and women faced exile.

Theoretically the Stoic creed did not prevent its followers from being loyal citizens of the empire; but in practice there was certain to be conflict. Their exaltation of virtue and their austere regimen in life were implicit rebukes to a luxurious emperor or court: the not uncommon actual abstention of Stoics from politics and their half-cynical attitude of independence gave further grounds for suspicion. Julius Canus offended Caligula by uncompromising argument, and Thrasea under Nero was charged with disbelief in the deification of Poppaea and with contempt for state-religion. Besides, the historical outlook of many Stoics as *laudatores temporis acti* tended to give umbrage in high imperial quarters. Revolutionary sympathies might not illogically be suspected in enthusiasts for 'Romans of the olden times.' It had been dangerous to call Cassius 'last of the Romans': it was scarcely less dangerous to drink toasts to the memory of Brutus and Cassius on their birthdays.[3] There lay significance in the fact that Helvidius Priscus, who had been banished by Nero, renewed under Vespasian his subversive propaganda in favour of what was termed democracy, but was really planned to be a government of Rome by the senatorial class in consonance with philosophical ideals.[4] It is scarcely surprising then that Vespasian expelled all philosophers except Musonius.[5] Only after Domitian did the imperial

[1] Epictet. *Diss.* III. x. 6: τὸ δὲ φιλοσοφῆσαι τί ἔστιν; οὐχὶ παρασκευάσασθαι πρὸς τὰ συμβαίνοντα; [2] Sen. *Epist. Mor.* xli. 2.

[3] Tac. *Ann.* IV. xxxiv; Juv. V. 36–37:
    'Quale coronati Thrasea Heluidiusque bibebant
    Brutorum et Cassi natalibus.'

[4] Dio Cass. LXVI. xii. 2 (ed. Bekker) says of Helvidius: βασιλείας τε ἀεὶ κατηγόρει καὶ δημοκρατίαν ἐπήνει.

[5] For prominent figures in opposition throughout the first century, see E. V. Arnold, *Roman Stoicism*, Camb. 1911; and G. Boissier, *L'Opposition sous les Césars*, Paris 1875.

government become reconciled with Stoicism, which in the second century was the prevailing creed of educated Romans and found one of its classic expositions in the Greek reflections of an emperor.

The concept of a Stoic opposition under the empire must not call up the picture of a regularly organised party of disaffection. The Stoic might, like Seneca, take service with a Caesar. But among several features of the empire which provoked hostility two at any rate stand out. A Stoic could not avoid feeling repelled at once by Caesar-worship, and by the development of a largely mechanical bureaucracy in which the individual lacked scope for the competent performance of duty. Now Stoicism claimed to supply the very competence for which there was little or no safe outlet in imperial employment. The strong tendency among Roman Stoics of the first century to accentuate the individual came less from an aggressive Cynic standpoint than, as in Seneca, from a conception of the inward development of personality effected by rigorous self-examination. It did not amount to an assertion of the individual as an absolute and independent entity; nevertheless, it encouraged that doctrine of self-sufficiency and that portion of disdain for others which can be illustrated from both Lucan and Persius.

Nor should the senatorial opposition under the Caesars be mistaken for lineal representatives of the nobles of the republic. The old families died out fast: some of their scions, as Tacitus and Juvenal show, lapsed into indigence and menial occupations. The patrician houses of the senate in Julius's day are almost extinct by Hadrian's time: Aemilii, Claudii, Fabii, Manlii and Valerii are gone: it is almost a surprise to find Cornelii. This disappearance of the ancient blood was due not so much to tyranny as to that voluntary childlessness which imperial legislation had attempted to discourage. A large proportion, then, of the new aristocracy was not of the old republican stock, but represented a fresh strain drawn from the industrial democracy of Caesar's age: it was destined in turn to collapse through its own prosperity.

Both on contemporary and on subsequent thought neo-Stoicism exercised an almost incalculable influence. The insistence on a moral order in nature to which man must conform made for salutary discipline, and the doctrine of the immanence of the divine reason ennobled the conception of duty. The recognition of moral progress, in contrast to the uncompromising tenet of sudden perfection held by the early Stoics, was a more practical, a more encouraging, a more human view, which possessed a tonic value beyond the reach of outworn paradoxes. Again, while the Stoic teaching on the brotherhood of man fostered kindliness, that on the equality of man fostered fairness of treatment.[1] These and other doctrines of value colour the deep Stoic influence on Roman law.

[1] The Stoic test of a man's worth was character: 'we all have the same source: no man is nobler than another, save he who has a more upright character,' Sen. *De Ben.* iii. 28.

In the field of religion, Stoicism proved ultimately to be a solvent of polytheism; for though Stoics might profess belief in the divinities of traditional paganism, they yet turned to allegory as an explanation of the myths, and thus tended to undermine an unquestioning acceptance of the gods. Stoicism, therefore, with its pantheistic trend contributed to the annihilation of traditional religion among the intellectuals without fully establishing monotheism to replace the polytheistic system.

Another of the more serious influences of the age, largely, though as we shall find not entirely, independent of rhetorical artifice, was the practical interest in learning of an encyclopaedic sort, exemplified in Celsus, the elder Pliny and the lost works of Suetonius. The discontent repeatedly expressed over men's waste of time is another reminder that the more serious thinkers were unlikely to reap permanent satisfaction either from social amenities or from vapid rhetoric. We have something like a gospel of work if we combine Phaedrus's scoffing remarks on the fussy *ardaliones*, Seneca's distaste for spending energy on trifles, the elder Pliny's nervous husbandry of hours for study, his nephew's grumblings about encroachments upon leisure, and even Martial's regrets over procrastination and lost opportunities – *soles . . . nobis pereunt et imputantur*, as he so humanly says.

Yet another influence which must not go unnoticed is that of the provinces, and especially the influence exercised by the old province of Spain.[1] With some claim to have developed a partially independent culture of its own, it spoke a Latin which naturally retained certain idioms, words and sounds used by previous generations of soldiers and colonists. Latin which had grown old-fashioned at Rome might still in these days be heard in Spain. It is not altogether fanciful to detect a Spanish note in parts of the Silver literature; for among Romano-Spaniards of the time were the Senecas and Lucan, Columella, Quintilian, Martial, besides several rhetors of standing. Trajan was a native of the Spanish Italica, where Hadrian's ancestors had lived since the days of the Scipios. It is significant of the contribution being made by the provinces to Rome that the Spanish influence is observable in the first century, to be followed by the development of an African Latinity in the second, and the flourishing of Romano-Gallic rhetoric in the third. The contemporary influence of Greece also acted externally upon Rome in so far as it was exerted by Greeks who taught or wrote in the city. History has recorded how responsive to personal contact with Greece itself were emperors like Nero and Hadrian; but the deeper Hellenic influence lay imbedded in the literature of the past, constantly lectured upon and assimilated generation after generation in Rome.

The wonderful variety of the Silver literature depends on the intermingling of such currents of influence, old and new. Tradition and inheritance, both Greek and Roman, operate side by side with fresh

---

[1] Strictly, two provinces under the Republic—three under the Empire.

problems and interests. It was no age of stagnation. Distinctive, though conventional, voices are heard in the epics of Lucan and of his three successors, Valerius, Statius and Silius, whether, as in the case of Lucan and Silius, they chose a historical theme, or, as in the case of the other two, they had recourse to mythology. Virgilianism acted there, as it also did in the eclogues by which Calpurnius Siculus transmitted pastoral poetry to Nemesianus. The drama of the day, never very great, has left, besides the *Octavia*, which is the single extant historical play in Latin, only Seneca's mythological tragedies based on the Greek dramatists. Far more individual power is shown in satire. Persius, a convinced young Stoic student of Horace, fulminates in crabbedly compressed sermonettes against moral backsliding; and later, Juvenal, proclaiming himself to belong to the literary lineage of Lucilius and Horace, displays his unsurpassable strength of invective. Satire may be said to have taken a new turn early in the first century when Phaedrus used the iambics of his beast-fables to suggest with mischievous irony the foibles of mankind, and once more a new turn when, in the last quarter of the century, Martial perfected the epigram with the stinging close after the fashion which has ever since made him famous. In the revival of the Menippean satire, formerly associated with the name of Varro, we again encounter the medley of verse and prose. This type is represented in Seneca's skit on the deification of Claudius and in Petronius's picaresque novel.

As regards prose style, the names of Seneca and Petronius mark two different tendencies traceable throughout the period – Seneca, usually artificial, though less so in his satire; and Petronius, as becomes a portrayer of manners, more influenced by the spoken Latin of his day. It might have been expected that encyclopaedic, scientific and technical learning should be uniformly conveyed in the simple style; but it is not always so. Straightforward expression, as a rule, characterised Celsus in the medical part of his encyclopaedia (and presumably also in the lost parts), as well as Columella in his agricultural treatise, and Frontinus writing about aqueducts; whereas one detects, on the other hand, the lure of the purple patch when the elder Pliny pauses for intervals of reflection in his gigantic *Natural History*. So too Pomponius Mela's geographical manual is needlessly decorated with flashes of intended eloquence; while Valerius Maximus's handbook of stories for rhetoricians would have been more entertaining had he told the stories in plainer style leaving embellishment to the rhetoricians for whom he collected them. In history restraint of style is far to seek. Velleius Paterculus is convicted by his excessive superlatives alone, though one forgives him much for his surprisingly original interest in certain aspects of literary history. Curtius Rufus, handling the grand subject of Alexander's campaigns, shows his ability in semi-romantic description rather than in historical inquiry. During the Neronian era, we meet the epigrammatic manner in Seneca's philosophy. The brilliant neatness of his sentences lent them a quotability which essayists in later literatures have loved. But this is a manner whose qualities cloy; and a revulsion from his style soon took place, when in the Flavian era Quintilian's lectures warned students against the seductions of Senecan prose and beckoned them back to Cicero's rounded periods as the true models for composition. A modified Ciceronianism is, therefore, visible in Quintilian, and a still more modified Ciceronianism in his pupil, the younger Pliny. It also marks Tacitus's early dialogue on oratory; but his characteristic style, that of his historical writing, is notoriously the triumph of an original genius in verbal parsimony. The closing phase of the Silver Age still exhibits the two tendencies side by side in Suetonius's business-like sentences and in Florus's feeble echoes of rhetorical utterance.

The language which was the medium for this literature may be briefly surveyed. Some aspects of Silver Latinity have been incidentally touched upon in connexion with the preponderating amount of poetry read at school, which bore fruit not merely in poetic phraseology and Virgilian imitations, but in constructions (like the familiar dative of the agent with a passive verb) now transferred from poetry to prose. No doubt some of the typical usages and idioms which we shall find illustrated in Silver authors are due to the inevitable change which any living language must undergo. Old words gain a new meaning:[1] new words are introduced. The Latin of Cicero could not have been, either in vocabulary or in sentence-structure or in grammar, the Latin of five generations later:[2] hence we are prepared to observe in Tacitus and other writers of the Silver Age alterations in the employment of the subjunctive mood, fresh meanings of prepositions (like *circa* and *citra*), new usages of and new positions for connective particles.[3]

In tracing differences between Silver and earlier Latin, it is difficult to assess the relative importance of the universal tendency in language towards change and of such special influences as the systematic drill in

[1] *E.g. interim* in sense of 'sometimes'; *subinde*, 'repeatedly' (Fr. *souvent*); *numerosus*, 'numerous'; *plerumque*, 'often'; *capere*, 'admit of' or 'be liable to'; *securus*, 'safe' (*subinde* and *securus* in these senses are found in Livy as well as in Silver authors).

[2] *E.g.* Cicero declared the superlative of *pius* to be un-Latin when used by Mark Antony, *Phil.* xiii. 43; but Sen. *ad Polyb.* vii. 4, has *piissimis*; *cf.* xv. 4, *piissime. Itaque* in Cic. is regularly at the beginning of a clause, in Sen. often after one or two words, though even in some writers of the Golden Age (Auctor ad Herennium and Livy) the Senecan practice is found occasionally. *Proinde*, once associated with imperative or subjunctive, comes to be used more and more, without any idea of command or exhortation, as an ordinary inferential word meaning 'therefore.' Among noticeable grammatical usages are the new Silver senses given to the fut. part. in *-urus*.

[3] For useful summaries of representative Silver features, see Furneaux's Introd. to ed. of Tac. *Ann.* and Summers's Introductions to *Select Letters of Seneca*, 1910, and to Tac. *Hist.* Bk. III, 1904. *Cf.* A. Dräger, *Ueb. Syntax u. Stil des Tacitus*, ed. 3, Lpz. 1882. For typical features of vocabulary, C. Paucker, *Vorarbeiten zur latein. Sprachgesch.* Berl. 1884, zweite Abt.: 'Uebersicht des der sogenannten silbernen Latinität eigenthümlichen Wörterschatzes,'

rhetoric and poetry. Some apparent changes such as are noticeable in the position of *igitur*, in a seemingly strange word, or strange meaning, or in the use of a mood, are in reality inheritances from one or two prose writers of the Golden Age, especially Sallust and Livy: what had once been an exception has become, if not the rule, at least much commoner. Apart, however, from the inevitable laws of development, the Latin language of the first century and a half of the Christian era was most deeply affected by three fixed attitudes of mind – the rhetorical passion for terseness, the rhetorical passion for novel modes of expression, and the rhetorical concentration of study upon poetic authors. Of these, compression was especially admired in the clause or phrase with epigrammatic point, but its pursuit was accountable not only for the shorter sentence in vogue, but for all sorts of ellipses[1] in grammar and for a copious employment of asyndeton. The avoidance of the stereotyped made for the introduction of new words and meanings, greater freedom in the handling of moods, and a departure from the more regularly balanced clauses and phrases of Ciceronian Latin. Many of the changes in vocabulary are due to the individual genius of prose writers who invented words, or, by adopting them from the common speech, gave them a literary *cachet*. Under this head, Tacitus is an excellent example both as innovator and as lover of the rare word. Probably few who use the term 'accumulator,' in speaking of modern apparatus, know that it was invented by Tacitus to describe one who heaps up wealth. The liking for the unusual which pervades his sentence-structure, his expression and his syntax descends into his selection of words. Thus, when there is a choice between noun-forms ending in *-men* and *-mentum*, he characteristically decides for the more uncommon form: he actually invents *imitamentum*, though *imitamen* had the poetic sanction of Ovid.

The wholesale invasion of prose by the poetic element already emphasised calls only for a few illustrations in a preliminary survey. It is poetic example that leads Seneca to write *senium* for *senectus*, *Venus* for *amor*, *iuuenta* for *iuuentus*, and leads Tacitus to use Lucretian words like *insatiabiliter*, Virgilian words like *breuia* ('shoals'), and adjectives like *indefessus* and *intemeratus* which both Virgil and Ovid had used before him. It is the poetic turn of expression also that fostered the increasing boldness of personification in prose, the use of abstract nouns in a concrete or personal sense,[2] and the substantival use of a neuter

---

[1] *E.g.* frequent omission of parts of *esse*; omission of *eo, tanto, potius* in comparisons, and of *utrum* or *-ne* before *an*.

[2] *E.g. ingenia*, 'men of talent,' 'geniuses' (Sen. *Ad Helv.* xix. 5; Tac. *Agric.* ii). The post-Augustan sense of *custodiae* as 'persons under guard,' 'prisoners,' in Plin *Ep.* X. xix, and Suet. *Tib.* lxi, *Nero* xxxi, Sen. *Ep.* v. 7, shows a complete change round from a previous extension of its meaning found in Cic., viz. 'persons serving as guards,' 'sentinels.' *Cf. inquisitio,* 'investigators,' Plin. *Ep.* X. xxx; *matrimonia,* 'wives,' Tac. *Ann.* II. xiii; *amicitia,* 'friends,' II. xxvii; *consilia,* 'advisers,' IV. xl; *affinitatibus et amicitiis,* 'kindred and friends,' *Agr.* xliv; *lectiones,* 'works to be read,' Quint. *I.O.* X, i. 45.

adjective.[1] Poetry affected the grammar of cases and tenses as well. Thus the Latin perfect used in a general sense like the gnomic 'aorist of experience' in Greek, was in Augustan Latin still a poetic usage of which Virgil was fond in the *Georgics*; but by Seneca's time it had passed into imperial prose.[2] These and other instances, too many for citation here, make it evident that the language no less than the literature of the Silver Age has the interest of possessing distinctive features of its own.

A few reflections may fitly form a summary and conclusion to this introduction. When considering the Silver Age, in style so easily contrasted with its golden predecessor, one must beware of so isolating its artificialities as to produce an impression that it teems with faults. The truth rather is that the Silver Age does by a natural process of literary evolution continue tendencies already present in Augustan times. There is in Horace an artificiality which in some measure anticipates Persius and Statius; there are in Ovid ingenuities prophetic of Seneca and Lucan; and in Sallust and Livy aspects of prose which foreshadow Tacitus. There was no violent break; but in time, if only by reason of a gradual and apparently cyclic exhaustion of genius, the changes become too obvious to miss. It is perfectly reasonable, it is indeed incumbent, to state the differences; but they must be so stated as to include not merely signs of stylistic variation but fresh notes of wider outlook in certain later writers who come close to the general human heart, perhaps because less exclusively aristocratic than the elder Romans. A catholic criticism must do justice to their strength as well as to their weakness.

Such a caveat is needful, because the factors of national deterioration, even though they worked slowly, were unquestionably manifold. They were not merely political and economic: they were physiological and, what is of deep significance for literature, they were psychological. Though it is easy to take an exaggerated view of vice under the empire, there is nevertheless significance in the fact that the most powerful voices in the whole period are the voices of protest raised by Juvenal and Tacitus: satire and irony inevitably flourished in such an environment. There is a strong temptation to see little but proof of decadence in the conventional imitators among the poets of the age, in its literary conceits, and unreal rhetoric, and even in its occasional recourse to the opposite tendency towards innovation, which French criticism has taught us to associate, as much as imitation, with decadent literature. Broadly the undeniable truth is that the Silver poets, whatever their literary skill, have fallen off in sheer artistic achievement. To turn from Lucretius and Virgil to Valerius Flaccus and Statius is to recognise an inferior quality of soul. The Silver poets have less whereon to feed man's higher nature. Virgil's profundity of feeling and reflection is something more

---

[1] *E.g.*, 'umido paludum,' Tac. *Ann.* I. lxi; 'lubrico paludum,' *ibid.* lxv: *cf.* 'occulta saltuum,' *ibid.* lxi; 'subiecta uallium,' *ibid.* lxv.

[2] *Ad Helv.* ii. 4: 'nulli tamen non magno constitit etiam bona nouerca.'

enduring than refinements based on rhetorical commonplaces. Enough
has, however, been said to lay stress upon the variety of the Silver Age,
and upon the unfairness of estimating it solely as an age of decadence.
One can no more affix a single label on a composite era than one can in-
dict a nation. If the feeble echo or the falsetto note is often heard, it is
not the only sound. The literature of the time must be judged positively
by its own appeal to the world. Under this aspect, the Silver Age has
its unique luminaries, the individuality of whose genius ensures them
permanent fame. The mark of the true classic is the power of giving
pleasure to the young and old of many generations through some fascinating and constantly renewed testimony to the indestructible continuity of human nature. Its interest is therefore universal, and its
popularity unrestricted to an epoch. Readers of different countries at
different epochs find in such work a source of eternal delight: it is not
alien to them, nor they to it. In so far as authors of the Silver Age can
address themselves successfully to mankind, and some of them beyond
challenge retain this power, their place is secure among the immortals.

Chapter II

ROMAN EDUCATION UNDER THE EMPIRE

Connexion of Roman education with literature – Evolution
through three periods – Emergence of three grades in education –
Some problems of elementary education – Suitable nurses and
reading-books – 'Secondary' training under *grammatici* – Province of 'grammar' – Exercises prescribed – Authors taught by
grammatici – The higher training in rhetoric – Exercises preliminary
to declamation – The *suasoria* – The *controuersia* – Ingenuity and
unreality combined – The broad basis of sound oratory – Subjects
included in Roman schemes of education – Spread of the traditional
system in imperial times – Decay of Greek in the West – Growth
of governmental interest in education – Attitude of emperors
towards provincial academies and the later fortunes of the old
education.

THE main clue to the literary qualities of Silver Latin is to be
found in education, and particularly in rhetorical education. No
social or political factor exercised so determining an influence
upon the literature of imperial Rome. It cannot be too clearly realised
how potent must have been the effect of a training which was undergone by the writers, speakers and civil servants of each generation, and
which had for its cardinal aims, first, to secure a thoroughly appreciative acquaintance with the best poetry in the literatures of Greece and
Rome, and, next, to equip students with the power of effective and per-
suasive speech. A connected account of the education in vogue is, therefore, a fitting prelude to the evidence for the rhetorical system which may
be drawn from such sources as the *Controuersiae et Suasoriae* collected by
the elder Seneca, Quintilian's *Institutio Oratoria*, Tacitus's *Dialogus de
Oratoribus* and the notes by Suetonius *De Grammaticis* and *De Rhetoribus*.

Roman education, viewed in its continuity, underwent certain well-
defined processes of evolution. Its history from first to last from simple
to complex, possesses the interest of showing how the primitive domestic
discipline made way for a cosmopolitan culture imparted in great
measure by skilful foreigners, and how the ancient training of what we
should call a primary type came to be amplified by a 'secondary' curriculum, and still further by advanced courses of a 'University' character.

Interesting, however, as is the whole of this development, it is with definite phases and periods that we are here concerned. One may, in fact, conveniently think of Roman education as falling broadly into three ages, ending, each in its turn, with the Punic Wars, the reign of Hadrian (A.D. 117–138), and the close of the Western Empire. Here we are mainly concentrating attention on the earlier generations of the Christian era; and what we find, as regards education, is that, before the opening of our period, scholastic training at Rome had gone through its most progressive stage, and, in range of subjects and interest, had left far behind the ancient parental instruction. That old type of instruction is best exemplified by the rigid, unromantic and severely practical method according to which the elder Cato brought up his son,[1] and which, despite limitations, was well adapted to the mind, body and estate of the older Romans. It was a grounding in the elements of reading, writing and arithmetic, coupled with sound physical and moral instruction, and had been entrusted by custom largely to those agents of education in the home whom Seneca happily calls the 'domestic magistrates.'[2] In those early times which the young Pliny[3] recalls with admiring regret, it was possible that every parent should be an instructor and that the intimate companionship between father and son should be relied upon to guarantee not only proficiency in the barest essentials of intellectual education, but also ability to serve in the army, knowledge of the laws and of religious rites, propriety of conduct and experience helpful in advising or controlling men.

As the ages passed, however, increased complexity of social conditions, together with the influx of Greeks whether bond or free, tended inevitably to relegate the work of equipping youthful minds to cultured slaves under parental supervision, and, at a later stage, very often to grammarians, rhetoricians and philosophers who settled in Rome eager to convey knowledge. Besides, the Romans, as conquest brought them nearer to world-dominion, were shrewd enough to recognise that a training which had suited the burgher of a city-state stood in need of generous extension, if it were to mould the citizens of a governing power charged with imperial responsibilities. The momentous agent of expansion in Roman education was the influence of Greece.[4] The expansion itself may be fairly gauged from the acquaintance with the principles of Greek rhetoric common among the upper classes at Rome by the middle of the second century B.C., and from the establishment of three distinct grades of education controlled respectively by the *litterator*, the *grammaticus* and the *rhetor*. These correspond roughly to the

---

[1] Plut. *Cato Maior*, xx: αὐτὸς μὲν ἦν γραμματιστής, αὐτὸς δὲ νομοδιδάκτης, αὐτὸς δὲ γυμναστής.
[2] *De Ben.* III. 11.
[3] Ep. VIII. xiv. 6: 'suus cuique parens pro magistro.'
[4] Some of its details are considered in the chapter entitled 'The Invasion of Hellenism' in Duff, *L.H.R.* pp. 68–86.

elementary, secondary, and university standards of modern days.[1] While, however, literary and rhetorical education had reached a high pitch of proficiency long before our period opens and ceased to alter much in method, there are, on the other hand, before our period closes, signs of a changed attitude towards education on the part of the imperial authorities – signs, in fact, indicating some amount of endowment and control by municipalities and by the Emperor.

Allusion has been made to the emergence of three grades of education. Of these, the 'secondary' and 'university' grades possessed under the Empire the deepest significance for their effects upon literature because of the attention bestowed upon the grammatical and aesthetic study of authors, upon rhetoric and upon philosophy. But while the bearing on literature is necessarily closer at these second and third stages in the educational fabric, still one cannot ignore the 'primary' training, which contained features of fundamental importance for thought and literary production. It is not germane here to consider, as Quintilian does in the first book of his treatise, the methods of conveying to children the rudiments of reading, writing and arithmetic,[2] or to comment on the awkwardness of the Roman numerals.[3] Perhaps, in passing, it may be worth remark that the proportion of illiterates in ancient Rome was less than many might be disposed to guess; for elementary education must have been fairly extensive by the time of Polybius to admit of the circulation of military orders in writing; and the scribblings on walls in Pompeii argue a widespread ability to read and write in the first century A.D. But two problems in the most elementary education are not to be passed over, for they appeared to ancient thinkers to be vital in their influence upon character and taste. These were the choice of a nurse, and, at a subsequent stage, the choice of books from which reading should be taught. To Quintilian both were matters of serious consideration. Although primitive custom preferred, and learned authors[4] argued, that mothers should suckle their own infants, and although the devoted care of a mother remained up to imperial times an appreciable and appreciated factor in shaping youthful lives,[5]

---

[1] Apul. *Flor.* IV. xx: 'prima cratera litteratoris ruditatem eximit, secunda grammatici doctrina instruit, tertia rhetoris eloquentia armat.'

[2] For instruction in reading, see L. Grasberger, *Erziehung u. Unterricht im klass. Alt.* II. (Würzburg 1875), pp. 256–300; writing, *op. cit.* II. 300 ff.

[3] Marquardt, *Das Privatleben der Römer*, ed. 2, 1886, pp. 97–104; or Fr. tr. *La vie privée des Romains*, 1892, I. 115–123.

[4] Early in the *De Liberis Educandis*, ascribed to Plutarch, it is laid down δεῖ δὲ (ὡς ἐγὼ ἂν φαίην) αὐτὰς τὰς μητέρας τὰ τέκνα τρέφειν καὶ τούτοις τοὺς μαστοὺς ὑπέχειν. Plut. *Mor.* 3C.

[5] Cic. *Brut.* lviii. 210–211: 'magni interest quos quisque audiat cotidie domi, quibuscum loquatur a puero, quemadmodum patres, paedagogi, matres etiam loquantur. Legimus epistulas Corneliae, matris Gracchorum; apparet filios non tam in gremio educatos, quam in sermone, matris'; *cf.* Tac. *Agric.* iv: 'in huius (*i.e.* matris) sinu indulgentiaque educatus per omnem honestarum artium cultum pueritiam adulescentiamque transegit.'

still there is evidence for the employment, at an early period in Rome, of both foster-mothers and dry nurses. At a later period the large number of household nurses may be inferred from inscriptions.[1] Their province, it was recognised, was not confined to sound alimentation; they helped to form character for better or worse, and to eliminate bad habits, mischievous notions and incorrect pronunciations. Hence the emphasis laid upon the selection of suitable nurses in Quintilian and in the treatise *De Liberis Educandis* ascribed to Plutarch.

The other matter in the elementary education which bears on literary equipment is the choice of reading-books. The scarcity of literary texts in Latin, which stimulated Livius Andronicus in the third century B.C. to translate the *Odyssey*, had long since ceased to trouble teachers; the difficulty came to lie rather in the embarrassing wealth of available material. Quintilian is emphatic in his counsel that for the earliest lessons good authors should be selected; and his preference is for Greek.[2] He believed in the stimulus obtainable from great literature, even where the pupils are too young to appreciate its full meaning and beauty. In any case there were simple fables and extracts from standard authors in abundance to serve as convenient lesson-books.

The second and third stages of education were entrusted to a *grammaticus* and a *rhetor* respectively; here the methods and subjects produced manifest effects upon literary men in Rome. Age-limits for the different grades of study varied considerably owing to individual capabilities and the overlapping of which Quintilian complained; but commonly a pupil passed from elementary instruction to the 'grammar school' at about twelve or thirteen, and then to the school of rhetoric at about sixteen. The function of 'grammar' was to train pupils in the intelligent and effective reading of standard authors both Greek and Latin; and the teachers themselves were of diverse origin and rank. Most of the series of *grammatici* mentioned by Suetonius were Greeks, and many were freedmen;[3] but there were native Romans quick enough to adopt the principles of criticism illustrated by Crates in his lectures upon Greek literature about 165 B.C., and to transfer them to their own poets, with the result that Naevius, Ennius and Lucilius speedily became school authors.[4] Though instances occurred of Roman knights taking up such work, still, as a rule, a profession of meagre returns and meagre repute attracted only a motley concourse of strange fellows – the retired apparitor, the unsuccessful pantomime-actor or the ex-boxer.[5] But that the demand for instruction was considerable is plain from the mention by Suetonius of the time when there were twenty flourishing grammar

[1] Consult 'monumenta columbariorum' in *C.I.L.* VI. 4352, 4457, 6323, 6324, 8941–8943; and the occurrences of 'nutrix' and similar words in the Indices to volumes ix and x of *C.I.L.* under 'parentelae et necessitudines.'
[2] *Inst. Or.* I. i. 12.
[3] Suet. *De Gram.* xv, xvi, xix, xx
[4] *Op. cit.* ii.   [5] *Op. cit.* ix, xviii, xxii.

schools in the capital.[1] Many Greek *grammatici* in Rome towards the end of the Republic added to their duties the teaching of Latin; thus, the freedman Ateius Philologus, a native of Athens, was called by Asinius Pollio *nobilis grammaticus Latinus*,[2] and Gnipho who taught Cicero was *non minus Graece quam Latine doctus*.[3] Specialism, however, in the one or the other literature was usual in the schools of the Empire, and the testimony of inscriptions proves the existence of separate masters for Greek and for Latin.[4]

The implications and functions of 'Grammar' were wider than with us. Its two main concerns, as we shall find in Quintilian, were the correct employment of language (*recte loquendi scientia*) and the appreciative criticism of poetry (*poetarum enarratio*).[5] The former comprised study of the parts of speech, accidence, metres, and faulty usages in word, idiom, pronunciation or spelling. The latter involved much more than knowledge of literature; for, since its aim was the elucidation of a poet's complete value and meaning, it demanded acquaintance with subsidiary subjects like music, geometry, astronomy, physics and philosophy.[6] One feature in the training which had lasting effects upon literature and which coloured diction under the Empire, is the signal preference for lecturing on poets rather than on prose-writers: this was an old tendency, for Cicero had raised his voice against the comparative neglect of history.[7] It is also of interest to recollect the attraction which even the drier and more detailed aspects of grammar possessed for many great Romans, for scholars like Varro, leaders of men like Caesar, and emperors like Claudius. Keil's *Corpus Grammaticorum Latinorum* may be said to establish the study as one of the monuments of the Roman genius; and such representative commentators upon Virgil as Macrobius and Servius are good examples of the mode in which capable grammarians were expected to annotate a classic.

The main exercises prove the attention given to composition. They included the re-telling of Aesop's fables by word of mouth or in writing, paraphrases, training in moral maxims (*sententiae*), extracts of ethical import (*chriae*), sketches of character (*ethologiae*), brief stories (*narratiunculae*) of a poetic order where the momentous thing was information rather than style.[8] The treatment of literature – on which ancient 'grammar' laid very great stress – embraced expressive reading (*lectio*) free from sing-song and provincialisms;[9] the elaborate explanation (*enarratio*) of subject-matter; textual criticism (*emendatio*); and literary criticism (*iudicium*).

---

[1] *Op. cit.* iii. [2] *Op. cit.* x. [3] *Op. cit.* vii.
[4] *E.g.*, 'Grammaticus Graecus,' *C.I.L.* II. 2236 (Corduba); VI. 9453, 9454; X. 3961 (Capua); 'Grammaticus Latinus,' II. 2892 (Tricio in Spain); III. 406 (Thyatira in Asia Minor, ΓΡΑΜΜΑΤΙΚΩ ΡΩΜΑΙΚΩ); V. 3433 (Verona), 5278 (Comum); VI. 9455 (Rome); IX. 5545.
[5] Quint. *Inst. Or.* I. iv–ix. [6] *Inst. Or.* I. iv. 4; I. x. [7] Cic. *De Leg.* I. ii.
[8] *Inst. Or.* I. ix. 6. [9] *Inst. Or.* I. viii. 2; VIII. i. 3; XI. iii. 30.

The authors taught by the professor of grammar were largely the same as those taught subsequently by the professor of rhetoric. The tenth book of Quintilian, therefore, gives a representative list, subject to the qualification that rhetoric required more prose than grammar did. The difference lay not so much in the authors as in the mode of treatment: the *grammaticus* taught literature, the *rhetor* taught oratorical effect. In Greek it was traditional to start with Homer, as in Latin, under the Empire, with Virgil. Other usual Greek authors were Hesiod, who was valued for his practical maxims; the lyric poets, in excerpts 'bowdlerised' to minimise the erotic element; the masters of Attic tragedy; and the comic writers, particularly Menander, in selections. Among Latin authors, Livius Andronicus's translation of the *Odyssey* into saturnians still held its ground when Horace went to school; and generations of schoolboys were reared on the older epic poets Naevius and Ennius, and on the dramatists Plautus, Caecilius, Terence, Pacuvius, Accius, Afranius. Virgil was introduced into the course by Caecilius Epirota, the freedman of Cicero's friend Atticus, and soon took a premier position. Horace, too, speedily realised his own alarmed anticipation of becoming a text-book; and a passion for novelty, combined with a revulsion from the archaic, helped to bring about lectures on the works of Lucan, Statius and Nero himself, while the authors were still alive. Reaction was a recurrent feature in Roman literary taste as in education. It was a protest against the predominance of the moderns in the second century A.D. that actuated the revived enthusiasm for ante-Augustan poetry. The poets, then, on the whole, played rather too oppressive a part at this stage of education; and it was inevitable that the rhetorician should adjust the balance, for his pupils were to be concerned mainly with prose as their medium. Cicero had become a model in his own day, and Quintilian regards him as a fine exemplar from the outset (*iucundus incipientibus quoque et apertus*). Of the historians, Quintilian prefers Livy to Sallust because the latter, he considers, demands a more advanced intelligence. Here it is but right to say he has in view especially the needs of students of declamation.

If we class philosophy, especially when pursued by Romans abroad, as a kind of 'post-graduate' study, we may regard the formal education in Rome as culminating in rhetoric. The training under the *rhetor* was designed to equip pupils for the vocations of public life – for deliberative and forensic oratory; and, despite obvious faults, it undoubtedly furnished in the best days of the Empire a constant supply of men of affairs, magistrates and lawyers, wielding speech with a standard of efficiency beyond the prevalent attainments of civil servants in modern times. The Roman, inheriting a native turn for oratory, had been easily drawn to the study of Greek rhetoric, which was based upon prolonged theorising and practice in Sicily, Athens and Asia Minor. So insistent appeared to be the demands of rhetoric that teachers were constantly tempted to initiate their pupils into it too soon,[1] when they ought to have been continuing grammar; and this overlapping was the natural occurrence in the old days before any line of professional demarcation had been drawn between the provinces of grammar and rhetoric.[2] But even much later, it often remained a point of honour with grammarians to give boys at the grammar school practice in rhetoric so that they might do themselves and their masters credit when they joined the rhetorical academy.[3] The training in rhetoric at Rome had been in touch with Greek methods from the second century B.C.; but education was profoundly affected by the introduction early in the first century B.C.[4] of the composition declaimed on a purely imaginary theme; and in time the Latin term *declamatio*, which had signified the forcible delivery of a speech, came to be applied to the academical exercise in rhetoric on an invented subject. Thenceforward declamation was the supreme test and crowning exercise in rhetoric, success in which was the ambition of pupils and the pride of parents.[5] Practice in it spread from Italy to the schools of the west, in Gaul and Spain.

Before students were matured for declamation, they had to pass through a prescribed series of preliminary exercises.[6] These included narratives less poetic in cast than those of the 'grammar school,' investigation of debatable questions in history, panegyric and invective, examination of good and bad laws, comparison of character, moral studies or 'commonplaces' (*communes loci*) serviceable for attacking vices, questions of a general type for debate (*theses, e.g.,* 'Is town life preferable to country life?' 'Is forensic or military renown the greater?'), and questions involving reasons for particular facts (*coniecturales causae*, which Quintilian recollected from his student days as entertaining exercises, and which he illustrates by the example, 'Why is Cupid winged and furnished with arrows and torch?').[7] Lectures on great masters in oratory and history were also requisite; and here models like Cicero and Livy might be studied with the maximum of profit. Quintilian maintained that the student should memorise passages from the masterpieces of standard authors instead of wasting energy on 'cold cabbage heated up' – the *crambe repetita* of the pupil's own show-pieces.[8]

The two most advanced exercises were the *suasoria* and the harder *controuersia* – the former intended to prepare for deliberative oratory,

[1] *Inst. Or.* II. i.
[2] Suet. *De Gram.* iv: 'ueteres grammatici et rhetoricam docebant.'
[3] Suet. *De Gram.* iv: 'ne scilicet sicci omnino atque aridi pueri rhetoribus traderentur.'
[4] Declamations were introduced at Rome perhaps by Molon of Rhodes about 84 B.C., as H. Bornecque thinks (*Les déclamations et déclamateurs,* etc., Lille 1902, p. 42).
[5] Juv. X. 114–117; Quint. *Inst. Or.* II. vii. i.
[6] *Inst. Or.* II. iv.
[7] *Inst. Or.* II. iv. 26; *cf.* Propert. II. xii.
[8] *Inst. Or.* II. vii. 1: Juv. vii. 154.

the latter for pleading in the law-courts.[1] Ample illustrations of their nature are furnished by the seven *suasoriae* and five books of *controuersiae* which have come down, along with excerpts from five lost books, out of the collection of the elder Seneca. Quintilian cites examples of stock themes, and there exist also the declamations of the pseudo-Quintilian and excerpts from Calpurnius Flaccus. The *suasoria* was an imagined consideration of the action suitable at a historical crisis: sometimes it was a supposed soliloquy, *e.g.*, 'Alexander deliberates whether he shall cross the ocean,' 'Agamemnon deliberates if he should sacrifice Iphigeneia,' 'Cicero deliberates whether he should burn his works to secure his safety from Antony';[2] sometimes it was a supposed joint deliberation, *e.g.*, 'The three hundred Spartans at Thermopylae consider whether they ought to retreat,' 'The Conscript Fathers discuss the propriety of surrendering the Fabii to the Gauls';[3] at other times it was a supposed address conveying counsel of the kind which Juvenal remembered offering to the dictator Sulla by way of exercise in the academy where he suffered the cane.[4] Similarly, many a junior aspirant after eloquence composed an advisory speech to Hannibal urging him to advance straight upon Rome after Cannae.[5] Seneca[6] records some interesting facts concerning Ovid's attitude to this exercise. After commenting on the influence of the schools upon Ovid's poetry and on the young poet's reputation as a declaimer, he tells us that Ovid rarely declaimed *controuersiae*, and in any case only those of a psychological nature (*non nisi ethicas*); his preference was for the *suasoria*, and he found arguing irksome.[7] These illuminating remarks explain both the aspect of Ovid's genius exhibited in the *Heroides*, and his failure to carry out his father's wish that he should become a lawyer.

---

[1] The Roman turn given to Greek rhetorical methods is marked by the change of terminology, which indicates a change in practice. The main exercises at first had been called *theses*, the Greek term (θέσεις) applied to general questions for debate, such as 'Ought a man to marry or remain single?' 'Is it better to take a share in public life or to mind one's own affairs?' Then came a business-like development or Roman condescension from general to particular whereby an approach to facts and reality was made in treating 'cases' such as those tried before a court; and, appropriately, these exercises were called by a Latin name, *causae*. Both terms were in use during Cicero's days, but early in his career there emerged the fashion of *declamatio*, the scholastic exercise in rhetoric based on but not identical with Greek models; and in course of time we read no longer of *theses* and *causae*, but of *controuersiae* and *suasoriae* – both, it will be noted, Latin, not Greek terms.

[2] Sen. *Suas.* i, iii, vii; *cf.* Quint. *Inst. Or.* III. viii. 16–19, *e.g.* 'Deliberat C. Caesar an perseueret in Germaniam ire,' etc.

[3] Sen. *Suas.* ii; Quintilian, *loc. cit.*

[4] Juv. I. 15–17.

[5] Juv. VII. 158–164; *cf.* X. 166–167:

> 'I demens et saeuas curre per Alpes,
> Vt pueris placeas et declamatio fias.'

[6] *Contr.* II. ii. 8–12.

[7] *Contr.* II. ii. 12: 'libentius dicebat suasorias: molesta illi erat omnis argᴅ mentatio.'

For entire success, it should be noted, this hortatory declamation required historical knowledge, psychological insight, some dramatic power, and distinct gifts of imagination and style.

In the *controuersia* one has passed from monologue to a debate which professed to represent the pleadings in an imaginary suit or criminal trial, where, as Addison's Sir Roger would have it, 'much might be said on both sides.' The students virtually acted an invented case in a sham court. They argued for or against – sometimes, to gain additional readiness and thoroughness, they argued first on one side, then on the other. Though there was a semblance of observing legal forms, yet the circumstances, the laws assumed to be applicable, and the standing characters were largely drawn from a realm of imagination which undeniably evoked marvellous ingenuity in argument, but merited the strictures in Petronius and Quintilian because of its divorce from actual life. Magicians, pirate chiefs, and their susceptible daughters, preternaturally hard-hearted fathers, and unconscionably cruel tyrants appear and reappear. Suetonius[1] cites two specimens of the less extravagant *controuersiae*. The first concerns the disputed ownership of a treasure which happens to be dragged up in a fishing-net after certain youths have, by way of speculation, purchased in advance that particular cast from the fishermen – are the purchasers entitled to the fish plus the gold, or to the fish only? The other concerns the disputed freedom of a slave from the East so valuable that the dealer disguised him and falsely declared him as a free man at Brindisi to escape the duty exigible by the Customs officers – has the slave been legally emancipated in virtue of his owner's declaration before witnesses?[2] In Seneca the situations are often more unreal. Take his very first case: One of two brothers who were at variance had a son; when his uncle fell into poverty, the kind-hearted nephew helped him, but was disinherited by his father for so doing: he was, however, adopted by his uncle, who luckily had a great estate left to him: meanwhile the young man's father came to want, and, though forbidden by his uncle, the lad now insisted on helping his father: in consequence, he is disinherited by his uncle – the question is, can he successfully impugn his uncle's decision?[3]

Such exercises, incredible though the situations might be, imparted, through the mental gymnastics involved, a nimbleness of mind, a quickness in propounding or refuting arguments, a versatility in treatment, and a finish of speech which again and again fell little short of the amazing. The adept could equip himself with skilful mastery from the whole armoury of rhetoric. Yet, whatever merits may be claimed for rhetoric here or in the chapter on the elder Seneca, the training had

---

[1] *De Rhet.* i.
[2] This case is similar to CCCXL in the shorter Quintilianean *Declamationes*, ed. C. Ritter (Teubner) 1884.
[3] *Contr.* I. i.

obvious drawbacks. For its range was narrow and unreal: it handled things and persons such as never were on land or sea: and these same unreal cases were handled an infinite number of times, so that the depressing round of declamation, as pupil after pupil rose from the bench, was calculated, Juvenal says, to bore luckless professors to death![1] Any ambitious pupil had to take refuge in innovations upon the threadbare theme; and his most promising chance lay in suggesting some *colour*, some ingenious line of defence undreamt of by any predecessor. Hence the far-fetched absurdities with which the pleadings teem. At any cost, old material had to receive a new dress, bedizened with all the frippery of rhetoric; and this compulsion produced an inordinate concentration upon tricks of expression to the detriment of matter and sense. A frequent result was an inartistic phantasmagoria of artificialities, conceits, antitheses and quibbles. Nor was the effect upon morals always better than upon aesthetics, for such a system was at times apt to engender a heedlessness of truth or falsity in fact, and callousness to the justice or injustice of a plea, provided only it could be made telling. Another dangerous fruit was pretentious glibness of speech of the kind which the staid author of the *De Liberis Educandis* repeatedly denounced as obnoxious;[2] and – most far-reaching of all the consequences – the rhetorical declamations were largely accountable for the unreal pose and mannerisms of the Latin literature of the Silver Age.

For such artificiality the best cure lay in extended knowledge. No sound critic ever based oratory on mere tricks of speech. Practised judges like Quintilian and Tacitus complained that true eloquence had deteriorated owing to the extravagance and ignorance of declaimers. Agreeing with Cicero, Quintilian views ideal oratory as founded upon a strong moral and intellectual basis; for to Quintilian, as to Cato generations earlier, the effective orator was the good man skilled in speaking (*uir bonus dicendi peritus*).[3] Mere plausibility or claptrap is ruled out by his insistence upon the orator's knowledge of the subject on which he is to speak. Put this way (*mihi satis est eius esse oratorem rei de qua dicet non inscium*), Quintilian's requirements seem more moderate than Cicero's sweeping demand for wide knowledge of all great subjects (*omnium rerum magnarum atque artium scientiam*);[4] yet Quintilian too believes in the study of subjects outside the professional training in rhetoric, especially ethics, physics and dialectic, law, and history.[5]

At a much earlier period, indeed, Romans of the better class had been expected to cover a wide field of knowledge. Cato, for instance, included

---

[1] Juv. VII. 154.
[2] *E.g.* τῶν δὲ πανηγυρικῶν λήρων ὡς πορρωτάτω τοὺς υἱεῖς ἀπάγειν, and later οἱ δ' αὐτοσχέδιοι τῶν λόγων πολλῆς εὐχερείας καὶ ῥαδιουργίας εἰσὶ πλήρεις, and again, σοφὸν γὰρ εὔκαιρος σιγὴ καὶ παντὸς λόγου κρείττων. Plut. *Mor.* 6A, 6C, 10E.
[3] *Inst. Or.* XII. i. 1. Quintilian insists on the moral excellence essential to great orators in I. *pr.* 9–10 and II. xv. 1, and to instructors in oratory in II. ii.
[4] *Inst. Or.* II. xxi. 14, where Quintilian quotes Cicero *De Or.* I. vi. 20.
[5] *Op. cit.* I. *pr.* 16; XII. ii. 10; iii; iv.

in his scheme oratory, agriculture, law, war and medicine. A century later, Varro's nine departments of education were grammar, dialectic, rhetoric, geometry, arithmetic, astronomy, music, medicine and architecture. In the first three of these one recognises the 'trivium' and in the next four the 'quadrivium' of the medieval education, while Cato's subjects of agriculture, law and war have come to be regarded as professional. Medicine would tend to be more and more superficially studied, by reason of the number of Greek practitioners who came to Rome. The inclusion of architecture in the list is a testimony to the interest taken in the principles of a fine art which constituted an integral portion of Roman civilisation, and reminds one of the broad education which Vitruvius believes should go to the training of an architect. But one may assume that architecture was in practice a special profession, and that an encyclopaedic education became less and less attainable, as knowledge deepened, although, under the Empire, writers like Celsus and Pliny still made an encyclopaedic appeal, at least to mature readers. It was, indeed, largely in philosophy that the abler youths followed 'post-graduate' courses, either at Rome itself, where Epicurean, Academic and Stoic thought had long been represented, or abroad, especially at Athens, as the time-honoured fountain-head of the schools. Under the later Republic, the custom of seeking breadth in education is well exemplified by the studies which famous authors had pursued. Thus Virgil, besides his literary reading, worked at rhetoric, philosophy, mathematics, medicine and law; and study at a 'foreign university,' which became common under the Empire, is illustrated in the careers of Caesar, Cicero and his son, Horace and Ovid.

Our present concern, however, is not with philosophy under the Empire but with grammar and rhetoric; and this for two reasons – firstly, grammar and rhetoric affected literary style more than philosophy ever did, deep though the influence of Stoicism was in imperial days; secondly, it was the time-honoured curriculum in grammar and rhetoric which was most widely diffused in the Roman world, and which was, especially at many Western seats of learning, taught to the absolute exclusion of philosophy. In the Greek portions of the Empire, the so-called 'Second Sophistic' was represented in the second century A.D. by itinerant rhetoricians presenting their displays of eloquence before audiences whose powers of criticism proved the continuance and diffusion of the ancient education.[1] In the Western portions, it is interesting to note that the ancient system of grammar and rhetoric came to be preserved particularly at Carthage in Africa and in the academies of Gaul. Marseilles, Autun, Lyons, Bordeaux, and, later, Toulouse, Narbonne and Trèves were typical centres of instruction. The educational

[1] S. Dill, *Rom. Soc. from Nero to M. Aurelius*, London 1904, p. 372; Mommsen, *Provinces of Rom. Emp.* Eng. tr. 1886, I. pp. 362–367; *cf.* Philostr. *Apoll. Tyan.* i. 7; *Vit. Soph.* i. 220.

movement was of old standing in Gaul, where Marseilles had long exercised a magnetic attraction. Memories of the sound education which he
had enjoyed at Marseilles doubtless weighed with Agricola when, about
A.D. 80, he established schools in Britain for the sons of chieftains;[1] and
there was in Britain doubtless a serious enthusiasm for Roman culture,
although Juvenal makes game of it by his jesting allusions to the influence of Gallic eloquence on British advocates and to the talk in the
'Farthest North' about establishing a chair of rhetoric.[2] Later in the
second century, the regular three grades with some amplifications are
illustrated in the studies of Marcus Aurelius; his early lessons from the
litterator were varied by others from an actor and a tutor who taught
both music and mathematics; next, he worked under professors of
grammar, one of Greek and three of Latin; and at the later stage he had
three Greek masters of rhetoric, among whom was Herodes Atticus,
and one Latin master, who was Fronto. He studied philosophy under
many teachers, and devoted much attention to law. Public declamation
also had an attraction for him.[3] The firm hold obtained by such courses
as we have described is plainly seen for many generations beyond our
period. Alexander Severus early in the third century passed through
just such a course as Marcus Aurelius had done.[4] The instruction which
many of the Christian Fathers underwent in youth was on the old pagan
lines, and the *Confessiones* of St. Augustine are typical from this standpoint, because they are the vivid reminiscences of one who had been a
student of rhetoric at Carthage and a professor at Milan. The conditions
of education in Gaul in the fourth and fifth centuries are best known from
the writings of Ausonius and Sidonius Apollinaris.[5] Christians and non-
Christians then found a bond of union in the literary studies familiar
during their 'college days'; so that some measure of vitality was left to
the old training despite the degeneration consequent upon its bondage
to unreal and conventional dexterities.

One life-giving element of our period, however, gradually vanished
out of the Western schools. That was Greek. Whereas Seneca includes
Greek arguments in his *Controuersiae*, and, whereas in the days of
Apuleius and Tertullian scholars knew Greek as well as Latin, yet by
the fourth century both in Africa and in Gaul it was little taught. St.
Augustine, for instance, had no liking for or proficiency in Greek and
read Plato mainly in Latin translations.[6] This severance of the two
literatures was prophetic of the approaching division of the Empire
and of the usual Latin curriculum in the Middle Ages.

A highly interesting feature in education during imperial times is

[1] Tac. *Agric.* iv. 4; xxi. 2.
[2] Juv. XV. 111–112.
[3] S.H.A., *M. Ant. Phil.* ii–iii.
[4] S.H.A., *Alex. Sev.* iii.
[5] S. Dill, *Rom. Soc. in last Cent. of W. Empire*, ed. 2, Lond. 1905, pp. 385–451.
[6] *Confess.* I. xi ii–xiv; VII. ix; VIII. ii.

the closer *rapprochement* of the government therewith. This was a growing, though a slowly growing, tendency. The state had shown solicitude over morality by enacting sumptuary laws and encouraging marriage, but had been reluctant to patronise education directly. The Caesars had, however, foreshadowed a new policy. Julius paid respect to erudition by granting citizenship to *peregrini* who settled in Rome as medical men or teachers of the liberal arts.[1] Augustus exempted teachers from an edict banishing foreigners, and he transferred Verrius Flaccus with his school to the Palatium at a handsome salary, so that he might instruct the imperial grandchildren.[2] Tiberius and Claudius were personally interested in grammatical studies; but the next practical step towards imperial patronage consisted in the fixing by Vespasian of an annual stipend of 100,000 sesterces for Greek and Latin rhetors. Whether Vespasian's decree was intended to apply beyond the walls of the capital, and how soon it actually came into force inside the walls is not quite clear; at any rate, Jerome says Quintilian was the first professor at Rome to receive payment from the *fiscus*, and he sets this down to a year in Domitian's reign.[3] Trajan, recognising the value of education as a means of training the future citizens of a state, decided to secure public instruction for five thousand poor boys.[4]

But it was left for Hadrian to take that new departure which constitutes his reign an epoch in educational history. Versed in literature, a skilled musician and painter, fond of declamation, the emperor had a taste for keeping learned men at Court, and fellow-feeling made him kind to them. Upon teachers who had grown too old for duty he conferred a retiring allowance.[5] At Rome he housed rhetoric handsomely in his famous Athenaeum, and in the provinces he founded schools, awarded them subventions, and made appointments of teachers to them. It is worth while to trace the tendency beyond the limits of our period. Hadrian's active policy of generous interest was continued by Antoninus Pius, who improved the status and income of professors of rhetoric and philosophy all over the Empire.[6] Furthermore, he exempted from certain state-imposts rhetors, philosophers, grammarians and physicians, defining the number of teachers entitled to such immunity in different towns – thus, the minimum *personnel* for the smallest place touched by his edict consisted of five physicians, three sophists and three grammarians.[7] This imperial measure bears witness to the connexion of both central and municipal authorities with a local educational staff. In fact,

---

[1] Suet. *Iul.* xlii.
[2] Suet. *Aug.* xlii; *De Gram.* xvii.
[3] Hieron. *Chron. Euseb.* ad ann. Abr. 2104: 'Quintilianus ex Hispania Calagurritanus primus Romae publicam scholam et salarium e fisco accepit et claruit.'
[4] Plin. *Paneg.* xxvi–xxviii.
[5] S.H.A., *Hadr.* xvi.
[6] S.H.A., *Ant. Pius* xi: 'rhetoribus et philosophis per omnes prouincias et honores et salaria detulit.'
[7] *Dig.* XXVII. i. 6.

the burden of maintaining local academies fell on the municipalities, and what an emperor did was by special benefits to stimulate local educational policy. It seems, therefore, natural that Marcus Aurelius in A.D. 176 should have devoted money towards the establishment of professorial chairs at Athens.[1] Beyond his reign it must suffice to indicate only the most significant symptoms.[2] Alexander Severus in the third century introduced a bursary system for deserving lads.[3] In the next century, repeated edicts exhibit emperors in the light of protectors of underpaid or irregularly paid teachers against the penurious economies and dilatory finance of local bodies. Beneficence had established rights of control: hence, at the end of the third century, when Constantius Chlorus nominated Eumenius as principal of the reorganised school at Autun, the town accepted the emperor's action as a matter of course. Julian in 362 explicitly claimed the prerogative of appointing professors to chairs, and, although he entrusted the sifting of candidates to the municipalities, he subjected them to the first definite restriction imposed by an emperor on local liberty of selection, when he forbade the teaching of literature by any Christian. Gratian's edict – which is of interest as showing the hand of his adviser and old tutor, the poet Ausonius – fixed the emoluments for different grades of teachers; thus, a rhetor was to be paid twice as much as a grammarian. Virtually in this way, although the Government did not make direct grants, yet money for educational salaries was earmarked in the municipal budgets. So the chronicle of the imperial organisation of public instruction proceeds; and, if it did little to affect the methods in vogue, still the patronage was of value in keeping learning alive. The last great event in this connexion was the establishment by Theodosius II at Constantinople of a university staff consisting of thirty-one professors. Little over a century later came the dissolution by Justinian.

[1] Dio Cass. LXXI. xxxi. 3 (ed. Bekker); Lucian, *Eun.* iii.
[2] For a fuller account see G. Boissier: 'L'instruction publique dans l'empire romain' in *Rev. d. deux Mondes* 1884.
[3] S.H.A., *Alex. Sev.* xliv.

C

PART I

Literature under Tiberius, Caligula and Claudius

A.D. 14—54

Chapter I

THE ELDER SENECA: ORATORS AND RHETORICIANS

Rhetoric in operation – The elder Seneca's life – Character and tastes – His surviving *Controuersiae* and *Suasoriae* – His marvellous memory – Value of the prefaces – Their portrayal of rhetoricians – Critical views – Unpractical nature of declamations – Recollections – The academic and the forensic – Seneca's method – Cases criminal, civil, social – Immoral, romantic, incredible elements – Sources – Literary ability – Effect of the exercises – Ingenuity – Interest of digressions – Silly arguments – Qualities of declamations in relation to Silver literature.

Speakers of two generations – The emperors Tiberius, Caligula and Claudius – Some rhetoricians and orators of the time – Informers.

A STUDY of the elder Seneca is invaluable, not merely for the light which he sheds upon the methods pursued by professional speakers, but also for his knowledge (illustrated by a wealth of anecdote and reminiscence) concerning the individual literary qualities or even mannerisms of orators and rhetors both Augustan and Tiberian. Acquaintance with the system represented in his collection of *Controuersiae* and *Suasoriae* is indispensable for an appreciation of the position and prospects of oratory reflected in Quintilian's treatise and Tacitus's dialogue. But Seneca's work is much more than an illuminating introduction to works about oratory: it constitutes the great exemplar of the Roman rhetorical education in operation, which must be grasped in order to estimate the stylistic merits or demerits of verse and prose in the Silver Age. Seneca is a gateway through which the history of Latin expression must pass towards Lucan as well as towards Tacitus, and to examine the academic exercises recorded by him is to go far on the path to understand the style of two centuries; for, like much subsequent prose and verse, they contain elements pointed to the degree of monotony, ingenious to the degree of unreality, and sometimes half-poetic in virtue of a spice of far-fetched romanticism.

L. Annaeus Seneca[1] was born at Corduba. An ancient Spanish town

---

[1] The MSS. give L., which may account for the confusion of his works with those of his more famous son. The argument for M. is not convincing.

which received Italian settlers in 152 B.C. and was granted later (perhaps by Pompey) the status of a Roman colony, Corduba had literary traditions in Cicero's time, and by Martial's day was able to boast of having produced three noted members of a single family, namely, the two Senecas and Lucan.[1] This provincial family had attained equestrian rank, as we learn from words assigned to the younger Seneca.[2] The elder Seneca was prevented by the civil war from hearing Cicero[3] declaim 'with his great pupils in their *praetextae*,' *i.e.*, during the consulate of Hirtius and Pansa in 43 B.C.; and, since the young Spaniard could not well have attended declamatory performances under the age of twelve, it is not likely that he was born later than 55 B.C. He was a boy (*puer*, *Contr.* I. *praef.* 3) when he first reached Rome, probably in 42 B.C., after the battle of Philippi. He may have come with his Spanish friend, Porcius Latro: in any case, they were class-mates in the rhetorical school of Marullus,[4] who was perhaps recommended to them by his Spanish origin more than by outstanding merit. But Seneca did not restrict himself to one teacher. He had Arellius Fuscus for one of his early masters, and he evidently made a practice of listening to all available speakers, if we may judge from his wide acquaintance with their modes of argument and expression in the *Controuersiae*. This implies long residence in Rome, though there is no proof to support his frequent designation as a 'rhetor.' Guess-work would assign to him the official duties of a procurator, and would by the call of such duties explain his return to Spain for a period. It was in Spain that he married Helvia, the mother of his three sons – M. Annaeus Novatus, who took the name of his adoptive father Gallio and, as pro-consul of Achaea, had the apostle Paul brought before him;[5] L. Annaeus Seneca, the philosopher; and M. Annaeus Mela, Lucan's father.

Clearly Seneca was in Rome at a date between 29 and 24 B.C., when he heard Ovid declaiming under Arellius Fuscus;[6] and still later in 17 B.C., when he heard Latro's embarrassing reference to the subject of adoption in the presence of Augustus and Agrippa.[7] He was back in Rome before Asinius Pollio died, A.D. 5; for he mentions having heard Pollio's youthful oratory and afterwards the oratory of his old age.[8] The date of his death is to be inferred approximately. His allusion to the extinction of the Scaurus family (*Suas.* ii. 22) cannot be earlier than A.D. 34; and we can feel reasonably sure that he outlived Tiberius; for the account of that emperor's death given by Suetonius[9] on the authority of 'Seneca' is plausibly referred to the lost historical work, which, as

[1] Mart. I. lxi. 7–8; Cic. *Pro Arch.* x. 26. In *Suas.* vi. 27, Senca calls the Spaniard Sextilius Ena from Corduba 'municipem nostrum.'
[2] Tac. *Ann.* XIV. liii.   [3] *Contr.* I. *praef.* 11.   [4] *Contr.* I. *praef.* 22.
[5] *Acts* xviii; *cf.* imaginary portrait of Gallio in Anatole France's *Sur la Pierre Blanche.*
[6] *Contr.* II. ii. 8.   [7] *Ibid.* II. iv. 12–13.
[8] IV. *praef.* 3: 'audiui illum et uiridem et postea iam senem.'
[9] Suet. *Tib.* lxxiii.

THE ELDER SENECA 39

we know from a fragment of the younger Seneca, his father composed. The outspoken criticism on the policy of burning books (*Contr.* X. *praef.* 7) suggests that publication did not precede Tiberius's death in 37. On the other hand, when the younger Seneca was banished in A.D. 41, his mother was a widow;[1] so that the father can be presumed to have died at an age well over ninety, between A.D. 37 and 41.

A man of old-fashioned austerity,[2] the elder Seneca recalls Cato the Censor, whom he admired. It is provincial virtue more than a love of rhetorical commonplace that speaks when he censures the moral decadence of the times; and one cannot but admire the straightforward sincerity in his manner of addressing his sons for whom he put together the *Controuersiae*. Even if public service interested him for part of his life, he can confidently be described as a scholar by preference. Not modern enough in his tastes to sympathise with the higher education of women, he discouraged Helvia from devoting herself to those philosophical studies in which their second son was destined to see a remedy for most of the ills of existence. Yet the attraction of the past did not render him hostile to the imperial system, which, under Augustus, he found compatible with reasonable liberty:[3] and, while repressive book-burning stirred his anger, he declined to waste pity on speakers who would give utterance to treasonable words at the risk of their lives.[4] His patriotism burned strongly enough to give him pleasure in pitting the epoch of his model Cicero against the oratorical claims of 'arrogant Greece.'[5] In general, he distrusted the smart levity of Greek rhetoricians,[6] and his occasional compliments to them were oftener than not accompanied with a qualification.[7]

Of his ten books of *Controuersiae*, five (III, IV, V, VI and VIII) are represented only by the headings and excerpts of a fourth-century epitomator,[8] with the fortunate addition, however, of the prefaces to books III and IV. The other five books (I, II, VII, IX, X) survived in spite of being summarised and give a reasonably full presentation of the arguments used in different declamations, though gaps are especially noticeable in the transcription of the debating points made in Greek.

[1] Sen. *Consol. ad Helv.* ii. 4.
[2] Sen. *Consol. ad Helv.* xvii. 3: 'patris mei antiquus rigor.'
[3] *Contr.* II. iv; cf. IV. *praef.* 5: 'illi clementissimo uiro' (referring to Augustus).
[4] Contrast X. *praef.* 5–7 with II. iv. 13: 'horum non possum misereri qui tanti putant caput potius quam dictum perdere.'
[5] I. *praef.* 6: 'insolenti Graeciae.'
[6] I. v. 12: 'Glyconis ualde leuis e Graecis (*v.l.* 'et Graeca' *uel* 'ut Graeca') sententia est.' There are commendations of Greeks in I. iv. 11–12, but then Albucius is said to surpass them.
[7] *E.g.* X. iv. 18 and 23. For Seneca's Roman preferences cf. praise of a Greek speaker of Roman type, Agroitas from Marseilles (*Contr.* II. vi. 12); glances at Greek unsavoury realism (I. ii. 22–23); record of Arellius Fuscus's views about Roman borrowers who improved on Greek originals (IX. i. 13); and Cestius's views on Cicero's surpassing 'arrogant Greece,' *Suas.* vii. 10, repeating Seneca's phrase in *Contr.* I. *praef.* 6.
[8] Galdi, *L'Epitome n. lett. lat.* p. 148.

The prefaces to these five books have also survived, except that the preface to IX is incomplete. The survival of excerpts for the fuller books enables us to survey the method followed in epitomising. The total number of subjects debated is seventy-four, of which, thirty-nine are represented by excerpts only. The number of *controuersiae* in a book varies from six to nine. There are seven *suasoriae* (perhaps part of a larger collection), of which the first has lost its beginning. These exercises have been defined and illustrated in the chapter on Roman education: it remains to examine Seneca's subjects, method and judgements.

This elaborate collection of arguments on rhetorical themes was the compilation of his old age, and evidence has been cited to show that some parts were written after A.D. 37. It does not follow, however, that the whole was put together at the beginning of Caligula's reign by a man over ninety:[1] it is more likely that the author had begun his task years before when his sons would be practically interested in rhetorical exercises, and that he spread its composition over the later period of Tiberius's reign without publishing until the emperor was dead. The *Suasoriae* were composed after the *Controuersiae*.[2]

Seneca's purpose is stated in his first preface, which is addressed to all three sons, and yet meant for the public at large.[3] It was to recall the manner and diction of declaimers of the older school, and to represent speakers whom his sons could not have heard. Impressing on these young men the wisdom of taking bygone rhetoric into account along with contemporary rhetoric, he is conscious of a decadence in oratory to be measured against the greatness of Cicero and his times. To the author the causes appear to be three: luxurious laziness; the fact that, since oratory came to offer fewer rewards, men turned to pursuits less honourable but more profitable; and a natural law of reaction. Realising the scarcity of works representative of the greatest declaimers and, still worse, the circulation of forgeries (*quod peius est, falsi*), he declares it his duty to rescue noble names from oblivion. Hence it is natural to respond with pleasure to his sons' request that he should undertake so extensive a task.[4] Only a marvellous memory could have achieved it; but Seneca possessed a Macaulay-like gift of remembrance, and, as he remarks with obvious truth, it was the distant past he recalled the more surely. There had been a time when he was capable of repeating a list of 2,000 names read over once.[5] This is partly the secret of his proficiency in citing arguments from about 120 different speakers, though one is not precluded from believing that he had preserved notes, and that he consulted published collections.

---

[1] I do not think Schanz has proved his conclusion, S.H. § 335: 'Die Abfassungszeit der Schrift fällt daher in die ersten Regierungsjahre des Caligula.'
[2] *Contr.* II. iv. 8: 'cum ad suasorias uenero.'
[3] I. *praef.* 10: 'populo dedicabo.'
[4] I. *praef.* 1; 'exigitis rem magis iucundam mihi quam facilem.'
[5] I. *praef.* 2.

The seven prefaces possess great interest. One may weary of the seventy-four themes and the often scrappy arguments, even although they are genially diversified by criticism, digression and reminiscences; but the prefaces are eminently readable in respect of subject-matter and style. They are valuable for characterisation of speakers, for critical judgements, and for their record of facts otherwise unknown to literary history: they are attractive for their entertaining stories. Besides, they give the best opportunity of weighing Seneca's own literary qualities in contradistinction to the text of his *themata*, where he is for the most part professedly reporting the words of others. His Latinity, in its pleasant freedom from artifice, is worthy of an author who consistently revered Cicero and was aware that an inferior type of eloquence had emerged. This alone would constitute him an important link between the Golden and the Silver Age. Indeed, the first preface shows his realisation of that change from oratory to declamation for which the principate was largely accountable. Commenting on the alteration of the Ciceronian *causae* into the later *controuersiae*, he proceeds to draw the distinction between the public speaking of an orator (*uera actio*) and the private exercise (*domestica exercitatio*) of a declaimer. The new declamation, he notes, was a product of his own period.

Each preface, as a rule, treats one rhetor prominently, and in the succeeding book that rhetor's arguments are reported with considerable fullness. Thus, the opening preface sketches a delightfully graphic picture of Seneca's friend, Porcius Latro, his bodily strength and strong voice, his ineradicable Spanish ways, his passion for work in defiance of the laws of digestion, his memory for written notes, his mastery over historical detail, and his method of practising the artifices of his craft. Such realistic portrayal cannot but rivet our attention upon his advocacy in the *controuersiae* which follow; and Seneca explains that the first controversy in his collection was so placed because he remembered it to be the earliest of Latro's declamations in the academy of Marullus. Similarly, the next preface describes Fabianus, the teacher of the younger Seneca, and in Book II a special effort is made to recall his arguments. The preface to III deals particularly with Cassius Severus; that to IV deals with a pair, Asinius Pollio and Q. Haterius; that to VII is mainly on Albucius; that to IX considers why Votienus Montanus did not practise declamation; and the last preface, when Seneca is tiring of his subject, gives rapid impressions of various speakers – Mamercus Scaurus (a great orator spoiled by laziness); Labienus, nick-named 'Rabienus,' a Pompeian in spirit who had his books publicly burned; Musa, objectionable for unnatural rhetoric; a group consisting of Moschus, Pacatus, Sparsus, Bassus, Capito; and finally the Spanish declaimers Gavius Silo and Turrinus Clodius.

Seneca's admirable criticisms are well seen in the second preface, in which he contrasts Fabianus with his own master Arellius Fuscus. Here he

c*

commends the study of rhetoric as a fitting pursuit for his favourite son
Mela, whose talents he rated more highly than those of his two brothers,
then preparing for public life. Among instructive features in the preface
to III are the demarcation of forensic from academic speaking, and the
explanation offered by Cassius Severus of his relative inferiority as a
declaimer. Severus, it may be noted, was a good extempore speaker, and
anger improved his pleading. After arguing that *non omnia possumus
omnes*, that the individual's gifts are often confined to a single field, that
Cicero's style was inferior in verse and Virgil's in prose, he accounts for
his success at the bar in words which implicitly censure the whole
method of declamation:

'I have been accustomed to address not an audience, but a judge;
I have been accustomed to answer not myself, but an opponent. I avoid
superfluous words as much as inconsistent ones. In scholastic speaking
what may not be considered superfluous, when the whole thing is a
superfluous practice?... When I speak in court, I am doing something;
when I declaim... I seem to be toiling in dreamland (*in somniis laborare*).
... Declaimers are like hot-house plants that droop in the open (*uelut
adsueta clauso et delicatae umbrae corpora sub diuo stare non possunt*).
... There is nothing to be said for testing an orator in such a childish
exercise. What would you think of judging a pilot on a fish-pond?'[1]
Seneca, then, is by no means blind to the unpractical nature of declamation. Elsewhere he records instances of the absurdity of some rhetorical figures in a law-court,[2] and the inability of even a practised
declaimer to plead in the forum under the open sky without the familiar
associations of four enclosing walls.[3]

Part of the charm in the prefaces depends on random recollections.
We grow familiar with Seneca's *Memini*.[4] It is not the least of their
merits that some of the reminiscences are humorous and satiric. He
takes care to chronicle Severus's amusing attitude to the conceited
Cestius, whose modern declamations students got up by heart, though
in Cicero they studied only speeches to which Cestius had composed
replies. 'One day' (says Severus) 'I remember entering his lecture-room
when he was to deliver a speech against Milo (*i.e.* a rejoinder to Cicero's
Pro Milone). Self-satisfied as usual, Cestius was saying, "If I were a
Thracian gladiator, I should be a Fusius; if I were a pantomime-actor, I
should be a Bathyllus." Unable to check my wrath I burst out, "Yes, and
if you were a drain, you'd be the main drain!" – huge guffaws from
everybody! The pupils gazed, curious to see what uncouth sort of creature I was. Cestius, ready to answer Cicero, had no answer for me!'[5]

Other interesting points occur in the preface to IV. They include a

---

[1] *Contr.* III. *praef.* 12–14.
[2] VII. *praef.* 7: 'schema dixi.'   [3] IX. *praef.* 3.
[4] *E.g. Contr.* II. i. 34; III. *praef.* 16; IV. *praef.* 10 and 11; VII. *praef.* 4 and
5; VII. iv. 10; IX. v. 15; X. *praef.* 8.
[5] *Contr.* III. *praef.* 16–17; here the 'memini' is in Severus's story.

glance at the select audiences of Asinius Pollio, who was the first to give *recitationes* before invited guests;[1] Seneca's recollection of Pollio's instructing his grandson how to look on both sides of a declamation; and references to the extempore declamations by Q. Haterius, 'the one among all Romans known to me,' he says, 'who transferred Greek facility to Latin.' His speed of utterance made Augustus remark, 'Our friend Haterius needs a brake put on' (*sufflaminandus est*). The sketch of Albucius in the preface to VII is diverting. He was fearless in his employment of words expressing *res sordidissimas*: 'sour wine' and 'flea-bane,'... 'latrines'[2] and 'sponges' came all alike to him in speaking. A chameleon orator, for ever adopting fresh styles, he sometimes proved unlucky in his figures, as when he asked rhetorically 'Why is a cup smashed if it falls, and why is a sponge not?', on which Cestius commented, 'To-morrow he'll give a declamation on why thrushes fly and gourds don't!' It was Albucius who, in the debate about a parricide set adrift in a boat, invented the far-fetched joke of calling the boat 'the wooden sack' (*culleum ligneum*) alluding to the sack used in the punishment of parricides.

The incomplete preface to IX resumes the criticism of declamation as unpractical. Seneca recognises the defects afterwards emphasised by Petronius and Tacitus,[3] when he points out that the dominant aim in declamation is to please, not to carry conviction (*non ut uincat sed ut placeat*). This is why it hunts for alluring ornaments (*lenocinia conquirit*) and avoids solid reasoning. Declamations composed on the assumption that one has only fools for opponents (*aduersarios quamuis fatuos fingunt*) must provide a poor training for a court of law. The conditions of practice are too easy in an academic exercise: gladiators, it should be remembered, train with heavier weapons than those with which they fight in the arena.

The final preface is notable for the author's frank confession that he has exhausted his recollections and they him (*fatebor uobis: iam res taedio est*). Indignant at the governmental revenge taken on the writings of Scaurus and of Labienus, he yet thanks heaven that these punishments of genius did not begin until genius itself was deteriorating. Musa's extravagance of language is illustrated and condemned:

> I remember his saying 'Birds that fly, fish that swim, beasts that run, find graves in our insides. Ask now why we men die suddenly – we live by deaths!'

Freeman though he was, Musa, in Seneca's view, richly deserved flogging like the veriest slave for such artificiality. 'Much, I consider, must be allowed to talent,' he adds; 'one must allow faults, but not monstrosities.'

[1] See Funaioli in P.W. *s.v.* Recitatio. The nature of Pollio's innovation is discussed by A. Dalzell in *Hermathena* lxxxvi (Nov. 1955) pp. 20–28.
[2] Accepting Bornecque's *latrinas* for *lanternas*.
[3] *Satyr.* 1–5; *Dial. de Or.* xxxv.

The traditional title *Oratorum et Rhetorum Sententiae Diuisiones Colores* indicates the method. On a case propounded, the sentiments (*sententiae*) and contentions of a number of speakers for or against are given, often mere jottings; then a skeletonic mapping out (*diuisiones*) of *quaestiones* involved; and, finally, a selection of more or less plausible conceptions (*colores*) designed to put a special complexion on certain acts under review. Invention and ingenuity find their best opening in the third group, but the ingenuity often overleaps itself into absurdity. A few extracts from II. i may serve by way of illustration. A rich man who has already disinherited no fewer than three sons, asks for a poor man's only son in order to adopt him: the poor man says 'yes'; but the son says 'no,' and is thereupon disowned by his father. Arguments from eleven speakers in favour of the son are cited, among them those of Porcius Latro and Arellius Fuscus, whose arguments on the other side are afterwards given. Latro opens for the youth: 'And this is my fate – disowned and adopted at the same moment! The home that sheltered my father up to old age cannot admit me! . . . (*To the rich man*) You suppose gold and silver to be riches, but they are the playthings of fortune. I give you warning: even if I come to you, I shall take care – and it is a very easy thing in *your* house – to get disinherited! Strange things do happen, but I never dreamt that my father would hate children, or the rich man want them. I desire no patrimony: happiness is a frail fleeting thing' – and he cites examples. Vibius Rufus makes the young man argue: 'The very father that does not like keeping his children, judges it necessary to have children! I invited his disinherited sons into our humble abode. Am I going to rob them of their home after promising them mine! What am I to do? If I obey, I shall get disinherited: if I don't obey, I shall get disinherited. I love my father: and that is my offence.' Among Fuscus's points are these: '(*To the rich man*) You ask for a son: well, there are crowds of youths without a father! (*To his father*) Lay on me any command you choose: I shall go to sea, go on war-service, provided that, wherever I am, I remain yours'; and much of his oration turns on the perils of wealth. Then Fabianus also declaims against the corrupting influence of riches, and uses his noted gift of description to contrast domestic decoration with natural landscape scenery, which is the possession of the poor. When Latro in turn argues for the father, he represents him as saying: 'If I did not know what an evil poverty is, I should understand it now: my son does not dread being disowned. The Metelli had access to the busts of the Fabricii; adoption amalgamated the families of the Aemilii and the Scipios. From the foundation of Rome to our own days our famous patrician nobility has depended on it. Adoption cures the wounds of fortune (*adoptio fortunae remedium est*).' The marshalling of arguments under the *diuisio* follows: *e.g.* Pompeius Silo begins, on behalf of the reluctant son, with the trite question, 'Is a father to be obeyed in all things? And even if in all things, does this include an act that would make him no longer one's father? Can a son be handed over for adoption against his will? If he cannot, can he be disowned for exercising his own will?' and so through logical alternatives on to his proof that the proposed adoption was, firstly, disgraceful; secondly, useless; thirdly, dangerous. When the *colores* are reported, Seneca comments on their risky allurements and adduces warning examples of silliness. He does not mince words when he disapproves. This is a *color* from Latro in defence of the young man, who is supposed to say: 'I was always friendly with the three disowned sons: I am their friend still. When they were disinherited, I advised them to keep quiet and by yielding soften their father. I told them, "As soon as you think it the right time, my father will entreat yours." Well, now they assure me that the most favourable moment is here. They are right: my father cannot find any more favourable moment for the reconciliation: the rich man is seeking sons.' And here is Latro's *color* when he spoke on the other side: 'This,' says the father to his son, 'is my aim: I want to hand you over for adoption, so that the disowned sons may be by your means more readily reconciled to their father.'

While the exact point at issue varies greatly in the *Controuersiae*, the general question under debate falls into one of three types – criminal, civil, social. The fourth book may illustrate this division, as well as the unlikelihood of the themes. Of its eight cases, three are criminal, three civil, and two involve questions of public status. The criminal cases are: (IV. i). A man is dragged from the grave of his three children by a wild young roisterer who plays upon him the prank of forcibly shaving him, dressing him in festal attire and compelling him to take part in a banquet; (iv) During war-time a man who has lost his weapons in battle seizes weapons from a hero's tomb, fights bravely and restores them: he is charged with sacrilegious violation of the monument; (vi) A man's wife dies in giving birth to a boy: the father marries soon after, and the boy borne by the second wife has a remarkable resemblance to his half-brother. Both are brought up in the country and become almost indistinguishable. After many years, on their reappearance in town, the father, who knows which is the elder, will not tell his wife which is her child: he is charged with cruelty. The civil cases are: (iii) The ravisher of a girl secures from her exiled father a command that she shall elect to marry him, but her brother at home insists on her claiming the culprit's death: the brother is disinherited for opposing his father's will; (v) A stepson, who is a doctor, declines to attend his stepmother, and his father disinherits him; (viii) A proscribed master in time of civil war is sheltered by a faithful freedman to whom he promises remission of all future claims on his service; when he is restored to his belongings, he makes demands on the freedman, which the latter resists. The two cases of status are: (ii) Metellus, in rescuing the

Palladium from the burning temple of Vesta, has lost his eye-sight: as a blind man, he is refused the right to exercise the priesthood; (vii) A man taken in adultery by a tyrant wrests his sword from him, kills him, and claims a public prize as a tyrannicide.

In the whole collection the criminal charges predominate: of the 74, there are 30 criminal, 26 civil, while 18 affect status. But many side issues are involved. There are about a score of cases concerning immoral relations such as adultery, seduction, outrage and prostitution: almost as many turn on the disinheriting of children; seven on poisoning; seven on tyrants, a theme more at home in Greece. Pirates add a mild flavour of danger to some, but again and again the imagined circumstances are hopelessly unnatural and bizarre, and encourage extravagance of treatment and style. Certain *controuersiae* sound like sketchy novels with impossible plots, and must have been so handled in the *narratio* of a clever rhetor, who aimed at the diversion of a leisured and *blasé* audience. One instance[1] combines the following episodes: a tyrant is slain; an illicit *liaison* results in homicide; a father's intercessions are rejected by a son, who is afterwards captured by pirates; they demand a ransom, but the unforgiving father replies that, if they cut off their prisoner's hands, he will pay twice the amount; the captive is eventually liberated by the gang; later the father falls into beggary; and finally his son refuses to help him. Anything may be expected in such a jumble – rhetorical outbursts, Homeric quotations, a plea of insanity, or the *color* devised by a professor with a voice like a hundred fellows roaring themselves hoarse (*centum raucorum uocem*) to the effect that the father's offer to the pirates 'You will be paid double for cutting his hands off' was merely a regrettable secretarial error (*librario una syllaba excidit 'non'*) for 'You will be paid double for *not* cutting his hands off!'

The ultimate sources of most of the themes are undiscoverable. Many had become stereotyped in Greek rhetorical schools, and, with little or no modification, were transmitted through generations at Rome. Thus, actual Greek history supplied material for the *suasoria* on Alexander's entry into Babylon, and Greek tragedy for Agamemnon's deliberation whether he shall immolate his daughter. Sometimes the historical kernel was of the smallest. It is, for instance, an invention that the Athenians deliberated about removing their Persian trophies under Xerxes's threat to return with his army. Sometimes the law invoked was a genuine one from the Attic code: often, however, it was a figment of the schools. An example is the debate on whether the priestess convicted of immorality who was thrown from a rock and survived might be subjected to punishment a second time: by Roman law a guilty priestess was buried alive. From Sulla's time onwards there had been a growing accumulation of material for the free use of declaimers either to thrash out on Greek lines or to fuse with Roman elements. The

[1] *Contr.* I. vii.

treatise *Ad Herennium* and Cicero's *De Inuentione* supply a long list of themes drawn from Roman as well as from Greek history; but details were liberally altered in declamations to secure rhetorical effect; for a good point counted more than historical accuracy. Mythology was also a source: and fertile imagination yet another.

Seneca's ability as a writer is shown both in his suggestive comments and in a Boswellian aptitude for reproducing the words and style of others. In criticism nothing could be sounder than his grasp of that psychological endowment which made Ovid successful in a *suasoria*, of the wilfulness which made that poet love the bizarre lines which others censured, and the quality in his lost oratory which made it poetic prose (*solutum carmen*, *Contr.* II. ii. 8). Most illuminating are the remarks on Montanus's passion for repetitions: he was 'the Ovid of orators' because he could not let well alone (*nescit quod bene cessit relinquere*, *Contr.* IX. v. 17). It argues a genuine feeling for style that Seneca, besides characterising good and bad speakers, can also represent their actual manner, such as Latro's exclamatory qualities in Book I or his outburst on Popillius's barbarity in killing Cicero in Book VII. Similarly in the case of the Roman official who had a man beheaded at a banquet to satisfy the curiosity of a *fille de joie*, Seneca reproduces Murredius's tetracolon which ended in nonsense 'to complete the rhythm' – 'Justice was subservient to the bed-chamber, a praetor to a harlot, prison to a banquet, day to night' (*Seruiebat forum cubiculo, praetor meretrici, carcer conuiuio, dies nocti*, IX. ii. 27). The heartlessness of the same scene is vividly brought home by Seneca's illustration of Vibius Gallus's realism, 'A toast was drunk to the headsman for his deft stroke' (*lictori quia bene percusserat propinatum est*, IX. ii. 23).

The pernicious effect of some of the subjects upon the morality of pupils may easily be overstated. It is doubtful whether there was more of the violent and the illicit in them than is illustrated on a modern cinema film, which does not provide an equal stimulus towards thought and expression. Much, indeed, in ancient declamations was morally sound and bracing, even if rather commonplace: there was a healthy spirit in the denunciations of luxury and of tyranny, which might pass safely in an academic exercise, but might spell ruin in a historical work under the Empire. It is, besides, doubtful whether students altogether failed to realise the unreality of their controversial world; even the far-fetched elements may be said to have been attempts to satisfy the perennial human desire for romance. With so many stock subjects common to the successive periods represented by Seneca, Quintilian and the pseudo-Quintilian, by Calpurnius Flaccus,[1] and later in Greek by Libanius, it was inevitable that sensible arguments should run dry,

[1] For parallels between subjects in Seneca, the pseudo-Quintilian and Calpurnius Flaccus, see T. S. Simonds, *Themes Treated by Elder Seneca*, Baltimore 1896, pp. 71–81.

and relief from the hackneyed should be sought either in artificial embroidery or in capricious invention. The incentive to invent operated
often without the check of common sense: so that one is reminded of
nothing so much as of the pedantically ingenious questions which were
devised by the fantastic imagination of the Troubadours to be pleaded
and decided in a Court of Love.

Ingenuity is so characteristic of the Silver Age that it deserves to be
noted in the making. It is most observable in the cunningly contrived
rebuttal of a charge. At first sight, one might condemn as beyond all
excuse the scandalous practical joke already mentioned which was
played upon a man at his children's grave. Subjected forcibly to a
fashionable toilette, the mourner had been presented by an unruly
young reveller to his boon companions and coerced into attending their
banquet in a neighbouring garden. What fair complexion shall an enter-
prising defence put upon such conduct? One answer to the prosecution
follows these lines: Was it not reasonable to be touched by the old man's
mourning and loneliness! Was it not heart-breaking to notice that he had
no kinsman to console him? Now when it is too late, the offenders, of
course, can see that his friends must have deserted him, because they
knew he was mad. In fact, 'all was meant in kindness' is the explanation
offered by this misunderstood young gentleman! 'It was a festive occasion, and I was entertaining some of my good friends, when one of
them said, "Why do we let that poor fellow in the cemetery kill himself
with grief? Nobody can make up his mind spontaneously to abandon
sorrow: people are bashful about it: they want compulsion . . ."' To
prove the continuance of his friendly attitude, the defendant assures the
complainant: 'I'm perfectly ready to give you more consolation of the
same sort – only, you'd just accuse me again!' The danger of such
smartness in rhetoric and in literature is that it constantly tends to be
overdone. Ingenuity of idea and phrase palls even in Ovid and in Lucan;
but, indulged in by the smaller mind of a rhetorician in quest of specious
argument or pointed epigram, it becomes grotesque, as Seneca shows
by his censures.

The seven deliberative exercises, or *Suasoriae*, exhibit similar rhetorical qualities to those in the *Controuersiae*, and furnish continued
proof of the attraction which digressive anecdotes, luckily for his readers,
possessed for Seneca. At times he conscientiously pulls himself up
(*longius me fabellarum dulcedo produxit; itaque ad propositum reuertar*,
Suas. i. 7); but to his deviations from the strict lines of argument we
owe interesting comments, *e.g.*, on Virgil's avoidance of bombast (i. 12);
Pedo's lines describing Germanicus's voyage (i. 15); Arellius Fuscus's
description of the moon in contrast with Virgil's simpler and happier
words (iii. 4); Gallio's amusingly nonchalant attitude towards im-
passioned oratory at which he jested as 'plena deo' (iii. 6–7); the records
of Pollio's hostility to Cicero's reputation (vi. 14); an extract from Livy

on the death of Cicero (vi. 17); Cornelius Severus's hexameters on the same subject (vi. 26); and Cestius's praise of Cicero's services in exalting the Latin language over Greek (vii. 10).

Seneca had not spared foolish arguments in the *Controuersiae*. Murredius, quoted in the seventh book for a foolish point regarding Popillius, the ungrateful murderer of Cicero, and for another ineptitude on a poisoning charge is declared in the ninth book to be 'as silly as ever.'[1] In the murder mystery, where a woman is found wounded, her husband killed, and a breach made in the wall between the house and the neighbouring one, Seneca justifiably stigmatised as fatuous the bit of description 'My father had holes made in him as if he were the wall' (*pater meus tamquam paries perfossus est*).[2] So it is with absurdities in the *Suasoriae*. The deliberations of the 300 Spartans in the pass whether to retreat or face the Persian are marked both by excellences and by inanities. 'Whither will you, hoplites, flee, who are yourselves the walls of Sparta?' – that, in four neat words,[3] is cited by Seneca as the best hit made by any Greek speaker in this *suasoria*. On the other hand, his strictures upon overstrained point are severe; for he says the prize-winner for puerility (*inter has pueriles sententias uidetur palmam meruisse*) was the speaker who played with the conceit that the inscription to the fallen Spartans was written in blood squeezed from their wounds – 'ink,' he exclaimed, 'worthy of a Spartan!' (where the Latin *atramentum* gives a more violent contrast to the red blood). The last *suasoria* concludes with two remarks from 'that most likeable fool' Gargonius, 'than which not even he had ever said anything sillier.' Turgid rhetoric receives corresponding castigation. The author, in making fun of his namesake Seneca 'Grandio' (ii. 17), so called because he liked everything big from sandals to a sweetheart, recalls his handling of the 300 Spartans at bay. Lifting his arms and rising on his toes (that was his way of making himself bigger!) he declaimed in swelling accents a Spartan's imaginary soliloquy: 'So all Greece has abandoned us. So much the better, I am glad, I am glad.' We wondered, remarks Seneca drily, what there was to be glad about. 'Why? Because I shall now have the Persian to myself. That monarch, Xerxes, who has stolen seas with his armada, who has confined the earth but extended the deep, whose orders impose a new aspect upon universal nature, that monarch may doubtless encamp over against the heavens; but I shall have the gods for comrades!' If the elder Seneca's good sense had been more widely shared, such bombast would have been frowned out of existence.

From these exercises, then, one may take an inventory, as it were, for the literary stock-in-trade of Silver Latin. There are exclamatory and high-flown outbursts typified in the apostrophe to the monster of cruelty who maimed foundlings to make money out of their begging;[4]

---

[1] *Contr.* VII. ii. 14, iii. 8; IX. iv. 22. [2] VII. v. 10.
[3] *Suas.* ii. 14: ποῖ φεύξεσθε, ὁπλῖται, τείχη ; [4] *Contr.* X. iv. 2.

commonplaces on themes like the mutability of fortune,[1] or the effect of calamity on the mind; *sententiae*, embodying ancient wisdom in proverbial form, such as 'The cure may be worse than the disease' (*quaedam remedia grauiora ipsis periculis sunt*), 'There are many paths to death,' 'Innocence is a protection in danger,' 'Nature has given none the breath of life for ever';[2] the purple patches in elaborate descriptions of ocean or tempest or natural scenery;[3] the brief and pointed epigram designed to surprise by ingenuity or paradox, 'Weeping is a modest curse directed against human calamity (*fletus humanarum necessitatum uerecunda exsecratio est*);[4] and the frequently allied antithesis, 'the greatest runaways among the brave, the greatest laggards among runaways' (*inter fortes fugacissimi, inter fugaces tardissimi*).[5] The indictment which lies against rhetoric for extravagance in the use of these and other artifices, and for its frequent self-divorce from real life, must not blind us to the good services which it rendered. Though but a simulacrum of the old free oratory, it was cherished by the Romans with almost pathetic assiduity, and from their devotion to it as an end in itself they gained at least sharpened wits and facility of expression. The rhetorical training maintained in the Empire a high standard of ability in the use of language. This was not its sole advantage. Declaimers were not, as a rule, politicians, but the declamations afforded a safe outlet for a certain amount of social criticism and even a certain amount of republican feeling. Some of the themes, we have seen, gave the mind the satisfaction of entering upon mildly romantic adventures. The very fact that the law assumed in a case was not the actual law of Rome aided the growth of a new sentiment of equity. Further, there was ethical value in the moral and humane reflections of an experienced declaimer, while the attacks made upon luxury and riches were in keeping with a literary exaltation of the poor and the humble, which implied a broadening conception of the worth of the individual. To suppose that the declamations produced merely expert phraseology and did not stimulate thought is a profound mistake.

Seneca places before us the speakers of two generations in Rome, who by their various nationalities – Italian, Greek, Spanish and Gallic – indicate the cosmopolitan hold obtained by rhetoric. Most of the older generation, as Augustans, are outside our present limits;[6] some speakers belong to both generations; and some definitely to the reign of Tiberius. Of the quartette (τετράδιον) placed by Seneca in the highest rank[7] –

[1] *Suas*. i. 9.
[2] *Contr*. VI. vii. 2; VII. i. 9, i. 10; *Suas*. ii. 2.
[3] *Suas*. i. 2; *Contr*. VII. i. 26 (in Greek); *Suas*. ii. 8 (Thermopylae).
[4] *Contr*. VIII. vi. 3.   [5] *Suas*. ii. 4.
[6] On Augustan rhetoricians see Duff, *L.H.R.* p. 456; Tfl. 268; S.H. 334–337.
[7] *Contr*. X. *praef*. 13.

Porcius Latro, Arellius Fuscus, Albucius Silus and Junius Gallio – the
first three had been recognised as eminent before the Christian era
began. Ovid studied under Latro and Fuscus, and doubtless a subtle
portion of their rhetorical influence descended through the poet to his
imitators in the first century. Fuscus also had for a pupil Papirius
Fabianus, a philosopher still more than a speaker, who taught the
younger Seneca. Gallio, whose arguments are often exemplified in the
Controuersiae, was noted for a jingle (*tinnitus*) of style in speaking. One
of his writings was an answer composed to Labienus's invective against
Bathyllus, the favourite of Maecenas; and other publications of his
were declamations and a treatise on rhetoric. He was exiled in A.D. 32.
Though Cestius Pius from Smyrna was pre-Tiberian, his pupils, Sur-
dinus, Aietius Pastor, Quintilius Varus (son of the general crushed by
the Germans in A.D. 9), formed a group towards the beginning of
Tiberius's reign; and Argentarius, his assiduous ape (*Cestii simius*), belonged clearly to the same time. Cestius had a swarm of followers who,
we have seen, learned by heart his speeches in preference to Cicero's.

In passing to speakers definitely under Tiberius, Caligula and
Claudius, it is worth while to remember that the emperors themselves
were by education products of the rhetorical system. Tiberius,[1] as a
student of rhetoric under Theodorus of Gadara, imbibed new principles
– very different from those which his predecessor Augustus had learned
from Apollodorus of Pergamum. The Apollodoreans, emphasising *nar-*
ratio, stood for regularity in the division and structure of a speech,
whereas the Theodoreans, eager for greater freedom, were content if the
argumentatio alone was adequately handled. Tiberius's years of retirement at Rhodes, before he was emperor, had perfected his acquaintance
with Greek rhetoric; and his skill in the diplomatic and even cryptic
use of language is apparent in the reports of his senatorial speeches given
by Tacitus.[2] In Latin, his tendency was to prefer archaic to foreign
words and to base his oratory on the manner of Messalla Corvinus.
Among his literary compositions were memoirs, while his verses showed
the influence of Euphorion and other Greek poets. His successor, C.
Caesar Caligula, from whose insane jealousy sprang his desire to anni-
hilate the works of Homer, and his scathing attacks upon Virgil as well
as Livy, did not publish works, though he was well trained in rhetoric,
capable as a speaker especially when stimulated by anger, and critically
contemptuous of the younger Seneca's style as 'sand minus mortar.'[3]
His uncle Claudius, the next emperor, was a voluminous writer in
Greek and Latin. An early taste which he evinced for history had been
fostered by Livy; and his learning in other fields was extensive. Now a
play, now a book on gambling, now an apology for Cicero against the

[1] Suet. *Tib.* lxvii, lxx ('artes liberales utriusque generis studiosissime coluit');
ibid. lxxi; *Dom.* xx; Sen. *Suas.* iii. 7.
[2] *Ann.* IV. xxxi; XIII. iii.   [3] Suet. *Cal.* xxxiv and liii.

strictures of Asinius Gallus, came from his pen. He even proposed three additional letters, the inverted digamma (Ⅎ) for consonantal *u*, antisigma (Ɔ) for *ps*, and the left half of H (Ⱶ) for the *y* sound between *i* and *u*.[1] Part of the speech delivered by Claudius before the senate in A.D. 48, supporting the admission of Gallic nobles to Roman offices, was found recorded on a bronze tablet at Lyons in 1524, and forms an interesting subject of comparison with the version by Tacitus (*Ann.* XI. xxiv). Claudius's consort, Agrippina, wrote memoirs, which the elder Pliny and Tacitus consulted.[2]

Of rhetoricians at least partly of the time of Tiberius, like the Asprenates, the Bruttedii, Turrinus and Capito, it is enough to distinguish the last for his declamation regarding Cicero's murderer Popillius, which remained in circulation and was erroneously ascribed to Latro.[3] Many speakers published collections of their speeches or manuals on speaking. Junius Otho, praetor in A.D. 22, was the author of four books on *Colores*;[4] and Rutilius Lupus, towards the end of Seneca's lifetime, brought out an abridged translation of a work on figures of speech by Gorgias, who taught at Athens in the first century B.C. Alfius Flavus, one of Cestius's pupils, wrote also in verse. Senatorial eloquence under Tiberius was (in addition to Junius Otho) represented by Asinius Gallus, son of Asinius Pollio, and inheritor of his caustic style; Aeserninus, Pollio's grandson; Valerius Messallinus Cotta, younger son of the Augustan Messalla Corvinus, and consul in A.D. 20, a pleasure-seeker with gifts in verse-making and in pleading (Ovid in exile had read a speech which he had delivered in court); Mamercus Scaurus, the easygoing aristocrat whose friendship with Sejanus and authorship of a tragedy, *Atreus*, proved his ruin; Q. Haterius, who died an old man in A.D. 26 and whose startlingly rapid delivery called forth Augustus's remark, already mentioned, that he needed a brake put on;[5] L. Arruntius, a man of ability at once academic and forensic; Votienus Montanus, from Narbo, who made his mark in an inheritance case for Galla Numisia, and was exiled for treason in A.D. 25; and L. Calpurnius Piso, one of the most dignified characters of the day, who alarmed Tiberius on one occasion by denouncing the infamy of informers and threatening to quit Rome in disgust.

To the time of Caligula and Claudius belongs Crispus Passienus, son and grandson of the two Augustan Passieni. His published speeches were among those familiar to students in Quintilian's boyhood.[6] It is notable that Caligula allowed the condemned works of certain Augustan

[1] Suet. *Claud.* xli; *Tac. Ann.* XI. xiv; Quint. *I. Or.* I. vii. 26.
[2] Plin. *N.H.* VII. 46; Tac. *Ann.* IV. liii.
[3] Sen. *Contr.* X. *praef.* 12.
[4] Sen. *Contr.* I. iii. 11; II. i. 33.
[5] Tac. *Ann.* IV. lxi; Sen. *Contr.* IV. *praef.* 7: 'sufflaminandus est.'
[6] *I. Or.* X. i. 24: 'nobis pueris insignes *Pro Voluseno Catulo* Domitii Afri, Crispi Passieni, D. Laelii orationes ferebantur.'

orators and historians, T. Labienus, Cremutius Cordus and Cassius
Severus, to circulate again.[1] Of these Cremutius belongs to the annals
of history. Labienus, more noted as an orator than as a historian, was
disliked for exceeding the due limits of free speech, and his enemies were
pleased when his books were given to the flames by senatorial decree
about A.D. 12.[2] The blow was one which he refused to survive. Cassius
Severus, another prominent orator in the *Controuersiae*, had offended
Augustus by libels upon men and women of high station, and died in
miserable poverty after twenty-five years of exile. There are reasons
for believing that his death happened about A.D. 37, five years later than
the date assigned by Jerome. Tacitus connects with his condemnation
the first application of the *lex maiestatis* to writings.[3]

Many orators were occupied rather as political accusers than as
literary creators, finding it lucrative to place delation at the service of
any emperor whose aim was to ruin the potentially dangerous scions of
aristocratic families, the so-called opposition under the Caesars. Some
were unquestionably able persons, like Domitius Afer of Nemausus
(Nîmes), who pleaded in the law-courts, occupied high positions in
several reigns, and was known for legal writings *De Testibus*, and for
published speeches mentioned by Quintilian. He had begun his career
as an accuser by A.D. 26, and lived into Nero's times (A.D. 59).[4] P.
Suillius, one of the dreaded informers under Claudius, eventually fell
himself under sentence of banishment. Vibius Crispus, already by
Claudius's time active in the nefarious intrigues of the delator, survived
until about A.D. 90, one of many links between this period and the
Flavian age.

[1] Suet. *Cal.* xvi: 'Titi Labieni, Cordi Cremuti, Cassi Seueri scripta senatus-
consultis abolita requiri et esse in manibus lectitarique permisit.'
[2] Sen. *Contr.* X. *praef.* 4–5 and 7.
[3] Tac. *Ann.* I. lxxii; IV. xxi; Sen. *Contr.* III. *praef.*
[4] Tac. *Dial.* xiii; *Ann.* IV. lii and lxvi; Plin. *Ep.* II. xiv. 10; Quint. *I. Or.*
V. vii. 7; VIII. v. 16; IX. ii. 20, iii. 66, iv. 31; X. i. 24 and 118.

Chapter II

VALERIUS MAXIMUS – A REPERTORY FOR SPEAKERS

Valerius Maximus – His date – His nine books and their aim –
A collection for rhetoricians – Method and arrangement –
National subject-matter and spirit – Sources – Survival of his
influence through abridgements – Limitations in historical outlook – Adulation of the Caesars – Moralising and sententious
reflections – His style a mirror of the period – The poetic element – Rhetorical exclamations and declamations – Balanced
structure – Artificial conceits – Language – Abstractions – Vocabulary and syntax.

LITTLE can be surmised regarding the life of Valerius Maximus,
the compiler of a significant repertory for rhetoricians; but that
little is enough to settle his period. Vossius,[1] rejecting the suggestion that he belonged to the third century A.D., proved that he must
be referred to the age of Tiberius; and there is not much to add to his
arguments. Aulus Gellius, in the second century, cites from the eighth
book of Valerius.[2] Further, what are almost the only explicit personal
reminiscences in Valerius's work afford evidence of date; for his great
friend, the eloquent Sextus Pompeius, with whom he visited Asia and
to whose kindly patronage he pays a tribute in his chapter on friendship,
is identical with one of the consuls in the last year of Augustus's and the
first year of Tiberius's reign, A.D. 14.[3] Pompeius was also a friend of
Germanicus, and the patron to whom Ovid addressed certain epistles
from Pontus:[4] he became proconsul of Asia about A.D. 27. Besides, the
tone in which Brutus and Cassius are charged with 'parricide' for their
share in the assassination of Julius Caesar savours of the repressive times

[1] *De Historicis Latinis* (1624) prefixed to many editions of Valerius.
[2] Gell. *N.A.* XII. vii; 'Scripta haec historia est in libro Valerii Maximi
Factorum et Dictorum Memorabilium octauo' (*i.e.* Val. Max. VIII. i. *sub fin.*).
[3] Val. Max. II. vi. 8; 'Asiam cum Sex. Pompeio petens Iulidem oppidum
intraui.' *Cf.* IV. vii. *ext.* 2: 'Pompeium meum . . . a quo omnium incrementa
commodorum ultro oblata cepi . . . qui studia nostra ductu et auspiciis suis
lucidiora et alacriora reddidit.'
[4] *Ex Ponto* IV. i. and v. For Pompeius as speaker, *cf. Ex Ponto* IV. iv. 37
('facundo ore'); Val Max. II. vi. 8 ('facundissimo sermone'); Tac. *Ann.* III.
xi.

of Tiberius.[1] Confirmatory impressions may be derived from Valerius's style; and, finally, if more precision in dates be desired for an author not so lavish in their use as Velleius Paterculus was, then two passages may be cited bearing on the time of composition. The prefatory remarks to his treatment of *pudicitia* must have been written before Livia's death in A.D. 29; and the denunciation directed against Sejanus (though it does not name him) must have been written after his downfall in A.D. 31.[2] Valerius's work, then, appeared at latest within a few years after the publication of Velleius's history in A.D. 30; for its dedication to Tiberius, who is the Caesar addressed[3] and often flattered, shows that it was not subsequent to the close of his reign in A.D. 37.

His work, *Facta et Dicta Memorabilia*, consists, as we have it, of nine books; and though his epitomator, Julius Paris, implies there were ten, this is most likely an error. The author's aim will be best understood in the light of a summary of the contents:

Book I. Religion, auspices, omens, prodigies and marvels, ranging from more to less awe-inspiring instances – from a mysterious utterance or miraculous intervention of a god, to such merely curious cases as those of the man who forgot how to read, or the princess with a double row of teeth, or a heart stuffed with hairs!

Book II. A *pot-pourri* of subjects, perhaps in this book more loosely interrelated than in any – marriage, magistracies, military regulations and discipline, public games, foreign customs, censorial strictness, and so on.

Book III. Mental and moral endowments, bravery, endurance, rise from humble origin to greatness, degeneracy, self-confidence, etc.

Book IV. Moderation, abstinence, conjugal love, friendship, generosity, etc.

Book V. Clemency, gratitude, ingratitude, filial duty, brotherly affection, patriotism, paternal love and severity.

Book VI. Chastity, outspoken retorts, strict punishments, weighty words and acts, justice, national honour, fidelity of wives and of slaves (where the comment *quo minus exspectatam hoc laudabiliorem fidem* speaks eloquently of the prevailing distrust felt by masters), and mutability of fortune.

Book VII. Good fortune, wise sayings or acts, smart sayings or acts, military ruses, defeat at elections, the straits of necessity, wills cancelled or ratified.

[1] I. v. 7, viii. 8; VI. iv. 5; *cf.* proceedings taken by creatures of Sejanus in A.D. 25 against Cremutius Cordus for having praised Brutus and Cassius, Tac. *Ann.* IV., xxxiv.   [2] VI. i. *praef.*; IX. xi. *ext.* 4.

[3] I. *praef.*: 'Te igitur huic coepto, penes quem hominum deorumque consensus maris ac terrae regimen esse uoluit, certissima salus patriae, Caesar, inuoco: cuius caelesti prouidentia uirtutes, de quibus dicturus sum, benignissime fouentur, uitia seuerissime uindicantur.' H. Peter, *Die Geschichtliche Lit. über d. röm. Kaiserzeit*, Lpz. 1897, I. p. 15, gives the date between A.D. 29 and 32. See S.H. 423 for the question of more precise dating.

Book VIII. A book covering an extensive range, but furnishing only a few brief examples under some of its headings – Acquittals and convictions in public trials, famous private law-suits, women who pleaded cases, testimony borne in court, those who committed faults which they punished in others, industry, leisure, eloquence, expression and gesture, striking effects of the arts, memorable old age, desire of glory, magnificent honours conferred.

Book IX. Luxury and lust, cruelty, anger and hatred, avarice, arrogance, perfidy, temerity, mistakes, vengeance, wicked sayings and doings, deaths out of the common, desire of life, enrolment in families by fraud.

This fairly full but not exhaustive list serves to indicate the author's intention to illustrate subjects likely to be touched on by an orator. The design relates the work to the rhetoric of the times. Here was ready for use a collection of noteworthy anecdotes constituting a serviceable *Vade mecum* for speakers or teachers. And this aim, easily discernible from a table of contents, is openly avowed by the compiler: his task, he tells us, was to make a handy digest of memorable deeds and sayings with a view to saving his readers the trouble of hunting among the scattered authorities whose writings he himself had to consult.[1] It is a fair guess that he was a professor of rhetoric.

Dividing each book into chapters on separate topics, Valerius generally subdivides each chapter into Roman and foreign examples. The latter (*externa*) are fewer and are sometimes omitted.[2] Occasionally he confesses to a sense of perplexity between the mass of available material (*sermo infinitis personis rebusque circumfusus*) and the claims of reasonable brevity:[3] and so he feels bound under certain heads to reduce the number of examples (*satietas modo uitanda est*).[4] Some parts of the work show little sign of systematic dovetailing: others exhibit closer interconnexion. From time to time he is at pains to indicate his method of grouping illustrations; thus, he exemplifies self-confidence, first in war, next in peace, then introduces the poet Accius avowedly as a link between Roman and foreign instances.[5] Or, again, just as he is about to pass to foreign examples, some insistent Roman illustration may arrest his attention with a demand to be recorded (*ad externa iam mihi exempla transire conanti M. Bibulus ... manus inicit*);[6] and equal emphasis marks

---

[1] I. *praef.* . . . 'ab illustribus electa auctoribus digerere constitui, ut documenta sumere uolentibus longae inquisitionis labor absit.'

[2] Some subjects are especially Roman, *e.g.* II. i, *De Matrimoniorum Ritu*, or VII. v, *De Repulsis*. It is inaccurate to say that 'each chapter' has the section on *externa* as was alleged in earlier editions of Teuffel, § 279, 2.

[3] IV. i. 12; *cf.* VI. iv, *ad init.*: 'ex abundanti copia nec parca nimis nec rursus auida manu.'

[4] III. viii. *ext.* 1.

[5] III. vii. 11: 'ut ab eo decentius ad externa transeamus, producatur in medium'; *cf.* transition from 'bona fiducia' to 'constantia,' III. viii, *ad init.*; and from praises of poverty to 'uerecundia,' IV. v, *ad init.*   [6] IV. i. 15.

his transition from Book IV to V – from generosity to its 'fit companions, humanity and clemency.' These and other such instances prove that he had an artistic regard for unity, and that it would be unfair to view him as an accumulator of higgledy-piggledy miscellanea.

In subject-matter, and in spirit no less, he is decidedly national. The predominance of examples from native life, custom and history makes this inevitable; yet it is, after all, but one aspect of the Roman in him. He is Roman in the practical aim wherewith he composed his digest for rhetoricians and their pupils; in the typical position assigned to religion at the forefront of the work; and in the conservative note upon which his text opens. This Roman conservatism animates his dignified pride in recording the ancestral habit of referring intricate ceremonial to pontifical wisdom, the sanction for action to augural observation, oracular responses to prophetic books, and the fit treatment for portents to the lore of Etruria. About illustrations from foreign history he is conscious that, if they do not make the same direct appeal as national examples, still they introduce a pleasant variety in the Latin subject-matter (*attingam igitur externa; quae, Latinis inserta litteris, ut auctoritatis minus habent, ita aliquid gratae uarietatis afferre possunt*).[1] No less patriotic is the enthusiasm with which, after mentioning the lays of ancient Rome once sung at banquets, he praises the old Roman training, and with a rhetorical climax turns his list of great families so educated into a compliment to the Caesars:

> *Maiores natu in conuiuiis ad tibias egregia superiorum opera carmine comprehensa pangebant, quo ad ea imitanda iuuentutem alacriorem redderent. Quid hoc splendidius, quid etiam utilius certamine? . . . Quas Athenas, quam scholam, quae alienigena studia huic domesticae disciplinae praetulerim? Inde oriebantur Camilli, Scipiones, Fabricii, Marcelli, Fabii: ac ne singula imperii nostri lumina simul percurrendo sim longior, inde, inquam, caeli clarissima pars diui fulserunt Caesares.*[2]

A similar spirit pervades his record of the honour secured for Latin as the official and imperial language everywhere,[3] his apostrophe eulogising Marius's disdain for Greek eloquence;[4] and his genuine admiration for the old national deliberative body: 'The Senate-house was the trusty deep-set heart of the commonwealth, fortified, walled all round with the healthiness of silence. As men crossed its threshold, they cast aside personal and put on national affections.'[5] So too one notes his pride in 'the most tenacious bond of military discipline,' which he pronounces 'the especial glory and mainstay of the Roman power, having been by salutary steadfastness kept untarnished and unscathed to the

---

[1] I. vi. *ext.* 1. [2] II. i. 10.
[3] II. ii. 2. [4] II. ii. 3.
[5] II. ii. 1: 'Fidum erat et altum reipublicae pectus Curia, silentiique salubritate munitum et uallatum undique: cuius limen intrantes, abiecta priuata caritate, publicam induebant.'

present time.'[1] It is the same with his panegyrics upon Rome;[2] his gratified consciousness of the progressive evolution from 'Romulus's small hut' (*paruula Romuli casa*) to 'the pillar of the world' (*terrarum orbis columen*);[3] his belief in the generosity of the Roman people;[4] his rhapsodic outbursts like *O munificentiam gentis Romanae deorum benignitati aequandam!*[5] or his satisfaction in Roman justice.[6]

In the absence of systematic acknowledgement of his borrowings, it is impossible to give an exact account of the sources of Valerius. Any reader will observe that Livy has been largely drawn upon, even though he is mentioned but once.[7] Cicero is mentioned oftener;[8] but the mere occurrence of his name is no gauge of the extent to which he was used. Varro must have been an authority in many instances.[9] We may also infer that he consulted Sallust and Asinius Pollio and, for foreign examples, Trogus.[10] Besides mention of such poets as Livius Andronicus and Accius, there are references to the historian Caelius (Antipater), to the *Collecta* of Pomponius Rufus, and to M. Scaurus's autobiographic *Memoirs*.[11] Cato's work on *Origines* is cited definitely in one passage,[12] and may elsewhere be reasonably thought to have supplied material. That work, as well as Cato's *Orations*, must have been in Valerius's mind when he wrote the words *ornata sunt ab eo* (sc. *Catone*) *litterarum Latinarum monumenta*.[13] About a score of Greek authors are cited. His treatment of sources varies. The original may be copied with fidelity, or paraphrased and rhetorically embellished, or condensed, or sometimes misrepresented thanks to bungling; for superficiality betrays him into many confusions.

Yet, blemishes notwithstanding, there are, as testimonies to a great measure of utility and vitality in his work, at least two well-known abridgements[14] of it – one by Julius Paris, made about the fourth century, and intended, like the ampler original, for schools; the other by Januarius Nepotianus, the extant form of which breaks off in the third book (III. ii. 7), but which was evidently drawn from a manuscript of the

[1] II. vii, *ad init.*   [2] II. vii. 6.   [3] II. viii, *ad init.*
[4] IV. viii. 4.   [5] V. i. 1.   [6] VI. v, *ad init.*
[7] I. viii. *ext.* 19. For literature on the sources see bibl. *re* p. 54. A. Klotz, *Herm.* xliv (1909) 198 ff. gives forty-one anecdotes as common to Val. Max. and Seneca, which he believes came from a book of 'Exempla' derived (possibly by Hyginus) from Livy, Antipater, Cato, etc. R. Helm, 'Val. Max. Seneca u.d. Exemplasammlung,' *Herm.* lxxxiv (1939) 130 ff., rejects the hypothesis of a pre-Valerian collection of 'exempla' and thinks that Val. Max. made his own collection direct from Cicero, Varro, and others.

[8] In Teuffel, § 279, 3, it is erroneously said that Cicero is 'likewise mentioned only once' (*i.e.* VIII. xiii. *ext.* 1); but see VIII. x. 3 and other passages.

[9] III. ii. 24: 'Nisi ea certi auctores, inter quos M. Varro, monumentis suis testata esse uoluissent'; *cf.* II. ii. 6, which may be based on Varro's information 'de senaculis' in his *De Vita Populi Romani*; *cf.* Varro, *De Ling. Lat.* V. 156.

[10] For Trogus as utilised by Val. Max., see R. B. Steele, *A.J.P.* xxxviii (1917) 19 ff.

[11] II. iv. 4; III. vii. 11; I. vii. 6; IV. iv, *ad init.*; IV. iv. 11.

[12] VIII. i. 2.   [13] III. iv. 6.

[14] Galdi, *L'Epitome n. lett. lat.* pp. 128–140.

original superior to any now extant, because it summarises the gap in the first book (I. i. *ext.* 4 – I. iv. *ext.* 1). Possibly the C. Titius Probus, to whom is ascribed in some MSS. the summary on Roman names at the end of Valerius, was an earlier epitomiser than Julis Paris and may have left an epitome afterwards combined with his; but, as the summary on names cannot by any stretch of imagination be called literature, there is scant profit in discussing the date of Titius Probus or his relationship to Julius Paris.[1] Suffice it to add that the existence of late abridgements and the number of MSS. of the full text which have come down are indications of its hold upon medieval education. Niebuhr, indeed, declares: 'Throughout the Middle Ages Valerius Maximus was considered the most important book next to the Bible; it was the mirror of virtues and was translated into all the languages of Europe.'[2] Teuffel[3] more cautiously remarks that he was not rarely read (*nicht selten gelesen*) in the Middle Ages; but even this modified statement is an illustration of the continued enthusiasm for Roman history.

His outlook on the world and his attitude towards historical questions do not argue a penetrating or independent genius. He relates omens and miracles in a spirit of unquestioning superstition; *e.g.*, after his record of prodigies sent by Jupiter to dissuade Pompey from resistance to Caesar, Valerius asserts that 'the overmastering principles of destiny prevented a heart not otherwise possessed by folly from weighing the prodigies aright.'[4] He is also uncritical in his acceptance of traditional stories; if they are ancient, he argues that antiquity should secure credit for them, while it is his own function not to reject as idle such tales as gained the sanction of famous literary documents.[5]

On many historical matters his attitude is distorted by bias. He is an apologist for Caesarism, animated by an unconcealable dislike for inflammatory agitations conducted by the tribunes of the people in the days of the republic.[6] Thus, although he admits the moderation of Tiberius Gracchus, he elsewhere brands him 'an enemy of his fatherland.'[7] Gaius Gracchus he regards as one who might have been a champion of the state, but who preferred to be its impious disturber.[8] Consistently with this anti-democratic leaning, his attitude towards the imperial family is throughout one of such fulsome adulation that the author deteriorates into a toady; and this without, so far as we know, the excuse which may be offered for the flatteries of his contemporary Velleius, on whose personal notice war had forced some of the admittedly able traits in Tiberius. Valerius's invocation had described

---

[1] Teuffel, § 279, 10; *cf.* Galdi, *op. cit.* pp. 141–144.
[2] B. H. Niebuhr, *Lects. on Hist. of Rome*, ed. L. Schmitz, ed. 3, Lond. 1853, vol. i. p. xcvi.
[3] Teuffel, § 279, 5. [4] Val. Max. I. vi. 12.
[5] I. viii. 7: 'nostrum sit inclutis litterarum monumentis consecrata perinde ac uana non refugisse.'
[6] III. viii. 3: 'furialis fax tribunicia.'
[7] IV. i. 8; IV. vii. 1. [8] VIII. x. 1.

the reigning emperor as one 'whose heavenly foresight guarantees a
kindly fostering care for the virtues about which I am to speak'; and he
delights to note that Tiberius has nobly united the blood of the Nerones
with that of the Livii (*in ortum salutaris principis nostri conflueret*).[1]
Again, he makes allusions to the blessings of contemporary life under an
excellent emperor;[2] but his enthusiasm embraces the whole kith and kin
of the Caesars – they are heavenly luminaries risen from the time-
honoured Roman training.[3] So Julius Caesar is mentioned or addressed
in terms of religious adoration, well seen in the apostrophe[4] *Tuas aras
tuaque sanctissima templa, Diue Iuli, ueneratus oro*, ending with an artificially balanced reference to the assassination: 'Then burst forth the
parricidal act of those whose design to subtract thee from the number of
mankind involved thine addition to the conclave of the gods!' Elsewhere
Caesar's good qualities are declared to have given him the *entrée* into
heaven, and his repurchase from pirate captors in earlier days is noted
as a strange transaction on the part of Fortune; for then she ordained
that a small ransom should buy back 'the brightest star in the universe':
why, then, should ordinary men complain concerning Fortune, if she
does not spare even the Caesars, 'sharers in her own divinity'?[5] This
commendation of Caesarism lasts up to the end of the work:[6] now the
author couples Julius and Augustus as *patrem et filium . . . diuinitatis
fastigio iunctos*;[7] now it is on Augustus that he concentrates attention;[8]
now on the palace, as a hallowed abode – *ad Augustam domum, bene-
ficentissimum et honoratissimum templum*.[9] Sycophancy reaches its
acme of enormity in his shameless association of Chastity with the
marriage-bed of the princess Julia.[10]

In another way the narrowness of Valerius's outlook is discernible.
He is given to moralising, a habit which in itself might afford a thinker
opportunities for philosophic criticism of men, conduct and events.
As it is, the actual pronouncements cannot hide the shallowness of the
author's intellect. His denunciations of luxury, partly perhaps sincere
and usually justifiable, are also partly perhaps suggested by conventional

---

[1] II. ix. 6. Tiberius was the son of Livia by Ti. Claudius Nero.
[2] *E.g.* II. i, *ad init.*; *cf.* V. v. 3.   [3] II. i. 10.   [4] I. vi. 13.
[5] VI. ix. 15: 'C. autem Caesar cuius uirtutes aditum sibi in caelum struxerunt.
. . . Parua igitur summa clarissimum mundi sidus in piratico myoparone rependi
Fortuna uoluit'; and, on Julius's care to fall with decency before his assassins,
IV. v. 6: 'in hunc modum non homines exspirant, sed di immortales sedes suas
repetunt'; *cf.* VIII. ix. 3; IX. xv. 2.
[6] *E.g.* IX. xv. 5: 'a Sullana uiolentia Caesariana aequitas reduxit gubernacula
Romani imperii.'
[7] I. vii. 2.
[8] I. vii. 1: 'diui Augusti sacratissima memoria'; IV. vii. 7; IX. xv. 3.
[9] VIII. xv, *ad init.* In II. viii. 7: 'qua postes Augustae domus sempiterna
gloria triumphant,' the allusion is to the old oak near Julius's house which furnished the wreath conferred for saving a citizen's life.
[10] VI. i, *ad init.*: 'Tu (*sc.* Pudicitia) palatii columen, augustos penates sanctis-
simumque Iuliae genialem torum assidua statione celebras': the reading 'Iuliae
gentis' does not greatly mend matters.

sententiae within the cognizance of all educated Romans. These reflections, many of them second-hand or ready-made, constitute practically all his philosophy. He takes few steps towards scientific history. Eagerness to make a point renders him indifferent to healthy doubt; for his aim is to teach, if not history, at least rhetoric, by examples.[1] With almost a fabulist's fondness for pointing a moral, he enjoys conveying lessons on the degeneracy of his fatherland. He has praise for the old-fashioned *probitas* and *continentia* once under censorial scrutiny and by him regarded as the righteousness that strengthens a nation – *quid enim prodest foris esse strenuum, si domi male uiuitur?*[2] Incidentally his protests afford glimpses of social history. He remarks on the advance in luxury at Rome since the days when Rufinus, an ex-consul, was struck off the senatorial roll for acquiring ten pounds' weight of silver plate;[3] and he glances at the contemporary craze for building-sites more extensive than the farm-lands of Cincinnatus.[4] So, too, after dating the growth of Roman pleasure-seeking from the close of the Second Punic War and the conquest of Macedon, he contends that the abrogation of the Oppian law regulating the expenses of women was the thin end of the wedge which made an opening for greater extravagance in adornment.[5] Another passage emphasises the spread of luxurious customs within a single generation – *cuius adulescentia priscos mores uidet, senectus nouos orsa est.*[6] Occasions are fastened upon to inculcate venerable saws on the 'riches of him who hath no desires' (*omnia nimirum habet qui nihil concupiscit*), or on the necessity of checking vice at the start (*neque enim ullum finitur uitium ibi ubi oritur*).[7]

His reflections, however, are not confined to the topic of effeminacy; for there is a wealth of general truths and half-proverbial sayings. They have the pointed expression suitable for clinching an argument or adorning a speech: *e.g.* 'Necessity makes the most effectual hardening for human weakness' (*humanae imbecillitatis efficacissimum duramentum est necessitas*), or 'There is a standing antipathy between valour and poltroonery' (*sic enerues animos odisse uirtus solet*).[8] Similarly, of Theramenes's bravado in toasting his enemy Critias out of the very poison he had been sentenced to drink, 'To face punishment with such ease is assuredly to free oneself from punishment' (*profecto est supplicio se liberare, tam facile supplicium perpeti*);[9] of the harm done to oneself by

---

[1] H. Peter, *op. cit.* I. pp. 15–16: 'indem er die effektvollere Überlieferung auswählt, selbst dann, wenn sein Gewährsmann (Livius) schon Zweifel an ihrer Glaubwürdigkeit angedeutet hatte, ferner selbständig die Pointe möglichst zuspitzt und dabei sich nicht scheut, wissentlich von der Wahrheit abzuweichen, die obendrein noch durch seine Oberflächlichkeit, seinen Leichtsinn und seine Gewissenlosigkeit schwer geschädigt wird; zahllose Anachronismen und Fehler hat er in die Erzählung hineingetragen.' *Cf.* Kempf, Prolegg. to 1st ed. 1854, pp. 26–34; W. Köhler, *Qua ratione Liuii annalibus usi sint historici*, etc., Göttingen 1860, pp. 13, 21 ff.

[2] II. ix, *ad init.*   [3] II. ix. 4.   [4] IV. iv. 7.
[5] IX. i. 3.   [6] IX. i. 5.   [7] IV. iv, *ad init.*; IX. i. 2.
[8] II. vii. 10 and 15.   [9] III. ii. *ext.* 6.

indulgence in angry passion (*dolorem cum inferre uult, patitur*);[1] or of
the altogether admirable bravery that comes from true philosophy
(*illa uehemens et constans animi militia*);[2] or yet again, of the vital interconnexion between home and country.[3] Among more elaborate passages
of this reflective cast is one (with a typical mixture of metaphors) upon
the fleeting nature of human blessings:

> 'Too perishable and frail, too much resembling the toy rattles of
> children, are your so-called human strength and human wealth.
> Their rising tide is as instantaneous as their ebb is sudden: at no
> place and in no person do they stand firmly fixed to steadfast roots;
> but, driven hither and thither by the wayward blast of fortune, they
> miserably plunge in an abyss of disaster those whom they have
> raised aloft and who are now deserted by an unforeseen recoil. And
> so things which by their loss double the bitterness of the hardships
> inflicted ought to be neither considered nor called blessings.[4]

To sum up, although he is superstitious, uncritical, time-serving and
in his moralising somewhat hackneyed, yet Valerius is not to be denied
credit for protesting against luxury, whether in an independent spirit
or from sympathy with the emperor's policy; and occasionally his
genuine appreciation of the greatness of Rome may condone his rhetoric.

This leads to a consideration of his style. Wearing the characteristic
guise of the period, it is rhetorical to the verge of bombast; it is metaphorical; it is, as we have seen, given to *sententiae* and marked by artifice especially in its penchant for the balanced and epigrammatic. At his
briefest he does not hold us – the curt paragraphs allotted to some illustrations are little better than a catalogue; and at times he is himself
conscious of the defects attendant upon this mode of treatment.[5]
Many examples are incidents compressed from such authors as Livy
and, it must generally be added, spoiled in the compressing. How much
more effective, for instance, and dramatic is Livy's handling of the
trick whereby a Roman cheated a Sabine out of a cow intended for a
sacrifice to bring good fortune![6] Still, justice compels the admission that
sometimes Valerius relates a story both briefly and well – particularly
where there is a neat dialogue to introduce. Such merits, however, as he
has fail to raise his conglomerate of anecdotes into an aesthetic whole.

[1] IX. iii, *ad init.*
[2] III. iii. *ext.* 1; the 'militia' is illustrated by examples of 'patientia' which
follow, III. iii. *ext.* 2–4.
[3] V. vi, *ad init.*
[4] VI. ix. *ext.* 7: 'Caduca nimium et fragilia, puerilibusque consentanea cre-
pundiis sunt ista quae uires atque opes humanae uocantur. Affluunt subito, repente dilabuntur: nullo in loco, nulla in persona stabilibus nixa radicibus consistunt; sed incertissimo flatu fortunae huc atque illuc acta, quos sublime
extulerunt, improuiso recussu destitutos, profundo cladium miserabiliter
immergunt. Itaque neque existimari neque dici debent bona, quae inflictorum
malorum amaritudinem desiderio sui duplicant.'
[5] II. vii. 5: 'non digna exempla quae tam breuiter, nisi maioribus urgerer,
referrentur.'   [6] *Cf.* Val. Max. VII. iii. 1, with Livy I. xlv.

The influence of the rhetorical schools dominates his poetic and ex-clamatory vein, and not seldom beguiles him into turgidity. A piece representative of his occasional touch of poetic fancy follows his story about the symbolic wheat-grains heaped by ants into the mouth of the sleeping infant, Midas:

> To the ants of Midas I incline with justice and reason to prefer the bees of Plato; for the former proved harbingers of a prosperity perishable and frail; but the bees foretold prosperity solid and ever-lasting, when they placed the honey inside the lips of the little child asleep in his cradle. On hearing of what had befallen, the inter-preters of prodigies declared that from his mouth should flow a dulcet eloquence unparalleled. Yet to my thinking it was not on Mount Hymettus, fragrant with thyme blossom, that these bees fed, but on the Heliconian mountain-slopes verdant with learning of every kind, and so by the inspiration of the goddesses they instilled into a noble genius the sweetest nourishment of the most exalted eloquence.[1]

Uncurbed by artistic repression, he indulges too freely in the ex-clamatory. This tends to inflation, and through over-employment be-comes wearisome. Take the outburst (*O spectaculum admirabile!*) on the preparations for carrying out the sentence of scourging passed by the dictator Papirius upon his insubordinate master of the horse; or the apostrophe to the dictator Postumius, who adjudged his own son to death for disobedience to a military command.[2] Touching the Mace-donian envoys to Rome, who volunteered to carry the funeral bier of Aemilius Paullus, the author exclaims:

> Twice did Macedonia show our city, Paullus, that you were an illustrious man; during your life, by its spoils; on your death, by its shoulders![3]

It is a forced point made at the expense of simplicity. The section on the praises of poverty ends in characteristic tones:

> Why then do we lacerate with daily invective a moderate fortune, as if that were an especial hardship for mankind? . . . Let us rather rise in spirit and with the memory of the olden times refresh our souls enfeebled by gazing upon money; for by the hut of Romulus, and by the modest dwellings of the ancient Capitol, and by the ever-lasting hearths of Vesta, content to this day with earthen vessels, I swear that no riches can be preferred to the poverty of such men![4]

If the passage were not so declamatory one might accept the suggested implication that the author's means were moderate; as it stands, its autobiographic significance may be doubted.

[1] I. vi. *ext.* 2.   [2] II. vii. 6 and 8.
[3] II. x. 3: 'Bis enim te, Paulle, Macedonia urbi nostrae illustrem ostendit: incolumem, spoliis suis; fato functum, humeris!'
[4] IV. iv. 11.

Akin to the rhetorical element in Valerius are the copiousness and boldness of his metaphors. Their free introduction without a semi-apologetic *uelut* or *quoddam* or *ut ita dicam*, if un-Ciceronian, is in a stylistic sense more modern. The metaphors may be violent, or over-done, or actually mixed. One of many instances occurs in the contrast between Euripides and a self-confident contemporary proud of his powers in rapid composition:

The writings due to the fertile rush (*fertilis cursus*) of the one have collapsed without reaching the first turning-posts of memory (*intra primas metas memoriae*); the work of the other, a product of the lamp and of the hesitating pen, shall be borne with the full sails of fame along the passage of all time.[1]

Again, the degeneracy of Scipio's son is 'a birth of darkness from the lightning' (*Di boni, quas tenebras ex quo fulmine nasci passi estis!*);[2] and the break in the even tenor of Polycrates's happiness is thus expressed: 'Once only did he change his expression, when it was shaken with a very brief jolt of sorrow' (*semel dumtaxat uultum mutauit perquam breui tristitiae salebra succussum*).[3]

The balance so representative of his time is a favourite device in summing up illustrations, as *inimicorum existimatione punitus, suo iudicio finitus* (of the death of Theramenes), or *ita alteri tectum mendacium, alteri ueritas aperta finis uitae fuit*,[4] or in his prologue to Book I, 'the other gods we have received, the Caesars we have given' (*deos enim reliquos accepimus, Caesares dedimus*). In a later book he remarks that in the *collegium poetarum* the difference between the dramatist Accius and a certain member of the Caesar family lay in books not busts (*ibi uoluminum non imaginum certamina exercebantur*), while of Verginius resolved to deliver his daughter from the designs of Appius Claudius he says: *puellam occidit pudicaeque interemptor quam corruptae pater esse maluit*.[5]

His artificiality is largely due to the inveterate habit of hunting for effective contrasts, and to a passion for the epigrammatic in expressing facts and reflections.[6] Overreaching his aim, he constantly falls into far-fetched conceits. Some of these smart sayings are as heartless and taste-less as the headlines of certain modern newspapers. Take his comment

---

[1] III. vii. *ext.* 1; *cf.* II. vii, *ad init.*: 'militaris disciplinae tenacissimum *uinculum* in *cuius sinu ac tutela* serenus tranquillusque beatae pacis status *acquiescit.*'

[2] III. v. 1. Other typical metaphors are: IV. vii. *ext.* 2, 'infulis misericordiae permulseris'; VIII. v. 4, 'quae decora ciuitatis umbone iudiciali repulsa sunt'; IX. ii. 1, 'Sulla . . . omnes Italiae partes ciuilis sanguinis fluminibus inundauit'; IX. iii, *ad init.*, 'ira quoque et odium in pectoribus humanis magnos fluctus ex-citant.'

[3] VI. ix, *ext.* 5.   [4] III. ii. *ext.* 6 and 9.   [5] III. vii. 11; VI. i. 2.

[6] *Cf.* VIII. i. 7: 'uictoriam in ipsa uictoria perdidit'; IX. i. 6: 'eodem tem-pore et in iisdem penatibus diuersa saecula habitarunt, frugalissimum alterum, alterum nequissimum.'

on the intended result of the punishments inflicted upon Romans who
had surrendered to a force of slaves: the object was, he says grimly,

> that those who had been lured by the desire for life into permitting
> runaways richly deserving crucifixion to set up trophies over them,
> those who had not blushed to have the ignominious yoke imposed
> upon their own liberty by the hands of slaves, should now find bitter
> their share in the light of day, and should now have a manly longing
> for that death of which they had felt a womanish dread.[1]

Here the final antithesis between *effeminate timuerant* and *uiriliter opta-
rent* is singularly unnatural and strained. He is scarcely less artificial
when he declares that 'from the gallant wounds' of Cato of Utica 'flowed
more glory than blood,' and that by falling on his sword he taught mankind 'how the upright should prefer honour without life to life without
honour.'[2] The tendency resembles Dryden at his earliest and worst,
and the riot of conceit during one phase of English literature in the
seventeenth century.

No less in the narrower aspect of vocabulary and constructions does
the Latin of Valerius Maximus bear the stamp of the Silver Age. His
prose shares the fondness noticeable in Phaedrus's verse for abstract
turns of expression. As Phaedrus uses *maiestas ducis* for 'the Emperor,'
so Valerius uses *mea paruitas* for 'my humble self.'[3] This liking for the
abstract, conjoined with abundance of metaphor, contributes to give his
phraseology a more modern ring than the strictly classical Latin idiom
has. When Marius is described as hostile to the upholders of ancient
lineage, Valerius merges such persons in the abstract term *uetustas*, and
the incompetent warriors who belittled successful men risen from lowly
origins are grouped under the phrase *militaris ignauia*.[4] He refers to
Aemilius Lepidus despatched by the senate to be a guardian for a
young Egyptian prince as *amplissimique et integerrimi uiri sanctitatem*.[5]
In similar fashion, he mentions 'men who have slipped into this deviation (of luxury) unknown to old-world temperance,' where a simpler and
earlier style of Latin might have said 'unknown to our temperate
ancestors.'[6]

As might be expected, new words rise into prominence and old words
are used in changed senses. For example, he appears to favour *sugillare*,
which, like *sugillatio*,[7] is a Livian word – a significant point when it is
remembered that Livy marks the transition between republican and

---

[1] II. vii. 9.
[2] III. ii. 14; cf. V. iii. 2, VII. vii. 1 ('togatam militiam').
[3] Prologue to Bk. I.   [4] II. iii. 1.   [5] VI. vi. 1.
[6] IX. i. 3: 'uiros in hoc priscae continentiae ignotum deuerticulum prolapsos.'
Cf. IV. iii. 14: 'quae quidem tam misericors continentia plebis tacitum crudelium
conuicium fuit'; IV. vii. 6: 'fideli mendacio obscuritate ipsa suffragante, Bru-
tum se esse simulauit.'
[7] *Sugillare* ('beat black and blue,' hence 'insult'), III. ii. *ext.* 1; VII. v. 5
and viii. 9; Livy IV. xxxv; *Sugillatio*, II. iii. 1; VI. ix. 12; IX. ii, *ad init.*;
Livy XLIII. xiv.

D

Silver Latinity.[1] Valerius gets the unusual and 'post-classical' word *uaframentum* ('a trick') into his head at VII. iii. *ext.* 2, and repeats it in the fourth and seventh paragraphs of the chapter. Indeed, he is given to this repetition of words and expressions which capture his fancy. Symptoms of the change coming over the language may be detected in his invention or acceptance of fresh meanings and fresh usages. Thus he widens the metaphorical use of words: *e.g. Cimonis incunabula opinione stultitiae fuerunt referta* (VI. xi. *ext.* 3) shows a more artificial employment of *referta* than Cicero's *uita undique referta bonis* (*Tusc. Disp.* V. xxxi. 86). The adjective *numerosus*, too, appears in its late Latin sense.[2] Nor are his constructions those of stricter days. As in Phaedrus and on rare occasions in earlier authors, *persuadere* is used personally in the passive; and infinitives are joined freely with verbs which in the Golden Age preferred a dependent *ut* and subjunctive.[3] In all such linguistic matters Valerius is as symptomatic of his age as when he serves the needs of disputants and declaimers, or makes his verbal obeisances before imperial authority. So, while he is not a thinker even to the limited extent that Velleius is, while he is casual in investigation, superficial in comment, and too often showy in style, yet, as a literary landmark, he possesses historical importance sufficient to justify an attentive examination of his work.

[1] Duff, *L.H.R.* pp. 480–481.
[2] III. ii. 24: 'numerosa donorum pompa'; II. ix. 1: 'posteritati numerosae.'
[3] III. viii. 1: 'persuasam'; V. ix. 4: 'persuasus.' For infinitives see, *e.g.*, V. x. 3: 'orationi meae uagari permittam'; VII. i, *ad init.*: 'malignitatis obliuisci sibi imperauit'; IX. i. 3: 'uehi permittebat'; *ibid.* 'quas imbecillitas . . . studium ad cultum hortatur conferre.' Usages like Quintilian's familiar 'fere solus legi dignus' (*Inst. Or.* X. i. 96) are already in vogue: *e.g.* II. ix. 1: 'puniri dignos.' For rare Golden Age uses of *persuadere* personally in the passive see *Ad Herenn.* i. 9 and 10; ps.-Caesar B. *Afr.* 55; Caesina apud Cic. *Ad Fam.* VI. vii. 2; Ovid *A.A.* iii. 679; Prop. IV. i. 146. Infin. w. *permitto* occurs in Cic. *N.D.* III. 4, Nepos, *Con.* 4 and Livy XXIV. xvi. 17 and XXV. xviii. 12; w. *impero* in early Latin and in Sallust *Cat.* 16 and *Iug.* 47; w. *hortor* in Cic. *Sest.* 7, *Invent.* ii. 17; Nepos, *Phoc.* 1; *Ad Herenn.* ii. 28; Sall. *Cat.* 5.

Chapter III

VELLEIUS, CURTIUS AND HISTORY

Minor historians of the period – Cremutius Cordus, Aufidius Bassus and others.

Velleius Paterculus – Ancestry – Interest in literature and in the East – Military service under Tiberius – Scheme of the compendium – Obligation to be brief – Sources – Subjective factors of interest in Velleius – Symptoms of Silver Latin – The rhetorical element – Epigrammatic antitheses – Literary conceits – Merits of style – Sententious sayings – Defects and merits as historian – Subjective historical method – Character-pieces – His picture of Tiberius – The close on an imperial note.

Q. Curtius Rufus – The puzzle of his identity – Probable date under Claudius – Eight surviving books – The attractive theme of Alexander the Great – Curtius, Plutarch and Arrian in relation to sources – Want of critical method and historical grasp – Gift of narration – The hero's character – A psychological study in deterioration – Fortune and Fate – Stoicism in Curtius – Freedom from superstition – Rhetorical element – Some features of style.

MINOR HISTORIANS

UNDER Tiberius, Caligula and Claudius history did not greatly flourish: under Nero, we shall find, it flourished still less. There are only two historians of note in the period – Velleius and Curtius. Before considering them, we may pause on a few minor names. Cremutius Cordus illustrates the danger of historical composition in the early Empire, especially if a writer gave offence to a powerful minister like Sejanus. Cremutius was charged with praising Brutus in his annals, and with calling Cassius 'last of the Romans.' He starved himself to death, and the senate had his books burned in A.D. 25, though Tacitus says copies were hidden and published.[1] Similarly, the downfall of the republic and the initial phases of the Empire occupied Aufidius Bassus in Tiberius's reign. He gave attention to Rome's wars with the Germans, and his work is cited by the elder Pliny in the *Natural History*, and was continued by him in a lost work entitled *A fine Aufidii Bassi*.[2] The elder Seneca's lost historical work has been

[1] Tac. *Ann.* IV. xxxiv–v; see also p. 53.
[2] Sen. *Suas.* vi. 18 and 23; Younger Sen. *Ep.* XXX. 1; Quint. *I. Or.* X. i. 103; Plin. *N.H. praef.* 20; VI. 27.

recorded as containing an account of the end of Tiberius. A later group includes Caligula's victim Gaetulicus, who governed Germany for ten years, but whose writings on Germans and Britons may, like other works of his, have been in verse; then, in Claudius's time, Servilius Nonianus who wrote on recent as well as contemporary history, and Bocchus who treated chronology and the marvels of Spain.

VELLEIUS PATERCULUS

The circumstance that C.[1] Velleius Paterculus was quaestor elect in A.D.6[2] warrants the inference that his birth took place not later than 19 B.C. After A.D. 30, the year of the consulate of M. Vinicius, to whom he dedicated his history and whom he often addresses in its course, we know nothing of Velleius; and, indeed, he seems to have played no prominent part in the reign of Tiberius, for throughout the sixteen years which elapsed after his nomination as a *candidatus Caesaris* for the praetorship in the year of Augustus's death[3] we have no information about him. Then comes the fact that he published his book; and as to his biography the rest is silence. For us, therefore, his activity lies within narrow limits of time: its outstanding feature, that which determined his outlook on history, was his career in the public and especially the military service during the first fourteen years of the Christian era.

He came of a family which, as he is at pains to remind his readers, had been strenuous in civic life and in the profession of arms. Dealing with the Italian franchise war, he declares that mistaken modesty (*uerecundia*) shall not deter him from doing justice to the part played by an ancestor (*atauus*), Minatius Magius, who in turn was the grandson of a notable Campanian, Decius Magius. This more distant forbear figures in Livy's pages at Capua as a stubborn advocate of fidelity to Rome despite the threats of Hannibal.[4] The author's grandfather, C. Velleius, a *praefectus fabrum*, had been honoured by Pompey and remained so keen an anti-Caesarian that he ran himself through with his sword, when by reason of years he felt unable actively to support Tiberius Nero (father of the future emperor Tiberius) after his defeat by Octavian: 'I shall not defraud my own grandfather,' says Velleius admiringly with a Johnsonian emphasis, 'of a testimony which I should give to a stranger.'[5] He notes elsewhere that his father, like himself, had been *praefectus equitum*.[6] Again, he records the assistance given by Capito, his uncle (*patruus meus*), a man of senatorial rank, to Agrippa in prosecuting

---

[1] The inscription *C.I.L.* VIII. 10311 would, if it referred to the historian, confirm the praenomen 'Gaius' of the *editio princeps*. But the inscription is probably post-Caligulan. See note in *C.I.L.* VIII *ad loc.*
[2] Vell. II. cxi. 3.
[3] II. cxxiv. 4.
[4] Vell. II. xvi. 2; Livy XXIII. vii–x.
[5] II. lxxvi: 'Quod alieno testimonium redderem, eo non fraudabo auum meum.'   [6] II. civ. 3.

C. Cassius after the assassination of Caesar.[1] To his brother, Magius
Celer Velleianus, he makes several allusions, chronicling his recognised
ability as lieutenant-general under Tiberius Caesar in Dalmatia and his
association with the author both in attending Tiberius's triumph, and
later as one among 'Caesar's candidates' for the praetorship.[2]

Concerning his formal education we have scant knowledge; yet considerable rhetorical training may be argued from his artifices of style;
and he must have imbibed an interest in books and authors, to judge
from his pronouncements on Homer, Hesiod and Cicero, and from
excursuses on literary men of the Gracchan, Ciceronian and Augustan
periods.[3] About the beginning of our era he was a young officer (*tribunus militum*) who had gained preliminary insight into military life
under Vinicius's father in Thrace and Macedonia, and was next on
service in the East.[4] Such service doubtless provided a stimulus towards
writing the now mutilated compendium upon Oriental and Greek
affairs near the outset of his history. Elsewhere, too, we meet transient
suggestions of Oriental colour and memories – as when he recalls his
good fortune in beholding a gorgeous durbar held on an island in the
Euphrates between C. Caesar and the Parthian monarch;[5] or when
there flashes on his inward eye the pleasant recollection of 'so many
events, places, nations and cities' of the East;[6] or when he recounts
Antony's luxurious chariot-ride through the streets of Alexandria as the
new Father Bacchus, 'ivy-wreathed, clad in a golden robe, thyrsus in
hand, and buskins on his legs';[7] or again when, *con amore*, he devotes
picturesque touches to his description of the extravagant mummery of
Antony's quondam friend, Plancus, who acted Glaucus 'naked and
painted sea-green, wearing a chaplet of reeds on his head, dragging a tail
after him and crawling upon his knees.'[8]

But no experience left upon his history so distinctive an imprint as
his military service under Tiberius. This meant contact virtually for
eight years on end with a powerful and able personality.[9] For his commander's greatness he conceived and expressed unbounded enthusiasm
in an almost eighteenth-century sense of the term. It is an enthusiasm

[1] II. lxix. 5. [2] II. cxv. 1; cxxi. 3; cxxiv. 4.
[3] I. v, vii; II. ix, xxxvi, lxvi. [4] II. ci. 3.
[5] II. ci. 2: 'quod spectaculum stantis ex diuerso, hinc Romani, illinc Parthorum
exercitus, cum duo inter se eminentissima imperiorum et hominum coirent
capita, perquam clarum et memorabile sub initia stipendiorum meorum tri-
buno militum mihi uisere contigit.'
[6] II. ci. 3: '. . . haud iniucunda tot rerum, locorum, gentium, urbium re-
cordatione perfruor.'
[7] II. lxxxii. 4, *sub fin.*
[8] II. lxxxiii. 2: 'caeruleatus et nudus caputque redimitus arundine et caudam
trahens, genibus innixus.'
[9] II. civ. 3: 'Hoc tempus (*i.e.* A.D. 4) me, functum ante tribunatu, castrorum
Ti. Caesaris militem fecit; quippe protinus ab adoptione missus cum eo praefectus equitum in Germaniam, successor officii patris mei, caelestissimorum
eius operum per annos continuos †VIII praefectus aut legatus spectator, tum
pro captu mediocritatis meae adiutor fui.'

which amounts to a bias for Tiberius in particular and for the Caesars in general. The question of the character of Tiberius may be with greater appropriateness raised in considering Tacitus; but at least more light and shade might have been expected from Velleius, if, as an actual observer (*spectator*), he aimed at producing an impartial and realistic picture of the man. What one can say without prejudice is that he had abundant opportunity for estimating the merits of Tiberius as a general, and that both the author and the subject of his eulogies were men of proved military experience. The future historian went out as a cavalry officer with Tiberius to Germany in A.D. 4; two years later, when quaestor-elect, he took charge of reinforcements despatched from Rome to Tiberius, who was then coping with the danger threatening Italy from Dalmatia and Pannonia; and even in the year of his quaestorship he acted as *legatus* under him.[1] 'What battalions of the enemy did we not behold in that first year?' exclaims Velleius proudly.[2] The ultimate surrender of Pannonia confined war-like operations to Dalmatia, where Velleius and his brother were assisting Tiberius.[3] Scarcely was Dalmatia pacified in A.D. 9 when the appalling disaster to the Roman arms under Varus in Germany summoned Tiberius thither to the rescue of imperial fortunes, or, to follow Velleius's artificial expression, as the *patronus* who took up the case of his client, the state: 'the never-failing champion of the Roman Empire undertakes the cause so familiar to him.'[4] With Velleius's attendance at Tiberius's triumph in the winter of A.D. 12–13 the record of his career as a soldier fittingly closes.[5]

It is natural that, like Livy on a larger scale, Velleius should treat with greater fullness events nearest to his own day; but his treatment of early history would look less disproportionate, if his compendium had come down in more perfect form. As it stands, Book I has lost its opening; and only eight chapters have survived to represent the affairs of the East and Greek and Tyrian enterprise before the foundation of Rome. An allusion to the rape of the Sabine maidens is interrupted by a gap of well-nigh six hundred years in the narrative, which is resumed in the second century B.C., at the period of the second Macedonian war. Then ten extant chapters of Book I include the fall of Carthage and Corinth, an account of Roman colonies and some grants of the franchise, reflections on the multiplicity of geniuses at certain epochs and remarks on

[1] II. civ. 3; II. cxi. 3.
[2] II. cxi. 4: 'Quas non primo anno acies hostium uidimus?' It was Burman who inserted 'non' for *nos*. Heinsius's conjecture of 'fudimus' is rejected by Kritz, who thinks it was approved 'sine iusta caussa' by Krause, Orelli and others.
[3] II. cxiv–cxv.
[4] II. cxx. 1: 'perpetuus patronus Romani imperi adsuetam sibi causam suscipit.'
[5] If the inscription C.I.L. VIII. 10311 (already mentioned p. 68 n. 1) had referred to the historian, then Velleius would have risen through tribunate or aedileship and through the praetorship to the post of legate of Legio III Augusta stationed in Africa.

Roman literature and oratory. Book II, in 131 chapters, ranges over more than a century and a half from Tiberius Gracchus to Tiberius Caesar. The last definite historical allusion is to the emperor's bereavement by the death of the dowager-empress Livia, which happened in A.D. 29.[1] The tone of encomium adopted towards Sejanus would prove, even if we did not know the date of Vinicius's consulate, that the work ended before his fall in A.D. 31.[2]

In reviewing the literary and historical qualities of Velleius, one must keep in mind the intentionally compendious nature of his work. Readers are indeed not likely to forget it; for he repeatedly pauses to explain that he is in haste, harping on the point till it sounds like a refrain among his themes. This brevity was a kind of literary fashion, comparable with that to which Phaedrus lays claim at the same period. Velleius seems desirous of illustrating the merits of his compendious system when applied to a serviceable digression upon Roman colonies (*non inutili rerum notitia in artum contracta*).[3] At another time, he feels impelled to digress on the recurrence of periods distinguished for special talent, although he is sensible that the 'headlong rapidity' of his composition, 'like the revolution of a wheel, or the downrush of an eddying torrent, admits of no halt, and involves rather the exclusion of necessary details than the acceptance of the superfluous.'[4] Similarly he realises the necessity laid upon him by his limits to deal succinctly with even such a subject as the greatness of Pompey (*operis modus paucis eam narrari iubet*);[5] while the greatness of Caesar forces him to stop despite his urgency (*quamlibet festinantem in se morari cogit*).[6] Again, he offers a condensed account of the outbreak of the Civil War in contradistinction to the copious volumes of others;[7] almost apologetically he regrets that his promise to be brief involves racing over details in Caesar's campaigns against the Pompeians;[8] with equal regret he exclaims that the boons conferred upon the world by the victory at Actium could not have justice done them in so rapid a survey as his abridgement;[9] and elsewhere he asserts the impossibility of describing adequately the magnificence of Octavian's triumphant return to Rome 'even in the compass of a regular history, let alone a work so abbreviated as this.'[10] But it is in connexion with Tiberius that he becomes still more insistent upon his obligation to be concise; thus, he promises to discuss in a

[1] II. cxxx. 5: 'cuius temporis aegritudinem auxit amissa mater, eminentissima et per omnia deis quam hominibus similior femina.'
[2] II. cxxvii–cxxviii.   [3] I. xiv.
[4] I. xvi. 1: 'intellego mihi in hac tam praecipiti festinatione, quae me rotae proniue gurgitis ac uerticis modo nusquam patitur consistere, paene magis necessaria praetereunda quam superuacua amplectenda.'
[5] II. xxix. 2.   [6] II. xli. 1.   [7] II. xlviii. 5.
[8] II. lv: 'admonet promissae breuitatis fides quanto omnia transcursu dicenda sint.'
[9] II. lxxxvi: 'in hoc transcursu tam artati operis.'
[10] II. lxxxix: 'ne in operis quidem iusti materia, nedum huius tam recisi digne exprimi potest.'

different work Pannonia, Dalmatia and other countries subdued by Tiberius;[1] he reserves, presumably for the same intended work, the circumstances attending that prince's withdrawal from Rome into temporary seclusion at Rhodes;[2] he looks forward to conveying an impression of the popular joy over his adoption 'in that regular history' (*in illo iusto opere*); so too with further Dalmatian and Pannonian victories and the Varian disaster which called Tiberius to Germany.[3] The alarming effect of Augustus's death he avers to be beyond description: 'I have no leisure in so precipitate a narrative to portray it, and he who has leisure is unable to do it.'[4] All this may savour of protesting too much on the part of one who would be brief; yet it has its importance as a proof that he had a conception of, and perhaps yearnings after, a different method of writing history; while, to some extent, his confessedly compendious aim disarms criticism or, at least, palliates certain blemishes and omissions. It is beside the point to reproach him with sketchiness when his plain object is to be sketchy; nor is it surprising that in his hurry he should be at times careless in composition, awkward in structure, conversational in tone, and given to tasteless repetition in word and phrase.[5]

In a work which makes no pretence to be exhaustive we cannot expect an enumeration of authorities. Some sources he does, in fact, mention; others we are left to infer. Discussing the foundation of Capua and Nola (in a manner half suggesting that he belonged to the former town[6]), he cites vaguely 'some authors,' and then descends in particular upon Cato, whose *Origines* he is certain to have found useful, and from whom he dissents 'with all due deference to his carefulness.'[7] He alludes to the *Annales* of Hortensius as authoritative upon the Italian war of Sulla's time; to an inscription, in proof of a religious ceremony performed by Sulla; to ampler details 'in the larger volumes of others' who had treated the outbreak of the Civil War; and to the autobiographic memoirs of Augustus.[8] The effect of the annalist's method is observable in his inclusion of a survey of Greek colonisation; and we may readily suppose, since the works of Atticus, Cornelius Nepos and Pompeius Trogus[9] were available, that he made use of them. Livy, who was

---

[1] II. xcvi: 'alio loco explicabimus, hoc opus seruet formam suam.'
[2] II. xcix. . . . 'iusto seruemus operi . . . in hoc transcursu dicendum est.'
[3] II. ciii. 4, *cf.* cxiv, cxix. 1.
[4] II. cxxiv: 'neque mihi tam festinanti exprimere uacat neque cui uacat potest.'
[5] *E.g.* fondness for the epithet *caelestis*, II. lx: 'spreuit itaque caelestis animus humana consilia'; II. lxiv: 'fulgentissimo et caelesti ore' (of Cicero); lxvi: 'caelestissimi oris' (of Cicero again); civ: 'caelestissimorum eius operum' (of Tiberius); cxxiii: 'animam caelestem deo reddidit' (of Augustus); or such recurrences as 'mihi contigit' in II. ci. 2, cxxi. 2, cxxiv. 4.
[6] Teuffel, § 278, 1. citing Vell. I. vii. 2; II. xvi. 2; II. lxxvi. 1.
[7] I. vii. 4: 'pace diligentiae Catonis dixerim.'
[8] II. xvi. 2, xxv. 4, xlviii. 5, lix. 1 (reading *praeuenit*).
[9] Duff, *L.H.R.* pp. 253–254, 309–312, 463–464.

republican enough to be dubbed 'Pompeian' by Augustus, would not possess the pro-Caesarian enthusiasm likely to commend him to Velleius.

The curtness of the specially compendious parts does not conduce to interest, and for this reason one welcomes occasions when summary gives place to slightly more spacious digressions such as those on colonies, on early Roman literature and the natural law regulating the emergence of genius, on literature and oratory in the Gracchan period, on great authors of the Augustan age, on Roman provinces, and on the boons of the Augustan *régime*.[1] But it is only fair to say that the general effect compares favourably with that of most compendium-writers in Latin. For instance, his compendium is of much greater force and individuality than that of Florus. Velleius can at least be spirited and interesting (even if over-enthusiastic), when he relates his personal impressions of Tiberius. This may be due to an excess of that subjectivity which is a characteristic of the Silver Age; but it has the merit of winning attention. He leaves us under no misapprehension as to his likes or dislikes. He is no democrat: he hates the 'pernicious' agitations of the Gracchi; he detests Marius and Cinna and the tribune of the people, Manilius (*semper uenalis et alienae minister potentiae*);[2] on the other hand, he is full of admiration for Marcus Cato, while his affection for the Caesars emerges at every opportunity, continuously from the chapter recording Octavius's birth, on through the appreciative comparison of Julius Caesar's achievements in Gaul with the subsequent exploits of Tiberius, until he reaches those passages where he sounds the praises of the *princeps* or of his minister Sejanus.[3] Now, while these antipathies and sympathies imply partiality, they by no means make the historian less entertaining. It is one thing to be trustworthy, and another to be readable. Besides, as we shall find, the very style, faults notwithstanding, has a good deal of colour and variety: it is no dead monotony in its choice of words and ideas.

Already in his prose there are evidences of the change which had set in towards Silver Latinity. Traces of such tendencies may be remarked in Livy,[4] but in Velleius they are more prominent; for the old massive and, on the whole, straightforward periods are largely replaced by briefer sentences where pointed phrase and emphatic contrast argue a style at once disdainful of absolute simplicity and ambitious of attracting notice to the manner of expression. Where he attempts the long sentence, the inferiority of his literary architecture becomes patent: it is often an ill-built fabric of clumsy patchwork. Thus, the character of Julius

---

[1] I. xiv–xv, xvii; II. ix, xxxvi, xxxviii, lxxxix.
[2] Gracchi, II. iii, vi–vii; Marius, II. xi; Manilius, II. xxxiii.
[3] Cato, II. xxxv; Octavius's birth, II. xxxvi; Julius Caesar, II. xxxix; Tiberius as soldier, II. xciv–xcvii, civ–cxv, cxx–cxxii (for his praises, esp. xciv, xcix, cxi, cxiii–cxv, cxx, cxxii, cxxiv, cxxix–cxxx); Sejanus, II. cxxvii.
[4] Duff, *L.H.R.* pp. 480–481.

D*

Caesar is portrayed in a rambling sentence where the first word 'hic' is separated from the closing verb 'elapsus est,' to which it is nominative, by nearly 130 words forming an overcrowded series of subordinate clauses and phrases.[1]

The evolution of Latin prose during the first century A.D. is so closely wrapped up with the educational training undergone by writers, that one instinctively looks for traces left by the rhetorical school upon Velleius. They are not far to seek among his plentiful exclamations and interrogations: *e.g.* the apostrophe denouncing Antony for Cicero's murder:

'You gained nothing, however, Mark Antony (for indignation bursting from heart and spirit compels me to depart from the regular form of my history), you gained nothing, I tell you, when you paid the hire for cutting off a divine gift of utterance and a most noble head, or when you procured for a ghastly wage the assassination of a man once the preserver of the commonwealth, once a consul so illustrious! You robbed Cicero on that day of a life of trouble, of an age in the yellow leaf, of an existence more pitiable under your domination than death could be under your triumvirate; but his reputation, the renown of his actions and words, these, instead of taking away, you enhanced. He lives and will live in the memory of all the ages; and as long as, whether framed by chance or providence or by what means soever, there shall endure unharmed this fabric of the universe, which he almost alone of Romans could see in the mind's eye, could grasp with his genius, and could illustrate by his eloquence, so long shall it carry the praise of Cicero as the companion of its own continuance. All posterity will admire his writings against you, and will curse your conduct towards him!'[2]

The poetic element in his diction is an allied feature; and another kindred symptom is an inordinate fondness for superlatives.[3]

But it is his habitual quest after the striking and epigrammatic that

---

[1] II. xli. 1–2; *cf.* the clumsiness of structure in I. xii. 4–5, 'bellum ... clementiae' with a characteristically awkward parenthesis; II. ii. 1–3, 'quippe . . . iuuenem'; and elsewhere *passim*.

[2] II. lxvi. 3: 'nihil tamen egisti, M. Antoni (cogit enim excedere propositi formam operis erumpens animo ac pectore indignatio), nihil, inquam, egisti mercedem caelestissimi oris et clarissimi capitis abscisi numerando auctoramentoque funebri ad conseruatoris quondam rei publicae tantique consulis inritando necem. rapuisti tum Ciceroni lucem sollicitam et aetatem senilem et uitam miseriorem te principe quam sub te triumuiro mortem, famam uero gloriamque factorum atque dictorum adeo non abstulisti ut auxeris. uiuit uiuetque per omnem saeculorum memoriam dumque hoc uel forte uel prouidentia uel utcumque constitutum rerum naturae corpus, quod ille paene solus Romanorum animo uidit, ingenio complexus est, eloquentia inluminauit, manebit incolume, comitem aeui sui laudem Ciceronis trahet omnisque posteritas illius in te scripta mirabitur, tuum in eum factum exsecrabitur.' For rhetorical interrogations, see II. liii. 2.

[3] *E.g.*, II. xxiii. 1 (of Marius): 'uir in bello hostibus, in otio ciuibus infestissimus quietisque impatientissimus.' The usual plethora of superlatives is well exemplified in II. xxix (character of Pompey).

classes Velleius's Latin as definitely Silver.[1] His antitheses – and some
are excellent – would impress one more, if they were fewer; their frequency palls, and amid such an embarrassment of material, one need
but select the examples first to hand. 'Scipio, by the destruction of
Carthage and Numantia, freed us from the dread of the one, and the
insults of the other' (*excisa Carthagine ac Numantia ab alterius nos metu,
alterius uindicauit contumeliis*).[2] A little more elaborate is the studied
contrast of nouns, adjectives and tenses observable in the following:

> *ne quid usquam malis publicis deesset, in qua ciuitate semper uirtutibus
> certatum erat, certabatur sceleribus, optimusque sibi uidebatur qui fuerat
> pessimus.*[3]

Another chapter contains a balanced summary of the rivals' position
at the outbreak of the Civil War:

> *alterius ducis causa melior uidebatur, alterius erat firmior; hic omnia
> speciosa, illic ualentia: Pompeium senatus auctoritas, Caesarem
> militum armauit fiducia,*[4]

in reading which one cannot help thinking of Lucan's famous anti-
thesis concerning the same struggle, *Victrix causa deis placuit sed uicta
Catoni*, and the fuller comparison between the protagonists which
follows that line.[5] So one might quote the distinction drawn between
Brutus and Cassius, or the portions of the chapter on Actium where
Velleius piles antithesis upon antithesis.[6]

Sometimes his artificiality lies in straining after an affectedly remote
way of conveying a mental picture; and such literary conceits may or
may not be combined with the trick of antithesis. He introduces a fanciful idea of the solace which the outcast Marius might derive from the
ruins of Carthage, each contemplating, each comforting the other (*cum
Marius aspiciens Carthaginem, illa intuens Marium, alter alteri possent
esse solacio*).[7] When Catulus asphyxiated himself, he found a death
rather after the wish than the design of his enemies (*mortem magis uoto
quam arbitrio inimicorum obiit*).[8] Similar anxiety to compass a smart
saying animates the conceit implying that Catiline's end had cheated
the executioner: 'gallantly fighting, he yielded up the breath of life
already due to capital punishment' (*fortissime dimicans quem debuerat
supplicio spiritum reddidit*).[9] So of Sextus Pompey, the son of the pirate-
crusher turned pirate, as Velleius must remind us: so, of the heroic
lady, who 'bringing about a premature death by swallowing live coals
was compensated for death by deathless fame' (*uiuo igni deuorato prae-
matura morte inmortalem nominis sui pensauit memoriam*).[10]

---

[1] For the palpable 'desire of Velleius Paterculus to write for the sake of fine
writing and to improve upon the diction of the Ciceronian era,' see E. G.
Sihler, 'On Velleius Paterculus,' *Tr. Am. Ph. A.* xxv (1894) pp. xlv–xlix.
[2] II. iv. [3] II. xxvi. [4] II. xlix. [5] Luc. *Phars.* I. 129–157.
[6] II. lxxii, lxxxv. [7] II. xix, *ad fin.* [8] II. xxii.
[9] II. xxxv, *ad fin.* [10] II. lxxiii, lxxxviii.

His prose style demands attention, both as a type of its period and as the subject of strictures which have sometimes been too unqualified. Although nowise comparable to the *lactea ubertas* of Livy, yet a careful examination will show that it cannot fairly be dismissed as absolutely meagre. There are qualities which recall Sallust: and that must be imputed to Velleius for literary virtue. His very artifices save him from baldness, while, as a military author, he displays, with all his faults and affectations, more sense of style than, for instance, the continuators of Caesar.[1]

His semi-proverbial sayings, which read like so many condensations of a reflective wisdom, rather heighten than otherwise one's opinion of him as an author. Such pronouncements as the following imply, not absolute invention, but a faculty of insight and expression: 'rivalry nurtures talent' (*aluntur aemulatione ingenia*); 'continuance at the height of perfection is hard' (*difficilis in perfecto mora est*); 'what one cannot overtake one ceases to follow' (*quod assequi non potest sequi desinit*); 'precedents do not stop where they start' (*non ibi consistunt exempla unde coeperunt*); 'men are indulgent critics of themselves' (*familiare est hominibus omnia sibi ignoscere*); 'any port in a storm' (*exitialem tempestatem fugientibus statio pro portu*); 'ease is the deadliest foe to discipline' (*res disciplinae inimicissima otium*); 'great tasks need great helpers' (*magna negotia magnis adiutoribus egent*).[2] On at least two occasions he propounds the ancient notion that those predestined to calamity are forced into foolishness by some higher power, be it 'God' or 'Destiny's force that none may wrestle against.'[3]

For his historical method at large profundity cannot be claimed. He does not appreciate great movements in history; he does not exhibit the essential nexus or continuous evolution between periods; and though his eye to their relationship in time is noticeable in the frequent insertion of a date, even this laudable habit is discounted by inconsistencies in chronology. On the other hand, if he shows no keen discernment for the causal link conjoining ages, he can grasp and criticise certain political, social or economic developments which constitute differences between them: thus, he remarks forcibly upon the increase at Rome of civil broils (II. iii), aestheticism (I. xiii), luxury (I. xi, xv),[4] and house-rents (II. x). And while the vital significance of great movements is not made luminous, he at least realises the duty of assigning causes, as in his

[1] Duff, *L.H.R.* pp. 301–302.
[2] I. xvii. 5; *ibid.* 6; *ibid.* 7; II. iii. 4, xxx. 3, lxxii. 5, lxxviii. 2, cxxvii. 2.
[3] II. lvii: 'Sed profecto ineluctabilis fatorum uis, cuiuscumque fortunam mutare constituit, consilia corrumpit'; *cf.* II. cxviii: 'ita se res habet, ut plerumque cui fortunam mutaturus est deus, consilia corrumpat.' It is the spirit of the later proverb, *quem Iuppiter uult perdere dementat prius*.
[4] I. xi, Metellus, who built the first marble temple at Rome, 'uel magnificentiae uel luxuriae princeps fuit.' In I. xv Velleius sympathises with the opposition of 'puritans' like the consul Scipio to the completion of a theatre by Cassius the censor at Rome.

speculation upon the contemporary emergence of great geniuses (I. xvii). It adds to his merits that he recognises the play of human passions and in virtue thereof remains no mere chronicler, but becomes a discerner and recorder of motives – as in the case of the outbreak of the Civil War, where he accounts for Pompey's attitude, or where he states the respective objects of Pompey, Caesar and Crassus in forming their triumvirate.[1] If, then, it may be admitted that Velleius writes history without deep penetration into what Teuffel calls 'the internal connexion of things';[2] yet it is going too far to say that 'his interest centres upon individuals only.' For, surely, his actual search for motives must relate the individual to his surroundings; and, as indicated, he is not entirely neglectful of the need for tracing causes. Besides, his serviceable digressions, already glanced at, arise expressly from his sense of the inferior force of isolated details in history as compared with their effect when grouped together.[3]

With these qualifications, however, the truth remains that his history is written mainly from a personal or subjective standpoint; and its cardinal method is the biographic, with some of the merits and most of the defects entailed. It is, then, not highly scientific or philosophic: on the other hand, though Velleius believes in the universal sway of fortune,[4] there is in such a character-loving method little danger of representing historical figures as mere puppets controlled by some indefinable but apparently inexorable 'Will of the Age.' With him prominent men are no tools of impersonal forces, but living actors who logicially deserve moral blame or commendation when their qualities come to be weighed. So, through his own interest in character, he increases his readers' interest in his personages and seldom leaves a doubt as to his opinion for or against a man. Strong sympathies, indeed, may be consistent with a claim to be candid and dispassionate.[5] Velleius is, however, too enthusiastic to realise the extravagance of his praises. Bias has blinded the judge. Tiberius was doubtless an able soldier, but Velleius damages the emperor's character by excessive eulogy. Perilously endowed with an inexhaustible capacity for laudation and an insatiable thirst for superlatives, he resembles a professional writer of testimonials in favour of the Caesars.[6]

The likes and dislikes are not confined to persons. He is almost

---

[1] II. xxx, xliv.

[2] Teuffel, § 278: 'Für den inneren Zusammenhang der Dinge hat er kein Verständnis, seine Teilnahme gilt den Personen.'

[3] I. xiv. 1: 'cum facilius cuiusque rei in unum contracta species quam diuisa temporibus oculis animisque inhaereat. . . .'

[4] II. cxvi. 3: 'utinam non maioribus experimentis testatum esset, quantum in omni re fortuna posset!'

[5] II. cxvi. 5: 'neque enim iustus sine mendacio candor apud bonos crimini est.'

[6] See remarks on Drusus, II. sxvii, and rapturous exclamations on Tiberius, II. cxi.

puritanic in his suspicion of art and wealth as detrimental to the community;[1] and yet this distrust of aestheticism does not conceal from him the crass ignorance (although he is too grave to see the humour) which Mummius showed in serving his celebrated notice upon the contractors for the removal of pictures and statues from Corinth to Rome, to the effect that any masterpiece lost must be replaced![2] He is scathing in his denunciathin of proscription, and sarcastic on the tendency to minimise contemporary greatness and on homage rendered to high place.[3] Still, it is upon his character-drawing that one should focus attention. His briefer character-pieces, containing many neat strokes, include, in the first book, that of Scipio (xii–xiii); in the second, Marius (xi); Mithridates (xviii); Cinna (xxiv); Cato, finely called 'the very likeness of Virtue' (*homo uirtuti simillimus*, xxxv); Clodius (xlv); Curio, 'a most ingeniously good-for-nothing person' (*homo ingeniosissime nequam*, xlviii); Caelius, who resembled Curio and was not *minus ingeniose nequam* (lxviii); Brutus and Cassius (lxxii); Lepidus (lxxx), Shakespeare's 'slight unmeritable man,' called by Velleius 'the biggest of fools without a single good quality to deserve the long indulgence of fortune'; Maecenas, whose voluptuous effeminacy during leisure-hours is noted in *otio ac mollitiis paene ultra feminam fluens*, and his sleepless vigilance at an emergency in the no less striking words *ubi res uigiliam exigeret, sane exsomnis* (lxxxviii). The sketch of Drusus comes later (xcvii). Fuller portrayals are given of Pompey (II. xxix) and Caesar (xli). Still more elaborate is the character of Tiberius conveyed in different chapters; and to this picture we now turn, remembering that a complete estimate of the real Tiberius involves the attitude of Tacitus. Tiberius is introduced in a comparison with Julius and Augustus;[4] but we get our first historical glimpse of him when, a child of two, he lay in the arms of his mother Livia, then a fugitive from the troops of the man whose consort she was one day to be.[5] Really, however, he enters on Velleius's stage in his nineteenth year, announced with a fanfare of praise as a quaestor of promise:

'Tiberius Claudius Nero . . . brought up on a system of the loftiest principles, a youth of high birth, good looks and imposing stature, thoroughly equipped with an excellent education and superior talents, who from the outset had awakened expectations equal to his present greatness, and even to the eye had proclaimed himself a prince.'[6]

For almost forty chapters Tiberius is the dominating figure; but it is

[1] I. xi, xiii.
[2] I. xiii. 4 . . . 'iuberet praedici conducentibus, si eas perdidissent, nouas eos reddituros.'
[3] II. xxviii, cii. 3: 'semper magnae fortunae comes adest adulatio.'
[4] II. xxxix.   [5] II. lxxv.
[6] II. xciv: 'Ti. Claudius Nero . . . innutritus caelestium praeceptorum disciplinis, iuuenis genere, forma, celsitudine corporis, optimis studiis maximoque ingenio instructissimus, qui protinus, quantus est, sperari potuerat uisuque praetulerat principem.'

mainly his career previous to his accession which Velleius describes; for it is only in five closing chapters that he touches briefly on his reign. This brevity is the more disappointing in view of the account which Tacitus gives in the *Annals*; and those at least who accept that account must charge Velleius with *suppressio ueri*. About twenty chapters are occupied with Tiberius as a soldier.[1] They contain material illustrative of his greatness, such as the indescribable enthusiasm for him as a general:

'The very sight of him drew tears of joy from the soldiers. They were all eagerness, with a sort of unexampled rapture in their salutation and a passion for touching his hand: they could not restrain themselves from immediately adding "Is it really you, General? Have we got you back in safety?" and then, "*I* was with you in Armenia, General," "*I* was in Raetia," "*I* had a reward from you in Vindelicia," "*I* in Pannonia," "*I* in Germany" – a scene not to be expressed in words, and perhaps scarcely capable of winning belief.'[2]

This forms an effective prelude to his military successes in Germany. Another impressive incident is that of the tall and aged German chieftain who in a native 'dug-out' paddled half across the river between the enemy and the Roman camp to request the privilege of looking upon Tiberius.[3] Tiberius's solicitude for the health of subordinates (his provision of an ambulance for sick officers is one illustration), and his self-discipline on active service, are among the admirable traits emphasised.[4] Apart, however, from handling his prowess, Velleius has ways of elevating his hero. He touches on Tiberius's dignified leisure at Rhodes, the disturbing effect exercised upon the peace of the world by this retirement, the widespread joy over his adoption by Augustus, and his modest reluctance to accept imperial sovereignty.[5] Then, looking back from A.D. 30 over Tiberius's years upon the throne, in a passage whose textual variations fortunately do not impair the sense, our author paints in *couleur de rose* his picture of the reign:

'Of the transactions of these last sixteen years, massed (*ingerantur*, Ellis; *inhaereant*, Kritz) as they are before the eyes and mind of everyone, who shall venture upon a detailed account! Our emperor secured the consecration of his sire not by authority, but by scrupulous reverence (*non imperio sed religione*); he did not simply give Augustus a divine title – he made him a god. Financial stability has been recalled to our public life and political disaffection cleared out of it (*summota*), as bribery has been from the elections, and strife from the senate-house.

---

[1] II. xciv–xcviii, civ–cxv, cxx–cxxii.
[2] II. civ. 4: 'At uero militum conspectu eius elicitae gaudio lacrimae alacritasque et salutationis noua quaedam exsultatio et contingendi manum cupiditas non continentium protinus quin adicerent, "uidemus te, imperator? saluum recepimus?" as deinde "ego tecum," imperator, in Armenia, "ego in Raetia fui," ego a te in Vindelicis, "ego in Pannonia," ego in Germania donatus sum," neque uerbis exprimi et fortasse uix mereri fidem potest.'
[3] II. cvii.   [4] II. cxiv, cxv.   [5] II. xcix, c, ciii, cxxiv.

Justice, equity, industry, long buried and cumbered with mould (*sepultaeque ac situ obsitae*), have been restored to the state. There has been an enhancement of prestige for the authorities (*magistratibus* instead of *militibus*), of grandeur for the senate, and of dignity for the law-courts. Rioting in the theatre has been put down, and upright conduct has been either the aim inspired in all or a necessity imposed upon them: integrity is honoured and irregularities are punished. The humble man respects the powerful without fearing him, while the powerful takes precedence of a humbler man without despising him. When were provisions more moderate in price? When was peace richer in blessings? Spread over the regions of east and west and everywhere within the bounds of south or north, the Augustan Peace to the uttermost corner of the earth preserves men immune from the dread of brigandage. Accidental losses sustained not only by individuals but by cities are made good through the generosity of our prince. Cities in Asia have been repaired; provinces have been secured against the wrongdoing of governors. Office is the ready reward of merit; crime is certain to meet with punishment, even if it comes late. Influence is surpassed by a fair claim, and intrigue by desert; for our best of princes by his own practice teaches his countrymen to act aright, and while he is greatest in power, he is even greater as an example.'[1]

Later we read his panegyric upon Tiberius composed in exclamatory fashion:

'With what precepts did he equip his dear Germanicus and imbue him with the principles of campaigning in his own company long before he welcomed him back as the conqueror of Germany! What were the honours which he heaped upon his young manhood, when the style of his triumph corresponded to the greatness of his exploits! How often has he honoured the people with donations, and how willingly, when he could do it with the approval of the senate, has he made good a deficiency in a senator's income without either offering inducements to extravagance or allowing honourable poverty to be deprived of dignity! . . . What a formidable war, stirred up by the Gallic chieftain Sacrovir and Julius Florus, did he suppress with a rapidity and a gallantry so marvellous that the Roman people found itself a conqueror before it was conscious of being at war, and the messenger of victory outstripped the news of danger! The highly alarming conflict in Africa, too, despite its daily increase in seriousness, was, under his auspices and direction, speedily laid to rest. What public works has he erected of his own (*sua* rather than *suo*), or in the name of his family! With what dutiful generosity, surpassing human belief, is he rearing a temple to his sire! . . . Anything that has at any time enjoyed eminent renown, he considers to have the claim of kindred upon his protection. With what

---

[1] II. cxxvi. The passage has genuine interest for the claims made on behalf of imperial government.

liberality on other occasions, but, especially at the recent conflagration on the Caelian Mount, has he out of his own patrimony relieved the losses of people in every rank! How little are the public disturbed when, without the consternation involved in a levy, he organises the raising of troops, a matter of prolonged and peculiar alarm!'[1]

Having thus belauded his talent for training youth in military science, his benefactions, energy, businesslike grasp, filial piety, and gift for organisation, Velleius proceeds humbly to protest his wonderment that the gods should permit plots to be formed against so good a ruler, and to bemoan the sorrowful bereavements and shameful domestic trials which have befallen the emperor.

So the historian praises not wisely but too well. There is no whisper about unfair treatment of Germanicus to besmirch the spotlessness of the emperor: nor is there a suggestion of fault in Sejanus, for the powerful minister had not yet fallen. In the pages of Tacitus we look upon a different portrayal of the emperor and his times. But with Velleius all is right in the Roman world. As an old soldier he is unflinching in loyalty to his *imperator*. He could not belong to the political opposition. From the first warmly affected towards the Caesars, he shows his favourable attitude to the Empire in his sketch of the benefits conferred by the Augustan *régime*.[2] Consistently with this feeling of approval a sense of the continuity of Rome animates and dignifies his closing prayer. This is an appeal for national preservation and defence addressed to Jupiter of the Capitol, to Mars as author of the Roman name and mainstay of its power, to Vesta as warden of the ever-burning fires, and finally to all those majestic divinities who had conferred imperial destiny upon Rome:

> *Voto finiendum uolumen est. Iuppiter Capitoline, et auctor ac stator Romani nominis, Gradiue Mars, perpetuorumque custos Vesta ignium, et quidquid numinum hanc Romani imperi molem in amplissimum terrarum orbis fastigium extulit, uos publica uoce obtestor atque precor: custodite, seruate, protegite hunc statum, hanc pacem, hunc principem.*[3]

Q. CURTIUS

A story is told about Alfonso V of Aragon and I of Naples and Sicily that once, when ill, he had Quintus Curtius's narrative of the exploits of Alexander the Great read to him, and that the result proved to be more than relaxation; for the King was cured. This anecdote of a ruler in the fifteenth century, notable for kindness to scholars who fled from Constantinople to escape the Turks, is one which indicates the right approach to Curtius. He is to be read rather for entertainment than for exact instruction; yet, after all, this is to certify his possession of a

---

[1] II. cxxix. 2–cxxx. 2.
[2] II. xxxvi (on Augustus), lxxxix (on Augustan *régime*). [3] II. cxxxi.

considerable literary gift. The manuscripts give his name as Q. Curtius Rufus; but details of his life are not forthcoming and his date is a matter of inference. There seems no way of settling his relationship to or identity with the Curtius Rufus[1] in Tacitus, said to have been the son of a gladiator, who gained the *insignia triumphalia* for overworking his soldiers at silver mines in Germany, beheld an ominous midday vision recorded[2] by both Tacitus and Pliny, and eventually became proconsul of Africa. It has been argued that, if he had been a writer, Tacitus would have mentioned the fact; that a proconsul might have been expected to be more proficient in military history than our Curtius is; and that an imperial official characterised by a 'sullen sycophancy towards superiors' (*aduersus superiores tristi adulatione*) would not have been so independent in criticisms on Alexander's arrogance, and on his courtiers' subservience – 'the perpetual curse of princes, whose power has been overthrown oftener by flattery than by foes.'[3] Plausible answers can be framed to each of these arguments; for example, it is unfortunately too innocent (and Sallust will serve as an instance) to assume that a writer's morality is equal to his moralising. But all things considered, no absolute conclusion can be reached. Rather more satisfactory is the contention that he wrote under Claudius; for the two contemporary references[4] traceable in his work best suit that period. One arises out of the siege of Tyre, 'now that prolonged peace restores all things, Tyre, reborn after her destruction, finds repose beneath the protecting clemency of Rome'; and the other contrasts the dissolution of Alexander's dominions after his death with the happier condition of the Roman Empire: 'Rightly does the Roman people acknowledge a debt of safety to a prince that shone forth like a new star of the night which wellnigh proved our last: most truly it was his rising, not the sun's, that restored light to a world in gloom (*caliganti*) when, deprived of their head, its members were in conflict and panic.' The first passage proves very little; the 'prolonged peace' is the *pax Romana* of the early Empire. The most satisfactory explanation of the second passage is that it refers to the night in January, A.D. 41, when Caligula was murdered and Claudius found himself suddenly elevated to the throne; and the suggestion has been made that *caliganti* is a play on the dead emperor's name. Moreover, if the historian is the Curtius Rufus given between Porcius Latro and Valerius Primanus in Suetonius's list in *De Rhetoribus*, then the order of names would suggest a similar date.'[5]

[1] H. Furneaux, on Tac. *Ann.* XI. xx, thinks it probable Curtius Rufus was father of the historian.　　[2] Tac. *Ann.* XI. xxi; Plin. *Ep.* VII. xxvii. 2–3.
[3] Curt. VIII. v. 6: 'adulatio, perpetuum malum regum, quorum opes saepius adsentatio quam hostis euertit.'
[4] IV. iv. 21: 'longa pace cuncta refouente . . .'; X. ix. 3–4: 'nouum sidus inluxit: huius, hercule, non solis ortus lucem *caliganti* reddidit mundo.'
[5] C. Hosius, *Rh.M.* xlviii, p. 303 ff., on 'Lucan u. seine Quellen' endeavours to suggest, on ground of analogies in description and resemblances in expression, that Lucan used Curtius. If proved, this would clearly bear on his date. But

Of the ten books which Curtius composed on Alexander's exploits, the first two are lost. Other gaps occur at the end of Book V and beginning of VI, and there is a break in the last book. Freinsheim in the seventeenth century wrote Latin supplements for the missing parts, drawing his material from many authors including Plutarch and Arrian. The eight surviving books narrate Alexander's career from 333 B.C., when he was twenty-three and had reached Phrygia in his Asiatic expedition, up to his death at Babylon in 323 with the resultant confusion and rivalries. Falling short of first-rate history, the work is yet a wonderful and often enthralling pageant of adventure, diplomacy, barbarity, kindliness, privation, battle and sieges with 'scapes i' the imminent deadly breach.' We need not read far in the existing Latin text before Alexander characteristically cuts the Gordian knot; and the will-power thereby displayed is soon triumphantly seizing the passes of Cilicia, winning the battle of Issus, and capturing the Persian queen and queen-mother (Book III). Tyre falls after protracted siege-operations calling forth many inventions. In Egypt Alexander visits the oracle of Jupiter Hammon, is declared the god's son, founds Alexandria, and on his return into Asia defeats King Darius at Arbela (IV). The great cities of Babylon, Susa, Persepolis, fall into the victor's hands, and Darius, to Alexander's indignation, is murdered by two of his own commanders (V). Oriental luxury increases its hold on the conqueror; and he has to face danger from conspirators (VI). An emissary is despatched to kill Parmenio, his general in Media, whose son had been, on insufficient evidence, put to death for treason. Then Alexander carries his conquests into the heart of Asia (VII). His murder of Clitus is the outcome of quarrelling over the wine-cups, and his domineering arrogance is depicted as on the increase. Besides, his espousal of an Oriental bride, Roxane, causes widespread disapproval. The next episode is the invasion of India, and a description of the country is attempted as a preliminary. The Indus is crossed and King Porus defeated (VIII). After continued operations in the Punjab, the army protests against proceeding farther and Alexander reluctantly sanctions withdrawal. Nearchus is told off to investigate the Indian Ocean (IX). Mutinous outbreaks hamper Alexander's schemes of universal conquest and at Babylon he dies. After much scheming and counter-scheming Perdiccas divides the lands overrun by Alexander as provinces to be ruled by different generals, and Ptolemy transfers the embalmed body of the monarch to Alexandria (X).

The barest summary of such achievements serves as a reminder,

---

Hosius's theory is examined and rejected, I think convincingly, by R. Pichon in *Les Sources de Lucain*, 1912, pp. 254–261.

I. Lana, *R.F.I.C.* 1949, p. 48–70, argues for the beginning of Claudius's reign. But Vespasian's reign is not impossible. If we do not press the play on words in *caliganti*, the passage X. ix. 3 could refer to Vespasian's accession. *Cf.* J. Stroux, *Philol.* lxxxiv (1929) pp. 233 ff.

though not as an explanation, of the greatness which the ages have conceded to Alexander. This unique personality remains an enigma: how much was due to personal ambition or actually to blood-lust, how much to thirst for adventure, how much to any definite or indefinite notion of disseminating Greek culture through the absorption of many ancient sovereignties into one far-extended empire, historians have found it hard conclusively to decide. But though the motives are beyond exact measurement, and though they palpably changed amidst the growing brilliance of repeated triumphs, the general results are unmistakable. Alexander's was a career destined to alter the course of civilisation, and open a new epoch for the world. Naturally, then, history has always felt the attraction of his name. Professional writers accompanied his expedition and, like modern war-correspondents, employed their eyes and ears to advantage; official records were kept of Macedonian affairs, of campaigns by land, of coasting voyages, and survived long enough to be documents for later research; so that, between authors with war experience and authors of the study, a gigantic literature was composed on the conqueror in the Alexandrian epoch. The theme in turn fascinated Rome. Livy, jealous of the Macedonian's fame, makes a patriotic digression[1] to argue that he would not have had the success against Rome that he had against Persia and India: and Livy's contemporary, Pompeius Trogus, concerned himself with Macedon, as is plain from the epitome by Justinus. Some realisation of the adventurous element in his career prompted the academic exercise recorded by the elder Seneca 'Alexander deliberates whether he should cross the ocean.'[2] Finally, the extent to which the glamour of his life fascinated the Middle Ages is shown in Chaucer's words:

The storie of Alisaundre is so comune
That everie wight that hath discrecioun
Hath herd somewhat or al of his fortune.

Curtius, therefore, entered upon a great inheritance. Yet he cannot be said to have made full use of his available sources. Only in two passages[3] does he name authorities: in both Clitarchus is mentioned, and in one of them Timagenes as well. It is possible indeed that he drew from Clitarchus (c. 300 B.C.) mainly through Timagenes (c. 55 B.C.). But, supposing he drew directly, Clitarchus was not a first-rate source; for it is an erroneous inference from Diodorus[4] and Strabo that he actually

[1] Livy IX. xvii–xix.   [2] Sen. Suas. i.
[3] IX. v. 21: 'Ptolemaeum, qui postea regnauit, huic pugnae adfuisse auctor est Clitarchus et Timagenes: sed ipse ... afuisse se ... memoriae tradidit.' IX. viii. 15, on number of Indians slain: 'Clitarchus est auctor.'
[4] Diod. Sic. II. vii: ὡς δὲ Κλείταρχος, καὶ τῶν ὕστερον μετ' Ἀλεξάνδρου διαβάντων εἰς τὴν Ἀσίαν τινὲς ἀνέγραψαν: cf. Strabo XI. v. 4, where Clitarchus's statement regarding the Amazon queen who visited Alexander and his record of a geographical distance in stades from the Caspian do not prove his participation in the expedition.

served under Alexander. Further, he was turgid rather than veracious, and Cicero[1] thinks poorly of him, counting it against Sisenna that he was content with imitating Clitarchus, an inferior model even had the imitation been successful. In many respects, Curtius seems to have less historical method than the two authors who not long after treated the same subject in Greek, namely, Plutarch and Arrian. Plutarch (born *c.* A.D. 40) at the outset of his *Life of Alexander* records his consciousness of the mass of material available, but is careful to add that he is writing 'not histories but biographies.' All the same, he shows more critical acumen than Curtius, and does not necessarily accept, on a disputed point, the opinion of the majority. Arrian (*c.* A.D. 90–170), the latest classical historian of Alexander, possessed qualities which made him on the whole the best. His training in Stoic philosophy under Epictetus, his experiences as a soldier, his ability to write on *Tactics*, and the good sense with which he amply fulfils the promise of his proem to rely upon the evidence of Aristobulus and Ptolemy, both of whom served with Alexander – all contribute to the success of his story.[2]

Most of Curtius's defects lie on the surface. His geography is not infrequently at fault, his accounts of military operations are less than satisfying, his understanding of politics is far from profound, and his speeches are not individualised, but sound the same rhetorical note irrespective of variations in nationality and character. Virtually he renounces all claim to be critical when, relating the tenacity wherewith an Indian dog even with amputated limbs holds on to a lion, he declares,[3] 'Certainly I transcribe more than I believe; for I cannot bring myself to affirm what I doubt, nor to suppress what I have received.' In connexion with the plain speaking of Scythian envoys[4] who reproached Alexander for rapacity, Curtius professes to give it accurately (*incorrupta*), adding 'though their speech be despised, our integrity ought not to be.' Laudable enough so far; but faithful reproduction of selected material (if indeed it was selected with discrimination) would for him preclude actual invention, and yet freely permit literary embellishment. Such negation of any high standard of critical inquiry is in keeping with his weakness of historical grasp. He takes no synoptic view of the meaning and results of Alexander's career: thus, although he does contrast

[1] Cic. *De Leg.* I. ii. 7: 'quem (Clitarchum) si assequi posset aliquantum ab optimo tamen abesset.' *Cf.* Quint. *I. Or.* X. i. 75: 'Clitarchi probatur ingenium, fides infamatur.'

[2] F. Reuss, in *Rh.M.* xxvii (1902) pp. 559 ff., maintains that Clitarchus lived about 260 B.C. and must have used Aristobulus; objects to the hypothesis of a history of Alexander by Timagenes; and ascribes the agreement in the account of the campaigns by Strabo, Plutarch and Arrian to a common source in the writings of Eratosthenes.

[3] IX. i. 34: 'equidem plura transcribo quam credo: nam nec adfirmare sustineo de quibus dubito, nec subducere quae accepi.'

[4] VII. viii. 8 sqq.

the posthumous dissolution of his power with the unity of the Roman Empire,[1] he never attempts to estimate the debt of civilisation to the wars of Alexander. Notwithstanding such limitations, he displayed literary virtue. Above all, he can tell a story well. He had an inkling of the romance inherent in so intrepid an invasion of the gorgeous but perilous East, and his incidents are telling, sometimes positively exciting. Rhetorical erudition prompts him to over-indulge in descriptions: so that he enters with zest into details of difficulties overcome – a river reckoned impassable, a jungle wellnigh impenetrable, a rocky hill-fort to all appearance un-scalable, the hazards of snowdrift and frostbite, or of sun-scorched wastes. He shows, however, to most advantage where he can best import dramatic movement; e.g. in V. xii, the treacherous conspiracy against Darius carried out at night when the monarch is deserted by his guards and a portentous silence broods over his tent; VI. vii–xi, the plot against Alexander, involving its thrill of intrigue and discovery, with the plead-ing for life before the army, the hideous tortures to extort confession, and a final spice of mystery concerning the guilt or innocence of Philo-tas; VII. ii. 12–27, the camel-ride of Polydamas disguised as an Arab across the desert, and his fulfiment of Alexander's crafty scheme of murdering Parmenio without trial as he reads a forged letter purporting to be from his son Philotas; VII. xi, the scaling of the rock-fastness in Sogdiana; VIII. i. 22–52, the fatal quarrel at the banquet when Clitus, annoyed at Alexander's boastfulness, quotes Euripides on Greek kings who monopolise the glory of others, and then with drunken licence goes on openly to denounce Alexander's murder of Parmenio and to mock at Alexander's claim to be a son of Zeus; VIII. vi, the scheme of the pages of the bedchamber to assassinate the king after a carousal, the long wait for the expected chance, and the melodramatic inter-ruption by a crazed prophetess and the ruin of the plan by a change of heart in one of the conspirators; and, in IX. ix, the struggle against an unforeseen tide from the ocean.

Another element of interest is furnished by Curtius's conception of his hero's character. From one standpoint the work is a psychological study in progressive deterioration caused by prosperity. Here is a favourable sketch of Alexander which comes in the first of the surviving books:[2]

[1] X. ix. 3.
[2] III. vi. 17–20: 'Namque haud facile dictu est, praeter ingenitam illi genti erga reges suos uenerationem, quantum huius utique regis uel admirationi dediti ei fuerint uel caritate flagrauerint. Iam primum nihil sine diuina ope aggredi uidebatur: nam cum praesto esset ubique fortuna, et temeritas in gloriam ces-serat. Aetas quoque uix tantis matura rebus, sed abunde sufficiens, omnia eius opera honestabat et, quae leuiora haberi solent, plerumque militari gratiora uolgo sunt: exercitatio corporis inter ipsos, cultus habitusque paulum a priuato abhorrens, militaris uigor; quis ille uel ingeni dotibus uel animi artibus ut pariter carus ac uenerandus esset effecerat.'

'It is not easy to describe, apart from their inborn reverence for their monarchs, how far the people surrendered themselves to an admiration for this monarch in particular, or, you might equally say, burned with affection for him. To begin with, it looked as if he could essay nothing without heaven lending assistance: as luck was everywhere at his side, his very rashness had turned to his glory. Then, even his years were scarcely ripe for achievements of such moment, and yet they were more than enough, for they threw a halo round all his exploits; and things that are commonly thought insignificant not infrequently find their way to the common soldiers' hearts. He took his physical exercise among them; his dress and style were little different from the ordinary man's; while he possessed true military energy. Such were the natural endowments or mental skill that had secured for him an equal share of affection and respect.'

Henceforward the author's task is to display the effect of constantly triumphant warfare on such a character: and his method throughout is to record noble and chivalrous qualities in Alexander, but at the same time to produce the impression that gradually, under the influence of success, luxury and drink, the king yielded oftener to arrogant, arbitrary and cruel impulses, so that Jekyll-like he found it increasingly difficult to return from his inferior to his better nature. Hence a sort of alternation between good and bad strikes the reader as the tale is unfolded. The demoralisation of the army at Babylon (V. i. 36–39) is a significant presage; still the conqueror feels qualms (V. ii. 13–15) about setting his feet on a table at which Darius used to dine, and he shows tactful respect for the feelings of the captive mother and children of Darius (V. ii. 18–22) when he apologises for his unfortunate, and to Persians impossible, suggestion that the Queen Mother and her granddaughters should work at woollen clothes as did royal ladies in Macedonia. Similarly the moderation which marked one part of his career (V. iii. 15, *moderationem clementiamque regis quae tunc fuit*) becomes evident in his mercy to enemies at the intercession of Darius's mother. Then falls a dark shadow: his fine traits of endurance, activity, honour and clemency are sullied by his insuperable passion for wine, and the drunken advice of the harlot Thaïs leads to the wanton burning of Persepolis, for Alexander's guests 'rise from table intoxicated to fire a city which they had spared when they had arms in their hands' (V. vii. 5, *surgunt temulenti ad incendendam urbem cui armati pepercerant*). In the next book, Curtius pronounces Alexander a victim of luxury; 'the man whom Persian arms had not broken was defeated by vice' (VI. ii. 1, *quem arma Persarum non fregerant, uitia uicerunt*); nevertheless he is still considerate towards captives (*ibid.*), and, out of courtesy to Artabazus, an old Persian in his ninety-fifth year, orders horses for himself and his aged prisoner, forgoing his well-known preference for marching on foot (VI. v. 5). It is noted that his outward appearance disappointed the

Amazonian queen (VI. v. 29), as it afterwards did the Scythian envoys (VII. viii. 9), being in both cases 'not at all proportionate to his reputation.' Meanwhile, Oriental tastes and habits (VI. vi. 1–8) were driving him in the direction of ostentatious pomp. Luxury, however, did not prevent the king from sharing the privations of his men. The same chapter (VII. v) which relates his merciless barbarity at Branchidae relates also his self-abnegation, despite the pangs of thirst, in declining water meant for some young men in the army. Yet this temperate warrior became an insufferable boaster in his cups, lauding his own exploits and belittling his royal sire Philip (VIII. i. 22). True, he undergoes agonies of remorse after his hasty murder of Clitus (VIII. ii. 1–12); but now that Clitus's unbridled tongue has led to his doom, frankness in presence of the king becomes impossible (VIII. iv. 30, *post Cliti caedem libertate sublata*). Alexander succumbs to the charms of Roxane, because 'amid fortune's subservience to him, he could less control his desires now' (VIII. iv. 24, *minus iam cupiditatibus suis imperantis inter obsequia fortunae*). Scheming to be proclaimed a god, he resents Macedonian objections (VIII. v. 5–24). 'His greed for glory and insatiate lust for fame grew intolerant of all obstacles' (IX. ii. 9, *auaritia gloriae et insatiabilis cupido famae nihil inuium nihil remotum uideri sinebat*). The chronicle reveals a grotesque chaos of pleasure and pain: immediately after the riotous Bacchanalian march of Alexander's army in the East, Curtius remarks 'This pomp had the executioner at its heel, for the satrap Astaspes already mentioned was ordered to be put to death: so true is it that cruelty is no bar to luxury, nor luxury to cruelty' (IX. x. 29–30). A similar strain is heard in the last book: 'He began to be impetuous in executing punishments, and likewise in believing ill of people. Prosperity, it is plain, has power to alter one's nature, it being a rarity for anyone to be sufficiently guarded in respect of good fortune' (X. i. 39–40). In the final summary of his character (X. v. 26–37) we read 'it is plain to all fair judges of the king, that his merits were due to nature, and his faults to fortune or his time of life,' and later in his estimate Curtius elaborates this. For on the one hand he attributes to 'fortune' failings such as Alexander's claim to equal the gods or his exaction of divine honours – sins of pride, in fact, generated by his victories; and on the other hand he views his irascibility and intemperance as slips of youth which time would have abated. 'It must, however, be allowed that while he owed a very great deal to merit, he owed more to fortune, whom he alone of mortal men held within his power.'

This raises a fundamental question touching the historian's concep- of Alexander's whole career.[1] The ascription of virtues to 'nature' and faults to 'fortune' takes us but a little way towards explaining a

[1] The conception deserves comparison with Florus's view of the Roman Empire as the outcome of a struggle between fortune and virtue.

great man. The antithesis resembles Plutarch's account of Alexander's success as due to fortune (τύχη) combined with generalship (*Alex.* xx), and it does not obviously fit into the Stoic view which Curtius elsewhere professes to be his solution for the enigma of life. 'Fortune' indeed counts for much with Curtius. It was what we should call sheer luck that the enemy did not attack and crush Alexander's troops while they revelled on Mount Meros. 'It is incontestable that glory is oftener the gift of fortune than of merit' is the comment (VIII. x. 18, *quis neget eximiam quoque gloriam saepius fortunae quam virtutis esse beneficium?*). So, too, of a week's Bacchanalian progress when the revelling host might have been an easy prey, 'Fortune who ordains the credit and value of things here also turned a military scandal into glory' (IX. x. 28, *fortuna quae rebus famam pretiumque constituit . . .*). Alexander's aims against Spitamenes were secured without exertion on his part, because 'fortune, never weary of favouring him, managed the matter without his presence' (VIII. iii. 1, *fortuna indulgendo ei numquam fatigata . . .*) – a personification like that implied in the 'homage paid by fortune' (*obsequia fortunae*, VIII. iv. 24) which, as already shown, rendered him less master of his passions when he met Roxane, the satrap's daughter. The king's quick decision to segregate the Macedonian grumblers over Parmenio's death proved, like everything else, fortunate for him, because they always afterwards fought gallantly to remove the stigma (VII. ii. 37, *consilium temerarium forsitan . . . sicut omnia alia felicitas regis excepit*): and in his last adventure oceanwards 'the one consolation of his rashness was his unfailing success' (*unum erat temeritatis solacium perpetua felicitas*). Little wonder, then, that Alexander should believe in his *felicitas* (VII. vii. 28) or his *fortuna* (*fortunam cui confidat*, VII. ix. 1, *fortunae suae confisus*, VII. xi. 27) like Julius Caesar after him.

In some of these instances Curtius may appear to imply little more than luck. But logically he is no believer in chance. He is a fatalist in his view of human life and is clearly influenced by Stoicism: so that his 'fortune' in the last resort would be merged in 'fate.' The inevitability of fate is a thought repeated in various contexts: of Alexander's risk of a wound he says, 'but to my mind, fate is unavoidable' (IV. vi. 17, *sed, ut opinor, ineuitabile est fatum*); of Darius's incapacity to take advice that would rescue him, he says, 'he is doomed to his own lot' (V. xii. 8, *destinatus sorti suae*); and of an intrigue to ruin an innocent man, 'destiny, whose appointment is inevitable, was at hand' (X. i. 30, *fatum cuius ineuitabilis sors est appetebat*). His theory of history is made explicit apropos of the failure of Patron, the Greek, to save Darius by warning him against the treachery of Bessus:

My belief may afford amusement to any who are convinced that human affairs roll on driven by blind haphazard. I favour the belief that every series of events follows by immutable law its course as the result of eternal ordinance and the nexus of mysterious causes long since preordained.[1]

An aspect of Curtius's thought commonly overlooked is a certain enlightenment of mind which argues his emancipation from some of the superstitious obsessions of antiquity. He condemns as unacceptable to the gods the ancient Tyrian sacrifice of a freeborn boy (IV. iii. 23): he remarks, on the recourse to a soothsayer about an accident to a crow, that Alexander's 'mind was not without its touch of superstition' (IV. vi. 12, *et erat non intactae a superstitione mentis*) and on the consultation of the oracle of Hammon that 'the prophet had set himself to flatter' (IV. vii. 26, *uates in adulationem compositus*). He dubs the employment of diviners for a military problem as 'the outcome of a superstitious mind' (V. iv. 1, *a superstitione animi*). A noticeable example occurs in the introductory description of the judicious Gobares who, after reminding the Persian satrap Bessus incidentally that a dog's bark may be worse than its bite and that still waters run deep, advocates coming to terms with Alexander: 'there was at the feast one Gobares, of Median nationality, more renowned for his profession of the magical art (if it really is an art and not a jest at the expense of the silliest) than for any knowledge thereof' (VII. iv. 8). Plainly Curtius would have one take note that such things mean weakness: it was when ill and confronted with serious menaces that Alexander, 'who had, since Darius's overthrow, given up the consultation of soothsayers and prophets, fell back on that super-stition – the delusion of mankind' (VII. vii. 8, *humanarum gentium ludibria*). It must have given Curtius satisfaction to record later how Alexander dismissed the warnings of a fortune-teller as unseasonable hindrances (IX. iv. 27–30).

Speeches and descriptions yield Curtius his readiest outlet for rhetoric. Not offensively overdone, it is most patent in the sententious remarks introduced into narrative and speeches alike. Of gallant fighting in a tight corner he says 'necessity, I hold, sharpens even cowardice, and despair is often the cause of hope' (V. iv. 31, *ut opinor, ignauiam quoque necessitas acuit et saepe desperatio spei causa est*). When Alexander tried to win indulgence for his Oriental luxury by generous gifts, the comment is, 'but, I hold, to the free the price of slavery is unwelcome' (VI. vi. 11, *sed, opinor, liberis pretium seruitutis ingratum est*). The story of a poor scion of a royal race brought from garden-work to a throne calls forth an almost Juvenalian cynicism: 'the cause of his poverty was as usual honesty' (IV. i. 20, *causa ei paupertatis, sicut plerisque, probitas erat*). Two instances may be given from a speech: 'Those bear afflictions

---

V. xi. 10: 'eludant fidem licet quibus forte temere humana negotia uolui agique persuasum est: equidem aeterna constitutione crediderim nexuque causarum latentium et multo ante destinatarum suum quemque ordinem immutabili lege percurrere.' But textually this is a vexed passage. The words 'equidem . . . crediderim' are a conjectural insertion.

best who conceal them' (V. v. 11, *optime miserias ferunt qui abscondunt*) and 'no man loyally loves one he disdains, for calamity is querulous and prosperity proud' (V. v. 12, *nemo fideliter diligit quem fastidit, nam et calamitas querula est et superba felicitas*). Some of the inserted epistles have a rhetorical ring, as in Alexander's haughty words to Darius: 'I know both how to conquer and how to consider the conquered . . . when you write to me, remember that you are writing not only to a king, but to your king' (IV. i. 10–14).

As regards the technique of his prose, Curtius's sentence-endings show a distinct preference for a cretic followed by spondee or trochee, a rhythm which perhaps no contemporary employs so often. An ending about half as often used – though still comparatively common – is the double cretic; next to that, the cretic followed by a tribrach, and then the double trochee.[1]

His style in general is influenced by Sallust, Virgil and, most of all, by Livy. But there is in him a sameness of expression for similar situations which becomes monotonous, and marks his inferiority in prose to Livy's brilliant variety. One cannot read far without noticing his pluperfect indicatives for sketching a situation, his employment of a future participle in Greek fashion to denote purpose, his loose ablatives absolute, his repetition of the connectives *ceterum* and *quippe*. Some rhetorical constituents of his style have already been illustrated. Yet it must be conceded that neither mannerisms nor the poetic strain in him debar him from being generally clear: not seldom he is even vivacious.

[1] For these four types of *clausulae* De Groot, *Prosarhythmus*, gives, over a number of observed instances, the following percentages – 31, 15, 12 and 8. The first and second types are favourites of Cicero; and the double trochee, preceded by a cretic or a molossus, is also common in Cicero.

Chapter IV

CELSUS: MELA: MISCELLANEOUS LEARNING

Cornelius Celsus – Contents of his encyclopaedia – The eight
books *De Medicina* – Sources – Relation to this times – Common
sense – Curiosities of Celsian medicine – Style.
The first Roman Geography – Pomponius Mela – The coasting
method – Some aspects of his treatment – Faults and merits –
Sources – Enlivening touches – Description of customs and marvels – Mela on tides – Rhetorical elements and his rhythm –
Miscellaneous learning of the age.

CELSUS

THE biography of A. Cornelius Celsus, the encyclopaedist, is a
blank; and, in the absence of details, inquiry must rest satisfied
with the guarantee of his gentile name through its occurrence in
Columella and the elder Pliny.[1] Celsus was a senior contemporary[2]
frequently mentioned by Columella, who belongs to the time of Nero.
Pliny's statement that Julius Graecinus made use of the agricultural
work of Celsus suggests that at least the books on farming were written
before the close of Tiberius's reign; for Graecinus was executed under
Caligula about A.D. 39.[3] The subsequent books on medicine may be
presumed to precede A.D. 47 or 48, when Scribonius Largus published
among his prescriptions a cure for quinsy, for which ailment Celsus
declares he has not found a remedy in any medical treatise.[4]

The encyclopaedic habit of Cato and Varro[5] descended to Celsus.
His labours included agriculture, medicine, military tactics, rhetoric,
jurisprudence and philosophy – all subjects of traditional importance in

[1] *E.g.* Col. I. i. 14; III. xvii. 4; Plin. *N.H.* XIV. 33: 'Graecinus qui alioqui
Cornelium Celsum transcripsit.' The praenomen has the authority of MS.
headings of the *De Medicina*.

[2] Col. III. xvii. 4: 'Iulius Atticus et Cornelius Celsus, aetatis nostrae cele-
berrimi auctores, patrem atque filium Sasernam secuti.'

[3] Teuffel, § 280, 1; 283, 4. Cichorius, *Röm. Studien*, 1922, pp. 411–417,
examines Pliny's citations and argues that the agricultural portion of Celsus was
written A.D. 25–26, and the medical portion soon after.

[4] IV. iv. 1: 'quamuis in monumentis medicorum non legerim'; *cf.* Teuffel,
§ 294, 2.

[5] Duff, *L.H.R.* pp. 191 ff. and 241 ff.

the higher education of a Roman. To each he devoted several books;[1] but the one surviving portion is the *De Medicina* in eight books. His military writings, whether in the encyclopaedia or in separate pamphlets, were consulted by Vegetius and perhaps by Joannes Lydus.[2] The books on philosophic systems, in which (Augustine informs us) the aim was rather exposition than refutation, may have been included in the encyclopaedia; but he evidently wrote other treatises on philosophy.[3] Quintilian, who bestows modified praise upon Celsus's style in discussing philosophy, cites his opinions on rhetoric, frequently to disagree with them.[4] This is not unnatural when it is remembered that Celsus's cursory treatment of rhetoric would not be calculated to satisfy a specialist like Quintilian; and it may be guessed that Celsus's rhetorical portion was in fact eclipsed by the fuller treatment of the great professional authority and so sank into oblivion.

Regarding the order of parts in this encyclopaedia, we can be certain that the five books *De Agricultura* opened the work, and that the *De Medicina* followed, forming Books VI to XIII[5] of the whole *corpus*.

---

[1] There were five books on agriculture, Col. I. i. 14; and, if he is the Celsus mentioned by the scholiast to Juv. vi. 245, there were seven books on rhetoric ('Celso: oratori illius temporis qui septem libros *Institutionum* scriptos reliquit'). His work on philosophy was in six books, Augustine, *De haeresibus* (Migne, *Patrolog.* xlii, 1861, p. 23), 'opiniones omnium philosophorum . . . sex non paruis uoluminibus quidam Celsus absoluit.'

[2] Veget. *De re mil.* i. 8; Lyd. *De Mag.* i. 47; iii. 33: καὶ συγγραφὴν περὶ τούτου μονήρη Κέλσος ὁ 'Ρωμαῖος τακτικὸς ἀπολέλοιπε, and 34. Vegetius says 'Cornelius Celsus' and presumably refers to the encyclopaedist (thus confirming Quintil. XII. xi. 24 that Celsus did write on things military). He gives no indication of date except that in a group of three authorities he places Celsus between Cato Censorius and Frontinus. If the passages in Kydus refer to the encyclopaedist, then Celsus must have been writing as late as Nero's reign, because Lydus (*De Mag.* III. 33 and 34) refers to a work on the Eastern campaigns of Corbulo. But Lydus's Κέλσος is more probably Marius Celsus, who brought Legio XV Apollinaris from Pannonia to join Corbulo in 63 (Tac. *Ann.* XV. xxv), and who figures in after Galba's fall. Lydus (*De Mag.* I. 47) makes Frontinus write before Κέλσος. That is a veritable 'howler' if Cornelius Celsus is meant; if, on the other hand, Marius Celsus is meant, it is a venial error, or might even be correct supposing Marius Celsus (about ten years older than Frontinus) to have written in his old age. On this whole question see S.H. § 474 (paragraph headed: 'Die Monographie über den Partherkrieg') and works there cited; also R. Syme, *Tacitus*, Oxf. 1958, vol. ii, pp. 682–3.

[3] Aug. *loc. cit.*: 'nec redarguit aliquem, sed tantum quid sentirent (*v.l.* sentiret) aperuit'; contrast Quint. *Inst. Or.* X. i. 124: 'scripsit non parum multa Cornelius Celsus, Sextios secutus, non sine cultu ac nitore.'

[4] *I. Or.* XII. xi. 24: 'Cum etiam Cornelius Celsus, mediocri uir ingenio, non solum de his omnibus conscripserit artibus sed amplius rei militaris et rusticae et medicinae praecepta reliquerit'; *cf.* II. xv. 22 and 32; VIII. iii. 35: 'neque enim accedo Celso qui ab oratore uerba fingi uetat.'

[5] In Cels. V. xxviii. 16, the mention of a prescription, 'as already recommended in case of cattle,' proves the agricultural portion preceded. The opening of the preface to what is now Bk. I, suggests that 'Agriculture' *immediately* preceded, 'ut alimenta sanis corporibus agricultura, sic sanitatem aegris medicina promittit.' This is confirmed by headings in many MSS., 'Celsi artium liber VI, idem medicinae I'; *cf.* Col. I. i. 14.

Detached from the encyclopaedia, they possess the unique importance of representing the healing art in classical Rome. At the close of an introduction, which is an epitome and criticism of prevailing tendencies in medical science, Celsus summarises his own position and announces his plan of handling first rules of health and next phenomena and cures of disease. To this end Book I is largely of diet; II of symptoms and therapeutics; III of fevers; IV of internal diseases, considered in order from the head to the joints of the feet; V and VI of drugs and ailments for which they are specifics (with numerous prescriptions); VII and VIII of surgical operations.

His sources are mainly, but not entirely, Greek; and among those the influence of Hippocrates and Asclepiades is pre-eminent. The authority of the former is recognised in the preface to Book II; his teaching on massage, Celsus notes, was in nowise superseded by the more diffuse Asclepiades; and again his magnanimous avowal of a professional mistake is admired, but without any such encomiastic fanfaronade as to justify the nickname 'Hippocrates's ape' sometimes given to Celsus.[1] Asclepiades is also in high favour: his books on preservation of health and on general remedies are cited; his cure for a tertian fever is approved for its rejection of the faulty method of Cleophantus; he is quoted in contrast with Erasistratus to show that doctors differ about the treatment of haemorrhage or about the stress to be laid on diet.[2] Erasistratus is another medical authority often mentioned.[3] Prescriptions are ascribed to an imposing array of practitioners – especially in the pharmacy of the fifth book.[4] Further, the punctiliousness with which Celsus introduces Greek synonyms indicates the origin of much of his reading.[5] Yet it would be a mistake to suppose that he confined himself to the older Hellenic sources. He had the work of recent practitioners, both native and foreign, like Cassius or Themison, to draw from; he had his own observation, though this plays no great part; so he introduces, sometimes with emphasis, his individual views and criticisms, and throughout displays a practical common sense which is typically Roman.

Some of these points demand attention, as illustrations of the author's relation to his times. Indeed, it is not surprising that Celsus, who in another field incurred the disapproval of Quintilian because of an

[1] II. *praef.* 1: 'non dubitabo auctoritate antiquorum uirorum uti, maximeque Hippocratis'; *cf.* II. xiv. 2, VIII. iv. 3. Rhodius, in a rambling *Vita* prefixed to Almeloveen's ed., records the nickname 'Hippocratis simiam.'
[2] IV. ix. 2: 'Asclepiades . . . auctor bonus'; IV. xi. 6, for Asclepiades and Erasistratus on haemorrhage; I. iii. 17: 'in eo uolumine quod de *tuenda sanitate* composuit'; II. xiv. 1: 'in eo uolumine quod *communium auxiliorum* inscripsit'; *cf.* III. xiv. 1–2 (tertian fever) and V. *praef.* 2 (diet preferable to medicaments).
[3] *E.g.* III. iv. 5: 'Commodeque Erasistratus dixit . . .'; IV. xxxi. 9; V. *praef.* 1, etc.
[4] V. xviii is a good example, particularly § 5 *sqq.*
[5] *E.g.* II. i. 8 (consumption): 'tabes quam Graeci φθίσιν nominant'; *ibid.* 12 (paralysis): 'resolutio neruorum, παράλυσιν Graeci nominant.'

'excessive passion for novelty,'[1] should have in medicine shown himself abreast of the latest tendencies and discoveries. Thus, though he does not always agree, he takes pains to record Themison's advice as something modern;[2] and in his preface remarks on the attitude of his followers (*Themisonis aemuli*) to the vexed question of theory *versus* practice. Cassius, again, is singled out for characterisation as 'the most talented leech of our age,' and is elsewhere mentioned as the proud discoverer of a remedy for disease of the larger intestine.[3] The opening remarks by Celsus upon the diverse views of contemporary schools, and subsequent comparisons between medical practices of his own day and those of predecessors, prove that he was alive to advances or at least changes in the healing art.[4] Sometimes he inserts original examples, such as the method of inducing perspiration pursued near Baiae.[5] At other times his personal opinions or results of his observation are stated with a dogmatism that would do credit to wide practical experience.[6] Scaliger, indeed, believed that Celsus practised; but this has been stoutly denied, and one notices nothing in him that a vigilant eye and a perusal of medical books might not have yielded. It is difficult to credit that, if he had been a practising physician or surgeon, he would have refrained from quoting cases which he had attended. Undoubtedly, however, he gains in interest by combining an individual note with a continual suggestion of his environment. It is Celsus himself who speaks when the increased recourse to bleeding is noted as a novelty, and especially when he proceeds with his cautionary remarks on its unsuitability in certain cases and its murderous results in others.[7] Like most contemporary writers, he feels impelled to stigmatise the two great moral and hygienic perils of the Empire – idleness and luxury.[8] As a whole, his background forms for modern readers an attractive

[1] *I. Or.* IX. i. 18: 'Cornelius tamen Celsus adicit ... figuras colorum, nimia profecto nouitatis cupiditate ductus.'

[2] *E.g.* I. *praef.* 11: 'Themison *nuper* ipse quoque quaedam in senectute deflexit'; III. iv. 6 (on food in fevers): 'At Themison *nuper*, non quando coepisset febris, sed quando desisset ... considerabat'; *ibid.* 17: 'Neque tamen uerum est quod Themisoni uidebatur'; *cf.* IV. xxii (cure for dysentery).

[3] I. *praef.* 69: 'ingeniosissimus saeculi nostri medicus, quem nuper uidimus, Cassius'; IV. xxi. 2: 'Est etiam medicamentum eius rei causa comparatum, quod κωλικόν nominatur: id se repperisse Cassius gloriabatur.

[4] *E.g.* II.xii(decreased use of injections); II.x.1 (increased use of blood-letting).

[5] II. xvii: 'quarumdam naturalium sudationum ubi terra profusus calidus uapor aedificio includitur sicut super Baias in myrtetis habemus.'

[6] III. xi. 2: 'Tum hoc *ego* puto temptandum'; III. xxiv. 3: '*Ego* ... praefero,' after citing Asclepiades and others on jaundice; III. xxi. 14, a treatment of dropsy introduced by Tharrias is 'still observed by many, I see' ('esse seruatum a pluribus uideo'). In VII. xii. 4 he cites a case known to him of an ineffective operation upon a tongue-tied patient ('Ego autem cognoui qui, succisa lingua,' etc.), and in VII. vii. 6 he says of a certain eye-operation that he remembers no successful case ('ego sic restitutum esse neminem memini').

[7] II. x. 11: 'quod si uehemens febris urget, in ipso impetu eius sanguinem mittere hominem iugulare est.'

[8] I. *praef.* 5: 'siquidem haec duo (*sc.* desidia et luxuria) corpora, prius in Graecia, diende apud nos, afflixerunt.'

index to other days and other lands. The risks to health in autumn are naturally important to one writing in Rome: the mention of a siesta at midday comes from a southern clime: the careful description of the way to extract an arrow revives pictures of ancient warfare: and the stress laid upon reading aloud as an exercise beneficial or injurious in certain bodily affections takes the reader back to the declamatory *recitatio* which once played its great part in the Roman social and educational system.[1]

The common sense noticeable in Celsus is in part an inheritance from earlier medical systems and ancient human experience; but in part an individual trait of tone and attitude. The wisdom evident in the preface must be credited to the author himself; for there, after an able statement of the issue between empirics and theorists in medicine, he holds the balance fairly, and votes for a combination of experience (*usus, experimenta*) with science (*rationalis ars*). Proposing, therefore, a *uia media* as likeliest to lead to truth, he sagely argues that the great doctors of the past were not made doctors by scientific investigation independently of practice, but were by the fusion made greater doctors still.[2] Among enlightened points in the same introduction are his freedom from the superstitious notion that diseases originate in divine wrath (a supposition logically denounced as a barrier to medical research and progress); his insistence upon the quest for true causes; and the emphasis laid upon anatomy and dissection. Celsus is indeed scientific enough to state principles which were ultimately to antiquate and supersede him: thus, under the head of dissection, he advocated the acquisition of a knowledge destined in due time to convict him of errors; for his anatomy, when he comes to it, is not beyond reproach. His remarks on vivisection are interesting. While he states the argument for experimenting upon condemned criminals, he also states with sympathy, and even some tenderness, the contrary argument on behalf of those surgeons who aim at 'cure, not kill' (*prudentem medicum non caedem sed sanitatem molientem*), who recognise that the chances of the arena or war or an affray often provide a view of internal organs during life without dependence upon the scalpel of some 'ruffian bandit of a doctor,'[3] and who are content 'to learn through pity what others have come to know by fiendish cruelty' (*idque per misericordiam discere quod alii dira crudelitate cognouerint*). His final verdict is that vivisection is superfluous, but

---

[1] II. i. 8–9, 15 (autumn); I. x. 3 ('somnus meridianus'); VII. v. 2 (surgical treatment of arrow-wounds); I. ii. 6, iv. 5, vii, viii. 3 ('clara lectio,' 'uoce contendere,' 'ut lectione aliisque generibus exerceatur,' 'clare legere').

[2] I. *praef.* 47: 'Verique simile est ... non ideo quidem medicos fuisse, uerum ideo quoque maiores medicos exstitisse.'

[3] His language (*ibid.* 42–43) pointedly suggests the parallel between the 'ruffian' vivisectionist and the 'ruffian' robber with violence: 'ita mortui demum praecordia et uiscus omne in conspectum *latrocinantis medici* dari,' and 'interdum enim gladiatorem in arena uel militem in acie uel uiatorem *a latronibus exceptum* sic uolnerari ut eius interior aliqua pars aperiatur, et in alio alia.'

dissection imperative.[1] On many matters his counsels may involve no more than an ability to profit by ordinary human experience and medical tradition; yet, they are counsels which require continual restatement and are violated in all ages. Instances may be found in his rules for preservation of health, in the limits assigned to bodily exercise, in the reduction of food after hard work, in the advantages of a rest cure,[2] or in the physiological restrictions incumbent upon the scholar's burning of the midnight oil – restrictions, more salutary,[3] if less romantic, than the enthusiasm of the student in Bailey's *Festus*,

> When night hath set her silver lamp on high,
> Then is the time for study.

With equal plausibility he advocates the benefits of change: it is good for a cough, while the climate that made one ill is the very worst for the invalid:[4] similarly a voyage is recommended for consumption. Undismayed by any thousandth-chance failure, he insists on the inferences as to the power of medicine that one can draw from countless successful cases.[5] There is, however, no attempt to overestimate the value of drugs; for he bears in mind the curative efficacy of nature,[6] and in another connexion declares the best medicine to be diet seasonably given.[7] Other illustrations of sound sense are his reminder of the tact requisite in a physician about to take an invalid's pulse, his admission that the confident quack may succeed with another's patients better than with his own (*quos ratio non restituit temeritas adiuuat*), and his suspicion of too rigid a theory concerning 'critical days' during an illness as being apparently due to the misleading influences of Pythagorean numbers upon medical calculations.[8] Throughout his work he gives the impression that he set himself in a business-like manner to illustrate the aims which Asclepiades ascribed to a capable physician and which Celsus approves as an ideal *uotum*, namely, 'to effect a cure with safety, despatch, and pleasantness' (*ut tuto, ut celeriter, ut iucunde curet*).[9]

The person likely to reap the maximum of enjoyment from Celsus would be a medical man with historical instincts and a liking for straightforward Latin. A perusal will not recompense the seeker after either

[1] I. *praef.* 74: 'Incidere autem uiuorum corpora et crudele et superuacuum est, mortuorum discentibus necessarium.'   [2] I. ii. and iii.
[3] I. ii. 5: 'Sin lucubrandum est, non post cibum id facere, sed post concoctionem.'
[4] II. i. 4: 'Pessimum aegro caelum est quod aegrum fecit'; IV. iv. 4: 'Utilis etiam in omni tussi est peregrinatio, nauigatio longa, loca maritima, natationes.'
[5] II. vi. 16: 'Non si quid itaque uix in millesimo corpore aliquando decipit, id notam non habet, cum per innumerabiles homines respondeat.'
[6] II. viii. 20: 'Scire licet, inter ea quoque quae ars adhibet, naturam plurimum posse.'
[7] III. iv. 6: 'Optimum uero medicamentum est opportune cibus datus.'
[8] III. vi. 6 (pulse); ix. 4 (a quack's temerity); iv. 11–15 (critical days).
[9] III. iv. 1.

E

elaborate style or unquestionably sound advice; but to any reader pass-
ably acquainted with modern medical theory and practice his pages
offer much in the way of interest, and occasionally of entertainment.
Celsus represents the stage of medical knowledge attained in the early
Empire, and the regimen and prescriptions found in his work indicate
the method of treating or maltreating Roman citizens unlucky enough
to need professional attendance. In a system so many centuries prior
to the germ-theory of disease or to antiseptic and anaesthetic surgery,
all sorts of quaint precautions and quaint remedies are advocated. There
is a difference of atmosphere which, once felt, exerts a fascination, partly
in spite of and partly in virtue of its errors. It is true that his teaching
on anatomy leaves much to be desired; but the lay reader soon forgives
mistakes such as those regarding the spleen.[1] His surgery takes one back
to a period ages before chloroform or ether, when one essential merit
of the operator was intrepidity sufficient 'to resist being influenced by
the patient's shrieks into hurrying more than the case demanded or
cutting less than was needful,'[2] and when, in an operation for cataract,
the head had to be held fast to prevent a movement which might be
permanently fatal to the eyesight.[3] Among curiosities of Celsian medicine may be cited blood-letting for the spitting of blood,[4] and a queer
precaution against headache, to wit, the avoidance of moonlight particularly before the conjunction of sun and moon.[5] Some pronouncements
on diet are extraordinary – pork is the lightest and beef the heaviest
of foods (*leuissima suilla est, grauissima bubula*).[6] His recipe for quinsy
is to eat a young swallow salted, burned, and administered as a powder in
hydromel; and his comment here implies by contrast that, as a rule,
book-knowledge rather than practice is the basis of his pharmacy –
'although I have not read this in medical treatises, still I believe it
ought to be included in this work of mine.'[7] The powdered liver of a
fox[8] for asthmatic troubles is comparable to the roast mouse still recommended in parts of Norfolk for whooping-cough. Not the least
interesting are those prescriptions which, like so many survivals from
primitive magic-healing, belong to what may be called excremental
medicine. Prominent ingredients in his pharmacopoeia are not only
such as deer's marrow, bull's suet, hog's lard, but also the ordure of
various animals. Lizard's dung and pigeon's blood are among the
purgatives; and the dung of lizard, pigeon, ring-dove, swallow and sheep
among caustics.[9] As an encyclopaedic summariser of previous and current medicine, Celsus could not be expected to go beyond his own age;
but at least this may be urged – that his emancipation from a number of
earlier superstitions and his sensible attitude on the combined merits

---

[1] IV. i. 5.
[2] VII. *praef*. 4: 'Non ut clamore eius motus uel magis quam res desiderat pro-
peret, uel minus quam necesse est secet.'
[3] VII. vii. 14c.   [4] IV. xi. 6.   [5] I. iv. 1.   [6] II. xviii. 7.
[7] IV. vii. 5.   [8] IV. viii. 4.   [9] V. v, viii; *cf*. V. xxii. 4.

of theory and practice were far-off presages of a time when medicine would abandon the copious blood-letting and clysterising of coprophagous patients. An illustration of the mark left by Celsus upon medicine was the implicit claim to have eclipsed him which was made in the name 'Paracelsus' assumed some four centuries ago by the clever Swiss alchemist and quack Theophrastus Bombast von Hohenheim. If in the twentieth century Celsian medicine lies under a cloud, it is mainly because, notwithstanding his professed anxiety to give fair-play to both theory and experiment, he does not convince practising doctors that he founded his work sufficiently upon observation. Book-learning and the experience of others do not, from the standpoint of science, counterbalance this absence of a commanding personal authority.

We have seen that Quintilian, who would be most prone to appraise Celsus by his work on rhetoric, did not consider him an author of eminent genius. Without, however, exalted merit, Celsus had a sanity which is reflected in his style. One aspect of his good sense is that gift of straightforward expression which differentiates him from the artificiality of contemporary Latin. He states a plain fact or counsel or argument in a plain way. Some, indeed, of his readers, attracted by the elegance of his brief sentences, have declared that more store should be set by his Latinity than by his medicine. It is an elegance which consists in no literary adornment beyond what comes of lucid, facile and neat exposition in sound Latin.[1] There is almost nothing in the way of literary allusion. Quite exceptional in this respect is the passing reference to the poets' accounts of Ajax or Orestes as illustrating the creations of a disordered imagination.[2] Apropos of swallow's blood prescribed for an injured eye he mentions the *fabula* which told how the old birds healed the eyes of their young with a herb, but *fabula* here may mean popular tradition rather than the literary fable. Signs of the usages of Silver Latin occur: *igitur* begins sentences in the manner of Sallust and Tacitus: *frequens* is used in its later sense: and occasionally he shows the tendency to use abstracts for concretes.[3] But he keeps clear of contemporary mannerisms. When he uses balance, as in his opening words, it is not so much for ornament as for clearness;[4] and herein he presents a strong contrast to such writers as Velleius Paterculus and Valerius Maximus. A well-sustained example of his style is his introduction, where he is free to discuss general subjects at some length and to state his views. In it, the sentences are short and direct – well adapted, without artifice,

---

[1] As a rule, he has too keen a feeling for exactitude to indulge often in a pleonasm like 'causa quae ante praecesserat' (I. *praef.* 70).

[2] III. xviii. 19: 'Quidam imaginibus non mente falluntur; quales insanientem Aiacem uel Orestem percepisse poetae ferunt.'

[3] IV. xxviii. 2: 'uitare autem oportet *cruditates*,' in sense of 'indigestible fare.'

[4] I. *praef.* 1: 'Ut alimenta sanis corporibus agricultura, sic sanitatem aegris medicina promittit.' *Cf.* I. *praef.* 36: 'Nec post rationem medicinam esse inuentam sed post inuentam medicinam rationem esse quaesitam,' where the antithetic order aims at clear emphasis, not rhetorical effect.

to the subject in hand. He is not concerned to avoid the repetition of a word or phrase by hunting after remote equivalents. Once, indeed, he seems to hesitate on a matter affecting his choice of words: it is, however, a hesitation animated not by rhetorical motives but by those qualms of modesty in expression which led many cultured Romans to avoid the Stoic outspokenness in 'calling a spade a spade' and to reject even innocent collocations of sounds capable of conveying indecent suggestion. The question from this latter standpoint is discussed in the well-known letter by Cicero where he furnishes a salutary motto in the opening phrase *amo uerecundiam*.[1] It will be readily gathered that the difficulty for Celsus arises not in collocations of sounds, but in terms which he feels he must use in certain delicate parts of his subject.[2] His quandary is to secure clearness with a due observance of the dictates of modesty and the requirements of medicine.[3] Finally he decides in the interests of health that his treatment must be open and exhaustive; and it is noteworthy that, while he regards Greek terms in such connexions as more acceptable, he prefers in fact to use Latin words.

One may conclude with a passage on the duties of a physician, where the *clausulae* of two sentences recall the Ciceronian *esse uideatur*:

> In the case of these (external injuries), it is beyond everything imperative upon a medical man to know which are incurable, which are difficult to treat and which are easier. For the wise doctor's duty is, first, to decline handling a patient ill beyond the possibility of recovery, and so avoid the appearance of having killed one who was already cut off by his own fate; next, where there is serious apprehension – falling short, however, of absolute hopelessness – to inform the relatives of the person in danger that hope is beset with difficulty, so that, if his skill is baffled by the malady, he may not produce the impression either of ignorance or of deception. But, just as this is the fitting attitude for a wise man, so on the other hand it is worthy of a charlatan to magnify a trivial case in order to produce the impression of a greater achievement.[4]

[1] Cic. *Ad. Fam.* IX. xxii (discussion by E. W. Fay in *C.Q.* I (1907) 13 ff.; Cic. *Or.* XLV. 154; Quint. *I. Or.* VIII. iii. 44–47 (on κακέμφατον), IX. iv. 33; *cf.* F. Ritter, 'Uebertriebene Scheu der Römer vor gewissen Ausdrücken und Wortverbindungen, *Rh.M.* iii (1835) 576 ff.

[2] VI. xviii. 1: 'Proxima sunt ea quae ad partes obscenas pertinent: quarum apud Graecos uocabula et tolerabilius se habent et accepta iam usu sunt, cum in omni fere medicorum uolumine atque sermone iactentur.'

[3] *Loc. cit.*: 'ut difficilior haec explanatio sit simul et pudorem et artis praecepta seruantibus.'

[4] V. xxvi. 1C: 'In his autem ante omnia scire medicus debet, quae insanabilia sint, quae difficilem curationem habeant, quae promptiorem. Est enim prudentis hominis, primum eum qui seruari non potest non attingere, nec subire speciem eius ut occisi quem sors ipsius interemit: deinde, ubi grauis metus, sine certa tamen desperatione, est, indicare necessariis, periclitantis in difficili spem esse; ne, si uicta ars malo fuerit, uel ignorasse uel fefellisse uideatur. Sed ut haec prudenti uiro conueniunt, sic rursus histrionis est paruam rem attollere quo plus praestitisse uideatur.'

POMPONIUS MELA

Pomponius Mela makes at least this claim on attention that his is the first Roman geography which has come down. A study holding a central position between natural sciences such as physics, astronomy, geology, zoology on the one hand and human sciences such as history, anthropology, ethnology, sociology on the other, might reasonably have been expected through its multifarious orientation to appeal to the didactic tendencies of Roman writers. One might have expected that upon the physical, mathematical and ethnographical foundations laid by the Greeks, imposing edifices would be raised by a people whose commercial and military interests opened the world to them, and that the continuous expansion of Rome beyond Italy would stimulate geographical inquiry. No doubt Varro did contribute to the subject, and Caesar, at any rate incidentally. But for generations systematic investigation remained in the hands of Greeks and made little advance upon the knowledge attained in the times of Alexander and Alexandria. It is significant, then, that at a date when the Romans held the greater part of Britain, they had added scarcely anything to the facts learned by the voyage in northern waters made by Pytheas of Massilia about 330 B.C. Much later, indeed, when Pompey's operations against Mithridates opened out the lands in Asia between the Black Sea and the Caspian, the opportunity for recording fresh geographical results had been seized not by any Roman but by the general's Hellenic comrade, Theophanes of Mytilene. Later still, the newly consolidated Roman Empire of the Augustan era received a systematic description from a Greek of Pontus, the renowned Strabo, who, friendly to Rome as he was, entertained but a poor opinion of Roman geographers, remarking that they imitated Greeks without much success, and without bringing to the subject much love of inquiry.[1] These considerations render such Roman works on the subject as exist the more noteworthy; and time has left to us only two, first, the *Chorographia* (or, as it is sometimes called, *De Situ Orbis*) by Pomponius Mela, largely an unoriginal compendium, and later, the portions in the *Natural History* of Pliny which handle geography in no very scientific manner, though their author has too high a regard for truth to acquit Roman writers of falsification or carelessness in their investigations.[2]

Pomponius Mela was, he tells us,[3] a native of Tingentera in Spain, not far from Gibraltar. A slight balance of evidence[4] suggests that he wrote his description of the world under Claudius and that he refers to

[1] Strabo, III. iv. 19: οἱ δὲ τῶν Ῥωμαίων συγγραφεῖς μιμοῦνται μὲν τοὺς Ἕλληνας, ἀλλ' οὐκ ἐπὶ πολύ· καὶ γὰρ ἃ λέγουσι παρὰ τῶν Ἑλλήνων μεταφέρουσιν, ἐξ ἑαυτῶν δ' οὐ πολὺ μὲν προσφέρονται τὸ φιλείδημον, κ.τ.λ.

[2] Plin. *N.H.* V. 12.

[3] Mela II. vi. 96: 'unde nos sumus, Tingentera.'

[4] Teuffel, § 296 n. 1.

that emperor and his triumph of A.D. 44, rather than to Caligula, when he says: 'About the nature of Britain and the nature of her sons it will not be long before more definite and better ascertained details are given. Closed for ages, Britain is now being opened up by the greatest of emperors,[1] victorious over tribes not only unconquered before his own day, but actually unknown. The evidence of its peculiarities which he aimed at in his campaign, he brings home to render clear by his triumph.'[2]

The method of Mela was prompted by the coasting survey of early travellers, and the tradition of such works as the partially genuine *Periplus* or 'Cruise' of Scylax[3] in the fourth century B.C. In the first two of his three books Mela follows the Mediterranean seaboard from west to east along the southern shores and then back from east to west along the northern shores: the third book is left for countries outside this scheme which, though it could not possibily be exhaustive, still with a certain appropriateness had for its hinge the Mediterranean, the ancestral home of geography. Thus, his brief introduction over, Mela deals in Book I with the main divisions of the world, and, after a general survey of Asia, Europe and Africa, turns to a particular description, starting with Morocco, and from Egypt and Arabia proceeding round Asia Minor by the coast of the Levant, Aegean, and Black Sea until in Scythia he reaches Europe. In Book II the course is in the main westwards from European Scythia by Thrace, Greece, Italy, Southern Gaul to Spain with a digression on islands of the Mediterranean suggested by the 'Gades insula.' Book III is concerned with coasts and countries outside the Mediterranean. The ocean brings him to the subject of tides, and he next follows the outer seaboard of Spain, proceeds by Gaul and the Baltic (his Codanian Gulf) to Germany, Sarmatia and Northern Scythia, then notices the islands of the ocean (including Britain and Thule), India, the Persian Gulf, and by a short circuit of Africa works his way back to the part of Mauretania bordering on the Atlantic, so that he ends where he began.

The Mediterranean (*nostrum mare*) is viewed as a continuous sea contracting at the Hellespont (Dardanelles), expanding in the Propontis (Sea of Marmora), narrowing again in the Bosporus, but once more widening into the Black Sea. The method of an imaginary voyage has the

---

[1] Norden, *Kunstprosa*, p. 305, imagines that in the Latin text, III. vi. 49, 'tamdiu *clausam* (*sc.* Britanniam) aperit ecce principum maximus,' there is a play on the name of Claudius.

[2] Literary histories (*e.g.* earlier edd. of Teuffel, 296, 1, and of Schanz, 443) used to combine this passage (III. vi. 49) with Mela's alleged mention (II. vii. 111) of Thia, an island not known before A.D. 46, to prove a later date. But G. Wissowa, *Herm.* li (1916), p. 89 ff., distrusts the reading in II. vii. 111, and argues that the future in *triumpho declaraturus* makes it imperative to take the triumph as a *terminus ante quem*. He rejects 46 and believes the beginning of 44 to be the date of composition.

[3] Bunbury, *Hist. of Anc. Geog.* I. p. 404; Tozer, *Hist. of Anc. Geog.* p. 119.

disadvantage of greatly neglecting interior countries (*e.g.* in Asia, Assyria); and Mela, in the later part of his work, feels compelled to leap eastwards to seas which shall secure him contact with India and Ethiopia. Being a Spaniard, he treats Spain with comparative fullness. In some other cases he holds that the reputation of a city or region dispenses him from elaborate description: Athens, for instance, is too famous to require notice (*clariores quam ut indicari egeant Athenae*), and Italy is handled in a matter-of-fact way without bursts of enthusiasm for the land of his adoption. He will be brief, he promises, concerning a country the treatment of which is demanded rather by the claims of system than by a need for exposition, since here 'all is known' (*nota sunt omnia*).

He blunders in thinking that the Danube flows into the Adriatic,[1] and he is unscientific in blending mythology with geography; but he has the merit of knowing about the north-western sweep of the Gallic coast and about northern seas and the Orkneys (*Orcades*).

Of Mela's sources we have scanty information. He quotes Cornelius Nepos twice,[2] and mentions a report by Hanno the Carthaginian after a voyage of discovery, for which Mela's authority may be Nepos. The knowledge of Spain acquired by Varro, when a Pompeian officer in that country, may possibly have been accessible to Mela,[3] who in turn became a source for the elder Pliny. He is cited on Ireland by one of the scholiasts on Juvenal and on the channels of the Ganges by Servius in opposition to Seneca.[4]

With something like a grudge the author in his proem declares that his task is of a sort which does not admit eloquent treatment; as it involves an array of names, its subject-matter is tedious rather than genial (*longa est magis quam benigna materia*). At the same time, it is well worth study (*aspici cognoscique dignissimum*) and calculated to recompense attention through the very thought put into it, if not through the talents of the author.[5] Though the work be dry and little susceptible of ornament (*facundiae minime capax*), Mela does grasp opportunities of embellishing and enlivening his theme; and the alert reader may, among geographical details, discover and even welcome a rhetorical word-picture or record of wonders.

---

[1] II. iii. 57; iv. 63. Elsewhere he knows of its presence in Eastern Europe. His mistake is a survival of the ancient belief that the Ister had two very distant outlets, one into the Adriatic and the other into the Black Sea. On this misconception see Tozer, *Hist. of Anc. Geog.* p. 120.

[2] III. v. 45 and III. ix. 90.

[3] J. Jung, *Grundriss d. Geographie von Italien u. d. Orbis Romanus* (Müller's Hb. III. iii. 1), ed. 2, Mun. 1897, § 36: 'Von römischer Seite ist zuerst Varro (116-27 v. Chr.) als geographischer Schriftsteller über Hispanien aufgetreten, das er als Legat des Pompejus persönlich kennen gelernt hatte.'

[4] *Scholia in Juv. vetustiora* (ed. P. Wessner, Teub. 1931) ad Juv. II. 159-160; *Servii in Verg. carm. commentarii* (ed. G. Thilo and H. Hagen, Lpz. and Berl. 1923) ad Virg. *Aen.* IX. 31.

[5] I *prooem.*: 'quod si non ope ingenii orantis at ipsa sui contemplatione pretium operae attendentium absoluat.'

One of these purple patches is the description of the cavern of
Corycus[1] in Cilicia, environed by charming greenery and entered by a
narrow and difficult footpath which descends among rustling trees and
dancing rivulets to a grotto within a grotto, darker and more mysterious,
filled with a sound as of crashing cymbals, where a great river seems to
issue forth only to vanish again: and beyond are the depths of the
cavern unmeasured and inexplorable. What otherwise would be a
catalogue is lighted up by passing allusions to famous battlefields,
scenes with historical, poetic or legendary associations, birthplaces of
celebrities, and monuments to the mighty dead; and no little entertainment may be got from his mention of customs[2] and of marvels. It is
not every geography that provides readable fare like the strange fountain
of the Sun in Cyrenaica which boils at midnight and is icy cold at noon
(I. viii); queerly illogical African tribes who curse the Sun both at his
rising and at his setting, and who have no individual names and are a
dreamless people; or cave-dwellers feeding on serpents; or headless
creatures with faces in their chests; the Pyramids (I. ix), and the Mausoleum of Halicarnassus (I. xvi) – representative wonders of the world;
birds that shoot their wing-feathers like arrows (II. vii); the land of
the midnight Sun (III. v); the rich pastures of Ireland on which flocks
might feed till they burst (III. vi); the island of 'hairy women' (presumably some species of apes, III. ix); and the well that brings on a
fatal laugh (III. x). One may read how to defy the serpents of Colu-
braria (II. vii, *ad fin.*); or may be half persuaded, apropos of the rocky
district of the Lapideum (Le Crau) in Southern France, to believe the
old fable that it once rained stones there (II. v). The attraction of the
marvellous is for Mela irresistible; Syracuse, for example, interests him
not for its situation or history, but for the legend of Arethusa: and
perhaps, if he could not be completely scientific, it was well that he
should thus frankly display his not unengaging limitations.

Yet he can be serious and perspicacious. He notes the German love
of war for little or no reason except the desire of having a desolation
round a country where might is right;[3] and he apologises that he cannot
give German geography exhaustively, because the names are too barbarous for Roman lips to pronounce (*quorum nomina uix est eloqui ore
Romano*, III. iii. 30). His description of the Atlantic tides,[4] with his
alternative theories about their cause, may be translated:

'A vast limitless sea, stirred by great tides (that is the term for its
movements) at one time floods the plains, at another uncovers them
widely and retreats. It does not work so on plain after plain in turn;

[1] I. xiii. 72.
[2] *E.g.* Egypt, I. ix; Pontus, I. xix; Scythians, II. i; Druids, III. ii.
[3] III. iii. 27: 'bella cum finitimis gerunt, causas eorum ex libidine arcessunt,
neque inperitandi prolatandique quae possident, nam ne illa quidem enixe
colunt, sed ut circa ipsos quae iacent uasta sint: ius in viribus habent.'
[4] III. 1. 1–2.

it does not by alternate advances sweep round in full rush first on these and next on those; but after pouring out from its centre upon the shores of all countries and islands alike, however far apart, it quits them, and again massing towards its centre returns upon itself. Such is the regular force of the incoming tide that it drives back even mighty rivers, and either overtakes land animals or leaves sea-creatures high and dry. So far there is no definite decision whether this is the action of the universe through its own heaving breath, attracting and repelling the waters everywhere (on the assumption of savants that the world is a single animate being); or whether there exist some cavernous depressions for the ebb-tides to sink into, thence to well out and rise anew; or whether the moon is responsible for currents so extensive.'

The traces of rhetoric are visible not only in descriptions, but also in balanced clauses and exclamatory parentheses which recall Valerius Maximus. Of the bridging of the Hellespont by the Persians he exclaims 'marvellous and mighty feat!' (*mirum atque ingens facinus!*), and of the devotion of the Carthaginian brothers buried alive to settle a boundary dispute in their country's favour, 'Marvellous feat most worthy of remembrance!' (*mirum et memoria dignissimum facinus!*).[1] But he is not long-winded, and indeed has caught some of Sallust's brevity, as where he remarks of the rivers Simois and Scamander near Troy that for them 'fame has done more than nature' and so gives pithy expression to a feeling which many a traveller on the Trojan plain must have shared. Nor is Mela a mere echo of others: his prose has a rhythm of its own. Even without careful enumeration one is struck in reading his Latin by the frequency of two Ciceronian *clausulae* (— ∪ — — ⏓ and — ∪ — — ∪ ⏓). Closer investigation has shown that while he quite remarkably avoids the double trochee endings which are so much more common in Celsus, Curtius, the Senecas, Tacitus and others, he almost as markedly exhibits a preference for closing on a cretic followed by an anapaest or tribrach (— ∪ — ∪ ∪ ⏓) or, to a lesser degree, on one of the favourite types of Greek *clausulae*, the double dactyl (— ∪ ∪ — ∪ ∪).[2]

MISCELLANEOUS LEARNING

In the miscellaneous learning of the age may be included its philosophy, criticism and grammar, jurisprudence and medicine. To take the last first, one recognises in Scribonius Largus, court physician to Claudius, a sort of pendant to Celsus; for in A.D. 47 or 48 he published his collection of medical prescriptions. The jurists included Ateius Capito's pupil, Masurius Sabinus, who gave his name to the 'Sabinian' school, and influenced legal thought through his three books on the *ius ciuile*. In contrast with him M. Cocceius Nerva, the emperor's grandfather,

---

[1] II. ii. 26; I. vii. 38.
[2] See tables of statistics in De Groot, *Prosarhythmus*, pp. 108–109.

E*

trained by Labeo, the great Augustan rival of Capito, was a forerunner of Proculus from whom the 'Proculians' took their name. Among the grammarians were Julius Modestus, Hyginus's freedman, who followed his master's broad conception of grammar; the strict purist Pomponius Marcellus;[1] and the successful but immoral teacher, Q. Remmius Palaemon (*flor.* A.D. 48), whose handbook (*Ars*)[2] had a great vogue, and with whom Persius and Quintilian studied. Columella drew from Julius Atticus and Julius Graecinus, both writers on vine-culture in the time of Tiberius; and the botanists Caepio and Antonius Castor were used by the elder Pliny.

Apicius, pre-eminent as the ideal gourmet, belonged to the reign of Tiberius. His culinary lore was, as we know from Seneca and from a note on Juvenal,[3] committed to writing. The work, however, on cookery in ten books which passes under his name (*Apicius de re coquinaria*)[4] is a compilation of some centuries later, poorly and even ungrammatically written, although entertaining for its astounding variety in ingredients and modes of dressing fish, flesh and fowl, as well as for such naïve receipts as that for improving honey: 'mix two parts of good honey with the bad and put on the market.'

In philosophy the austere morality of the Sextii, father and son, in the Augustan age, had been transmitted through their adherent Papirius Fabianus to the youthful Seneca. Celsus, as we have seen,[5] also wrote on philosophy. Theoretical speculation, however, might prove politically disastrous; for the uncompromising arguments of Julius Kanus, or Canus, led to his being sentenced to death by Caligula:[6] it was a philosopher who attended him to the place of execution, Julius undertaking that, if he discovered the condition of souls in the other world, he would revisit his friends to inform them. But the Stoics in the time of Nero form a more powerful group of thinkers, and, as we shall see, left a permanent mark on literature.

---

[1] Suet. *Gr.* 22: 'sermonis Latini exactor molestissimus.'
[2] The extant *Ars Palaemonis* (Keil, *G.L.* v. 433 ff.) is spurious.
[3] Sen. *Ad Helv.* X. 8; Schol. Juv. IV. 23.
[4] Vollmer (in his edn. w. Giarratano of Apicius, Lpz. 1922) has argued that the 'Caelius,' sometimes added to Apicius's name, should be dropped as an erroneous expansion by Renaissance scholars of what they found on the title-page of the archetype MS.
[5] *Cf. supra*, p. 92–3.   [6] Sen. *De Tranq. An.* xiv. 4; *cf.* 9.

Chapter V

PHAEDRUS AND FABLE: POETRY OF THE TIME

Phaedrus – His Life – Books of Fables and 'Appendix' – Text
incomplete – His Greek exemplar – Relationship to Aesop –
Novelties introduced by Phaedrus – Anecdotes based on Roman
life – Political allusions and prosecution by Sejanus – The gentle
art of making enemies – The injustices of life – Human weaknesses
– The serious and the humorous – Perennial interest in fable –
Realism – Phaedrus as man of letters – Fable in the later Roman
world – Style – Art – Phaedrus and La Fontaine – Metre – A
concluding view.

The poems of Tiberius – Germanicus Caesar's *Aratea* – Mythological Astronomy – Albinovanus Pedo – Decadent forms of
drama – Mime, Atellan farces and *Fabulae Salticae* – Pomponius
Secundus.

PHAEDRUS: THE FABULIST OF ROME

PHAEDRUS, the fabulist of Roman literature, was an alien
slave of Thracian, or, to use his own adjective, 'Pierian' origin.
The lines[1] in which he laid claim to birth 'almost in the very school
of the Muses' are to be taken, according to the spirit of the context,
in the strict geographical sense and not as a metaphorical anticipation
of the Tennysonian conception that 'the poet in a golden clime is born.'
Perhaps the plain prose of the matter is that his birthplace was the
Roman colony of Philippi. Evidently he was brought to Italy when young;
for he refers to studying Ennius in boyhood.[2] His Latin and Greek
education followed the customary routine, to judge from the fact that,
although fables do not readily lend themselves to a display of erudition,
yet his yield proof of acquaintance with such authors as Virgil, Euripides and Simonides.[3] Hardly mentioned in classical literature, his

---

[1] III. *prol.* 17 *sqq.*; L. Schwabe, *Rh.M.* xxxix (1884) p. 476, proves against
E. Wölfflin (*ibid.* p. 157) that the lines are meant literally.
[2] III. *epil.* 33–35:
    'Ego, quondam legi quam puer sententiam
    "Palam muttire plebeio piaculumst."
    Dum sanitas constabit, pulchre meminero.'
Line 34 is from the *Telephus* of Ennius.
[3] III. *prol.* 27–28; IV. vii. 6 *sqq.*; IV. xxii (xxiii) and xxv (xxvi).

name first appears as a nominative, 'Phaedrus,' in a prefatory letter of Avianus;[1] but some have argued that it is more in accord with linguistic usage and inscriptional evidence to call him 'Phaeder.' Inasmuch, then, as he became a freedman in the household of Caesar Augustus, one may consider his full name C. Julius Phaeder or Phaedrus.[2] Concerning the limits of his life, and its scanty details, we are dependent upon deductions from his writings. There is a prevalent consensus among critics that the first two of his five books were published during the reign of Tiberius,[3] perhaps together, perhaps separately as Ellis supposed,[4] and that the third book appeared under Caligula, some time between A.D. 37 and the beginning of 41. Now, since passages[5] in that book suggest that the author was already conscious of approaching age, there is justification for guessing that he was born some fifteen years before the Christian era.[6] Although in Book III he had decided to relinquish authorship, he explains his change of mind in the prologue to the next book,[7] and even after that we possess a fifth, the product of his advanced years.[8]

The two opening books, which explain in their prologues the relationship between the present fables and those of Aesop, may be regarded as dedicated to readers at large;[9] but the rest were dedicated to individuals; namely, Book III to Eutychus, plausibly identified with the chariot-driver of the Greens prominent under Caligula;[10] IV to one Particulo, for whom Phaedrus entertained a respect enhanced, doubtless, by gratification at being quoted in his compositions;[11] and Book V to a certain Philetes, or Philetus, who is pointedly expected to see the applicability to the aged author of the tale about the old hunting-dog past its best:

[1] Avianus, *praef.*: 'Phaedrus etiam partem aliquam quinque in libellos resoluit.'
[2] Plessis, *Poésie lat.* p. 484. Ellis (*Fables of Ph.*, Inaug. lect., Lond. 1894, p. 3) thinks the rare by-form 'Phaeder' less likely.
[3] The emperor seems to be referred to as alive in II. v. 7, where he is 'Caesar Tiberius'; contrast 'a diuo Augusto' of Augustus, III. x. 39.
[4] Ellis, *op. cit.* p. 2. Bk. I is more strictly 'Aesopian' or Hellenic; Bk. II obviously introduces Roman matter.
[5] III. *epil.* 15–19; III. i. 7.
[6] L. Havet (ed. of 1895, p. 242 ff.) favours later dates for his birth and for chronology of the works. According to his arguments – which present difficulties – Book III was written under Claudius, IV under Nero, and V as late as Vespasian's time. Havet's hypothesis depends primarily upon his transposition from Book III of the second part of the prologue (ll. 33–63) to the epilogue of Book II.
[7] III. *epil.* 1; IV. *prol.* 1–10.
[8] V. x. 9–10. That Phaedrus here alluded to his own advanced years was the view of Ribbeck, *Gesch. der röm. Dichtung* iii. p. 27.
[9] *E.g.* II. *prol.* 11. Havet claims that prol. and epil. of Bk. III were addressed to an unknown Illius at a date not earlier than A.D. 43.
[10] F. Bücheler, *Rh.M.* xxxvii (1882) pp. 333 ff.
[11] IV. *epil.* 4: 'uir sanctissime'; *prol.* 17–19:

> 'Mihi parta laus est, quod tu, quod similes tui
> Vestras in chartas uerba transfertis mea
> Dignumque longa iudicatis memoria.'

> You praise our past, if what we are you blame:
> Nicely, Philetes, you can grasp my aim.[1]

In addition to these five books, for which (discounting the recorded readings of the lost *Remensis* and three imperfect codices) only a single manuscript[2] is extant, there is an 'Appendix' of about thirty fables. These, although they look tinctured with medieval colour and show signs of having been supplemented from the Greek collection of Babrius, are considered to have been drawn by Perotti in the fifteenth century from a subsequently lost abridgement of Phaedrus.[3] Twenty so-called 'New Fables', gained from the prose paraphrases associated with the name of the medieval Romulus, appeared in Nilant's edition early in the eighteenth century. The traces discernible therein of their original verse-form led scholars like Dressler and Lucian Müller to rewrite them in metre.[4] Recently Zander in his *Phaedrus Solutus* has reclaimed thirty fables which he has rewritten in senarii after a careful investigation of the three prose-collections – the Ademarian, the Wissemburgensis and 'Romulus.' Zander has aimed at separating Phaedrian and non-Phaedrian elements in the prose paraphrases; he has isolated the traces of fifth-century or sixth-century Latin comparable with what is to be found in Salvianus or Gregory of Tours; and, following principles of Phaedrian metric expounded by Havet, he has made a rather more successful iambic reconstruction of missing fables than some of his predecessors in this field.

Much of Phaedrus, then, is lost. This is a safe conclusion, if only from gaps in our existing text and from the disproportionate length of the books – the total of ninety-three fables in the five books being made up of the constituent numbers thirty-one, eight, nineteen, twenty-five and ten. Besides, an objection of the imaginary matter-of-fact critic forestalled by Phaedrus[5] is that 'not merely beasts but trees do speak' in his fables; yet, in such of the surviving tales as are incontestably by Phaedrus, trees nowhere appear among the interlocutors.[6]

[1] V. x. 9–10:
> 'Quod fuimus, laudas, si iam damnas quod sumus:
> Hoc cur, Philete, scripserim, pulchre vides,'
where the reading of P is *fili te*, and of R *fili² de*.

[2] L. Müller's ed. 1877, Introd. pp. xiii–xxxvii; Plessis, *op. cit.* pp. 488–491.

[3] Ellis (*op. cit.*) gives a useful account of MSS. and early history of the text. Janelli, the editor of the 'Perottine' fables in 1811, has been supported by Cardinal Mai, Orelli, Lachmann, L. Müller, Hervieux and Ribbeck in accepting their descent from Phaedrus. Ellis (*op. cit.* pp. 25–28) gives reasons against crediting this, and compares the impression left by these fables to that left by various imitations of Ovid, the *Nux* or the *Consolatio ad Liuiam* or the spurious poems among the *Heroides*.

[4] For Müller's opinion of Dressler's iambic composition see his ed. of 1877, pp. xxxviii–xxxix.   [5] I. *prol.* 6.

[6] The account of trees favoured by different deities in III. xvii is not an example; but in *Fab. Nouae* (Müller's ed., no. xiii), the oak admits to the ash that they were justly cut down because they had ordered the wild olive to supply a man with an axe-handle.

If Phaedrus had been asked what was the origin of his material, he would have answered 'Aesop' without hesitancy or qualification. Yet the true answer is not so simple. On the one hand, the well-springs lay far deeper in primeval Aryan tales than Phaedrus could have dreamed, and on the other hand the fables which he assumed to be by Aesop consisted largely of accretions subsequent to Aesop's time. The primitive beast-story, so widespread an element in folklore, becomes literary when it is shaped either to satiric or to moral purpose. Some such shaping of the beast-fable lies at the root of the renown of the Samian slave, the actual 'Aisopos,' who flourished in the middle of the sixth century B.C. From tradition and experience – that great repository of practical morality – the Greek observer drew his store. But in the history of literature 'Aesop' became gradually a vague name; for later tales were freely ascribed to him as a kind of father of fable, and such tales enjoyed wide popularity among Greek democracies both as a convenient cloak for social criticism and as a simple form of amusement. In this respect, then, there is an 'Aesopic' just as there is a 'Homeric' Question. The supposed Aesopic fables (λόγων Αἰσωπείων συναγωγαί) were gathered about 300 B.C. by Demetrius of Phalerum, once tyrant at Athens, and afterwards *savant* at Alexandria, where he did much to establish the great library. This Greek prose collection it was – altered and interpolated by Alexandrine scholars – which formed the basis of Phaedrus's neat version in Latin iambics. The same collection, it may be inferred from the reappearance of several stories in Plutarch (or in writings attributed to him), was a source common to Phaedrus and Plutarch (or the pseudo-Plutarch).[1] Further, there is ground for holding that the modern 'Aesop' contains actually more of Phaedrus than of Aisopos, thanks to the influence exerted by Phaedrus in medieval times, mainly if not entirely through the prose-forms to which his verses had been reduced.

Phaedrus was not the first who used the fable in Roman literature. It had been employed incidentally by Ennius, Lucilius and Horace.[2] Phaedrus, however, was the first to compose separate volumes of fables in Latin: this was the one Hellenic form not yet taken over. Drama, epic, didactic, elegy, lyric, history presented no fresh openings; but a limited claim to originality might be based on free poetic adaptations of Greek prose-fables current under the name of 'Aesop.' The attitude of Phaedrus to 'Aesop' was not one which paused critically to examine the implications of the name, but evidently accepted 'Aesop' as the personality responsible for the fables ascribed to him. Phaedrus,

---

[1] Otto Crusius, *Rh.M.* xxxix (1884) p. 603; Ellis, *op. cit.* p. 4; *cf.* W. G. Rutherford, *Babrius*, Introd. p. xi.

[2] Aul. Gell. II. xxix; Hor. *Epist.* I. i. 73 *sqq.* (the sick lion, previously in Lucilius 980 *sqq.* Marx); I. vii. 29 (the *uolpecula* that raided the bin); I. x. 34 (horse securing man's help against stag); *Sat.* II. vi. 79 (town mouse and country mouse).

therefore, felt that, however much he might modify or add, he individually owed Aesop a debt for the substance at least of the fables; and this relationship to the Greek sage is proclaimed at the outset:

> Matter which first old Aesop did rehearse
> Hath Phaedrus polished in iambic verse.
> Two boons my book hath: it can laughter raise
> And give sage counsel in life's wildering maze.
> Howbeit, should one think to criticise,
> Since beasts, nay even trees, here sermonise,
> Let him remember that in fables we
> Divert ourselves with unreality.[1]

Indeed, throughout we are continually being reminded of his model. The epilogue to the second book – an *envoi* to the volume which began with the piece just cited – gives utterance to his admiration in the sentiment which possessed a strong attraction for De Quincey:

> To Aesop Athens reared a statue great,
> And set on lasting marble base a slave—[2]

a proof, says Phaedrus, that the pathway of honour lies open to all and that glory depends on merit instead of birth. If he follows in Aesop's steps, it is in no spirit of envy, but in one of fair emulation:

> If Latium shall countenance my task,
> More authors shall she have to match with Greece.[3]

The prologue of the next book shows that this ambitious desire of bringing honour to Roman literature harmonises with his own patriotic appreciation of Hellenic traditions:

> If Phrygian Aesop by his genius,
> If Scythian Anacharsis could by his
> Build deathless glory, why should I, who am
> Of nearer kin to literary Greece,
> Forsake in idle sleep my country's fame?[4]

[1] I. *prol.* 1–7:
> 'Aesopus auctor quam materiam repperit,
> Hanc ego poliui uersibus senariis.
> Duplex libelli dos est: quod risum mouet
> Et quod prudenti uitam consilio monet.
> Calumniari siquis autem uoluerit,
> Quod arbores loquantur, non tantum ferae,
> Fictis iocari nos meminerit fabulis.'

[2] II. *epil.* 1–2:
> 'Aesopi ingentem (*v.l.* ingenio) statuam posuere Attici
> Seruomque aeterna collocarunt in basi.'

Ingenio is most likely. This is one of a few cases in which N and V preserve by their reading ('Aesopi ingenio') the right tradition against the older manuscript P and the record of R. P gives 'Aesopo ingentem (*m. pr.* Aesopi ingento). . . .'

[3] II. *epil.* 8–9:
> 'Quod si labori fauerit Latium meo,
> Plures habebit quos opponat Graeciae.'

[4] III. *prol.* 52–55.

In a later poem, he pictures Aesop brought out in 'the fresh buskins' of the tragic trimeter;[1] elsewhere,[2] he protests against carping detractors who set successes among the fables to Aesop's account but failures to Phaedrus's own account. The last prologue offers the explanation that he employs Aesop's name to recommend his works, as great artists' names might be inscribed on productions not by themselves: this is virtually to amplify his remark in another place that the fables are 'not Aesop's, but Aesopian.'[3]

It may well be, as Lucian Müller suggested,[4] that Phaedrus used a more complete Aesop than is now available, and that we therefore cannot know how much he owed; but, however extensive his debt, it does not amount to servile borrowing. Independence is not surprising in an author who explicitly recognises individuality in literature,[5] and who, while he undertakes to imitate Aesop's principle of instruction through examples, at the same time engages to introduce novel and diverting anecdotes:

> The sage's method I shall keep with care:
> Yet should it please me add some incidents
> Whereby variety may charm the taste,
> I pray thee, reader, take it courteously.[6]

By such promised anecdotes, some from bygone Greek life, some from contemporary Rome, and by allusions to current events sufficiently caustic to bring trouble upon his head, Phaedrus added greatly to the living force of his work. Bent on his twofold purpose of amusement and counsel, he could not, without becoming a dull second-hand plagiarist, shut his eyes to his own times. Occasionally, indeed, the Roman setting is plainly revealed. It is so in the case of the too credulous father who slew his son under a misapprehension, and then by his suicide left his suspected wife to be haled before the *centumuiri*: it is so in the tale of the conceited flute-player called 'Princeps,'[7] who used to play accompaniments to the *pantomimus* Bathyllus and who, with sublime assurance, mistook for plaudits in his own honour the acclamations of the theatre intended for the real *princeps*, the emperor. Equally Roman, or at least Italian, is the atmosphere in the entertaining tale about the peasant who competed in pig-squeaking on the stage against a professional ventriloquist, and, despite his ingenious precaution of keeping a live porker

---

[1] IV. vii. 5: 'Et in cothurnis prodit Aesopus nouis.'   [2] IV. xxi (xxii).
[3] IV. *prol.* 11: 'Quas Aesopias non Aesopi nomino.'   [4] Ed. 1877, p. 98.
[5] IV. *prol.* 7-8:
> 'Sua cuique cum sit animi cogitatio
> Colorque proprius.'
[6] II. *prol.* 8-11:
> 'Equidem omni cura morem seruabo senis;
> Sed si libuerit aliquid interponere,
> Dictorum sensus ut delectet uarietas,
> Bonas in partes, lector, accipias uelim.'
[7] Bücheler, *Rh.M.* xxxvii (1882) p. 332.

hidden beneath his clothes to be pinched surreptitiously, was howled down by the audience as defective in realism! The closing situation is one of delicious irony when he turns the laugh against his judges by openly displaying the authentic grunter:

> Look ye, this shows what critics you must be.[1]

Again, the painted 'history' of the warfare between mice and weasels[2] seems to allude to wall-paintings of a comic or burlesque nature such as can be illustrated from Pompeii. Another instance is a hit at the *ardaliones*,[3] the fussy triflers and ineffectual meddlers of Roman society. They are derided under the semblance of an officious slave who, by forcing his gardening labours upon the attention of his imperial majesty, tried hard to curry favour and possibly win the ceremonial slap (*alapa*) that conferred liberty:

> A tribe of busy-bodies live at Rome,
> Hot-headed bustlers, pressed 'mid idleness,
> Panting *sans* effort, and with much ado
> Effecting naught, a plague unto themselves
> And most detestable to other men.
> This tribe, if I but can, I would reform
> By this true tale, which will repay your care.
>   Tiberius Caesar once, when Naples-bound,
> Had reached his villa at Misenum's Cape,
> Which, by Lucullus on the headland built,
> Gazes far over the Sicilian main,
> And looks right down upon the Tuscan Sea.
> The Prince was strolling 'mid its pleasant glades,
> When one of his high-girt domestic slaves,
> Whose tunic of Egyptian linen fell
> Loose from his shoulders with its drooping fringe,
> Started with wooden watering-pot to spray
> The droughty ground, and for parade of work
> Got laughed at. Then by well-known cuts he gained
> Another terrace, quick to lay the dust.
> Caesar observed the man and grasped his game
> Of counting on some profit to be earned.
> 'Come here!' the Emperor cried; the knave skipped up,
> Brisk with the joy of sure gratuity.
> Then his Imperial Highness had his jest:
> 'You've not scored much, and all your fuss is lost:
> Far more with me the slaps of freedom cost!'[4]

But Phaedrus's satire was not merely social: it invaded politics. In

---

[1] For these instances, see III. x; V. vii; V. v.
[2] IV. vi. 2: 'Historia quorum et in tabernis pingitur.'
[3] *Ardalio, ardelio, ardulio* are spellings found in glossaries. Nettleship inclined to favour *ardalio, Contribns. to Lat. Lexicography*, Oxf. 1889, p. 267.
[4] II. v.

one passage he refers to fable as a literary invention which might be of
service when one dare not be outspoken;[1] and though it would be an
exaggeration to consider him an organ of political opposition, he clearly
did give umbrage in high quarters by criticisms. There are always people
ready to fit the satiric cap on their heads; and much in Phaedrus could
be deemed offensive by a bad conscience. Some doubtless detected a
political allusion where none was intended; yet there were lines which
inevitably summoned up before the mind recent chapters in Roman
history. No one, for instance, with republican sympathies in his heart
could avoid putting his own interpretation and comment upon the lines:

> Amid a change of government in states
> Poor folk change nothing but their master's name.[2]

Besides, certain fables definitely entered on dangerous ground. Thus,
the familiar tale of the Wolf and the Lamb is explicitly levelled at false
accusers, deriving special significance from the increase of informers
(*delatores*), eager to secure convictions for treason, and encouraged by
the authorities.[3] Nor is hatred of *delatores* under Tiberius far to seek
in the story of the evil end which befell the Wolf who bore false witness
to support the Dog as plaintiff in his invented claim against the Sheep
for a loan.[4] Indeed, there is a good deal of fun in the fables at the expense of law-courts and judges. The problem whether the emperor liked
the anecdote (previously translated) concerning his snub administered
to the officious slave must remain undetermined; and equally insoluble
is the question whether he recognised his portrait in the dread King
Water-snake sent to succeed King Log, the *roi fainéant* against whom
the Frogs had petitioned;[5] but, at any rate, for the emperor's minister
Sejanus there was decidedly unpalatable reading in the first two books.
Sejanus was very like the upstart Jackdaw in peacock's feathers and his
projected alliance with Livia, widow of the Emperor's son Drusus,
possibly lent a sting to the protests of the Frogs against the marriage of
the Sun who, even as things were, dried up the pools: 'what will result if
he have progeny?'[6] Whichever may have been the offending fables in the
volume of Bad Beasts, Sejanus assuredly did institute proceedings against

---

[1] III. *prol.* 33–37:
> 'Nunc fabularum cur sit inuentum genus
> Breui docebo. Seruitus obnoxia,
> Quia quae uolebat non audebat dicere,
> Adfectus proprios in fabellas transtulit
> Calumniamque fictis elusit iocis.'

[2] I. xv. 1–2:
> 'In principatu commutando ciuium
> Nil praeter domini nomen mutant pauperes.'

[3] I. i. 14–15:
> 'Haec propter illos scriptast homines fabula,
> Qui fictis causis innocentes opprimunt.'

[4] I. xvii.   [5] I. ii.
[6] I. vi. 9: 'Quidnam futurumst si crearit liberos?'

the author, who resented the indignity of suffering 'calamity' at such hands.[1] There is no evidence as to the punishment inflicted – whether it was banishment or imprisonment or even a return to slavery – but Phaedrus's tone proves that it left him sore; and the incident is one among many illustrations of the repressive influence of the imperial *entourage*, a circle where few dared say the thing they felt.

It was not only through political strictures that Phaedrus made enemies. As we shall find, his very style, his love of brevity and pith, incurred hostile criticism, and, like Terence, he felt bound to devote portions of his prologues to answering detractors. Annoyance was also given by the manner in which his fables upheld honesty and justice:

> Hard task it is one's feeling to restrain,
> When, conscious of sincere integrity,
> 'Tis badgered by the insolence of knaves.
> 'Who are they?' you will ask: well, time will show.
> There is a motto which I learned at school:
> 'An open growl from common folk is crime.'
> While I have wits, I shall remember well.[2]

Perhaps he is over-insistent on the didactic element in his work and on the lessons derivable from regarding him seriously:

> You take my work for jest; with naught to do
> More grave, I wield an airy pen, 'tis true.
> Howbeit, scan my trivial lays with care:
> How great the profit you will gather there![3]

It is an important aspect of his relation to his times, and a powerful factor in his social criticism, that he emphasises the ubiquitous presence and frequent triumph of injustice. It would be too much to call him gloomy or pessimistic; yet his figures move in a beast-world where, notwithstanding the moral sermonettes, much hardship and unfairness are perforce endured. The Wolf tyrannises unmolested: the Lion insists that the whole spoil is his 'share' and defies his allies to demur: the Ass, captured by robbers, feels no worse for the change of owner than, as a rule, Rome might when she gets a new emperor.[4] When the great

---

[1] III. *prol.* 38–43:
> 'Ego porro illius (*sc.* Aesopi) semita[m?] feci uiam,
> Et cogitaui plura quam reliquerat,
> In calamitatem deligens quaedam meam.
> Quodsi accusator alius Seiano foret,
> Si testis alius, iudex alius denique,
> Dignum faterer esse me tantis malis.'

[2] III. *epil.* 29–35.
[3] IV. ii. 1–4:
> 'Ioculare tibi uidemur, et sane leui,
> Dum nil habemus maius, calamo ludimus.
> Sed diligenter intuere has nenias:
> Quantam sub illis utilitatem reperies!'

[4] I. xv. 2.

fall out, humble people have to suffer – so argue the Frogs about the battles of the Bulls.[1] In a life so troublous, resignation is assumed to be a wise precaution – the Frogs, oppressed by their terrible King Watersnake, after lazy King Log, come to realise that it is best to let well alone, or, even if things are not well, to bear the ills one has.[2] Accordingly, there is much acceptance of fate. This is a wicked world, and must be recognised as such; for so far are rogues from infallibly getting their deserts that their success is often a good advertisement for villainy (*successus improborum plures allicit*, II. iii. 7).

Phaedrus, however, looked beyond the Rome of his day to that wider sphere of human nature which the best fables always illustrate and to which they owe much of their perennial attraction:

> My scheme will brand no individual,
> But life itself and human ways describe:
> 'A heavy task to promise,' one may say.[3]

This relation to life at large comes to a great extent under the second of his professed objects – sound counsel. For example, it is with becoming seriousness that he treats the idea of the two wallets for human shortcomings familiar in Catullus's allusion and forming the ancient analogue to Burns's aspiration:

> Oh wad some power the giftie gie us
> To see oursels as others see us!

In Phaedrus it takes this shape:

> Two wallets Jove on us hath slung –
> One stuffed with faults ourselves have made
> He set upon our back; and hung
> Before our breast the other, weighed
> Down with all other people's vice.
>   Hence our own frailty 'scapes our eyes:
>   Let neighbours slip – we criticise![4]

With similar seriousness of tone he uses the instance of the treasure-dragon to introduce his impressive apostrophe to the miser.[1] In another

[1] I. xxx.
[2] I. ii. 31: 'Hoc sustinete, maius ne ueniat, malum.'
[3] III. *prol.* 49–51:

> 'Neque enim notare singulos mens est mihi,
> Verum ipsam uitam et mores hominum ostendere.
> Rem me professum dicet fors aliquis grauem.'

[4] IV. x:

> 'Peras imposuit Iuppiter nobis duas:
> Propriis repletam uitiis post tergum dedit,
> Alienis ante pectus suspendit grauem.
> Hac re uidere nostra mala non possumus;
> Alii simul delinquunt, censores sumus.'

Cf. Catull. xxii. 21: 'Sed non uidemus manticae quod in tergo est.'
[1] IV. xx (xxi). 16–26.

poem we find the wise pilot's advice for voyagers across the ocean of life:

> Rejoice restrainedly and murmur slow;
> For life is one long blend of weal and woe.[1]

There is also a note of pathetic truth to human experience and of wistful yearning in the little piece on the rarity of affection in ordinary life:

> The name of friend is common; friendship, rare.
> When a small home was built by Socrates
> (I would not shun his death to win his fame,
> I'd yield to odium, if but cleared when dust),
> One of the people – name unknown, of course –
> Asked 'Why so small a house for one so great?'
> The answer came ''Twill hold my real friends.'[2]

Yet it would be unfair to leave the impression that even in his satire on human nature Phaedrus constantly wears a sober face. He does not forget that one of his objects is amusement; and although there may be little enough of the 'laughter' which he promised, still many subjects are treated lightly and pleasantly. In such manner he handles the recurrent foibles of humanity exemplified in braggarts, in public gullibility, in interested advisers, in the old lady with a weakness for drink, and so forth.[3] Here is his glance at good-looking and lucky fools:

> Sir Reynard once a tragic mask espied:
> 'How fine a face to have no brain inside!'
> Said he. And so with those to whom their fate
> Gives rank and glory, but an empty pate.[4]

Here again, a little more fully than in the Horatian *parturiunt montes, nascetur ridiculus mus*, we have a vivid illustration of 'much cry and little wool':

> A mountain once was brought to bed
> With frantic groans of labour torn.
> Earth in excitement lost its head –
> When lo! a tiny mouse was born!
> This story is designed for one
> Of mighty threats, fulfilment none.[5]

There is humour, too, as of some irresolute Sir Roger de Coverley, in Mr. Justice Ape's summing up of a case where prosecutor and defendant are alike disreputable and there has been unscrupulous cross-

---

[1] IV. xvii (xviii). 9–10:
  'Parce gaudere oportet et sensim queri:
  Totam aeque uitam miscet dolor et gaudium.'
[2] III. ix: 'Vulgare amici nomen, sed rarast fides. . . . '
[3] I. xi, xiv, xxv; III. i.   [4] I. vii.
[5] IV. xxiii (xxiv): 'Mons parturibat, gemitus immanes ciens,' etc. *Cf.* Hor.
A.P. 139.

swearing. After hearing two clever but conflicting perorations, the
Justice pronounces with Gilbertian comicality for both sides:

> 'You, Wolf, it seems, ne'er lost what now you claim:
> I find, glib Fox, you stole it all the same!'[1]

One must not overlook another source of charm. Good fables have a
right to be read for the story alone. Now, as has been pointed out, much
in Phaedrus comes down through Aesop from the primitive beast-
story and folklore of the Aryans: much is but the residuum of what
prehistoric fancy was capable of inventing and believing in far-off times
when quadruped, reptile and bird were supposed to talk. Phaedrus gave
classic expression in verse to tales which have appealed to countless
generations of children and which hold their own in the modern nursery.
For, as Reinach would like us to believe, our youngsters love such tales
because they are unconscious totemists![2] To read Phaedrus, therefore,
is like meeting friends that everyone must know, because the stories
illustrate the common experience of mankind. So, granted a judicious
ability to overlook the obtrusion of a moral first or last in a fable, one
never tires of The Wolf and the Lamb, The Jackdaw in Peacock's
Feathers, The Lion's Share, The Ambitious Frog and the Ox, The
Sham Hospitality of Fox and Stork, The Mule with the Load of Gold
and the Mule with the Load of Barley, The Wolf at Large and the Dog
with a Collar,[3] The Pearl in the Dung-heap, Aesop tossing Nuts or All
Work and No Play, The Fox and the Sour Grapes, The Viper and the
File, The Snake in the Bosom, The Forelock of Opportunity, and
Old Bald-pate with the Fly or Adding Insult to Injury.[4]

Human realism, in fact, has been imparted to the beast-fable. Constantly forgetting that one is reading about animals, one does not care
if the doings and sayings are inconsistent with the laws of physics or
natural history. It matters little that a swimming dog is unlikely to see
his reflexion in the water, and that cats do not habitually eat young pigs.[5]
The passions, wiles and talk of the animals are convincing because of
the resemblance to mankind. In this sense, how natural it all is – how
true to life! The cynical ingratitude of the bitch after borrowing shelter
for herself and whelps; the mortally wounded pride of the old lion who
endures a double death (*bis uideor mori*) when kicked by the ass; the
much to be suspected outburst of sudden generosity on the part of de-
signing persons in contrast with the staid fidelity of a watchdog; the

[1] I. x. 9–10.   [2] S. Reinach, *Orpheus*, Eng. ed., 1909, p. 16.
[3] III. vii. Havet's theory (*R.E.A.* 1921) that this fable represents an actual
dialogue in A.D. 16 between Arminius the Cheruscan warrior and his Romanised
brother Flavus cannot be either proved or disproved.
[4] The most famous line in Phaedrus is probably V. iii. 5:
> 'Iniuriae qui addideris contumeliam.'
[5] I. iv; II. iv. Lessing in the one case and Ellis in the other criticised adversely
Phaedrus's accuracy. For similar mistakes, see J. J. Hartman, *De Ph. fabulis
commentatio*, Leiden 1890.

dignified contempt wherewith the boar declines to avenge a lewd insult (*inquinari nolo*) – these[1] and many such have close parallels in actuality. Little wonder, then, that contemporaries not infrequently beheld themselves under the disguise. So entirely apposite were many stories that, as already seen, offence was sure to be taken where none was meant.

Without being among the great in achievement, Phaedrus yet exhibits the genuine attitude of a man of letters. He is intensely sensitive to unfriendly criticism; he repeatedly makes retorts on cavillers;[2] he is proud of literary qualities like brevity;[3] believes he has his place as the introducer of a new form in Roman literature;[4] and has confidence in the survival of his writings.[5] He takes pleasure in his vocation; for it is with obvious satisfaction that he recounts the value of literature to Simonides.[6] Yet, equipped as he was with talent and self-reliance, and likely to secure an initial recommendation from his connexion with the imperial court, he admits that he made his way with difficulty. The admission occurs in the passage where, after mentioning his birth, he avows his disdain for wealth and his devotion to poetry:

> I came to birth on that Pierian hill,
> Whereon the hallowed dame, Mnemosyne,
> Nine times a mother, bore to Thunderer Jove
> The Muses' Choir. Though almost in that school
> I first saw light, though from my breast I have
> Erased all lust for gain, and with fair fame
> Undimmed, have set my heart on my career,
> Still 'tis but grudging welcome I receive.[7]

In face of opposition, however, he feels the superiority of his own unappreciated pearls: it is like throwing them on a dunghill to offer fables to unresponsive readers:

> Once in a dung-heap, as for food it sought,
> A barnyard fowl a pearl to light had brought:
> 'Ah, what a gem to lie so low!' he cried;
> 'If found by one for thy true worth keen-eyed,
> Long since thou hadst regained thy pristine pride.
> But I, thy finder, much prefer my food:
> Nor I to thee, nor thou to me dost good!'
> I mean the present fable to allude
> To those who Phaedrus have not understood![8]

[1] I. xix, xxi, xxiii, xxix.
[2] *E.g.* II. *epil.* 10–14; III. ix. 4; IV. *prol.* 15; IV. vii; IV. xxi (xxii).
[3] *E.g.* II. *prol.* 12; IV. *epil.* 7. III. x closes with explanation that the story has been fully told because his brevity has offended some.
[4] II. *epil.* 1–9.
[5] III. *prol.* 32; IV. *epil.* 5–6:
> 'Particulo, chartis nomen uicturum meis,
> Latinis dum manebit pretium litteris.'
[6] IV. xxii (xxiii) and xxv (xxvi).
[7] III. *prol.* 17: 'Ego, quem Pierio mater enixast iugo,' etc.   [8] III. xii.

The tardy acceptance of his writings during his lifetime seems in harmony with the silence regarding him in the classics at large. Seneca, writing about A.D. 43, pronounces the fable to be work 'unattempted by the *Roman* genius.'[1] Possibly in this remark he may definitely have the Greek Phaedrus in mind, though he does not name him. Quintilian, while he finds a place for fable in his scheme of education,[2] does not mention Phaedrus. Before Avianus, who wrote in the fourth century, the single allusion generally cited as applicable to him, namely Martial's *an aemulatur improbi iocos Phaedri?* is not beyond dispute. While it is appropriate in Martial to call the fables *ioci*, as their author does, the epithet *improbus*, if it seriously means 'shameless,' is remarkably inappropriate as a fair description of our moralist, even when we grant that he can be coarse. It is just possible that the coarsest in him has not survived; but unless one adopts a supposition of this sort, there is a temptation to fancy that the Phaedrus whom Martial meant may have been some obscure writer of mimes.[3] More justice was done to his reputation in later centuries when abridgements were in vogue; and in the Middle Ages he may be said to have had his revenge.

This is a suitable point at which to note briefly the later fortunes of fable in the Roman world. It was not till after the time of Augustus that a group of Indian beast-stories with ethical applications was brought to Alexandria by a Cingalese embassy. Translated as the 'Libyan Fables' of one 'Kybises,' they had pithy conclusions pointing the moral to be deduced. In the days of Marcus Aurelius, a rhetor at his court, Nicostratus, formed a *corpus* out of the old Greek collection of Demetrius and the Libyan collection of 'Kybises.' This body of fable from the nearer and the farther East was next turned into Greek choliambics by Valerius Babrius, about whose date there has been considerable dispute, but who probably wrote before the end of the second century after Christ. It is the Libyan element, rather than the Aesopic, which predominates among the forty-two fables done into Latin elegiacs by Flavius Avianus in the fourth century; and his uninspiring verses close

---

[1] Sen. *Ad Polyb.* viii. 3 . . . 'fabellas quoque et Aesopeos logos, intemptatum Romanis ingeniis opus.' Most scholars take this to imply either an ignorance or an ignoring of Phaedrus on Seneca's part. But Seneca was writing to a Greek freedman, and remembering that Phaedrus was Greek too, he compliments his correspondent by remarking that fable writing was a sort of literary work which *Romans* had not tried. I have argued in *C.R.* xxix (1915) pp. 252–253, that there is no need to implicate Seneca in a wilful falsehood. See also J. P. Postgate who discusses (*C.R.* 1919, p. 19 ff.) some parallels between P. and Seneca.

[2] *Inst. Or.* I. ix. 2.

[3] Mart. III. xx. 5. This is Friedländer's suggestion *ad loc.* Teuffel, § 284, 3, dismisses it summarily as against probability ('ohne Wahrscheinlichkeit'). But Plessis, *Poésie lat.*, p. 487, agrees with Friedländer. Ellis (*op. cit.* p. 8) takes Martial to mean the fabulist, and *improbi* to allude to fables such as I. xxix; III. i; III. iii; IV. xv (xvi); IV. xviii (xix). G. Thiele, in *Philol.* lxx, 1911, pp. 539–548, proposes to read in Martial 'an aemulatur improbi *logos* Phaedri?' taking *logos=apologos* (*cf.* Sen. *Ad Polyb.* viii. 3) and *improbi*='audacious' applied to political allusions in the fables.

the ancient records on this subject. With the later and more fascinating
history of fable we are not concerned, except to observe that in the
Middle Ages it was Phaedrus who was especially read and paraphrased
among fabulists. About eighty of his fables were collected in prose, perhaps in the ninth century,[1] and went under the name of 'Romulus.' The
prose collection which once belonged to the monk Ademar of Chabannes
or Chabanais,[2] and was possibly written by himself early in the eleventh
century, possesses the historic interest of preserving some portions
of Phaedrus otherwise lost; elsewhere among its contents are prose
versions of existent verse fables in Phaedrus with but slight alterations.[3]

The outstanding qualities of the style and art of Phaedrus are his
direct simplicity of language and unpretentious neatness of phrase and
line. On brevity, as already indicated, he plumed himself, though on
occasion he is half-apologetic over it. Brevity, we know, is not necessarily
simple; but his brevity is. With him, condensation was not purchased
at the expense of clearness; for his style is on the whole flowing and easy.
Its natural turns, which seem to grow out of the nature of the subject,
are at once appropriate to his animal speakers and a contrast to the artificial rhetoric beginning to inundate Latin literature. At the same time,
he was aware of this increasing tendency towards the high-flown and
the far-fetched; for in a passage[4] where he makes telling retort on the
hypercriticism launched at him, he composes a specimen of the tragic
manner, and proclaims the impossibility of pleasing a fastidious Cato[5]
of a critic by means of either *fabellae* (fables) or *fabulae* (plays). It is, then,
vastly to his credit that, while he thus affords proof of what he could
do in aping tragic diction, he yet so avoids inflation and preciosity as to
attain a strict and almost Attic sobriety of style comparable with the clear-
cut and restrained work of Terence in the drama or of Caesar in prose.
His use of antithesis, which is not tediously overdone, may be cited in

[1] The process of abridgement, mutilation and transformation of Phaedrus
took place between the time when Avianus must have read the fables in verse-
form (*i.e.* with intervals marked between lines), and the ninth or tenth century,
when the *Pithoeanus* has them without any mark to distinguish them from prose.
Ellis (*op. cit.* pp. 9–10) argues that the abridgement 'may have been executed
in the 5th or 6th cent., and that the gradually declining knowledge of ancient
language and metre, which the unsettled state of Europe produced, caused the
iambics of Phaedrus to be written in prose. As prose they were probably read
by the Carlovingian scholars.'

[2] 'Ex libris bonae memoriae Ademari grammatici' is part of a note in the MS.,
which was written in the Abbey of St. Martial de Limoges.

[3] The influence of Phaedrus, and especially the strong influence of the Romulus collection, upon the MS. of Ademar, are discussed by G. Thiele, *Der illus-
trierte lateinische Aesop* (*Codices Graeci et Lat.*, suppl. iii, Leiden, 1905); *cf.*
C. M. Zander, 'De generibus et libris paraphrasium Phaedrianarum,' *Acta Univ.
Lund.* xxxiii (1897); *Phaedrus Solutus*, 1921.

[4] IV. vii.

[5] IV. vii. 21–22. Cato is, of course, the type of the austere literary judge, *e.g.*
in the Petronian epigram, 132:

> 'Quid me constricta spectatis fronte, Catones?'

illustration of his restraint; *e.g.*,

> Strangers he gulls, but friends make fun of him
> (*Ignotos fallit, notis est derisui*, I. xi. 2)

> Bores to themselves, a loathsome tribe to others
> (*Sibi molesta et aliis odiosissima*, II. v. 4).

In a certain fondness for abstract[1] turns of expression one remarks a resemblance to the style of Valerius Maximus, and therefore a symptom of the movement in the language towards Silver Latinity. In general, despite his foreign origin, the Latin of Phaedrus obeys correct canons, though there are occasional vulgarisms and instances of loose grammatical usage.[2]

He does not possess in any remarkable degree the artist's eye. The picturesque may be said to begin and end for him in a few vivid synonyms like 'long-ears' (*auritulus*) for an ass, 'the wizened one' (*retorridus*) for an old mouse, or in epithets like those in 'branching antlers' (*ramosa cornua*) of a stag, or 'lightning-flashing tusks' of the wild boar (*fulmineis dentibus*).[3] He may pause to give a condensed description; but it is rare to find anything so full in this kind as Juno's summary of the peacock's advantages:

> Thou bear'st the palm for beauty as for size;
> The gleam of emerald illumes thy neck;
> A tail thou spread'st with brilliant plumes begemmed.[4]

Nor does he trouble, we have seen, to keep true to nature; except in wonderland, cow, she-goat and sheep make a curious triple alliance for a lion on a carnivorous expedition. Really, Phaedrus is in Roman fashion bent upon moralising so that his readers shall reap benefit (*utilitatem*);[5] and this domination of the moral is one factor which prevents any free and accurate study of animals. Not one of the world's mighty sages, he has rather a thin philosophy to propound; and on his narrow stage the beasts sometimes display no more vitality than wooden

[1] *E.g.* I. xiii. 12: 'Tum demum ingemuit corui deceptus stupor';
  II. v. 23: 'Tum sic iocata est tanti maiestas ducis';
  III. v. 9: 'Sed spes fefellit inpudentem audaciam';
cf. the personification in I. xxvii. 6:
    'Poenas ut sanctae Religioni penderet';
and in IV. xi. 4:
    'Repente uocem sancta misit Religio.'

[2] On vulgarisms, see H. von Sassen, *De Phaedri sermone*, Marb. 1911, p. 8. 'Persuasus' occurs III. v. 8 (*cf.* I. viii. 7) but see *supra*, p. 66 n. 3.

[3] I. xi. 6; IV. ii. 16; I. xii. 5; I. xxi. 5. The epithet *fulmineus*, applied to *dens* or *os*, is shared with Ovid and Statius.

[4] III. xviii. 6–8:
    'Sed forma uincis, uincis magnitudine;
    Nitor smaragdi collo praefulget tuo
    Pictisque plumis gemmeam caudam explicas.'

[5] IV. ii. 4. A case in point is the threefold lesson, each, as it were, numbered and labelled, from the story of the thief who stole an altar-lamp, IV. xi. 16–21.

marionettes. This renders his psychology too naïve – his animals reason in a manner patently subordinate to the intended lesson. The doves, for instance, harried by the kite, see at last the error of their ways and acknowledge the justice of their punishment:[1] and the outcome has a smack suggestive of a death-bed repentance in accord with the distinctly self-regarding morality inculcated.

Although the parallel of La Fontaine's fables must cross the mind insistently during a study of Phaedrus, yet any elaborate comparison between the two would be futile. There is so much that is incommensurate. The claim of Phaedrus had been to polish in iambic verse the prose of 'Aesop'; and it may be granted that his fables have more picturesque turns than their Greek originals. But they pale before the masterpieces of the French writer. Phaedrus does not possess the knowledge, the penetration, the dramatic power, the sense of style – he has not, in short, the genius which makes La Fontaine a great poet at a great epoch, and *par excellence* the thinker and artist among fabulists. The Russian fabulist Kriloff, who is manifestly under obligations both to La Fontaine and to Aesop, may in one striking way be said to continue the Phaedrian tradition; for, whereas La Fontaine's fables are impersonal, Kriloff's had a frequent and pointed bearing on affairs and circumstances in the Russia of his time.

The metre of Phaedrus is the iambic senarius throughout. It is not the iambic line favoured by Catullus, Bibaculus or Horace, but broadly that employed by the ancient comic writers. He may have been influenced by Publilius Syrus, to whose sententious manner the moral of a fable often bears resemblance. We meet with a different type of iambic trimeter in Seneca, who, owing to Ovidian influence,[2] composed lines unlike the early Roman tragic iambic; for neatness and monotony have in the Senecan iambic replaced the strong rough lines of Ennius, Pacuvius and Accius. But it is the ancient iambic line, as used in comedy by Plautus and Terence, which descends lineally to Phaedrus. Only, while he may offend a fastidious ear by admitting spondees in the second and the fourth feet, he is generally careful to avoid overloading his verse with long syllables and to secure variety of sound by occasionally introducing three-syllabled feet[3] and by attention to elision.

Regarding the fables as a whole, Mackail contends that 'their chief interest is as the last survival of the *urbanus sermo* in Latin poetry';[4] but perhaps this view too exclusively estimates them from the linguistic and stylistic side. Slight from the standpoint of purely literary merit, the fables of Phaedrus do however possess considerable historical

---

[1] I. xxxi. 13: 'merito plectimur.'
[2] Butler, *Post-Aug. P.* pp. 70–71.
[3] His usage with regard to various feet is discussed in Müller's ed., 1877, pp. ix–xiii. Consult also the careful essay on metre and prosody in Havet's ed. of 1895.
[4] *Lat. Lit.*, 1895, p. 160.

importance. They hold their place in the chronicle of European fable-literature; they form a chapter in the book of Rome's debt to Greek models; they contain a significant amount of original material, with a virile bearing upon contemporary life; and, farther, it is not the least of their claims to attention that they wielded a potent influence in medieval times, and, if only as one of those lesson-books which sink deep into the memory, they have been beloved by many generations of readers.

POETRY OF THE TIME

To the exiguous body of minor poetry during his own times Tiberius contributed a lyric lament on the death of L. Caesar, and poems in the late Greek manner.[1] It has already been observed that the emperor had profited by his studies in rhetoric, under Theodorus and others, enough to acquit himself proficiently in speaking and in writing, though he cultivated at times a halting and obscure manner. Towards the close of Augustus's reign, Manilius[2] had written his *Astronomica*, viewing the universe on Stoic principles and displaying a style not uninfluenced by Ovidian dexterity.

A famous but ill-starred prince has a niche in the history of that particular type of didactic poetry which descended from Cicero and Manilius. The emperor's nephew and adopted son, Germanicus (15 B.C.–A.D. 19), added to military ability a command of his own language as speaker and poet.[3] He wrote Greek comedies which have perished, and in both languages elegiac epigrams, a few of which have been preserved, including a Latin one on a boy who met with a fatal accident on ice. To him are usually assigned the hexameter translations or adaptations of Greek poems on astronomy and weather-signs which have come down, some 700 and 200 lines respectively, under the name of 'Claudius Caesar.' The larger portion on astronomy represents with varying degrees of fidelity Aratus's *Phaenomena* 1–732. The lines on weather forecasts have no relation to Aratus. There is ancient authority for the ascription to Germanicus; Lactantius, for instance, quotes a line from 'Germanicus Caesar in his Aratean poem.'[4] An apostrophe to Augustus in the poem (l. 558) implies the death of that emperor, and *genitor* in l. 2 is applicable to his adoptive father Tiberius. Rutgers's advocacy for the authorship of Domitian (who did not take the title 'Germanicus' until after his campaign against the Chatti in A.D. 84) has found little acceptance.

---

[1] Suet. *Tib.* lxx. Probably most, if not all, of Tiberius's poetry was composed before his accession. Certainly this is true of the lament on L. Caesar (*ob.* A.D. 2).
[2] Duff, *L.H.R.* pp. 450–454.
[3] Suet. *Cal.* iii; Tac. *Ann.* II. lxxxiii; Plin. *N.H.* VIII. 155: 'fecit et diuus Augustus equo tumulum, de quo Germanici Caesaris carmen est.'
[4] Lact. *Div. Inst.* V. v. 4: 'ut Germanicus Caesar in Arateo loquitur carmine: "Nec consanguineis fuerat discordia nota."'

Astronomy formed in antiquity an integral part of a liberal education: a cultured Roman in reading about the heavens was far from being so helpless as is the average reader of today, nor was the ancient so ignorant when he looked at the starry sky. The work translated and amplified by Germanicus is, in effect, an indication of a different type of knowledge, requirement and interest from that usual in modern times, and its compound of astronomy and mythology cannot retain the attraction which it once exercised. A heavenly body is not merely mentioned in its position or for its influence: it is connected with the legend from which its name is derived, and so the didactic is lit up with faint gleams of poetry, in which perhaps Germanicus excels his original. Thus the deteriorating ages of the world appear as in Ovid and the name of a constellation like Andromeda leads away from science into fancy:[1]

> The picture of her woe abides: she still extends
> Her arms as once when bound to cruel cliff.

Long ago, Frey[2] pointed out the prince's free treatment of his Greek original, his correction of mistakes in the light of later knowledge, and his insertion of passages of his own composition, somewhat in the fashion observable in Coleridge's rendering of Schiller's *Wallenstein*. If time-honoured legends are not subjected to critical examination, they are at least sometimes introduced apologetically: 'if an old tale may find favour,' 'if in truth Jupiter was suckled as a child,' 'if in truth Atlas upholds the realms of Jove.'[3] This independence of method and spirit is one of the features which distinguish Germanicus's version of the *Aratea* from the preceding attempt by Cicero and the later one by Avienus in the fourth century.

A poem concerned with Germanicus may appropriately be mentioned here, because it connects the age of Augustus and that of Tiberius. It is a fragment in hexameters which stops short in the twenty-third line as quoted by the elder Seneca[4] to illustrate Latin power in describing the ocean. The verses are by Albinovanus Pedo,[5] a poet of Ovid's set, who had written a *Theseid* among other things some years earlier than this poem on the expedition under Germanicus into the North Sea. Tacitus has described the storm which befell this same expedition in the *Annals* (II. xxiii). In turgid style Pedo aims at conveying the nervous alarm of adventurers braving the unknown hazards of high

---

[1] 205–206:
> 'Sed poenae facies remanet districtaque pandit
> Bracchia ceu duri teneantur robore saxi.'

[2] *De Germanico Arati Interprete*, 1861.

[3] ll. 31, 165, 264: 'ueterist si gratia famae,' 'si uere Iuppiter infans . . .' etc.

[4] *Suas.* i. 15.

[5] Duff, *L.H.R.* p. 449. The name Albinovanus Pedo suggests a possible relationship with Albinovanus Celsus mentioned by Horace, *Epist.* I. viii. 1. He accompanied Tiberius to Armenia in 20 B.C.

latitudes, with a sense of being exiled (*extorres*) beyond the known limits of the globe into sunless realms where Ocean 'bears enormous monsters 'neath its sluggish tides': They exclaim:

> Heaven calls us back, forbidding mortal eyes
> To know the boundary of the world: why force
> With oars those alien seas and haunted waves?[1]

Though Pedo is mainly Augustan, his declamatory lines composed under Tiberius possess the interest of forming a link between the rhetorical qualities observable in Ovid and the epic poetry of the Silver Age.

The rarity of names of contemporary playwrights is a reminder that the drama, usually at Rome outrivalled by less intellectual entertainments, had fallen upon evil days. The popular dramatic performances, in favour of which comedy[2] had virtually disappeared, were now the mime and the Atellan farce. The mime, realistic and often coarse though it was in its picture of life, yet, according to the opinion of so staid a philosopher as Seneca, shared with ancient classical tragedy and comedy the merit of conveying impressive lessons of practical wisdom;[3] and there is a familiar anecdote told of the death-bed scene when Augustus asked those around him whether he had played the 'mime' of life well, capping his query with Greek verses which solicited their applause.[4] A writer of Caligula's time named Catullus composed mimes, two of which were *Phasma* ('The Spectre') and *Laureolus*, whose title-rôle of a bandit was on one occasion sustained by a wretched criminal who underwent a real crucifixion upon the stage.[5] The Atellan farce held its ground during several reigns,[6] and was presumably all the more acceptable because some line or lines might strike the audience as covertly directed against an emperor.

Tragedy can scarcely be said to have had a real survival in the atrophied forms of *fabulae salticae* and dramatic recitations.[7] The *fabula saltica* expressed action, feeling and character, sometimes no doubt with marvellous dexterity, through the dancing, gesture and garb of a

---

[1] ll. 20-22:

> 'Di reuocant rerumque uetant cognoscere finem
> Mortales oculos: aliena quid aequora remis
> Et sacras uiolamus aquas?'

[2] The chief authors of comedy traceable during the Silver Age are the Pomponius Bassulus recorded in an inscription at Aeclanum (*C.I.L.* IX. 1164) as a translator of Menander as well as a writer of original plays, and the Vergilius Romanus of Pliny's letters who composed comic dramas after the old fashion. These, it may be guessed, were not intended to be acted. See S.H. § 417.

[3] Sen. *Ep.* viii. 8.

[4] Suet. *Aug.* xcix.

[5] Juv. VIII. 185-187; Suet. *Cal.* lvii; Jos. *Ant.* XIX. i. 13: μῖμος εἰσάγεται καθ' ὃν σταυροῦται λῃστῶν ἡγεμών.

[6] Suet. *Tib.* xlv; *Galba* xiii. See *infra*, pp. 222-223.

[7] Lucian, *De Saltatione*; Friedländer, *Sittengesch.* II. iii. 3; Butler, *Post-Aug. P.* pp. 26-28.

pantomimus, while the words of the play were assigned to a chorus. Had the librettos come down, some might conceivably have entered into literary history: we know, for instance, that Lucan wrote fourteen such librettos; and, later, Statius wrote an *Agaue* for the dancer Paris. Many pieces, however, were based on the most unsavoury stories in mythology, and represented a Pasiphaë, a Myrrha, or a Leda. As regards the pathetic recitations whether extracted from plays or composed specially to be recited, this mutilated or attenuated form of drama became one of the great amusements of Nero both as writer and performer.

Dramatic composition under the Empire was in reality no safer for authors than history was. If a mere line about a ruler's folly in a tragedy apparently so remote from contemporary politics as his *Atreus* involved the downfall of Mamercus Scaurus,[1] it is hardly matter for surprise that an equivocal jest in an Atellan farce should lead Caligula to have its luckless author burned in the amphitheatre.[2] The friendship of P. Pomponius Secundus[3] with a son of Sejanus had rendered him suspect under Tiberius, and for years he remained under surveillance with enforced leisure for literary creation. Outliving Tiberus, he again became a public figure. The elder Pliny speaks of him as of consular rank, served under him against the Germans, and wrote his biography. Why the mob in the theatre attacked Pomponius in A.D. 47 is not clear. Quintilian, at any rate, considered him far the best tragic poet he had seen. Of his plays only a single title survives – the *Aeneas*, presumably a *praetexta* dramatising portions of the legendary history of Rome.[4]

[1] Dio lviii. 24: ἑάλω διὰ τραγῳδίαν . . . ᾿Ατρεὺς μὲν τὸ ποίημα ἦν, κ.τ.λ.
[2] Suet. *Cal.* xxvii.
[3] Tac. *Ann.* V. viii, XI. xiii; *Dial.* 13; Plin. *N.H.* VII. 80, XIII. 83, XIV. 56; Plin. *Ep.* VII. xvii. 11; Quint. X. i. 98. Interesting light is thrown on his life and qualities by Cichorius, *Röm. Stud.* pp. 423-432, where it is shown that Pomponius lived till late in Nero's reign.
[4] Attraction to the Troy-saga may explain the tragic songs which Paetus Thrasea rendered at the *cetaria*, or festival, in honour of the Trojan Antenor at Padua, where Thrasea came from, Tac. *Ann.* XVI. xxi; *cf.* Charisius (Keil, *G.L.* i. 125), quoting Pliny, *i.e.* presumably the lost *Dubius Sermo*.

PART II

Literature of the Neronian Period

A.D. 54—68

Chapter I

COLUMELLA AND AGRICULTURE

Columella's works – His date – Subjects treated in *De Re Rustica* – His outlook on agriculture – Vivid glimpses of farm-life – Attitude to sources – Prose style – Feeling for colour – His verse book on gardens – Things useful and things beautiful.

THE *De Re Rustica* of L. Junius Moderatus Columella is our best witness to methods of husbandry in the earlier Empire. A Spaniard by birth – his native place was Gades[1] (Cadiz) – he took both a family and a personal interest in farming. His uncle, 'the most diligent husbandman in the province of Baetica,' whom he several times cites with respect, gained great experience in land-owning:[2] and when Columella himself acquired estates in Italy,[3] he added practical knowledge to his study of Greek, Carthaginian and Roman writers on the subject. An inscription[4] tells that he was of the Galerian tribe and served as an officer in the *legio sexta ferrata*; so it is a reasonable conjecture that, when that legion was stationed in Syria, he took the opportunity of observing agricultural operations which he recalled when he came to write.[5] Besides his *De Re Rustica* in twelve books (originally designed to end with the tenth book which is in verse), he had previously written a manual on agriculture, of which the second book, *De Arboribus*, is left. A work now missing was his counterblast to fortune-telling, *Adversus Astrologos* (XI. i. 31); and he at least had it in mind to compose[6] an account of rituals followed in farming, which would have been of great value for a student of Roman religion.

He wrote after Julius Graecinus and Cornelius Celsus (the agricultural part of whose encyclopaedia he often quotes), but before the elder Pliny,

[1] VIII. xvi. 9: 'in nostro Gadium municipio'; X. 185: 'et mea (*sc.* lactuca) quam generant Tartesi litore Gades.'
[2] II. xv. 4; V. v. 15: 'uir illustribus disciplinis eruditus ac diligentissimus agricola Baeticae prouinciae'; VII. ii. 4; XII. xxi. 4: 'patruus meus, illustris agricola.'
[3] III. ix. 2.
[4] *C.I.L.* IX. 235 (=Dessau 2923): 'L. Iunio L. f. Gal. Moderato Columellae, trib. mil. leg. VI ferratae.'
[5] II. x. 18: 'hoc idem semen Ciliciae Syriaeque regionibus ipse uidi mense Iunio Iulioque conseri et per auctumnum . . . tolli.'
[6] II. xxi. 5–6.

who in turn used Columella. One other chronological point can be determined, which shows he was writing in Nero's reign. In the third book of the *De Re Rustica* he mentions Seneca, 'a person of excellent genius and learning,' as holding a Nomentan estate[1] not far from his own; and, as Seneca acquired this late in life but must have already held it long enough to make it known for its abundant vintage-yield, the inference is that this book was written not much before Seneca's death in A.D. 65.

Briefly these are the subjects of the twelve books:

I, General rules for country life, *e.g.* on choosing land, securing water and staffing a farm; II, treatment of land, ploughing, manuring, various crops; III-IV, vineyards and vines; V, land dimensions, elms, olives, fruit-trees; VI, cattle, horses, mules; VII, sheep, goats, and (after a chapter on cheese-making) swine and dogs; VIII, poultry and fish-ponds; IX, wild cattle and bees; X, gardens (in verse); XI, duties of a farm-bailiff, work for different months, and gardens (in prose); XII, duties of a bailiff's wife – provisions, pickling, fruit-preserving; on mead, cheese, figs, raisins, making and treatment of wines, savoury olive marmalade, salting swine's flesh.

From the mere headings one can see at once that such work is technical rather than literary; yet there is much in it to recreate important aspects of the environment of the Romans in the first century. Columella was conscious that agriculture, the traditional strength of Rome, was being sapped by the multiplication of parks and country-seats and by wasteful mismanagement of estates through incompetence. He is very insistent on the abuses due to absentee landlords, and equally insistent on the need for practical farming and personal control. The owner who manages for himself ought to secure better returns than he would by letting to tenant-farmers, though this latter method avoids some of the risks consequent on running the farm by slave-labour under a farm-bailiff.

A summary examination of his preface to the first book illustrates his general outlook and his advocacy of restored attention to agriculture, for which he has imbibed a traditional Roman veneration. The old Roman practice, he says, of land-tilling in which a consul or a dictator used to take personal delight, the pursuit which might be called 'own sister to philosophy' (*quasi consanguinea sapientiae*), has fallen on evil days. There are teachers for all other sciences and arts, including trumpery, luxurious, and even disreputable ones; but, he adds, 'of agriculture I know neither self-professed teachers nor pupils.' Mother earth is foolishly alleged to have declined in fertility, whereas the true reason

---

[1] III. iii. 3: 'Nomentana regio . . . quam possidet Seneca uir excellentis ingenii atque doctrinae.' See discussion hereon in relation to Plin. *N.H.* XIV. 49–51, by V. Barberet, *De Columellae Vita et Scriptis*, 1887, pp. 23–25. Cichorius, *Röm. Stud.* pp. 417–422, makes it probable that Columella served on the expedition to Cilicia Tracheia in A.D. 36 (II. x. 18), and was at Rome in 41 (III. viii. 2).

is that skilled labour is not being devoted to her. Feeble old town-slaves will be banished to do country work, although rural toil demands both knowledge and 'green age' capable of standing fatigue. In contrast with olden times, we Romans 'have crept (*correpsimus*) inside the city-wall and ply our hands rather in circuses and theatres than among crops and vineyards.' We misspend our days and nights and 'consider ourselves lucky because we never see a sunrise or a sunset.' Things are come to such a pass that 'in this Latium and Saturnian land we let out by public auction the importation of corn from our provinces.' Agriculture is no easy thing to excel in; but the right attitude is not despair in face of its vast variety (*tam uariae tamque uastae scientiae*), but determination to use the knowledge handed down by Greek and Roman writers (many of whom Columella names),[1] and to make diligent practical experiment. As he remarks in his first chapter, 'practice and experience are masters in the arts': books and rules are only auxiliary: nothing benefits the farm so much as the master's own presence.

Naturally the didactic value in such work outweighs the artistic; but there is a great deal of old-world information which can hardly fail to interest, though it may but concern the right contrivance of an old Italian hen-house, the food proper for poultry, recipes for preserving pears, the way to make mead of the very best honey, or the mode of reasonably encouraging treatment which Columella found efficacious with his slaves. It is something to have thus brought home to the mind what life meant on farms in the imperial period, to learn that a shepherd's dog should be white so that it could be distinguished on dark mornings or at evening twilight from the dangerous wolf, to note the frugality and energy laid down as ideally requisite in a competent farm-bailiff, to admire the methodical regularity declared to be equally essential in the farm-bailiff's wife as in a chorus of singers or (as the author says, no doubt with a touch of personal reminiscence) in the army. One of the truly Roman features in Columella is his maintenance of a standard of hard work, fortified by his citation from Cato, 'by doing nothing men learn to do evil.' It is true his science is far from impeccable: some of his cures are appallingly foolish, and his astronomy is little likely to produce a sound calendar. But then even blunders may have the merit of affording amusement; and, besides, there is in him a modesty which half disarms criticism. It appears very prettily in his final sentence, when, now an old man, and conscious of the magnitude of his theme, he comes to say good-bye to it:

As a conclusion of my work now accomplished, I think it not improper, Publius Silvinus, to declare to my readers (if truly any be found who deign to take cognisance of such affairs) that I nowise doubted the existence of wellnigh an infinity of matters capable of being ingrafted upon this subject, but that I judged it right that only

[1] I. i. 7–14 (7–11 Greek; 12–14 Roman).

such as seemed most necessary should be handed down to remembrance. Nature has not, however, bestowed even on grey hairs insight into all things; for even whosoever have been esteemed the wisest of mortals are said to have known many things, but not all.[1]

Columella's sources include, besides Greek authorities and Mago the Carthaginian, whose work the senate of the republic had ordered to be translated into Latin, Cato,[2] the Sasernae (father and son), Tremellius Scrofa, Varro, Virgil, Hyginus, and among later writers Graecinus, Julius Atticus and Cornelius Celsus. The two last he characterises as 'the most celebrated authors of our age.'[3] He often adduces Celsus's opinions, just as he often quotes Virgil's *Georgics*. Columella is noticeably more specific, in fact more honest, touching his sources than many writers of antiquity were. Nothing could be more open than his introductory remarks on bees and beehives. It is solely for the sake of completeness, he explains, that he must include the theme: for on it 'no precepts can be given more carefully than have been delivered by Hyginus, nor more gracefully than by Virgil, nor more elegantly than by Celsus.'[4]

Columella writes on a practical subject in a practical way. Of course there must be rare technical words drawn from operations that fall to be described, like *adnodare* ('trim down to the knot.' IV. xxii. 4, IV. xxiv. 10), *decacuminare* ('cut tops off,' IV. vii. 3, V. vi. 12), *canteriatae* (of vines supported by trellis-work, V. iv. 1, cf. *canterius*, IV. xii. 1), *impedatio* ('propping,' IV. xiii. 1), *scabrata* (of a vine roughened by pruning IV. xxiv, 22), *glocire* (of a hen's clucking, VIII. v. 4).[5] His sentences are clear and business-like, though without the archaic and bare jerkiness of Cato. Generally his most polished style appears in his prefaces; and, where he aims at finish, the influence of Cicero can be traced. Even without exact statistics, the ear detects the cadences of his *clausulae* – a liking for cretics (or resolved cretics) followed by trochee or double trochee, spondee or double spondee. One feature anyway is refreshing: he does not weary his reader with purple patches or with the artifices of his age. There are allusions to Spanish habits and Spanish names, but there is no Spanish rhetoric. When he is enthusiastic, his enthusiasm is natural, and that is why one can honestly welcome a certain poetic vein in him. Independently of his constant quotations from Virgil, and his verse-book on gardens, an artistic sentiment stirs within the author,

---

[1] XII. lix. 5: 'Clausulam peracti operis mei, P. Siluine, non alienum puto indicem lecturis (si modo fuerint qui dignentur ista cognoscere), nihil dubitasse me paene infinita esse, quae potuerint huic inseri materiae: uerum ea quae maxime uidebantur necessaria, memoriae tradenda censuisse. Nec tamen canis natura dedit cunctarum rerum prudentiam. Nam etiam quicunque sunt habiti mortalium sapientissimi, multa scisse dicuntur, non omnia.'

[2] See Duff, *L.H.R.*, for Cato, pp. 191–193; for Varro, pp. 249–251.

[3] III. xvii. 4.   [4] IX. ii. 1.

[5] Other examples are given by W. C. Summers, *Silver Age of Latin Lit.*, p. 286.

and his eye does not fail to mark nor his pen to convey the colours of an Italian vineyard in autumn:[1]

Even the greatest stranger to rural life, should he come into your grounds planted in due season, must with a transport of pleasure marvel at the kindliness of Nature, to see match each other, there the Bituric vines rich in fruitage, and here their rivals the pale yellow vines. . . . Bounteous earth, rejoicing over the annual return of the season, as it were some eternal childbearing, offers to mankind her breasts distended with new wine. Amidst all, while Bacchus favours the pregnant vine-branches whether of the white kind or golden and ruddy, or agleam with purple brightness, everywhere doth Autumn shine lustrous, laden with parti-coloured fruits.

This feeling for colour is met with again in his verses:

> Then paint your land
> With many-coloured blooms, those stars of earth –
> The fair-tress'd daffodil and lion's maw
> Fierce gaping, lilies too that keep
> Their greenness in grey baskets, hyacinths
> Or snowy-white or blue. Add violets
> Pale-creeping or with gold and purple proud,
> And roses over-full of modest blush.[2]

His treatment of horticulture in the tenth book, like his motive for writing it, was partly utilitarian, partly, but only partly, poetic. He was scarcely free enough in soul to take a garden, as Bacon did, for 'the greatest refreshment to the spirits of man'; nor would Bacon's threefold division of 'a greene in the entrance, a heath or desart in the going forth, and the maine garden in the midst' ever have occurred to Columella. The luxury of contemporary banquets shocked him, he says in his preface; no poor man could afford such extravagance. Yet thrifty use might be made of a garden, and this would have been handled in prose but for Silvinus's request that Columella should write in verse what Virgil expressly bequeathed in the fourth book of the *Georgics* for literary posterity. Parts of the subject seemed so insignificant that the author feared its treatment might resemble 'making ropes out of sand'; and thus throughout the 436 hexameters there may be traced a sort of conflict between the desire to give serviceable advice concerning a market-garden and an artistic yearning after beauty. Columella, indeed, succeeds, as Martial did after him, in making some at least of his vegetables

[1] III. xxi. 3–4.
[2] X. 96–102:

> 'Pingite tunc uarios, terrestria sidera, flores,
> Candida leucoia et flauentia lumina caltae
> Narcissique comas et hiantis saeua leonis
> Ora feri calathisque uirentia lilia canis,
> Nec non uel niueos uel caeruleos hyacinthos.
> Tum quae pallet humi, quae frondens purpurat auro,
> Ponatur uiola et nimium rosa plena pudoris.'

poetic. Flowers are a godsend to him. Besides, there are Virgilian echoes from *Eclogues*, *Georgics* and *Aeneid*, but also occurrences of compound adjectives proportionately rather more frequent than in Virgil.[1]

The start is made on useful topics – soil proper to a garden, trees indicative of suitable ground, the wall or fence, the undesirability of statues save of the protective wooden Garden-God; then, after a pause to utter a conventional invocation, the author advocates digging and ploughing regardless of mercy for 'mother earth.' The season

> When nesting swallows twitter 'Spring is come'[2]

calls for the employment of manure, hoe, rake and spade, and for the planting of gay flowers, as in the passage already translated. Herbs of various potency, different kinds of cabbage, watering of young plants and the management of a dry hill-plot lead to his insistence on work at the right moment:

> Be wakeful, men! noiseless the Seasons ply
> Their pace, and all the year turns round unheard.[3]

Then follows a procession of vegetables – parsley, leeks, parsnips and lettuces, with a side-glance directed to the 'thousand hues' secured by the skilled gardener, till the fertility of spring wakes a rhapsody on the dominion of Venus as reminiscent of Lucretius and Virgil, as it is anticipative of the *Peruigilium Veneris*:

> Hence ocean, hence the hills, hence all the world
> Do keep spring-time; hence lust in man and herd
> And fowl: the fire of love lit at the heart
> Rageth within the marrow, till o'ercloyed
> Venus fulfils the fruitful frame and gets
> Manifold offspring, peopling still the world
> With young, lest in a barren age it faint.[4]

Here, however, the poet checks himself: let such themes be reserved for a bard inspired to sing of nature's mysteries: he must answer the call to humbler matters:

> Knit strains with slender thread such as 'mid toil
> The pruner, bending o'er his shrubs, may sing
> Attuned, or gardener in his pleasaunce green.[5]

---

[1] *Nubigenae, uersicoloribus, pestifer* are Virgilian: *frugifero* and *nubifugo* are not, though the former was used by Ennius.
[2] X. 80: 'Veris et aduentum nidis cantabit hirundo.'
[3] X. 159–160:
> 'Inuigilate, uiri: tacito nam tempora gressu
> Diffugiunt nulloque sono conuertitur annus.'
[4] X. 209–214. Cf. Lucr. I. 1–49; Virg. *Georg.* II. 323–345.
[5] X. 227–229:
> 'Et secum gracili conectere carmina filo
> Quae canat inter opus Musa modulante putator
> Pendulus arbustis, holitor uiridantibus hortis.'

So we find ourselves among cresses, artichokes, pomegranates and beet; till again the brilliant array of spring-blossom fills the poet with glee over the flower-harvest:

> Yea, harvest presseth on with scented blooms;
> Now is spring gaudy, now the bounteous earth
> Is glad to deck her brows with coronal
> Of all the proud-pied increase of the year.
> Now Phrygian lotus shows its gem-like face,
> And violet-beds unclose their winking eyes.
> The 'lion' yawns and, tinged with nature's blush,
> The rose unveils her maiden cheek to pay
> The gods due worship and their sanctuaries
> Perfume with blended scents of Araby.[1]

So for the moment he is on the verge of fairyland invoking the nymphs.

Then comes the thought that in workaday Italy and in its market towns there is money to be made from the produce; so one must remember the tasks appropriate as the day lengthens and the southern heat increases: one must be on guard against inroads of insects and danger to ripe fruits from rain and hail, and must grow cucumbers and melons, plums, peaches and figs, not forgetting Vulcan's feast in autumn. But, at this autumnal allusion, the vintage beckons us away from gardens to obey the summons of Bacchus, and with that Columella finishes his task self-imposed in pursuance of the behest of Virgil, the Roman Hesiod,

> Who sang through Roman towns the Ascraean lay.[2]

[1] X. 255–262.
[2] X. 436 (the closing line): 'Ascraeum cecinit Romana per oppida carmen,' echoing Virg. *Georg.* II. 176: 'Ascraeumque cano Romana per oppida carmen.'

F*

Chapter II

PETRONIUS: NOVELIST AND POET

The remains of the *Satyricon* – The name Petronius Arbiter –
The Petronius of Nero's time – Identity of the author – Menippean form – Earlier adventures of three ne'er-do-wells in the extant text – The banquet of Trimalchio – Arrival of guests and
host – Courses surprising and excessive – Conduct of the host –
His blunders and egotism – Talk of the guests – Adventures
resumed after the banquet – Sea-voyage and shipwreck – The impostors at Crotona – Love-episodes and closing scenes – The
dramatic date – Sources and the author's originality – Traces of
literary convention even in first realistic romance – Morals and
realism – Elements picaresque and sensual – Qualities anticipative
of modern novels – Certain contrasts with Apuleius – Latin of the
Satyricon – Plebeian speech – Examples in Petronius – Contrast
with certain contemporary tendencies – His poetry – *De Bello
Ciuili* – Short poems attributed to him – Nature and love.

A N intensely interesting, though fragmentary, work, now by
most scholars ascribed to Nero's reign, is usually entitled
the *Satyricon* or *Satiricon* (originally a Greek genitive plural),
though the fragments are in the manuscripts also called *satirae* or *satyri*,
and referred to Petronius Arbiter as author. Like the *editio princeps* of
about 1482, several editions appeared without the famous 'Banquet of
Trimalchio,' which was recovered at Trau in Dalmatia only in the
middle of the seventeenth century. In that unique manuscript (*Tragu-
riensis*) an entry had been made to the effect that the contents belong
to Books XV and XVI of Petronius's 'Satyri'; if this is trustworthy,
then merely a fraction of a long work has come down to us. Since that
thrilling discovery at Trau, all claims to have found additions have
proved to be based on forgeries, like the passages published at Rotterdam in 1692 by Nodot, who pretended they were contained in a manuscript from Belgrade.

Quotations from 'Arbiter' or 'Petronius' are made by several ancient
scholars (*e.g.* Diomedes, Servius, Priscian); Fulgentius cites him as
'Petronius Arbiter'; Terentianus Maurus calls him 'Arbiter disertus,'
and Sidonius Apollinaris classes him among renowned masters *eloquii
Latini*: but the process of excerpting (like epitomising, often fatal to an
original) probably accounts for the disappearance of the complete work

about the seventh century. The limited Petronius now extant was pre-presumably the portion known to Eugenius Vulgarius in the tenth century, to John of Salisbury in the twelfth, and to Vincentius of Beauvais in the thirteenth.

Niebuhr's opinion that the work was of the third century and Beck's that it belonged to the time of Augustus or Tiberius have by general consent given place to the established belief that it was written in Nero's age.[1] Its social atmosphere, its style, its echoes of Seneca, Lucan and even of the emperor, all point the argument in the same direction. Likewise it is in the highest degree probable that the author is the Petronius whose death is dramatically recorded by Tacitus and whose character is attractively idealised by Sienkiewicz in 'Quo Vadis?' Gaius (or as Nipperdey[2] preferred, Titus) Petronius was one of a series of Nero's victims in A.D. 66, and Tacitus devotes two chapters[3] to the career and end of a very remarkable man:

With him day passed in sleep, night in the duties and amusements of life. Energy makes some men's reputation, but idling had made his: he was considered, not a debauchee and spendthrift like most squanderers of their wealth, but a man of polished luxury. The freer his sayings and doings and the more seeming carelessness they displayed, the more cordially were they construed as looking like straightforwardness. Yet when governor of Bithynia and afterwards when consul, he showed himself alert and a match for business. Then, falling back on vice or aping vice, he was selected by Nero to be one of his small inner circle, his judge of etiquette (*elegantiae arbiter*); for the emperor thought nothing charming and elegantly voluptuous, unless Petronius had given him approval of it.

As ill luck would have it, he roused the dangerous jealousy of Tigellinus, who proceeded to compass his ruin through a false charge. Nero was in Campania when Petronius received an ominous command to confine himself to Cumae. He was not the man to tolerate fluctuations of fear and hope: on the other hand he was little disposed to fling life away by precipitate suicide: so he alternately opened and bandaged his veins, exactly as he chose, held receptions for his friends and indulged in conversation neither serious nor suggestive of stoical virtue.

[1] See Th. Studer, 'Ueber das Zeitalter des Petr. Arb,' *Rh.M.* ii (1843) p. 50, and works listed in S.H. § 397. More recently U. E. Paoli has argued for a date later than the time of Martial (*Studi Ital. di Filol. Cl.* 1937, p. 3 ff.); rebutted by G. Funaioli (*Rendic. Accad. Bologna* 1937, p. 46 ff.) and E. V. Marmorale, *P. nel suo tempo*, Naples 1937. In 1948 Marmorale, abandoning his position of 1937, argued powerfully for a date at the end of the 2nd or beginning of the 3rd century (*La Questione Petroniana*, Naples 1948). The defenders of the traditional date sprang to arms: e.g. A. Maiuri ('Petroniana' in *Parola del Passato*, 1948, 101 ff.); R. Browning ('The Date of Petronius' in *C.R.* 1949, 12 ff.); N. Terzaghi ('Ancora sull' età di Pet.' in *Anales de Filologia Classica* (Buenos Aires) IV, 1947–1949, p. 115 ff.); E. Paratore ('P. nel iii secolo?' in *Paideia* iii (1948) p. 261 ff.).
[2] Relying on Plin. *N.H.* XXXVII. 20; Plut. *Mor.* 60E.
[3] Tac. *Ann.* XVI. xviii–xix.

He listened as they repeated, not views on the immortality of the soul or on the theories of philosophers, but light poetry and sportive lines. To some of his slaves he gave generous gifts, to others a flogging. He went in to dinner, then indulged in sleep so that, though forced upon him, his death might appear the result of chance. Even in his will he did not, like most doomed men, flatter Nero or Tigellinus or any other powerful personage; instead, he wrote a description of the prince's scandalous excesses, prefixing the names of the profligates and the women concerned, and detailing every immoral novelty; then sealed the document and sent it to Nero.

This *chronique scandaleuse* written in Petronius's last hours cannot, as some have hastily surmised, be the *Satyricon*, a far more elaborate production, which must have demanded prolonged leisure for its composition. But the *Satyricon* enables one to imagine the pith and realism of the terrible indictment hurled at the depraved despot by one who had been his minister of amusements. Certainly, in the qualities ascribed to Petronius by Tacitus, there is nothing to render it unlikely that the ascription of the fragments in the manuscripts to Petronius Arbiter refers to any other person than the Petronius who is called by the historian the emperor's *elegantiae arbiter*. It is immaterial that Tacitus did not allude to any previous literary work by him: the historian's grave judgement might not have considered its tone worth mention, and, in any case, it is not his way to record the writings of historical figures. We should never, for instance, have known about Seneca's voluminous compositions from Tacitus. On the positive side it may be affirmed that the Tacitean portrait of Petronius wears the very features to be expected in the author of a novel depicting low and vicious life in tones which argue intimacy of knowledge and at the same time the almost cynically detached spirit of a spectator. This Mephistophelean *insouciance* of attitude has the artistic merit of leaving the wickedest and vulgarest characters of the story to act in an absolutely natural way, and exactly fits the brilliant courtier for whom, in spite of a spasmodic energy suggestive of higher capacities, the favourite business of life was the invention, organisation and criticism of sensuous enjoyments. A psychology thus complex may well have baffled his closest friends. It might amuse so great a master of facile accomplishment to surprise Rome by an unsuspected talent for administration abroad. The controller of the revels may have been able at will to listen with assumed gravity to philosophical discussions and rhetorical performances, or even take part in what might one day furnish material for satire; in all probability he narrowly observed Seneca and Lucan at court as potential 'copy'; but his real affair was to be the ultimate authority on pleasures for exalted society, and, with a defiant unconcern, to live the life of an expert in everything that could contribute towards passing time gaily away.

What remains of the *Satyricon* is (like the contemporary *Apocolocyntosis* by Seneca) in the form of the Menippean satire taken over into Roman literature by Varro[1] from the Cynic philosopher Menippus of Gadara, and therefore in prose interspersed with verses. Its story of adventures, many of them unutterably disreputable, is related by Encolpius, one of a trio on a round of escapades among the half-Greek cities of Southern Italy. His fellow-wanderers, rogues like himself, are Ascyltus, a young freedman, and Giton, a handsome serving-boy, who is a bone of contention between them. The narrative is diversified with a few entertaining tales – about a werewolf, about witches substituting a straw changeling for a boy, and the famous one of the widow of Ephesus[2] – digressive stories within a story, which long remained a convention of the novel, like the history of 'the man of the hill' in *Tom Jones*.

Our present text opens somewhere on the coast of Campania – perhaps, if indeed it is necessary to locate the scene, at Cumae,[3] though Naples, Puteoli and Misenum are among the rival suggestions. Encolpius, a student of rhetoric for the time being, is delivering a tirade against the unreality and futility of a rhetorical education totally divorced from the business of the actual world. Professor Agamemnon, who is in his company, argues in defence that teachers have to suit current taste or close their academies. The faulty training of the day he ascribes to parents' insistence on an easy and quick road to proficiency; and, breaking into verse, he recites choliambics on the simple life advisable for an orator, and hexameters on the needful study of Socratic philosophy and Demosthenes. Meanwhile Ascyltus has slipped off, and a crowd of students pour into the colonnade. Encolpius starts in pursuit of his comrade; asks his way of a greengrocer-woman, who guides him to a disorderly establishment, where he discovers his friend, and soon afterwards enters on one of a series of jealous wrangles with him over Giton. In the market-place the pair meet with exciting experiences, told in Latin so admirably natural as to place everything before our eyes. A brawl breaks out because the pair are taxed with being in possession of a stolen cloak (*pallium*), and because at the same time they challenge a countryman wearing a lost tunic of their own, threadbare

[1] Duff, *L.H.R.* pp. 244–246.
[2] §§ 61–62, 63 and 111–112.
[3] This was Mommsen's view ('Trimalchios Heimath u. Grabschrift' *Herm.* xiii (1878) p. 114 ff.=*Gesam. Schr.* vii. p. 191 ff.), which some think incompatible with Trimalchio's reference to seeing the Sibyl in a cage at Cumae (*Satyr.* 48). For other views see S.H. § 395. After the sea-voyage, from § 116 to the end, the scene is definitely at Crotona. Some missing incidents may have occurred at Massilia; for Servius (ad Virg. *Aen.* III. 57) ascribes to Petronius the story of a human scapegoat there in time of plague (*cf.* Sid. Apoll. *Carm.* XXIII. 155–156: 'et te Massiliensium per hortos sacri stipitis Arbiter colonum . . .' But it is too impetuous to infer therefrom, as some have done, a Gallic origin for Petronius, or to regard his *Satyricon* as the beginning of the French novel!

indeed but very precious for the secret stock of gold coins sewed into it. Folk are much puzzled with the strangers' willingness to renounce the cloak for the shabby tunic. They just escape arrest, and, when they have reached their inn, are visited by one Quartilla, who, preceded by her servant and attended by a little girl, has come to declare that they owe her penance for disturbing her ritual in the chapel of Priapus. Later, the scene changes to her house, where an orgy leads to general drowsiness, broken at length by the entry of two burglars. When their depredations are interrupted, the robbers pretend to snore, and the convivial licentiousness is renewed.

Then (in our text, after a gap in the story) comes the morning of Trimalchio's banquet (§§ 26–78) – a free repast secured for the adventurers through Agamemnon. Out of the existing total of 141 sections, over 50 are concerned with this episode, whose details vividly recreate an extravagantly vulgar dinner-party given by a wealthy *parvenu* of the freedman class to people of similar standing and to uninvited guests. It reads like an excursion into an ancient and not unreal land of Cockaigne. There is scarcely a dull piece among all the kaleidoscopic changes from incident to incident between the opening glimpse of the host,

> a bald old man in a reddish shirt, playing at a game in which he never stooped to pick up a ball, if it touched the ground, but had a slave to supply fresh ones from a bag,

and the final scene during which, amidst the confusion caused by the irruption of the fire-brigade, Encolpius and his friends, surfeited and bored, made good their escape.

Four decorated lackeys precede the great man's litter, which brings him home in a scarlet woollen wrap from the preliminary bath, while a musician plays small pipes close by, so that Trimalchio shall have music wherever he goes. The guests reach the entrance:

> There stood a porter in green, with a cherry-coloured belt, shelling peas in a silver dish. Over the doorway hung a golden cage and a spotted magpie in it greeted arrivals.

These splashes of colour make a fitting prelude to the exuberant profusion throughout. Everywhere is a lavish parade of wealth and such an over-plentiful variety of viands that one feels of Trimalchio as of Chaucer's frankeleyn:

> It snewed in his hous of mete and drinke,
> Of alle deyntees that men coude thinke.

Trimalchio is drawn as the representative of a new rich class whose social aspiration in any community must always be entrance at all costs into the envied circle of people of quality – that old caste which it must ape in default of manners and traditions of its own and whose culture it must affect with a nervous sense of inferiority imperfectly concealed under blatant self-assertion. A huge chained dog painted on the wall with large letters above, 'CAVE CANEM,' played on guests the same mild joke as the familiar mosaic at one of the thresholds in Pompeii. This was, however, merely an introduction to other decorations, which represented Trimalchio in the slave-market, Trimalchio guided to Rome by Minerva, Trimalchio learning book-keeping, Trimalchio appointed steward, Trimalchio at various stages in his successful rise, 'and just where the wall-space of the colonnade gave no more room, Mercury had lifted him by the chin and was hurrying him to his elevated official dais (as a *sevir Augustalis*).' No wonder that Fortune should be there with a horn of plenty and the three Fates spinning golden threads. Trimalchio was one of those who find in their own career a substitute for ancestors. His name reappears incessantly inscribed on as many things as possible: one part of the dining-room door-posts ended in a sort of ship's beak bearing the legend 'presented by the steward Cinnamus to Gaius Pompeius Trimalchio, priest of the college of Augustus'; besides, silver dishes might be noted with the host's name and their weight scrupulously engraved on the edges.

The diners take their places and have *hors d'oeuvres* served without Trimalchio, who arrives purposely late to the strains of music, his shaven head peeping out above a scarlet cloak and a fringed napkin round his neck – an irresistibly funny figure at which any guest off his guard was sure to laugh (*expressit imprudentibus risum*). His display of rings, bracelet and bangle indicated no better manners than his explanation to his guests that it was inconvenient for him to come so soon, but that he had sacrificed his own pleasure to avoid keeping them waiting. Even so, he means to finish his game with crystal pieces on a draughts-board of terebinth wood.

From this point the banquet proceeds through a whirl of surprise courses and surprise incidents. The pea-hen's eggs distributed from under a wooden hen prove, though doubtful-looking at first, to contain a fat beccafico wrapped in spiced yolk of egg. A slave-boy is boxed for troubling to pick up a silver entrée-dish that had fallen – by orders of the host it must be thrown down again and swept away. To ensure a fair field as in war ('*aequum*' inquit '*Mars amat*'), he has arranged that each guest shall have a separate table; 'so the stinking slaves won't make us so hot by crushing past us' (*obiter et putidissimi serui minorem nobis aestum frequentia sua facient*). When his fine old Falernian, labelled one hundred years in bottle,[1] is produced, he indulges in one of his ill-bred remarks. 'Yesterday I didn't supply such a good brand, and there were far more

---

[1] *Sat.* 34: FALERNVM OPIMIANVM ANNORVM CENTVM.
The year of Opimius's consulate 121 B.C. was famous for its vintage. If the dramatic date of the novel is A.D. 50–60, *annorum centum* is an understatement. The idea of labelling the age, as well as the date, of the wine is absurd (the label would have to be changed every year). It further brings out the gaucherie of Trimalchio's ostentation. He is proud that his wine has scored a century!

genteel people at dinner' (*heri non tam bonum posui, et multo honestiores cenabant*). The old wine, like other incidents of the dinner, sets the host moralising. 'Ah me, so wine lives longer than poor mankind; so let's have a good "wet" (*tengomenas*). Wine is life': but next moment a slave brings in another reminder of death, a mechanically jointed silver skeleton, on which Trimalchio reflects in verse:

> Alack for us poor men! man's little all
> Is naught: so shall we all be when we pass
> Below. Then let us live while luck allows.[1]

One can but summarise, without entering into details, the fare provided. A Zodiac dish with symbolic dainties above for each of the twelve signs (on which the host insisted on giving a rambling astronomical lecture afterwards) has much finer delicacies concealed underneath. A wild boar on a tray is attended by huntsmen and hounds, and when the boar is opened, the birds begin to fly – thrushes, to wit, limed by fowlers in the dining-room for the astonished banqueters. Three white pigs are driven in, one of them to be turned into a dinner on the spot. Soon after, a pig is served up, to all appearance ungutted, and when by a prearranged jest, the seemingly negligent *chef* has been stripped for punishment, a stab at the animal releases a tumbling mass of cooked sausages. What promises to be a last course (*epideipnis*) consists of thrushes of fine meal stuffed with raisins and nuts, followed by quinces stuck all over with little spikes to resemble hedgehogs; but to their horror and loathing the sated guests are next confronted with what looks to be a fat goose garnished with fish and different birds, and yet all made, as Trimalchio boasts, by his expert cook Daedalus out of the same ingredient, namely, hog's flesh! Suddenly two slaves fall a-fighting and smash the waterpots that hang round their necks, thus revealing oysters and mussels to be handed round presently in competition with snails offered by the cook on a silver grid-iron.

Still more entertainment is derivable from the conduct and talk of the diners than from the conglomerate *menu*. The host at one time inflicts on his guests a hideous tune from a mime; he must crack his joke in shouting 'Carve 'er!' (*Carpe*) at his slave 'Carver' (*Carpus*); he talks very plainly on subjects customarily thought delicate; he needs to be told by his wife to remember his dignity; and yet later in the meal he lets a favourite slave mount on his back and slap him. Loving to create astonishment, he has an enormous hoop let down from an opening in the ceiling to convey golden crowns and perfume-boxes as souvenirs; and he has cakes and fruits prepared to spurt out saffron. After acrobatic performances come Homeric reciters clashing spear and shield.

[1] *Sat.* 34:
> 'Eheu nos miseros, quam totus homuncio nil est!
> Sic erimus cuncti, postquam nos auferet Orcus.
> Ergo uiuamus, dum licet esse bene.'

Trimalchio tries to follow their Greek in some sort of Latin *Iliad*, until he thinks fit to explain the situation by his own fatuous version of the tale of Troy:

'You know the story they're doing? Diomede and Ganymede were two brothers. Their sister was Helen. Agamemnon ran off with her and palmed off a hind on Diana in her place. So Homer is now telling of the fighting between Trojans and Parentines. Of course Agamemnon won, and married his daughter Iphigenia to Achilles. That's what drove Ajax out of his mind, and he'll make the sequel clear in a second.'[1]

And so a charger is carried in bearing a calf boiled whole and helmeted for a raving 'Ajax' to slash at and divide on the point of his sword among the onlookers.

Another curious recitation is that by a young slave-boy of Habinnas's, who, with his wife Scintilla, had arrived late in the evening, mellow from a wake. The boy starts with the opening line of *Aeneid* V, but, being a foreigner, soon makes blunders and actually sandwiches in between Virgilian pieces scraps from Atellan farces 'so that for the first time in my life,' comments the smart Encolpius, 'even Virgil hurt my finer feelings' (*ut tunc primum me etiam Vergilius offenderit*).[2] This production is, however, in keeping with Trimalchio's own standard of attainment; for it is one of the signs of his vulgarity that he pretends to a learning which he does not possess. He attempts literary talk with the professor present, claiming culture on the ground that he owns two collections of books – one Greek, one Latin.[3] He used to read Homer when a boy, he adds; and with what effect is evident from the 'howlers' in his story of the origin of Corinthian bronze, which bears some resemblance to that of Charles Lamb regarding roast-pig:

'When Troy fell, that charlatan and big rascal Hannibal heaped all the statues of bronze, gold and silver on to a single funeral pile and set them on fire: they turned into one amalgam of bronze. From this mass artificers took pieces and made cups, dishes and statuettes.'[4]

Such mixed history prepares one for his mixed mythology when he boasts of his ownership of a round hundred beakers.

'engraved with Cassandra killing her children – and the little boys are lying dead so naturally that you'd think they were alive.[5] I have also a thousand cups, which Mummius left to my late master; and on them Daedalus is shutting Niobe into the Trojan Horse.'

[1] § 59.   [2] § 68.   [3] § 48.   [4] § 50.
[5] § 52: 'et pueri mortui iacent sic ut uiuere putes.' Squire Western is equally confused in his recollections of the metamorphosis of Actaeon into a stag: 'I'd rather be run by my own dogs as one Acton was that the story-book says was turned into a hare and his own dogs killed un and eat un.' Fielding, *Tom Jones*, Bk. XVII. ch. 3.

The proud egotism of the self-made man who has risen in the social scale is admirably made to betray itself by such means as the engagement-book displayed prominently, the daily gazette of events on his estates read at dinner,[1] his narrative of how he got on in business, or even his attempts at pathos by reading his will, the directions for his tombstone and his own epitaph:[2]

HERE RESTS

C. POMPEIVS TRIMALCHIO MAECENATIANVS:

NOMINATED TO THE AUGUSTAL PRIESTHOOD
IN ABSENCE, HE MIGHT HAVE BEEN MEMBER
OF ANY CIVIL GUILD IN ROME, BUT DECLINED.
DUTIFUL, BRAVE, FAITHFUL,
HE STARTED WITH LITTLE, BUT LEFT THIRTY MILLIONS:
YET HE NEVER HAD A COLLEGE EDUCATION.
FAREWELL BOTH HE AND THOU!

The talk of the guests makes a refreshing change from what would otherwise be intolerable gorging. Here the author proves his dramatic realism by drawing from the spoken Latin of the day, introducing its colloquialisms and faulty grammar. A few translated extracts may suggest the off-hand character of the conversation:

'I couldn't eat any more so I turned to my neighbour to get all the news I could, and started raking up stories and asking him who the woman was that was bustling up and down. "That's Trimalchio's wife," says he, "her name's Fortunata, and she measures her shekels by the bushel. And what was she just a little while ago! Well, you must excuse my saying it, but you wouldn't have taken a bit of bread from her hand. Now – I can't say why or wherefore – she's in the seventh heaven: she's Trimalchio's *factotum* (*topanta*). The truth is, she's only got to tell him at high noon that it's dark, and he'll believe it. He hasn't a notion of what he owns – he's such a plutocrat; but this lynx of a woman keeps a look-out on everything, even where you wouldn't think it."'

And he proceeds to describe her as sober and thrifty, but a shrew and capable of inflicting, like Mrs. Caudle, curtain-lectures on her husband (*est tamen malae linguae, pica puluinaris*).[3]

Nowhere do we hear more of the true ring of chatter than when the hosts's temporary retirement removes all restraint:[4] Dama bawls for an extra tankard:

'Day doesn't count: it's night before you can turn about. So the best you can do is to go right from bed to dinner. And nice chilly weather we've had. Hot baths has scarcely warmed me up (*uix me balneus calfecit*). After all, hot drinks is equal to an overcoat. I've had

[1] § 53.   [2] § 71.   [3] § 37.   [4] § 41.

some good pulls, and am absolutely tight (*plane matus*). Wine'sh
gone to my head' (*uinus mihi in cerebrum abiit*).

Seleucus breaks in – he has been at a funeral:

'Well, well, he's joined the majority (*abiit ad plures*). The doctors
did for him, or rather his evil stars has done it (*immo magis malus fatus*).
A doctor's only a comfort to the mind. Still he had a fine funeral
. . . and the mourning was jolly good – he left several slaves their
freedom – even if the widow was stingy with her tears. What if he
didn't treat her over well? Woman taken all round is a bird of prey.
One should never do a good turn: it's just like chucking it down a well.
But an old love nips like a crab.'[1]

One bore is interrupted by another; 'Let's remember the living,'
shouts Phileros, but he too is soon talking about the dead man and his
brother. Next Ganymedes insists on having his growl over profiteers
and high prices until Echion, the rag-merchant, the optimist of the party,
brings him to book:

'Do give up whining. Now it's this way, now it's that, as the
countryman said when he'd lost the spotted pig. What one doesn't
get today, one will tomorrow – that's how life pushes on. S'help me,
ye couldn't mention a better country, if only it had the right people.
. . . If you emigrate, you'll be telling how pigs trot round at home
ready-cooked. And, mark ye, we're going to have a smashing gladiatorial show (*munus excellente*) in three days more – the public
holiday.'[2]

And reckless of grammar, he rattles on about gladiatorial matches, till
he takes to chaffing the professor:

'Now, Agamemnon, I fancy you're saying "what's this bore
blethering about?" Folks like you that's able to speak doesn't. You
don't belong to our sort, and so you jeer at the remarks of we 'umble
people. We know as how much learning doth make you mad.'[3]

With their escape from this maelstrom of junketing, the youths re-
commence their adventures. It was no easy task after hard drinking to
find the way back to their inn in the dark through a strange town. Luckily
Giton had made chalk-marks on columns in the daytime, and the white
could be seen.

Renewed quarrels between Encolpius and Ascyltus give place to a
fresh set of incidents. Encolpius in a picture-gallery has met a shabbily
dressed and unprincipled old poet Eumolpus. He can talk effectively on
the decay of art[4] owing to the disappearance of the ancient times of

---

[1] § 42.   [2] § 45.
[3] § 46: 'Videris mihi, Agamemnon, dicere "Quid iste argutat molestus?"
Quia tu, qui potes loquere, non loquis. Non es nostrae fasciae, et ideo pauperorum uerba derides. Scimus te prae litteras fatuum esse.'   [4] § 88.

rivalry in hard work, when unselfish toil for posterity contrasted with the modern love of wine, women and wealth. Seeing Encolpius interested in a picture of the taking of Troy, he recites sixty-five iambics on this *Troiae Halosis*, introducing the Trojan horse and Laocoon with the serpents as in *Aeneid* II, and thus briefly handling a theme which had interested Nero. His verses have a way of bringing a shower of stones about his head, but he remains an incorrigible versifier, even later when in imminent danger from shipwreck. Encolpius has deemed it wise to share Giton's favour with Eumolpus, and the three have made their way aboard ship when Encolpius discovers to his alarm that the ship belongs to an old enemy, Lichas, and that he, with Tryphaena, another deadly enemy made in a lost part of the story, is actually on the vessel. To avoid detection, Encolpius and Giton agree to be shaven and branded to look like slaves; but a sea-sick passenger notices in the moonlight the shaving – an evil omen at sea – and discovery follows, with a free fight in which passengers and crew take part until a treaty of peace is made. Then there are rejoicings aboard, and Eumolpus indulges in elegiacs and hendeca-syllabics on the tonsure of the youths, for whom wigs and false eye-brows have to be obtained. To illustrate fickleness, Eumolpus recounts the tale of the apparently inconsolable widow of Ephesus and the kindly soldier. In a storm Lichas is blown overboard and drowned, and the voyage ends in shipwreck.

The closing scenes are laid in Crotona, whither Encolpius and Giton accompany Eumolpus with much bravado and assurance to practise fraud and wilful imposition for their livelihood. Legacy-hunting is the great industry of the city (*nam aut captantur aut captant*, 116). The strangers have decided that Eumolpus shall act the part of a fabulously wealthy landed proprietor from Africa who has unfortunately been shipwrecked, but who can presumably more than repay in the long run any hospitality received at Crotona. Before the impostors set to work, a pause in the narrative permits Eumolpus to propound critical doctrines on historical poetry in his remarks introductory[1] to nearly three hundred hexameters[2] upon the *Bellum Ciuile* of 49 B.C. It is in the mouth of Eumolpus that the author places the famous phrase about the studied grace of Horace (*Horatii curiosa felicitas*).

Adventures are to the adventurous; and Encolpius, now called Poly-aenus, is not long in Crotona before a serving-maid makes amorous overtures to him on behalf of her mistress, and his introduction[3] to this fair Siren named Circe is related with a romantic beauty which deserves to be linked with a less unsavoury intrigue:

'It was not long before she ushered her mistress from her hiding-place and escorted to my side a lady perfect beyond all dreams. There is no language that can contain her charm: words of mine must fall short – her tresses all over her shoulders, a cascade of nature's own curls; a low

---

[1] § 118.   [2] §§ 119–124.   [3] § 126.

forehead with the hair turned back from it; eyebrows running on to the line of her cheeks and, between the eyes, almost united again; eyes brighter than the gleaming stars when there is no moon; just a curve on the nose; and sweet lips such as Praxiteles imagined Diana had. And then her chin, her neck, her hands, and the whiteness of those feet set in a tiny band of gold – she had eclipsed the marble of Paros. I had long loved Doris: I thought nothing of Doris now.'

The meetings with Circe end, however, disastrously for her lover, whom her servants finally expel with ignominy as an unsatisfying swain. Other troubles are in store when he has the misfortune to kill one of three sacred geese, but the imperfections of the text give a disjointed effect to the remaining episodes, which close with a very natural uneasiness on the part of the tricksters lest they be found out, and the grim jest which Eumolpus plays upon expectant beneficiaries under his will by making it a condition in one of the clauses that his heirs shall after his death slice him up and eat him!

While the period of composition may be taken as Neronian, the time of the events related is most likely not much earlier. Though Mommsen put the dramatic date under Augustus, Friedländer prefers the close of Claudius's reign or beginning of Nero's; and this proposition fits the case of Trimalchio 'Maecenatianus,' freed in boyhood by his patron Maecenas, who died in 8 B.C. Petronius describes Trimalchio as old (*senem caluum*, 27) at the time of his entertainment; hence it may be imagined to have happened about the middle of the first century.

On possible literary sources of the *Satyricon* perhaps too much has been written, in view of the fact that whatever the borrowing, suspected or unsuspected, the work remains a monument of originality for its realistic portrayal of certain grades of contemporary Italian life. The debt to that human fund of material and to the author's unique genius for artistic handling eclipses any debt to literary sources. Of these sources the most obvious concerns his method of relieving prose with verse after Varro's Menippean fashion: and to this particular medley (without any claim to the Varronian spirit) the title of *saturae* may allude. There are also a few burlesque echoes of epic,[1] although, in the absence of the missing books, one cannot be justified in accepting the theory of 'The Wrath of Priapus'[2] as a motive comically analogous to a Homeric 'Wrath of Poseidon,' and thereby imagined to link the escapades into a unity suggestive of an obscene Odyssey. Persecution by an offended deity of sex-lust may plausibly be considered to operate for part of the story in the spirit of the lines,

[1] *E.g.* Giton concealed under the bed is compared to Ulysses under the ram; one of Encolpius's enchantresses is Circe, etc.
[2] E. Klebs, 'Zur Composition von Petr. Satirae,' *Philol.* xlvii (1889) p. 623, considers this wrath as the *Leitmotiv* of the whole romance.

Angry Priapus of the Dardanelles
Hunts me on earth and where grey Ocean swells;[1]

but it remains problematic whether it dominates the whole.

Other literary forms have been put forward as credible sources of influence on the *Satyricon* – the serious heroic romance, stories of adventure implied in certain rhetorical exercises among the elder Seneca's collection, the prologue of comedy, and, with more plainly apposite bearing, the mime[2] for its realism, and the erotic Milesian tales[3] in Greek if not in Sisenna's adaptations from Aristides. The hypothesis that Petronius travestied such Greek love-romances as are represented by the Ninos story[4] recovered on a first-century papyrus can scarcely hold good where we find no structure clearly suggesting parody to a reader: manifestly the tone of Petronius is far removed from that of the conventional courtships, piracies, voyages, shipwrecks, separations and reunions in the love-stories of later Greek literature.[5] Time has even been spent on an endeavour to prove that picaresque Greek novels existed from which Petronius might have borrowed his rascally heroes. No doubt he owed much: there is equally no doubt that he created the realistic novel; for before him such prose fiction as had appeared in the form of fable, parable or anecdote fell far short of a sustained romance well filled with incident and characterisation.

But just as the *Satyricon* as a whole, however original in spirit, owed something to literary convention, so the *Cena Trimalchionis* repeats stock-features of Greek banquets like the performances by acrobats and reciters, the appearance of the uninvited guest (Habinnas), the quarrel, and the dog-fight.[6] The *Cena* in Roman satire had a tradition beginning perhaps in Ennius, but certainly established by Lucilius and developed by Horace; and between Nasidienus's banquet in Horace and Trimalchio's dinner-party there are points of resemblance[7] enough to prove how fresh and independent Petronius could be even when he handled

---

[1] § 139:   'Me quoque per terras per cani Nereos aequor
Hellespontiaci sequitur grauis ira Priapi.'

[2] On influence of mime, see K. Preston, 'Some Sources of Comic Effect in P.,' *C.P.* 1915, p. 260 ff. and F. Moering, *De P. mimorum imitatore,* Münster 1915.

[3] The type is seen in the Widow of Ephesus (*Satyr.* §§ 111–112). On Milesian tales see Norden, *Kunstprosa,* II. 602, 604 n.; E. Rohde, *Der griech. Roman* (1900) 586, and 'Zum griechischen Roman,' *Kl. Schr.* (1901) II, 25 ff. (rp. from *Rh.M.* xlviii (1894)); H. Lucas, 'Zu den Milesiaca des Aristides,' *Philol.* lxvi (1907) 16 ff.

[4] See on this subject S.H. § 395; F. F. Abbott, *Common People of Anct. Rome,* pp. 128–133; C. W. Mendell, 'P. and the Greek Romance,' *C.P.* 1917, 158 ff.

[5] V. Chauvin, *Les romanciers grecs et latins,* Paris 1862.

[6] For traditional features from banquets in Greek lit. see J. Geffcken, 'Studien zur griech. Satire' in *Neue Jb. K. A.* xxvii (1911) 395 and 484; and, in general, F. Ullrich, *Entstehung u. Entwickelung d. Litteraturgattung des Symposion,* Würzb. 1908.

[7] A. Collignon, *Étude sur Pétrone,* p. 254 ff.; J. Révay, 'Horaz u. Petron,' *C.P.* xvii (1922) p. 202 ff.; L. R. Shero, 'The *Cena* in Roman Satire,' *C.P.* xviii (1923) p. 126 ff. esp. pp. 134–139.

a tralatician idea like that of a rich and ill-bred parvenu, or reckless
extravagance, or an accident at the feast, or the efforts of guests to
smother laughter at their host, or their obvious freedom from restraint
during his temporary withdrawal.[1]

A sentence written in the eighteenth century makes a good introduction to much of the criticism passed on Petronius: 'I told him that,
in my opinion, he wrote with ease and vicacity, but was withal so lewd
and indecent that he ought to find no quarter or protection among
people of morals and taste.' So Smollett makes Roderick Random answer
Earl Strutwell when he has raised the question of Petronius's 'taste in
love' as 'generally decried and indeed condemned by our laws.'[2] The
judgement has the interest of occurring in a novel which presents a
parallel to the *Satyricon* in its spirit of adventure into more than questionable companies and in its background of rascality and immorality.
Petronius's own line,

You damn a work of fresh outspokenness[3]

may be taken as an anticipation of the attitude of many. In this faithful
picture of seamy aspects of Italian life and manners there is much that
is loathsome, but there is much that is merely vulgar, much that is
innocuously humorous, while as a true presentment all of it retains
its value in the history of society. It should be noted too that if Petronius
does not condemn, neither does he commend. As a recording spectator
with a nobleman's half-amused cynicism and a jaded voluptuary's thrill
from contemplating low life in contrast to court ceremonial and luxury,
he was justifiably conscious that he had inaugurated something new in
literature.

Any who may entertain misgivings about the title of Petronius's
work to rank as a realistic romance would do well to consider Guy de
Maupassant's preface to *Pierre et Jean*. There he states and defends the
position of the realistic artist among novel writers. The realist, because
misunderstood, is sometimes injudiciously condemned. No mere slavish
copying of contemporary life will produce an adequate sense of simple
reality; for an endeavour to incorporate within the limits of a book the
whole truth and nothing but the truth would inevitably result in desperate
entanglement among an endless number of insignificant details. So the

---

[1] Hor. *Sat.* II. viii. 77–78:
'Et soleas poscit: tum in lecto quoque uideres
Stridere secreta diuisos aure susurros.'
Petr. *Sat.* 41: 'ab hoc ferculo Trimalchio ad lasanum surrexit. Nos libertatem
sine tyranno nacti coepimus inuitare conuiuarum sermones.'
[2] Among the manuscript titles is *Petronii arbitri affranii Satirici lib. incip.*,
where the at first puzzling appearance of the name of Afranius indicates Petronius's resemblance to that writer of togata-comedies *in puerorum foedis amoribus*
(Teuffel, § 305, 1).
[3] *Sat.* § 132: 'damnatisque nouae simplicitatis opus.'

artistic realist, as surely as he values art and under pain of becoming a commonplace verbal photographer, must select characteristic details only, must communicate some meaning which underlies the bewildering miscellany of apparently incongruous incidents, and must, by his readjustment of actualities, compose a synthesis more intelligible and more cogent than life itself. This is a task which genius alone has power successfully to achieve; and, indeed, so subtle is the genius demanded that the higher order of realists must, as Maupassant suggested, prove themselves to be illusionists. In this connexion, one conceives that Petronius's presentment of Trimalchio's dinner-party is more effective and more memorable than the exact record of an actual dinner-party would have been. The quality of the host's character and motives is grasped best from the artist's manipulation of incidents; for without recourse to elaborate psychological analysis there can be unmistakably conveyed, by means of such conversation, behaviour and gestures as the author's foresight has introduced, a convincing picture of the mental endowment of persons under observation. And, if this is the case with character, so too the events may be chosen and marshalled in such a way as to suggest their special significance in the narrative. These a realist like Petronius will choose and marshal with unabashed candour, disdaining nothing that is common to humanity, and unhindered by qualms of gingerly prudishness.

It is his mode of representing life that places Petronius in the company of Rabelais, Fielding and Smollett. His is a gay, outspoken, unashamed sensuality, flitting naturally from pleasure to pleasure and accepting for his characters without hesitancy the experiences of the world which come their way. This is the true spirit of the picaresque romance. Now one thinks of Gil Blas as a parallel, now of some of Dumas's adventurers. An amour, a fight, a theft, a carousal, come all alike to Encolpius; and it is among the author's distinctive merits that without pointless embroideries or reflective digressions he uses an accumulated experience of cities and men to fashion a straightforward and life-like story. It is briskly told, and because its characters seem flesh and blood it smacks of truth. Its living people reveal themselves in part through their doings or misdoings, in part through natural talk; they are, in fact, the sport of their own weaknesses, whether they be the wandering rogues Encolpius and Ascyltus or the self-satisfied profiteer Trimalchio or some of his fellow-freedmen in affluent or in reduced circumstances. From the pen of an adept in sternly realistic treatment of figures and situations the reader must expect the shocking as well as the mirth-provoking; so that frank avowals and naked abandonment of reticence give to the *Satyricon* some of that kind of realism which is discoverable in certain French and Russian novels. The sensuality is, however, by no means sexual only. There is something Gargantuan, as there is certainly intended to be something satiric, in the overdone profusion which marks Trimalchio's hospitality; and yet its variety and surprises imply that sort of sensual delight in good food which animates Anatole France's description, in his *Histoire Comique*, of the Castelnaudary stew a-cooking twenty years till the added ingredients in the pan imparted a quality like that in the women's amber-flesh of old Venetian masters. This Roman, this Gallic interest in food is not understood in England, where people do not talk about meals as they did at Rome and do in France; but then the renown of England does not lie in her cookery.

It is as a novelist that Petronius must be appreciated. A full judgement on his achievement is prevented by the loss of much the greater part of his work, though enough survives to prove his mastery of some qualities felt to be most enjoyable in the modern novel; such as his humour of situation and dialogue, often as pronounced as in Dickens; his restrained irony of attitude, not tragic as in Hardy, but verging towards Meredith's comic spirit; his creation of incidents lively and varied, carrying the reader along as rapidly as in Dumas; and his management of pervading atmosphere in consonance with incidents and characters – a great secret in all the most effective tales. But in these light chapters of ancient life let no reader look for depth of thought or passion, or any of that pity and tenderness which make the strength of some of the greatest modern fiction.

The *Metamorphoses* or *Golden Ass* of Apuleius in the second century is the only other fictitious narrative in Latin prose. One must place in a separate category *The Marriage of Philology and Mercury* written by Martianus Capella in the fifth century. That work was designed by Capella to precede his educational encyclopaedia on the *triuium* and *quadriuium*. It follows the Menippean form, as the *Satyricon* did, but is a pedantic allegorical fantasia. *The Golden Ass* and *the Satyricon* are alike of a higher imaginative order than the stereotyped romances of erotic adventure which subsequently became common in Greek; but, though they are both more readable than the loves of Theagenes and Chariclea in Heliodorus's *Aethiopica* or of Daphnis and Chloe in Longus's elegant prose pastoral, the *Satyricon* excels *The Golden Ass* because of its greater originality and its more typically Roman colour. *The Golden Ass* betrays more of the influence of Greek Milesian tales, notably in its long[1] but charming episode of *Cupid and Psyche*; and, while it may be considered a satiric romance in its mockery of contemporary superstition, priestly imposture, and a weak police-system under which brigands enjoyed too much licence, still its atmosphere of the marvellous and the magical is widely dissimilar to the prevailing realism of the *Satyricon*, which, except in incidental tales concerning werewolf or witches, seldom departs from fidelity to actual life. Lucius, the hero of the later romance, whose lubricity and prying are responsible

[1] Apul. *Met.* iv, 28–vi. 24.

for his transformation into an ass, is, no doubt, as the victim of the
mismanaged spell, brought into contact with different classes of individuals, different homes, and different religious rites including the
mysteries of Isis so finely described towards the close; but the realism
is less telling in Apuleius than in Petronius, because the incidents are
related in a bizarre African style, whose colour and ring contrast markedly
with the natural Latin of the *Satyricon*.

This Latin of the *Satyricon* has a natural ring, partly because, even
where Petronius writes in literary Latin, he is, as a rule, simple, direct
and non-rhetorical; partly because he constructs a life-like framework
of easygoing remarks; partly because he employs the actual words of
everyday conversation. His style is not a unity. He is master of two
styles – one educated, the other colloquial.[1] Encolpius, like the rhetorical professor Agamemnon and the poet Eumolpus, expresses himself usually in the polished urbane Latin, which, without being over-
formal, is still distinct from the vulgar Latin in which the freedmen
speak. Even within this latter sphere, difficulties have been encountered
in rigidly demarcating ordinary colloquial elements from plebeian and
possibly dialectic elements. It is unlikely that Petronius took pains to
manufacture an accurate mosaic of Campanian words: enough, that
through broad strokes imitative of the locutions of humble folk he produced an effect like that of the 'racy genuine language' which Borrow
somewhere admires in criminals' accounts of themselves; and, in fact,
there are echoes as of an ancient Newgate Calendar. This dialogue is
as true to life as the talk in Kipling's 'Soldiers Three' or in Conrad's
'Nigger of the Narcissus.' One of the great values, therefore, of Petronius
is that his realistic novel, along with comedy, satire and the less formal
letters of Cicero, affords examples of that popular Latin which is so
important for understanding the genesis of the Romance languages.
To take the most familiar instance, it is significant that *caballus*, which
descends as the word for 'horse' into Italian, Spanish, Portuguese,
French and Roumanian, should be found in writers like Lucilius,
Horace and Juvenal as well as in Petronius.[2]

This *sermo plebeius*, then, Petronius causes to live again for his readers
with just admixture enough of Greek[3] to remind us that we are supposed
to be in Campania. And so the freedmen, while they dine and revel,
speak slangily and ungrammatically, uttering their thoughts in too
casual and disconnected a manner to trouble about logical subordination
of clauses or periodic form, and interspersing their talk quite appropriately with saws or scraps of popular wisdom, rare compounds and

[1] Even the grammar is intentionally varied; *e.g.* the correct accusative, *Nicero-
tem*, 61, contrasted with Trimalchio's *Niceronem*, 63.
[2] *Sat.* 117; 134.
[3] *E.g.* athlum, 57; phantasia, 38; philologia, 39; polymitus, 40; synoecio, 93;
apoculare, 62 and 67 (= ἀποκυλίω); and hybrids like bilychnis, 30 (=bis+
λύχνος); percolopare, 44 (= per + κόλαφος); lupatria, 37; excatarissasti, 67.

diminutives,[1] irregular inflectional endings and false genders. The sententious is rolled off by Trimalchio with a negligence of grammar which can be paralleled, if not exactly echoed, in English:

'My friends, even slaves are human beings, and they has drunk the same milk as us, even if their evil stars has downed them.'[2]

Commending his wine, he declares 'Fishes must swim' (*pisces natare oportet*). Ganymedes grumbles 'This district's going down as the calf's tail grows' (*haec colonia retrouersus crescit tanquam coda uituli*). 'One good turn deserves another' (*manus manum lauat*) says the next guest, who concludes in Latin less commendable than the sentiment, 'Education's a treasure and culture never dies' (*litterae thesaurum est et artificium nunquam moritur*, 46).

The spoken language, being conservative no less than innovating, retained, as it does in many countries, a proportion of archaisms, so that Petronian diminutives and other formations find parallels in early Latin writers. *Gaudimonium*, 61, and *tristimonium*, 63, remind one of words like *mercimonium* in Plautus; and there is an old-fashioned sound in *sestertiarius*, 45; *dupunduarius*, 58 and 74; *linguosus*, 43 and 63; *dignitossus*, 57; with adverbs like *improbiter*, 66; *largiter*, 71; and *urceatim*, 44. Similarly, several frequentative and intensive verbs are of the sort used by comic authors, and may be referred to the *sermo cotidianus* rather than to the *sermo rusticus*.[3] Plebeian speech was also, like comedy, rich in intransitives of the first conjugation (*e.g. naufragare*, 76; *aginare*, 61); and in compounds (*recorrigere*, 43, shared with Seneca and Tertullian; *adcognoscere*, 69; *domusio*, 46; *caldicerebrius*, 45, *nesapius*, 50). To the vulgar speech we may set down most of the departures from classic grammatical form, such as 3rd declension nouns transferred to 1st, *e.g.* the Greek words *schemas*, 44; *stigmam*, 45, 69; 2nd declension nouns transferred to 1st, *triclinia*, 71; *intestinas*, 76; 1st to 2nd *margaritum*,[4] 63; 3rd to 2nd *uasus*, 57; *pauperorum*, 46. *Bouis*, 62, and *Iouis*, 58 appear as nominatives: so too *lacte*, 38, which with the adjective in *munus excellente*, 45, is almost Italian. Changes of gender are seen in *caelus*, 39, 45; *uinus*, 41; *balneus*, 41; *fatus*, 42, 71, 77; *fericulus*, 39 (=*ferculum* with epenthetic vowel from vulgar pronunciation); *lorus*, 57. Notable verb-forms are *uinciturum*, 45, for *uicturum*; *fefellitus sum*, 61; *faciatur*, 71; *mauoluit*, 77. Alterations in voice occur; *e.g.*, *potes loquere*, *non loquis*, 46; *pudeatur*, 47. As might be expected, old words are

---

[1] *E.g. amasiunculus*, 45; *amasiuncula*, 75; *lamellula*, 57; *cor(i)cillum*, 75; *manuciolum*, 63. The loss of force in popular diminutives is plain from 'hominem . . . ualde audaculum,' 63 ='a mighty bold fellow.'

[2] § 71: 'amici,' inquit, 'et serui homines sunt et aeque unum *lactem* biberunt, etiam si illos malus *fatus* oppressit.'

[3] Guericke (*op. cit.* in bibl.), p. 34.

[4] The neuter form, instead of the usual *margarita*, was used by Varro, Tacitus (*Agr.* xii) Suetonius and Tertullian, and probably by Pliny (*Ep.* V. xvi. 7).

used in new senses: *e.g. notaui*, 6 (='I noticed'),[1] and departures are made from standard syntax; *e.g. temptemus si adhuc sorbilia sunt*, 33; *persuadeo hospitem*, 62.[2]

True as he is to certain phases of life and speech, Petronius is yet a contrast to contemporary literary tendencies. In this very realism of his he is independent, and in large measure it must have rescued him from the risk of indulgence in the rhetorical artificialities of the period. He is, besides, a sort of flippant Epicurean counterfoil to the grave Stoic thought in Seneca's treatises, and he is out of sympathy with Lucan's manner in composing a historical poem.

Petronius is himself one of the figures in the poetry of the Neronian age. His own poetical attainments were considerable. The mere skill is evident from the varied verse-passages, long or short, in the *Satyricon*. Some of these have a literary bearing like Agamemnon's didactic lines on the training of an orator, or Eumolpus's iambics *On the Sack of Troy* – uninspired in face of the inevitable comparison with Virgil, but undeserving of that shower of stones which Petronius merrily makes the reciter earn. The longest piece consists of 295 hexameters to illustrate Eumolpus's dogmas concerning the dangers which beset a poem on the *Bellum Ciuile*. Without naming Lucan, these pronouncements imply a criticism on his epic, especially in their objection to taking actual facts for poetic material and in their advocacy of divine interventions (*deorum ministeria*) which the *Pharsalia* had eschewed. The poem itself cannot be read without thoughts of Lucan, particularly in its description of portents and panic. The alarm in Rome over Caesar's approach is described in a passage characterised by rhetoric, artificialities and monotony in phrase and metre,[3] while it contains pithy sentences recalling Lucan's style: *e.g.* 'as each man fears, so great his flight' (*quantum quisque timet, tantum fugit*), and 'slays, if prayers could slay, his absent foe' (*absentem uotis interficit hostem*).

More poetic feeling is shown in some of the shorter pieces, such as the lines picturing the love of Circe and Encolpius in a flowery setting like that of Mother Earth in Jove's embrace:

> Forth flashed rose, violet, and iris soft,
> And from the meadow green white lilies laughed:
> So bright the ground that to the lush grass called
> Our love: and day grew fairer to befriend
> Our hidden sighs.[4]

[1] It is an easy development from the physical sense of *notare*, 'to note' or 'mark down,' and the transition is found in Cicero.   [2] *Cf.* p. 66 n. 3.

[3] *Sat.* 123, ll. 209–232: *tantum fugit* (221) is echoed by the corresponding metrical position of *tantum trahit* (231); *maerentia tecta relinquunt* (225) by *maerentia pectora iungant* (229); *relinquunt* ends 225 and *relinquit* 227. On Petronius and Lucan, see S.H. § 392.

[4] *Sat.* 127:   'Emicuere rosae uiolaeque et molle cyperon,
>   Albaque de uiridi riserunt lilia prato:
>   Talis humus Venerem molles clamauit in herbas,
>   Candidiorque dies secreto fauit amori.'

Apart from verses in the *Satyricon*, there are short poems which, with different degrees of authority and in different number, have been considered Petronian. Bährens gives 37.[1] Sixteen pieces follow the epigrams assigned to Seneca in the Codex Vossianus Q. 86, and include two guaranteed as Petronian by Fulgentius, who quotes from them; eleven others were drawn by Binet from a now lost MS. which apparently ascribed them to Petronius, from whom Fulgentius in any case cites one; and they were followed by eight in regard to which at most a stylistic argument can be used; while four more (including, however, two from our mutilated *Satyricon*) are entitled as by Petronius in a different MS., Codex Vossianus F. 111. There is fair reason to believe that these, with a few possible exceptions, are his work, and they may be excerpts from vanished portions of the *Satyricon*. Not unnaturally they vary in theme, metre and style, so that an appropriate motto is furnished by the couplet:

> Find here what each desires: men's pleasure goes
> Strange ways: one pulls a thorn and one a rose.[2]

The fear that created gods, the emigrant with the world before him, the triumph of worthlessness, an old man's torrent of tears, betrayal of secrets, perils of the sea, nature's infinite variety, sympathy in suffering, a sweetheart's gift of apples, a parrot from India, and a theory of dreams, are among the subjects. A few end in epigrammatic manner with a line which has some of the point though not all the sharpness of Martial. Nowhere, however, can we more readily believe that we have the genuine accents of Petronius than in poems which imply a cordial delight in natural beauty. It is more than a sated epicure's itch for change from town, because in some a truer poet speaks than in the pastorals of his contemporary Calpurnius Siculus. Thus, Petronius leads his brief description of an autumn scene up to a neat final line:

> All the year's promise stood before our eyes.[3]

Or he pictures his simple country house lovingly indeed, but with a sense of disillusion and an almost Senecan consciousness of wasted time:

> Care-free the shelter of my cottage-roof;
> And wine-rich clusters hang from fertile elm.
> Red apples and ripe cherries load their boughs;
> Pallas' own olive breaks with fruited branch. . . .
> Go to now: sell the fleeting hours of life
> For rich repasts! I pray my waiting end
> May find me here to answer for my hours.[4]

[1] *P.L.M.* iv. nos. 74–108, 120–121.
[2] *Ibid.* 74:
    'Inueniat (?inuenias) quod quisque uelit: non omnibus unum est
        Quod placet: hic spinas colligit, ille rosas.'
[3] *Ibid.* 75, l. 5: 'Ante oculos stabat quidquid promiserat annus.'
[4] *Ibid.* 81:
    'Paruula securo tegitur mihi culmine sedes
    Uuaque plena mero fecunda pendet ab ulmo,' etc.

In another poem he hails the sea-side with rapture

> O strand more sweet to me than life! O sea!
> Blest he who visits oft thy neighb'ring shores.
> O beauteous day! Once in this scene I used
> To rouse the Naiads with alternate stroke.
> Here's depth of pool, there's seaweed from the bay,
> Here trusty haunt for passion unrevealed.
> My life is lived; for grudging fortune ne'er
> Shall filch from me what happier hours bestowed.[1]

But he has nothing finer than his sonnet-like poem in fourteen lines on the tyranny of love:

> In night's first silence couched, scarce had I found
> Repose and given to Sleep o'erwearied eyes,
> When cruel Love clutches my hair and cries:
> 'Keep vigil thou, I say, for all thy wound.
> Canst thou, my slave, by thousand amours bound
> Alone, alone, thou block, lie sluggard-wise?'
> Thereat, barefoot, with tunic loose, I rise
> And try all paths, but follow no path round.
>
> I run, I slacken speed, I half retrace
> My tracks, then in the highway blush to wait.
> Lo! hushed are human sounds and traffic's roar,
> And note of bird and trusty pack that bays.
> Alone of all, both sleep and couch I hate,
> Heeding, great Cupid, thy imperial lore.[2]

[1] *P.L.M.* iv. no. 84:
> 'O litus uita mihi dulcius, o mare! felix
> Cui licet ad terras ire subinde tuas,' etc.

[2] *Ibid.* 99: The English verse is from J. Wight Duff's 'Sonnets from the Antique' in Quatercentenary number of *Alma Mater*, Aberdeen Univ. Mag., 1906.

The elegiacs show in the eighth and tenth lines Petronius's departure from the rigorous Ovidian disyllabic ending in the pentameter:
> 'Lecto compositus uix prima silentia noctis
> Carpebam et somno lumina uicta dabam:
> Cum me saeuus Amor prensat sursumque capillis
> Excitat et lacerum peruigilare iubet.
> "Tu famulus meus," inquit, "ames cum mille puellas,
> Solus io solus, dure, iacere potes?"
> Exsilio et pedibus nudis tunicaque soluta
> Omne iter incipio, nullum iter expedio.
> Nunc propero, nunc ire piget, rursumque redire
> Poenitet et pudor est stare uia media.
> Ecce tacent uoces hominum strepitusque uiarum
> Et uolucrum cantus turbaque fida canum.
> Solus ego ex cunctis paueo somnumque torumque
> Et sequor imperium, magne Cupido, tuum.'

Chapter III

SENECA THE PHILOSOPHER: MISCELLANEOUS LEARNING

SENECA THE PHILOSOPHER

THE jungle of literature which has grown up around Seneca testifies to the manifold inquiries stimulated by his personality and works. The bare enumeration of representative treatises or essays on Senecan subjects becomes oppressive. In Latin and in many modern languages they have dealt with problems of his life – the cause of his exile, his moral character, his inconsistencies, his political significance and control or want of control over Nero; they have dealt with the chronology of his writings; with his theology, philosophy and cosmology, so that what he thought of God, man and the world has been scrutinised in relation to Stoicism as well as to those eclectic modifications which were always typical of the practical Roman; they have dealt, too, with his science, with aspects of his style, his characteristic prose, his gift of piquant satire, his poetic and tragic powers; with difficulties, still unsolved, in his text; with questions of his influence upon Christian literature, European drama and modern essay-writing. There is, then, no lack of Senecan themes, and his influence makes him one of the most prominent figures in the history of letters.

The Seneca family belonged to Corduba, the chief city of Baetica, which was the most civilised province of Spain. There, about 4 B.C.[1]

[1] The conjectural date is based on *De Tranq.* xvii. 7; *Ep.* cviii. 17 and 22; *Nat. Q.* I. i. 3. H. Lehmann, *Claudius u. Nero*, Gotha 1858, 152, prefers 8 B.C. Ch. Favez, in ed. of *Ad Helv.*, supports the earlier date because of Seneca's recollection of Asinius Pollio recorded *De Tranq.* xvii. 7; Pollio died in A.D. 5.

L. Annaeus Seneca,[1] second son of the so-called 'rhetor,' was born.
His mother Helvia, we learn in the *Consolatio* sent to her by her exiled
son, had a philosophical bent – a contrast in this respect to her husband,
whose interest lay in rhetoric. The family was well-to-do and talented.
The elder Seneca and Helvia had three sons. The eldest was M.
Annaeus Novatus, to whom his brother dedicated his treatises *On Anger*
and *On A Happy Life*: he became 'Gallio' through adoption by L.
Junius Gallio, the orator, and, when governor of Achaea in 51–52, happened to have the apostle Paul brought before his tribunal.[2] The second
son, who alone of the three retained the cognomen 'Seneca,'
became, as a statesman and writer, the most famous member of
the family. The youngest son, M. Annaeus Mela, of whose ability his
father[3] held a high opinion, was of a more retiring disposition, but,
without courting senatorial honours, proved himself a successful
money-maker, and possesses his best title to fame as the father of
Lucan.

Seneca was brought when a child, in the arms of an affectionate aunt,[4]
to Rome, whither his parents either preceded or followed him. His preliminary training under a *grammaticus* left him with a memory of much
barren detail and a pronounced distaste for verbal criticism or the
minutiae of book learning;[5] his subsequent training in rhetoric by such
masters as Mamercus Scaurus, Gallio, Musa, Julius Bassus,[6] and under
the auspices of his father, made an indelible impress upon his genius.
No doubt his true intellectual love was reserved for philosophy, and
he saw the weaknesses of declamation;[7] but we have his father's evidence
that all three sons were captivated by rhetorical *sententiae*,[8] and Seneca's
own style – disconnected, pointed, antithetic, metaphorical and piquant
– is the best proof of its own origin. With his philosophical studies came
a fuller satisfaction for intellect and spirit. Seneca was thoroughly
Roman in emphasising the practical aspect of philosophy. 'Philosophy,'
he says, 'consists not in words but in realities. She sits at the helm and
steers the voyage through the hazards of the waves.'[9] More and more
Seneca was drawn to it, not merely as a guide to conduct, but as something that filled a profound need of the soul. To him it signified the
divine way, truth, and life: it made, especially through the Neo-
Stoicism which he accepted and developed, a religious appeal. For the

---

[1] He gives his full name, *De Ben.* IV. viii 3. For his birthplace see Mart. I. lxi.
7–8.
[2] *Acts* xviii, 11–17. Anatole France gives a lively account of Gallio in *Sur la
Pierre Blanche*, as already mentioned, p. 38 n. 5.
[3] *Contr.* II. *praef.* 4.
[4] *Ad Helv.* xix. 2.
[5] *Ep.* lviii. 5, lxxxviii. 3 *sqq.* and 37, cviii. 24; *De Br. Vit.* xiii. 2.
[6] *Contr.* X. *praef.* 2, 8, 9, 12.
[7] *Ep.* xx, 2: 'facere docet philosophia, non dicere'; cxv. 1: 'quaere quid
scribas non quemadmodum.'
[8] *Contr.* I. *praef.* 22; IV. *praef.* 1; VII. *praef.* 9.
[9] *Ep.* xvi. 3.

elect there was a turning away from the world,[1] a disdain of earthly
things,[2] the duty of self-examination,[3] the joys of conversion,[4] the
apostolic call to enlighten others.[5] There were ascetic privations,[6] hard
at first in their disciplinary stringency, although afterwards joyously
welcomed: there were ecstatic possibilities of drawing close to God.[7]
The boy might not at once grasp all the implications of the higher
teaching, and in life he may have practised very imperfectly the doctrines to which he gave eloquent and noble expression; yet it is certain
that from the outset his philosophical masters exercised a deep influence upon him. They were three disciples of the Sextii – Sotion, Attalus
and Fabianus. Sotion, arguing on Pythagorean principles, persuaded
Seneca to become vegetarian; Attalus, the Stoic, with a contempt for
luxury, induced him to renounce perfumes, wines, oysters, mushrooms
and a soft bed; while Fabianus, who had given up a career as a speaker
to devote himself to philosophical discussion, conveyed to him much of
his own enthusiasm. Seneca was the first to arrive for a lecture, and
last to leave: his abstinence and fasts were so rigorous that his health,
never of the best,[8] began to suffer, and his father intervened with the
timely reminder that he might be mistaken for a devotee of the foreign
superstitions which Tiberius had endeavoured to extirpate about A.D.
19. If Seneca sighed as a theorist, he obeyed as a son. Fits of melancholy drove him to thoughts of suicide, which Stoicism permitted in
certain circumstances: only regard for his father prevented him from
losing control over himself. The state of his health may have accounted
for visits to Pompeii and to Egypt, where an aunt was wife of the
governor.[9] One of his early works, a lost treatise on Egyptian religious
practices (*De Ritu et Sacris Aegyptiorum*), must be put down to his
stay in the country. His aunt was more than a good nurse; she could
use her influence for her nephew, and on his return to Rome about A.D.
31 helped to secure the quaestorship for him. Then his career as a
speaker at the bar began. Some years passed, and his oratorical performances drew upon him the jealousy of Caligula, who, not content
with sneering at them as 'mere competitive exercises' and 'sand without lime,'[10] would have put Seneca to death but for the whisper from
one of the emperor's favourites that he was in any case doomed to die
soon from consumption.[11] Theatened men, however, live long, and

[1] *Ep.* xix. 1, xxii. 1 *sqq.*, xcviii. 13.
[2] *Ep.* iv. 10–11, xvii. 3–4, xxxi. 10. [3] *De Ira* III. xxxvi.
[4] *Ep.* vi. 1 (sign of grace to see one's faults); viii. 3.
[5] *Ep.* vi. 4 ('gaudeo discere ut doceam'), viii. 3 ('rectum iter . . . lassus
errando aliis monstro'), xxxiv. 1 ('adsero te mihi: meum opus es'), xlviii. 7–8.
[6] *Ep.* xviii. 5–9, cviii. 13 *sqq.*
[7] *Ep.* xxxi. 11, xli. 2, xcv. 50.
[8] *Ep.* liv. 1, lxxvii. 9, lxxviii. 1, civ. 1.
[9] *Ad Helv.* xix. 2 and 4–6.
[10] Suet. *Cal.* liii: 'commissiones meras . . . harenam esse sine calce.'
[11] Dio LIX. xix. 7 . . . πιστεύσας ὅτι φθόης τε ἔχοι κακῶς καὶ οὐκ ἐς μακρὰν
τελευτήσοι.

G

Seneca's future fame lay in other fields than the dangerous one of oratory.

By degrees his own preference turned him to literature and philosophy.[1] Some of his lost works belong to this period – collections of discourses and poems, a physical treatise *De Motu Terrarum*, a biography of his father, who died about A.D. 39, and perhaps the *Consolation to Marcia*. Most likely, too, the material for the three books *On Anger* was collected about the same time, and published, with its bitter allusions to Caligula,[2] soon after that emperor was safely dead. Seneca was not a recluse: a measure of self-effacement may have been judicious under Caligula, but Seneca's own choice was to make the student's loneliness alternate with social engagements. 'There should be a blend, an alternation of solitude and society: the former will cause us to want human kind, the latter to want ourselves. And the one will be a cure for the other: solitude will heal dislike for a crowd, a crowd will heal the weariness of solitude.'[3] The school of the world was essential to the thinker on wisdom. He was a good business man, able to advance his financial interests; and he had gifts of elegant expression which fitted him to mix with the highest circles in Rome. At Claudius's court, after Caligula's murder, Seneca occupied a prominent position as an asset in the party of the princesses, Julia Livilla and Agrippina, daughters of Germanicus and nieces of the emperor. His happiness was short-lived. A charge was brought against him of an immoral intrigue with Julia.[4] Messallina, the unscrupulous empress, is not unreasonably suspected of having for political reasons invented the accusation to weaken a rival faction. It involved Julia's death ultimately, and Seneca's trial before a subservient senate, where the death-sentence was at Claudius's suggestion commuted to banishment. So for eight years, from 41 to 49, he underwent the punishment of 'relegation' in Corsica.

In writing his *Consolation to Helvia*, probably a good many months later, he endeavours to cheer his mother by philosophical arguments that exile is quite tolerable, and very much what the exiled person makes it; but his real feelings of weary despondency are expressed in certain epigrams and in his *Consolation to Polybius* of A.D. 43, when his sympathy proffered to Claudius's learned Secretary for Petitions (*a libellis*) and his cringing flattery of the emperor were designed, though in vain, to facilitate his recall. Certainly, he had books and literary pursuits to occupy his mind; slaves may have been in attendance; and his friend Caesonius Maximus seems to have stayed with him for a time; but there was much that was depressing. He had lost his father, his wife and a child: like

---

[1] *Ep.* xlix. 2.

[2] *De Ira* I. xx. 8–9; II. xxxiii. 3 *sqq.*; III. xviii. 3–4 and xix.

[3] *De Tranq.* xvii. 3: 'miscenda tamen ista et alternanda sunt, solitudo et frequentia: illa nobis faciet hominum desiderium, haec nostri; et erit altera alterius remedium; odium turbae sanabit solitudo, taedium solitudinis turba.'

[4] Dio LX. viii. 5–6; schol. ad Juv. V. 109.

other ancients, he could take little pleasure in rugged scenery: and there
was a limit to his interest in the ethnology of the island. For a capitalist,
diplomat and courtier, for a literary man with social instincts, banishment meant the same poignancy of suffering as Ovid knew on the shores
of the Black Sea. But relief came for Seneca as it never came for Ovid.
The year 48 saw the execution of Messallina, and in 49 Seneca was recalled and made praetor, through the influence of Agrippina, Claudius's
new consort, who realised that a man of his literary reputation would
make a suitable tutor for her boy Nero.[1] The young prince's education
consisted of all available subjects of culture, with two chief limitations
according to Suetonius: Nero's mother disapproved of philosophy for a
future ruler, and Seneca jealously discouraged the study of the old
orators, so that his own modern style might remain Nero's ideal.[2] When
Claudius was done to death in 54, it fell to the imperial tutor to compose
a suitable panegyric for his pupil, the new emperor, to deliver; and so
began the period of five years – the *quinquennium*[3] praised long afterwards by Trajan[4] – during which Seneca, aided by the good sense of
Burrus, prefect of the guard, kept Nero on paths of comparative decency
and moderation.[5] Part of Seneca's policy was directed towards keeping
Nero free from undue interference on the part of his imperious mother,[6]
who hotly protested against 'the claim of the cripple Burrus and the
exile Seneca to govern mankind with a maimed hand and a scholar's
tongue.'[7] At this period Seneca's influence as a statesman reached its
zenith; and it is a reasonable conjecture that for a time he contrived to
mould governmental policy in the spirit of his own broad-minded cosmopolitanism. It was of some service to the world that the author of the
De Clementia, addressed to Nero when he was eighteen, should now be
his chief adviser. Dio himself, who is usually a hostile witness where
Seneca is concerned, gives to him and Burrus credit for able and fair
administration.[8] There were, however, black crimes which Seneca,
whether privy to them or not, had to condone. Britannicus, the true
heir to the purple, had been got rid of by poison at the emperor's table
in 55; and in 59 came Agrippina's murder by her son's command.
State policy, the historical cloak for many infamies, might argue a case
on behalf of both acts: the one removed a rival and secured the throne,
the other ended a woman's ascendancy and secured the emperor's
freedom.[9] It was Seneca who composed for Nero the statement to be

---

[1] Tac. *Ann.* XII. viii.   [2] Suet. *Nero* lii.
[3] The *quinquennium* is here used in its customary sense, and not the less likely
one in which J. G. C. Anderson applied it to the last five years of Nero's reign
on the ground that the Golden House scheme and rebuilding after the Great
Fire were the achievements which aroused Trajan's admiration. (*J.R.S.* I
(1911) p. 173 ff.)
[4] For Trajan's admiration, see Aurel. Victor, *De Caesaribus* v.
[5] Tac. *Ann.* XIII. ii, vi, xi.
[6] *Ibid.* v and xiii.   [7] *Ibid.* xiv.
[8] Dio LXI. iv. 1.   [9] Tac. *Ann.* XIII. xvii; XIV. vii and xi.

read in the Senate respecting his mother's death. One can only guess what acquiescence meant for a man who could both think and feel. To his credit be it said that he seems at least to have pleaded with Nero to save his cruelly maligned empress Octavia in A.D. 62.

That was the year of Burrus's death and of Tigellinus's elevation,[1] when Nero had begun to lean upon worse advisers, who urged him to shake off his mentor.[2] The mentor himself, recognising that his influence was undermined, placed before Nero his request to retire.[3] The wealth of a professing Stoic made an easy target for criticism,[4] and a tempting lure for an avaricious emperor. Seneca's speech, therefore, at his interview, as reported by Tacitus, took mainly the form of an *apologia pro diuitiis suis*. His wealth amassed in these years of service was an index surely of his Majesty's bounty; and, now that he was old, it should return to his Majesty. Nero, adroitly setting his ability in repartee to the credit of his excellent teacher, declared that Seneca was not nearly so old that his imperial pupil could think of dropping his pilotage; moreover he could not possibly accept his wealth – for what would people say?[5] Fair dissembling words did not deceive Seneca. From that day he changed his mode of life: he no longer kept open house or made public appearances attended by troops of friends. He had some three years yet to devote to studious retirement: and to this period, A.D. 62–65, can be assigned with confidence his essay *On Leisure* (*De Otio*), his elaborate *Moral Letters* (*Epistulae Morales*), the seven books of the *Quaestiones Naturales*, and with less certainty some other works. Once again he made an offer of his substance to the emperor: it was in A.D. 64 when he proposed to help in repairing the devastation caused by the burning of Rome.[6] He was not however destined to escape the despot. In 65, on an allegation of complicity in Piso's conspiracy – and there were some who said that the next emperor was intended to be the philosopher[7] – the old man was ordered to put himself to death. What Tacitus records of the last hours of Seneca, his dignified calm, his reliance upon philosophy, his farewell advice to friends, his devoted wife's desire to die with him, the too slow ebbing of life from the chill attenuated frame, is an account few can read unmoved.[8]

The character of Seneca presents anomalies comparable to those which are notorious in Lord Bacon's case. If Seneca does not merit to the full the absolute superlatives which Pope applied to Bacon, 'the

[1] On Burrus's death two *praefecti* were appointed for the praetorian guard, Ofonius Tigellinus and Faenius Rufus; the former soon gained an evil ascendancy.
[2] Tac. *Ann.* XIV. lii: 'exueret magistrum.'   [3] *Ibid.* XIV. liii–liv.
[4] Seneca had been attacked by Suillius in A.D. 58, *Ann.* XIII. xlii; for attacks in 62 see *ibid.* XIV. lii and lxv.
[5] *Ibid.* XIV. lv–lvi.
[6] *Ibid.* XV. xlv; Dio LXII. xxv. 3.   [7] Tac. *Ann.* XV. lxv.
[8] *Ibid.* XV. lx–lxiv. The wife referred to was Pompeia Paulina, Seneca's second wife.

wisest, brightest, meanest of mankind,' still the noble grandeur of his theoretical morality was deplorably sullied by lapses in actual life. Many of the charges date from his own time; and never was the calumny of enemies more rife, more gross, more readily believed than in the days when creatures like Suillius threw their slanderous mud. Among the historians, Dio is too biased to be trusted in his enumeration of the immoralities and inconsistencies laid to Seneca's account. The story of improper relations with Julia so obviously served Messallina's machinations that it cannot be accepted as incontrovertible fact, while the suggestion of an amour with Agrippina is even more incredible. That Seneca was privy to the deaths of Claudius, of Britannicus and of Agrippina was whispered and repeated, but the rumours can be neither proved nor disproved. His weak condonation of such deeds very naturally subjects him to suspicion. That he advocated the contempt of wealth and yet accumulated it is not to be gainsaid; even so, and granted that he lent money on interest, we are not bound to believe Dio's statement[1] that Seneca caused an insurrection in Britain by suddenly calling in the huge sum of forty million sesterces. If he was a thrifty financier all his life, he at least thereby escapes the accusation of a vicious abuse of his money in an age of luxury.

While, however, some of the blackest charges may be parried as not proven, one count in the indictment is beyond denial, even if it be capable of extenuation. Outside the study, he lacked true moral bravery. Nothing could transcend the elevation of his ethical theory; but this emphatic assertor of moral principles tamely saw them trampled upon at court. Circumstances overbore his protests, perhaps even his qualms: his wisdom failed in courage and his prudence degenerated into pusillanimity. A voluptuous court, it must be allowed, had no atmosphere of bracing discipline in which an austere philosopher could practise virtue: its extravagant opulence and titanic depravity were better calculated to stifle the moral sense with a rankly perfumed sultriness. The danger was twofold: at one time, the aesthetic taste and social charm of Nero might lull the conscience to rest; at another, his tigerish nature might unnerve any counsellor. Let it be admitted that Seneca was incapable of maintaining an impolitic opposition, and that he was, in Carlyle's words, 'so wistfully desirous to stand well with Truth and yet not ill with Nero' that he remains 'our perhaps niceliest proportioned half-and-half, the plausiblest plausible on record.' Such scathing words may be glibly repeated by critics who are safe from Nero. But is no allowance to be made, if Seneca failed to transfer the dogmatism of the schools to an emperor's acts? The philosopher's heart at least was on the side of goodness. Nero's court, life, policy must have often caused inexpressible pain to a believer in the Fatherhood and Providence of God, the brotherhood of man, the divine spark within all, the sovereign excellence of

[1] Dio lxii. 2.

virtue, the vanity of worldly goods, the sin of luxury; and it must have
been hard to adapt to Neronian orgies Seneca's own ascetic preferences
and practices. But a personality endowed with philosophic will, like
Seneca's, aimed sincerely at a higher life for himself and a better world
for others: it could not choose but exert some influence. When one complains of Seneca's inconsistencies, is one prepared to say that he would
have served Rome better by avoiding court? To say this is to forget the
good he did. To his credit stand Nero's promising *quinquennium*, a
policy of toleration in religion, and an endeavour to lessen cruelty in
gladiatorial shows: besides, he preached clemency in life, as the author
of the *Octauia* makes him do in the play. Nero's deterioration after
Seneca's retirement is in itself a testimony to his previous authority.

Perhaps it is not merely fanciful to trace a dynamic evolution in
Seneca's character determined by his continuous struggle against
hindrances and failures. If a worldling like Petronius came in time to
feel out of touch with the vanity of court life, what of Seneca, who
realised its vanity from the outset? In spite of much to disillusionise and
to disgust, he persevered at court until his prospects of influencing
Nero faded into nothingness, and his offered renunciation of riches had
been hypocritically declined. His very faults made him in a sense a
better man, and so acquired a spiritual value; for a recognition of his
own backsliding and cowardice showed the force of temptation and
taught indulgence towards human frailty. This is why Seneca is less
bigoted, less overbearing than most of his fellow-Stoics. His habit of
self-examination must have often revealed his faults to him, so that one
outcome was a tolerance which might well be imitated in judging him.
'We have all done wrong,' he says in the *De Clementia*[1] – *peccauimus
omnes*. It is, then, more charitable, as well as more profitable, to forget
his imperfections and omissions in favour of positive qualities like his
humility[2] and humanity – to forget his timidities in favour of his bravery
at the end. In one of his later years he wrote to Lucilius: 'Before old
age my aim was a good life; in old age my aim is a good death.'[3] And in
another letter there is an utterance of dignified courage on which the
hour of trial set the final seal of validity:

> Without dread, then, I am composing myself for that day on which,
> laying aside shifts and subtleties, I shall have to judge respecting my-
> self whether I merely speak or really feel as brave men should,
> whether all my insolent words hurled against fortune were mere
> pretence and mumming. Discount man's opinion: it is uncertain and
> partial. Discount the philosophical pursuits of a lifetime: it is death
> that is to pass judgement on you. 'Tis true: discussions, literary con-
> versations, words collected from the precepts of sages, and learned

[1] I. vi.
[2] *De Vita Beata* xvii. 3: 'Non sum sapiens'; 4: 'ego in alto uitiorum omnium
sum'; xviii. 1: 'cum uitiis conuicium facio, in primis meis facio'; *Ep.* lvii. 3:
'multum ab homine tolerabili, nedum a perfecto absum.'   [3] *Ep.* lxi. 2.

discourse do not exhibit the true strength of the mind. The greatest cowards can talk big. What you have achieved will then be made plain when you come to die. I accept the terms: I do not shrink from the decision.[1]

Besides his tragedies, short poems and the satire on Claudius, which are to be considered in another chapter, the following prose works by Seneca are extant – twelve so-called *Dialogues*, two books *On Clemency*, seven *On Benefits*, seven books of *Natural Problems*, and 124 *Moral Epistles*. His works that are lost, or survive only in fragments, trenched on the provinces of geography, physics, natural history, biography and ethics. Among these were *De Situ Indiae, De Ritu et Sacris Aegyptiorum, De Motu Terrarum, De Forma Mundi, De Piscium Natura, De Vita Patris, De Superstitione, De Matrimonio, De Immatura Morte, Moralis Philosophiae libri*. Some of his *Orationes* and additional books of *Letters* also circulated. The twelve *Dialogi* collected in the Ambrosian MS. are given in the following order: *De Prouidentia, De Constantia Sapientis, De Ira libri III, Ad Marciam de Consolatione, De Vita Beata, De Otio, De Tranquillitate Animi, De Breuitate Vitae, Ad Polybium de Consolatione, Ad Heluiam Matrem de Consolatione*. Unfortunately, these are not in the sequence of composition: had they been so, fuller light would have been shed on the author's intellectual development. Much labour has been spent on the chronology of the works, and respecting some of them at any rate the conclusions reached by inquirers are vain and conflicting. Several avenues of approach have been explored along the lines of internal evidence drawn from statement, expression or rhythm. But contemporary allusions (apart from those sometimes merely imagined in the searcher's enthusiasm) are scarce in Seneca, as if to remind us that the treatises are concerned with themes which are independent of the years. Similarities of thought yield inconclusive criteria of contemporaneous composition in an author who, on some subjects, expressed himself in much the same manner from first to last throughout his career, but who conversely, on other subjects, contradicted himself within the range of the same treatise. Then, again, statistics, like Bourgery's, showing relative frequency of definite metrical sentence-endings form an unsubstantial foundation on which to base theories of earliness or lateness in composition. Pichon[2] in 1912 considered that, on the chronology of the works, Gercke in his *Seneca-Studien* of 1895 had to a great extent superseded Jonas's dissertation of 1870; and in 1924 it was suggested[3] that Albertini had made it almost unnecessary to consult

---

[1] *Ep.* xxvi. 5–6: 'non timide itaque conponor. . . .'

[2] *J. Sav.* 1912, p. 213: 'Les travaux récents sur la chronol. des œuvres de Sén.'

[3] See J. D. Duff's notice of E. Albertini's *La Composn. dans les ouvrages philos. de Sén., C.R.* xxxviii (1924) p. 89. Albertini states with admirable clearness the difficulties of the problem and indicates the variety of answers given. His conclusions are often in agreement with Gercke's.

Gercke. If one constructs a table to exhibit the dates assigned by different critics to the works, the variation of opinion is at first sight bewildering. For instance, the *Consolatio ad Marciam*, which Lipsius placed after the exile, was, according to others, written during it (41–49): and, according to Albertini, before it (40). All three books of the *De Ira* were, according to Jonas, published in 41, but, according to Lehmann and Rossbach, in 49 after the recall; or – to take what marks perhaps the maximum of divergence – the *De Prouidentia*, in which Waltz sees a similarity of tone linking it with the *De Constantia*, is referred by him to the first months of exile, 41–42, while Albertini, agreeing with Gercke that it belongs to Seneca's last years, gives 63. For dating the tragedies, opinions are equally at variance. The general proportion of uncertainty is so great that one is tempted to fall back upon Madvig's dictum of 1873, *librorum Senecae praeter paucos tempora incerta sunt*.[1] Yet, after all, there are points on which we can lay firm hold. Few of the extant prose works were written before Seneca's exile in 41, and most of the best-known ones belong to the sixteen years which he had to live after his recall, when he was well over fifty years of age. There is much to say for believing that the *Consolatio ad Marciam* is the oldest of the surviving treatises (A.D. 40), and that at least two books of the *De Ira* were composed in 41. We can be quite certain that the other two *Consolations*, namely *Ad Heluiam* and *Ad Polybium*, belong to the early part of the exile, the one to 41–42, the other to 43. No other work can be, without challenge, ascribed to this Corsican period, although some authorities think that to it belong the *De Breuitate Vitae* as well as the *De Constantia* and the *De Prouidentia*. As to the period after Seneca's recall in 49, there is no doubt that the *De Clementia* was written early in Nero's reign, probably in 55 (Albertini thinks 56). It is generally agreed that the *De Otio*, *Epistulae Morales*, and the *Quaestiones Naturales* follow the retirement of A.D. 62, the composition of the last two works speading over more than one year.

Realising, then, that a full and exact chronology is unattainable, we proceed to a brief survey of the works.[2] Of the twelve *Dialogi*[3] it may be convenient to consider the three *Consolations* first, then the three books *On Anger*, and finally the remaining half-dozen treatises. The *Consolations* are not spontaneous expressions of sympathy, but literary efforts following broadly a scheme. It was a Greek invention thus to cure one of the maladies of the soul – grief; and the philosophers of different schools[4] who composed such exercises were in time joined by the rhetoricians, so that two streams of influence converged in what was a kind

---

[1] *Aduersaria Critica*, Vol. II, Copenhagen 1873, p. 344.
[2] The logical sequence and arrangement of topics in the treatises (other than *N.Q.*) and letters are examined by Albertini, *op. cit.* pp. 51–146.
[3] Only one, the *De Tranq.*, has a form suggestive of 'dialogue' in the true sense.
[4] Favez, ed. of *Ad Helv.* p. xxxviii ff.

of popular philosophy, with general features of similarity. Among these
features were eclecticism in argument; insistence upon our inability
to control external circumstances in contrast with the possession of our
own reason and will; the employment of rhetorical *loci communes* and
historical examples, as in a declamation; and a typical structure. Usually
this structure consisted of an introduction, on the evil to be remedied;
the main body of the consolation, on the cause of the affliction and the
person afflicted; and a conclusion. It is evident that this species of moral
pharmacy, based on an established science of consolation, possessed its
time-honoured conventions alike in plan and thought. While, therefore,
in Seneca the colour borrowed from Stoics and others is pronounced, it
is fruitless to endeavour to trace his sources in detail. What gave a *Consolation* its distinctive value was very much what gives value to any work
of art – the genius of its author and his power, within the limitations of an
old form, to achieve a fresh result. The special circumstances deplored,
the personality of the individual consoled, sometimes even digressions
indulged in, and the signal mastery of style displayed, might all open
up paths to an original effect.

The *Ad Marciam* is addressed to the brave daughter of Cremutius
Cordus, who published some of the writings of her dead father, one of
Sejanus's victims. Its design is to console her in her continued mourning for her son, whom she had lost three years earlier. Between its
exordium and its peroration it contains a fairly systematic reasoning
based on examples of other mothers in grief and on precepts for the
control of grief.

Seneca's hand, however, is surer in the *Ad Heluiam*, the most
regularly arranged and, at the same time, the cleverest and most
readable of the three *Consolations*. Once he has passed the exordium
and a recapitulation of the troubles which have already taught his
mother, Helvia, to be courageous, he addresses himself to the immediate
task of consoling her for the loss of her exiled son – himself. The situation, it will be observed, is unique: for the person whose loss is
mourned comforts the mourner. His ingenuity and prevailing Stoicism
are apparent in the defence of the two main positions. On the one hand,
the exile himself is not really unfortunate, because he has been trained
not to mind the deprivation of external blessings; banishment is but a
change of place which cannot affect virtue; enforced poverty does not
hurt the sage (an argument which gives a handle for invectives against
luxury); and the disgrace of exile lies only in man's opinion. On the
other hand, his mother is not really unfortunate; it cannot be that she
laments her son's support, since her affection has always been dis-
interested; her natural pangs over the separation give her an excellent
chance of displaying fortitude after the manner of other courageous
women whom Seneca proceeds to cite; her melancholy can be dispelled
through her favourite studies in philosophy, and through the affection of

G*

the dear ones who are left. Seneca's recognition here of ordinary human feelings outside the chill reason of the Stoics makes the one truly touching portion of his *Consolation*. For himself, he is happy to have leisure both for the study of the universe and for light literary work. In the *Ad Polybium*, written about the middle of A.D. 43, he is far less cheerful. Here the object is to comfort Polybius, a learned and influential freedman at court, on the death of a brother. Apart from the reasoned consolation, two features stand out – the author's acknowledgement of his misery in a remote corner (*angulo*) of the world, where his very Latin might suffer,[1] and his flatteries of the emperor in the hope of securing a remission of his sentence. The inconsistency with his previous fortitude and the undignified abasement in respect of Claudius have made all Seneca's admirers wish that he had never written this treatise. Diderot's denial of Seneca's authorship in the eighteenth century has, however, received only slight support in modern times. The manner is Seneca's, and there are not wanting memorable sayings; *e.g.*, on the obligations of high rank, 'great fortune is great servitude' (*magna seruitus est magna fortuna*, vi. 5); on a dilemma for mourners, 'to lament one in bliss is jealousy; to lament the non-existent, insanity' (*beatum deflere inuidia est, nullum dementia*, ix. 3); on life as a torture (*omnis uita supplicium est*, ix. 6), at the beginning of a fine passage on the troublous ocean of life whose one final haven is death; respecting the dead man, 'he has not left us but gone before' (*non reliquit ille nos sed antecessit*, ix. 9); and on the grumbler under a reversal of fortune, 'the man who gives to the close of a spell of pleasure the name of injustice has no gratitude' (*ingratus est qui iniuriam uocat finem uoluptatis*, x. 2).

The three books *De Ira* (which have certain gaps) were dedicated to Seneca's brother, Novatus. They investigate the characteristics, uselessness and curability of anger. The plan, although the author several times indicates his line of treatment and his transitions, is not satisfactory.[2] There are repetitions and contradictions,[3] and the relation of Book III to the preceding couple presents difficulties. The work must be later than Caligula's reign; for it contains frank criticism on his mad anger, I. xx. 8–9, and on his barbarities, III. xviii. 3–4 and xix. 1–2. In the last passage Seneca indulges in the bitter climax: 'Caligula tortured his victims by means of all the grimmest things in the world, with the cord, boot, rack, fire, and with that face of his (*uultu suo*).' Possibly the first two books were written, as Albertini suggests, in 41, just before the banishment; and Book III, which reads as if it came from Nero's preceptor, may have been added in 49 to the work interrupted eight

---

[1] *Ad Pol.* xiii. 3, xviii. 9.
[2] H. W. Müller, *De Sen. librorum de ira compositione*, Lpz. 1912; P. Rabbow, *Antike Schriften üb. Seelenheilung u. Seelenleitung*, Lpz. 1914.
[3] Albertini, *op. cit.* pp. 61–63.

years before. Seneca's handling of so unfortunately common a human
frailty could not fail to possess interest. He reminds us that ungovern-
able rage is the one passion that seizes a nation as a whole and so
leads to war.[1] The gift of apt illustration which marks the *Letters to
Lucilius* is already noticeable. Irascible men, he suggests, ought not to
meddle with the more exacting sorts of task, or, if they do, should stop
short of weariness: their tempers need to be softened with milder pursuits; 'for who does not know that clarions and trumpets are irritants,
just as some airs are lullabies to soothe the mind? Green is good for
wearied eyes (*confusis oculis prosunt uirentia*), and some colours are rest-
ful for weak sight, while the brilliancy of some is dazzling.'[2] There is the
gift too of graphic description and anecdote. A reader never forgets the
opening chapter, where, after citing the sage who called anger 'a brief
insanity,' the author gives his tellingly repulsive portrayal of the outward symptoms of mad wrath leading up to his words of dismissal,
'You could not tell whether the vice is more hateful or ugly.'[3] Nor does
one forget the idle Sybarite who was annoyed over seeing a labourer
hard at work, and who complained about the discomfort caused him by
the rumpling of some of the rose-leaves on which he lay.[4]

Years elapsed before Seneca indited to the same brother the now imperfect *De Vita Beata*. Novatus had become Gallio by adoption, as the
superscription *Ad Gallionem* shows: most likely his governorship of
Achaea was over. Two main questions are propounded – what makes
life happy? and what is the way to the happy life? Happiness for Seneca
consists not in what the many, but in what Stoic sages, think happy.
It is 'to live according to nature,'[5] in possession of a sound mind, true
courage, true patience, and a true estimate of things, so reaping 'an
immense joy, unshaken and equable, along with peace and harmony of
spirit, greatness of mind and gentleness; for all savagery is the outcome
of weakness.'[6] From another point of view, happiness is to practise
virtue. Against pleasure a polemic is directed, although Seneca takes up
a broadminded attitude towards the Epicurean system when properly
interpreted (ch. xii). The mode of attainment to happiness is not clearly
formulated, but the essay develops a spirited retort to those who yelp
(*conlatrant*) at philosophy on the ground that philosophers do not perform what they preach.[7] In particular a defence is needed for the ownership of wealth by the sage who affects to despise it. For himself Seneca

---

[1] *De Ira* III. ii.   [2] *Ibid*. III. ix. 1–2.   [3] *Ibid*. I. i. 3–4.
[4] *Ibid*. II. xxv. 2: 'questus est quod foliis rosae duplicatis incubuisset.' A
longer anecdote, admirably told, is that of Augustus twitting Asinius Pollio
with keeping in his house 'the wild beast' Timagenes, *ibid*. III. xxiii.
[5] *De Vita Beata* iii. 3: 'quod inter omnis Stoicos conuenit, rerum naturae
adsentior'; viii. 2: 'idem est ergo beate uiuere et secundum naturam.'
[6] *Ibid*. iii. 4.
[7] *Ibid*. xvii. 1: 'Quare ergo tu fortius loqueris quam uiuis?'; xviii. 1: 'aliter
(inquis) loqueris, aliter uiuis'; xx. 1: 'non praestant philosophi quae loquun-
tur.'

can reply that he does not claim the virtuous perfection of the sage, but a wise use of wealth justifies its retention. Even in high estate a virtuous life may be led. Since the impression is given that the author is answering criticisms levelled at him as a rich man, a plausible date is 58 or 59, after Suillius's attack upon Seneca.

The three treatises *De Constantia Sapientis*, *De Tranquillitate Animi*, and *De Otio* were addressed to a recipient, whose name, Serenus, fits the tenets conveyed. Annaeus Serenus died as prefect of Nero's *uigiles* during one of Seneca's later years: he had been accommodating enough to lend himself as a screen to prevent Agrippina from detecting Nero's passion for the freedwoman Acte. Waltz,[1] following Hense, has pointed out that the three treatises mark progressive stages of philosophical attitude in Seneca's pupil. In the *De Constantia* Serenus is Epicurean; in the *De Tranquillitate*, he is already Stoic in sympathy, though restless; in the *De Otio*, he is a convinced disciple. The fuller title for the *De Constantia* states its theme, 'that the wise man can receive neither wrong nor insult' (*nec iniuriam nec contumeliam accipere sapientem*). Not unnaturally, considering its subject, some have referred it to the early months of exile; but a reference to a recent discussion on Cato[2] implies Rome rather than Corsica as the place of writing. As the purpose is to prove a paradox – admittedly a hard saying for Serenus – Seneca begins by explaining that Stoic doctrine is too manly to aim at attractiveness. The answers to the supposed adversary's objections involve a good deal of hair-splitting; but there is a fine confidence in the emphasis laid upon the calm of the sage amidst the storm of war; 'for no siege-engines can be invented to shake the well-established mind' (*nulla machinamenta posse reperiri quae bene fundatum animum agitent*), and he sums up:

> See, then, Serenus, that the perfect man, full of virtues human and divine, can lose nothing: his goods are girt with solid and unscalable ramparts. You cannot compare with them the walls of Babylon which Alexander entered, nor the battlements of Carthage or Numantia. . . . Those which protect the sage are safe from fire and invasion: they yield no passage: they tower impregnable, equalling gods. You have no ground for saying, as you are wont to do, that this sage of ours is nowhere found. We invent no such unreal glory of human genius (vi. 8–vii. 1).

At the opening of the *De Tranquillitate*, Serenus confesses his uneasy

---

[1] Ed. *De Otio*, Paris 1909. According to C. Marchesi, *Seneca*, 1920, all three were written about 62. Dessau's view, *Herm.* liii, 1918, p. 192 ff. is that they were composed after Serenus's death, late in Seneca's career, as a memorial recreating three stages in a dead friend's advance towards and in Stoicism. Waltz stands not alone, as Dessau said, but has Münscher's support (*op. cit.* in bibl., p. 10), for dating the *De Const.* early in Claudius's reign, about 42. Most concur in putting all three somewhere in Nero's reign; *e.g.* 54–56, *De Const.*; 59, *De Tranq.*; 62, *De Otio.*

[2] *De Const.* i. 3: 'Nuper cum incidisset mentio M. Catonis . . .'

vacillation in the pursuit of peace of mind. What, for instance, should
be the attitude of man amidst luxury? What are the claims of leisured
retirement against the worries of public life? What satisfaction comes
from literary fame? The answer gives Seneca's views on the attainment
and maintenance of such an unruffled course that the mind shall take
pleasure in itself and in its surroundings. An extraordinary amount of
human wisdom is contained in this treatise, which seeks to provide a cure
for ennui and nerves. Among the interesting topics are failures in life;
the restless traveller in quest of change; the teacher who performs genuine social service (*in priuato publicum negotium agit*, iii. 3); the value of
friendship (*nihil aeque oblectauerit animum quam amicitia fidelis et
dulcis*, vii. 3); property as a source of anxiety (a theme illustrated with
characteristic fertility); foolishness in book-collecting (*multoque satius
est paucis te auctoribus tradere quam errare per multos*, ix. 4); the defiance
of fortune; the vanity of human wishes; the interest in the condition of
spirits beyond death; the proper estimate of human failings and sorrows;
the torment of an artificial life; and the advisability of a little nonsense
now and then to obviate the dullness produced by all work and no
play (*danda est animis remissio . . . nascitur ex assiduitate laborum ani-
morum hebetatio quaedam et languor*, xvii. 5).

The *De Otio* (mutilated at beginning and end) defends the moral
value of leisure from affairs, in reply to Serenus's statement of the
strict Stoic position. Seneca's plea is that at every age it is permissible
to renounce action for philosophical meditation; but most of all is it
permissible for those who have grown old in active service. Amid general
corruption, such withdrawal is countenanced on both Stoic and Epicurean principles. We all belong to two commonwealths, and in retreat the
sage may usefully serve the universal cosmopolis, the world at large,
through his speculative life in accord with nature. Especially may he
with profit devote himself to satisfying that inquiring disposition
implanted in man by Nature herself. Nature has produced us to be
spectators of her vast works: her beauty and complexity are not meant
to pass unobserved. So by the right path of research, man must 'discover something more ancient than the world itself' (*aliquid ipso mundo
inueniat antiquius*, v. 5): for 'our thought bursts through the battlements
of heaven, dissatisfied with knowing merely what is shown' (*cogitatio
nostra caeli munimenta perrumpit nec contenta est id quod ostenditur
scire*, v. 6). The scientific impulse here is that which animates the
Quaestiones Naturales, and the general tone befits the statesman who
has resigned all responsibility for public policy.

The theme of the *De Otio* leads us to the much earlier *De Breuitate
Vitae*, in which the final advice to Paulinus, controller of the grain-supply
for Rome and probably the father of Seneca's second wife,[1] is that he
would make the best use of life by retiring to cultivate philosophy. Such

[1] See P.W.: *s.vv.* Pompeius no. 99, Pompeia no. 130.

advice could hardly come with full effectiveness from an exile, languishing in involuntary retirement; and that Seneca wrote the dialogue after his recall is proved by a passage (xiii. 3) where he mentions a lecture, certainly in or near Rome, which he heard a few days before composing the dialogue. This passage dates the dialogue more precisely still; for the lecturer is recorded as stating that Sulla was the last Roman to extend the *pomerium* of the city. The *De Breuitate Vitae*, therefore, must have been composed before Claudius extended the *pomerium*, which he did sometime between January 25th 49 and January 24th 50. The date lies therefore between Seneca's return from exile early in 49 and January 24th 50, the latest possible day for the Claudian extension of the *pomerium* – probably in the spring of 49[1] before Seneca was designated praetor; for unless (as is possible) his praetorship was a sinecure, he could hardly advocate retirement for Paulinus while accepting a magistracy himself.

The treatise is full of good things. Nowhere in literature are there to be read pithier remarks on the value of time. The first century of our era displayed a peculiarly keen sense of the way in which days are wasted. Under Tiberius, Phaedrus, we have seen, made fun of those fussy triflers, the *ardaliones*; and late in the century Pliny chafes against the petty but innumerable inroads made on leisure, while Martial betrays the same nervous spirit. Here Seneca speaks for the Neronian period. Life is short: yes, but it is we who make it so: life is long enough, if well employed. The general blindness to the worth of time is amazing: men will resist encroachments on land or money, but will let people trespass freely on their time, which is in reality their life. They are spendthrifts with the one thing in which greed is honourable (*profusissimi in eo cuius unius honesta auaritia est*, iii. 1). We live, in fact, as if we were to live for ever. You hear men coolly postponing leisurely reflection till after fifty or sixty: should they not blush to reserve for the sovereign duty of reflection the mere remnants of a life no longer fit for business! Drusus[2] once declared that he was the only person who had never had holidays even when a boy: precocity like that must have an evil end. But the really great man will not let his hours be filched away from him; and his life will be long because devoted to self-improvement. Many a wrinkled grey-haired man has merely existed, not lived, a long time (*non ille diu uixit, sed diu fuit*, vii. 10). Yet for all men's extravagance with this most precious of things, confront them with the

[1] 49 is the date accepted by Jonas, *De Ordine Librorum Sen.*, Berlin 1870; by Gercke, *Seneca-Studien*, Lpz. 1895, p. 289 ff; by Albertini, *Composn.* etc., p. 21 ff; by P. Grimal, *R.E.L.* 1947, p. 164 ff. (a very clear statement), and by others. See S.H. § 461. H. Dessau, *Hermes* 1918, p. 188 ff. finds difficulties in this date and would prefer to put the dialogue in 62, *i.e.* nearer to Seneca's own retirement. He is followed by Marchesi, *Seneca*, p. 214, and by L. Herrmann, *Latomus*, 1937, p. 109 ff. Herrmann and Grimal reiterated their respective views, *R.E.L.* 1948, p. 222 ff. and 1949, p. 178 ff.
[2] Tribune, 91 B.C. Mysteriously murdered the same year.

peril of death, and how they plead for more time! For what purpose?
To learn how to live and how to die demands a lifetime; but the paramount concern is laid aside in favour of toilsome exertions for a future
on which no one can count. Thus the true life suffers from that procrastination which is the thief of our todays (*exspectatio, quae pendet ex
crastino perdit hodiernum*, ix. 1): so old age comes as a surprise, and
death as a terror, to those who have been busy (*occupati*) over the wrong
things, and have squandered time on luxury, affectation or vice. That
man has true leisure who has the sense of leisure: its secret lies with
philosophy, through whose study one may master centuries that are past
and commune with all the ages and all the sages. Those great thinkers –
not the arrogant snobs whom some court in Rome – constitute the true
society of the world; and yet, Seneca reminds us (like Ruskin long afterwards in *Sesame and Lilies*), none of those great thinkers will refuse
access to him. The communicable wisdom of the ages points the
right path towards immortality, and what philosophy has hallowed is
beyond the reach of injurious time.

The remaining dialogue is the *De Prouidentia*, given first in the
Milan MS. It is addressed, like the *Naturales Quaestiones* and the
Epistulae, to Seneca's friend Lucilius, a man with literary tastes,[1] who
had held procuratorial offices in various parts of the Roman world,
including Sicily, and in whom some have seen the author of the *Aetna*.
The subject of the *De Prouidentia* is summarised in the fuller title – why
any misfortunes befall good men, when a Providence exists (*quare
aliqua incommoda bonis uiris accidant, cum prouidentia sit*). From the
Stoic doctrine of a providential government of the universe, it follows
that suffering must serve a good purpose. Discipline is one of the ends
subserved: misfortune is a school for virtue, and a spectacle noble
enough for the gods to witness is that of good men struggling with
adversity – *non miror si aliquando impetum capiunt spectandi magnos
uiros conluctantis cum aliqua calamitate . . . ecce par deo dignum, uir fortis
cum fortuna mala compositus, utique si et prouocauit* (ii. 7–9). The last
clause 'especially if he has actually thrown out the challenge,' is an addition symptomatic of a rhetorical over-statement too common in this
essay. The imperfect way in which some points in the argument are
worked out has led certain critics to hold that a portion is lost at the end.[2]

Of the *De Clementia*, once in three books, we possess the first and a
portion of the second. The idea of writing on clemency was suggested
to Seneca through recollecting Nero's words, when he reluctantly
signed a death-warrant, 'Would that I had never learned to write!'[3]
If one is tempted to jeer at Seneca's compliments to Nero and his

---

[1] *N.Q.* IV. *praef.* 1 and 12. Seneca quotes a hexameter from a poem of his,
N.Q. III. 1; iambics, *Ep.* viii. 10; another hexameter, *Ep.* xxiv. 21.
[2] Schanz does not think so (S.H. § 454). On the other hand, Albertini, *op.
cit.* p. 102, says: 'Je suis de ceux qui croient que la fin du *De Prouid.* est muti-
lée.'   [3] *De Clem.* II. i: 'Vellem nescire litteras!'

expectations that a better era had dawned, one must in fairness remember the high hopes entertained and in some measure realised during the earlier years of the young prince's reign. Book I discusses the need for clemency in a ruler. The emperor, as war-lord, is urged to recognise his responsibilities. He should follow the model of the gods: things a subject might do, a monarch cannot, in the full light that beats upon a throne (*multa contra te lux est, omnium in istam conuersi oculi sunt*). Cruelty makes a tyrant; but the affection of subjects is a stronger defence for a prince than their fear. Book II degenerates into tedious attempts at the definition of *clementia* in contrast with what the Stoic condemns as weaknesses – mercy (*misericordia*) and pardon (*uenia*).

The seven books *De Beneficiis* addressed to Aebutius Liberalis were not issued together. An allusion towards the close of Book I[1] shows that Claudius was dead, and it is likely that the first four books appeared some years after 54; being followed by the remaining books,[2] perhaps by V and VI together, as Gercke thinks, before the retirement of 62, and by VII still later.[3] The praise of Demetrius in VII. viii–xii best suits Seneca's closing years. Based upon Hecaton, Panaetius and other Stoics, the treatment of *Benefits* is marked by insight into human nature and generosity of impulse rather than by strict method. It may be too much to say that the work is incapable of analysis,[4] but it is safe to say that an attempted analysis shows the absence of exact system.

There are repetitions and anticipations, apparently because the author, instead of punctiliously exhausting a particular aspect of his subject, preferred to record, as they came, in characteristically concise and striking language, his thoughts upon points which he left himself free to illuminate again as occasion might offer. He is not unaware of such repetitions.[5] He is aware, too, of his digressions, on which he imposes a closure in such terms as, 'Let us now return to the theme set before us,' or 'My enthusiasm is carrying me away rather too far, for the subject is a tempting one.'[6] Even his initial definition of a benefit is unduly

---

[1] *De Ben.* I. xv. 6.   [2] *Ibid.* V. i. 1.

[3] *Seneca-Studien*, p. 308 ff., supported and developed by F. Préchac (*Comptes rendus de l'Acad. des Inscrns.* 1914, p. 111 ff.). Bourgery (*R. Ph.* 1910, p. 167 ff.) would place Bks. VI and VII, as exhibiting an increase of regular *clausulae*, some time after the other books. Pichon (*J. Sav.* 1912, p. 212 ff.) asks why, if that metrical criterion holds for VI and VII, one should not apply it to Bk. V. Bk. V is credited with only 41 per cent. of regular clausulae, and so by Bourgery's test should be earlier than I and II which have about 50 per cent. But Bourgery takes Bk. V as a collection of notes previously made or a hastily composed addendum. However Bourgery himself seems later to have abandoned his metrical arguments; cf. *Sén. Prosateur*, 1922, p. 60 n. 1, where he concludes, 'Il est même douteux qu'un intervalle appréciable sépare, dans la composition du *De Beneficiis*, le livre vii des six autres.'

[4] Paul Thomas, *Morceaux choisis de Sénèque*, ed. 8, 1918, p. 145, says: 'il serait aussi difficile que peu utile d'en donner une analyse.'

[5] E.g. *De Ben.* I. vii. 2: 'ut dixi.'

[6] *Ibid.* I. xiv. 1: 'ad propositum nunc reuertamur'; I. x. 1: 'sed longius nos impetus euehit prouocante materia.'

deferred (I. vi. 1) until after five somewhat rambling chapters. Such traits, although they may be adjudged faults in logic, actually contribute to the easiness and readability of his work.[1] Besides, some of his best thoughts are repeated in such varied form that they cannot fail to arrest the attention and impress themselves on the memory. Despite, then, a dearth of method, no man can rise from the most casual reading of a tractate by Seneca without having grasped its spirit. The redoubled beats, so keen and insistent in their staccato, ensure that effect.

The commonness of ingratitude is in Book I put down largely to the wrong mode of conferring benefits. The essence of a benefit lies in the attitude of the giver; and two points need consideration, the kind of benefits to be conferred and the mode of giving. The latter point is dealt with in Book II which turns to the mode of receiving, a topic involving that of the ungrateful disposition. Book III continues the subject of ingratitude, stating and answering problems: 'Can ingratitude be prosecuted?' No. 'Can a slave benefit a master?' Yes. 'Can children confer on a parent more benefits than they have received?' Yes. Book IV, dealing with aspects of benefits and gratitude, puts the query, 'Should one benefit the ungrateful?' The later books, from their investigation of *quaestiones*, are casuistic in character, but by no means uninteresting. Book V asks 'Is it a shame to be surpassed in benefits?' then takes up the Stoic paradoxes 'No one can be ungrateful,' 'All are ungrateful'; and proceeds to find fresh puzzles, 'Must a son be grateful for benefits done to his father?' 'Is that a benefit which was not intended?' Among the problems in Book VI are 'Do we owe gratitude to one who has benefited us against his will?', or 'without knowing it?', or 'incidentally in furthering his own interests?', and in the last book 'Can one benefit the sage who possesses all?' and 'What is the position where the giver has forgotten the benefit conferred?' Although many of the problems end in unfruitful refinements, there is much to treasure in Seneca's permanently valuable and shrewd criticism of human conduct. He is genuinely anxious to correct by his counsels one of the most detrimental and heartbreaking mistakes made in life; for he well realises how much pain is caused by ignorance in conferring or in receiving a benefit. A few citations from Book I will illustrate some aspects of his attitude:

'I should find it hard to say whether it is meaner for the recipient to repudiate a benefit, or for the giver to press for its repayment, inasmuch as a benefit is a sort of loan whose return absolutely depends on the spontaneous action of the debtor.' (I. i. 3).

'We find many people ungrateful; yet we make more people so, because at one time we are insistent and harsh in our claims for return, at another time we are fickle enough to regret our generosity.

[1] *Cf. Argumentum* to Bk. I in the ed. (Paris 1827) of M. N. Bouillet in Lemaire's *Bibliotheca Cl. Lat.* (no. 73): 'libri boni sunt sed mehercule in ordine et tractatu confusi, quem uix est uel adnitentem expedire.'

... By such conduct we spoil the whole favour. ... A benefit is felt to be a debt in the same spirit as that in which it is bestowed.' (I. i. 4 and 8.)

'If a man does not give because he does not receive, he must have given in order to receive, and that justifies ingratitude. How many there are who are unworthy of the light of day, and nevertheless the sun rises.' (I. i. 10–11.)

'Persevere in your generosity. ... Assist one with your means, another with credit, another with your favour, or your advice, or a word in season. ... Is he ungrateful for one benefit? After receiving a second, perhaps he will not be so. Has he forgotten two? Perhaps the third kindness will bring back the recollection of those that slipped his mind.' (I. ii. 4 and 5.)

'The reality of a benefit lies not in gold, nor silver, but in the goodwill of the giver.' (I. v. 2.)

'What is a benefit? It is the doing of a kindness which gives pleasure and in the giving gets pleasure. ... The spirit animating the act is what exalts trivial things, throws lustre on ordinary things, while it can discredit great and highly valued ones.' (I. vi. 1 and 2.)

The *Naturales Quaestiones* is in Seneca's eyes an excursion into the highest speculation; for such physical inquiries concern God's universe, whereas moral philosophy concerns man. The subject had occupied Seneca in Corsica,[1] and for many years he must have collected material to be combined (not over methodically) in these seven books. At the opening of Book II he gives his threefold division of the knowledge of nature into astronomy, meteorology, and geography, according as the investigation is directed to phenomena in the heavens (*caelestia*), or between the heavens and earth (*sublimia*), or upon the earth (*terrestria*). He does not, however, treat these subjects equally or in order, as a glance at the contents of the different books will prove. Indeed, the order of these books is much disputed.[2] It is possible that Seneca never finally settled their succession; for the work may have been ultimately issued by Lucilius, to whom it was dedicated. The time of composition can be determined within limits. Book III shows that it was the work of the author's old age after his retirement in 62, and the opening of Book VI records the earthquake at Pompeii in February of 63.

The main themes are distributed among the books thus: I, Fire (meteors, rainbow, mock sun, etc.); II, Air (Thunder and Lightning); III, Water in various forms; IV, The rise of the Nile and (after a sudden break) snow, hail, and rain; V, Wind and atmospheric movement; VI, Earthquakes; VII, Comets.

The historical importance of the work is considerable. Here Seneca is in the succession to the Augustan Sextii, who had some reputation

[1] *Ad Helv.* xx.
[2] A table of varying rearrangements is given in S.H. § 466. The last book (VII) is put first by Gundermann, and the first last by Schultess and Gercke. Diels, Müller and Gercke begin with III, which Bourgery would put at the end according to his metrical tests.

for scientific inquiry. Their influence and that of the 'pneumatic' physicians, who took a Stoic view of the mechanism of physiology, contributed to keep physical speculation alive in the first century. Science, however, was still too much a literary manipulation of material bequeathed by predecessors to facilitate real advance. This in the main applies to the compiler of the *Naturales Quaestiones*. Although he undoubtedly developed germs of independence (*e.g.*, in ridiculing the divination with which he could not irrevocably break), he is not possessed by his subject, as the Epicurean poet Lucretius was. For Western Europe, in default of direct access to Aristotle, the work remained during the Middle Ages the prevalent authority on cosmology; but scientific, according to modern standards, it certainly is not. The absence of the exact equipment nowadays available rendered nice experiment impossible, and with the best will in the world the observer was exposed to all the risks attendant on the inaccuracy of sense-perception. To the utmost of his ability, nevertheless, Seneca sought to secure trustworthy data; *e.g.* with respect to a comet (VII. ii); he was a searcher after causes, and stated fairly the points of conflicting theories; eclectic by preference, he even rejected the explanations of his own Stoic school when he deemed them incorrect; and he realised that generations of workers might be needed to reach truth in complex subjects (VII. xxv). On the other hand, he never learned to divorce ethics from physics, and consequently some of the most interesting parts of the *Naturales Quaestiones* are his unscientific digressions. Thus, lightning suggests other presages and leads to discussions on fate and religion in Book II. Closing the same book, he recognises that some would rather be delivered from the fear of lightning than know its origin, and, conceding that a moral should attach to every study, he proceeds to reason against the dread of death. Again, the chafing of the sea, he believes, indicates that Nature will ultimately inundate the world to make a new world. Lucilius is admonished at the beginning of Book IV that he must not be arrogant, although governor of Sicily; for the island is 'a province, not an empire'; and the topic of snow occasions one of his tirades against the despicable luxury of effeminate Romans who would bathe in it or use ice to cool their thirst. In such passages the physicist has reverted to the moral philosopher.

Much labour has been spent in arguing that the 124 *Epistles to Lucilius* were not real letters. In the last resort, the question is hardly a vital one; for supposing the form were proved to be fictitious, Seneca must at least have meant the collection to be taken for a budget of correspondence despatched by him to his friend, because he introduces references to letters received.[1] Several scholars[2] have followed Lipsius

[1] *E.g. Ep. Mor.* xlviii. 1, lxxi. 1, lxxv. 1.
[2] *E.g.* Hilgenfeld, Gercke, Schanz, Bourgery (refs. in S.H. § 467). Albertini thinks the letters real, and discusses the problem, *op. cit.* pp. 132–146. I accept his views.

in his denial of the reality of the correspondence; but it is more satisfactory to accept the epistles as representing a real correspondence subjected to the author's editorial suppression of the regular opening or
closing phrases, of very intimate passages, and of certain personal names.
They were written in A.D. 63 and 64, and sent, as written, to Lucilius.
At different points in the collection a subject is often reopened, and there
are inconsistencies in thought, so that no logical order is to be looked
for, although it is possible to trace certain chronological groups[1]
according to Seneca's change of reading or residence. Thus, the model
of Epicurus's letters to Idomeneus especially pervades the first twenty-
nine letters, most of which close with an Epicurean maxim sent to
Lucilius under some such jocular labels as 'a little gift' (*munusculum*),
'a windfall' (*lucellum*) or 'toll' (*portorium*). Similarly, we note the effect
of his concurrent study of Posidonius in many letters after No. 78.
About forty letters (Nos. 49–87) seem to have been composed in Campania, and the subsequent letters in Rome or its neighbourhood. Some
are brief notes: others treatises many pages long. Seneca remarks on the
difference between Cicero's epistolary notes[2] about current politics and
his own letters discussing moral and intellectual problems. Promising
Lucilius a literary immortality[3] through the publication of the correspondence, he keeps his eye fixed on posterity as firmly as ever the younger
Pliny or Madame de Sévigné did.

The variety of interest is great, when it is remembered that the prevailing object is the consideration of philosophical points, and that,
therefore, many personal details were intentionally excluded. Nothing
stands out more, throughout a perusal, than Seneca's faith in the eternal
and inestimable value of philosophy, for which everything should be
sacrificed. Philosophy is the guide of life (xvi) and its joy (xxiii): more
vital than any physical exercise, it promotes the health of the mind (xv),
guarantees a pleasant old age (xii), and teaches how to face death (a recurrent topic): it offers the glory of literary immortality (xxi), and deserves to be made a man's life-work (lxxii). Hunger and povery must be
endured cheerfully in the quest after wisdom (xvii), and social pleasures
rigidly renounced to win the needful seclusion (*recede in te ipse quantum
potes*, vii. 8). Such seclusion involves hard mental toil, not for oneself
but for posterity (viii), to increase the store of human wisdom. Philosophy must be studied earnestly in Stoic writings as a whole, not in
merely convenient anthologies (*flosculi*, xxxiii. 1): for Stoics decline to
practise window-dressing (*ocliferia*: 'We don't trick a purchaser, so that,
when he has entered the shop, he'll find nothing beyond what was hung
up in front,' xxxiii. 3). The time-honoured traditions of philosophy

---

[1] Various attempts have been made: *e.g.* Bourgery, *R.Ph.* xxxv (1911) pp.
40–55; Albertini, *op. cit.* p. 44 ff.
[2] *Ep. Mor.* cxviii. 1–2.
[3] *Ibid.* xxi. 5.

stamp it as a gradual achievement of civilisation (xc). It is no self-regarding morality, but has duties to discharge – the reclaiming of backsliders (xxv) and help for the wretched (xlviii). Genuine philosophy is in touch with human kind (v), despite the risk of debasement from mixing with the mob (vii): truly democratic, it is no respecter of pedigrees (*stemma non inspicit*, xliv. 1), and it is an occupation of the heart, not a pose marked by outward peculiarities (v).

His counsels are couched in terms of winning modesty. He is not perfect, he confesses (xxvii); if he ventures to prescribe remedies, he is in the same infirmary (*ualitudinario*, xxvii. 1) talking with other moral invalids about common ailments of the soul and their cure. This note of sympathy with frailty in utter forgetfulness of dogmatic Stoicism is one of the most likeable traits in Seneca: it increases his hold over us and his power of doing us good. So he preached self-control (xviii) more effectively than many a bigoted champion of total abstinence; recommended the right behaviour for travel (*i.e.* learn to be at home everywhere as a citizen of the world, xxviii. 4); and pleaded the duty of kindness to slaves ('"They are slaves" you say – nay, our humble friends: "slaves!" you repeat – nay, our fellow-slaves, if you remember that Fortune has the same rights over masters and slaves alike,' xlvii. 1). He was too sensible to be misled by Stoic paradoxes about the self-sufficing sage who had no need of a friend (ix and cix): there had to be a *uia media* between contamination amidst the madding crowd (vii) and deterioration in solitude: alone with oneself, he reminds us, one might be in bad company (x). Thus he writes:

> When friendship is made, one must trust; before it is made, one must judge. There is a topsy-turvy confusion in your folk who, in disobedience to the rule of Theophrastus, judge one after making a friend of him instead of making him their friend after judging him. Ponder long whether a given person is to be admitted to your friendship: when you have decided that he is to be so, welcome him with all your heart. Converse with him as boldly as with yourself (iii. 2).

The human appeal of the letters is intensified by the light thrown on contemporary life. They place before us the loathsome butchery at gladiatorial shows (vii), the seductions of a seaside resort (li), the arrival of mailboats from Alexandria (lxxvii), the pleasure of travelling light in contrast to the overpowering magnificence of some travellers (lxxxvii). No less enlivening are personal details which bring the author nearer to us – even his asthma (liv) and other ailments (lxxviii), depressing attacks of fever, and his decision to be careful out of consideration for his wife's solicitous feelings (civ), sea-sickness on a trip in the Bay of Naples (liii), an outing in a litter (lv), trying experiences during a day of mud and dust in a tunnel near Naples (lvii), lodgings over a noisy public bath (lvi), feelings on the death of a friend (lxxviii and lxiii. 1 and 4, 'at a friend's loss the eyes should be neither dry nor streaming . . . let us see to it that the recollection of our lost ones is a pleasant one'), attendance at philosophy lectures when old (lxxvi), thoughts suggested by a wrestling-school or Scipio's villa (lxxxvi). Here the work on Italian fields is put before us ('It's late June . . . this very day I noticed peasants harvesting beans and sowing millet,' lxxxvi. 16); and another letter gives Seneca's own experiences in vine-grafting (cxii). Elsewhere we find reminiscences of his teachers with entertaining anecdotes (cviii), or a hint to Lucilius that he must climb Aetna (lxxix). His attitude to the government of the day appears in exhortations to practise circumspection and avoid offence (xiv). It is noteworthy that he says nothing to indicate whether he looked back with satisfaction upon his public life. No doubt, his own tastes preferred the serene detachment of an onlooker portrayed in the following passage :

> You dun me for more frequent letters: let's compare accounts – you'll not be solvent! The bargain, of course, was that *you* were to start – *you* were to write, I was to write back. But I'm not going to make difficulties: I know you're safe for credit, and so I'll pay in advance, and not do as that master of style, Cicero, tells Atticus to do – write anything that rises to his lips, even if he has got no news. I can never be at a loss for matter, though I skip all the details that fill Cicero's letters – what candidate is in difficulties; who is fighting with other people's backing, who with his own; who is standing for the consulship in reliance on Caesar or on Pompey or on a money-chest; what a skinflint Caecilius is, out of whom his own relations can't shift a penny at less than twelve per cent. No, it's better to handle one's own troubles than other folk's, better to examine oneself, and see for how many things one is a candidate. . . . This, my dear Lucilius, is the noble line – the line that means tranquillity and freedom – to compete for nothing, and entirely to give the elections of fortune the go-by. How great do you take the pleasure to be when the assembly of the tribes has been summoned, when the candidates are on tenterhooks within their respective quarters, when one is offering money, another acting through an agent, another smearing with kisses the hands of folk to whom he'll refuse his handshake after election, when all are waiting in dumb amazement for the crier's voice – how great the pleasure to stand at one's ease, a spectator of that Vanity Fair (*nundinas*) without either buying or selling anything?[1]

The discussions frequently bear, like St. Paul's epistles, the mark of the Stoic diatribe. Objections are supposed to be raised (*inquis*) by Lucilius or by an imaginary opponent to be scrutinised and refuted. And there is something Bionean in sharp sarcasms recalling those of the *Apocolocyntosis*. The philosopher makes great game of the futile queries raised by pedantic teachers (lxxxviii. 7–8 and 37); of brainless pleasure-seekers in Rome, the human 'antipodes' who turn night into day (cxxii);

---

[1] *Ep. Mor.* cxviii. 1–3.

of an outrageously vulgar parvenu freedman who purchased highly educated slaves to enable him to parade learning by proxy (xxvii); of a
philosophical lecturer's rapid delivery, which was too like the glibness of
a cheap-jack (xl. 3, *istam uim dicendi rapidam atque abundantem aptiorem
esse circulanti quam agenti rem magnam ac seriam docentique*); or of
luxurious baths hot enough to parboil a condemned criminal (lxxxvi. 10).

The remarks on style in various letters are instructive, as coming
from one whose own style has provoked severe criticism in ancient and
modern times. Letter 84 discusses the assimilation of reading, and
states a theory of style in the making: bee-like we should gather widely,
but the combined products must finally be made our own. In Letter 100,
writing for the soul is contrasted with writing for the ear, and Seneca distinguishes the prose of Fabianus from the artificially inverted prose of
the day. Letter 114 examines decadence in style, which is explicable on
the hypothesis that it is a mirror of morals. Seneca's citations here illustrate the loose and undisciplined compositions which, he argues, reflected the character of Maecenas. With the spread of luxury the affected
manner in literature keeps pace, and eccentricity of expression captures
the cultivated public as well as the common herd. There is no absolute
standard: fashion sways style. While some ape the diction of earlier
generations, others cannot abide the old-fashioned; and Seneca points
the distinctions between the long rhythmic sentences of Cicero and the
terse abruptness of Sallust. In the next letter, 115, he warns Lucilius
not to be over-anxious to attain to a fine style: matter is more than
manner – the question should be 'what?' not 'how?' Then, anticipating the famous *Le style est l'homme même*, he declares that style is the
yield of a man's mind (*oratio cultus animi est*).

This raises the question of Seneca's own prose. The stress laid on
the 'what,' rather than the 'how,' goes some way, though not all the way,
towards explaining why he wrote, as many would have it, so badly.
Quintilian, the champion of a phase of restored Ciceronianism in the
next generation, may be taken to speak for the hostile critics. In a well-
known passage[1] he examines Seneca's merits and demerits. In Quintilian's eyes Seneca's style was spoilt by all sorts of blemishes, and he
felt it his duty to point his students to stricter standards of taste. Tacitus
afterwards recorded Seneca's power of appealing to his contemporaries.[2]
This very attractiveness Quintilian recognised, but feared: 'he charmed
because of his faults only' (*placebat propter sola uitia*). Conceding
Seneca's ready and rich intellect, his learning and versatility, brilliant
sententiae and moral value, he at the same time indicates his weaknesses –
liability to be misled by those who 'devilled' for him in scientific inquiries (*aliquando ab his quibus inquirenda quaedam mandabat deceptus est*);

---

[1] *Inst. Or.* X. i. 125–131.
[2] Tac. *Ann.* XIII. iii: 'ingenium amoenum et temporis eius auribus accom-
modatum.'

want of strict accuracy in philosophy; and a style all the more pernicious because full of fascinating faults (*eo perniciosissima, quod abundant dulcibus uitiis*). Yet Quintilian considers that, in spite of wilful manner- isms, Seneca is safe reading for those of maturely trained judgement, for he allows there is much in him to approve and to admire. Next century, when an archaising movement had set in, Fronto[1] condemns his style more sweepingly for its 'fever-producing plums' (*febriculosis prunulis*), while Gellius[2] records some readers' dislike for his glib vulgarity as well as other alleged defects, and censures Seneca for having, in the now lost twenty-second book of the *Epistles*, dared to pass unfavourable criticisms on Ennius, Cicero and Virgil.

It is clear that a lover of Cicero's polished amplitude will not feel drawn to the Senecan sentence which, by comparison, must appear offhand, and, despite frequent use of pointed balance, to a large extent formless. In order that a sententious thought might go home impressively and might be easily recalled and quoted, a premium was set upon its smart and brief formulation. The literary fashion was everything by fits and starts and nothing long; for the copious rounded periods of the older oratory had for the time lost their power of attraction. So eloquence no longer flowed in a full broad stream, but glittered iridescent like intermittent jets shot into sunlight from a cleverly contrived fountain. Seneca himself writes[3] that he would like his *Letters to Lucilius* to be as natural in tone as if he were chatting with his friend seated or walking at his side; and so colloquial words and phrases do not surprise us. Indeed they fit the easygoing argument, as homeliness fits some sermons. But Seneca adheres to this simple model no more rigidly than Words- worth to his theory of 'a selection of the language really spoken by men.' Seneca is far from avoiding the artificial; and his style, like his character, has complexities and inconsistencies. It is intelligible, then, that critics should distinguish good and bad qualities in his composition, but perhaps it is more profitable to ask whether, with his style, he ful- filled his main object in writing. He had to face the fresh problem of composing readable tracts on ethical questions mainly Stoic: so, as an experimenter and innovator, he was sure to depart from traditional lines. Yet sometimes it looks as if he were censured for not being another Cicero. In literature, however, there are many mansions. The opening for Seneca was to create the Latin philosophical essay; and here he is, on the whole, a success.

To this success his power of awakening interest greatly contributed; for he is not a dull writer. He secures varied effects by neglecting logical method, so that he becomes pleasantly discursive; he diversifies his

[1] *De Orat.* i. § 2 (Naber 155).
[2] *N.A.* XII. ii. The passage is full of quotations from the lost book xxii.
[3] *Ep.* lxxv. 1: 'qualis sermo meus esset si una sederemus aut ambularemus, inlaboratus et facilis, tales esse epistulas meas uolo quae nihil habent accersitum nec fictum.'

science with rhetorical descriptions; he illuminates a point with wonderful fertility in examples; and he holds the attention by his lively manner in arguing a question. Homeliness of expression alternates with elevation of thought. It is a personal and unmistakable style, crowded with those disconnected, jerky, antithetic and epigrammatic sentences which made Macaulay say: 'to read him straightforward is like dining on nothing but anchovy sauce.' After all, those same forcible and quotable sentences have the merit of leaving Seneca's position clear. Now the virtue of an essay, in the true and original sense, lies largely in this, that, while it may not exhaust a subject, it must, if a good essay, convey a lucid impression. The qualities here noted are parallel to those in the writings of Montaigne and Bacon, and constitute Seneca one of the most admirable essayists in the world.

Everywhere we meet with such terse sayings as these:[1] 'A life is not incomplete, if it is honourable'; 'it is not an important matter to live – it is important to die honourably, wisely, courageously'; 'as a play, so is life – it matters not how long but how good the acting is'; 'success is a restless thing . . . it intoxicates in more ways than one' (*res est inquieta felicitas . . . mouet cerebrum non uno genere*); 'a humiliating and grotesque sight is an old man at his A B C' (*turpis et ridicula res est elementarius senex*); 'old age is an ailment for which there's no cure' (*senectus insanabilis morbus est*). There are paradoxes like 'some people have stopped living before they could start' (*quidam ante uiuere desierunt quam inciperent*); or balanced clauses, 'in a multitude of books is distraction – so, as you can't read all you've got, its enough to have as much as you can read'; or pieces of workaday wisdom, 'what's the good of meeting one's trouble halfway? You'll have the trouble fast enough when it comes' (*quid iuuat dolori suo occurrere? satis cito dolebis cum uenerit*), or 'if you don't want a man to lose his head in a crisis, you should give him practice beforehand.'[2]

Superabundant terseness of this sort leaves the reader dazzled and fatigued. Seneca's is a prose which produces an effect analogous to that of his nephew Lucan's hectic verse.

His language,[3] as we might expect, is an amalgam of the literary and the vulgar. On the one hand, there is the contribution of rhetoric and learning – poetic words, archaisms, philosophical terms, Hellenisms; on the other hand, the contribution of spoken Latin. A good deal of his vocabulary he shares, not with the more literary authors, but with Varro, Columella and the elder Pliny. From trade come such words as *botularius* ('sausage-maker') and *libitinarius* ('undertaker'); and from agriculture, such as *folliculus* ('pod') and *retorridus* ('parched up').

[1] *Ep.* lxxvii. 4, 6 and 20, xxxvi. 1 and 4, cviii. 28.
[2] *Ep.* xxiii. 11, ii. 3, xiii. 10, xviii. 6.
[3] Summers, *Select Letters of S.* p. xlii ff. gives a careful study; *cf.* Bourgery, *Sénèque Prosateur*, pp. 206–305.

There are colloquial words like *pilicrepus* ('ball-player,' found in inscriptions), *scordalus* ('brawler,' in elder Seneca and Petronius), and diminutives like *punctiuncula* ('a wee jab'). There are also rare words, not known before Seneca, like *collatrare* ('yelp at') and *perpessicius* ('much enduring'). To other words he gives a new meaning.

Traces of Seneca's influence are found in Juvenal and Tacitus; and early Christian writers[1] like Tertullian, Lactantius and Jerome were attracted by the spirit and words of one who was for long believed to have corresponded with St. Paul. His prose style is definitely echoed in Tertullian's *Apologeticum*; for its peroration, fiercely triumphant in its eulogy upon martyrdom, contains antitheses, exclamations, historical instances and short crisp utterances which ring as if they might have come from a converted Seneca.

If only as the exponent of Latin Stoicism, Seneca deserves lasting fame. The spirit of the later Stoicism can be gathered from his Latin essays and epistles, and in Greek from the *Discourses of Epictetus* recorded by Arrian and from the *Meditations* composed by the Emperor Marcus Aurelius. In the eyes of all three, the Stoic mode of thought guarantees healing for the wounds of life. But internal peace can be attained only by hard-won victories over self and over circumstance, by persevering progress towards virtue – a progress which, Seneca wisely insists, is in itself virtue – by trust in Providence, by acceptance of the Divine Will, by harmonising oneself with Nature. The precept of Epictetus, 'endure and abjure' (ἀνέχου καὶ ἀπέχου), expresses much of this ascetic faith. The tranquillity which the stricter Stoics of Greece would confine to the perfect sage is, in the more sensible Roman spirit, claimed by Seneca for him also who is advancing and has made some headway. It is a hard fight to advance, he says, but 'you are sworn to make yourself a good man'[2] and the very striving is virtue.[3] This is typical of the Roman rejection of the more pedantic early Stoicism. In Seneca the system has become an enlightened and broadened one, too practical to mistake paradoxes for genuine intellectual or moral sustenance. So too Seneca's breadth of sympathy indicates the widening of the moral ideal; for cosmopolitanism has transcended the old opposition between Greek and barbarian. The claims of others are infinitely heightened, when in each fellow-man there is recognised, notwithstanding imperfections, some spark of an all-pervading divine essence. Forbearance, kindliness and true humanity are the fruits of such a creed: so out of a once rigid and unbending system disdainful of feeling, intolerant of human frailty, was evolved the Neo-Stoicism which could not but be moved by the sorrows and follies of the world and could

---

[1] *E.g.* Lact. *Div. Inst.* I. v: 'Annaeus quoque Seneca, qui ex Romanis uel acerrimus Stoicus fuit, quam saepe summum Deum merita laude prosequitur!'
[2] *Ep.* xxxvii. 1.
[3] *Ep.* lxxxix. 8: 'ad uirtutem uenitur per ipsam.'

not look upon a distressed gladiator or a sick slave without seeing a kinsman deserving commiseration. It was a great gain for the world that at Rome the strength of Stoicism had grown less harsh, its exaltation less arrogant, its integrity less priggish, its calm less unfeeling.

At first it is not unnatural that in the restrained and self-confident Stoic philosophy a reader might seem to encounter a remote and even repellent quality as of a system too unreal to be literally practical. Yet in fact this is a mistake. The Roman Stoicism of the first century was no mere theoretic elaboration: it was a faith which offered genuine consolation amidst desperate afflictions. Upon a believer it could confer the victory in defiance of the most malignant arrows of fortune. In such a faith some men could steel themselves, for the sake of the state, to help the work of government in trying times, and some could die triumphant over human injustice. History bears the clearest testimony to the inspiring vitality of the creed; and it is from this standpoint that one can best observe the human side of Seneca. Behind his preaching of Stoic doctrine there worked a powerful earnestness which goes far to justify the iteration of counsels throughout the massive corpus of his treatises and letters.

The very seriousness of this philosophy, then, related it to life: it is in part the outcome of actual and often dangerous experience in dark times. It is a seriousness which makes the lighter human touches rarer and more precious. No doubt the sage cannot descend so easily to earth from an Olympian superiority as the ordinary *littérateur* who may be content to view mankind from the plain rather than from the heights; and one realises that it was easier for Cicero and Pliny to unbend in their *Letters* than for Seneca to do so in his. It is, then, all the more to the credit of Seneca's good sense, as it certainly adds to his interest, that, though the *Letters* primarily subserve the purpose of permanent ethical instruction, he is by no means wanting in 'small talk' and humour. The same breadth of mind that saved him from being a rigid dogmatist taught him to discover material for comment everywhere – vegetarianism, study in rowdy surroundings, slops for an invalid, the invasion of a dining-room by kitchen appliances to keep dainties hot.[1] He can make fun of and, at the same time, defend the Stoic annihilation of emotion: with a touch of mischief he reports the young man's question to Panaetius, 'Should the good Stoic fall in love?'[2] Never interested in logic, he jests at syllogisms more than once:[3] they are not applicable, he insists, to the supreme question of human good and human conduct: 'such subtleties make savants rather than saints' (*non faciunt bonos sed doctos*). A similarly jocular vein at the expense of pedants runs through his letter on virtues viewed as *animalia*,[4] where he leads the Stoic argument by a *reductio ad absurdum* to the conclusion that to make a wise speech in

[1] *Ep.* cviii, lvi, lxxviii. 23 and 25.
[2] *Ep.* cxvi. 5. [3] xlviii, cvi. [4] cxiii.

the senate is an 'animal.' Referring to his sea-sickness, he remarks facetiously that if he had regularly to be put ashore, as he was after one brief
trip on the Bay of Naples, then a voyage anywhere would take him twice
as long as Ulysses's wanderings lasted, and with mock seriousness he
affects to think that we owe the elaborate *Odyssey* ultimately to the hero's
mal de mer.[1] So, too, he drops the philosophic mantle to give us vivid
pictures like that of his picnic with a friend,[2] or a tissue of exaggerations
in satirising the luxury of the day: 'We have reached such a pitch of
luxury that we decline to tread on anything but precious stones' (*eo
deliciarum peruenimus ut nisi gemmas calcare nolimus*, lxxxvi. 7).

Such ordinary human notes strengthen Seneca's power over us when
we turn to his grave and elevated thought. He does not work out systema-
tically for us the whole body of the Stoic doctrines; but few can rise
after reading in his books without feeling the better for it. A tonic bracing
of the spirit comes from the serene forbearance advocated in the *De
Ira*; the uncalculating generosity so estimably pervading the *De Beneficiis*; the princely, if Stoically guarded, clemency recommended in the
De Clementia; the widely sympathetic understanding of human nature
evident in the *Letters*; the virtuous conquest of desire proclaimed as the
secret of bliss in *The Happy Life*; and the complete mastery of the soul
indispensable for *The Constancy of the Wise Man* or for *The Tranquillity of the Mind*. The closing words of his last letter to Lucilius show the
true Stoic independence of worldly standards:

> I shall give you in brief a rule whereby to measure yourself,
> whereby to gauge your development: in that day you will come to your
> own, when you realise that the successful are of all men most miserable.
> Good-bye.

MISCELLANEOUS LEARNING

After the study of achievement so many-sided as Seneca's in philosophy, oratory and natural science (apart from his contribution to
satire and drama), a brief sketch of contemporary learning is appropriate.
In history the Neronian period did not shine. The impressions of
Domitius Corbulo in Asia, of C. Suetonius Paulinus in Mauretania, of
Ti. Claudius Balbillus in Egypt, and of L. Antistius Vetus in Germany
made little mark. Agrippina, the emperor's mother, composed memoirs
which the elder Pliny and Tacitus quote. Works by jurists were not
directly literary; but they were so frequently influential on Roman
thought and its formulation that it is right to record the names of the
younger Nerva, father of the future emperor; Proculus from whom the
'Proculians' took their name, and, among their 'Sabinian' rivals, C.
Cassius Longinus. Much philosophy continued to be written in Greek,
as was done by Musonius Rufus and by Cornutus, who also was the

---

[1] liii.   [2] lxxxvii.

author of works on grammar and rhetoric. But Latin was employed
for philosophical purposes not only by Seneca but by Papirius Fabianus
and Celsus. Stoicism, whether in formal exposition or in the actual lives
of its professors, became one of the mighty intellectual and moral forces
of the time. The independence of spirit, too, which the system fostered
made its followers suspect: some of their tenets might readily be misconstrued as those of a political opposition, while a defiantly courageous
manner of dying gave to many victims of an emperor's cruelty a semi-
religious halo of martyrdom. Among such victims were Barea Soranus,
and Paetus Thrasea of Patavium, author of a panegyric upon the younger
Cato which Plutarch used. Thrasea's ruin in A.D. 66 involved his son-
in-law Helvidius Priscus in banishment; but Helvidius returned when
Galba had succeeded Nero, impeached twice unsuccessfully his father-
in-law's accuser, and brought upon himself a second exile under
Vespasian.

It was to Nero that Caesius Bassus dedicated his metrical treatise:
he may, as mentioned elsewhere, be identical with Persius's poet-friend.
Scholarship was also represented by Q. Asconius Pedianus (probably
10 B.C.–A.D. 76) and M. Valerius Probus of Berytus. The former proved
himself a thorough investigator into the subject-matter and meaning of
classical writers in his *Liber contra obtrectatores Vergilii* and his commentaries upon Cicero's speeches. We possess, in impaired form, his
commentaries on five speeches.[1] One most valuable portion is his introduction to the *Pro Milone*. On Cicero's Verrine orations notes of a very
different character, as superficial as the genuine Asconius is satisfying,
and as grammatical as he is historical, have come down along with the
other comments, but are usually referred to a 'Pseudo-Asconius' of the
fifth century. The eminent grammarian Valerius Probus belongs to the
Neronian period, though he outlived it by many years.[2] His provincial
education had brought him under the influence of older Latin books,
and as a teacher in Rome he retained that interest in the style of
the past which guaranteed linguistic equipment for his editions
of Latin authors. He left a miscellany of notes upon archaic Latin;[3]
and Gellius, who often cites him, shows that he delivered lectures to his
pupils on the subject. He elucidated, with critical notes, Terence,
Lucretius, Virgil, Horace and Persius.

The oratory of the day recalls the names of the Stoic speakers in the
Senate, Paetus Thrasea and Helvidius Priscus. Eprius Marcellus made
himself notorious as a *delator*; the rhetorician Julius Africanus we shall
find praised by Quintilian[4] and coupled with Domitius Afer; Galerius
Trachalus had his talents used by the Emperor Otho in the composition

[1] On the lost *Pro Cornelio* and *In toga candida*, and on the extant *In Pisonem*, *Pro Scauro* and *Pro Milone*.
[2] Mart. III. ii. 12; *cf.* Gell. I. xv. 18. He is to be distinguished from the gram-marian Probus of the 4th cent.
[3] Suet. *Gr.* 24.
[4] X. i. 118.

of speeches.[1] Fabricius Veiento, who was accused in A.D. 62 for his satiric codicils directed against senators and priests, was banished by Nero, and had his books burned, but was in Rome again practising delation under Domitian. Among the professors of rhetoric were Clodius Quirinalis from Arelate (Arles); Antonius Liberalis who maintained a feud with Palaemon; and Verginius Flavus, the eminent teacher, who had Persius for a pupil.[2]

[1] Tac. *Hist.* I. xc.
[2] Tac. *Ann.* XV. lxxi: 'Verginius studia iuuenum eloquentia fouebat.' He is mentioned or cited by Quintilian as Verginius,' *I. Or.* III. i. 21; III. vi. 45; IV. i. 23; VII. iv. 24; as 'Flavus,' VII. iv. 40; as 'Flavus Verginius,' XI. iii. 126.

Chapter IV

SENECAN SATIRE AND POETRY:
DRAMA OF THE AGE

Apocolocyntosis – A summary – Title and conclusion – Spirit and purpose of the skit – Menippean qualities – Style and metres. Seneca's short poems – The nine tragedies – Authenticity – When written – Not intended for the stage – Contrast with Greek spirit – Sources of the tragedies – Deviations in plot from Greek originals – Influence of previous Latin dramatists – Influence of Euripides – Outstanding defects – The unintentionally ludicrous – Effective qualities of style – Thrust-and-parry lines – The epigrammatic – Poetry – Philosophical passages – Stoicism – Roman colour – Metre – Seneca's influence on Italian and French drama – Seneca and Elizabethan tragedy – Transmission of stock characters and horrors – A quieter stream of influence.

The *Octavia* play – Date and authorship – Historical content – Misplaced erudition.

Comic drama of the age – Emperor and theatre – Curiatius Maternus and other tragic poets.

SENECAN SATIRE, POETRY AND DRAMA

THE *Apocolocyntosis*, or 'pumpkinification' of the Emperor Claudius, being, as a Menippean Satire, to some extent in verse, is a convenient link between Seneca the prose-writer and Seneca the poet. Many light and flippant touches in this skit, coupled with the metrical facility shown when prose is dropped, enable us to believe that he could have also written the verse-epigrams ascribed to him. A summary may convey some notion of its contents and spirit.

'I wish,' he begins, 'to record the proceedings in heaven on October 13th in the new year which opens this fortunate era. No concession is to be made to malice or favour. It's simple truth.' Then the author pokes fun at historians, philosophers and poets. One may inquire if this is to be a true story of Claudius's translation. But whoever demanded witnesses from a historian? The exact hour of day? Well, you may expect philosophers will say the same thing before clocks will! Was it afternoon? Oh, these poets! not content with raving about a sunrise or a sunset, they must interfere with our noontide:

Now Phoebus' ear had passed its mid career.

That was the very time when Claudius lay dying, and he was an unconscionable time over it. Mercury had to remonstrate with one of the Fates: 'Isn't the poor wretch ever to have a rest? Why, it's sixty-four years since he started gasping. What grudge have you got against him and the nation?' But Clotho remarked, 'I wanted to give him a tiny bit of time longer, till he should confer Roman citizenship on the two or three left without it! . . . ' However, she consents to leave a few foreigners in the world, just as a kernel (*in semen*):

> Round the foul spindle then she twined the thread
> And snapped the life-span of Prince Dunderhead.

Meanwhile Lachesis has a new golden thread to manipulate – Nero's; and Apollo is there to chant approval:

> Ye Fates, cut not this short: let him outlive
> The span of mortal life, like me in face,
> Like me in grace, my peer in voice and song. . . .

'Nothing loth to look kindly on a handsome man, Lachesis went on spinning by the handful, and presented Nero with many extra years, on her own (*annos de suo donat*). Just then Claudius bubbled forth (*ebulliit*) the ghost, and consequently ceased to convey even the impression of being alive! He breathed his last as he was listening to a company of comedians, so there's good reason for dreading *them*!'

(*The scene shortly after changes.*)

'Now listen to what took place in heaven. My informant will guarantee my accuracy (*fides penes auctorem erit*). Jupiter had got word that a person had arrived – a rather tall person and rather grey: he was theatening something or other, it was thought, for he was constantly shaking his head: he dragged the right foot. They'd asked what his country was, but couldn't make his answer out. He wasn't a Greek; he wasn't a Roman – didn't belong to any known race, in fact.'

So, at Jupiter's suggestion, Hercules, who had travelled the whole world over, was told off to interview this outlandish stranger. Greatly troubled, Hercules thought a thirteenth labour was upon him! Still, the new arrival looked like some sort of human being (*uisus est quasi homo*), he tried him with Greek – a line from Homer. Claudius was belighted to find savants (*philologos*) in heaven; there would therefore be some room for his own works on history! So he answered in Greek, and, Roman-like, claimed Troy as his place of origin. Unluckily for this remark, the Goddess Malaria, who had attended him from Rome, interrupted with a flat contradiction, 'It's an absolute lie. He was born at Lyons: he's a genuine Gaul: so, of course, he took Rome – the proper thing for a Gaul to do!' Thereat Claudius blazed out in anger and (like the Queen of Hearts in *Alice in Wonderland*) shouted, 'Off with her head!' But you might have fancied the bystanders were his own freedmen for all the notice they took! Thereupon Hercules called him to order: 'You just mark my words. Drop playing the silly ass. You've come where mice nibble iron. Make a clean breast of it – else I'll bang the *sottise* (*alogias*) out of you.' And to make himself more terrifying, Hercules assumed the tragic role, and declaimed:

> What place of birth you vaunt, be quick to show;
> Else felled to earth this club shall lay you low.
> This club has often butchered fiery kings!
> Why babble these uncertain murmurings? . . .

Claudius's reply, so far as it could be understood, was an attempt to mollify Hercules, reminding him of days spent by the emperor on law-cases near his temple.

His success in this attempt must have been described in a passage now lost; for we are suddenly present at the debate in heaven concerning Claudius's eligibility for deification. Some deity is quizzing Hercules on his proposal:

'Only do tell us what sort of a god you want that creature made. He can't be an Epicurean god; for such a one *ne dérange ni soi-même ni les autres* (οὔτε αὐτὸς πρᾶγμα ἔχει τι οὔτε ἄλλοις παρέχει). There's a bit of the Stoic deity in him, I can see; for he's got neither heart nor head. . . . Is this person to make our crooked ways straight? Why, he doesn't know what to do in his own bedroom, and now he 'scans the purlieus of the sky' – wants to be a god! He's not content with having a temple in Britain and with savages for worshippers!'

At this point Jupiter 'spies strangers' in the House, and in accordance with the rules Claudius has to retire. Janus, on being asked to express his views, makes a long speech too fast for the shorthand writer to keep up with (*quae notarius persequi non potuit*). Arguing that the honour of being a god must not be given to the *canaille*, he proposes a motion of exclusion in general terms. The next speaker, Diespiter, moves that Claudius be made a god in view of his relationship to Augustus and Augusta,[1] and in view of Romulus's need for a comrade in devouring boiled turnips! Many speeches are made and Hercules canvasses the gods in Claudius's favour; but Augustus opposes in an oration of scathing irony:

'I call you to witness, Conscript Fathers, that since I was made a god, I have never uttered a word. I always mind my own business. But I can no longer disguise my feelings. Was it for this that I secured peace on land and sea? . . . Words fall short of my indignation. . . . This man, Conscript Fathers, who looks as though he couldn't disturb a fly, used to kill folk as readily as a dog squats down.'

Claudius is then denounced as a murderer of Augustus's descendants, and is apostrophised with the question why he passed death-sentences in cases that were untried:

---

[1] *I.e.* Livia, wife of Augustus and by her previous husband grandmother to Claudius. Claudius's other grandmother was Octavia, sister of Augustus.

H

'Where is this usual? It's not done in heaven. Look at Jupiter. He's been ruler for ever so many years, but Vulcan's the only person whose leg he has broken. . . . He lost his temper with his wife and hung her up, but he didn't kill her, did he? . . . Who's going to worship Claudius as a god? Who's to believe in him? Make a god of such as he is, and nobody will believe you are gods yourselves!'

Augustus's motion for deportation is carried, and Claudius is haled off to the lower regions by Mercury. As they pass down the Via Sacra, they can see Claudius's funeral in progress – a lovely (*formosissimum*) funeral and an extravagant one, obviously the obsequies of a god (*plane ut scires deum efferri*). And now Claudius realises that he is dead, since there is din enough for him to hear the anapaestic dirge:

> Pour out your weepings, your sorrows make known:
> Deafen the forum with many a groan! . . .
> > O weep for the dead, for none had the head
> > To settle suits faster, and every point master,
> > Tho' only one side of the case had been tried,
> > And oft he had heard from neither a word!
> > Who now the whole year will processes hear?

All this was most enjoyable. Claudius would have liked to watch his funeral longer, but he is hurried off below. Now, who should be in the lower world to meet him but his freedman Narcissus, spick and span, fresh from his bath? He had got ahead by a short cut (*antecesserat compendiaria*), and says he, 'What have *gods* to do with mere mortals?' But Mercury breaks in: 'Be sharp and tell them we're coming.' Narcissus flies off faster than you could say the word. Everything slopes in hell, you must know: it's easy going down. So Claudius, gouty though he was, arrived at Pluto's door in a twinkle. Cerberus, 'the hundred-headed brute' to use Horace's phrase (*ut ait Horatius, belua centiceps*), was on the scene; and it was a little trying to face a shaggy black monster-dog after being used to a small whitish pet-bitch (*subalbam canem in deliciis habere adsueuerat*). But Narcissus shouted the announcement 'Claudius is coming!' and immediately there was a throng of his victims to give him a reception! Then, as they crowd round, consuls, prefects, relatives and freedmen, the absent-minded emperor remarks, '*Voici mes amis partout!* How did *you* come here?' to which they answer, 'Who but yourself sent us, you assassin of all your friends? To court with him!' So he is brought before Aeacus, and statistics are produced of those he had put to death: and Aeacus, being a person of perfect fairness, judges Claudius on Claudian principles; that is, he hears only the case for the prosecution! The verdict is 'Guilty.' What should the sentence be? A new sort of penalty is wanted, and, after discussion, Aeacus decrees that Claudius must rattle dice for ever in a box with no bottom. The convict had already begun this fruitless task, when all of a sudden Caligula

appeared on the scene to claim him as a slave. Witnesses prove that they
had seen Caligula thrashing him: so clearly he must have been in servitude, and is therefore assigned to Caligula, who gives him as a gift
to that most righteous judge, Aeacus: and Aeacus hands him over to his
Greek freedman Menander to be a law-clerk in attendance upon cases
for evermore.

So the satire ends. Some critics will not allow the author to be funny
in his own way, and they express dissatisfaction. They gravely point out
that Claudius is not turned into a pumpkin, a metamorphosis which
they understood was promised in the title: therefore they urge that
perhaps the real conclusion is lost, or perhaps the real pumpkinification
belonged to another pamphlet altogether.[1] There is no need to be so
literal: Claudius, an imperial applicant for divine honours, is sufficiently
metamorphosed when he is degraded from heaven to a trumpery post
in hell, and when throughout the satire he is treated as a silly pumpkin-
head[2] of a man. The title in the best MS. (Sangallensis) is *Diui Claudii
incipit Apotheosis* (spelt 'Ἀποθήοσις) *Annei Senece per satiram*, which does
not, at first sight, square with the title *Apocolocyntosis* recorded by Dio
Cassius.[3] Yet, on examination, the MS. title betrays a confirmatory corruption. It is tautological, as it stands, for one does not deify a deified
emperor; all, however, is intelligible if it be, as Bücheler guessed, a
contamination of an original superscription *Diui Claudii Apocolocyntosis* with a gloss, *Apotheosis per satiram*, to explain the parody implicit
in the rare word.

The conclusion has been otherwise impeached.[4] Some have thought
the Caligula episode illogical after Claudius had been sentenced to perpetual dice-playing: others have thought the end too abrupt to be
effective. Logic, however, is not to be demanded from a merry jest,
and the fun lies exactly in its inconsequent suddenness. So far is the
dénouement from being pointless that in reality its point is double.
Firstly, it represents a ruler who had yielded excessive power at his
court to freedmen, as being now adjudged a slave, and transferred, like
the veriest chattel, to be a freedman's underling; secondly, it represents
one who had a passion for acting the judge on earth as doomed to

---

[1] Th. Birt, *De Sen. Apoc. et Apoth. lucubratio*, Marb. 1888, thinks Sen. wrote
not only the existing political satire, but a lost philosophical *Apocolocyntosis*.
A. Stahr, *Agrippina*, Berl. 1867, p. 343, also refuses to identify the *Apotheosis* with
the *Apocolocyntosis*, but further denies S.'s authorship of the extant skit. J. J. Hartman, *Mnem.* xliv (1916), holds that the pumpkinification was contained 'in
aliquo colloquio' distinct from the extant 'Ludus.'
[2] The Greek title ἀποκολοκύντωσις is from κολοκύντη = Lat. *cucurbita*. For
the satiric use of *cucurbita cf.* Pet. *Sat.* 39; Juv. XIV. 58; Apul. *Met.* I. xv. The
title *Ludus de morte Claudii Caesaris* is in inferor MSS., and involves an un-
Latin use of *ludus*.
[3] lx. 35: συνέθηκε μὲν γὰρ καὶ ὁ Σενέκας σύγγραμμα, ἀποκολοκύντωσιν αὐτὸ ὥσπερ
τινὰ ἀπαθανάτισιν ὀνομάσας.
[4] E. Bickel in 'Der Schluss d. Apoc.,' *Philol.* lxxvii (1921), defends the ending
as it stands.

remain a mere law-clerk (*a cognitionibus*) in the infernal regions till the
end of time. Several references to Claudius's freedmen in the body of the
satire are in keeping with this conclusion, especially the ironical gibe
at their contemptuous disobedience;[1] similarly, there are previous
references to his performances in law which make the finale perfectly
appropriate.[2]

The question of Seneca's authorship involves different problems. Is
the satire a likely product of his genius? How could he consistently write
such an attack after his grovelling adulation of Claudius in the *Consolatio
ad Polybium*,[3] and after composing the funeral laudation for Nero to
pronounce at the ceremonial sanctification of Claudius?[4] The two questions of ability and consistency must be kept separate. About Seneca's
versatility and control of brilliant style there can be no doubt, while
humorous and satiric qualities are not wanting in his *Letters*: about his
consistency it must be allowed that this never was his strong point.
Few philosophers are more vulnerable than the Stoic who amassed
wealth and the moralist who drafted exculpatory orations to be delivered
by a tyrant. Modern feeling cannot but see indecency in this bitter
invective against a deceased sovereign. Seneca laughs mercilessly at the
dead emperor's frailties, mental and physical – his pedantic stupidity,
offensive absent-mindedness, capricious temper, unreasoning tyranny,
shambling gait, and stammering utterance. The unprepossessing picture
is painted with increasing bias until in Augustus's denunciation of
Claudius the author takes full opportunity for venting his spleen. There
is no intention of being any fairer than Aristophanes was to Euripides or
Socrates. One must expect nothing about the better aspects of Claudius's
policy or scholarship, or about the building schemes of his reign, nor
any pity for the deep damnation of his taking off. Cunningly his contemptuous dismissal by the Fates is set in juxtaposition with Apollo's
praise of his young successor. A feeble dotard had gone: with the new
princeps a golden era would return. Ignoble we may call it, but it can at
any rate be explained. Years before, to suit his own longings for recall
from exile, Seneca had resorted to gross flattery of Claudius in addressing Polybius: recently he had by request composed a formal speech on
the dead emperor to suit the immediate state-occasion: but now
he was quick enough to see that no reverence was shown to Claudius's
memory. His own oration, spoken by Nero, had been received with un-
disguised merriment when it mentioned 'the foresight and sagacity'[5]

---

[1] *Apoc.* 7: 'putares omnes illius esse libertos: adeo illum nemo curabat.'
[2] *E.g.*, *Apoc.* 7: 'ante templum tuum ius dicebam'; 10: 'antequam audires,
damnasti'; 12: 'discere causas una tantum parte audita, saepe et neutra'; *cf.*
in the finale 14: 'illum altera tantum parte audita condemnat.'
[3] Diderot argued that either Seneca's adulation was sarcastic or that the *Consol.
ad Polyb.* was written by someone else to damage Seneca's character.
[4] Tac. *Ann.* XIII. iii.
[5] Tac. *Ann.* XIII. iii: 'postquam ad prouidentiam sapientiamque flexit
nemo risui temperare.'

of the departed prince; and Nero's conscience over the poisoning of
Claudius troubled the emperor so little that he came to joke[1] about
mushrooms as food for the gods – had not Claudius gone by that means
to heaven? On the whole, however, it suited the poisoners, Nero and
Agrippina, that Seneca should take an opportunity of adopting their
official version of the death and say nothing awkward about mushrooms.
At the same time, if he depreciated Claudius and magnified Nero, so
much the better: the predecessor would be the less missed and the
successor the more commended on the threshold of his reign. So at last
Seneca's chance came for unmasking his true attitude. He detested
Claudius:[2] he had an old score to wipe out: he probably felt a sincere
contempt for his pedantry: and thus a clever and venomous pasquinade
was written by a man of flesh and blood, a Spaniard who could let his
feelings – especially those of hatred – go. It rings as if it must have been
written very soon after the official deification which it burlesques, *i.e.*
soon after the middle of October, A.D. 54.[3] The latest occurrence to
which the author refers is the death of the imperial freedman Narcissus,
whose removal followed hard upon that of his master.

The idea of a visit to the other world was familiar in ancient epic and
drama, and could be made to serve either a serious or a comic purpose.
The gods are treated by Seneca cavalierly; but Lucilius, Lucretius, even
Cicero, had accustomed readers to such literary irreverence, and in
Seneca no systematic attack on state religion was contemplated. Combined with the spirit and form of Menippean satire, such a framework
and such an attitude gave excellent promise of burlesque effect; for the
Menippean satire, thanks to Cynic traditions, encouraged the outspoken, the abrupt, the inconsequent, the startling in manner. Inherited
from Menippus of Gadara and transmitted through Varro, it could be
employed as an irresponsible and defiant medley. Seneca's satire is less
akin to the generally good-natured outlook of Varro[4] than to that
Cynicism in Menippus which is the secret of the Gadarene's attraction
for Lucian.[5] But while Seneca shared in the spirit and conventions of the
traditional Menippean, his place in this succession must not obscure
his originality. The *Apocolocyntosis* is far too fresh and lively, too direct
in its satiric bearing upon an actual personality, to be anything but work
of an individual stamp. Obviously it is in many respects a contrast to the
contemporary Menippean of Petronius. It had its own descendants, too:

---

[1] Dio lx. 35: τοὺς γὰρ μύκητας θεῶν βρῶμα ἔλεγεν εἶναι. *Cf.* Suet. *Nero* xxxiii.
[2] Tac. *Ann.* XII. viii: 'infensus Claudio dolore iniuriae credebatur.'
[3] Bücheler dates the *Apoc.* immediately after Claudius's death. Hirschfeld (*Kl.
Schr.* 1913, p. 481, n. 4) connects the composition with Nero's annulment of
Claudius's consecration (Suet. *Claud.* xlv). Bickel (*op. cit.*) accepts Hirschfeld's
date.
[4] For examination of Seneca's relationship to Menippean satire, see O.
Weinreich, *Senecas Apocol. . . . Einführung, Analyse und Untersuchungen, Übersetz-
ung*, Berl. 1923.
[5] R. Helm, *Lukian u. Menipp*, Lpz. 1906.

long after the classic age, two definite imitations of Seneca's satire appeared; one, Lipsius's *Satura Menippea* towards the end of the sixteenth century; the other Cunaeus's *Sardi Venales* in 1612.

Critics have differed about the style of the *Apocolocyntosis* in comparison with that of Seneca's philosophical works. But two things have to be remembered; Menippean satire does not claim the finish of style that suits philosophy; on the other hand, so expert a writer as Seneca had the ability to produce a fresh type of prose, if necessary, and to sprinkle it with homely proverbs, colloquialisms, slang plebeian grammar and a plebeian want of syntax.[1] Adroitness in turning from higher to lower style is nowhere better seen than in his contemporary Petronius.

The versification is that of a skilled hand. The interspersed hexameters are comparable in quality with those of the epigrams and minor poems ascribed to Seneca. Behind the anapaestic dirge on Claudius lies the author's facility gained in writing choral odes for his tragedies,[2] and even the fourteen iambic *senarii* exhibit the same fondness for anapaests[3] which marks the speeches and dialogues of his plays.

Seneca as poet must be judged not only by his dramas but by a collection of brief pieces in the *Anthologia Latina* compiled at Carthage in the sixth century. Of the opening seventy-three poems three are assigned by the MSS. to Seneca; but most, or indeed all, of the seventy-three may be his. Except a few in hendecasyllables, the poems are elegiac. They touch on miscellaneous themes – the mutability of things, a quiet life, the hardships of exile, republican heroes like Cato and Pompey, the true friendship of such as Crispus (presumably Passienus Crispus, the able orator who was consul a second time in A.D. 44), the false friendship of the great, imperial victories, luxury, riches, and the evils of civil warfare. While the reader is prepared for Stoic lines on simplicity of life and the dissolution of the universe, he is perhaps surprised to find erotic poems in the collection, until he realises that Seneca was no exception to the common practice whereby Romans amused themselves with composing verses inferior in morality to their authors' actual behaviour.[4] Even in the amorous pieces, however, it is a moralist that professes to speak – he sets limits to immodesty, and admires the fair one who relies on natural rather than artificial charms (*naturae simplicitate ualet*). There is, at the same time, in other poems much that fits the true Seneca – lines to his native Corduba (xix), a reference to his

---

[1] *E.g.* (proverbs) 1: *aut regem aut fatuum nasci oportere;* 9: *manus manum lauat;* (colloquialisms) 1: *dicam quod mihi in buccam uenerit;* 3: *in semen relinqui;* (slang) 4: *animam ebulliit;* 9: *mapalia* (Punic='shanties'); (parataxis) 2: *si dixero mensis erat October;* 10: *dic mihi . . . quare damnasti.* The diminutives *nummariolus, ciuitatulas, auriculam,* and a few more, occur.

[2] Weinreich, *op. cit.* pp. 65–66, considers that he travesties his own *Herc. Fur.*

[3] Five out of these fourteen lines have an anapaest in the fifth foot.

[4] Plin. *Ep.* V. iii. 5.

two brothers (v. 14), and one to his little nephew, plausibly identified
with Lucan:

> Our sweetly prattling Marcus will, I pray,
> Challenge both uncles' eloquence some day.[1]

He curses Corsica, the island

> That terrifies at summer's earliest glow,[2]

and can be yet crueller as the season advances. Amidst a plentiful lack
of blessings, there are only two things to find there, 'the place of exile
and the exile's self' (*exsul et exsilium*). He asks merely for an undis-
turbed existence: 'Let the praetorship fall to those who wish it,' he
says, and it is significant that Seneca had not risen higher than quaestor
before his banishment. His fulsome and repeated eulogies on Claudius's
victories are partly redeemed by their romantic association with distant
Britain 'severed by the dreary sea' (*uasto disiuncta Britannia ponto*),

> Where the chill constellation of the North
> Outshineth aye the stars that do not set.[3]

The nine plays ascribed to Seneca in the Codex Etruscus and other
MSS. of the same family are given in the following order: *Hercules*
(*Furens*), *Troades*, *Phoenissae*, *Medea*, *Phaedra*, *Oedipus*, *Agamemnon*,
Thyestes, *Hercules* (*Oetaeus*). Inferior MSS. give the alternative titles of
Thebais for *Phoenissae* and *Hippolytus* for *Phaedra*. They add the
Octauia, which cannot be by Seneca for reasons to be mentioned later.

The testimony to the manysidedness of Seneca[4] is so strong that there
is no need to pay attention to Sidonius Apollinaris's blunder in separating Seneca the dramatist from Seneca the philosopher. It is true that
Quintilian does not give Seneca's name in his list of dramatists; but he
certifies his interest in tragic diction (VIII. iii. 31), and quotes part of a
line from the *Medea* as Seneca's (IX. ii. 8). Six plays, *Medea*, *Hercules
Furens*, *Troades*, *Phaedra*, *Agamemnon* and *Thyestes*, are cited by Latin
authors or grammarians. The remaining three, *Oedipus*, *Phoenissae* and
Hercules Oetaeus are, like the others, regarded in the MSS. as by Seneca.
These three have had their authenticity attacked, but scholars generally
accept all but portions of the *Hercules Oetaeus*. This last play extends, as
we have it, to nearly 2,000 lines, and its very length, along with echoes of

---

[1] li. 5–6:
> 'Sic dulci Marcus qui nunc sermone fritinnit,
> Facundo patruos prouocet ore duos.'

[2] ii. 5: 'Corsica terribilis cum primum incanduit aestas.'

[3] xxxvi. 5–6:
> 'Qua frigida semper
> Praefulget stellis Arctos inocciduis.'

[4] Quintil. X. i. 128: 'tractauit etiam omnem fere studiorum materiam: nam
et orationes eius et poemata et epistulae et dialogi feruntur'; *cf.* VIII. iii. 31;
Tac. *Ann.* XIV. lii; Plin. *Ep.* V. iii. 5.

previous plays, arouses suspicion: further investigation into such a feature
as its double chorus (in which it resembles Seneca's *Agamemnon*) or into its
change of scene leads to the conclusion that it is a patchwork due, in part,
to other hands than Seneca's. The attribution of the plays as a whole to
Seneca is confirmed by internal evidence. The short pointed *sententiae*
both in form and in expression resemble his prose: and there are
frequent parallels in thought, especially if, as often occurs, the thought
assumes a Stoic cast.[1]

The question when Seneca wrote the tragedies is one which has received various and inconclusive answers. Birt[2] in 1911 dogmatically
asserted that most of them were composed after 54 and none before 49.
Later,[3] fresh emphasis was laid on Quintilian's recollection of hearing
praefationes in which the propriety of a phrase for tragedy was discussed between Seneca and Pomponius Secundus. The plausible suggestion was made that these *praefationes* were spoken, not written, introductions to public readings of tragedies. Quintilian mentions the incident as a reminiscence from his youth, and, as he was born about A.D.
35, this implies a date in the early fifties of the first century. The point
bears on the two problems whether Seneca's dramas were meant for the
stage and when they were composed. It may be that some of Seneca's
plays, like some by Secundus, were read, if they were not written, in the
early fifties, and a desire to foster in his pupil Nero an interest in adaptations from the Greek might explain why Seneca should give tragic
readings about that period: but it does not follow that all the plays are to
be so dated. Pomponius Secundus had been in Germany in 50 and 51,
and his debate with Seneca may therefore have followed his return. He
had, however, produced plays or at least some kind of dramatic compositions before, as we know from the storm raised against him in the theatre
in 47.[4] So too Seneca, who returned from banishment in 49, may
have written plays during his years of enforced leisure in Corsica. It is
not surprising that this is the period of his life to which prevailing guess-
work has ascribed the tragedies. But the problem appears insoluble;

---

[1] Examples may be found in P. Schäfer, *De Philosophiae Annaeanae in Senecae
tragoediis vestigiis*, Jena, 1909.
[2] Th. Birt (*Neue Jb. K. A.* 1911). F. Jonas, *De ordine librorum Sen.*, 1870,
had aimed at a closer determination of dates, *e.g. Med.* and *Tro.* soon after
Seneca's return from exile in 49, *Herc. Fur.* after 57, *Oed.* after the Parthian
war of 58, *Thyest.* after Seneca's retirement in 62. Weinreich (*Senecas Apocol.*,
1923, p. 65), founding on Münscher's metrical analyses, remarks with airy confidence, 'Daran denkt man heute nicht mehr dass die Tragödien, ganz oder zum
Teil, in der Jugendzeit oder während des Exils entstanden seien.' Weinreich
maintains that Seneca wrote *Thyestes, Herc. Fur.* and *Tro.* before he composed
the anapaests of the *Apoc.* in 54. He gives Münscher's dates for the remaining
plays: 54 or 55, *Phaedra* and *Medea*; a year or two later, *Agam.*; 57, *Oed.*; 64
or 65, *Herc. Oet.* and *Phoen.*
[3] C. Cichorius, *Röm. Stud.* pp. 426–429; Quintil. VIII. iii. 31. For further
chronological discussion see O. Herzog, 'Datierung der Tragödien des Sen.,'
Rh.M. 1928, p. 51 ff. Herzog places four plays in the period of exile, 42–49.
[4] Tac. *Ann.* XI. xiii. *Cf.* p. 127 *supra.*

there was abundant time for Seneca to have written tragedies even before he was exiled, a man of over forty, and there are elements in the tragedies more nearly akin to a clever student's rhetoric than to philosophical maturity. Nor would it be easy to disprove a contention that some at least of the plays consisted of early material worked over and touched up at a later date.

That Seneca intended his dramas for the stage is incredible. No doubt there were still in the Neronian period tragic representations, but many of Seneca's elaborate speeches would have been unsuitable in a theatre, and some scenes would not act as they stand. It was one thing for Seneca merely to imagine Medea slaying her children in public, but another thing to have this shown before actual Roman audiences, accustomed though they were to horrors. The sufficiency of three actors, apart from the chorus, for all the characters of a play is not so much an attempt to meet theatrical conditions as an adherence to Greek convention. On the other hand, the rhetorical dexterity and descriptive power exhibited in the tragedies suited the taste of literary coteries before whom dramatic compositions could be read with effect.[1]

As an adapter of Greek tragedy, Seneca was attracted most to the blend of realism and romance which characterises Euripides. Out of nine plays his model is definitely Euripides in four, *Hercules Furens*, *Troades*, *Medea* and *Phaedra*. Besides, in the imperfect and inconsistent remains of the *Phoenissae*, Euripidean material is drawn from the Greek play of that name, though there are also contributions from Aeschylus's *Seven Against Thebes* and Sophocles's *Oedipus at Colonus*. On Aeschylus was based the *Agamemnon*, and on Sophocles the *Oedipus* as well as the drearily long *Hercules Oetaeus*, whose authenticity has most been called in question. The *Thyestes* has no equivalent among extant Greek plays. These Latin plays are in no sense versions of the Greek: Seneca did not feel himself bound to adhere to the original plot in detail, but either introduced departures or followed Roman predecessors in their departures.[2] The essential contrast, however, is one of spirit, which no reader can fail to realise, if he turns from Aeschylus's *Agamemnon*, Sophocles's *Oedipus Tyrannus* and Euripides's *Medea* to their Senecan descendants. In the Latin plays one has entered a new world, where genius has been replaced by cleverness, and an eminently classic directness of expression by rhetoric. Despite the recurrence of philosophical sentiments, there is no longer felt, like a pervasive force, the old Aeschylean preoccupation with fundamental themes of life and destiny, an atmosphere of altitude in thought and emotion whence a poet can survey the deepest problems concerning God and man, sin

[1] Recent attempts to maintain that the tragedies were intended for the stage are unconvincing. See M. Coffey in *Lustrum* ii (1957) pp. 162–163.

[2] Differences in plot or structure between the Latin and corresponding Greek plays are exhibited in the comparative analyses appended to Miller's edition (Loeb). The chief differences are summarised in S.H. §§ 369–377.

H*

and suffering; there is no longer that combination of serenity and of
tense drama which makes the *Oedipus Tyrannus* one of the greatest of
plays; nor is there any longer the wide Euripidean humanity to win
full sympathy for the outraged wifehood of Medea.

The most cursory comparison of Seneca's plays with extant originals
will indicate the nature and sometimes the object of his alterations. The
Hercules Furens dramatises the hero's madness which is with terrible
irony turned upon his own wife and children after his triumphant return
from the underworld in time to rescue them from the tyrant Lycus.
For the sentence of death against the absent hero's sons in Euripides the
Roman dramatist has substituted a compulsory, and defiantly refused,
offer of marriage from the tyrant to Hercules's wife Megara; and he has
introduced Theseus, not towards the close, as in the Greek play, but
much earlier, so as to facilitate a long description of adventures shared
by Theseus with Hercules during their raid upon the infernal regions.
Another significant contrast is that Seneca treats Hercules's slaying of
wife and children as an exhibited part of the dramatic action, and not as
material for narration in accord with Greek usage.

The *Troades*, on afflictions which befell the captive dames of Troy,
combines material from the play of the same name by Euripides with
parts of his *Hecuba*. In fact, Seneca's play is cited under the title of
Hecuba by Probus. The sacrifice of the princess Polyxena, which the
ghost of Achilles demands shall be made at his tomb before the Greeks
sail away, is based on the *Hecuba*. To it Seneca adds from the *Troades*
the Greek precautionary execution of Astyanax, the little son of Hector
and Andromache. The extent of Seneca's originality in what is one of
his best plays cannot be absolutely assessed without more knowledge
than we are ever likely to obtain of two lost plays by Sophocles – the
Polyxena and the *Captive Women* (Αἰχμαλωτίδες).

The presence among Accius's plays of an *Astyanax* and a *Troades*
raises the question of a possible influence of the older Roman tragic
writers upon Seneca. It is certain that in his prose works Seneca occasionally cites them, either from direct knowledge or indirectly through
Cicero. Some doubt may be felt whether earlier Roman tragedy retained
all the prestige ascribed to it by Ribbeck; for, though it may not have
entirely vanished from the stage, the taste of the Neronian age was
even more pronounced than that of the Augustan in regarding it as old-
fashioned and uncouth. If the fragments of Accius indicate departures
from Euripides in which Seneca resembles him, this does not prove
positively the influence of the earlier Latin poet: they may have used
a common source in Sophocles. At best, however, all this is conjecture,
though it has been gravely made material for learned tractates.[1] There

---

[1] F. Strauss, *De ratione inter Sen. et antiquas fabulas Romanas intercedente*,
Rost. 1887 (combats Ribbeck's views on ancient Roman tragedy); K. Liedloff,
Die Nachbildung griech. u. röm. Muster in Senecas Troades u. Agamemnon,

remains the obligation to remember that one need not find a source for every departure made by Seneca from extant Greek plays. He is entitled to credit for a measure of originality and a desire to entertain readers or hearers with inventive variations of his own on a familiar plot as well as with ingenious rhetorical points. This is his express theory of literary borrowing; for he advocates, it will be remembered, a bee-like diligence in blending borrowed materials into a new and distinctive flavour, so that even if the original source is manifest, the product shall be something different.[1]

The fragmentary *Phoenissae* presents puzzling features. The title suggests that Seneca contemplated importing from the Greek a chorus of Phoenician damsels. Its 664 lines fall into two portions. The earlier portion presents, as in Sophocles's *Oedipus at Colonus*, the self-blinded and self-exiled king wandering under the guidance of his daughter Antigone, who has vowed never to desert him. With a rhetorical echo of Roman Stoicism, he claims volubly the right of self-murder, a right which, during three years of misery, he has not exercised and which Antigone is at pains to refute by argument. A sudden break, where a choral ode might have been expected, leads to a brief episode in which Oedipus bitterly prays that his sons, Eteocles and Polynices, at war with each other, may act worthily of such a miserable father. From l. 363 a new episode, partly akin to the situation in Aeschylus's *Seven against Thebes*, represents Antigone as now in Thebes, no longer with her father, but with her mother Jocasta, who has not committed suicide as in Sophocles's *Oedipus Tyrannus* or in Seneca's *Oedipus*, and whose feelings are torn between the two brothers at enmity:

> But though I love both sons with equal warmth –
> Where pulls the stronger cause and poorer luck,
> There bends a heart that ever aids the weak.
> Woe makes the sufferer dearer to his kin.[2]

The hopelessness of her attempt to conciliate the pair is seen in Eteocles's theory of power which is propounded, and in Senecan manner expanded, towards the close of the fragment:

> Who fears being hated wills not to be king.[3]

A reference to the literature[4] on the *Phoenissae* shows how some have held these passages are excerpts from one or more completed dramas;

Grimma 1902; R. Schreiner, *Sen. als Tragödiendichter in seinen Beziehungen zu den griech. Originalen* (contains bibliography), Mun. 1909; L. Tachau, 'Die Arbeiten üb. d. Tragödien des Sen. in d. letzten Jahrzehnten,' *Philol.* xlviii (1889) p. 340. R. B. Steele, 'Some Roman Elements in the Trag. of S.,' *A.J.P.* 1922, p. 1 ff.

[1] Sen. *Ep.* lxxxiv. 5 . . . 'in unum saporem uaria illa libamenta confundere, ut, etiam si apparuerit unde sumptum sit, aliud tamen esse quam unde sumptum est appareat.' [2] *Phoen.* 383–386.
[3] *Phoen.* 654. [4] S.H. § 371. *Lustrum* ii (1957) p. 132.

others that they are fragments of one or more dramas never completed; others again that they are only dramatic studies or sketches not designed to be worked up into play-form.

The main differences of plot-construction which distinguish Seneca's *Medea* from Euripides's play are that, for the chance visit of King Aegeus to Corinth when he promises to protect Medea during her imminent exile, Seneca substitutes a scene in which Medea's wonder-working powers are described; and that, while in the Greek play the children of Jason and Medea are sentenced to exile along with their mother, in the Latin she begs in vain to be allowed to take them with her. Jason's confession that he could not live without his children suggests to her the most terrible part of her revenge:

> Thus doth he love the boys? 'Tis well. He's caught.
> The spot for wounding him hath been laid bare.[1]

How far these and other changes either in plot-management or in expression are due to Seneca himself is past finding out. Medea's story, dramatised half a dozen times in Greek, was a theme that attracted several Latin writers. Long after Ennius and Accius it had been handled by Ovid, both in the *Heroides* and in a play now lost; later, in Seneca's time, it occupied the attention of his nephew, Lucan, and of Curiatius Maternus. Seneca's admiring imitations of Ovid, demonstrable elsewhere in his writing, render it likely that here too he owed him much.

A subject not nearly so congenial to Roman tastes as Medea's revenge was the guilty passion of Queen Phaedra for her stepson Hippolytus, an almost puritanic devotee of the chase, for whom life in the open air meant everything and woman nothing. The extant version of this romantic theme by Euripides is his famous *Hippolytus* of 428 B.C., which has been designated *Hippolytus Crowned* ('Ἱππόλυτος στεφανηφόρος or στεφανίας) to distinguish it from his previous and less successful drama *Hippolytus Veiled* ('Ἱππόλυτος καλυπτόμενος). It is an interesting literary point that Seneca seems to have been attracted to the earlier version;[2] for he restored in the plot of his *Phaedra* what Euripides apparently cancelled in deference to Athenian censure – the personal avowal of her love by Phaedra to her stepson. In the extant play by Euripides the nurse takes it upon herself to open Hippolytus's eyes to the queen's feelings; and, after his horrified recoil, the shame-stricken Phaedra strangles herself, leaving a note with false charges against the innocent youth. But in Seneca, as she has in person confessed her love, so in

[1] *Med.* 549–550:

> 'Sic natos amat?
> Bene est – tenetur. Vulneri patuit locus.'

[2] So too Ovid in *Her.* iv (Phaedra's epistle to Hippolytus) seems to follow the earlier Euripidean version rather than either the later one or Sophocles's lost *Phaedra*. For a study of the sources of the Phaedra, see U. Moricca, 'Le Fonti della Fedra di S.', *S.I.F.C.* 1915, p. 158 ff.

person does she malign him to her husband Theseus; and so again, when Hippolytus has met an undeserved death, it is Phaedra in person (not, as in Euripides, the goddess Artemis) who reveals her crime and clears Hippolytus.

In incidents, structure, and spirit, the *Oedipus* is a woeful falling off from Sophocles's thrilling development of the steps in the revelation of the king as the unwitting murderer of his father. In Sophocles the seer Teiresias is sent for in time of crisis, and, when forced to speak, declares, though he is not believed, that Oedipus is the criminal sought for: in Seneca much space is laboriously wasted upon the description of gloomy sacrifices and necromancy. Instead of announcing, as in the Greek, the suicide of the queen, Seneca towards the close brings face to face the two chief victims of tragic circumstance, before Jocasta openly kills herself. But the very construction of the play is inferior. Devoting over 300 lines to lyric portions and over 200 to details of sacrifices and necromancy, the Roman writer has left himself only some 500 lines for the disentanglement of a complicated dramatic story.

Equally disappointing, when contrasted with its renowned Greek original by Aeschylus, is the *Agamemnon*. The disproportion of 1012 Latin lines to 1673 Greek could be compensated for by nothing short of vastly superior literary power; and of that there is no sign. The prevailing absence of genuine thought and feeling in choric songs and invocations based on a frigid mythology is in strong contrast to the profound reflections in the choruses of Aeschylus. It may be that, as Leo thinks,[1] this was Seneca's first essay in drama, and the *Oedipus* his second. In any case, the deviations from Aeschylus are noticeable. Instead of the watchman, who in the Greek announces the beacon-sent tidings of Troy's capture, there is substituted a much more typically Senecan figure – the ghost of Thyestes, filled with the spirit of revenge against his hated brother Atreus, father of Agamemnon, and therefore urging Aegisthus, the queen's paramour, to perform his destined part in the hour of Agamemnon's triumphant return from war. Clytemnestra, in the episode which follows, seems disposed to listen to the advice of her nurse – another typically Senecan figure – and abandon the design of murdering her husband. Less strong-willed than the Aeschylean Clytemnestra, she is confirmed in her purpose by Aegisthus. A further Senecan trait is the detailed description by the herald of the appalling storm which overtook the Greeks on their homeward voyage. Appearing late in the play (l. 782) – considerably after the band of captive Trojan women led by Cassandra – Agamemnon makes his exit less than 30 lines further on. One misses the famous and symbolic scene of the purple carpet in Aeschylus: it is replaced by brief and unheeded warnings of Agamemnon's impending death from Cassandra. One misses too the single line of

[1] F. Leo, *De Sen. tragoediis observationes criticae* (*i.e.* vol. 1 of his edn. of Sen.'s *Trag.*) 1878, p. 133.

final anguish from the victim within. The Latin play represents Cassandra, not as murdered along with her captor, but as relating outside the palace the crime that is being perpetrated. An exciting moment occurs when Electra hurries from the palace and succeeds in sending her young brother Orestes, the future avenger, away into safety under the care of King Strophius, who has opportunely arrived in his chariot on his way home from an Olympic victory. Aeschylus represents the boy as already staying at the court of Strophius. His sister Electra, who at the close of Seneca's play is sent to imprisonment while Cassandra is sent to her death, makes no appearance in the *Agamemnon* of Aeschylus. Some of these variations are foreshadowed in the fragments of Livius Andronicus's *Aegisthus*, and Accius's *Clutemestra*[1] – a coincidence which suggests either Seneca's knowledge of the older Latin plays, or his use, in common with Andronicus, of a Greek play by a dramatist junior to Aeschylus.

There is no surviving Greek original with which to compare Seneca's *Thyestes*,[2] a gruesome play on the fiendish revenge wrought by Atreus upon his ambitious and adulterous brother Thyestes. But some parts at least of this dark story touching the accursed house of Pelops, son of Tantalus, had been dramatised by Sophocles and Euripides in plays entitled *Thyestes*. It was a common theme for Roman writers. Three at least had handled it before Seneca: Ennius in his *Thyestes*; Accius in his *Atreus*, containing the cynical words *oderint dum metuant*; and, more famous still, Horace's contemporary Varius in his *Thyestes*, which was praised by Quintilian as worthy to be set beside any of the Greek tragedies.[3] Whether the earlier Latin plays influenced Seneca or not, it is barely conceivable that he should have missed reading Varius. But even after Seneca the subject continued to attract. Under Vespasian, Curiatius Maternus composed a *Thyestes* as he did a *Medea*, and in the *Dialogus de Oratoribus* is rallied by Aper for wasting his time on such material. Presumably the Ligurinus addressed in Martial III. 45, and certainly the Bassus twitted by him in V. 53, had handled the theme of Thyestes.

Occasional brilliance in expression and occasional loftiness in thought fail to outweigh those bombastic utterances and those innovations in incident or character-drawing which rob the *Hercules Oetaeus* of the delicacy exhibited by Sophocles in the *Trachiniae*. As we have it, patched by Seneca himself or another,[4] it runs to a length of almost 2,000 lines

---

[1] Strauss, *op. cit.*, esp. pp. 44–57.

[2] P. J. Enk's article entitled 'Roman Tragedy' in *Neophilologus* xli (1957) p. 282 ff. contains (291–304) an interesting analysis and study of the *Thyestes*. Enk considers it one of Seneca's best works.   [3] *Inst. Or.* X. i. 98.

[4] Leo considers it in part spurious, see his edn. of Sen.'s *Trag.*, vol. i, 1878, p. 74; *cf.* W. C. Summers, *C.R.* xix (1905) p. 40. E. Ackermann maintains the genuineness of the whole, 'De Senecae Hercule Oetaeo,' *Philol.* Suppbd. x (1907) pp. 323–428; *cf.* his 'Der leidende Hercules des S.,' *Rh.M.* lxvii (1912) pp. 425–471.

– over 700 more than there are in Sophocles's play. In particular, the character of Deianira has suffered under Roman hands. From a heroine who was in the beginning tenderly attracted with Hellenic sweetness towards the captive Iole, and who was only by degrees tempted into jealousy, she is transformed by Seneca into one who hates at first sight – 'like to one maddened and with lowering gaze,' in her uncontrollable anger 'a tigress' or 'a Maenad,'[1] full of malevolence towards rival and husband. It is impossible to give to Seneca's Deianira the sympathy felt for the broken-hearted wife in Sophocles when she realises too late that the promised love-charm must mean death to Hercules. Other additions are the introduction of the hero's mother, Alcmena, to bewail his sufferings, and the incorporation into the play of his deification at the burning pyre on the summit of Oeta. There are, besides, signs that Seneca drew from Ovid's *Heroides* and *Metamorphoses*.[2]

Even the brief glances here directed at Seneca's deviations from well-known Greek originals serve to suggest many of his characteristics. His affinity with Euripides already indicated is significant. In truth, Seneca may be said to have, in great measure, although with inferior dramatic genius, pursued the path along which Euripides led. There was much to link together those two spirits, separated though they were by four centuries. There was above all a common interest in speculative philosophy and in live humanity. Already in Euripides there is the same craving after variety and effect, betrayed in situations intended to be telling, in pathetic or even harrowing detail, in picturesque descriptions, in smart argument, in sententious reflections. Here, if in any field, Seneca's rhetorical training equipped him. Even when he breaks away from Euripides, he is but following his example in the quest of variety. The more he changes, the more he imitates. It would, therefore, be difficult to overrate the Euripidean influence upon him, and this should be remembered in any estimate of Senecan influence upon the literature of the Renaissance. On the other hand, while historically carrying on a late development in Greek drama, Seneca is the child of his own age, imbued with Latin rhetoric, and capable of using it alike with imposing and with futile effect. It cannot be contested that in his free treatment of borrowed material he leaves his individual impress for good or bad upon his plays. There is a Senecan ring, for which he must himself accept credit or discredit, in his curtailment or expansion of plots, his elaboration of descriptions, his choice of impressive dramatic moments, and in that aim at heightened colour which is betrayed by his fondness for the weird, for ghosts, for incantations, and by his introduction of death as an integral part of the action.

His faults lie on the surface. Mythological conventionality in plots which were already, despite variations, fully exhausted in Greece;

---

[1] *Herc. Oet.* 237–253.
[2] Schreiner, *op. cit.* p. 9.

feebleness of moral significance; monotony of character;[1] lack of nature's infinite variety and lack of fidelity to much of the human nature selected for portrayal – such defects hinder the plays from powerfully enchaining the interest. The positive influence of rhetoric too is responsible for many far-fetched dialogues, high-flown declamations, and pedantic recitals. Seneca's Medea may be regarded as an epitome of his method. Barbaric though she is by hypothesis, she is yet in Seneca too little a woman and too much a sorceress: we miss the more natural evolution of character given in Euripides: from the outset her fury is rhetoric, and, while we loathe the craven ingratitude of Jason, her wrongs fail to move us fully, because her transports of insane hatred are demonstrably manufactured. Medea can pause to weigh her anger mythologically:

> What Scylla, what Charybdis swallowing
> Italian or Sicilian tides, or what
> Mount Aetna o'er a gasping Titan poised,
> Shall boil with threats like mine?[2]

Mythology is one of Seneca's besetting perils. Jason is extravagantly praised as handsomer than Bacchus or Apollo;[3] and the choric song praying that he may never be a victim of misfortune like his Argonautic comrades is too learnedly allusive,[4] though not so irrelevant as the chorus upon the labours of Hercules which follows the tardy and brief appearance of Agamemnon in the play bearing his name. One mythological group of which Seneca never can have enough is that of the familiar sufferers of punishment in Hades – Ixion, Sisyphus, Tantalus and Tityos: mentioned in the *Medea* without Tityos, they recur in at least four other plays, and are taken over for literary ornament by the author of the *Octauia*.[5] This may be a little tiresome, but nothing to the dreary boredom which reigns over long speeches like Medea's catalogue of the charms needed for her murderous purposes, in which the author is determined that his acquaintance with ancient geography and legend shall be unmistakable. Some such over-elaboration, some such

---

[1] These three points are taken up by Enk (*op. cit.*). On mythological conventionality he says: 'The Greek matter is undoubtedly the substratum, but that substratum is permeated by stoic ethic-psychological ideas and by a Roman pathos of suffering and willingness to die, which was the outcome of what severely tried humanity went through and experienced under Caligula, Claudius and Nero.' Against feebleness of moral significance must be set pp. 214–215 *infra* (on Stoicism in the tragedies). Enk finds strong moral significance in the Thyestes: *e.g.* the long-term consequences of evil: in the first scene 'Megaera compels Tantalus, against his will, to a disastrous deed; here we see clearly before us the meaning of this philosophic tragedy. When the spirit of evil, the will to do evil, has polluted a generation, the evil spreads further.' On monotony of character Enk argues that such a criticism does not take into account psychological changes, *e.g.* in Phaedra and Medea.
[2] *Med.* 408–410.
[3] *Med.* 82 *sqq.*
[4] *Med.* 607–669.
[5] *Med.* 744–747; *H.F.* 750–756; *Phaed.* 1230–1237; *Agam.* 15–21; *Thy.* 1–12; *Oct.* 619–623.

inability to tell a plain and simple tale, explains the account, too ludicrous to be pathetic, of the piecing together of the mutilated remains of
Hippolytus as if they were a jigsaw puzzle:

> CHORUS. The scattered limbs of that torn frame do thou,
> His sire, in order set, and straggling parts
> Put duly back; here for his strong right hand
> Is place; here set the left, skilled guide of reins;
> Of his left flank I recognise the marks.
> How great a part is missing for our tears!

> THESEUS. My nervous hands, be firm for task of woe:
> Be dry, my cheeks, and stay the flowing tear,
> The while a father portions to his son
> His limbs and makes a body. What is this –
> Shapeless and ugly, maimed with many a gash?
> What piece of thee, I know not: yet 'tis thine.
> Here put it – not in place, but where there's room.[1]

It is a dangerous realism which produces unintentional comicalities. What
shall we say about the ghost of Thyestes who, because during his life
he had been served with the hideous meal of his slaughtered children,
could grotesquely claim to be 'full of three sons buried in me?'[2] No less
peculiar is the chorus on the universal sway of love which reaches the
climax of absurdity among enamoured whales and elephants:

> Love holds the raving sea's leviathan,
> Love holds the Lucan kine.[3]

A similar desire to be at once literal and smart leads to the silliness of
Hercules's words on recovering his wits after he has slain his family:
'I have lost all,' he cries, 'lost soul, arms, honour, wife, children,
strength – and madness too!'[4] A deeper sense of humour would have
made Seneca more tragic. Further, more self-criticism in the light of
common sense would have spared us much of what fatigues us in him –
the pedantry, the senseless bombast,[5] the epigrams which so inevitably
come, no matter who is speaking; for a nurse will talk like a manual of
rhetoric or like Seneca the moralist.[6] When Phaedra's nurse sagely

---

[1] *Phaed.* 1256 *sqq.* P. J. Enk (*Neophilologus* xli (1957) pp. 304–305) defends
Seneca on the ground that it was a religious duty to piece together the mutilated
body for burial and that the dramatist would be expected to portray or describe
this action. But need Seneca have entered into such realistic detail?

[2] *Agam.* 26–27.

[3] *Phaed.* 350–351:
> 'Amat insani belua ponti
> Lucaeque boues.'

[4] *H.F.* 1259–1261.

[5] *E.g. Phoen.* 313–319.

[6] *E.g. Phaed.* 132–135. There are many *sententiae* in her speech of remon-
strance, 129–177. The nurse in Euripides's *Hippolytus* is similarly philosophical
(Eur. *Hipp.* 190–198, 252, 447–450). Euripides was criticised by Aristophanes
(*Frogs* 948–950) for making everyone of whatever station equally eloquent.

reflects on love-madness and on inordinate desire as the companion of high estate, she adorns her remarks about luxury with semi-proverbial wisdom, and proceeds, through a contrasted picture:

> Why dwelleth hallowed love in lowly homes?

to her epigrammatic conclusion

> Excessive power seeks power beyond its power.[1]

As in set speech or soliloquy, so too in dialogue, there is displayed an allied and wonderful cleverness, but it is preternatural. The reader is not captured, as he should be, by the dramatic illusion: he never quite forgets that beings of real flesh and blood are not so ingenious in tragic situations. He is, besides, positively wearied with Ovidian elaboration of the same picture by fresh strokes, or choral platitudes ringing changes on the same idea.[2]

Yet all is not exaggeration in sentiment and style. When the worst has been urged against Seneca, there remain speeches that are spirited, descriptions that are effective, and thoughts that are memorable. The style is in general lucid, and, if epigrammatic, is founded on pure Latin and on harmonious versification. Perhaps no better example of the dramatic speech in Seneca can be given than that from the *Troades* in which Agamemnon pleads against the proposed sacrifice of the Trojan maiden Polyxena at Achilles's tomb. The arguments, put with clearness and vigour, are characteristically fortified by *sententiae* and antitheses:

> Why stain with murder foul the noble shade
> Of that illustrious chief? First shouldst thou learn
> What victor ought to do, what vanquished bear.
> None keeps a sway of violence for long:
> 'Tis self-restraint endures. The higher Chance
> Hath raised and magnified the power of man,
> The more 'tis fitting he should curb his joy
> And quake at chequered circumstance, afraid
> Of gods too kind. Conquest hath taught me how
> A moment ruins greatness. And doth Troy
> Swell us with over-daring pride? We Greeks
> Stand on the spot Troy fell from. Once, I own,
> Self-willed I bore my kingship haughtily.
> But Fortune's smile, in others cause belike
> For pride, hath tamed in me such arrogance.
> Thou, Priam, mak'st me proud – but frightened too! . . .
> I will confess (thy pardon, Argive land,
> For these my words!) tho' wishing Phrygian foes

---

[1] *Phaed.* 211: 'cur sancta paruis habitat in tectis Venus?'
    215: 'quod non potest uult posse qui nimium potest.'

[2] *E.g.* conception of a tranquil sea, expressed three times over in *Tro.* 199–203; or notion of the abasement of the proud repeated again and again, *Agam.* 79–107.

Mastered and crushed, yet ruin, that hath laid
Their town in dust, I fain had warded off . . .
Enough, and more, of penalty is ta'en.
That now a royal maid should fall, a gift
Given to a tomb, and with her blood bedew
Dead ashes, yea, that crime so hideous
Be called a marriage, I will ne'er allow.
On Agamemnon comes the guilt of all.
Who stops not crime, tho' able, orders it.[1]

A few other illustrations chosen from the same play are the more appropriate because nowhere so much as in the *Troades* does he hold his own in rivalry with his Greek sources. It is characteristic that the agonised mother, Andromache, concealing her boy in her husband's sepulchre with the hope of eluding the murderous foe, should make the antithetic point:

If fate helps misery, here is escape:
If fate deny thee life, here is thy tomb.[2]

There is plausible rhetoric in the alliterative excuse which Helen proffers for luring Polyxena into an expectation of marriage when she is really to be executed:

Death without dread of death is welcome death;[3]

[1] *Tro.* 255 *sqq.*:
'Quid caede dira nobiles clari ducis
Aspergis umbras? noscere hoc primum decet,
Quid facere uictor debeat, uictus pati.
Violenta nemo imperia continuit diu,
Moderata durant; quoque Fortuna altius
Euexit ac leuauit humanas opes,
Hoc se magis supprimere felicem decet
Variosque casus tremere metuentem deos
Nimium fauentes, magna momento obrui
Vincendo didici. Troia nos tumidos facit
Nimium ac feroces? stamus hoc Danai loco
Vnde illa cecidit. fateor, aliquando impotens
Regno ac superbus altius memet tuli;
Sed fregit illos spiritus haec quae dare
Potuisset aliis causa, Fortunae fauor.
Tu me superbum, Priame, tu timidum facis! . . .
Equidem fatebor (pace dixisse hoc tua,
Argiua tellus, liceat) affligi Phrygas
Vincique uolui: ruere et aequari solo
Vtinam arcuissem . . . exactum satis
Poenarum et ultra est. regia ut uirgo occidat
Tumuloque donum detur et cineres riget
Et facinus atrox caedis ut thalamos uocent
Non patiar. in me culpa cunctorum redit:
Qui non uetat peccare, cum possit, iubet.'

[2] *Tro.* 510–512:
'Fata si miseros iuuant,
Habes salutem; fata si uitam negant,
Habes sepulchrum.'

[3] *Tro.* 869: 'Optanda mors est sine metu mortis mori.'

and Helen's own plea for her guilty self is a clever appeal suggesting that she was more sinned against than sinning:

> Was I the cause of wars and all the wreck
> That came on Troy? . . .
> Yet if triumphant Aphrodite gave
> Helen to be a guerdon to her judge,
> Then pity that poor prey;[1]

nor does one lightly forget the single utterance by the doomed boy – *miserere, mater*.[2] One wonders, too, whether Seneca was thinking of his own almost miraculous rescue from Caligula's death-warrant when he declared:

> This cause alone hath fended many a man
> From doom – belief that he was dead.[3]

Another dramatic feature often dexterously managed consists of the thrust-and-parry strokes in single lines – the Greek *stichomythia*. A suitable example comes from the passage where the nurse urges Medea to drop her daring resolution:

> MEDEA. Fortune doth dread the brave: cowards she quells.
> NURSE. Courage that finds its hour must win applause.
> M. Never can courage fail to find its hour.
> N. For ruined cause no hope reveals a way.
> M. With naught to hope, of naught should one despair.
> N. Thy Colchians are gone; thy lord is false;
>   Of thy resources naught is left to thee.
> M. Yet is MEDEA left: in her thou hast
>   Sea, land, sword, fire and gods with thunder-flame!
> N. Beware the king!
> M.   My father was a king.
> N. Fear'st thou not arms?
> M.   Not though from earth they rise.
> N. 'Tis death!
> M.   I wish it.
> N.   Flee!
> M.   Flight I've forsworn.[4]

An allied neatness of expression, not uncommonly strengthened by antithesis, marks the sententious epigrams found in isolated verses throughout. The following are a few from three plays:[5]

---

[1] *Tro.* 917–922.
[2] *Tro.* 792.
[3] *Tro.* 489:   'Haec causa multos una ab interitu arcuit,
          Credi perisse.'
[4] *Med.* 159 *sqq.*
[5] *Agam.* 115: 'Per scelera semper sceleribus tutum est iter.'
       130: 'Quod ratio non quit saepe sanauit mora.'
       144: 'Vbi animus errat, optimum est casum sequi.'
       259: 'Nec regna socium ferre nec taedae sciunt.'

Crime ever finds its safest path through crime.
What reason cannot, oft delay hath cured.
Best follow hazard when the mind's at fault.
Nor throne nor bridal bed brooks rivalry.
Too late to be on guard in peril's hour.
To wish for healing is the half of health.
Success gives certain crimes the stamp of right.
Light pangs are eloquent: deep pangs are dumb.

Sometimes the whole of a character's attitude in a given dramatic situation is summed up in a single line, as in Medea's words,

My crime-won home I must in crime forsake,

or her appeal to Jason later in the play,

Hold thou her sinless who has sinned for thee![1]

Compared with such a plethora of ingenious epigram, the flights into poetry are rare. Yet Seneca's eye was not closed to nature. He paints daybreak in its colour and its human significance:

Dawn sprinkles red on thorny brake
And Phoebus' sister doth forsake
            Till night the sky:
Hard toil uprises and doth wake
A world of cares and housefolk make
            Their work to ply.[2]

Some instinct, too, as of a seer, may have inspired his well-known prophecy:

Late in the years an age will dawn
   When Ocean must all things unseal,
And earth lie ope like one great lawn,
   When Tethys must new worlds reveal
   And Thule be Earth's End no more.[3]

  Thy.   487: 'Serum est cauendi tempus in mediis malis.'
  Phaed. 249: 'Pars sanitatis uelle sanari fuit.'
           598: 'Honesta quaedam scelera successus facit.'
           607: 'Curae leues loquuntur, ingentes stupent.'
[1] *Med.*   55: 'Quae scelere parta est, scelere linquenda est domus.'
          503: 'Tibi innocens sit quisquis est pro te nocens.'
[2] *H.F.* 135–138: 'Aspersa die dumeta rubent
                Phoebique fugit reditura soror.
                Labor exoritur durus et omnes
                Agitat curas aperitque domos.'
[3] *Med.* 375–379: 'Venient annis saecula seris
                Quibus Oceanus uincula rerum
                Laxet et ingens pateat tellus
                Tethysque nouos detegat orbes
                Nec sit terris ultima Thule.'

In view of the doubt sometimes needlessly cast upon Seneca's authorship of these dramas, it is of importance to note the strong tincture of philosophic thought which colours many of the speeches and choral odes. The *Troades* presents us with a chant on the doctrine of utter annihilation:

> Can it be truth that we utterly die?
> Is there no part of us left, when the soul
> At the final breath-flicker soars into the air,
> Mingling with cloudland so soon as the torch
> Lays fingers of fire on the corpse lying bare? . . .
> After our death there is naught. Death is naught;
> The mere finishing goal of a race quickly run. . . .
> The way into Hell and the cruel King's realm
> And Cerberus guarding the Perilous Gate
> Are idlest of gossip and meaningless words –
> A fable that sounds like a feverish dream.
> Dost thou ask where thou liest when death sets thee free?
> Thou shalt lie where the things lie that have not been born.[1]

A familiar Stoic dogma suggested the lines upon true kingship in the *Thyestes*:

> Treasures do not a monarch make,
> Nor garb of Tyrian hue,
> Nor diadem on royal brow,
> Nor portals bright with gold.
> A king is whoso quelleth fear
> And cursèd guilt of heart,
> Who mid ambition's wild caprice
> And mid the wayward cheers
> Of hot-head mob abides unmoved;

and a little later the sage's serenity is limned:

> Set in security of place,
> He vieweth all beneath:
> With a will he meets his fate
> Nor murmureth to die.[2]

Similarly Stoic are the notions of freedom, of equality with monarch and with God, and of the right to abandon life at will, which are propounded in the *Agamemnon*:

---

[1] *Tro.* 378–381, 397–398, 402–408; esp. 397–8 and 405–8:
> 'Post mortem nihil est ipsaque mors nihil;
> Velocis spatii meta nouissima. . . .
> Rumores uacui uerbaque inania
> Et par sollicito fabula somnio.
> Quaeris quo iaceas post obitum loco?
> Quo non nata iacent.'

[2] *Thy.* 344 *sqq.*

All slavish bonds he'll burst in twain
Who can capricious gods disdain,
Who on black Acheron's countenance
And on the Stygian gloom can glance
Untouched by gloom himself, who dares
To fix the close of earthly cares.
Peer of a king – of gods, is he.
Know how to die and so be free![1]

It is this creed of the open door leading out of life on which Oedipus
harps in the *Phoenissae*[2] and which the guilty queen proclaims in the
Phaedra,

Death ne'er can fail the man who wills to die.[3]

As we should expect, it is stated in the prose works[4] of Seneca, and so
brings him into touch with contemporary history; for it is but the
theoretical formulation of that right to suicide which many of the Roman
Stoics in opposition during the darkest days of imperial tyranny not only
claimed but exercised.

While, however, much of the philosophic colour in the plays reflects
their author's Stoicism, Seneca is dramatist enough to introduce non-
Stoic views also. He allows, for instance, the chorus in the *Phaedra* to
adopt an Epicurean and pessimistic attitude. It comes in an ode addressed
to Nature and to 'Olympus's Lord,' beseeching a solution to one of the
riddles of the universe – why it is that external nature is so regularly
controlled by law, whereas the Ruler of all things appears to be indifferent to man, and human affairs appear to be a chaotic realm of
chance.[5]

Philosophy, whether Stoic or not, is, after all, one of the personal
notes imported by Seneca into his adaptations from Greek drama. Like
his yet more pervasive rhetoric, it is of Roman cast, and, if anachronistic
in its Hellenic environment, it is but an additional sign of his independence of his originals. He is not at pains to avoid national colour: and thus,
reckless of inconsistency, he puts into the mouth of Mycenaean elders
certain terms redolent of Roman political history; turns the thought of a

---

[1] *Agam.* 605–611:

> 'Perrumpet omne seruitium
> Contemptor leuium deorum,
> Qui uoltus Acherontis atri,
> Qui Styga tristem non tristis uidet
> Audetque uitae ponere finem.
> Par ille regi, par superis erit.
> O quam miserum est nescire mori!'

[2] *E.g. Phoen.* 89–103, 146, 151–153.
[3] *Phaed.* 878: 'mori uolenti desse mors numquam potest.'
[4] *E.g. Ep.* xii. 10, where 'patent undique ad libertatem uiae multae, breues,
faciles' significantly resembles *Phoen.* 153, 'mille ad hanc (*sc.* mortem) aditus
patent'; xiii. 14, lviii. 36. Seneca disapproved of a merely capricious suicide,
Ep. xxiv. 25, xxx. 15.
[5] *Phaed.* 972–988.

Theban chorus towards the *clientes* and *patroni* of Rome, and, later in
the same play, towards a Roman rather than a Greek holiday; represents
the ex-king of Thebes as quoting, like a *paterfamilias*, his power of life
and death;[1] and – more surprising still – not merely fuses into a Corinthian marriage-hymn elements in the bantering Fescennine spirit
('rarely against our lords is license legalised'), but actually, a few lines
further on, where the metre has become hexameter, names that familiar
feature of a wedding at Rome:

> Let glib Fescennine hurl its merry gibes.[2]

Another national trait lies in his debt to Latin predecessors. This is
especially observable in his relation to Virgil and Ovid. To the former
he owes much in language and in idea: one cannot, for example, read
Theseus's description in the *Hercules Furens*[3] of his descent into the
Lower World, nor Andromache's account in the *Troades*[4] of her vision
of the dead Hector, without noticing reminiscences of *Aeneid* VI in the
one case and of *Aeneid* II in the other. Ovid, to whose rhetorical abilities
Seneca's early attention must have been directed by his father, is the
ultimate inspirer of many of his epigrams and mannerisms as well as
of some of his metrical characteristics. Seneca, however, though a
borrower in most fields, remained in part original and inventive. This
holds good of his choice of words. Such compounds as *luctificus* and
fatidicus he would, like other poets of his century, inherit from Virgil;[5]
and similarly such words as *securiger* and *multifidus* from Ovid. But some
compounds it would be hard to find in other authors, *e.g. incestificus*
and *superbificus*, and *nidificus* too, although the verb *nidificare* rises to
the mind in connexion with a famous tale of Virgil's readiness in verse-
making. *Pacificus*, used by Cicero once, Seneca seems to have originated
in verse and bequeathed through his nephew and Martial for its most
familiar use in the Vulgate version of the Beatitudes.

The iambic trimeter used by Seneca for dramatic speeches and dialogue is in his hands a finished line more akin to that of Greek tragedy
than to the rugged senarius of the oldest Latin dramas. Like the Augustans, and in all likelihood under the influence of Ovid's lost *Medea*, he
would regard the verses of Ennius, Pacuvius and Accius as uncouth.
Seneca, for instance, does not imitate the heavy Ennian line with its
spondees in second and fourth feet, and at least before a cretic ending
shows a preference for elision. But the general effect is a polished monotony, towards which contributing factors are scarcity of the more subtle

---

[1] *Thy.* 396–400 ('Quiritibus . . . plebeius'); *H.F.* 164, 839; *Phoen.* 103
('ius uitae ac necis').
[2] *Med.* 109: 'rara est in dominos iusta licentia,'
and 113: 'festa dicax fundat conuicia fescenninus.'
[3] *H.F.* 650–829.   [4] *Tro.* 442–491.
[5] Before Virgil *luctificus* was used in Cicero's poetry, and *fatidicus* in Varro
(*De L.L.*) and Cicero's prose.

elisions, want of varied pauses, and a pronounced liking for either spondee or anapaest in the fifth foot. According to Lucian Müller, in all Seneca there are only six examples of a double iambic ending to a line,[1] and statistics indicate that the anapaest in the fifth place, as a variant for the spondee, occurs rather oftener than once in every five lines. Seneca's iambic trimeter is at its neatest, as it is at its sagest, in the *stichomythia* of the dialogue. When in long speeches the sense too often closes with the end of each line, the sharp ring which is suitable in *stichomythia* becomes mere jerkiness. His trimeter – indeed the Latin trimeter in general – never attains the charm which can be illustrated from any Greek tragedy. Herein it contrasts with the Latin hexameter, which possesses a beauty and nobility rivalling any effect achieved in Greek. Trochaic tetrameter is used in three passages,[2] amounting to a total of 34 lines, based rather on the Greek model than on early Latin septenarii. But one departure is the admission of a dactyl in the sixth foot – a practice metrically analogous to the favour shown for an anapaest in the fifth foot of an iambic trimeter. Of choral measures he employs a considerable variety, some being feeble imitations of, others unfortunate departures from, Horace. The mixed metres in the *Agamemnon* and *Oedipus*[3] are such failures that some, forgetting how much of an experimenter Seneca was in dramatic composition, have denied that he wrote those plays. The sum of the matter is that the choruses, lacking strophic arrangement and often dull in theme, suffer from the wearisome continuance of the same line without the break of a shorter closing one. Long passages in Sapphics without an Adonic, or in Asclepiads without a Glyconic, or in anapaestic dimeter without a monometer, almost madden the reader because of their sameness; and, unluckily, while Seneca declines to afford the relief of a Glyconic among longer Asclepiads, he has no qualms about perpetrating a run of Glyconics for seventy or eighty lines on end.

Time, however, has not judged Seneca by the monotony of his choral metres. In literature it is not too much to say that he has been a world-wide influence; for without him the history of the drama in most countries would have run an entirely altered course. By the fourteenth century his influence upon writers in Italy was evident – on Mussato, for example, whose iambic tragedy *Ecerinis* was a literary triumph in 1314 or 1315.[4] Seneca's historical function was to be a link between the incipient modern drama and Hellenism, which could not be directly accessible, or indeed intelligible, so long as Greek study was in its infancy. As a force at the birth of modern drama he completely eclipsed

---

[1] They are all cases of words of four syllables, like *nepotibus, Med.* 512. W. R. Hardie, *Res Metrica*, 1920, p. 83, adds from *H.F.* 20 *nuribus impiis*, if that is the right reading.

[2] *Med.* 740–751; *Oed.* 223–232; *Phaed.* 1201–1212.

[3] Butler, *Post-Aug. P.* pp. 41–42, 71.

[4] R. Ellis, *Catullus in XIVth Cent.*, Oxf. 1905, pp. 10–11.

the other dramatists of antiquity: Sophocles counted for very little, Aeschylus for less, and Euripides mainly for as much of his spirit as operated through Seneca. When, therefore, Latin plays gave place to Italian tragedy in Cammelli's *Filostrato e Panfila*, Seneca was reckoned an appropriate personage to pronounce the prologue. At the period of the revival of learning, his plays had become renowned over Europe – Scaliger, it should be noted, rated him above Euripides – and his authority, except for Trissino's preference in favour of Greek models, was riveted on Italy. In France it was the Latin plays which Buchanan and Muret wrote for their scholars to act that introduced the Senecan model and pointed the way towards the French tragedy of the Pléiade. In contrast to comedy, over which Terence's influence did not retain its hold, French tragedy continued for three centuries to follow the foreign classical exemplar with the strictness observable in Corneille and Racine.

The immense popularity of Seneca in England during the sixteenth century is illustrated by the production of his *Troades* at Trinity College, Cambridge, in 1551–52, as well as by frequent translation and frequent imitation. A reason is easily found. English playwrights, confronted with the task of shaping the amorphous native drama, saw in his plays orderly patterns to suit their purpose. Here was a type of drama which was a descendant of the ancient Greek, with still less action than in the Greek, with choruses even more divorced from the action, but conveniently demarcating the play into definite episodes or acts; while, in spirit, this type of drama exhibited what was for the Elizabethan playgoer an acceptable store of moral reflections and harrowing situations. One could accordingly combine the satisfaction of hearing good talk about rectitude one moment, and of revelling in horrors the next. Morality could be blended with melodrama. The leaven worked rapidly after Heywood began a series of translations of Seneca's plays in 1559. Our first English tragedy, *Gorboduc*, 1561, is framed on the Senecan model, which had already captured the playwrights of Italy, France, and, in a measure, Germany. The division into five acts and the introduction of choruses (as lyric interludes rather than as integral parts in the drama) show Seneca's influence upon the form of such plays as *Gorboduc* and *The Misfortunes of Arthur*. Dramas, however, that can be called fairly and fully Senecan are not numerous in English; for the drama in England was turned into a freer course by Marlowe and Shakespeare, as it was in Spain by Lope de Vega and Calderon. The more lasting influence of Seneca on drama in France is largely attributable to the closer affinity between the Senecan and the French taste for rhetorical finish. But even where the model was not closely followed in England, the spirit of Seneca was operative; for it should be realised that it acted on the romantic drama no less than on the classical.

Thus, stock characters like the nurse, the ghost, the tyrant – each of

them borrowed from Greek by Seneca, but each slightly modified –
are handed on to the English drama. The nurse is a feature in five of the
ten plays which Elizabethans ascribed to Seneca;[1] in a sixth, *Thyestes*,
there is an attendant on Atreus who hears his secrets and gives advice,
while in a seventh, *Oedipus*, the blind Teiresias's daughter, Manto,
fills the office of trusted attendant on her father, like Antigone in the
Phoenissae. Such figures are prototypes of the nurse in *Romeo and Juliet*
and the confidante of the French stage. Thyestes's ghost designed in the
Agamemnon to personify a Spirit of Revenge is the ancestor of the murdered Andrea's ghost in Kyd's *Spanish Tragedie* and the ghost of the
hero's father in *Hamlet*. The ruthless Lycus in *Hercules Furens*, Medea
resolute in her contemplated barbarity, and Atreus openly avowing
villainy, are types of character that descend to Elizabethan literature –
to Barabas in Marlow's *Jew of Malta*, to Lorenzo in Kyd's *Spanish
Tragedie*, and to 'Crookback the Tyrant' in Shakespeare's *Richard III*.
There is indeed much that is Senecan – as if we were to fancy that some
old Spanish traits in Seneca were being revived – in *The Spanish
Tragedie*, a ghastly medley of blood and thunder, ghosts and horrors.
Its lurid description of the road to hell is after the manner of Seneca's
eeriest passages. This aspect is handed on to plays like *Titus Andronicus*,
and persists in Webster's *Duchess of Malfi* and *The White Devil*.
Richard III, too, has many Senecan lineaments besides that already
mentioned. One of the tragedies of blood, it has a multiplicity of ghosts:
it has even a Senecan tendency to that rant from which Shakespeare
did much to rescue drama; while the old tones of repartee, subtly
developed in Athenian tragedy and transmitted through Seneca to the
moderns, ring out in the dialogue between Richard and the Queen
Elizabeth in Act IV, Scene iv.

This *stichomythia* is the chief feature common to the popular playwrights of Shakespearean times and an author who represents a widely
divergent line of Senecan tradition – namely, Sir William Alexander,
Earl of Stirling. He followed the more classical Seneca, the Seneca of
argument, description and apophthegm. Tyrannical wickedness and
inflated bombast make room in his plays for discussions and reflections.
When Ben Jonson's *Sejanus* and *Catiline* had failed to keep Seneca on
the boards of the playhouse, scholars turned to write dramas, as Seneca
himself had done, for the study. Independent of popular taste, they were
free to copy the quieter, the less wildly romantic, side of Seneca, to
restore the chorus, to banish action, and create monuments of unreadable dullness. Works, however, like Alexander's are interesting contrasts to such dramas of the theatre as displayed Seneca's influence in
almost hypertrophied vitality.

---

[1] *E.g.* Thos. Heywood and others, *Seneca: His Tenne Tragedies*, Lond. 1581.
(The *Octauia* is included, wrongly.)

DRAMA OF THE AGE

The *Octauia*, in 983 lines, is the one surviving Roman historical drama. We have only more or less fragmentary traces of eleven other *praetextae* – Naevius's *Clastidium* and *Romulus*, Ennius's *Ambracia* and *Sabinae* (if we can be sure these two were plays), Pacuvius's *Paulus*, Accius's *Brutus* and *Decius*, Cornelius Balbus's *Iter*, and, under the Empire, the *Aeneas* of Pomponius Secundus and the *Domitius* and *Cato* of Curiatius Maternus. It is difficult to see why the traditional ascription of the *Octauia* to Seneca ever deceived anyone. That Seneca should have introduced himself on the stage is barely credible; but that he, or anyone, should, during Nero's lifetime, have ventured to portray the emperor as a heartless monster[1] to mother and wife, as well as a vindictive tyrant to his people, is absolutely incredible. It has long been recognised, too, that the dramatic prophecy of Nero's doom is too circumstantially accurate to have been composed till after the event in A.D. 68; and Seneca had died three years before. The play no doubt recalls his manner. It has a ghost: it has a couple of nurses: it has, like the *Agamemnon* and *Hercules Oetaeus*, a couple of choruses: but its doleful repetitions are too many and its epigrams too few for Seneca. Also, the metre, in spite of certain similarities, such as the liking for an anapaest in the fifth foot, shows significant differences; for example, though Seneca was not so careful as the Greek dramatists in linking lines together, he did not allow hiatus and a *syllaba anceps* at the close of lines nearly so often as the author of the *Octauia*. This is a further reason, if further reason be needed, for repudiating Seneca's authorship.[2]

Many conjectures have been made about the date of its composition, which has been put arbitrarily as late as the fourth century, not to speak of the absurd notion that the play was invented ten centuries later. The case for a date early in Domitian's reign has been argued solemnly[3] with little regard to the likelihood of such a publication under such an emperor. So too critics have cast around for an author and lighted upon Maternus, who, we know, wrote *praetextae*. These guesses take us nowhere. The most that can be said is that the author is unknown, but that he plainly studied Seneca; and that an extremely probable, because suitable, date is one of the years immediately succeeding Nero's fall.[4]

[1] *E.g.* 152, Nero is called 'iuuenis infandi ingeni.'

[2] Hardie, *Res Metr.* p. 67; *cf.* p. 84 n.

[3] G. Nordmeyer, *De Oct. Fab.*, Lpz. 1892. For views on this over-discussed question, see S.H. § 380 and next footnote. *Cf.* also *Lustrum* ii, 1957, pp. 174–189 for survey of 'Octavian' literature 1922–1955.

[4] *Cf.* P. J. Enk's conclusions, in *Mnem.* liv (1926) 'De Octauia Praetexta,' that the play was written not long after Nero's death and by an author well acquainted with Seneca's tragedies. These conclusions are similar to those of L. Herrmann, *Octavie 'tragédie prétexte'*, Paris 1924, that it was written in the reign of Vespasian by one who had been a pupil of Seneca. R. Helm (*Sitzb. Berl.* xvi, 1934, pp. 283–347) produces fresh arguments, largely metrical and stylistic, against the Senecan authorship, and puts the play in Domitian's reign.

The scene is laid in Nero's palace, and the time is A.D. 62. The play opens with a lyric lament by Nero's neglected empress, Octavia, who 'outwails the sea-bred Halcyons' in her grief over the criminal follies of her dead mother Messallina, and over the wickedness shown by her stepmother, Agrippina (now also dead) in poisoning her imperial husband, Claudius, Octavia's father, and in taking Octavia from her betrothed, Silanus, to marry her to young Nero. To these enormities and to the poisoning of Octavia's brother, Britannicus, rightful heir to the throne, the melancholy heroine and her nurse repeat their sombre allusions until they cease to be artistically effective. Nero's barbarity in murdering his mother, mentioned many times and once fully described,[1] and his maltreatment of his wife, leave the unhappy Octavia nothing to hope for but death. On one occasion she is goaded into half a threat, which the nurse, however, unable to take it seriously, answers with scorn:

OCT. Let Nero kill me too, lest I slay *him*!
NURSE. Nature hath not bestowed on thee such strength.
OCT. Pain, hate, grief, wretchedness and woe will serve.
NURSE. Nay, by compliance win thy cruel lord.
OCT. To give me back my brother, foully slain?
NURSE. To be thyself unharmed, and yet restore
      Thy father's tottering house with babes of thine.[2]

The nurse, like her mistress, is versed in mythology and endeavours to console Octavia for Nero's infidelities by relating Jupiter's misdemeanours as Swan or Bull or Golden Shower. The next choral chant recites a rumour that Nero has decided to espouse a new consort, and in the following episode Seneca enters soliloquising on the dangers of prosperity, on his own greater safety as an exile 'amid the cliffs of the Corsican sea,' and on the deterioration of mankind. Nero arrives blustering angrily and issuing orders to his prefect for two executions. Seneca's vain appeal for clemency is succeeded by his equally vain expostulation against the projected marriage with the wanton Poppaea. Nero declares his resolution to make the morrow his wedding-day. On his departure, the ghost of his mother appears in order to symbolise the vengeance that must come, and her speech contains the prophecy of Nero's doom (619–631), on which rests the conviction that the play is later than his death. Another choral ode precedes a scene between Poppaea, distraught by alarming dreams, and her nurse. Then to the chorus of Poppaea's sympathisers enters a messenger reporting a revolt in favour of Octavia. The emperor reappears, breathing merciless fury and

---

However the Senecan authorship has been recently defended by S. Pantzerhielm-Thomas, *Symb. Osl.* 1945; T. H. Sluiter, ed. of *Oct.*, Leiden 1949; B. M. Marti, 'Sen.'s Apocol. and Oct.: A Diptych,' *A.J.P.* 1952, 24 ff. H. Bardon (*Latomus*, 1939, p. 253 ff.) tentatively suggests Lucan as the author.

[1] *Oct.* 310–375.   [2] *Oct.* 174 *sqq.*

determined to revenge himself on Octavia, who in the final scene is
exhibited under an armed guard bound for exile and death. She came
with a wail and she goes with a wail.

Although one cannot withhold sympathy from the victim of Nero's
heartlessness, the many feeble repetitions, the tiresome lamentations, and
a minimum of incident, make the *Octauia* unforgivably dull. Even
Agrippina's ghost is unimpressive. If the reader wonders what business
mythology has in this particular galley, he must remember the Senecan
tradition. But, obviously, mythological lore removes all chance of
making a historical drama realistic. It is grotesque when the nurse
whitewashes Nero by giving a list of Jupiter's lapses from connubial
rectitude, or when Octavia herself, in railing against her wicked husband,
opines that Mother Earth did not produce a worse monster in Typhon.
Instead of all this, one would have liked a historical play to stir the
feelings with abuse of Nero in good set terms and in plain Latin. And
so with pity no less than indignation. If we are to sorrow with Octavia,
she must first (as Horace would remind us) sorrow herself – naturally
too, not uttering the artificial question, 'What nightingale can match
with plaints my tears?'[1] But the incubus of learning is sometimes
historical as well. The chorus take occasion to cite, as instances of the
disastrous results of popular favour, the Gracchi and Livius Drusus,
regretting that present grief prevents them from giving additional
examples – presumably by ransacking historical or rhetorical manuals
like the collection of *exempla* by Valerius Maximus. More perhaps than
any other handicap, such misplaced erudition balks this tragic story in
its intended emotional appeal.

The place occupied in the early Empire by *fabulae salticae*, *mimi*, the
performances of *pantomimi*, and recitations excerpted from standard
tragedies or composed for the occasion, has been already touched upon.
Literary comedy fared no better than literary tragedy: mimes and
Atellan farces had displaced it. The same thing holds good in the next
period as in the Neronian age; such a comedy as the younger Pliny
tells us[2] he heard Vergilius Romanus reading was modelled on classical
lines and stood no chance of winning popularity. The mime, on the
other hand, when it sketched ordinary life, had the spice of realism,
united sometimes to that wisdom of experience which Seneca recognised
as truly philosophic, and which, he suggests, it shared with writers of
tragedy and *togatae*.[3] It is interesting, in this connexion, to note that
Afranius's old *togata* of 'The House on Fire' (*Incendium*) was played in
Nero's time, truth to life doubtless being enhanced by the permission
granted to actors to keep any furniture which they saved from the
flames.[4] The Atellan farce had the additional and dangerous spice of

---

[1] *Oct.* 915–916, and she uses the Greek word ἀηδών.
[2] Plin. *Ep.* VI. xxi. 2.   [3] Sen. *Ep.* viii. 8.   [4] Suet. *Nero* xi.

veiled jest at exalted personages; but Suetonius gives us to understand
that Nero showed surprising indulgence towards offending authors, so
that joking allusions to the deaths of Claudius and Agrippina involved
no more serious penalty than exile.[1]

The variety of public amusements with which serious drama had to
compete may be estimated from several passages in Suetonius's *Life of
Nero*. It was at best but a spurious drama that found its way to the
boards. Nero liked appearing on the stage as a tragic character.[2] The
matricide Orestes, the blinded Oedipus, the mad Hercules were parts
that appealed to him;[3] and it may be inferred that, like Lucan, he wrote
the words to be recited or chanted. The quinquennial contests of the
'Neronia,' even if established from vainglorious motives, proved his
interest in poetry and music, and stimulated production of a kind.
The emperor's final performance on the stage was in an iambic chant
from *Oedipus in Exile*, a theme similar to that of the opening part of
Seneca's *Phoenissae*; in this piece, however, Nero used Greek.[4]

Pomponius Secundus, who had made his *début* as author long before,
as already recorded, lived far into Nero's reign. Whether the riot in the
theatre over his *carmina*[5] in Claudius's reign implies that he merely
wrote verses for actors, or whether he put complete tragedies on the
stage, one cannot say. Curiatius Maternus,[6] a famous orator who renounced public life for poetry and whose house is the scene of Tacitus's
Dialogus, had written his first play in Nero's time. One of his two
praetextae, entitled *Domitius*, was concerned with an ancestor of Nero's
who opposed Julius Caesar and died fighting at Pharsalia. His other
historical play, *Cato*, had just made a great stir in Rome at the time
in which the *Dialogus* was laid, A.D. 74–75. Like Seneca he wrote
tragedies on the Greek subjects of *Medea* and *Thyestes*.

It is clear then that, whether or not complete tragedies continued to
be represented on the stage, tragic poets at least continued to compose,
if only in a dilettante manner. But no real survival of tragedy can be
inferred from the shadowy list of names and titles yielded by allusions
in Juvenal and Martial[7] – *Alcithoe* by Paccius, *Thebae* (or *Thebais*) and
Tereus by Faustus, *Atreus* by Rubrenus Lappa, *Hercules* and *Hecuba*
(or *Troades*) by Scaeva or Scaev(i)us Memor, who belongs to the reign
of Domitian. It is one of literature's little ironies that Memor should be
addressed by Martial as 'the glory of the Roman buskin' (*Romani fama
cothurni*).

---

[1] *Ibid.* xxxix.
[2] *Ibid.* x: 'declamauit saepius publice; recitauit et carmina non modo domi
sed et in theatro.'
[3] *Ibid.* xxi.   [4] *Ibid.* xlvi.
[5] Tac. *Ann.* XI. xiii.   [6] Tac. *Dial.* ii, iii, and xi.
[7] Juv. VII. 12 and 72–73; Mart. XI. ix and x; *cf.* vet. schol. ad Juv. I. 20;
Ribbeck, *T.R.F.* p. 269. It has been previously indicated that Martial connects
Ligurinus and Bassus with a *Thyestes*, p. 206 *supra*.

Chapter V

PERSIUS: STOIC SATIRE

The *Vita* by Valerius Probus – Persius's friends – Cornutus, his
Stoic teacher – The six satires – Sources of Persius – Horatian and
Bionean influences – The charge of obscurity – Vivid pictures –
Other features of his style – His hexameter – Did he assail Nero?
– Varying judgements upon him.

PERSIUS

THE essential facts of the short life of Aulus[1] Persius Flaccus are
preserved in a biography taken from the commentary on the
poet by Valerius Probus.[2] Persius was born at Volaterrae in
Etruria, and lived nearly twenty-eight years, from December, A.D. 34,
to November, 62. Jerome, who felt attracted to his thought, corroborates
both dates on the Abrahamic system of chronology. When about six
years old, the boy lost his father, a man of equestrian rank; and his
mother, who bore the Etruscan name Sisennia, remarried, but lost her
second husband Fusius, a municipal knight, a few years later. It is
recorded of the youth that he was of gentle and modest character, good-
looking, and affectionate to his female relatives, his mother, sister and
aunt. Till he was twelve he was brought up in Etruria; his education
at Rome began in A.D. 46. First he studied literature under the able but
unprincipled Remmius Palaemon, and, even if temperamentally and
morally antipathetic to this famous teacher, Persius would at any rate
learn the technique of poetry in a school where the authors specially
taught included Terence, Horace and Virgil. Later he worked at rhetoric
under Verginius Flavus, whose renown for eloquence earned Nero's
hatred and who was banished at the same time as Musonius Rufus the
Stoic. There is little to support Lehmann's hypothesis[3] that republican
tendencies were conveyed by Verginius to Persius; but at least the
rhetorical method, practised though it apparently was by Verginius
with some modifications, must have influenced Persius through such
features as its search for striking phrases and its introduction of *communes loci*. All the same, Persius had been schoolboy enough to play

---

[1] MSS. give the Etruscan form *Aules*.
[2] Printed in many editions of Persius, *e.g.* Jahn, Owen, Cartault: see Bibl.
[3] H. Lehmann, 'Zur erklär. d. *Sat.* des P.,' *Philol.* vi (1851) p. 432.

truant from rhetorical exercises, which he found unprofitable and dis-
tasteful: a touch of oil might produce an appearance of weak eyes and
enable him to shirk the recitation lesson and so avoid declaiming some
fine dying speech of Cato. Dice or a top might be preferable to the
suasoria.[1]

Among his friends was the lyric poet Caesius Bassus, addressed in his
sixth satire, who became his posthumous editor. He respected like a
father Servilius Nonianus, ex-consul, orator and historian, who one day
by the plaudits of his audience attracted the Emperor Claudius to a
reading which he was giving near the Palatine Hill.[2] Persius's relationship to the younger Arria brought him into touch with her husband, the
Stoic senator Thrasea, whose *Life of Cato* was a source for Plutarch, and
who, though not in active opposition, wore a look of gravity equivalent to
a permanent rebuke for Nero.[3] Neither Thrasea nor Nonianus would
necessarily have inculcated upon Persius hatred of the imperial system,
and yet one may guess that Thrasea's conservatism had its influence on
his sympathies and tastes. He had composed juvenile verses on the death
of the elder Arria;[4] and he mixed in Stoic circles. At sixteen he began a
close and uninterrupted friendship with the Stoic teacher Cornutus,
and through him became acquainted with two Greek philosophers of the
day, Claudius Agathurnus (or Agathemerus) and Petronius Aristocrates,
and with the young poet Lucan, like himself one of Cornutus's pupils.
Lucan's admiration for his friend's talent was enthusiastic: Persius's
writings, he declared, were genuine poetry, and his own mere sportive
pieces (*illa esse uera poemata, sua ludos*). To Seneca, Lucan's uncle,
Persius was not drawn:[5] the courtier's pliant and adaptable Stoicism
evidently did not commend itself to this young devotee. Literature
apart, the most vital influence on Persius came from the intimacy and
instruction of Cornutus,[6] to whose philosophic power his pupil's satires
are the best surviving testimony. Cornutus was also a tragic poet, grammarian and author of a commentary on Virgil. Already, no doubt, suspect as a professor of Stoicism, he was banished for the suggestion that
Nero's projected epic on Roman history would be too long in 400 books.

Affectionate gratitude towards his master is one of the winning traits
in Persius and adds greatly to the human interest of the fifth satire,

[1] *Sat.* III. 44–51.
[2] Plin. *Ep.* I. xiii. 3: Tac. *Ann.* XIV. xix; *Dial.* xxiii.
[3] Suet. *Nero* xxxvii.
[4] The elder Arria was the wife of Caecina Paetus. When he was condemned
to death in A.D. 42, she encouraged his suicide by stabbing herself and handing
him the dagger with the words 'Paete, non dolet'. Plin. *Ep.* III. xvi; Mart. I.
xiii. The younger Arria was their daughter; and, when her husband Thrasea
was condemned in 66, she wanted to emulate her mother; but Thrasea dis-
suaded her. Tac. *Ann.* XVI. xxxiv.
[5] *Vita Persii*: 'Cognouit et Senecam sed non ut caperetur eius ingenio.'
[6] Cornutus: *Cornuti Theol. Graecae Compendium*, C. Lang, Lpz. 1881;
R. Reppe, *De L. Annaeo Cornuto*, Lpz. 1906; F. Villeneuve, *Essai sur Perse*,
pp. 47–102; P. Descharme, *La critique des trad. relig. chez les grecs anciens*, 1905.

I

which is addressed to him. On quitting boyhood, Persius relates he had been welcomed to 'the Socratic bosom' of Cornutus, and had all moral twists straightened by a rule applied with subtle skill:

> What share, sweet friend Cornutus, of my soul
> Thou art, 'tis joy to show. Strike it and test
> With care what part rings true, what is but paint
> And plaster of the tongue. Here would I ask
> A hundred voices to proclaim clear-toned
> Thy firm enlodgement in my bosom's folds,
> And let my words unseal the secret love
> Deep-hid unutterable in my heart . . .
> Just when my way grew puzzling, when, unversed
> In life, my ignorance let nervous thoughts
> Stray down the branching cross-roads, I consigned
> Myself to thee, and thou, Cornutus, tookst
> To thy Socratic breast my tender years.[1]

A few lines later he rejoices in their close union in relaxation and toil:

> With thee I wore away long sunny days
> And with thee culled the early bloom of night
> For banqueting, I can recall; we twain
> Were one in work, with one set time for rest,
> O'er modest board unbending gravity.
> Doubt not hereof – our lives by law ordained
> Accord, both guided by a single star.[2]

Persius died of an ailment of the stomach on his estate about eight miles out of Rome along the Appian Way. Possessed of considerable wealth (2,000,000 sesterces), he bequeathed a collection of books, including 700 volumes by the Stoic Chrysippus, as well as money and silver plate, to Cornutus, who accepted the library but renounced the other legacies in favour of his pupil's relatives. Persius left only a small amount of literary work, for the *Life* remarks that he wrote seldom and slowly (*scriptitauit et raro et tarde*), as might be inferred from his style. His juvenile works included a *praetexta*, a book of travels[3] (if *Hodoeporicon* is the true reading in the *Vita*), and his lines already mentioned on the heroic Arria. All these were, after his death, destroyed by the advice of Cornutus, who made slight corrections on the half-dozen satires before entrusting their publication to Caesius Bassus.

---

[1] V. 22–29, 34–37, reading in 34–35:
> 'Cumque iter ambiguum est et uitae nescius error
> Diducit trepidas ramosa in compita mentes.'

V. 41–46:
> 'Tecum etenim longos memini consumere soles,
> Et tecum primas epulis decerpere noctes. . . .'

[3] These may have been sketches of the nature of Lucilius's *Journey to the Sicilian Straits* or Horace's *Journey to Brundisium*. Lucilius III (Marx); Hor. *Sat.* I. v.

There is much to make Persius an interesting study. He was the first Stoic verse satirist of Rome; he was possessed by a moral earnestness almost preternaturally beyond his years, and died comparatively young; with his one book, as Quintilian remarked,[1] he earned genuine glory; he has throughout the ages attracted some and repelled others; he is undoubtedly difficult to understand, and yet he has exerted a great influence on thinkers.

His six satires amount only to 650 hexameters: the shortest (iv) being 52 lines long, and the longest (v) 191. None but the first, for which it is said he received stimulus from reading Lucilius, can be strictly called a satire: the other five are 'sermons,' rather in the modern than in the Horatian sense. Besides, there have come down fourteen choliambic lines, appearing in some MSS. as a prologue, in others as an epilogue. They may well be neither, but the single piece saved from Persius's other poems – a mock-modest disclaimer of inspiration which need not be taken literally as containing solemn misstatements by the poet about himself.[2]

Satire I, on the right and wrong spirit in current literature, is combined with the important secret (*opertum*) that everybody is an ass (*auriculas asini quis non habet?*) – a jocular offgrowth of the Stoic creed that all but the sage adept are fools. This initial attack on the corruption of literature furnished hints for the first satire of Juvenal. Persius in his imagined dialogue with a friend judges decadent literary taste to be a symptom of moral decay, and this stings him to pungent criticisms upon the foppery and ostentation of public recitations by authors who titillate the inward parts of a depraved audience with their licentious poetry. Private dinner-parties end in listening to insipid trash about a Phyllis or a Hypsipyle – but can a host get honest opinions on his poems from his guests? Heroics are attempted by writers who could not describe a simple rural scene, and there is a mania for archaisms and archaic poets, like Accius and Pacuvius.[3] What is the good of artificial oratory and polished antitheses, if there is a plain charge of theft to meet? And surely the manhood of the old Roman past has vanished when poetry apes nerveless stuff like,

Grim horns they filled with Mimallonean booms.[4]

[1] *Inst. Or.* X. i. 94: 'Multum et uerae gloriae, quamuis uno libro, Persius meruit.'

[2] A. Pretor, *C.R.* xxi (1907) p. 72 ff. argues that the choliambics are a prologue, and, being intended as a blind to safeguard the author against Nero's vengeance for alleged allusions to the emperor, contain deliberate untruths, *e.g.* that the writer has no capacity for authorship and is only half-educated or at least provincial (*semi-paganus*). For further study see A. Cartault, *R.Ph.* 1921, p. 63 ff.; L. Herrmann, *R.E.A.* 1932, p. 259 ff.; and S.H. § 383.

[3] I. 76–78.

[4] I. 99–102: 'Torua Mimalloneis inplerunt cornua bombis,' etc. The lines have been ascribed to Nero, but more probably are Persius's own parodies on the Catullan and pre-Augustan type of poetry favoured by many contemporaries who were court-favourites.

The poet's friend remonstrates: such unpopular truths may win a chilling reception for him in high society. By way of answer, Persius recalls the outspokenness of Lucilius and Horace's winning pleasantries at the expense of human foibles.[1] Is it sacrilege for Persius to mutter the truth and confide his little whispered secret, this joke of his own (*hoc ridere meum*), to the safe-keeping of a hole in the earth – 'All the world's got donkey's ears'? He asks for readers who have drawn an inspiring breath from the masters of the old Greek comedy – Cratinus and Eupolis and the 'Grand Old Man' (*praegrandi sene*) of comic drama, Aristophanes. This satire, then, is a manifesto of literary independence in contrast to the prevailing mode and of censorial independence after the ex mple of Lucilius. The remaining five contain his Stoic message to his generation.

Satire II, on praying aright, is a brief disquisition addressed to a learned friend, Macrinus, on a similar theme to that in Juvenal's tenth Satire. If Persius cannot rival Juvenal's brilliant rhetorical skill and force, he at least surpasses him in the impression which he leaves of moral dignity and almost religious fervour. Condensed and scathing in its denunciation of the immorality and foolishness of petitions brazenly offered to the gods though unfit to be overheard by men, the poem rises to a noble elevation at its close upon the spiritual value of true worship:

> O souls bent earthward, with no heavenly spark,
> What good to take our human thoughts to prayer,
> Judging God's pleasure from this sinful flesh? . . .
> It sins, flesh sins, yet gains by sin; but say,
> Ye priests, what profits gold in holy place?
> As much as maiden's dolls at Venus' shrine!
> Give we the gods what from his lordly plate
> Messalla's blear-eyed scion could not give –
> Duty to God and man in soul well blent
> And stainless inmost thoughts and noble heart
> In honour steeped – these let me to the shrine
> Convey, and humble meal will win my prayer.[2]

Satire III, on right living and right thinking, expostulates with laziness which childishly fails to face the serious purposes of life. It opens with a concrete picture of lounging: 'already bright morning enters the windows, widening the narrow chinks with light,' and yet we go on snoring off last night's debauch. Is it not a scandal to pass an unworthy existence like a Natta? – Only, his vice is ingrained hopelessly:

> He feels no guilt; knows not his loss; deep-drowned
> He makes no bubble at the surface more.[3]

[1] I. 114–118.   [2] II. 61–63; 68–75.
[3] III. 33–34:

> 'caret culpa, nescit quid perdat, et alto
> Demersus summa rursum non bullit in unda.'

May the Great Sire inflict on monsters of wickedness no other punishment than a revelation of virtue as she is:

Let them see Virtue – pine for Her they've lost.[1]

Then the poet commends the wisdom derivable from true philosophy in spite of the guffaws of the unsympathetic soldier:

Learn; and, poor souls, the causes grasp of things;
Grasp what we are, what life we're born to live;[2]

and from the same Stoic system one must learn the way at turning-points in one's career, the limits of wealth and of desire, the claims of fatherland and kin, and the part God has ordained one to play.

Satire IV, on the right knowledge of oneself, opens with a brief Socratic examination of the claim made by 'great Pericles's ward' (Alcibiades) to guide the state. Of course, wisdom comes before he has a beard! (*ante pilos uenit*). He ventures to advise the 'Quirites' (a Roman touch in what is a Greek situation) on delicate problems of policy, while making mere enjoyment his chief good and having no higher conceptions than those of an old vegetable-woman of the streets (an allusion that recalls the crone in the *Satyricon*, who was Encolpius's conductress to a haunt of vice).

How few to sound their own true nature try!
Inside the bag of one in front they pry;[3]

and yet the popular estimate of your character is worthless; you must retire within yourself and examine the state of your soul:

Dwell with yourself: learn your scant furnishing.[4]

Satire V, on the right freedom conferred by Stoic principles, has already been cited for its cordial acknowledgement of the poet's debt to the guidance of Cornutus. The model on which the whole is based is the seventh satire of Horace's second book. In contrast to the unity of feeling between himself and Cornutus, Persius notes the variety of aims in the world:

Motley is life: thousand the sorts of men.[5]

Men will not learn the one true lesson: they are in perpetual quest after a tomorrow which is never reached. What man needs is freedom – not the merely civic sort granted when a Roman praetor turned a slave into a freedman by formal stroke of the rod, but the true freedom guaranteed by moral reason:

[1] III. 38: 'Virtutem uideant intabescantque relicta.'
[2] III. 66–67:
    'Discite, et, o miseri, causas cognoscite rerum;
    Quid sumus et quidnam uicturi gignimur.'
[3] IV. 23–24.
[4] IV. 52: 'Tecum habita: noris quam sit tibi curta supellex.
[5] V. 52: 'Mille hominum species, et rerum discolor usus.'

> 'Twas not a praetor's task to give to fools
> Fine sense of duty or grant power to use
> Our fleeting life: you'd sooner teach the harp
> To any hulking clown.[1]

Without reason, which enables a man to distinguish good from bad, his every act is sin (one of the hard sayings typical of orthodox Stoicism):

> Reason has granted naught to thee: put out
> A finger: *that* is wrong. Yet what so slight?
> But never frankincense will win thy prayer
> That e'en a short half-ounce of right shall dwell
> In fools. God sunders right from foolishness.[2]

And so, if you have passions within that master you, or if you feel the rival claims of avarice and luxury, then you are a slave. The two hooks pull opposite ways. If you escape once, you may still drag your chain. The truly free man is he who can inhibit himself from an evil impulse and disentangle himself from weaknesses like ambition or superstition.

Satire VI, on the right use of wealth, is not so decidedly a Stoic homily as its four predecessors. Wintering at Luna on the Ligurian coast by the Tuscan Sea (*meum mare*), Persius addresses to Caesius Bassus his claim to spend money on reasonable objects, supporting it by an argument with a supposed heir who desires to have the fortune saved intact. The statement by the biographer that some lines were removed from the last book (*uersus aliqui dempti sunt ultimo libro*) is best understood to imply that this final satire is incomplete.[3]

The subject of the sources of Persius is one of considerable complexity. His material was largely provided by his education, associates, and his own tastes. Stoic by training and conviction, he was more orthodox and more dogmatic than most Romans, and so took over and restated with scant argument some of the extreme paradoxes of the School. His studies under rhetoricians who preferred the classic Augustan models account for the opposition which he displays in his first satire to the revived Alexandrinism of Rome, and for his borrowings from Virgil and, beyond all others, from Horace. Along with Horace he adopted for imitation Horace's outspoken master in satire, Lucilius.[4] His Horatian debts are visible everywhere, in reminiscent word or phrase or idea, all retaining the mark of their origin despite Persius's

---

[1] V. 93–95.   [2] V. 119–122.

[3] Macleane's is a plausible theory that 'uende animam lucro' (vi. 75) begins a new branch of the subject which is left unfinished. See his ed. of P. and Juvenal, Lond. 1857. Pretor (Introd. to his ed. in Catena Classicorum series, Lond. 1868, xix–xxii), argues that the gap comes earlier in Sat. vi. O. Jahn, who considered Sat. vi to be among the first composed and our Sat. i to have been among the last, believed that the sixth is complete as we have it and that the incompleteness is in Sat. i (Proleg. to his ed.).

[4] Fiske regards Lucilius as a source for Persius second in importance only to Horace. *Tr. Am. Ph. A.* xl, pp. 121–150.

inveterate habit of contorted involution, which of set purpose departs from Horace's clear straightforwardness. Thus, the simple rule of pathos in the *Ars Poetica*, 'If you would have me weep, you must yourself grieve first,' is by Persius elaborated into

> He who would bow me down with woeful plaint
> Must shed true tears, not tears prepared o'ernight.[1]

The reappearance of Horatian names gives an added effect of imitation, *e.g.* Pedius (i. 85), Nerius (ii. 14), Natta (iii. 31), Craterus (iii. 65), Bestius (vi. 37). Even a partial consideration of Persius's sources shows that his aim was to express Stoic thought in language largely Horatian – a *tour de force* bound to fall short of perfect success; for no writer could hope to wed the suppleness of Horace to Stoic rigidity. Jahn emphasised the influence of the mime on Persius in addition to that of Horace; and there is a possibility that the dramatic realism of mime-writers like Sophron acted on the satires.[2] To these must be added the influences of rhetoric and of the Cynico-stoical disputations. Rhetoric accounts for many of the diverse elements in his style, such as literary reminiscence, academic common-place, and argumentative artifice. Stoic preaching, which had for long been abandoned either to professional orators or to popular speakers, was now brought by Persius into literature. He might easily have imbibed the style of the Stoic diatribe ($\delta\iota\alpha\tau\rho\iota\beta\acute{\eta}$), or polemic disputation, from Cornutus; and at Thrasea's house he could have heard expositions by a Stoic like Musonius or by a Cynic like Demetrius.[3] Cynic inspiration had already operated on Roman literature through Varro's Menippean satires, and Horace alludes to the bitter wit of Bion.[4] The Bionean diatribe, given to blending learned argument with forceful words from popular speech, was likely to win attention from a writer fired, like Persius, almost to proselytising ardour; and Greek Cynic literature had itself inherited and in turn bequeathed elements from Socratic dialogue and drama and rhetoric which contributed to the

[1] Hor. *A.P.* 102:
> 'Si uis me flere, dolendum est
> Primum ipsi tibi';

Pers. I. 91:
> 'Verum nec nocte paratum
> Plorabit qui me uolet incuruasse querela.'

Other phrases in Persius's first satire which may be instructively compared with their Horatian bases are l. 43: 'nec scombros metuentia carmina nec tus' (*cf.* Hor. *Ep.* II. i. 269–270 and Catullus xcv. 7); ll. 64–5: 'ut per leue seueros effundat iunctura ungues' (*cf.* Hor. *Sat.* II. vii. 86 and (?) *Sat.* I. v. 32 and *A.P.* 294); l. 106: 'nec pluteum caedit nec demorsos sapit ungues' (*cf.* Hor. *Sat.* I. x. 71).

[2] Villeneuve, *Essai sur Perse*, p. 179 ff.

[3] Villeneuve, *op. cit.* p. 165.

[4] Hor. *Epist.* II. ii. 60: 'Bioneis sermonibus et sale nigro.' The varied linguistic elements and polemic artifices of the lost moral disquisitions of Bion are partially discernible in the remains of Teles, an obscure Cynic of the 3rd cent. B.C. For Bion, see Villeneuve, *op. cit.* pp. 130–135.

vigorous presentation of a philosophical argument. Just as the argumentative manner of certain of St. Paul's epistles is affected by the Stoic
diatribe, so Persius keeps up a similar tradition when he develops a
theme by answering an objector implied or definitely introduced.[1]

Worked on by influences thus complex, enamoured of condensation,
of allusiveness, of subtle borrowings, jerky in his management of dialogue so that a change of speaker is sometimes difficult to detect, Persius
developed a crabbed manner of expression which makes him the hardest
of Latin poets to read. Enjoyment is apt to vanish amidst the toil of disentanglement. Conscious as he was of the mission to proclaim salutary
truths, he yet seems to have forgotten the effective force of clearness, and
his curiously laboured style is certainly not that of the Cynico-stoic disquisition. The failure to support by connected argument dogmatic
tenets, in themselves possibly intelligible enough, and the departure
from a logical order of thought in the structure of some satires further
contribute to his obscurity. Strictures upon him date from ancient times.
Johannes Lydus, whose record of Persius's imitation of Sophron, though
challenged, has some facts in its favour, added that Persius surpassed
the obscurity of Lycophron.[2] In the time of Louis XIV Nicolas Chorier
in his *Aloisia* imagined a letter apostrophising Persius: 'You wrapped
yourself in blind night . . . You did not want to be understood, per-
chance you too did not understand! . . . You lurked inside yourself, lest
the painstaking sagacity of learning might discover you. You were
your own envelope.'[3]

The obscurity often lies in expression. A notoriously difficult line
occurs at iv. 49:

si puteal multa cautus uibice flagellas,

which, even supposing it is to be translated 'if craftily you scourge the
exchange with many a lash,' still leaves the sense cryptic. Excessive
compression may prove puzzling, as 'While I pluck forth old *grandams*
from your breast,'[4] meaning 'grandmotherly notions'; or, on testing
the true meaning of applause, 'Shake out thoroughly all this "*bravo!*"
(*belle hoc excute totum*); what does it not hold inside?' Another example
turns on Janus's luck in having two faces so that he cannot be mocked
behind his back by persons pretending to be storks pecking him, or
suggesting by mimicry that he had donkey's ears, or shooting out the
tongue to show disrespect:

---

[1] Pers. I. 44: 'Quisquis es, o, modo quem ex aduerso dicere feci'; *cf.* I
Corinthians xv. 35–37.
[2] Lyd. *De Mag.* I. 41: Πέρσιος δὲ τὸν ποιητὴν Σώφρονα μιμήσασθαι θέλων τὸ
Λυκόφρονος παρῆλθεν ἀμαυρόν.
[3] 'Obuoluisti ipse te caeca nocte. . . . Nolebas intellegi, forte et tu non intel-
legebas! . . . Latebas intra te, ne te curiosa et erudita inueniret sagacitas. Eras
ipse inuolucrum tibi.'
[4] V. 92: 'Dum ueteres auias tibi de pulmone reuello.'

O Janus, whom the stork ne'er pecks behind,
Nor hand that nimbly apes white donkey-ears,
Nor tongue as long as parched Apulian dog's,[1]

where strangely enough the essential key-notions of mockery and of
putting out the tongue are omitted. Occasionally an idiom may pull the
reader up, for example his liking for infinitives in substantival meanings.[2]
Thus it is not at first obvious either to readers or commentators that
iratus mammae lallare recusas is intended to signify 'pettishly refuse
your nurse's lullaby.'[3] Elsewhere the difficulty may lie in the disconnected course of his thought and the suddenness of his transitions;
so that one is kept on the alert by what is no light reading for tired
heads.

There are, however, compensations. The test is whether under a
cloud of difficulties there remains something real and sincere. Immediate delight is not obtainable from Persius: there are no flights of
pleasant fancy, no ideal scenes, no passages of sheer beauty; and, if the
reader is transported to no ideal world, he may be tempted to doubt –
some critics have doubted – whether the world of the young satirist is a
real world, whether his exposure of human weakness smacks more of
Stoic books than of actual life. Persius did not write for the crowd:
he in particular does not yield his secret except to the intimacy and sympathy of a thinking mind. His very obscurity is a fruit of a half-cloistered
delicacy which shrank from revealing itself in ordinary modes of expression, and therefore adopted a composite style in which Lucilius and
Horace, the mime and the argumentative Stoic diatribe, are all ingredients.
At the same time there has too often been a disposition to regard him
mainly as a youthful zealot, fanatically fervent in his Stoicism, who had
not mixed with his fellow-men. Sometimes it is forgotten that while
he can be provokingly obscure, he can also be vivid, and, though his
range is not wide, can show a power of observing life around him.

Among his sketches memorable for realism are those of the affected
reciter;[4] the laziness of the debauchee snoring as the sunshine pours
through the shutter-chinks and the shadow touches the fifth line of the
sundial;[5] the fretful struggle to get to work with book and ink and pen;[6]
the truant's games;[7] the centurion's idea of philosophers as

lugubrious Solons
With head bent down, pinning their eyes to earth;[8]

---

[1] I. 58:

    'O Iane, a tergo quem nulla ciconia pinsit,
    Nec manus auriculas imitari mobilis albas,
    Nec linguae quantum sitiat canis Apula tantae.

[2] *E.g.* I. 9: 'istud uiuere triste'; I. 27: 'scire tuum'; I. 122: 'hoc ridere
meum'; *cf.* Hor. *Epist.* I. vii. 27: 'reddes dulce loqui: reddes ridere decorum.'
[3] III. 18.   [4] I. 15–21.   [5] III. 1–6.
[6] III. 10–14.   [7] III. 43–51.   [8] III. 78–85.

I*

a national holiday on the occasion of a victory over the Germans;[1] a
shipwrecked friend who

> Lies on the beach himself, with gods hard by –
> Huge figures off the vessel's stern – and ribs
> Of his maimed ship now in the seagulls' path;[2]

or the funeral of a Roman master by whose last will and testament his
favourite slaves have been emancipated:

> Doorwards he stretches heels now stiff and cold;
> Then cits, made yesterday, in freedom's cap
> Shoulder the corpse.[3]

Vigour also characterises his metaphors. A warning against offending
high society by outspokenness is given thus:

> Beware, please, lest the doorsteps of the great
> Turn cool to you (*limina frigescant*).[4]

A kindred vigour produces violent expressions like 'purveying titbits
for other people's ears' (*auriculis alienis colligis escas*), or the forcible
personification of money spent on costly sacrifices in an unrewarded
pursuit after wealth:

> Till the last coin, now hopeless and befooled
> At the purse-bottom heaves its sigh in vain.[5]

A passage in the fifth satire[6] is illuminating as to Persius's own opinion
of his style. There Cornutus is imagined to tell the poet that his forte
lies not in mouthing high-flown tragedy, nor in foolish cawing (*corni-
caris*) of mysterious nonsense, nor in straining his puffed cheeks with
rhetoric till they go bang with a *pop*,[7] but, as he declares in Latin words
which intentionally echo Horace, 'Nay, you follow the language of
ordinary life, dexterous in the subtlety of your phrase-making' (*iunctura
callidus acri*);[8] or, in other terms, it was for Persius to cultivate plain
satire instead of dramatising any mythological supper of horrors. The
words *iunctura callidus acri* provide a clue both to his merits and to his
defects; for his phrase-making, at times strikingly successful, at other times
overleaps itself and becomes one factor in his Browningesque obscurity.

The ring of Persius's hexameters differs from that of Horace's,
which were constructed without regard to the high-sounding epic
tradition and designedly lowered in tone to suit the half-conversational
character of his *sermones*. It is natural that Persius, who interpreted
his Stoic message as lofty and severe, should not write with so easy a

---

[1] VI. 43–49.   [2] VI. 29–31.   [3] III. 105–106.
[4] I. 108–109.   [5] II. 50–51.   [6] V. 5–18.
[7] V. 13: 'nec *scloppo* (? stloppo) tumidas intendis rumpere buccas.' The loan-
words from vulgar Latin in Persius (*e.g.* diminutives and obscenities) are such
as occur in comedy and satirists like Lucilius and Horace. He also shares colloquialisms (*ebullire*, etc.) with contemporaries like Petronius in the *Satyricon* and
Seneca in the *Apocolocyntosis*.   [8] *Cf.* Hor. *A.P.* 47–48 and 242.

movement, but should adopt a more mechanical structure and more conventional cadence. There is in Persius a smaller number of spondaic words, a different management of *caesurae*, and a rarer use of monosyllabic endings; but, like Horace, he freely admits elision, and so presents a contrast with one of the features of the hexameters parodied in his first satire, as well as of the contemporary verse of Calpurnius Siculus, of the Einsiedeln eclogues and of the *Laus Pisonis*.

A hypothesis maintained with different degrees of detail by different commentators would make Persius not merely a mouthpiece of Stoicism but a political satirist who ventured to assail Nero. In the *Vita* a closing paragraph of unsettled authenticity affirms that in his fulminations against the modern school of literature he included an attack on the emperor.[1] This contained the expression *auriculas asini Mida rex habet*, which Cornutus altered for safety to *auriculas asini quis non habet?* to prevent Nero from thinking he was aimed at. Then the scholia gave varying accounts of the source of the hexameters in the first satire at which Persius jests, but one view was that they were Nero's; and so ancient commentators began to see throughout the satire a series of allusions to the emperor. Casaubon maintained that in Satire IV Alcibiades, the would-be statesman, stands for Nero, and though Jahn does not follow him here, as he does regarding Satire I, Casaubon has had supporters in Pretor and others.[2] Lehmann has gone further. He has claimed to find covert but stinging allusions to Nero in Satire V, the very satire which to most readers must appear remarkable in that, while it handles freedom, it avoids all political aspects of the question. The more the hypothesis grows by accretion of hitherto unrecognised allusions, the weaker it seems. Why should Nero alone be attacked? Why should the author have been so unphilosophical as to single out for constant censure an individual, when all the world fell far short of Stoic perfection? Might not Persius well remember that Horace, his model, left politics on one side? And are we to be asked to believe that Cornutus took the trouble to alter the words 'King Midas' to avoid giving possible offence to the emperor, and yet left in the text not merely copious hits at his Majesty more or less veiled, but actually lines of Nero's own composition of which the satirist made fun?

Opinions have varied greatly concerning Persius. His fellow-student Lucan, as already mentioned, praised him whole-heartedly, and his satires on publication won immediate esteem.[3] He was popular with the

---

[1] Specified in the Latin of the *Vita* as *Neronem principem illius temporis*.

[2] R. Pichon, *Litt. lat.* p. 553: 'Sans nommer Néron en toutes lettres (la chose eût été impossible) Perse le met en scène sous le nom d'Alcibiade.' R. Waltz, *Vie de Sénèque*, p. 9 n. 1, 'L'Alcibiade de sa quatrième satire est Néron, comme l'a pensé Casaubon: on peut admettre que Socrate y représente, dans une certaine mésure, Sénèque lui-même.' R. C. Kukula's *Persius und Nero* (Graz 1923) treats the first satire as containing a definite attack on Nero.

[3] *Vita*: 'Editum librum continuo mirari homines et diripere coeperunt'; *cf.* Quintil. X. i. 94; Mart. IV. xxix

Fathers of the Church for his strong advocacy of virtue and his *anima naturaliter Christiana*, and he has attracted enthusiastic commentators since the days of Valerius Probus in his own century. Isaac Casaubon wrote of his own unsparing labours on him: *in Persio omnem ingenii conatum effudimus*. On the other hand, Joseph Scaliger remarked sarcastically about that same commentary: *au Perse de Casaubon la saulce vaut mieux que le poisson*. It is common literary knowledge that he left his mark on Rabelais and Montaigne, on Ben Jonson and Boileau, which argues in him something deeper than what Nisard saw – the knack of reproducing servilely in verse ready-made philosophical ideas. Simcox thinks he improves upon every reading, and a French editor[1] declares *je quitte Perse avec un sincère regret et comme on quitte un vieil ami*; whereas a German scholar is delighted to lay him down: *mit Freuden legen wir den Dichter aus der Händen*,[2] and another writer discovers in the satires a sea of darkness.[3] It may be a half-cynical suggestion that editors come to love Persius in proportion to the toil which he has cost them, but one may fairly take leave to doubt whether an exponent of doctrines with which he hopes to better his fellow-men is justified in being so far from plain. It is true that a modern editor sought to acquit him of obscurity, arguing that he is difficult but not obscure.[4] Most students will hold that he is both, and that it must be largely a matter of disposition whether a reader will resent or not the trouble involved. Even that very earnestness in preaching morality which has gained him champions may appear to others the priggishness of a bookish young recluse. Still, in justice to Persius, it should be remembered that his lack of knowledge of the world may be easily overstated: his very education in rhetoric would open his eyes to evil; he had travelled; and many of his pictures show that he had observed life.

Persius set himself the task of presenting Stoic homilies in Horatian guise – a task perhaps harder, perhaps involving more incompatible elements even than that which Lucretius undertook when he wedded Epicureanism to the heroic hexameter. But whatever their obstacles, Lucretius attained his goal triumphantly, whereas Persius cannot be said to have won that perfect mastery over form and material which begets the greatest literature. Yet, obscurities notwithstanding, his voice has influenced the world and its thinkers; for it has at least been understood that there breathes through Persius no light-hearted complaisance with the frivolities of life, but a stern urgency always beckoning towards an austere ideal.

[1] E. Rousse, *Perse*, Paris 1884, p. 135.
[2] M. Schanz, edn. of 1913, § 384. Schanz's reviser C. Hosius says much the same: 'Mit einem Gefühl der Erleichterung legt er den Dichter aus der Hand,' S.H. § 384.
[3] J. Sorn, *Die Sprache des Persius*, Laibach 1890, p. 31: 'es ist ein Meer von Dunkelheit.'
[4] G. C. Ramsay, *Juv. and Pers.* (Loeb) 1918, Introd. pp. xxx–xxxii.

Chapter VI

LUCAN: HISTORICAL EPIC

The author of the *Pharsalia* – Authorities for his life – His
career – Relations with Nero – Lost works – The *Pharsalia* –
Summary of the ten books – What was its contemplated length? –
The three books first issued – Daring in choice of subject –
Originality in epic treatment – Lucan's sources, historical, philosophical and literary – Historical value – Mis-statements and anti-
Caesarian bias – Stoicism – Influence of previous poets – How
rhetoric affected him – Erudition – Realism – Speeches – Pointed
style in *sententiae* – A vein of poetry – His hero.

LUCAN

PRECOCITY and enthusiasm were eminent characteristics of the
young poet who first throve under Nero's favour and finally succumbed to that emperor's jealousy. Byron, dying at thirty-six,
is reckoned a fertile genius; but when Lucan had to face death at an
age earlier by more than ten years, there stood to his credit an almost
equally wonderful mass of work – letters and speeches, epic and drama,
miscellaneous verse, court-poetry, panegyrics and satires, as well as
librettos for mimes. Of all these, however, time has spared only his
Pharsalia, broken off in the tenth book. The determining factors in
his career were his descent from two prominent Spanish families and his
rhetorical education; for upon these depended the success and failure
of his life, and the main qualities of his thought and style.

Lucan's maternal grandfather was Acilius Lucanus, a Corduban
speaker of note. His paternal grandfather was the elder Seneca, well
known to Roman literary circles in the reigns of Augustus and Tiberius;
his father was Annaeus Mela, an *eques*, apparently something of a
philosophic recluse,[1] while his uncles were M. Annaeus Novatus (the
'Gallio' of the Acts of the Apostles) and the philosopher L. Annaeus
Seneca. To the latter he owed his introduction to court-life, which
proved an incentive to brilliant achievement but ultimately compassed
his ruin.

---

[1] Vacca, *Vita Luc.* mentions his 'studium uitae quietioris.' Vacca's *Vita* and
Suetonius's are contained in Reifferscheid, *Suetonii . . . reliquiae*; F. Weber,
Vitae Lucani collectae, Marb. 1856; also in edd. of Lucan by Francken, by
Hosius, and (of Bk. I) by Lejay. See Bibl. *re* p. 237.

While the impersonality of epic precludes the *Pharsalia* from yielding details about Lucan's life, yet from it alone sure inferences could be drawn as to his training in literature, rhetoric and philosophy, his anti-Caesarism, his self-confident and impetuous spirit. We are not, however, without definite biographical sources. There are two lives of importance, one imperfect and inimical, manifestly the basis of Jerome's entry[1] regarding the death of Lucan, and, since the days of Joseph Scaliger, concluded with justice to come from Suetonius's *De uiris illustribus*; and the other life a fuller and appreciative one, assigned to Vacca, a grammarian of the sixth century. Statius and Martial were admirers of Lucan and joined with his widow Polla in keeping his memory green; hence the *Genethliacon Lucani* of the former and several short pieces by the latter poet supply additional information.[2] The record of Lucan's connexion with the Pisonian conspiracy is in Tacitus, who also in the *Dialogus* ranks Lucan as already a classic alongside of Horace and Virgil.[3]

M. Annaeus Lucanus (A.D. 39–65) was born, about the year of his grandfather Seneca's death, at the 'Patrician Colony' of Corduba, itself for generations a centre of intellectual importance in Spain. The infant, when eight months old, was brought to Rome; for it was natural that his father Mela should migrate in response to the lure of the great city, where already his own father and brother had made their mark. Later, there are interesting references by the philosopher Seneca to the child. In the *Consolatio* addressed to his mother Helvia he writes about a nephew, who must be Lucan, as a winning boy whose merry playfulness and talkativeness would keep anyone amused (*ad cuius conspectum nulla potest durare tristitia . . . cuius non lacrimas illius hilaritas supprimat?*)[4] and an epigram of his prays that one day this prattling child (*dulci Marcus qui nunc sermone fritinnit*) may rival his uncles in eloquence.[5] His education under the best teachers was directed towards the realisation of that very wish. Grounded in literature and in the traditionally wide range of learning subsidiary to 'grammar,' he proceeded in due course to the study of rhetoric and philosophy. His declamations in Latin and Greek were of astonishing ability, eclipsing the efforts of his fellow-students, if not of his masters, and commanding the applause of his hearers. Such brilliance was at once a result and a cause of self-confidence: and the habitual desire to win attention confirmed him in many artificial conceits inseparable from the rhetorical system. Some philosophy he derived from his uncle; but he had at least one other famous Stoic teacher in Cornutus, at whose lectures, if we may trust

[1] Hieron. *Chron. Euseb.* ad. ann. Abr. 2079; 'M. Annaeus Lucanus Cordubensis poeta in Pisoniana coniuratione deprehensus bracchium ad secandas uenas medico praebuit'; cf. Suet. *Vit. Luc.*: 'bracchia ad secandas uenas medico praebuit.'

[2] Stat. *Sil.* II. vii; Mart. I. lxi; VII. xxi, xxii, xxiii; X. lxiv; XIV. cxciv.

[3] Tac. *Ann.* XV. xlix, lvi, lvii, lxx; *Dial.* xx.

[4] *Ad Helv.* xviii, 4, 5.

[5] Bährens, *P.L.M.* IV, p. 77: cf. p. 199 *supra*.

Probus, he met Persius.[1] For Persius's poetry Lucan expressed cordial admiration – a noticeable tribute from one whose precocious fertility had led him to compare himself favourably with Virgil.[2]

Quite early in his reign[3] Nero had his attention drawn by Seneca to a nephew so talented. Little is known precisely regarding the development of his relations with the emperor; but we read of a visit paid to Athens from which Nero recalled him to join his *entourage*, and of honours conferred, such as the quaestorship before the regular age of twenty-five, and an augural priesthood. In A.D. 60, when twenty-one, he achieved his first public literary triumph in his *Laudes Neronis* at the quinquennial festival of the *Neronia*, then newly established, and at this date Nero and his youthful panegyrist were evidently on the best of terms. But Lucan's position became insecure as Nero's dislike for Seneca grew pronounced. It was perilous to vie with a clever and conceited imperial egotist prone to arrogate a principate in arts as well as in state, and an award of the prize to Lucan in a competition where he had the hardihood to enter against Nero rankled in the ruler's heart. Suetonius implies that the final breach arose from Lucan's sensitive fancy that Nero's attitude towards his recitations was deliberately insulting, and from the poet's unbecoming ridicule of the emperor's verses. Vacca ascribes the quarrel to Nero's jealousy of Lucan's powers, and declares that he was forbidden further poetical production or forensic pleading. Thus silenced, except for covert satire, his passionate and wounded genius was driven into the Pisonian conspiracy, in which he took a prominent part,[4] indulging, according to Suetonius, in ferocious threats against the tyrant and in rapturous praises of tyrannicide. When, however, this over-ripened intrigue was unmasked, disaster revealed the weakness of his character; for, oblivious of his professed Stoicism, he descended to abject entreaties, and, in anxiety to save his life, made confessions involving among his accomplices his apparently innocent mother. That at least is what Suetonius records.[5] But pusillanimity did not capture Nero's indulgence. Lucan was ordered to die; and after a sumptuous repast had his veins opened. Then he recollected, and recited as his last words, a piece of his own about a soldier similarly

---

[1] Probus took Persius and Lucan to be of the same time of life; but Persius was Lucan's senior by about five years. Prob. *Vita Persii*: 'Cognouit per Cornutum etiam Annaeum Lucanum, aequaeuum auditorem Cornuti. Lucanus adeo mirabatur scripta (Persii) Flacci ut uix retineret se recitante eo cum clamore quin illa esse uera poemata diceret, sua ipse ludos faceret.' (*v.l.* 'recitante eo de more.')

[2] Suet. *Vita Luc.*: 'ut praefatione quadam aetatem et initia sua cum Vergilio comparans ausus sit dicere "et quantum mihi restat ad Culicem!"'

[3] Vacca, *Vita Luc.*: 'puerili mutato in senatorium cultum et in notitiam Caesaris Neronis facile peruenit.'

[4] Suet. *Vita Luc.*: 'ad extremum paene signifer Pisonianae coniurationis exstitit.'

[5] *Ibid.* 'matrem quoque innoxiam inter socios nominauit'; cf. Tac. *Ann.* XV. lvi. Vacca mentions no such incident.

bleeding to death. This dying quotation, although Tacitus's words[1] might very well suggest that it belonged to a separate poem, has been sought for in three[2] different places in the *Pharsalia*, and by some[3] identified with a passage from the ninth book:

> His tears were blood; and, where the ooze can find
> An outlet, wells abundant gore; the mouth
> And open nostrils stream: his sweat comes red:
> And every limb is drenched from teeming veins.
> So the whole body is a single wound.

Thus, when 'the mad despot's crime' (*rabidi nefas tyranni*) cut short the poet's career, his epic was incomplete and only in part published. 'Why doth a cruel lot debar greatness from old age?' asks Statius in his tribute to Lucan's memory.[4]

Thirteen of Lucan's lost works were known to Vacca, and five of these are alluded to by Statius, who adds the *Adlocutio ad Pollam*.[5] Suetonius, who confirms the other two authorities regarding the *Laudes Neronis*, mentions also a lampoon on Nero. The sagacious Vacca is clear that his thirteen are minor works compared with the epic on the civil war, but still 'not all to be disdained';[6] and one might guess that the most important are those common to Vacca and Statius – the *Iliacon* from the Trojan cycle, the *Catachthonion*, a descent into the underworld, the *Laudes Neronis*, and the *Orpheus*. Naturally, although in all likelihood less important, the *Adlocutio* to Lucan's wife Polla is mentioned by Statius in his poem addressed to her in widowhood; but we do not know whether it was in prose or verse, unless its inclusion immediately after the *De Incendio Vrbis*, the one prose composition in Statius's list, raises a presumption that it likewise was in prose. The remaining items in Vacca's list are the *Saturnalia*, on the gaieties of December,[7] ten books of miscellaneous *Siluae*, the unfinished tragedy of *Medea*, fourteen *Salticae Fabulae*,[8] *Epigrammata*;[9] and in prose (besides his account of the Great Fire at Rome) a series of *Epistulae ex Campania* (which, if they had survived, ought to have proved a fascinating addition to our specimens of ancient letter-writing) as well as a speech for and one against Octavius Sagitta. These *orationes* suggest that Lucan in A.D. 58, perhaps

---

[1] *Ann.* XV. lxx: 'recordatus carmen a se compositum, quo uolneratum militem per eiusmodi mortis imaginem obisse tradiderat, uersus ipsos rettulit, eaque illi suprema uox fuit.'

[2] *Phars.* III. 638–641; VII. 608–615; IX. 811–814.

[3] *E.g.* by May in the *Life* prefixed to his translation.

[4] Stat. *Sil.* II. vii. 92: 'Cur saeua uice magna non senescunt?'

[5] *Sil.* II. vii. 54–63.

[6] *Vita Luc.*, *ad fin.*: 'non fastidiendi quidem omnes, tales tamen ut *Belli Ciuilis* uideantur accessio.'

[7] H. Genthe, *De L. uita et scriptis*, p. 61, plausibly refers to the *Saturnalia* the coarse line quoted by Martial, X. lxiv. 6.

[8] What Schanz (S.H. § 390) calls 'Tanzstücke,' citing Jahn's description 'in usum pantomimorum scriptae,' Proleg. to his ed. of Persius, p. xxxiv.

[9] That is a possible correction of *appāmata* in the best MSS.

filled with the detective instinct characteristic of not a few literary men,
seized upon one of the most exciting murder trials of the day[1] as material
for two clever rhetorical show-pieces in proof of what a versatile genius
could say on both sides of a case complicated by cross-swearing and by
an innocent freedman's self-accusation.

The number of these works would be reduced by one on the suggestion which has been made[2] that the *Catachthonion* and *Orpheus* may
be identical. But this seems impossible. True, both concern the underworld and are in hexameters;[3] but Statius makes separate allusions to
them, and they are mentioned at different points in the *Life* by Vacca in
the sixth century, when Lucan's works were, as his words imply, still
extant.

The ten books of the *Pharsalia*,[4] on the war which broke out in 49
B.C. between Caesar and Pompey, amount to over 8,000 hexameters,
but do not complete the poet's design; for the tenth book, about 150
lines shorter than the next shortest, ends abruptly, leaving Caesar at
war in Egypt.

Book I, though in many respects powerful, might have had more epic
force had it plunged at once into the narrative. As it is, the action is
delayed by the announcement of the theme, a remonstrance on the
iniquity of civil warfare, the comforting reflection that but for that warfare Rome would have had no Nero, the fantastic picture of the emperor
as a god, and a fawning address to him as sufficient inspiration for the
poet without need to invoke Apollo or Bacchus. The ensuing sketch of
the causes of strife omits the burning question between the Senate
and Caesar concerning Caesar's command, but contains a vivid glance
at the motives and characters of the two protagonists, spurred by rival
claims (*stimulos dedit aemula uirtus*):

> Caesar could brook no man in front of him,
> Pompey none by his side.[5]

Referring to Pompey's lack of recent campaigning, Lucan unduly stresses
his advanced age.[6] Now in his fifty-seventh year, he was only four years
older than his opponent, and, as Lucan more than once reminds us, had
become Caesar's son-in-law by marrying Julia, whose death rendered

---

[1] Tac. *Ann.* XIII. xliv. Sagitta in presence of a freedman killed a woman who
would not marry him: the freedman sought to take the guilt on himself, but a
maid revealed the truth, and Sagitta was brought to trial.

[2] Pichon, *Les Sources de Lucain*, p. 53, footnote: 'ces deux poèmes n'en forment
peut-être qu'un seul.' In noticing Pichon's valuable work (*C.R.* xxvii (1913),
pp. 25–28), I mentioned what appeared to me the incredibility of this hypothesis.

[3] Bährens, *F.P.R.* pp. 365–368. W. Morel, *F.P.L.* p. 128.

[4] 'Pharsalia' is borrowed from IX. 985; the title in MSS. is *De Bello Ciuili*.

[5] I. 125–126:
> 'Nec quemquam iam ferre potest Caesarue priorem
> Pompeiusue parem.'

[6] I. 129–130.

the breach between them more likely. In Pompey the poet, warmly
though he espouses his cause, discerns a man over-confident in his
previous record, who

> Finds not new strength, but trusting much past luck
> Stands there the shadow of a mighty name.[1]

The contrasting figure of Caesar is drawn with force, though not with
sympathy:

> His manhood knew
> No rest – his only shame to lose a fight.
> Keen and untamed, where hope or anger called,
> He turned his hand, nor quailed to stain his sword . . .
> To make a path by havoc was his joy.[2]

Strict narrative begins with Caesar's passage of the Alps (l. 183),
bringing his big plans to the small river Rubicon – the antithesis in
adjectives is Lucan's – to be confronted with the majestic image of his
native country protesting against further advance:

> The waters of the little Rubicon
> Were won, when, in the general's sight, arose
> The mighty Phantom of his land, dismayed,
> Clear through the darkling night, most sad of look,
> Letting her grey locks stream from head that wore
> A crown of towers: so, with her tresses torn,
> Bare-armed she took her stand hard by and spoke
> Words blent with groans: 'Men, whither press ye on?
> Where bear my standards? If with right ye come,
> Or if as citizens, thus far ye may.'
>
> Then thrilled a shudder through the general's frame,
> Stiffening his hair, and on the river's brim
> Curbing his march a languor held his steps.
> Forthwith he prayed: 'O Thou, that lookest forth
> From the Tarpeian Rock down on the walls
> Of our great city, O Thou Thunderer,
> And Phrygian Home-Gods, . . . Vestal Fires, and peer
> Of highest Godhead, Rome, bless my design!
> Not thee do I pursue in frenzied arms.
> Lo! I am Caesar, lord on land and sea,
> O'er all the world, and with thy leave e'en now
> Thy champion.[3]

The Rubicon crossed, Ariminum is taken; Caesar is met by Curio,
tribune in the preceding year, and by the Caesarian tribunes of 49
expelled from Rome. A summons sent for troops from Gaul gives occasion for digressions on Gallic tribes, tides and Druids: then a description

---

[1] I. 135: 'stat magni nominis umbra.'
[2] I. 144 sqq.: 'sed nescia uirtus stare loco . . . gaudensque uiam fecisse ruina.'
[3] I. 185 sqq.

of panic in Rome at Caesar's approach leads to the introduction of prodigies and expiatory rites. The book ends gloomily amidst presages
of disaster. Lucan, it will be noted, while he removes from his historical
poem the conventional gods of epic, supplies their place by the supernatural, as represented here by the symbolic figure of Roma, by portents,
and by the prophetic second sight of both an astrologer and a matron
so weirdly possessed that she has power to behold Pompey already
lying dead.

A hesitant note of philosophy opens Book II. Stoics were perpetually
confronted with the problem of reconciling belief in fate with divination.
Why, asks Lucan, is man allowed knowledge of future woes through
omens? Then, with a transient departure from Stoic dogmatism, he
speculates on the operation of cause in the world. Is it the outcome of
law or chance? Yet he clinches this old debate with the Epicureans by
uttering the prayer,

> Thy will be done forthwith: let human thought
> Be blind to coming doom: grant hope 'mid fear![1]

Mourning, as at a death, falls on Rome: men pray for the peril of
foreign attack in preference to internecine strife. It is a passage typically
rhetorical in the tumid declamation of its earlier portion and the argumentative point of its close:

> Make Rome the foe of all the nations, but
> Spare us a civil war! Let Dacians hem
> Us here and Getae there; one rival should
> Meet Spain, the other turn his standard 'gainst
> The quivers of the East. And let thy hand,
> O Rome, have no relief from toil! Or, if,
> Ye Gods, ye will to blast th' Italian name,
> Then let all ether, fallen into fire,
> Crash manifold in lightning on the earth!
> O wrathful Father, in one instant smite
> Both sides, both leaders, ere they yet have earned
> Their doom! From such a crop of novel crime
> Seek they to prove which shall be lord at Rome?
> Scarce had it been worth while to stimulate
> A civil war, if neither were to rule.[2]

The chief incidents of the book are the remarriage to Cato of his former
wife, Marcia, widow of Hortensius; the resistance to Caesar offered by
Domitius (pointedly introduced because an ancestor of Nero) and the
retreat of Pompey southwards to Brundisium and thence overseas to
Epirus. What Heitland frankly calls 'padding' consists in digressions

---

[1] II. 14-15:
> 'Sit subitum quodcumque paras: sit caeca futuri
> Mens hominum fati: liceat sperare timenti.'

[2] II. 52-63.

on the civil wars between Marius and Sulla and on the rivers of Italy. The figure of Cato is of significance in relation to Book IX, where he plays a commanding part. In Lucan's eyes Cato is the incarnation of virtue, hitherto guiltless of his country's blood, but now, as Brutus tells him, drawn perforce into the struggle:

> Thy virtuous past shall have this one reward –
> War makes thee guilty as it finds the rest
> (*Accipient alios, facient te bella nocentem.*)[1]

Full of admiration for Cato's ascetic ordering of his life, the poet proudly depicts his Stoic ability to combine a self-sufficing virtue with altruistic claims.

> To keep the Mean and hold due boundary,
> To follow Nature, spend a life for Rome,
> Deeming his birth was for the world, not self:
> For him to stifle hunger was a feast:
> Whate'er but warded storm from roof-tree was
> For him a lordly palace: richest garb
> For him to draw i' the old way round his limbs
> The Roman burgher's shaggy gown. . . . But ne'er
> Did selfish joy creep in to steal a part
> In Cato's deeds.[2]

Book III, mainly concerned with Caesar's doings on his return to Rome and during his siege of Massilia, is impoverished by a wearisome list of Pompey's eastern allies and an incessant series of too ingeniously horrible deaths which befall the combatants. But among compensating passages are the descriptions of Pompey's farewell to Italy and of the eerie forest near Massilia. The former opens the book with a note of poetry and pathos:

> The South Wind fell upon the yielding sails
> And sped the Armada till its argosies
> Ploughed through the midmost deep: each mariner
> Kept steadfast outlook for the Ionian Main.
> Pompey alone ne'er turned his eyes aside
> From Italy, but all the while he watched
> The homeland havens fade away and shores
> That ne'er would meet his sight again, and peaks
> Cloud-wrapt, and scarce distinguishable hills.[3]

The second passage, a study in the sombre touched with the spirit of Celtic romance, describes the grove of the Druids. Here we are in a haunted twilight wood, polluted with inhuman rites, shunned by bird and beast as by sylvan deities, and though windless yet a-quiver with a mysterious thrill in its leaves (*arboribus suus horror inest*) – a forest of

---

[1] II. 258–259.   [2] II. 381 *sqq.*   [3] III. 1–7.

black waters and misshapen images of eldritch gods, awesome through a wan aspect of decay and nameless terrors, where caverns resound with the rumble of the earthquake, where the hewn death-yew comes to life again, where flame plays among branches that do not burn and serpents hold the oak in their embrace.[1]

Three episodes constitute most of the action in Book IV – Caesar's Spanish operations against Afranius and Petreius near Ilerda; the failure of one of three Caesarian rafts to escape the Pompeian blockade in Illyria; and the descent of Curio, in Caesar's interest, upon Africa, where he is defeated by Juba and meets death. The pangs of thirst suffered by Pompeians in Spain prompt one of Lucan's denunciations of luxury,[2] while the counsel of Volteius to his men on the trapped raft that they must slay each other rather than surrender is argued in the overstrained manner of the schools, and is an ingenious combination of special pleading and boastfulness. When the crew carry out their dreadful compact of mutual slaughter, like the offspring of the teeth of mythical dragons, characteristic realism is indulged in to describe the crawling writhing bleeding agony of the lacerated men. But this virtual suicide closes in a reflection that consoled many of Nero's subjects as well as Lucan – death is a ready way of eluding tyranny. Here it is still the Stoic who speaks; for Stoicism, while recognising the theoretical obliquity of suicide, admitted that it was in certain circumstances defensible:

> Despite such lessons shown of manliness,
> Yet craven peoples will refuse to learn
> How smooth the path of valour which the hand
> Can make to 'scape from bondage; but a King
> Is dreaded for his steel; and liberty
> Is galled with cruel arms, in ignorance
> That swords were given that none might be a slave.
> Ah Death! That thou mightst scorn to take from life
> Cowards, and but the brave be free to die![3]

The African expedition suggests the only long deviation of this book, on the legend of the earth-born Antaeus strangled by Hercules. Curio's soliloquy before battle reflects his not unnatural nervousness as commander of soldiers who had become Caesarians only by surrendering at Corfinium:

> 'Tis daring cloaks great fear: myself shall first
> Seize arms, and let my men, while yet mine own,
> March down to level ground; for idleness
> Aye bringeth changeful mind. End plots by fight!
> When blood-lust prompts and sword is firmly gripped,
> The helmet covers qualms. Who minds to weigh

---

[1] III. 399–421. Possibly the miraculous fire in the forest was suggested to Lucan by Sen. *Thy.* 674–5: 'excelsae trabes ardent sine igne.'
[2] IV. 373 *sqq.*
[3] IV. 575–581.

Oppos*è*d leaders then or balance claims?
Each backs the side he stands on; as at shows
Within the fateful amphitheatre,
No ancient grudge makes combatants engage –
Pairs hate at sight.[1]

The apostrophe to Curio after his death leads up to the familiar line which implies that his desertion to Caesar's side turned the scale of history:

Momentumque fuit mutatus Curio rerum.

Though Book V opens in Epirus with the assembly of the Senate friendly to Pompey and closes with his decision to send his wife Cornelia for safety to Lesbos, yet Caesar is the dominant figure, especially when he cows the mutineers (who express their grievances with pointed rhetoric), and recrosses the Adriatic in a small boat on a tempestuous night to bring Antony to his aid. The action is delayed by a digression of about 150 lines on the Delphic Oracle consulted by Appius.

Caesar's will-power is well brought out in his defiant braving of the storm despite the fisherman's warning. He is content to have Fortune for his sole attendant (*sola placet Fortuna comes*) in crossing the sea to ensure the transport of his troops from Italy; for

Mad-set on battle-mellay was his heart.[2]

But the storm proves an irresistible temptation to Lucan. Having exhausted his list of contending winds, he turns to hyperbole – mountains long buffeted in vain now at last succumb, and portentous waves new to those seas roll in from the encircling ocean. Next he elaborates the description by a resort to mythology. Much more human, however, is the concluding episode, in which Pompey, deeply affected, can scarcely bring himself to tell his wife that for her safety they must part:

Words fail him, though his purpose be resolved;
And so he fain would clog what is to come,
Indulge delay and moments steal from doom.
All slumber banished and the night far gone,
Cornelia clasps his breast that teems with care,
And seeks fond kisses from her lord now turned
Away. She marvels that his cheeks are wet,
And, smitten with a wound mysterious,
She dare not find great Pompey shedding tears.
He sighing said: 'My own, more dear than life –
I mean the life of happier times, not this
That burdens me – the woeful day hath come,
Which we postponed too little, yet too much:
Caesar is nigh, all eagerness for fight!'[3]

[1] IV. 702–710.
[2] V. 476: 'Caesaris adtonitam miscenda ad proelia mentem.'
[3] V. 731 *sqq.*

Overloaded with digressions, besides detail of Caesar's scheme to en-
close his enemy at Dyrrhachium, and hyperbolical praise of the centurion Scaeva's repulse of Pompey's attempt to break through, Book VI
is not on the whole successful. The plan to construct gigantic lines of
investment is at first as little grasped by Pompey

> As wild waves boiling on the Kentish shore
> Rave all unfelt by Caledonians.[1]

In time, he is driven to counter-movements, and would have made a
victorious sortie but for the prowess of one outstanding Caesarian, on
whom, with incredible exaggeration, the whole fighting is made to
concentrate. This champion is not to be dislodged save by a war-engine;
he bristles with a thick forest of missiles in his chest; he offers the resistance of an African elephant; and, tearing out his eyeball along with the
arrow which pierced it,

> Stamps on the weapon and his eye as well![2]

This and much more is neither poetry nor common sense. The rest
mainly concerns the temporary discomfiture of Caesar, who retires upon
Thessaly followed by Pompey. If only Pompey had been a Sulla, reflects
Lucan, and had used his advantage for an immediate descent upon Rome,
there would have been no Pharsalia. The mention of Thessaly is responsible for digressions on geography and magic; and, though the wizardry
and witches of Thessaly appear more convincing in the pages of
Apuleius, yet Lucan, when he leaves off cataloguing the astounding
potency of Thessalian enchantments over love, weather, rivers,
mountains and laws of the universe, does achieve an effect of gruesome
diablerie through Sextus Pompey's morbid longing to learn the future,
not from oracles but, like Saul at Endor, from necromancy. After he
and his attendants have made their way past ruined tombs towards the
sunless and hell-like cavern where the sorceress Erichtho sits crooning
her malignant spells, he holds a midnight *séance* with the hag. Conceding
his request, she scares off birds and beasts of prey from the battlefield,
and selects a fallen warrior to be revivified by loathsome ingredients and
eerie incantations for the purpose of revealing prophetic messages from
the other world. The revelation is that the shades await both Sextus's
father and his house; Caesar's daring, on the other hand, delights the
spirits of dead Roman revolutionaries, but his triumph will be short.
With such ominous responses Sextus returns to his father's camp before
daybreak.

Book VII is not free from turgidity and extravagance, but it is the
greatest book of the poem, and describes the feelings of both rivals
before Pharsalia as well as their fortunes in the culminating battle. With

---

[1] VI. 67–68.   [2] VI. 191–192, 198–199, 205, 208, 219.

an outburst of enthusiasm, Lucan predicts the enduring power of his
subject to engross readers:

> 'Mid tribes in far-off years, 'mid folks unborn,
> Haply by fame alone to time bequeathed,
> Or haply profited by such renown
> As e'en my toiling pen can lend the great,
> When men shall read of war, this tale shall still
> Move hope and fear alike, or futile wish.
> Spellbound each reader still shall fancy doom
> Is yet to come, not past and gone, and so
> Will favour thee, great Pompey, to the end.[1]

In the famous passage on Pompey's dream, he is fancied to be once
more receiving the plaudits of the Roman people in his own theatre:

> In dreamland Rome seemed his. Break not that sleep,
> O camp-watch! Ne'er let bugle strike his ears!
> To-morrow's ghastly night, sad to recall
> The day, brings naught but deadly battle-lines.[2]

He awakes to realities. The Pompeians clamour for the fray and
criticise their leader's caution:

> In Pompey's camp 'Pharsalia!' was the prayer.[3]

Unhistorically Cicero, who was not present, is introduced as urging
him to give battle. He consents under protest and his men have their
will; but

> On many a face was paleness as of death
> To come – a look most eloquent of doom.[4]

Amidst other presages of disaster, Lucan's bias insinuates that Caesar
sacrificed to the infernal powers. The harangue to his followers is some
of it plausible argument, some of it rhodomontade, but, by reason of its
vigour, all very readable. Observing the disposition of Pompey's troops
(Lucan's account of which does not agree with that of other authorities),
and seeing his wish fulfilled in the enemy's descent upon the plain,
Caesar confidently addresses his soldiers as the true arbiters of his
destiny:

> No need for prayer: woo fortune now by fight,[5]

and continuing his alliterative rhetoric:

> Wave but the blade and bring the whole world low.[6]

With corresponding alliteration, and not without bravado, Pompey's
speech to his army expresses his reasons for confidence:

---

[1] VII. 207 *sqq.*   [2] VII. 24 *sqq.*   [3] VII. 61.   [4] VII. 129–130.
[5] VII. 252: 'Nil opus est uotis: iam fatum accersite ferro.'
[6] VII. 278: 'Et primo ferri motu prosternite mundum.'

Our better cause bids hope for help from Heaven.'[1]

But in vain. Tyranny, in Lucan's view, was triumphant at Pharsalia. Why did Rome ever know freedom, if she was to lose it?[2] Surely, the gods' apathy had led through civil warfare to the creation of new deities and a new religion in emperor-worship![3] Refraining from details of individual horrors on the battlefield, Lucan contrasts the fugitive Pompey looking back upon lost greatness with Caesar, whose adversary is henceforward not Pompey but freedom,[4] and who to discerning eyes might well be an object of pity – ''twas worse to win' (*uincere peius erat*). The picture of the conqueror is not flattering. According to Lucan, Caesar encouraged his men to plunder, was leader of the really guilty side, was hunted Orestes-like by avenging furies, callously surveyed the dead, and withheld from the rotting corpses that cremation which would not be refused (and here a piece of far-fetched Stoicism is dragged in) by the universal conflagration at the end of the world.

The main interest of Book VIII lies in Pompey's flight to Egypt and his murder as he is about to land: it is broken by reflections on and apostrophes to both Egypt and Pompey. A prey to nervous fears, alarmed at the rustle of woodland leaves in the wind,[5] the defeated warrior escapes in a frail craft to Lesbos, where he endeavours to console his swooning wife:

> Thy husband's woe alone may win thee praise.
> Take heart: let thine affection strive with fate
> And love me for myself, a vanquished man.[6]

He sets sail with her in anxiety great enough to make unnatural his converse with the pilot upon astronomy. By the Levant he reaches Cilicia, the scene of his old victories over piracy, and holds council with his remaining supporters on the policy, cunning but unprincipled, of playing East against West. Why not entangle and weaken Parthia by inducing her to fight in Rome's civil wars? This proposal of Pompey's is scouted as dishonourable by Lentulus – why not rather, he argues, keep the conflict within the Roman world, and try Egypt, whose king, Ptolemy, owed his throne indirectly to Pompey? So he sails to meet the death prepared for him by Ptolemy's cynical adviser Pothinus, whose contention is that expediency must be preferred to right and that it is wisdom to side with the conqueror:

> Freedom in crime protects a hated sway. . . .
> Who would be good must quit a royal court:
> Virtue and sovereign power do not accord.
> Blush to be cruel and you'll always fear![7]

In the offing at Pelusium, overmastering fate secured that Pompey

---

[1] VII. 349: 'Causa iubet melior superos sperare secundos.'
[2] VII. 440–445.   [3] VII. 457–459.   [4] VII. 695.
[5] VIII. 5–6.   [6] VIII. 76–78.   [7] VIII. 491; 493–495.

should be enticed from his high-sterned vessel into a small boat, where, within sight of wife and son, he was stabbed by the traitor Septimius. Achillas, that 'Pharian satellite,' claimed the right to carry the victim's head to the young king. Having noted the majesty of Pompey's looks as preserved in death, Lucan yields to his besetting passion for realism and spoils the pathos of the scene. Instead of Virgil's dignity of sorrow, or beauty of simile, we have the repulsive details of the still gasping mouth and the drooping neck laid cross-wise on a boat-thwart to be hacked through; there are sinews and veins to cut; there are bones to break; it all takes time (*diu*); for the art of whirling off the head at a single blow, Lucan remarks (with his thoughts perhaps on Caligula), had yet to be developed – *nondum artis erat caput ense rotare.*[1] Such realism is rendered superfluous by what follows:

> To let the cursèd boy prince know the dead,
> Yon manly wealth of hair by kings admired,
> The locks which graced that noble brow, were seized,
> And, while the features lived and sobbing breath
> Yet moved the lips to murmur, while the eyes
> Unclosed were glazing, on a Pharian spear
> Was fixed that head whose word for war had rung
> The knell of peace, the head that swayed our laws
> In *campus* or from *rostra* eloquent.
> This face, O Roman Fortune, pleased thee once![2]

The headless body is recovered from the sea in the moonlight by Cordus, one of Pompey's Roman attendants, and, after an incomplete crema-tion, for which the material has to be supplied by the somewhat ludi-crous device of theft from a conveniently deserted funeral pile, it is buried hastily; for the dawn has surprised Cordus at his ceremonial. But the lonely grave on the beach cannot confine one so illustrious:

> The Roman name and the wide realms of Rome
> Mark the true boundary of great Pompey's tomb.[3]

Imprecations upon Egypt follow – futile, because Lucan's curse of barrenness, if it could have been fulfilled, would have closed the chief granary of Rome. With further wild rhetoric on the burial-place the book ends.

Pompey's apotheosis begins Book IX:

> Not in Egyptian ashes lay his soul:
> A little dust held not so great a shade.
> Spurning the tomb and quitting limbs half-burned
> And the unworthy pyre, it makes for Heaven.

The lamentations of Cornelia, her announcement of her husband's in-junction that unceasing war must be waged for liberty against Caesar, the

[1] VIII. 673.   [2] VIII. 679–686.   [3] VIII. 798–799.

vengeance on Egypt threatened by Pompey's elder son when he learns
of his father's murder, and Cato's dignified praise of the dead leader are
preliminary to the chief theme of the book – the heroism of Cato. He will
have none of the argument that continuance of war is criminal, now that
Pompey is dead. Expostulating with reluctant Pompeians, he sarcastically declares that Caesar will believe they did him an intentional benefit
by running before him at Pharsalia – here and in other passages erroneously called Philippi. As their next objective is Juba's kingdom, Lucan
is enabled to describe the treacherous quicksands of the Syrtes, a storm
that imperils Cato's fleet, and the swamps of Triton which most of the
ships reach in safety. The resolution to march across the desert to
Mauretania occasions a digression on Libya as well as passages recounting Cato's marvellous endurance[1] of thirst, and his refusal to consult
the oracle of Hammon (whose misplacement is one of the not uncommon geographical blunders in Lucan). Labienus would have the will of
Jupiter ascertained by this austere captain of men:

> The laws above have ever ruled thy life,
> And thou dost follow God. Lo! now the leave
> Is thine to speak with Jove. Ask of the doom
> That waits accursed Caesar, and hold search
> Into thy country's future character.[2]

Cato, however, in tones worthy of the oracle itself, scouts the idea,
criticising it on Stoic principles:

> What should be asked? Whether I'd rather die
> Free, arms in hand, or look on tyranny?
> Whether a life is naught, e'en when prolonged?
> Or if years make a difference? Or if
> A good man can be hurt by any blow?
> Does Fortune drop her threats when Virtue fights?
> Is it enough to wish what merits praise?
> Does right ne'er grow by gain? All this we know:
> Jove cannot plant it deeper in our heart.[3]

Cato's inspiring fortitude during the march with his soldiers is almost
smothered beneath the mass of irrelevance expounding the origin of
serpents in Africa, and catalogues enumerating not only various species
of serpents but also various sorts of death from snake-bite. Late in the
book Caesar reappears on a voyage which brings him to the ruins of
Troy; and Lucan's confidence in his own literary immortality prompts
an apostrophe to poetry as conferring eternal renown:

> Hallowed and mighty toil of bards empowered
> To rescue all from fate and grant the gift

---

[1] Cato, as hero of the desert, receives an epithet found nowhere else – *hareni-
uagus*, IX. 941.
[2] IX. 556–559.   [3] IX. 566 *sqq.*

> To mortal nations of eternity!
> Grudge not, O Caesar, fame to heroes old –
> If Latin poësy may promise aught,
> Then, long as Homer's honours shall endure,
> Peoples to come will read both thee and me;
> For our[1] *Pharsalia* will live, and time
> Shall ne'er damn Lucan to obscurity.[2]

Caesar's veneration of his ancestral gods at Troy would have received more sympathetic treatment from Virgil. Lucan is content to record his coasting voyage along Asia Minor and his crossing by Rhodes to Egypt, where, amidst his hesitation whether to land, one of Ptolemy's courtiers comes aboard ship with the head of Pompey. To Lucan his grief over his rival's murder is hypocrisy: now that he had ocular proof of the crime and thought it safe to be a good father-in-law (*tutumque putauit iam bonus esse socer*),

> Some tears he shed that fell not of freewill,
> And forced his moanings from a joyful heart.[3]

Book X, on Caesar in Egypt, would fit better into an epic on the mighty Julius himself than into the *Pharsalia*. Yet it has energy, in spite of a divagation on Alexander the Great, against whom Lucan inveighs as a 'successful bandit' (*felix praedo*), and a longer excursus on the Nile. The principal incidents are Caesar's visit to Alexander's tomb, his amour with Cleopatra, her magnificent banquet after a reconciliation with Ptolemy, the plot of Pothinus to kill Caesar, and the attack at dawn with Caesar at bay:

> He dreads the onset, yet disdains to dread:
> So roars some noble brute in cage confined
> And gnaws his prison till he breaks his teeth.[4]

Before the book is broken short, his arch-enemies, Pothinus and Achillas, are dead; but the renewal of resistance by Ganymedes brings him again into imminent danger. There we leave the Caesar of Lucan. In the opinion of so Pompeian a poet, he cannot be fittingly punished by any blow from Egypt:

> Not till his country's swords transfix the heart
> Of Caesar, shall great Pompey be avenged.[5]

This reference to the postponement of a fated penalty has in some eyes lent colour to the view that the poem was designed to continue Caesar's history up to his assassination in 44. The tenth book is on the face of it incomplete; even were that not obvious, we should detect an unfinished scheme from the assurance given to Sextus Pompey that his

---

[1] *I.e.* fought by you and told by me.   [2] IX. 980 *sqq.*
[3] IX. 1037–1039.   [4] X. 444–446.   [5] X. 528–529.

fate would be foretold by the shade of his dead father.[1] That promised episode, a parallel to Anchises's prophecy uttered to Aeneas, would have come into one of the unwritten books. A likely chronological limit would be Thapsus and the suicide of Cato in 46 B.C. That is Pichon's view,[2] which seems more commendable than his associated argument that, as the necromancy of *Pharsalia VI* corresponds in weirdness to the descent into the lower world in *Aeneid VI*, therefore twelve books must have been planned to answer to Virgil's twelve. Much closer parallelism between the several books of *Pharsalia* and *Aeneid* would have to exist before this contention had validity. In the seventeenth century, the historian Thomas May, whose works in verse and prose are all forgotten save his translation of the *Pharsalia*, believed that Lucan meant to carry his epic as far as Caesar's death. To fill the gap, May composed a *Supplementum*, which Hallam ventured to call 'the first Latin poetry which England can vaunt.' The whole matter is, however, conjectural; and the arguments for a contemplated prolongation to 44 B.C. are not of compelling cogency.

Another point on which there is divergence of opinion concerns the three books issued first according to Vacca's *Life*. Ussani thinks they were I, VII, IX; Pichon thinks II, VII, VIII. One might defend I, II, VII as a more likely group than either, if one took certain mistakes in VII to prove its comparative earliness and were to offer a plausible explanation of its touching-up with anti-Caesarism. In all the suggestions, however, there are difficulties concerning Lucan's attitude to Caesar and Nero; and waverers may do worse than fall back on the traditional view, which presents at least as few difficulties, and is the most natural interpretation of Vacca's words, namely, that I, II, III constituted the *tres libros quales uidemus*.

The seven books not published till after Lucan's death may have been already known to literary circles from the author's readings; for the composition of the *Pharsalia* presumably extended over several years before A.D. 65. If one is satisfied that Lucan even in his first book,[3] as well as in others, borrowed from Seneca's *Naturales Quaestiones* (belonging to A.D. 62 and 63), then that circumstance may be taken to limit the period; but Vitelli's endeavour still further to narrow the time of writing seems unconvincing.[4]

Let us realise the audacity of this youthful author. Himself in touch with an imperial court, he dared write a long poem glorifying the

---

[1] VI. 813–814.

[2] *Op. cit.* p. 270. A. H. Cruickshank, Professor of Greek in Durham, 1910–1927, saw a possible limit in the reference to Munda (45 B.C.) as the last battle of the civil wars, I. 40. But some take *ultima* there as 'most distant,' and Lucan, in spite of *ultima*, goes on to refer to Mutina (43) and Perusia (41 B.C.). R. T. Bruère (*C.P.* 1950, p. 217 ff.) thinks Lucan intended to reach 29 B.C.

[3] *Cf.* the language regarding portentous constellations in *Phars.* I. 527–529 with Sen. *N.Q.* VI. iii. 3 and VII. xx. 3.

[4] For summary of evidence, see S.H. § 390.

opposition to the founder of the imperial principle at Rome. Possibly, in an age of ingenious and bizarre compositions under a clever sovereign, he imagined that his work might pass muster or evade censure as an artistic *tour de force*, and that a generous interpretation would be placed upon a historical thesis handled with epic talent and oiled with introductory adulation. But Lucan must have been sufficiently intimate with the arbitrary despotism of Nero to recognise that in taking such a risk he played a game involving the highest of stakes. A consciousness of genius and an independence of spirit combined with the impetuosity of youth to drive him upon a hazard, in which perhaps he was keen to welcome the fascination of double danger. It was jeopardy enough to challenge the ruler of the world by rivalry in any field of literary eminence; but it was still more perilous to champion the defenders of the ancient republican system. Theirs had been a lost cause; and yet Lucan by setting himself to make idols of Pompey and Cato threw down the gauntlet to Caesarism again. Several factors contributed to this anti-Caesarism. Corduba, the Spanish home of his family, acknowledged a traditional allegiance to Pompey; Lucan's own boyish imagination conjured up roseate visions of the republican past; his reading in the Pompeian books of Livy confirmed his attitude; and the sense of Nero's intolerable unfairness in trying to silence him eventually turned intimacy into detestation.

This independence of spirit has its literary side, where Lucan proves himself an original genius. Apart from possession of a distinctive style, he refused to be encumbered by tradition. His originality lay not in the choice of a Roman historical theme – for there had been many epics, renowned and unrenowned, on national history – but in the decision to treat his theme without the conventional introduction of gods as controllers of the action. This novel method of treatment is, we know, criticised in Petronius.[1] Well aware of the intrinsic greatness of the figures in a colossal struggle, Lucan relied for his effects more on history than on romance. In his theme he thus broke away from Virgilian precedent, and substituted for legendary glamour the interest of a fierce human conflict waged in comparatively recent times.

His equipment for his task may be indicated by a sketch of his sources – historical, philosophical and literary. As regards history, the theory which holds the field is that certain lost books of Livy are the wellsprings of Lucan's subject-matter.[2] This thesis, the outcome of a hint given by Reifferscheid to Baier, his pupil, was maintained by the latter in a work published in 1874. It was reaffirmed by Pichon,[3] whose skill, in a most comprehensive study of Lucan's sources, addressed itself to

---

[1] *Satyr.* 118.
[2] Livy's books from the outbreak of the civil war to Caesar's death were cix–cxvi.
[3] G. Baier, *De Liuio . . . Lucani auctore*, 1874; Pichon, *Les Sources de L.*, 1912.

the emancipation of Baier's hypothesis from the exaggerations of Ziehen and Vitelli, and to its defence against the objections of Westerburg and Ussani. For the accessory material in his digressions Lucan no doubt went elsewhere: serpent-lore he could draw from Macer, who had copied Nicander; geography, in which he is inaccurate, from some general treatise; and data about Egypt in particular very likely from Seneca's missing work on that country. Much of his merely allusive and decorative matter could be furnished from the standard academic learning, amplified by his own experience – he had been a quaestor, he was an augural priest, and he had travelled. But for details of his main theme there lay open at that time the complete decades of Livy, who had derived information from Caesar, Posidonius and others. Material contemporary with the civil war could thus be reached through Livy as an intermediary. By Livy it had been to a large extent already Pompeianised. Lucan was not temperamentally likely to follow Caesar's own account; he would distrust Asinius Pollio, as one too active on Caesar's side; and although he might well have found facts to recommend the writings of Cremutius Cordus, we do not know that Cordus related the struggle between Caesar and Pompey. On the other hand, Livy was an author for whose literary power the Senecas expressed warm admiration, and Lucan, while subscribing to the opinion entertained by his grandfather[1] and his uncle,[2] felt the special call of political sympathy.

Lucan's historical value must remain a debatable question. It is comparatively easy, though it costs time, to construct a formidable list of his inexactitudes and deliberate departures from fact.[3] It is also easy to illustrate his strong bias against Caesar. The bias may be readily explained; but it is not always so easy to be sure that the unhistorical in him is due either to bias or to ignorance. When, for instance, he introduces Cicero, contrary to truth, in Pompey's camp before Pharsalia, is he simply careless, or has he yielded to a half-poetic, half-rhetorical desire to insert a speech from the orator? The almost infectious enthusiasm of Pichon for Lucan, while it makes him too tolerant of his wearisome digressions, too laudatory of poetic merit in his rhetoric, too appreciative of the originality of his borrowings, at the same time makes him perhaps too ingenious in finding excuses for his mis-statements. Yet the defence is at times justifiable. For example, as regards the frequently criticised epithets applied to Gallic tribes, their appropriateness is plausibly supported on historical, philological and archaeological grounds.[4] Again, on the alleged confusion between Arverni and Aedui

---

[1] Sen. *Contr.* X. *praef.* 2; *Suas.* vi. 22.
[2] Sen. *Ep.* c. 9.
[3] See Heitland's Introd. to Haskins's ed.
[4] Pichon's explanation (*op. cit.* p. 29) of the *picta arma* of the Lingones as 'une allusion aux boucliers ornés d'émail que l'on fabriquait à Bibracte' must interest anyone who has seen the Aeduan antiquities from Mont Beuvray at Autun.

(I. 427), Lucan's language need not involve the mistake commonly supposed, if proper stress be laid on both verbs in the line,

Aruernique ausi Latios se fingere fratres.

Certainly, to construct against Lucan a laborious indictment of error is quite misleading. It should, in any case, be noted that his additions are fewer than his omissions, and many alterations of historical fact charged against the *Pharsalia* may be due to Livy. One may surmise that Lucan himself is responsible for the silence about Caesar's pacific overtures, for the sinister misconstruction laid upon Caesar's clemency, and for the undervaluing of Caesarian bravery; because Livy, writing near the events, could hardly have risked such falsification of history. But, to hazard a guess – and here it is all guesswork – if Livy recorded generous acts by Caesar with some reserve as to their motives, then Lucan might conceivably drop them out because he did not think them sincere; and if characteristic episodes of bravery among the Caesarians were recorded, as we might expect, by Livy, then Lucan might with a kind of Stoic casuistry decline to take them over, because it would be evil to praise valour so ill employed. On the other hand, the elimination of Pompeian bloodthirstiness is presumably a feature already occurring in Livy;[1] and it is highly probable that incidents which put Pompey in an unfavourable light would be toned down by the historian who was twitted with having proved himself a good 'Pompeian.' In short, Lucan's suppressions and transpositions of fact are sometimes those of a partisan (and herein Livy preceded him), sometimes those of the artist who is interpreting history in a poet's way.

One result of his choice of subject, it will thus be seen, is that some questions affecting Lucan are not literary questions at all, but concern historical value and mis-statements intentional or unintentional. There is a risk of harbouring an exaggerated estimate of his historical acumen. Granted that he is at least scientific enough to note certain causes of the civil war, yet he betrays no conception of the vital constitutional principles involved, of the extent to which past abuses rendered the conflict inevitable, or of the real significance of the victory for the destinies of Rome and the world. Though in some aspects very Roman, Lucan is without Virgil's profound insight into the mission of the Empire. Readers will concede that he is sensitive to the nefarious horror and enormity of civil strife, for he calls shame upon it in exclamatory outbursts repeated till we weary; but this fervour arises less from social or moral or even vaguely humanitarian considerations than from his ingrained rhetoric. One should not presume to blame him: we have little right to demand scientific history from a poet. Although he selected a historical subject and so must remain, faults notwithstanding, a source

[1] Pichon believes this 'sans doute,' *op. cit.* p. 145.

of history,[1] yet it is not by historical standards than Lucan must be judged, nor, despite his Livian basis, could we unreservedly use his text to supply some of the missing matter of Livy. Frank allowance must be made for prejudices and inconsistencies, which are but natural to juvenile ardour and emotion. He had definitely taken his side, and it is absurd to look for a dispassionate attitude to Caesarian or Pompeian. Interested in philosophy without being a philosopher, he was not concerned to reflect how un-Stoic it was, and in any case, how futile, to reproach Caesar, the man of destiny, for being also a man of blood. Here, as so often, he lets feeling speak.

What philosophy appears in the poem is Stoic. Remembering the poet's family and his training alongside of Persius, we should expect nothing else; but it should also be remembered that the philosophical colour is incidental, and that the *Pharsalia* must, in the last resort, be judged less for its history or its philosophy than for its poetry. Critics like Heitland make as great a mistake in claiming a systematic character for Lucan's Stoicism as Souriau does in over-emphasising its contradictions. To demand rigid consistency in his thought is to end in the negative conclusion of Lejay – that Lucan had no philosophy. If a lapse into pessimism caused him to wonder whether the world is guided by the Stoic Providence or by blind chance, it was a very human aberration from his normal creed; and if, poet-like, he used the older mythological beliefs, such literary decoration must be no more pressed against him than against Lucretius.

Lucan's literary training implied acquaintance with the classics of the past. It would be far too much to call him a disciple of Virgil: his spirit is alien to the Virgilian, and yet his debt to the great epic poet was inevitable owing to the education of the times. Here the truth lies between Merivale's astonishing opinion that Lucan was in style practically independent of Virgil and Heitland's that Lucan was 'steeped' in Virgil's language. The debt is seen in borrowed words and locutions (like *felix qui potuit*, IV. 393, and *uenit summa dies*, VII. 195), in a fresh use of Virgilian epithets and phrases, in a heightening of Virgilian simplicity to achieve strong effects, and in imitation of Virgilian episodes. Conscious and subconscious echoes are so plentiful and obvious that one cannot feel like Merivale 'almost tempted to imagine that he had never read Virgil.' At the same time, there is no need to hunt for parallels where no parallels exist. Many of the alleged analogies in Heitland's elaborate list are too vague and faint to be reckoned as definite

[1] Lucan's influence on Appian, Dio Cassius and Orosius, asserted by V. Ussani (*Sul valore storico del poema Lucaneo*, Rome 1903) is denied on good grounds by Pichon (*op. cit.* p. 81 ff.). Westerburg (*Rh.M.* xxxvii (1882) p. 34 ff.) maintains that Florus drew from Lucan, and so did not simply summarise Livy. Against this theory powerful arguments are arrayed by Pichon (*op. cit.* pp. 69–81). Postgate (ed. Bk. VIII, postscript to Introd.) remarks that much of the difficulty would be removed by the assumption that the epitomator of Livy used Lucan as well as Livy and that Florus used the epitome.

K

borrowings; and even Pichon, who adopts a sounder attitude regarding the Virgilian influence, scarcely convinces us in his claim that the vanishing of Julia's ghost is modelled on that of Creusa, or that a father's anguish over a dying son is modelled on Anna's grief over Dido.[1]

Horace influenced Lucan slightly, Ovid very considerably. Sharing his uncle's admiration for Ovid, he not only borrowed mythological material from him but also inherited much of his rhetorical dexterity. The Ovidian gift of repeating an idea in surprisingly new ways reappears in Lucan, and accounts for Fronto's criticism that in his first seven lines he simply rang the changes on the one idea of 'worse-than-civil wars.'[2] He has not Ovid's wonderful lightness and facility, but in the smoothness and monotony of his versification it can be seen that the rhythms of the *Metamorphoses* have told upon him. Resemblances to earlier poets like Ennius[3] are not distinct enough to base conclusions upon; and a similarly negative result, many will agree, comes from the evidence adduced by Hosius[4] to detect verbal influences exerted by Manilius, by the author of *Aetna*, by the earlier books of Livy and by Q. Curtius. This inquiry has considerable interest in its bearing on works so conjectural in date as the *Astronomica*, *Aetna* and the *History of Alexander*; but unfortunately the evidence rests upon slight similarities and amounts to little. Some of the not very impressive resemblances between Curtius and Lucan are due to analogy of facts (deserts, for example, are much alike the world over, and prompt similar terminology); other resemblances may be ascribed to community of source; and others are simply part of the common stock of Latin expression. One exceptional case is that of Seneca, some of whose works, particularly the tragedies, appear (after allowance has been made for the wide prevalence of the same mythology and the same rhetoric) to have affected Lucan. This hypothesis, if accepted, would prove the anteriority of the tragedies and support their attribution to Seneca.

Far more important, however, than the discovery of verbal similarities is the consideration of the action of rhetoric on Lucan's genius. When it is remembered that the essential aim in academic declamation was to appear clever and striking at all costs, the central characteristic of his epic is at once grasped. The dominant note is one of display. The object, not to be natural, but above everything to be piquant and impressive, is pursued with marvellous vigour and with mastery of all effective artifices. To his training, therefore, and to his aim we owe the parade of erudition which leads him into digressions[5] and enumerations: the descent into realistic detail which is calculated to cause a shudder;

---

[1] Pichon, *Sources de L.* p. 226; Heitland's Introd. to Haskins's ed. p. cviii ff.
[2] Fronto, *De Orat.* § 5 (Naber 157): 'is initio carminis sui septem primis uersibus nihil aliud quam *bella plus quam ciuilia* interpretatus est.'
[3] Heitland, *op. cit.* p. cxxviii.
[4] *Rh.M.* xlviii (1893) p. 393 ff.; Pichon, *Sources de L.* p. 235 ff.
[5] References are given in Heitland, *op. cit.*

the subtlety of argument which makes a debating speech cogent; the
tendency to hyperbole which is bound to arrest attention; the love of
point, epigram, antithesis which produces memorable phrases; and the
recollection or invention of pithy maxims which embody human experience. His erudition is in part encyclopaedic, based on the science of the
day, and in part mythological, based on the ancient literary education.
The former accounts for excursuses on subjects like astronomy and geography,[1] many of which are out of place; the latter appears in allusions
or descriptions. The allusions may be straightforward, as when the preparations for Pharsalia are likened to those before the giants' war, and
when Caesar haunted by ghosts is likened to the matricide Orestes;[2] or
they may be slightly more recondite, as when the olive-branch is called
'the leafage of Cecropian Minerva,' and when Marius is said to 'gather
Libyan wrath,' because, like the giant Antaeus, he drew fighting-force
from the soil of Africa.[3] Myth in Lucan's eyes yields opportunities for
exhibiting book-knowledge and so overpowers his philosophy upon
occasion. Certainly in a critical mood he would, Stoic-like, reject the
legends. It is the free-thinker that speaks through Cornelia's guarded
promise to follow her husband 'through hell, if hell there be' (*per
Tartara, si sunt ulla*, IX. 101–102). But should the old traditional colour
seem requisite, Lucan makes no scruple about its introduction: thus
Julia's ghost, expelled from Elysium (III. 12), knows that Tartarus is
being enlarged to punish human misdeeds. His attitude is, in fact, not
consistent: On the one hand, when Pompey reaches Cyprus, Lucan
resists the attraction of the tale which long after inspired Botticelli's
'Nascita di Venere,' and so surrenders to rationalism with the unpoetic
caveat 'si numina nasci credimus':[4] on the other hand, he is romantic
enough to discern in the story of Antaeus or of the Golden Apples a
chance for a telling description:[5]

> None but a churl insults time-hallowed eld
> And summons bards to tell plain truth. There was
> Once on a time a forest all of gold
> Whose wealth weighed down its boughs with yellow fruit.
> A troop of maidens watched that radiant grove:
> And round the trees, 'neath ruddy metal bowed,
> A serpent never doomed to slumber coiled.

Realism in Lucan is now natural, now morbid, now grotesque. Too
often it is coupled with the desire to harrow by dwelling on the horrible.
Hence he revels in describing tortures, the agonies of the wounded, the
repulsive ghoulishness of a witch, the still twitching mouth of Pompey

---

[1] VIII. 161–184; X. 172 *sqq.*   [2] VII. 144 *sqq.*; *ibid.* 777 *sqq.*
[3] II. 93; III. 306. So it involves a little mythological lore to understand why,
among omens of trouble, the flame announcing the close of the Latin festival is
said to be parted into two, 'copying the Theban pyres' (I. 550–552).
[4] VIII. 458 *sqq.*   [5] IV. 589 *sqq.*; IX. 359 *sqq.*

after his head has been hacked off, revolting aspects of cremation, and equally revolting aspects of putrefaction.[1] So zealous is he in making a point that he again and again overshoots the mark, as in his account of a crowd of victims mutually smothering each other;[2] or of an old man's reminiscence of searching among the slain during the Sullan Terror for a body whose neck would fit his brother's head, which he was carrying;[3] or of Curio's slaughtered men in Africa having no room to fall:

> Hemmed by the throng each corpse still kept its feet
> (*Compressum turba stetit omne cadauer*, IV. 787).

When the realism is strained to breaking-point, it becomes unreal, as in the carnage during the sea-fight at Massilia. There the devilish ingenuity in inventing bizarre modes of death fails to make the struggle truly heroic, because the artificiality detracts from strong simplicity and pathos.[4] The poet, having caused smiles by far-fetched conceits, only just succeeds towards the end in striking a note of human feeling when he relates the parting of the mortally wounded Argus from his father.[5]

Good examples of Lucan's management of speeches are those of Caesar and Pompey in Book VII, where the two great opponents are made to express themselves in the author's forceful, if rather bombastic, rhetoric. In Volteius's speech in Book IV, encouraging his men to slay each other, we have virtually a thesis supported by the tricks of the schools and transferred to verse: the men by their death have to make a spectacle of themselves and the speech is correspondingly spectacular. The same rhetoric, often powerful and ingenious, invades parts of the epic where there is no set speech, but where the poet becomes declamatory, rendering his work, Quintilian thought, *magis oratoribus quam poetis imitandus*. Thus the reflections upon Pompey's grave in Book VIII are composed after the fashion of a special pleader in a *controuersia*. The smartness in shifting positions and the disregard for consistency argue little solidity; and even where, as in this passage,[6] the author's favourite Pompey is concerned, the limited depth of feeling is comparable to nothing so much as that of a versatile advocate. One is naturally reminded of Lucan's lost prose speeches for and against Sagitta.

Hyperbole is among his most noticeable rhetorical tendencies. He overstates and, in pursuit of overstatements, is drawn into the kind of elaboration which characterises the storm in Book V.[7] But the exaggeration is often confined to a single idea: so, to convey the notion of Caesar's immense lines of circumvallation near Dyrrhachium, Lucan avers that, inside them, rivers run their whole length from source to mouth,

---

[1] II. 173 *sqq.*; IV. 566 *sqq.*; VI. 529–569; VIII. 667–691; VIII. 777–778; IX. 766–781.
[2] II. 201 *sqq.* [3] II. 172. [4] III. 567 *sqq.*
[5] III. 723–751. [6] VIII. 851 *sqq.* [7] V. 593 *sqq.*

> There many rivers rise and speed their course
> Till yet within the lines they join the sea;[1]

and, of Thessaly polluted by the slain,

> What crop shall rise unstained with tainted blade?
> Thy plough shall ever wound a Roman ghost![2]

One of the great secrets of Lucan's brilliant rhetoric is his subtle power of expressing thought in terse[3] pointed form, often assisted by antithesis. When this subtlety is not carried to excess, the results are extraordinarily effective in producing memorable lines and phrases, epigrammatically summarising a character or a situation or, in the older meaning of *sententia*, a general truth. Even his less natural conceits have a way of clinging to the memory, like his paradoxical manner of suggesting that when Caesar's ships lie helpless on a still sea the crews would prefer a watery grave to being thus becalmed: 'all hope of shipwreck vanishes' (*naufragii spes omnis abit*).[4] Typical commonplaces admirably expressed in his neat Latin are those on the peril of success,

> Greatness is wrecked upon itself: the gods
> Have set that limit on prosperity
> (*In se magna ruunt: laetis hunc numina rebus*
> *Crescendi posuere modum*, I. 81–82);

on the danger of delay,

> Postponement ever hurts the well-prepared
> (*Semper nocuit differre paratis*, I. 281);

on famine as a cause of revolt,

> A starving people knows not fear
> (*Nescit plebes ieiuna timere*, III. 58);

on the secret happiness of death,

> From those who are to live the gods conceal
> The bliss of death; so they endure their life
> (*Victurosque dei celant ut uiuere durent*
> *Felix esse mori*, IV. 519–520);

on condonation of a widely supported fault,

> The sin that many share goes unavenged
> (*Quidquid multis peccatur inultum est*, V. 260);

---

[1] VI. 45–46. [2] VII. 851–852.
[3] He carries condensation too far, *e.g.* II. 35, *diuisere deos* = 'they divided the gods,' *i.e.* Roman ladies took their prayers to different temples; or he uses an over-fanciful conceit, *e.g.* II. 72, *depositum* applied to Marius, the exile, as 'the deposit' entrusted by Fortune to the marshes. But such phrases have at least the intended quality of being striking.
[4] V. 455.

on death, as viewed in Pompey's last words,

> In life success is mutable: in death
> Man meets not misery
> > (*Mutantur prospera uitae,*
> *Non fit morte miser*, VIII. 631–632);

on the true attitude to death,

> The brave man's finest lot
> Is knowledge how to die; next, death enforced
> (*Scire mori sors prima uiris, sed proxima cogi*, IX. 211).

Alliteration is noticeable in some of the examples cited. Lucan does not use it so sparingly as Heitland suggests: on the contrary, much of his verse gains additional emphasis from being alliterative, as does his best known line,

> Heaven loved the winning cause, Cato the lost
> (*Victrix causa deis placuit sed uicta Catoni*, I. 128);

or the simile descriptive of a storming charge by African horse,

> The loud sound shook the land: from shattered earth,
> High as the dust the Thracian whirlwind drives,
> A cloud dimmed heaven and drew the darkness down
> (*Tum campi tremuere sono: terraque soluta*
> *Quantus Bistonio torquetur turbine puluis,*
> *Aëra nube sua texit traxitque tenebras*, IV. 766–768).

A scrutiny of Lucan's feverish mannerisms and wilful faults must not blind one to his merits. It is true that he is rhetorical and sensational; and that behind his clever artifices lies no mystery. He is able half to surprise, half to weary us with dazzling tricks of style; but he seldom enchants us with beauty. Yet, when all his inaccuracies, distortions, conceits, digressions and tediousness have been urged against him, his great passages prove that, in spite of artificiality, he can be fiery[1] and wellnigh irresistible. He would have gained extraordinarily by compression: that is to say, he shows to most advantage in extracts. His best rhetoric is something intensely stirring, though it is a style more appreciated in France than in England. Nor, even if he seldom is deeply poetic, should the vein of poetry that is in him be overlooked: it appears in passages such as that on Pompey's last look at Italy, or on Cornelia in love with sorrow:

> Locking in fast embrace her cruel grief,
> She hath her joy in tears, enamourèd
> Of woe that henceforth is her lord
> > (*Saeuomque arte complexa dolorem*
> *Perfruitur lacrimis et amat pro coniuge luctum*, IX. 111–112).

---

[1] Quint. X. i. 90: 'ardens et concitatus.'

Some have submitted that the *Pharsalia* is an epic without a hero, or alternatively an epic with three heroes. Perhaps it is truer to argue that Lucan in a real degree rose to the inherent greatness of his theme by so portraying Caesar that, while Pompey was his formal hero and Cato his spiritual hero, Caesar, however much disliked and maligned by the author, was and still is the practical hero of the poem in virtue of the defiant egoism and the untiring energy summarised in the line,

> Thinking naught done while aught remained to do
> (*Nil actum credens cum quid superesset agendum*, II. 657).

Chapter VII

CALPURNIUS SICULUS AND MINOR POETRY OF THE NERONIAN AGE

Calpurnius and Nemesianus – Calpurnius belongs to Neronian period – Is 'Meliboeus' Seneca? – The seven Eclogues – *Panegyric on Piso* possibly by Calpurnius – Identification of the patron eulogised – Some aspects of style.

The Einsiedeln Eclogues – Uncertain date and authorship of *Aetna* – A blend of dullness and enthusiasm – The best passage – The *Latin Iliad* – Latin translations from Homer – Suggested acrostics bearing on authorship – Why was the Latin Homer called 'Pindar'? – Departures from the Greek original – Nero as poet – The lesser lights.

CALPURNIUS SICULUS

THE importance of the eclogues of T. Calpurnius Siculus rests as much upon their testimony to the continuance of one aspect of Virgil's influence as upon intrinsic poetic value. Eleven eclogues for long went under his name; but the edition by Angelus Ugoletus about 1500 cites the authority of a manuscript now lost for assigning the last four to Nemesianus, who wrote late in the third century. There is, in any case, good internal evidence for the separation; for, in the last four, elision is much commoner; more unclassical shortenings of final *o* appear; the parenthetic insertions of *memini* and *fateor* frequent in the first seven are absent; nor are there any of the allusions to the emperor which were familiar in the previous group. Besides, the ninth eclogue imitates parts of the third, though its taste is more questionable; and there are stylistic resemblances between the final eclogues and the undoubted work of Nemesianus on the chase – his *Cynegetica*.

Whether the epithet 'Siculus' means that he came from Sicily or that he was a follower of the Sicilian pastoral of Theocritus cannot be decided. His date too has been the subject of debate. The older theory of Wernsdorf, Gibbon and Bernhardy, that Calpurnius wrote under the Emperor Carus and his sons in the third century, has been rejected by most modern authorities for cogent reasons which combine to fix the eclogues early in the reign of Nero. The ruler they mention is young

(i. 44; iv. 85, 137; vii. 6),[1] good-looking (vii. 83–84),[2] divine (i. 84 *ipse deus*; vii. 6) and eloquent (i. 45; iv. 87). This applies to Nero satisfactorily.

The contemplation of a better time as in prospect (i. 42, 54),[3] and of fairer treatment of the senate (i. 62) is in keeping with the actual relief and confidence felt in the opening reign of Nero, when contrasted with the closing years of Claudius. The comet described in the first eclogue is most plausibly identified with that which, according to the elder Pliny, Suetonius, and Dio Cassius, betokened the death of Claudius and lasted into Nero's reign.[4] The scene of the games described in the seventh eclogue is not the Colosseum (which was not begun till the reign of Vespasian), but the wooden amphitheatre of Nero's time mentioned by Tacitus and Suetonius.[5] No other epoch, then, suits all these references so well as the early Neronian.

How far we can rely on Corydon's mention of a brother or of poverty for autobiographic information about the poet is extremely doubtful. The reference to Meliboeus as a patron who saved him by assistance from the need of going to Spain[6] may have a personal bearing, and the question of identifying the patron has been much discussed. Granted that he is a historical figure, Sarpe's[7] contention that Meliboeus was Seneca is

---

[1] iv. 84:

> At mihi qui nostras praesenti numine terras
> Perpetuamque regit iuuenili robore pacem,
> Laetus et augusto felix arrideat ore. . . . '

vii. 6: 'Quae patula iuuenis deus edit harena.'

[2] vii. 83–84:

> '. . . Ac nisi me uisus decepit, in uno
> Et Martis uultus et Apollinis esse putaui.

[3] i. 42:

> 'Aurea secura cum pace renascitur aetas,
> Et redit ad terras tandem squalore situque
> Alma Themis posito, iuuenemque beata sequuntur
> Saecula, maternis causam qui uicit Iulis' (*v.l.* in ulnis!).

[4] *Ecl.* i. 77–83; Pliny, *N.H.* II. 92; Suet. *Claud.* xlvi; Dio lx. 35.

[5] *Ecl.* vii. 23–24:

> 'Vidimus in caelum *trabibus spectacula textis*
> Surgere, Tarpeium prope despectantia culmen';

Tac. *Ann.* XIII. xxxi (A.D. 57): 'nisi cui libeat laudandis fundamentis et *trabibus* quis molem amphitheatri apud campum Martis Caesar exstruxerat uolumina implere'; Suet. *Nero* xii: 'munere quod *in amphitheatro ligneo* regione Martii campi intra anni spatium fabricato dedit. . . .' The games instituted by Nero are mentioned in Suet. *Nero* xi. [6] iv. 36–42.

[7] G. Sarpe, *Quaest. philol.*, Rostock 1819. C. H. Keene, in Introd. to his edn. p. 12, agrees. Summers, *Silver Age of Latin Lit.* p. 91, thinks that to identify the patron with Seneca or Calpurnius Piso is sheer caprice. See also S.H. § 386a, paragraph entitled 'Die Personennamen.' A recent study is 'Les Pseudonymes dans les Bucol. de Calp. Sic.' by L. Herrmann (*Latomus* 1952, p. 27 ff.). He makes Meliboeus Calpurnius Piso, and Tityrus not Virgil but Lucan. Corydon, as is generally agreed, is Calpurnius Siculus himself; Ornytus and Amyntas are his two brothers. Herrmann then identifies eleven other shepherds with literary personages of the time. *E.g.* Lycidas=Persius; Iollas=Cornutus; Thyrsis=Silius Italicus, Micon=Seneca; Stimicon=Statius.

K*

more satisfying than Haupt's identification of him with Calpurnius Piso, who in the *Laus Pisonis* is spoken of as under the patronage of Apollo. The fourth eclogue[1] describes Meliboeus as a poet under the auspices of Apollo and the Muses; and further it is suggested that he is an authority on winds and weather. Both references suit Seneca, who was a tragic poet and an observer of physical phenomena in his *Quaestiones Naturales*. Meliboeus is evidently a personage of exalted influence, and the idea of his acting as intermediary between the rustic singer and the emperor[2] is consistent with Seneca's high position at the imperial court.

The seven eclogues range in length from 84 lines (vii) to 169 (iv), and amount to 759 hexameters altogether. They are smoothly composed; and the echoes of Virgilian thought, expression, and poem-construction are obvious. Other Augustans are also laid under contribution. The whole effect, allowing for the artificiality and conventionality inseparable from the pastoral, is pleasing rather than forceful. The poet as 'Corydon' is conscious that to seek to be a second Virgil ('Tityrus') is an ambitious task, and so he represents Meliboeus as saying:

> High aim'st thou, Corydon, if Tityrus
> Thou striv'st to be. He was a bard inspired
> Who on the reed-pipe could outplay the lyre.[3]

Eclogue I is modelled loosely on the so-called Messianic eclogue of Virgil. Two rustics, Corydon and Ornytus, are sheltering from the scorching heat of the noontide,

> Where 'neath its very root the beechtree keeps
> Guard o'er the bubbling waters of the brook
> And casts a tangled shade with swaying boughs,[4]

when they find, carved on the bark of a tree, a prophecy by Faunus which heralds the dawn of a new golden age of peace and clemency associated with the accession of a young ruler, 'a very god, who will take in his stout arms the weight of the Roman empire.' Eclogue II, after the manner of Virgil's seventh eclogue, contains an amoebean contest in quatrains in which a shepherd and a gardener praise Crotale, the object of their admiration, and make rival offers in this wise:

> *Idas.* Lambs countless bleating 'neath the teat I feed;
> Countless Tarentine ewes yield wool for me,
> And all the year my snow-white cheese is press'd.
> Come, Crotale! This store shall all be thine.

[1] iv. 53 *sqq.*   [2] iv. 158–159.
[3] iv. 64–66:

> 'Magna petis, Corydon, si Tityrus esse laboras:
> Ille fuit uates sacer et qui posset auena
> Praesonuisse chelyn.'

[4] i. 11–12:

> 'Bullantes ubi fagus aquas radice sub ipsa
> Protegit et ramis errantibus implicat umbras.'

Astacus. Who seeks to count the apples which I pick
Below my trees, will sooner count fine sand;
Winter nor summer checks my crop of herbs.
Come, Crotale! The garden all is thine.[1]

In III, Iollas searching for a lost heifer meets Lycidas, who tells how
jealousy has driven him to lose his temper so far as to beat his sweetheart, Phyllis. Penitently he now would woo her love back in song, and
the poem ends with Iollas's undertaking the part of peacemaker. 'Out-
and-out country, and clownish at that' (*merum rus idque inficetum*)
was Scaliger's sweeping judgement on the eclogue, which has however
redeeming touches of delicacy and chivalry. Eclogue IV, much the
longest, is full of eulogy for the youthful emperor, whose services to
the world are chanted in responsive verses by Corydon and Amyntas
before their patron Meliboeus, who is besought to bring the verses
under the eye of his imperial majesty:

Corydon. O how my lines that run in slender strain
Would, Meliboeus, then resound, if e'er
Men said I had a home among those hills,
If e'er I chanc'd to see a farm my own!
For oft unkindly poverty would pluck
My ear and say 'The sheepfold is thy task.'
Yet, Meliboeus, should'st thou think my lays
Worth noticing, then bear them to our Lord;
For heaven grants thee right to pass within
The Palatine Apollo's holy walls.[2]

Eclogue V is more reminiscent of the *Georgics* than of the *Eclogues*, and
therefore savours more of work than of the idealised recreation which is
the feature of pastorals. It is extravagantly praised in the hexameter
summaries of Brassicanus's edition, to the effect that the agricultural
writers Varro, Palladius, Columella, Cato and Virgil himself were all
outdone here by the brief precepts enjoined by Mycon upon his young
pupil Canthus. The precepts largely concern the management of sheep
and goats.

The subject of VI is a not very entertaining wrangle between a pair
of shepherds over a decision which one of them had pronounced in a
musical contest between two other swains. The wrangle, it is proposed,
might be settled by a poetic competition between the disputants; but
their bad temper and abuse force the selected umpire to decline to act.
The last poem, VII, with a similarity in scheme to Virgil's first eclogue,
possesses a special archaeological interest by reason of the description
which the countryman Corydon, newly back from town, gives of the
wooden amphitheatre in Rome, where a 'young god' of an emperor
exhibited thrilling and surprising contests. The variety of rare animals

[1] ii. 68–75. [2] iv. 152–159.

and quick scenic changes had filled the rustic eyewitness with wonderment; and at a distance he could see the emperor himself:

> Unless my eyesight lied, one face methought
> Combined Apollo's look with that of Mars.[1]

It will be noted that these poems are not all strictly pastoral: under a bucolic guise the first, fourth, and seventh are essentially court-poetry with semi-political flavour and no little adulation. And in any case, whether they contained flatteries of the emperor or not, poems so artificial, as pastorals must be, were more likely to appeal to courtly readers than to any other audience of their day. The literary influence of Calpurnius Siculus was transmitted through Nemesianus to later centuries than the third, reappearing in the Renaissance pastorals of the Italians, Baptista Mantuanus, Sannazaro, and Andrelinus, and in the more prosaic French scholar Arnolletus (Arnoullet) of Nevers.[2] The first among these, the 'good old Mantuan' cited in *Love's Labour's Lost*, printed ten eclogues in 1498, and through them affected many authors of the sixteenth and seventeenth centuries, including Alexander Barclay's 'egloges' and, more memorable still, three 'aeglogues' in the *Shepheardes Calender* of Spenser.

A Panegyric on Piso (now generally taken to be C. Calpurnius Piso, the figurehead in the abortive plot against Nero in A.D. 65) has been claimed by some as the work of Calpurnius Siculus.[3] The 261 hexameters *De Laude Pisonis* are carefully composed, and, like those of Calpurnius's eclogues, contain few elisions.[4] The passage where the panegyrist addresses Piso as his Maecenas and a passage in Calpurnius's fourth eclogue addressed to Corydon's patron Meliboeus resemble each other in the application of the epithet *tereti* (probably 'slender') to verse; but the coincidence does not make irrefragable proof of unity of authorship.[5] The utmost that can be said is that the identification is plausible. The ascription to Virgil, reported from a lost manuscript of the whole poem, is impossible; while the ascription to Lucan in a manuscript of extracts results from a copyist's blunder; and such resemblances

---

[1] vii. 83–84.

[2] The influence of Calpurnius is illustrated in W. P. Mustard's notes to his edns. of *The Eclogues of Baptista Mantuanus*, 1911; *The Piscatory Eclogues of Sannazaro*, 1914; *The Eclogues of Andrelinus and Arnolletus*, 1918.

[3] M. Haupt, *Opusc.* I. p. 391; *cf.* Lachmann's comm. on Lucretius, ed. 3, 1866, p. 326, 'laudator Pisonis Calpurnius.' H. Schenkl (Ed. of Calp. Sic., Lpz. 1885, p. ix), F. Skutsch (P.W. *s.v.* Calpurnius, no. 119) and L. Herrmann (*Latomus* 1952, p. 27 ff.) are among the supporters of the Calp. Sic. theory.

[4] There are three instances, two in the first foot (*atque illos*, 24; *quare age*, 81) and one in the third (*et te credibile est*, 168), among the 261 lines; there are eight elisions, all in the first foot (eleven, if three doubtful cases be admitted) among the 759 lines of Calp. Siculus.

[5] *De Laude Pis.* 248: 'Tu mihi Maecenas tereti cantabere uersu.' Calp. Sic. iv. 152: 'tereti decurrent carmine uersus.'

in diction to the *Pharsalia* of Lucan as can be traced[1] in the panegyric
are due to identity of period rather than of authorship. As conceivable
authors of the poem three other names, Ovid, Saleius Bassus and
Statius, have been put forward, of whom the first lived too early and the
second and third too late to write it.

More certain ground is reached regarding the person eulogised. The
poet, who declares himself under twenty summers old (261), poor,
but ambitious for literary fame in preference to wealth (219–221),
directs his praises to a youthful patron, eloquent, courteous, generous,
musical, fond of games, and especially expert on the draught-board.
Such characteristics accord with the description of C. Calpurnius Piso
in Tacitus[2] and with Juvenal's 'Piso bonus' of Satire V. 109, where the
old scholium recounts Piso to have been such a celebrity for his playing
with *latrunculi* that people flocked to watch him. The panegyric was most
likely composed earlier than the eclogues of Calpurnius Siculus; and it
does not follow, though the 'Maecenas' of the one poem is C. Calpurnius Piso, that the 'Meliboeus' in the other poems need be the same
patron.

The laudation tends to monotony, though it never becomes absurdly
fulsome. Piso, whom the poet more than once addresses as *iuuenis
facunde* (32, 109), is honoured for having renounced the martial glory
of his ancestors to

> Wage kindly war before a legal judge;[3]

for ability to stir the emotions of the court,

> if thou sayest 'weep,'
> He weeps, then smiles if forced by thee to smile;[4]

and for captivating clients by his courtesy,

> thou dost show the path
> Of deference, and loving courtest love.[5]

Judged by the test of style alone, the piece has the ring of the first
century, and the spirit of the references to oratory is unmistakably post-
Augustan. It should be pointed out that the repeated use of *chelys*
for the 'lyre' suggests a similar period.[6] But reliance on internal stylistic
evidence is ancillary rather than essential, where the recipient of the
panegyric has been definitely identified.

[1] For such resemblances, see *Laus Pisonis* by Gladys Martin, Cornell Univ.
diss., 1917. However the ascription to Lucan has found modern support, *e.g.*
B. L. Ullman, *C.P.* 1929, p. 109 ff., and R. Verdière in his edition of Calp. Sic.
etc., Brussels 1953. For record of theories up to 1935 see S.H. § 387.
[2] *Ann.* XV. xlviii.
[3] l. 29: 'Mitia legitimo sub iudice bella mouere.'
[4] l. 47: 'Flet si flere iubes, gaudet gaudere coactus.'
[5] l. 132: 'Obsequiumque doces et amorem quaeris amando.'
[6] *De Laude Pis.* 166, 171, 242. *Chelys* is, except for Ovid's use, post-Augustan;
e.g. Calp. Sic. iv. 66, and in Statius often.

MINOR NERONIAN POETRY

Further examples of the bucolic verse of Nero's age are furnished by the Einsiedeln Eclogues. These are two brief pieces contained in a tenth-century manuscript at Einsiedeln. The first, in 49 hexameters, is a contest of the conventional type between two shepherds who praise the emperor's dexterity on the *cithara*, the one likening him to Apollo and the Thunderer, the other alluding to his poem on the burning of Troy. The umpire's decision is wanting. The other piece, 38 lines long, rejoices over the return of the Golden Age,

Saturni rediere dies, Astraeaque uirgo,

in the spirit of Calpurnius Siculus's

Aurea secura cum pace renascitur aetas,

and must belong to the happier opening years of Nero's reign. Beyond this there is no certainty about date or authorship, though considerable learned speculation[1] has been expended on two rather inconsiderable eclogues. The frail argument, for instance, has been used that Seneca's expression *fas sit uidisse* in Letter 115 (probably 64 B.C.) must refer to and so be later than *fas mihi sit uidisse deos* in the first poem. The higher literary quality of the second piece has appeared to some sufficient reason for assuming dual authorship: others[2] have in both seen lost eulogies by Lucan on the emperor: others still ascribe them to C. Calpurnius Piso,[3] laying stress on the way in which the first words of the second poem *Quid tacitus, Mystes?* seem to be echoed in the first words of Calpurnius Siculus's fourth eclogue, *Quid tacitus, Corydon?* Since the speaker there is Meliboeus (identified by some scholars, as we have seen, with Calpurnius Piso), the idea is that he may be quoting from a production of his own. One metrical feature may be pointed out: in the 49 lines of the first eclogue there are fully twice as many elisions as in the 261 lines of the *De Laude Pisonis*, and about as many as in the whole of Calpurnius Siculus.

According to the opinion of many, though the opinion is by no means unchallenged, this same Neronian period produced the *Aetna*, a didactic poem in 644 hexameters on the volcano. Traditionally, it came down among the minor works attributed to Virgil, although even by the time of Donatus doubt had been thrown on the attribution. While, then, it cannot be omitted in an account of the *Appendix Vergiliana*,[4] it equally calls for mention in a review of the later age to which many

---

[1] S.H. § 388.

[2] *E.g.* L. Herrmann, *Melanges P. Thomas*, Bruges 1930, p. 432 ff.

[3] E. Groag, in P.-W. *s.v.* Calpurnius no. 65; F. Bücheler, *Rh.M.* xxvi (1871) p. 235.

[4] Duff, *L.H.R.* pp. 360–362, for previous discussion of *Aetna*.

prefer to assign it. There have not been wanting modern attempts to
prove an early date: Kruczkiewicz[1] supported by Vessereau[2] has re-
asserted the Virgilian authorship, and Alzinger[3] has argued for the earliest
date of all, about half a dozen years after Lucretius's death in 55 B.C.
Independently of obvious imitations of Lucretius in the poem, its
general style alone would point to some subsequent generation: techni-
cally and after a ponderous manner, the hexameters are Virgilian in cast,
and Bücheler[4] would put them at least later than Ovid and Manilius.
One cannot but be struck with the frequency of the elisions, if one
turns to the *Aetna* straight from Calpurnius Siculus. The extreme inferior
limit of time, on the other hand, is A.D. 79, the year of the eruption of
Vesuvius, because in *Aetna* 424–431 the fires of the sulphurous lands
round Naples are regarded as extinct – a view impossible after the
renewal of volcanic activity.[5] Scaliger, accepting the authority of certain
fifteenth-century MSS., believed that Cornelius Severus was the writer;
but a common theory since Wernsdorf[6] has been that the author was
Lucilius Junior, the correspondent of the philosopher Seneca and
imperial procurator in Sicily. To Lucilius Seneca addressed his moral
epistles, the first book of his so-called dialogues, and his *Quaestiones
Naturales*. We know from Seneca that he wrote verse and had literary
tastes. We know too that Seneca wrote to Lucilius intimating that he
expected from him a description of his tour round Sicily, and urging
him to climb Aetna and send him information about the mountain:[7]

> But you were sure to indulge your own weakness, without a sug-
> gestion from anybody. There's no fear of your failing to describe
> Aetna in your poem (*ne Aetnam describas in tuo carmine*) and so
> touch on this commonplace of all the poets. Virgil's previous treat-
> ment was no hindrance to Ovid's handling the theme; and a pair of
> predecessors did not frighten Cornelius Severus off it. . . . Aetna is
> making your mouth water (*Aetna tibi saliuam mouet*), or I don't know
> you! You're bent on writing something fine (*grande*) to match former
> attempts.[8]

The terms of the letter, it should be observed, suggest not so much a

[1] *Poema de Aetna monte Vergilio auctori praecipue tribuendum*, diss., Krak.
1882. C. Brakman, 'De Aetna Carmine,' *Mnem.* li (1923) p. 205 ff. holding that
the treatment is based on Posidonius and that style and metre are Lucretian,
marshals internal evidence to support a date about 30 B.C.
[2] *L'Etna* (Budé) 1923.
[3] *Studia in Aetn. collata*, Erlangen 1896.
[4] *Rh.M.* liv (1899) p. 7.
[5] O. Gross, *De metonymiis sermonis Latini a deorum nominibus petitis* (*Dis-
sertationes Hallenses*, xix. 4 (1911) pp. 286–410) seeks (p. 305) on ground
of resemblances between *Octauia* and *Aetna* to suggest that the poet of the
Aetna was the borrower, and wrote between A.D. 69 and 79.
[6] Ed. of *P.L.M.* vol. iv, Altenburg 1785.
[7] Sen. *Ep. Mor.* lxxix. 4–7.
[8] A recent supporter of the Lucilius theory is J. H. Waszink ('De Aetnae
carminis auctore,' *Mnem.* 1949, p. 224 ff.).

separate poem as the insertion of a description to form an episode in a poem on which Lucilius was at work; and the arguments advanced, taken as a whole, do not avail to place the problem completely outside the range of question.

Should the author ever be indisputably unearthed, his literary reputation will not be vastly enhanced by the discovery; for there is little in the poem to relieve its dullness; textual uncertainties apart, it is not seldom obscure; and, despite the author's professed search for causes, it makes but indifferent science. So one finds difficulty in understanding Teuffel's apparently serious criticism of it as 'very attractive';[1] but there is no accounting for taste. At the same time, the author must be credited with an earnest enthusiasm for the study of certain natural phenomena and a disdain for legendary subjects, which at the outset he dismisses as hackneyed, though he himself lapses inconsistently into mythology where he portrays Jupiter as amazed at Aetna's fiery crashing menace and as alarmed lest the giants are once again to make war on heaven (ll. 202–203).

Men tour the world to see places celebrated in story, he points out, and then scornfully asks, 'Do you think such things worth visiting? Study the mighty work of nature the artificer' (*artificis naturae ingens opus aspice*, l. 599). Far less extended, however, than this maxim should imply, his own theme is a single circumscribed corner of nature, almost trivial compared with the *De Rerum Natura*, just as his spirit is one of remarkably tempered seriousness compared with the passionate ardency of Lucretius. Unfortunately the volcanic fire of which he wrote did not transmit itself to his style; and for his lack of interest in mankind he has paid the penalty of failing to engage a reader's interest. Significantly, he is most impressive when he leaves off theorising about the subterranean action of water, wind and fire, or describing ominous hidden rumblings and engulfing lava-streams, in order to show how the danger might affect human beings and elicit high moral qualities. This he does towards the close by introducing the episode of two brothers who rescue their father and mother during a volcanic eruption. The passage, though a little exclamatory and tautological, remains deservedly the best-known part of the poem. The following are excerpts translated from it (604 *sqq.*):

> Once Aetna burst its caves and glowed with fire;
> As if its inmost furnaces were wrecked,
> One wave of sweeping heat poured forth afar. . . .
> Ablaze were crops in fields, and like their lords
> Rich acres burned, and wood and hill gleamed red. . . .
> Then each man, as his will or strength to snatch

---

[1] *Gesch. d. röm. Lit.*, 1910, § 307: 'ein inhaltlich sehr anziehendes kleines Lehrgedicht.' His reviser in the 1920 edition is not so enthusiastic: 'ein inhaltlich anziehendes, aber schwer verständliches kleines Lehrgedicht.'

Might prompt, essayed to save his property.
One groans 'neath gold; another, gathering arms,
Puts them once more around his foolish neck.
One, faint with seizing things, is burdened by
His verses: lightly-laden run the poor! . . .[1]
    All is the prey of fire that spareth none
Or spares the good alone. Yea, once a pair
Of noble sons, one named Amphinomus,
And both brave-hearted in the task they shared,
When fires roared close upon their homestead, saw
Their father and their mother, bent with eld,
Alas, sink on the threshold wearily.
Cease, men of greed, to lift your spoils beloved!
Mother and father were *their* only wealth:[2]
This spoil they'll snatch, and through the midmost flames,
That gave them confidence, they haste to flee.
O sense of loving duty, best of goods,
Surest salvation for an upright man!
The fire-flames blushed to touch the pious youths,
And wheresoe'er they turned their steps, retired.
Blest was that day: the ground they trod unscathed:
Grim burning reigned to right and blazed to left.

The title of *The Latin Iliad* (*Ilias Latina*), though it might well raise
great expectations of literary achievement, is conferred upon 1070
hexameters of condensed paraphrase rather than of translation from the
long Homeric epic. Judged solely as a summary, its representation of
its original is most disproportionate; for over half the Latin total is
given to the first five books of the Greek twenty-four. Whereas several
of the earlier books get over 100 Latin lines, several of the later get under
10; the fifth book, for instance, gets 149, the seventeenth only 3. The
work must have been designed for an educational textbook, and to its
employment in schools it doubtless owed its survival, and, what is
notable in a production of no outstanding power, its happy chance of
materially aiding the knowledge of letters in post-classical times; for in
the dark medieval centuries, when Greek was forgotten in Western
Europe, this 'Latin Homer,' if only with faint and borrowed light, had
the incontestable merit of reflecting some of the old radiancy of 'the
tale of Troy divine.'
Although by no means the sole attempt to give a Latin dress to the

[1] 616–617:
     'Defectum raptis illum sua carmina tardant:
     Hic uelox minimo properat sub pondere pauper.'
I should like to give the poet the credit of sarcastically regarding poems as heavy
enough to be a hindrance; but the *carmina* are possibly charms or spells to which
recourse might be had in terror.
[2] 628–629:
     'Parcite, auara manus, dulces attollere praedas;
     Illis diuitiae solae materque paterque,'

epics of the Trojan cycle, in which the Romans by virtue of their fabled descent always felt a national interest, the *Ilias Latina* is yet the only one which has come down. Other workers in the same field have left of their performance fragments only, or nothing. Roman literature indeed may be said to have dawned with the translation of the *Odyssey* into Saturnian verse by Andronicus.[1] In Sulla's time, Cn. Matius, and probably also in the first century B.C. Ninnius Crassus, had rendered the *Iliad* into hexameters[2] without making any great mark. Then two attempts of imperial date may be mentioned besides the *Ilias Latina*. Attius Labeo, whom the scholiast on Persius declared 'unscholarly' (*indoctus*) – exactly the opposite epithet, by the way, to that which Aulus Gellius applied to Matius – turned both *Iliad* and *Odyssey* into Latin hexameters.[3] Persius calls his *Iliad* 'drunk with hellebore' (*ebria ueratro*),[4] and mercifully time has taken all save one line of it. The other attempt was in prose and was the composition of the Emperor Claudius's influential freedman Polybius. Seneca, in the *Consolatio* addressed to him, refers to this production twice[5] in commendatory terms. Apparently Polybius had translated Homer into Latin and Virgil into Greek; for Seneca says:

> Homer and Virgil have been benefactors of mankind as much as you have been a benefactor of these poets and of everyone in deciding to make them known to a wider circle than that for which they wrote,

and, again,

> Take in your hands the poems of either of the two authors [Homer and Virgil] – poems, the fame of which the abundant toil of your genius has enhanced, and which you have paraphrased (*resoluisti*) in such a way that, although their metrical form has gone (*quamuis structura illorum recesserit*), the charm is nevertheless preserved; for you have transferred them from one language to another so well as to secure that most difficult effect, the bringing of all the beauties of the original over into a foreign speech.

The *Ilias Latina* can with good reason be referred to some date earlier than Nero's death, because its author has introduced into it a passage coloured with loyal Roman sentiment which could have been composed at no time except under the Julian dynasty of the Caesars:

---

[1] Duff, *L.H.R.* 89 ff.; Bährens, *F.P.R.* p. 37 ff. W. Morel, *F.P.L.* p. 7 ff.
[2] Bährens, *F.P.R.* pp. 281 and 283; W. Morel, *F.P.L.* pp. 48 and 51; Duff, *L.H.R.* pp. 91 n. and 179.
[3] S.H. § 393.
[4] Pers. i. 50; *cf.* i. 4 and Schol. The surviving line:
        crudum manduces Priamum Priamique pisinnos,
was intended to translate *Il.* iv. 35 :
        ὠμὸν βεβρώθοις Πρίαμον Πριάμοιό τε παῖδας.
[5] Sen. *Ad Polyb.* viii. 2, xi. 5.

Had not great Ocean's ruler saved the prince [=Aeneas]
To flee and build New Troy in happier lands,
Raising a stock majestic to the stars,
The clan Rome loves would ne'er have come to stay.[1]

Its hexameters are post-Ovidian, and Plessis[2] ventures not over-convincingly to fix its composition as early as in the era of Tiberius, in which case the author must have been contemporary not with Lucan, but with Phaedrus. This author he believes to have been Italicus – not Silius, but another of previous date; and in that belief is involved the question of alleged acrostics at the beginning and end of the poem, which has attracted the curiosity and ingenuity of certain commentators. The initial letters of the first eight lines spell *Italices* and of the last eight lines *scqipsit*. A conjectural change in the seventh line gives *Italicus* and a mere transposition of words gives in the latter case *scripsit*. Some are content to leave the opening seven lines unaltered and read *Italice*, either as a vocative, or an adverb ('he wrote Italian-wise'). But the idea of the vocative has prompted tamperings with the next few lines to extract *Sili*, so that the poem would address Silius Italicus. To the acrostics[3] is added the further elaboration of finding, after the caesurae in the first six lines, the letters of a mesostich, *Pieris*, to mean 'The muse wrote it.' Such coincidences, however, in each case partly engineered, lead to no sure ground. Even if 'Italicus' were accepted, the style of the *Ilias Latina* is so unlike[4] that of Silius Italicus in the *Punica* that believers in the acrostic have had recourse to guessing it to be a work either of his youth or by someone else bearing the same name.

Another puzzle has arisen on the title 'Pindarus' which MSS. of the Middle Ages imposed on the Latin Homer. Why should two very different Greek poets have been thus confused? Referring to Lucian Müller's[5] attempted explanation of this alternative title as based on the coupling of Homer with Pindar in Horace's *Odes*,[6] Tolkiehn has suggested that the

[1] ll. 899–902:

'Quem nisi seruasset magnarum rector aquarum,
Vt profugus laetis Troiam repararet in aruis
Augustumque genus claris submitteret astris,
Non carae gentis nobis mansisset origo.'

[2] *Poésie lat.* p. 528 ff.
[3] For a record of the discussions on the acrostics see S.H. § 394.
[4] J. Tolkiehn, *Homer u.d. röm. Poesie*, Lpz. 1900, p. 101, quotes treatises by Paul Verres (1881) and by Altenburg (1890) to suggest that the metre of *Ilias Lat.* is better than that of Silius's *Punica*. The contention is that Silius would not have written his *magnum opus* in less careful style than an epitome of the *Iliad*. L. Herrmann (*L'Antiquité Classique* xvi (1947) p. 241 ff.) makes *Il. Lat.* a work of Silius Italicus's youth, even fixing the date at A.D. 45 or 46. Galdi, *L'epitome n. lett. lat.* p. 244, takes the view of Schanz that *Il. Lat.* is a free and brief rehandling of the Homeric *Iliad* by a dilettante fond of Virgil and Ovid ('innamorato di Virgilio e di Ovidio'). A real epitome would have had more Homeric colour.
[5] *Rh.M.* xxiv (1869), 492 ff.
[6] Hor. *Od.* IV. ix. 5–6; *cf.* Petron. *Sat.* 2.

intrusion of 'Pindarus' may have been due to the presence in earlier MSS. of 'Thebanus,' a possible epithet for Homer in respect of his legendary association with Thebes in Egypt.

As in the *Aratea* of Germanicus, new matter, though on a smaller scale, is sometimes introduced by the translator. An example of inserted Roman sentiment has been already cited. The last eight lines addressed to Calliope and other powers constitute the translator's personal fare-well to his task, and some of his departures from events or details, as narrated in the Greek, may be caused by his reminiscences of Virgil and Ovid or by his trusting to memory. The modifying influence of Virgil is traceable in a simile here and there; in his making Aetna the forge of Vulcan (856–857), which is not Homeric; and in many turns of expression.[1] There are, besides, positive inexactitudes, such as the assignment of some of Ulysses's words to Nestor (ll. 151 *sqq.*), or the slaying of Democoon by Agamemnon (ll. 372–373) instead of by Ulysses as in Homer. These very additions and negligences acquit the author of having been a slavishly close translator. His Latin possesses the virtue of straightforward clearness, and his versification a consider-able share of easy grace.

Nero also was among the poets, although he was one of the friends from whom literary men might reasonably pray to be saved. His educa-tion had been to some extent warped; for his mother Agrippina pre-vented the future emperor from studying philosophy deeply, and Seneca had in eloquence directed his pupil less to the old standard oratory than to the modern school in which the tutor himself cut a prominent figure.[2] It was observable that, unlike previous emperors, he preferred to have his speeches composed for him,[3] and Seneca could at least check the tasteless bombast of which he sometimes betrayed signs. Towards poetry he had a bent, though he missed supreme success. One may conclude that caprice and mannerism outweighed Nero's readiness and technique, without believing that the lines ascribed to him by the scholiast on the first satire of Persius are genuinely his. Seneca[4] commends for its ele-gance his line about the play of light on a dove's neck as it moves (*colla Cytheriacae splendent agitata columbae*); and Nero certainly displayed versatility in sportive, satiric and erotic verses, in monologues of a tragic character suitable for his own recitation on the stage, and in his epic *Troica*, whence may have come the episode of 'The Taking of Troy' which scandal alleged he chanted to the cithara while Rome was in flames.[5] His establishment in A.D. 60 of the quinquennial competition

[1] For reminiscences of Virgil and Ovid, see Plessis, *op. cit.* p. 532.
[2] Suet. *Nero* lii.
[3] Tac. *Ann.* XIII. iii.
[4] *N.Q.* I. v. 6.
[5] Mart. IX. xxvi. 9; Suet. *Dom.* i; *Nero* xxi, xxiv, xxxviii; Tac. *Ann.* XV. xxxix.

of the *Neronia* arose fully as much from his own ambition to win the prize in public as from any desire to patronise music and poetry.

Caesius Bassus, one of Persius's senior friends, was a lyric poet of whom Quintilian thought highly.[1] He may be the same as the author of a work on prosody dedicated to Nero. Seneca's friend Vagellius,[2] who had some reputation as a poet, the satirical versifiers Antistius (Sosianus) and Curtius Montanus mentioned in Tacitus,[3] and the Serranus included by Quintilian among epic authors may close the list of those who were lesser lights in Neronian poetry, unless the fact that Serranus is coupled by Juvenal with Saleius implies that he lived somewhat later.[4]

[1] *Vita Pers.* (see *supra*, p. 224 n. 2); schol. ad Pers. vi. 1 (see Jahn's ed. of Pers.); Quint. X. i. 96.
[2] Sen. *N.Q.* VI. ii. 7.
[3] *Ann.* XIV. xlviii (A.D. 62), XVI. xxviii (A.D. 66).
[4] Quint. X. i. 89; Juv. VII. 79–81.

PART III

Literature of the Flavian Period

A.D. 69—96

Chapter I

THE ELDER PLINY:
FLAVIAN SCIENCE AND HISTORY

Life – His public appointments – Eruption of Vesuvius – Avidity for knowledge – Six lost works – Contents and arrangement of the *Natural History* – Sources and method – Pliny's list of authorities – *Quellenkritik* – Some of its services – Variations in use of Greek and Latin sources – Difficulties as to minor authorities – Pre-eminent authorities – A few contrasts with modern science – Obvious weaknesses – Historical value of the encyclopaedia – Attractive features – Information pleasantly conveyed – Stoic outlook – Nature and man – Mother-earth – Human society – Human progress – Political views – Literary qualities – Rhetoric, sarcasm, epigram – Pith of expression – Purple passages – The common-place and the poetic – Sentence-structure – Survival of influence.

Flavian historians (a) under Vespasian, (b) under Domitian.

THE ELDER PLINY

WHAT everyone knows about an author is not necessarily of supreme importance; but the two most familiar facts about the elder Pliny – that he composed a massive *Natural History* and that he perished while investigating an eruption of Vesuvius – lie in their implications at the very roots of his title to fame. A meagre life by Suetonius has to be supplemented by information from the colossal work which is his imperishable monument and from his nephew's admiring testimony in four of his letters.[1] C. Plinius Secundus was born of an equestrian family at Novum Comum in A.D. 23 or 24,[2] and his birth near Lake Como led him to claim Catullus as a fellow-Northerner (*conterraneum meum*).[3] He must have come early to Rome, because Nonianus, whom the boy saw in his consulate,[4] held the office in A.D. 35. If we know little about his education, we can see from his style that rhetoric was not omitted; and, while there is no proof that

[1] Plin. *Ep.* III. v, account of his uncle's works; V. viii, history compared with oratory; VI. xvi, his uncle's death; VI. xx, continued account of eruption of Vesuvius.
[2] *Ep.* III. v. 7, states that he died in his fifty-sixth year; this was in August, A.D. 79.
[3] *N.H. praef.* 1, *i.e.* like Catullus a native of Gallia Cisalpina, though not, as some have argued, a fellow-townsman from Verona. [4] *N.H.* XXXVII. 81.

the poet Pomponius Secundus formally trained him in literature, we can at least be sure that he deeply influenced the younger man, who was destined to write his biography. Pliny's allusions to Pomponius are full of respect, and he recalls how on one occasion he saw at Pomponius's house specimens – then about two centuries old – of the handwriting of the Gracchi.[1] Similarity of disposition may have linked them together; for, like Pliny, Pomponius showed ability to combine literary with official duties. Pliny's youthful pleading at the bar was followed by military service. When twenty-three or twenty-four he was a cavalry officer under Corbulo in Germania Inferior, and his first book was written on the use of the javelin by mounted troops. His comradeship (*castrense contubernium*) which he mentions[2] with the future Emperor Titus may have happened ten years later, about A.D. 57, when he was in the army of Pompeius Paulinus,[3] again in Germania Inferior. Several allusions attest experiences among peoples near the northern frontier of the Empire;[4] no doubt it was personal knowledge that united with historical instinct to suggest his lost work on the wars in Germany.

Full detail, however, regarding his life before the accession of Vespasian is not available. It is true that he gives us a few interesting reminiscences: he saw for himself the harbour works in progress at Ostia about the beginning of Claudius's reign; he could remember Claudius's Empress Agrippina wearing a mantle of woven gold at a sham naval fight exhibited by the Emperor; and he witnessed the building of Nero's 'golden house' after the fire of 64.[5] On the other hand, we should like to be sure whether he had official connexion with the East. Was he ever procurator of Syria? Did he serve against the Jews as a staff officer under Titus? Was this the service which he calls *castrense contubernium*? Could he have been present at the siege of Jerusalem in 70? These questions might all be answered in the affirmative, if Mommsen's hypothesis were accepted that Pliny is alluded to in a Greek inscription from Aradus.[6] But the balance of authority prefers to hold that in 70 Pliny was in Gaul, and that this year began for him a series of procuratorships in Gallia Narbonensis, Africa, Gallia Belgica and Hispania Citerior.[7] Administered, according to Suetonius, with the

---

[1] *N.H.* VII. 80; XIII. 83. Pliny calls Pomponius 'consularis poeta' and 'uates ciuisque clarissimus.' [2] *N.H. praef.* 3.
[3] *N.H.* XXXIII. 143. This Pompeius Paulinus was probably the son of the person addressed in Seneca's *De Breuitate Vitae*. See *supra*, p. 173 and P.W. *s.v.* Pompeius no. 100.
[4] XII. 98 ('. . . qua Rhenus adluit uidi'); XVI. 2; XXII. 8.
[5] IX. 14–15; XXXIII. 63; XXXVI. 111.
[6] *I.G.* III. 4536; *Hermes* xix (1884) p. 644. Since Hirschfeld in 1887 (*Röm. Mitt. d. deutsch. archäol. Inst.* ii, p. 152) opposed Mommsen, several scholars, including Münzer, have also attacked the identification. Fabia and Detlefsen support it. See S.H. § 490.
[7] *N.H.* II. 150: 'ego uidi in Vocontiorum agro'; VII. 36: 'ipse in Africa uidi'; XVIII. 183: 'in Treuerico agro . . . '; Plin. *Ep.* III. v. 17: 'cum procuraret in Hispania.'

highest integrity, these offices at the same time widened his horizon, even though they were all held within the western half of the Empire.

While at Rome, Pliny kept in close contact with the imperial house. A well-known letter by his nephew tells us that it was his custom to visit the palace before daylight to interview Vespasian and then return to his daily task.[1] He was on duty as admiral of the fleet at Misenum on that summer afternoon in 79 which the younger Pliny's account of the catastrophe has made memorable. A pine-shaped cloud of smoky vapour rising above the neighbouring mountains betrayed alarming volcanic activity, and the phenomena, pointed out to him by his sister, the younger Pliny's mother, were too tempting for an ardent student of nature to miss, even though he was elderly, stout and busily engaged in reading after his midday siesta.

'He called for his shoes and climbed some high ground from which that uncommon sight could best be viewed. Looking at it from this distance, one felt uncertain from what mountain the cloud was rising, though later it was known to be Vesuvius. . . . It was white at one moment, at another grimy and spotted, as if it had carried up soil or cinders. A man of my uncle's learning saw that the phenomenon was significant and deserving of closer survey. He ordered a light vessel to be got ready and gave me the chance of going with him, if I wished.'[2]

Appeals for help reached him: large galleys had to be launched: and the scientific admiral made for the danger zone from which others were fleeing. His nephew's letter pictures him dictating observations, braving the rain of stones upon the bay, and by his coolness heartening his friend Pomponianus, in whose house at Stabiae (Castellamare) he supped and stayed overnight. The next day, one of preternatural darkness, amidst terrific concussions and sulphurous gas-fumes which put his friends to flight, he was left by the seashore and, troubled as he had been with his breathing, succumbed to asphyxiation. When, a day later, light was restored to the land, his body was found uninjured, wearing the appearance rather of sleep than of death (*quiescenti quam defuncto similior*).

An insatiable desire for knowledge and indefatigable industry in amassing it are the outstanding characteristics of Pliny. A hard-working official, he could never have completed so many volumes on intricate subjects without marvellous self-denial and an extraordinary faculty for dispensing with sleep. The small hours after midnight found him ready to begin study long before the time came for repairing to the Emperor Vespasian – another early riser. His very meals could be utilised for listening to a trained reader: during leisure hours, as he basked in summer sunlight, he would have a book read aloud, and take notes or extracts. A favourite, but very risky, remark of his was that there was no book so bad as not to contain something profitable.[3] In the country

[1] *Ep.* III. v. 9.   [2] *Ep.* VI. xvi.   [3] *Ep.* III. v. 10.

only bathing-time was exempt from study, and immediately after a bath, while he was being rubbed down, he listened to a reader, or himself dictated. In winter the close attendance of a secretary, with hands gloved against the cold and equipped with books and tablets, ensured that nothing should impede the acquisition and distribution of knowledge. Once at dinner a book was being read aloud, when one of the guests stopped the reader for mispronouncing some words and made him repeat them; upon which Pliny said, 'You understood him, surely?' 'Yes,' replied the friend. 'Then why did you stop him? We have lost more than ten lines by this interruption of yours.' *Tanta erat parsimonia temporis* is the summary of the younger Pliny.[1]

On another occasion he remonstrated with his nephew for taking a walk: 'You might,' said he, 'have avoided wasting those hours.' The nephew, in recalling the incident long afterwards, made the comment that his uncle thought all time lost that was not devoted to study.[2] By dint of this intense application he left to the younger Pliny no fewer than one hundred and sixty volumes of extracts written on both sides and in an extremely small hand, which, as the embarrassed legatee realised, was 'tantamount to increasing their number.'[3] It is rare for so passionate a student to fill so many practical offices, and there is a legitimate force in the younger Pliny's question, 'Who among the lifelong devotees of letters must not, when compared with him, blush for yielding to slumber and sloth?'[4]

Of the half-dozen lost works by Pliny, of which his nephew gives a chronological list,[5] one was a technical military manual, one a biography, two were on language under oratorical or grammatical aspects, and two were historical. They mark that all-roundness of interest which reappears in the *Natural History*. His literary career began when, as a young officer, he wrote his handbook on the use of javelins by cavalry, *De iaculatione equestri*.[6] The two books *De uita Pomponii Secundi* were intended for a tribute of affection to the memory of one who was both a literary friend and Pliny's commanding officer in Germany.[7] The *Bellorum Germaniae XX Libri* gave an account of the wars between Rome and the Germans. The idea came to the author on one of his German campaigns when he dreamt that the ghost of Drusus asked that his fame should be rescued from oblivion.[8] Tacitus quotes the work, which seems to have been in existence as late as the time of Symmachus in A.D. 396.[9] *Studiosi III Libri*, 'The Student,' or, according to Gellius, 'The Students,'[10] had each of its three long books divided into two volumes. Like Quintilian

---

[1] *Ep.* III. v. 12.   [2] *Ibid.* 16.
[3] *Ibid.* 17: 'qua ratione multiplicatur hic numerus.'   [4] *Ibid.* 19.
[5] *Ibid.* 1–6.   [6] *N.H.* VIII. 162.
[7] *Ibid.* XIV. 56.   [8] Plin. *Ep.* III. v. 4.
[9] *Ann.* I. lxix; Symm. *Epist.* IV. xviii. 6. M. Lehnerdt, *Herm.* xlviii (1913), pp. 274–282, discusses the possible survival of a copy in Germany in the fifteenth century.
[10] Gell. *N.A.* IX. xvi. 1.

after him, Pliny treated the education of an orator from infancy (*ab incunabulis*). Choice specimens from controversial declamations were included. The work impressed Quintilian on the score of carefulness, and therefore surprised him all the more by incidentally introducing fantastic views upon the secret of the long gown which Cicero used to wear and on the advisability of tidy or untidy hair for a speaker.[1] It was in the latest years of Nero's reign, when even learning had to walk warily, that Pliny turned to a grammatical subject[2] in *Dubius Sermo*, 'doubtful forms in language.' He thus made his contribution, as Julius Caesar had done, to the conflict between anomaly and analogy in linguistic forms, though Pliny's love of variety made him a less rigid stickler for analogy than Caesar had been. Its eight books carried weight with many grammarians including Charisius.[3] Next, in the thirty-one books *A Fine Aufidi Bassi* Pliny went back to history, continuing the work of Bassus. It is, however, not clear when that historian stopped: what we do know is that of three definite citations of Pliny's history by Tacitus,[4] the earliest refers to A.D. 55. The guess has been made – and opposed – that the thirty-one books treated annalistically the equal number of years from Caligula's fall in 41 to the triumph of Vespasian and Titus in A.D. 71.[5] Fabia, who, like Nissen, sees in the lost work a principal source for the *Histories* of Tacitus, suggests that Pliny started from the later years of Claudius's reign. Unfortunately, the surviving fragments[6] are too scanty to aid a decision; but, touching the *terminus ad quem*, it should be pointed out that Pliny's words show that he certainly treated Nero's last year, and suggest that he carried this history of his own times well into the reign of Vespasian.[7] Completed by A.D. 77, the work was left for publication by the younger Pliny, who notes in his uncle's historical composition the same scrupulous exactitude[8] that struck Quintilian in his oratorical treatise. Care alone, however, does not create literature; and no one can now say how far Pliny's methods in political and social history differed from his methods in natural history. That Tacitus by writing on the same period eclipsed and superseded him as artist and historian we may be quite sure. But it is likely enough that, even if he was no historical genius, we have lost much

---

[1] *I. Or.* III. i. 21; XI. iii. 143, 148.   [2] *N.H. praef.* 28.

[3] For Pliny's influence on Nonius Marcellus, H. Nettleship, *J.Ph.* XV. 189 (rp. in *Lects. and Essays*, Oxf., 2nd ser. 1895, pp. 145–171), 'Study of Lat. Gram. among the Romans in 1st Cent. A.D.'; on Gellius and others, J. W. Beck, 'Studia Gelliana et Pliniana,' *Fleck. Jb.* Supplbd. xix (1892).

[4] *Ann.* XIII. xx (early in Nero's reign, A.D. 55); XV. liii (Piso's conspiracy, A.D. 65); *Hist.* III. xxviii (sack of Cremona, A.D. 69).

[5] For the theories see S.H. § 494, 6.

[6] Peter, *H.R.R.* p. 110; *H.R.F.* p. 310.

[7] *N.H.* II. 199: 'anno Neronis principis supremo, sicut in rebus eius exposuimus'; *praef.* 20 (of Vespasian and his sons): 'Vos quidem omnes, patrem te fratremque, diximus opere iusto, temporum nostrorum historiam orsi a fine Aufidi Bassi.'

[8] *Ep.* V. viii. 5: 'historias et quidem religiosissime scripsit.'

attractive material in the shape of Pliny's first-hand impressions and experiences during a period with which he was contemporary.

The supreme memorial to his energy is his one extant production, the *Naturalis Historia* in thirty-seven books, admirably characterised by his nephew as 'a diffuse work, learned, with a variety equal to nature's own.'[1] The author found a patron, to whom he might address it, in the prince Titus – himself the composer of a poem on the appearance of a comet. Although dedicated to Titus in A.D. 77,[2] it was published, at least in the main, posthumously. Probably, either the first decade alone was issued in 77,[3] or even it may have been subjected to alterations after being presented to Titus: there is general agreement that the author during the last two years of his life continued his task, but did not succeed in giving a final revision to the remaining books. The arrangement is as follows. Book I, which is preceded by an epistle dedicatory, forms an introduction consisting of an exhaustive table of contents book by book (expressly designed to save time and trouble for busy readers)[4] with an imposing array of authorities employed in each: II, the single physical book, giving Pliny's cosmography in relation to God, the universe and its elements: III–VI, on the geography and ethnography of Europe, Africa and Asia, starting in the west at the Pillars of Hercules and, after two books allotted to countries on the northern side of the Mediterranean, restarting eastwards from Mauretania for India and Mesopotamia: VII, his anthropological section, treating man and human physiology: VIII-XI, four books on zoology – land animals (with the elephant first, because biggest), sea creatures, birds, insects receiving each a book: XII–XIX, eight books on botany, under which come forest trees and fruit trees and (in XVIII) agriculture: XX–XXVII, eight books devoted to materia medica from botanical sources: XXVIII–XXXII, five books devoted to materia medica from zoological sources: XXXIII–XXXVII, mineralogy and metallurgy, embracing a survey of their application to medicine and the fine arts, so as to bring in the healing properties of metallic substances, artistic productions in gold, bronze or other metals, the manufacture of colours and achievements of great painters, stones and their employment by architects and sculptors, precious stones and their value.

The arrangement is not illogical in broad outline, though the treatment of medicaments got from the animal kingdom is, with a curious

---

[1] *Ep.* III. v. 6.

[2] *Praef.* 2 addresses Titus as 'sexies consul.' His poem on the comet belonged to his fifth consulate, *N.H.* II. 89.

[3] This is Urlichs's view (*Chrestomathia Pliniana*, Berlin 1857, Introd. p. xiv): 'Vermuthlich gab er deshalb vor der Abreise nur die erste Dekade vollständig heraus. Bks. XI and XII in the codex Riccardianus and the last six bks. in the Bambergensis bear the words 'editus post mortem.' *Cf.* D. Detlefsen, *Untersuch. üb. d. Zusammensetzung der Naturgesch.*, Berlin 1899, p. 18; A. Klotz, *Herm.* xlii (1907) pp. 324–325.

[4] *Praef.* 33.

lack of symmetry, deferred until both the vegetable kingdom and its medicaments have been treated at great length. That the plan of division was the author's own is manifest from cross references within the text.[1] Even a brief summary of the scheme shows how much the subject is related to human concerns. In addition to thirteen predominantly medical books, the mineralogical portion contains a large amount bearing on the healing of man's ailments: and it was the human factor that fortunately prompted – what would not have occurred to many writers on mineralogy – a valuable digression on the history of art.

Pliny calculated that his work was a repertory of twenty thousand facts, or what he took for facts, compiled from about two thousand volumes and one hundred selected authors.[2] This last number, however, does not cover his obligations to all sources, because the lists or indices of Roman and foreign authorities, which he appends to his table of contents for each book, yield totals of 146 Roman and 327 foreign authors, or something approaching 500 in all. The discrepancy between this total in the indices and the hundred *exquisiti* is more apparent than real. It was a professed point of honour with Pliny, though not with ancient writers as a rule, frankly to own obligation to all from whom literary material had been derived: 'I hold it for courtesy and ample proof of an honourable modesty to acknowledge by whom one has profited.'[3] Therefore he feels gratitude not only to his hundred special authors, but to earlier writers whose knowledge they have enabled him to use. This avoidance, however, of any suspicion of plagiarism has been turned against him. Attempts have been made to charge him on this score with an empty parade of learning,[4] as if, even without his nephew's explicit testimony, any reader should fail to see that the author had drawn upon multitudes of books. He carries out his promise of acknowledgement to all authorities by recording their names (with subjects sometimes, but only sometimes, specified) in his indices for each book and to a less extent by mentioning authorities in the text. Here, however, he considers himself dispensed from systematic or exhaustive mention of the authors given in the lists: some are cited on incidental or isolated points, others can be inferred to be of more importance, and occasionally others are said to be followed for a considerable portion of the work.[5] Usually when an author is cited the information is

[1] *E.g.* XXXIII. 22, he makes a reference forward to his book on precious stones (viz. XXXVII): 'sicut dicemus in gemmarum uolumine.'

[2] *Praef.* 17: 'ex exquisitis auctoribus C.'

[3] *Praef.* 21: 'est enim benignum, ut arbitror, et plenum ingenui pudoris fateri per quos profeceris.'

[4] G. Montigny, *Quaestiones in Plin. nat. historiae de animalibus libros*, Bonn 1844, p. 7: 'uana eruditionis ostentatio.' Rabenhorst, 'Die Indices auctorum u. die wirklichen Quellen der N.H.,' in *Philol.* lxv (1906), sees in Pliny's desire to acknowledge literary obligations merely a rhetorical trick.

[5] VIII. 43–44: 'Aristoteles . . . uir quem in his magna secuturus ex parte praefandum reor,' *i.e.*, Aristotle is for zoology his great authority, and Pliny proceeds to mention his summary of 50 volumes of Aristotle ('collecta in artum').

indirectly reported in dependence upon such phrases as *Fenestella tradit* (IX. 123), *scribit Annaeus Seneca* (IX. 167), *Varro auctor est* (XVIII. 307), *L. Piso prodidit* (XXXIV. 30); but there are passages where authors are quoted *verbatim* for some lines on end, *e.g.* Trebius (IX. 93), Nepos (IX. 137) and Cato (XXIX. 14). One cardinal misfortune is that Pliny did not decide expressly to distinguish among principal, secondary, and still more remote authorities, such as those Greek writers who were known to him solely through intermediary writers, Greek or Roman. If he had even revealed the names of his hundred *exquisiti*, we should have possessed a canon for his main authorities, and thereby known which were subordinate, although the degree of their subordination might still have been perplexing to determine. Again, if we could have been certain of the principle underlying the order of names in each author-list, much would have been clearer about the origin and value of the material. Brunn's well-known pamphlet of 1856,[1] which has had great influence in Plinian criticism, laid it down that the order of names in each list broadly corresponded with the order in which the authors were originally used in the particular book to which the list was applicable. Unluckily, this principle, as Brunn himself saw, is not so simple as it looks; and on examination it is burdened with so many exceptions due to Pliny's subsequent insertions and to disturbances in the text, intentional or accidental, that one must reluctantly doubt its validity.[2] Another puzzle lies in the figures given after most of the tables of contents to represent totals of 'facts, stories, and observations' (*res et historiae et obseruationes*). The figures vary considerably (417 for Book II, but 2214 for VI), while they are absent for III–V.[3] They may have been taken over from the excerpt-books containing Pliny's raw material.

Such uncertainties engender speculation, and, since Montigny's tractate of 1844 examined the relation of Pliny to Aristotle,[4] a formidable mass of books or brochures has appeared on the sources of the *Natural History*. This subject of *Quellenkritik*, though dry, is not barren, because it bears on the progress of human knowledge in antiquity and on Pliny's mode of work. At the same time, a salutary reminder is given in Teuffel's

---

Klotz points out that the words in VI. 49, 'Demodamas ... quem maxime sequimur,' only mean that Pliny's material at this point goes back in the last resort to Demodamas ('in letzter Linie zum grössten Teil auf D. zurückgehen,' *Herm* xlii (1907) p. 327).

[1] H. Brunn, *De auctorum indicibus Plinianis disputatio isagogica*, Bonn 1856.

[2] On the relation between the order of authors' names in the special indices and the order followed in a general index common to Pliny's books on closely allied subjects, see Klotz, *Herm.* xlii (1907) p. 323, and his *Quaestiones Plinianae Geographicae*, Berlin 1906, p. 4 ff.

[3] Numbers often constituted a difficulty in the MSS., and uncertainty led to gaps. Klotz, *Herm.* xlii, p. 325, cites Dicuil, *De mensura orbis terrae*, as aware of imperfections in Pliny MSS. On the figures, *cf.* Th. Birt, *Das antike Buchwesen* Berl. 1882, p. 333.

[4] Montigny, *op. cit.*, showed that Pliny often named in his indices authors whom he had not directly consulted.

Geschichte der römischen Literatur that sure ground is likeliest where the
inquiry deals with authors whose works still exist in whole or in part –
Aristotle, Theophrastus, Cato, Varro, Virgil, Ovid, Vitruvius, Celsus,
Mela and Columella – and that, where intermediary or original authorities are lost, modern research has had wide room – and used it freely –
for the play of imagination.[1] This play of imagination accounts for some
arbitrary and extreme positions. Rose, for example, declared Pliny to be
an untrustworthy compiler who never handled Aristotle in Greek; Birt
was confident that Pliny used Aristotle only through Pompeius Trogus
(whereas others have laid much stress on King Juba, Nigidius Figulus,
and Varro as intermediaries); Koebert uncompromisingly denied to
Pliny the slightest intelligence in art criticism; Rabenhorst scrapped
Pliny's author-lists along with Brunn's attempted explanation of their
order, to make way for his theory that Pliny did apparently little else
than plunder the encyclopaedia of Verrius Flaccus.[2] Some proportion,
however, ought to be observed in theorising. Common sense refuses to
believe that all Pliny's authenticated toil could have been spent on summarising and annotating scores of authors for his excerpt-rolls, if his
Natural History were merely a compilation from Verrius Flaccus's
rerum dignarum memoria libri. Other reasons, if necessary, could be
advanced to demolish such a contention; but we may rest content with
the argument that the man who filled a series of distinguished offices
with absolute integrity (*procurationes splendidissimas et continuas summa
integritate administrauit*, Sueton.) would scarcely in his writing stoop,
under an assumed cloak of gratitude, to a fraudulent invention of authorities to whom he in reality owed nothing.

In fact, throughout an investigation which has to a great extent become a controversy, three schools of criticism are discernible – one,
radical in its attitude to Pliny, which, with Montigny, Rose, Rabenhorst
and others, would dismiss his lists as totally untrustworthy; a second,
conservative in attitude, which with Brunn, Urlichs, Gruppe and Detlefsen, would champion Pliny against a charge of pedantic or dishonest
parade; and a third, probably now represented by the majority of
scholars, moderate in attitude, which would admit that Pliny's list of

---

[1] Teuffel, 313, 3: 'Im übrigen hat die Phantasie des modernen Quellenforschers
hier, bei dem Verlust der meisten Quellen, weiten (auch reichlich benutzten)
Spielraum.'
[2] Rose, *Aristoteles Pseudepigraphus*, Lpz. 1863 ('ipsius nunquam Aristotelis
Graecos libros adhibuit'); Th. Birt, *De Halieuticis Ouidio poetae falso adscriptis*,
Bonn 1878 (criticised by Aly, *Zur Quellenkritik*, 1885, pp. 17–18); H. Koebert,
'Das Kunstverständnis des Pl.,' pp. 134–146, in *Abhandln. . . . W. v. Christ
. . . dargebracht*, Mun. 1891; M. Rabenhorst, *Der ält. Pl. als Epitomator des Verrius Flaccus*, Berl., 1907, and 'Die indices auctorum u. die wirklichen Quellen
der N.H.,' *Philol*. lxv, 1906 (examined by Klotz, *Herm*. xlii, p. 324 ff., who
declines to regard Pliny as a miserable humbug, 'elender Windbeutel' and
swaggerer, 'Aufschneider.') For brief account of Verrius Flaccus, see Duff,
L.H.R. pp. 458–460; Trogus, *ibid*. pp. 460, 463–464; Figulus, *ibid*. p. 253; Juba,
ibid. p. 485.

L

authorities cannot be taken at their face-value, but require minute sifting so as to discover, as far as is feasible, the relative importance of the authors named.

Yet amidst a welter of hypotheses, sometimes mutually destructive, real service has been rendered to learning. Brunn's rule, already mentioned about the order in the author-lists, was well worth formulating as an endeavour to disentangle Pliny's system of quotation. Aly made temperately stated contributions to the subject of the zoological sources, and Münzer has illuminated in particular Pliny's employment of Latin authorities like Cato and Varro, and their dependence in turn upon Greek originals. He has argued that Juba was for Pliny a channel for much of the older Greek learning, as Varro was for much of the older Latin learning.[1] In tracing sources for the fine arts treated in Pliny's last books, progress has been made on the lines laid down by Otto Jahn,[2] who, after detecting the homogeneous nature of many of the art-criticisms, indicated their immediate Varronian authorship and ultimate Greek origin. Since Brieger[3] made the first attempt to determine the names of the Greek writers whose opinions Varro had latinised, a series of scholars have developed or modified the views of the pioneers in this subject.[4]

Looking broadly at the whole vexed problem, one cannot find compelling reasons against believing that Pliny sometimes went back to the Greeks, and sometimes did not. In detail, if for a moment one considers zoology alone, there is ground for thinking that Pliny in certain parts of his work used the Greek *Zoica*[5] which passed for Aristotle, and in other parts used intermediary authors either Greek or Latin. It is a large assumption to make that a learned industrious Roman of the Flavian age never consulted the original Greek sources. Pliny probably obtained Aristotelian and Theophrastian material both indirectly through different intermediaries and directly from the Greek. As regards Latin authors, we know that he used Cato both directly and indirectly; for we find that a quotation in Varro refers him to a passage in Cato, whom he then evidently consults by way of verification, because he quotes

---

[1] F. Aly, *Zur Quellenkritik des älteren Pl.*, Marb. 1885; F. Münzer, *Beiträge zur Quellenkritik der Naturgesch.*, Berl. 1897.

[2] O. Jahn, 'Über die Kunsturteile des P.' (in *Berichte d. Sächs. Gesellschaft d. Wissenschaften*, 1850, pp. 105–142).

[3] A. Brieger, *De Fontibus Librorum XXXIII–XXXVI Nat. Hist. Plin. quatenus ad artem plasticam pertinent*, diss., Greifsw. 1857.

[4] This is well summarised in E. Sellers's introd. to *The Elder Pliny's Chaps. on Hist. of Art*, 1896, where attention is directed to relevant works by Schreiber, Furtwängler, Oehmichen, Robert, K. L. Urlichs, his son H. L. Urlichs, and others. Münzer, 'Zur Kunstgesch. des Pl.,' *Hermes* xxx (1895) pp. 499–547, examined the Greek bases for Pliny's history of art. To this list may be added A. Kalkmann's *Die Quellen der Kunstgesch. des Pl.*, Berl. 1898. He denies Pliny's indebtedness to Pasiteles of Naples included in the indices, and maintains that Pliny here relied instead on a chronological compilation by Apollodorus as well as a current catalogue of artists.

[5] Aly makes this probable, *op. cit.* pp. 18–19.

more of Cato's passage than Varro did.[1] A presumption is thus raised in favour of believing that a parallel desire for verification would at times carry Pliny back from Roman authors to Greek authors whom they cited. An apposite instance occurs in a passage[2] where divergent views of Aristotle and Trogus are contrasted, suggesting the inference that Pliny had both the Greek and the Latin author in front of him. Elaborate as have been the pains devoted to the inquiry,[3] one cannot hope fully to recreate the working methods of an omnivorous excerptor and annotator like Pliny;[4] but one may picture his closely written note-books packed with extracts, comments, and references, under appropriate headings or rubrics.[5] Beyond that, to descend into *minutiae* is guesswork. Pliny's arrangement in those overflowing excerpt-rolls[6] and his way of serving up material for his *magnum opus* are alike matters of speculation, not of dogma. Much of his grouping came from predecessors – categories of animals, for example, classified, unscientifically enough, according to their environment as terrestrial, aquatic, aerial, were ready found for him; but how many tables of interesting points, more or less relevant, Pliny himself added as fruits of discursive reading can only be faintly conjectured. We can fancy his notebooks contained countless headings like 'Earthquake, miraculous accidents due to,' 'Fortune, examples of mutability in,' 'The Sea, wonderful things observed in,' 'Death, signs of,' 'Elephants, remarkable traits in,' 'Of Tritons and Nereids,' 'Eagle, a strange case,' 'Wood, valuable kinds of,' 'Diet – for a man's health,' 'Headache, remedies for,' 'Crabs, what they cure,' 'Mining, methods of,' 'Gold, ancient uses of,' 'Colours, natural and artificial,' 'Precious stones, tests for'; many such are echoed in the *Natural History*. As to actual writing, his procedure was probably variable – involving now concentration upon one author or a very few authors, now dispersion among many authors or extracts from them. For larger and well-defined portions of his subject he would rely on one or more authors of highest importance – his authorities of first rank to be reinforced by others of inferior weight. Some such kind of hierarchy of sources has been sketched for the zoological books. Aly[7] has maintained that, whatever Pliny's reliance upon Roman sources by preference, this reliance does not hold for Books VIII–XI. Here in zoology, according to his argument, the Aristotelian tradition reigned supreme,

---

[1] *N.H.* XIV. 44–47. Münzer, *Beitr. zur Quellenkrit.* pp. 12–13.

[2] *N.H.* XI. 273–276.

[3] *E.g.* on Pliny's 'Arbeitsweise,' Aly, *op. cit.* pp. 19–21; Münzer, *op. cit.* pp. 3–133; Klotz, *Herm.* xlii. 323–329.

[4] Plin. *Ep.* III. v. 10: 'adnotabat excerpebatque.'

[5] Furtwängler, 'Pl. u. seine Quellen üb. die bildenden Künste,' in *Fleck. Jb.* Supplbd. ix, 1877, p. 4 ff., regards Pliny's mode of compilation as having been 'nach einer unter Rubriken geordneten Excerptensammlung.'

[6] *Cf.* his nephew's description, *Ep.* III. v. 17: 'electorum commentarios ... opisthographos quidem et minutissime scriptos.'

[7] *Op cit.* pp. 20–21.

and no Latin author could compete; but Pliny liked patriotically to adduce the authority of his fellow-countrymen, and he therefore on special subjects turned from Aristotle – on domestic animals to Varro and Columella, on bees to Hyginus. Other authorities in this second rank were Nigidius, Trebius Niger, and Trogus, who themselves had drawn copiously from Aristotle. To ensure a spice of attractive variety, Pliny resorted to sources of a third rank, and thus imported anecdotes from the royal dilettante Juba,[1] or the travelled consular Licinius Mucianus. Enlivening items could also be hunted up in Roman annalists, antiquaries, poets, and jurists, or, if already entered in the notebooks, could be fitted into a suitable place in the big work. Besides, there was the added personal touch due to Pliny's own recollections and comments.

For want, however, of any exact criterion, we are left with a double difficulty in absolutely pronouncing, firstly, which authorities are minor, and, secondly, what is the relative importance of different minor authorities. It is obvious that some writers must have been very seldom used: thus in the second book, on the universe, we should assume from the nature of its contents that Livy, Nepos, Sebosus and Caelius Antipater, though named in the author-list, are not primary authorities on physics: very likely Nepos and Caelius are included solely in virtue of the incidental citations from them regarding the circumnavigation of Africa.[2] Again, how can we assess Pliny's debt to Vitruvius and Valerius Maximus? Both names appear in a few of the author-registers, but they are never named in the text. Yet Pliny beyond a doubt used both, and, as they were post-Varronian, used them, not through Varro, but by direct consultation. In this connexion, it is judicious to observe that even as to pre-Varronian writers in Latin, though his debt to Varro is great, the exact amount of his independent research must remain undetermined. His reading in Roman literature earlier than Varro's time may have been considerably wider than some critics of late have given him credit for. Pliny was not a lazy man.

From this preliminary consideration of problems involved in the study of Pliny's sources we pass to a brief mention of his outstanding authorities for the principal branches of his work. In Physics he took over the inherited teaching of a large number of Greek thinkers, of whom he names, in his list for Book II, twenty-six as compared with seventeen Romans. He shows keen interest in such problems of Greek mathematicians as the size of the earth or distance of heavenly bodies. Enthusiasm evokes outbursts of praise for the wonderful scientific attainments of Greeks like Aristarchus and Hipparchus.[3] Matter is drawn from

---

[1] Since Aly wrote in 1885, the claims of Juba as a source have been pitched higher: Münzer, *op. cit.* 411–422.

[2] II. 167–170.

[3] *N.H.* II. 54: 'macti ingenio este, caeli interpretes, rerumque naturae capaces . . .'; 95: 'Hipparchus nunquam satis laudatus'; 118: 'ista plures sine praemio alio quam posteros iuuandi eruerunt.'

Posidonius; and Varro's authority acts influentially here, as in most books – it is rare to find his name absent from the author-lists. One cannot but think it peculiar that neither the *De Rerum Natura* of Lucretius nor the *Quaestiones Naturales* of Seneca earned for their authors a mention in this list, though their names appear later in the work. In Geography[1] Varro was supplemented by Agrippa's wall-chart of the known world which Augustus had completed. Pomponius Mela and Juba were also used, but not Strabo. An important Greek source was Eratosthenes, who flourished early in the second century B.C. and drew from Pytheas, Hanno, and Nearchus. The book on mankind was specially indebted to Varro, Trogus and Verrius Flaccus. Coming to the twenty-five books (VIII–XXXII) assigned to Zoology and Botany under various aspects, one does well to remember, with regard to the Greek sources, that Alexandria had shown less interest in the 'descriptive sciences' than in Physics, Mathematics and Astronomy. Zoology and Botany had been subordinated to the art of healing, and it is not without significance that Pliny devotes so large a space to their medicinal side. The development of technical applications appealed to the practical Roman temperament, which preferred empirical concentration upon externals to a Hellenic quest after universals. Doubtless Pliny often felt spiritually more at home with Roman writers – with Vitruvius's applications of mathematics rather than with Euclid's theorems, and with actual Roman achievements in engineering rather than with the problems of Archimedes. Thus in Zoology, while Aristotle's influence remains paramount, it acts also through intermediaries like Nigidius Figulus, Trogus, and Juba. In Botany, material is borrowed from Theophrastus (who had given close attention to the healing properties of plants) but also from Varro, Juba, and Sextius Niger (whose "Υλη – for he wrote in Greek – was a source common to Pliny and Dioscorides). Alongside of a clear respect for many Greek writers on botany, it is noticeable that Pliny shows fondness for Latin works with botanico-pharmacological contents: phrases like *proximi herbarii nostri* or *quidam e nostris* mark his national interest. On bees, Pliny, as we have noted, used Hyginus; on medicine, Celsus, Pompeius Lenaeus, Pompey's freedman, who made available Mithradates's lore on poisons, and Antony's freedman, Antonius Castor, a man of high renown in botany;[2] on agriculture, Cato, Varro and Columella. The Carthaginian Mago's treatise on husbandry had long been accessible through the Latin translation authorised by the Senate. Mineralogical material was first collected in the fourth century by Theophrastus; but Pliny, who used

---

[1] See list of works on the subject by Oehmichen, Gruppe, Detlefsen, Cuntz, Klotz and others in S.H. § 492.

[2] *N.H.* XXV. 9: 'cui summa auctoritas erat in ea arte nostro aeuo.' M. Wellmann 'Beiträge zur Quellenanalyse des älteren Plinius,' *Herm.* lix (1924) p. 129 ff, has endeavoured to awake fresh interest in Castor as a Latin source and in Solon of Smyrna as a Greek source for Pliny's medical botany.

his work on stones, is our principal surviving authority. In art, Pliny's chief guide to Greek authorities was Varro, whom he often cites. Varro had taken occasion to sketch the history of art in connexion with architecture, an important branch in his scheme of education (*disciplinae*). The three ultimate Greek originals were Durius of Samos, born about 340 B.C., and his juniors Xenocrates[1] of Sicyon and Antigonus of Carystus. From the first of these came biographic and anecdotic matter concerning artists, from the second a sketch of developments in art with information about workers in bronze and colour, and from the third miscellaneous items of aesthetic interest. In more than one index appear the names of Pasiteles as a writer on wonderful works and of Heliodorus as a writer on monuments dedicated at Athens. Cornelius Nepos, Fenestella, Vitruvius, and Seneca are among Latin authors in the art-lists. The contemporary general and historian Licinius Mucianus supplied the author with facts bearing on art in Asia Minor.

Among questions affecting this elaborately stratified fabric of ancient knowledge, the temptation may arise to inquire what is its scientific worth today. Certain drawbacks lie on the surface. One sees that the author was too bookish to be original, too receptive to be experimental, too acquisitive to be discriminating. He tended rather to be overpowered by his enormous material than to marshal it with unerring critical control. We hear in him no Baconian trumpet-call towards research as a condition of intellectual advance; but, then, can experiment be demanded at a stage when, in spite of mechanical discoveries in Alexandria and Rome, scientific instruments and appliances were as yet imperfectly developed? It is, in truth, easy, though not over-helpful towards a just estimate, to criticise Pliny for all his weakness in science when compared with standards of the present. Modern conceptions have, however, left much in the thought of less than a hundred years ago hopelessly antiquated – still more so an encylopaedist of the first century. The gap between ancient Rome and ourselves is perceived the moment that we think of contemporary theories on the constitution of the universe, on astrophysics, on the properties of matter, on energy, on the meaning of life, on the origin of species, on disease, and on art. Such terms as electromagnetics (*electrum* is only 'amber' for Pliny), spectrum analysis, radioactivity, relativity, anthropology, evolution, bacteriology and anaesthetics have no place in this old encyclopaedia. One has only to pick out a dozen names like Galileo, Newton, Laplace, Faraday, Huxley, Kelvin, Linnaeus, Lamarck, Lyell, Darwin, Mendel and Pasteur, and associate with them their teaching, to see at once how far Pliny has been outdistanced in Physics, Natural History and Medicine.

---

[1] This Xenocrates, the statuary who wrote *de toreutice*, is to be distinguished from Xenocrates, a physician of Aphrodisias in Cilicia, whose name appears in many previous author-lists, and from whose recent compilation Pliny borrowed remedies of a superstitious character.

Today any visitor to Como, the birthplace of the Plinys, might readily fancy that the city itself bears witness to the advance in scientific achievement since the *Natural History* was written. In the façade of the cathedral are statues of both uncle and nephew, and a piazza not far away contains a statue in honour of another native of Como, the re-nowned Volta, who heralded an era of electricity. Along with electricity the sciences most conspicuously absent in the *Natural History* are Chemistry, Geology and Biology. All this is a reminder that, if defects are pointed out, many of them were inevitable in Pliny's time, and to enter into minute detail would be implicitly to rehearse the history of scientific thought between then and now.

Pliny's physics, being pre-Copernican, give a geocentric plan of the universe; and no deeper explanation of the constitution of matter is vouchsafed than the doctrine of the four elements. His geography is un-scientific, in some respects untrustworthy, and too much of a dry cata-logue, in which many chances of winning interest are missed. In justice it should be said that he prepares us for this, and apologises indeed for his brevity.[1] How disappointingly unentertaining he can be is clear from the bald treatment of such an island as Sicily, or of such a country as Italy, which ends in his matter-of-fact dismissal of the subject, *haec est Italia, dis sacra, hae gentes eius, haec oppida populorum.*[2] Only at the outset does he let himself go regarding Italy; but a panegyrical excursus[3] does not atone for sins of omission. It is notorious that in his zoology there are many vulgar errors, and yet there is no dearth of the valuable and attractive. Here in the main the worth of what had been handed down from his master Aristotle ensured that much in Pliny must live; for Aristotle was a first-hand observer and exact recorder of the animal world, at any rate within the Aegean area which he knew: if he was overtaken by fable and fantasy, it was usually in the case of distant and semi-romantic regions. His fame as a naturalist has grown almost in inverse proportion to the decline of his fame as a physicist; for, whereas Copernicus and Galileo overturned his physics, the labours of men like Cuvier and Richard Owen have established his greatness in zoology. Of this Aristotelian tradition Pliny, though a less acute observer than his predecessor, inherited enough to win the grateful admiration of Buffon, just as his avowedly encyclopaedic aim won the sympathetic regard of von Humboldt. Neither in zoology nor in botany can his classifications be accepted today: nor yet are his descriptions, although many have merit, exhaustive or accurate. If we find cities confused in geography,[4] we are prepared for still worse confusion in the animal and

[1] *N.H.* III. 2 : 'locorum nuda nomina et quanta dabitur breuitate ponentur'; III. 39: 'nec ignoro ingrati ac segnis animi existimari posse merito, si obiter atque in transcursu ad hunc modum dicatur terra.' In the latter passage, where he is about to expand, he seems to realise his general unceremonious brevity.
[2] III. 138.   [3] III. 39-42.
[4] A. B. West, 'Multiplication of Cities in Anct. Geog.' *C.P.* xviii (1923) 48 ff.

vegetable kingdoms. To treat the elephant first of land animals or the whale first of sea creatures – at least after Tritons and Nereids! – is a negation of scientific order. Unfortunately, too, Pliny revived some of the fabulous element largely rejected by Aristotle. But here and there gleams betoken conceptions of the future. For example, had facts been more scientifically grasped, the assertion of sex in plants and the account of artificial fertilisation among date-palms might have carried the author far further. About his medicine what can be said? The quite imaginary healing powers ascribed to a vast assemblage of animals, plants and substances prove a great deal of his pharmacology to be a farrago of old-world and superstitious remedies. Still, here again the qualification of a critical sense is not entirely absent, inasmuch as Pliny realises that the absurd claims of wonder-workers[1] tended to discredit the genuine virtues of herbs. His credulity has its limits. While Pliny, like many a Stoic, accepts portents, as is plain from his record of monstrous births in Book VII, he, on the other hand, rejects the werewolf fable (*homines in lupos uerti rursusque restitui*, VIII. 80) as only to be believed if all tales are true! Supposing, then, he ever read the excellently told story of the werewolf in Petronius, he read it in the same spirit as a modern reader would.

No number of shortcomings, however, can rob this encyclopaedia of its historical value. The most comprehensive document on the current science of imperial Rome, it is at the same time an index to the attainments of previous epochs in man's pursuit after knowledge. Tested by its sources, it represents the intellectual stage reached through the manipulation and amplification of Greek – especially Aristotelian – knowledge by Alexandrian and Roman savants. Defects notwithstanding, it therefore abides an irremovable landmark. Admittedly a great deal of the *Natural History* is neither literature nor science: its style, which has yet to be considered, is often forbidding, and only under serious reservations can it be credited even with that informative quality which marks the literature of knowledge. Much of it, as we have seen, would be disowned by science. Yet its worst mistakes bear a significance in the chronicle of human thought. On the positive side, we owe an infinite amount of instruction to it and to it alone. Think as we choose of Pliny – picture him merely as an intelligent, painstaking, sincere official eager to know but limited in acumen, and dismiss, as we may by modern standards, his science as contemptible – we have still to place to his lasting credit the merit of seeing that the world around teemed with curious things of fascinating interest which demanded record, though they might elude explanation. Besides, the human note (quite apart from the book devoted to man) rings out again and again. Whatever he might during moments of despondency write in disparagement of mankind, Pliny recorded enough by way of entertaining stories to place man in strange and sometimes romantic settings. Much that would otherwise have

[1] XXVI. 18: 'magicae uanitates.'

perished was rescued by him from oblivion. Some of the toilers for
human progress in the distant past would be unknown but for his
mention, and important details about Rome itself and Roman ways can
be learned from no other ancient witness. Dreary tracts of second-hand
matter redolent of the lamp rather than of nature are compensated for
by information, often the fruit of Pliny's personal experience, concerning such a miscellany of subjects as German forests and Spanish mining,
animals imported for table-delicacies or public shows in the capital,
harbour-works, roads, embankments, bridges, the sewage system, aqueducts with other great engineering feats of which he is justifiably proud,
and (not always, it must be owned, without mistakes) the artistic treasures of the author's day.

While there is a sense, then, in which Pliny remains in part true
knowledge, he also remains literature in part, because a good deal of
of him can be read with pleasure. He is not, of course, to be continuously
perused: his own recommendation, if needed, is against any such
attempt, and Roman common sense would have prescribed for a work
of reference exactly what a character in Ennius prescribed for philosophy
– sips in preference to a sousing plunge.[1] For anyone not too rigidly
concerned with Pliny's Latin, an excellent way to enjoy him would
be to prop Philemon Holland's folio translation on a table, and browse,
as one lists, among the big pages that give a feeling of spacious leisure-
liness by their size no less than by their generously expanded allowance
of quaint English. An appropriate attitude finds a certain charm in
anachronisms whereby the *ager Gallicus* has become 'the French pale
about Ariminum,' or a Roman emperor in an inscription has been, as
Pontifex Maximus, turned into an 'Archbishop.' So *Diuus Augustus* is
'Augustus Caesar of happie memorie' and Eratosthenes 'a great
clerke verily for all kind of literature.' But even in Pliny's own Latin
there is often the attractive feature of readability. He has a knack of
recounting familiar things with freshness, and so one reads without
boredom about the marvellously indiscriminate digestion of an ostrich
(*concoquendi sine dilectu deuorata mira natura*, X. 2) and its foolish notion
that, its head once hidden, its whole body is out of sight (*cum colla
frutice occultauerint latere sese existimantium, ibid.*). His passage on the
nightingale is, no doubt, in essence incommensurable with Keats's *Ode*,
but it will be felt that no one has ever described in prose with more
enthusiasm than Pliny the musical variations in the bird's minstrelsy,
the marvel of sound so loud from so small a throat, the marvel of notes in
rise and fall so true to perfect harmony.[2] Judged solely by its information,

---

[1] *N.H. praef.* 33: 'Tu per hoc et aliis praestabis ne perlegant, sed ut quisque
desiderabit aliquid id tantum quaerat'; Gell. *N.A.* V. xvi: 'degustandum ex
philosophia censet, non in eam ingurgitandum.'
[2] *N.H.* X. 81–82: 'tanta uox tam paruo in corpusculo . . . in una perfecta
musica scientia modulatus editur sonus. . . .' The lavish measure of Holland's paraphrase is apparent here: three Latin words, *infuscatur ex inopinato*, become 'anon

L*

that is to say its facts and anecdotes, apart from manner of telling –
which is variable – the *Natural History* is one of the half-dozen most
interesting books in the world. To turn over its pages almost casually
will prove this. Now we read about Nature's wonderful equipment of the
mosquito (XI. 2-3), now about products of civilisation, whether, like
paper,[1] essential in Pliny's opinion, or less so, like citronwood tables
(*mensarum insania*, XIII. 91-95), or oysters brought from Brindisi
and refattened in the Lucrine lake (IX. 169). Again, we are told that
soap or *sapo* – not, by the way, a Roman word or invention – was originally produced for reddening the hair in the form of a Gallic pomade,
which was compounded of tallow and ashes, might be hard or soft, and
gained more popularity in Northern Europe with men than with women
(XXVIII. 191). Here we chance upon an account of the ways to find
gold (XXXIII. 66 *sqq.*), and there a case of a military officer being fool
enough to take 12,000 lb. weight of silver plate with him on a com-
paign against barbarians (*ibid.* 143). One gets to know what the eyes of
five emperors were like (XI. 143-144), how madly fond Tiberius was of
Lysippus's statue, the 'Apoxyomenos,' and how Nero spoiled Lysippus's 'Alexander' by gilding it (XXXIV. 62-63). Or it may be only
isolated scraps that we note – what ship brought the Egyptian obelisk
to the Vatican, who first served a boar whole, who first served goose-
liver at Rome, when bakers first came to the city, who was the earliest
doctor. Or the subject may be, as it is in Book XIV, famous vineyards
and vintages – what Augustus's favourite brand was, what was a good
invalid wine, what the wines at Julius Caesar's banquets, what the evils
of drunkenness or next morning's feelings after a debauch – 'a cask's
breath from the mouth, oblivion of almost everything, the death of
memory.'[2] It is all the more entertaining that his individual impress is
left on some at least of his catalogues. Thus his sketch of the imposing
structures of Rome,[3] interspersed with outbursts of commendation as
well as censures upon luxury, can hardly fail to amuse the modern reader
by its picture of the supposedly dignified Roman people whirling through
the air in two reversible theatres and actually cheering at the risk it
ran (*ad periculum suum plaudens*, XXXVI. 118).

Pliny's outlook on life was largely determined by his Stoic sympathies.
Epicurean, Academic and Neo-Pythagorean grains had fallen upon his
mind, but had not taken root there as did Stoicism. There was much to

---

all of a sudden, before a man would think it, she drowneth her words that one
can scarce hear her.' His 'descant between the plain song' and 'crotchets,
quavers, semiquavers and double semiquavers' add to the general effect of rich
freedom in his tribute to the bird.

[1] The chapters on *papyrus* are specially treated by K. Dziatzko, *Untersuch. üb.
ausgew. Kapitel d. antiken Buchwesens*, mit Text übers. u. erkl. von *N.H.*
XIII. 68-69, Lpz. 1900.

[2] XIV. 142: 'ex ore halitus cadi ac fere rerum omnium obliuio morsque
memoriae.'

[3] XXXVI. 101-125.

draw him to the system. He knew the most high-souled of its adherents, Paetus Thrasea, and he had studied Seneca.[1] A philosophy which pointed towards the study of nature, and was yet more engrossed in the attainment of virtue through wise conduct, could not but appeal to a grave, diligent, self-sacrificing spirit like Pliny's. It claimed to hold the solution for the riddle of Providence and the universe; and its ascetic position of disdain for pleasure so suited his own simple tastes and laborious days as to confirm him in a heart-felt dislike of luxury and of fools. His characteristic views, then, those to which he most regularly adheres, regarding God, the world and nature, man and society, are traceable to, or at least consistent with, Stoicism. Thus he is inclined to believe in a providential government of the world, whose soul is a divine power acting beneficently on earth as among the stars above.[2] Only human weakness could seek to associate God with an image made by human hands:[3] there is one God and, echoing Xenophanes's conception that 'He is all eye, all thought, all ear,' Pliny believes Him to be a mighty principle of Life and Soul, beside whom the manifold deities of Greece or Rome are simply a jest; for such diversity of gods makes 'the population of heaven outstrip mankind!'[4] With this pantheistic creed Pliny sees around him a divine organism at work for human good; and something noble animates his perception of godhead in the service of humanity. For mortal to help mortal, he feels, is to rise to the rank of divinity and to glory everlasting.[5] A sense of piety, then, must have lightened his own toil upon the encyclopaedia, since his explicit aim therein was to help his fellows and posterity.[6]

The same ultimate belief underlies his attitude to nature and to the earth, which are not always in his mind absolutely distinguished, and which logically indeed must be partially identified in respect of the divine element ascribed to both. Despite a few inconsistencies, there is no mistaking his general position; but the profundity of a philosopher is not to be expected from him. An honest simple-minded observer, Pliny did not arrogate to himself a power of penetration into the innermost recesses of nature. Perhaps he is chargeable with having been over-readily content to contemplate merely the outward appearance of things – their phenomenal existence. Yet this was at least sincerer than bedimming nature under a misty cloud of unwarrantable hypotheses. On the whole, he saw life and the world with remarkable clearness: finding in it matter for wonder, indignation, and pity, he did not stay to analyse the momentous theories logically implicit in such sentiments.

[1] I think it not unlikely that 'mola tantum salsa litant qui non habent tura,' *praef.* 11, is an echo of Persius II. 75, 'farre litabo.'
[2] *N.H.* II. 13: 'hunc esse mundi totius animum. . . . '
[3] *Ibid.* 14.
[4] *Ibid.* 15–16: 'maior caelitum populus etiam quam hominum intellegi potest.'
[5] *Ibid.* 18: 'Deus est mortali iuuare mortalem, et haec ad aeternam gloriam uia.'
[6] *Praef.* 16: 'qui . . . utilitatem iuuandi praetulerunt gratiae placendi, idque iam et in aliis operibus ipse feci.'

His criticism is at best on the surface: and he is more fully satisfied with a rapturous apostrophe or a puritanic tirade or a moralising reflection than with any systematic pursuit of a *vera causa* or any attempt to read the enigma of the universe. So he is not strictly consistent even with regard to this mighty 'Nature' whom he personifies as a Universal Mother. In one mood, thinking of man, poor wretch, whom she lays all naked upon the earth on his very birthday to wail in helplessness,[1] Pliny wonders whether after all she may be only a grim Stepdame (*parens melior homini an tristior nouerca*, VII. 1). But the mood does not last. As a rule, he is enamoured of Nature rather than of man: she does everything well, whereas man abuses and degrades her products. This spirit prompts Pliny's repeated invectives against the refinements of pleasure. From his standpoint the herbal dyes of Gaul are more innocent that the purple got from the *murex*, because the former are ready to hand, while the latter must be sought in the unfathomed depths of the sea (*intacta etiam ancoris*, XXII. 3). So then man is at fault. Man's pride is but folly after his lowly start at birth; man's inhumanity to man makes most of the world's mourning: man perverts the kindly boons of nature.[2] In contrast with his folly, his ingratitude, his extravagances, Nature is the inspired artificer whose perfect workmanship ought never to be improved upon.[3] Virtues in herbs are so many proofs that Nature produces nothing without some secret reason – really for the sake of man.[4] Her simple remedies far excel his artificial drugs.[5] Her infinite and joyous variety is such that painting cannot do justice to her festive hues.[6] In keeping with such affectionate enthusiasm, the author has a characteristic retort for scoffers at his devoted toil upon the *Natural History*, when he claims the consolation of suffering neglect in company with Nature the beneficent (XXII. 15, *plerisque ultro etiam inrisui sumus ista commentantes atque friuoli operis arguimur, magno quamquam immensi laboris solatio sperni cum rerum natura*). Finally, if we can take the text as authentic, it is to her that he addressed a pious farewell as he laid down his pen:

[1] VII. 2: 'hominem tantum nudum et in nuda humo natali die abicit ad uagitus statim et ploratum.' *Cf.* Lucret. V. 222–227.

[2] VII. 3: 'Heu, dementiam ab his initiis existimantium ad superbiam se genitos!' 5: 'At, hercule, homini plurima ex homine sunt mala'; XVIII. 3: 'ferro ipsi nocentius aliquid damus, nos et flumina inficimus, et rerum naturae elementa ipsumque quo uiuitur in perniciem uertimus.'

[3] XXII. 117–118: 'parens illa ac diuina rerum artifex. . . . Naturae quidem opera absoluta atque perfecta gignuntur. . . . Scrupulatim quidem colligere ac miscere uires, non coniecturae humanae opus sed impudentiae est.'

[4] XXII. 1 . . . 'nihil ab rerum natura sine aliqua occultiore causa gigni'; XVIII. 1: 'si quis aestimet uarietatem, numerum, flores, odores coloresque et sucos ac uires earum (*sc.* herbarum) quas salutis aut uoluptatis hominum gratia gignit.'

[5] XXIV. 1: 'sacra illa parente rerum omnium nusquam non remedia disponente homini'; 4: 'haec sola Naturae placuerat esse remedia parata uolgo,' etc.

[6] XXI. 1–2 . . . 'inenarrabili florum maxime subtilitate, quando nulli potest facilius esse loqui quam rerum naturae pingere lasciuienti praesertim et in magno gaudio fertilitatis tam uariae ludenti . . . ne pictura quidem sufficiente imagini colorum reddendae.'

'Hail, Nature, parent of all things, vouchsafe thy blessing on the work
of one who alone of Romans has celebrated thee in thine every phase'
(XXXVII. 205).

A parallel attitude is adopted towards Earth, whom with some forgetfulness of nature's beneficence he regards at once as part of nature, and
yet as a mother enfolding man when finally cast off by the rest of nature.
The typically Plinian eulogy translated below appears to ignore nature
as parent of all:

'The Earth is the one portion of nature on whom for her singular
services we have conferred a surname expressive of revered motherhood. She is to man as the heavens to God. She welcomes us at birth,
feeds us when born, and once we have issued into this world supports
us continually: at the last she folds us in her bosom when the rest of
nature has abandoned us, then most our mother as she covers us: in
none of her services more blessed than in that which makes us also
blessed – even bearing our monuments and titles, prolonging our name,
and extending our memory in despite of quick-passing time. Her final
power we men in our anger pray should lie heavy on an enemy who is
now no more,[1] as though we knew not that she is the only one never
angry with mankind. The waters steal into rain-clouds, harden to hail,
swell in waves, dash headlong in torrents: the air thickens in mist and
raves in the storm-blast. But Earth is bountiful, tender, indulgent. Ever
the handmaiden of mortal needs, what does she breed at our compelling,
what yield at her own will – what scents and savours, what juices, what
things to touch, what wealth of colour! How true her honesty to repay
with interest a loan entrusted to her! What plenty she maintains for
our sake!'[2]

When at the beginning of his book on agriculture he renews his
praises of Earth, it is to this passage that he refers, as one in which he
has already championed her cause.[3] Yet man has repaid her bounty with
gross maltreatment: 'with iron, wood, fire, stone, and crops she is
tortured every hour, and much more to serve our pleasures than our
needs. . . . How many hands are worn to enable a finger-joint to glitter
with a gem! If there were a hell, the excavations of greed and luxury
would have dug it up by now!'[4]

How empty, he reflects, is all man's striving. This Earth, the theatre
of our ambitions, is but a speck in the universe (*mundi punctus*). To those
who are avaricious for land he preaches a sermonette on the vanity of
human wishes, anticipating Juvenal's *sarcophago contentus erit* on the
close of Alexander's career.[5] In a gayer mood, however, he overlooks the

---

[1] The imprecation would be 'sit tibi terra grauis.'   [2] II. 154–155.
[3] XVIII. 1: 'Patrocinari terrae et adesse cunctorum parenti iuuat, quamquam inter initia operis defensae.'
[4] II. 157–158.
[5] II. 174–175 . . . 'cum ad mensuram auaritiae suae propagauerit, quam
tandem portionem eius defunctus obtineat.'

tortures of Mother-earth by crop-raising, and fancifully assigns as one explanation for the ancient fertility of the soil that it liked being ploughed by ex-generals of the Cincinnatus type, whereas in later days it underwent the ignominy of cultivation by slaves instead of retired dictators.[1]

Pliny's exaltation of nature proportionately depresses his views on man, society and progress. Good men, he thinks, are due to nature's kindness in providing the antidote with the poison:

'Some men too are born poisons. Like the black dart of the serpent's tongue, their venomous souls blight what they touch. They denounce everything, and, comparable with unhallowed birds, begrudge their own darkness, and disturb the quiet of night itself with their howls – the only utterance they have – so that their mere encounter, as much as that of ill-omened creatures, paralyses action or kind-heartedness. Universal hatred is the one known gain from their loathsome breath. But in this sphere too the majesty of nature has produced good and honest men, just as she is more fertile in plants that heal and nourish. Rejoicing in the esteem of the good, we will abandon such human scum to the bitterness that burns within them, and proceed to make life fairer (*excolere uitam*): and this with firmer resolution, as our aim is the pleasure not of reputation won but of service rendered' (XVIII. 4–5).

As to the related subject of human society, Pliny is disappointed with the heedlessness of contemporary Romans, the lack of serious desire for knowledge, the flippant passion for luxury. This latter theme never tires him, though it tires his readers. Historically he connects the inroads of luxury with the conquest of Asia.[2] Widened maritime control had endangered the old Roman character: 'we are not merely fed by risks at sea, we are clothed as well:' even shellfish had involved a devastation of morals (*populatio morum*), and, as regards the parade of wealth in pearls, 'it is not enough to wear them – people must walk on them!'[3] Censuring the expenditure of fortunes upon costly incense for funeral pyres, Pliny claims that the old salted cake of simple worship used to win more divine grace, and complains that millions on millions of sesterces are drained out of the Roman Empire annually by China, India and Arabia in return for Oriental exports like silks, pearls and scents – 'a dear price to pay for our extravagance and women' (*tanti nobis deliciae et feminae constant*).[4] Elsewhere, he ranks perfumes as the most superfluous of luxuries: 'pearls pass to an heir: garments enjoy a respite: but perfumes breathe their last on the spot – they die in what may be called their own hour: their chief recommendation is that, as a lady passes by, the scent may draw the attention of those who have other business on hand.'[5] Forced fruits and vegetables share his condemnation with iced water that only the rich could procure.[6] We have

[1] XVIII. 19–21.
[2] XXXIII. 148: 'Asia primum deuicta luxuriam misit in Italiam'; XXXIV. 34: 'usque ad deuictam Asiam, unde luxuria.'   [3] IX. 104–105, 114.
[4] XII. 82–84.   [5] XIII. 20.   [6] XIX. 52–55.

seen that he prefers natural dyes from Gallic plants to other sorts; Gaul therefore does not need to ransack the ocean for purples which the vicious use for seductive purposes. Gravely he adds that these more innocent vegetable dyes will not wash; and then, avoiding a detailed homily, pulls himself up with words that amusingly anticipate the medieval student's song *Mihi est propositum in taberna mori*.[1] The same liking for simplicity comes out in his admiration for the ancient plainness of the oak wreath (*ciuica corona*) conferred for life-saving in war – a custom worthy of deathless memory, because rescue of a citizen must not be matter for gain.[2] Pliny's own frugal habits of life and industrious husbandry of time give point to his protests against the shallowness of his day: he grieves in particular that the discoveries of the past are neglected and sound knowledge contemned owing to a pernicious worship of money (*auaritiae tantum artes coluntur*). In spite of free intercommunication throughout the Empire and the advantages of peace for quiet study, ground has been lost: preoccupation with the means of enrichment has engendered a lethargic attitude to antiquity as well as a brood of social evils.[3] Early in his work he had struck a similar note of regret over the unrewarded toil of ancient investigators (*sine praemio alio quam posteros iuuandi*), the contemporary failure to add to learning (*nihil addisci noua inquisitione*), and the cramping concentration on lucre (*lucri non scientiae gratia*).[4] The same revulsion against the carelessness of voluptuaries acts along with his ever-present desire for knowledge and his humanitarian regard for the thousand ills that flesh is heir to (*millia morborum singulis mortalium timenda*) among the motives which underlie Pliny's enthusiasm for the healing art.[5]

Bias in favour of simplicity and belief in nature's perfection combined to produce a curious anomaly in Pliny's attitude towards life. This appears in a distrust of inventions which, if pressed logically, would argue actual hostility to human progress. One is prepared to find his discontent with contemporary society impelling him, like Rousseau, to conceive an ideal picture of primitive tribes: and so his raptures[6] on the charming innocence of unsophisticated man, supposing there were no mines in a wicked world, will not deceive a modern reader into fancying a dainty existence among Hottentots or Andaman islanders. When, however, he denounces the audacious manufacture of *linum* into sails (XIX. 4–6), and a Roman admiral has thus declared war on ships, one asks how far this is merely a conventional pose. It is at least infinitely

[1] XXII. 4: 'Non est nunc propositum ista consectari.'
[2] XVI. 14 'O mores aeternos qui tanta opera honore solo donauerint. . . .'
[3] XIV. 2–6.
[4] II. 117–118.
[5] XXV. 22–23: '. . . fortassis aliquis curam hanc nostram friuolam quoque existimaturis: adeo deliciis sordent etiam quae ad salutem pertinent . . . misereri sortis humanae subit.'
[6] XXXIII. 3: 'Quam innocens, quam beata, immo uero etiam delicata esset uita, si nihil aliunde quam supra terras concupisceret.'

ridiculous when contrasted with Sophocles's famous ode on man as greatest of wonders, first and foremost because he 'fares across the white sea before the stormy South.'[1] By degrees we realise that Pliny, in spite of his passion for knowledge, was not sympathetic towards daring exploration or scientific discovery. Well aware that nature has her secrets, he is yet chary about probing too deeply. We have seen that he has no inkling of the fundamental conceptions of pure science. Nor could applied science ever have obtained his benediction or thriven on his cautious methods. He would have been out of touch with an age of rapid industrial development and mechanical improvements. Upon his reflections about the evil uses of iron,[2] Philemon Holland appends a marginal note: 'O Pliny, what wouldest thou say if thou diddest see and hear the pistols, muskets, culverines and cannons in these daies?' To transpose the Elizabethan apostrophe to more modern times, what would he have said of inventions like photography, tele-graph, telephone, electric light, electric transmission of force, gramo-phone, cinematograph, anaesthetics, bacteriological tests, X-rays, wireless broadcasting, television, and, after his objections to navigation, what would he have said about aeronautics and space travel?

His political views may be in a measure divined from his close inti-macy with the Flavian house, the tone of his preface to Titus, and allu-sions like that to the *salutaris exortus Vespasiani* (XXXIII. 41). Accept-ing the imperial system as indispensable to Rome, he is grateful for the security guaranteed by a world-wide order (*immensa Romanae pacis maiestate*, XXVII. 3). It is in virtue of this system that Italy holds the principate on earth and rules the nations aright (XXXVII. 201). Never-theless his patriotism is wider than a single political system: he is intensely national and proud of Rome as Rome. He therefore feels him-self free to praise the qualities which constituted the moral strength of the republic (XVI. 14); and, without Livy's dominant bias for the aristocracy, he still venerates the renowned families who made history. Cincinnatus, Curius Dentatus and the elder Cato are among his heroes – men who could take a lead in defending the state and its land. The decline of agriculture was in his eyes the most painful symptom of the deterioration of Rome (XVIII. 21 and 35). Literary judgements are not germane to his subject, but his reverence for Homer, Cicero and Virgil can be observed.[3] It was part of his patriotism that, as already noted, he made the fullest possible use of Latin authorities in collecting the substance of his work. His preference for the writers of Rome is inten-sified because of his conviction that foreign influences had damaged the nation. Great as had been the intellectual services of Greece to the

---

[1] *Antig.* 332 sqq.: πολλὰ τὰ δεινὰ κοὐδὲν ἀνθρώπου δεινότερον πέλει, κ.τ.λ.
[2] *N.H.* XXXIV. 138.
[3] Homer, VII. 108: 'pretiosissimum humani animi opus'; XVII. 37: 'fons ingeniorum Homerus'; eulogy on Cicero, VII. 116–117, XVII. 38: 'Cicero, lux doctrinarum altera'; Virgil, VII. 114.

world, Pliny quotes with gusto the warning from Cato which ends like the jest about the Scots' revenge for Flodden: 'That country (*i.e.* Greece) will present us with her literature, and corrupt everything – even more so, if she sends her physicians here. They have sworn to kill off every non-Greek with medicine!'[1]

Pliny's literary qualities form an extraordinary and somewhat irritant mixture. If one had to characterise his style, one might call it piebald; for there is an enormous difference between his lack-lustre catalogues and his intentional purple passages. Certain ingredients too are drawn from authors whose words have been worked into his text. In his preface he avows that he makes no claim to write an elevated style: his theme, he points out, is a dry one, calling for unadorned treatment, giving few opportunities for amusing a reader (*neque admittunt . . . iucunda dictu aut legentibus blanda*), and necessitating in some portions the use of words from country life or from abroad (*rusticis uocabulis aut externis, immo barbaris*) to suit the subject-matter.[2] But, in general, his writing bears unmistakably the imprint of the Silver Age: alongside of the usual rhetorical paraphernalia such as antitheses, exclamations, questions and figures of speech, it exhibits the presence of poetic colouring and a particularly formless structure of sentence. At the same time there are elements of individuality. Though Pliny can be insufferably dull, he can also furnish a lively description and tell a good story. The former gift may be illustrated by his sketch of a struggle between an eagle and its prey, condensed in jerky jingling clauses,[3] or by the account in Book X of the bee-republic, the spider's web, and organisation among ants. Among many stories which Pliny, better than his promise in the preface, introduced to secure variety of interest, one may refer to Cleopatra's boastful bet that she could spend ten million sesterces at a banquet and her way of doing it (IX. 119–121); the schoolboy of Baiae who used to bathe with a tame dolphin (IX. 25, followed – 26 – by a similar tale which the younger Pliny[4] seems to forget having found in his uncle's work); the cobbler's pet raven and why it got a public funeral (X. 121–122); the freedman who raised far better crops than his neighbours and who, when arraigned for sorcery, exhibited in court his implements and workmen with the words, 'These be my spells!' (XVIII. 41–43, *ueneficia mea, Quirites, haec sunt.*) One of the best Roman examples shows appreciation of the sardonic flavour in Tiberius's joke about invalid wine from Surrentum: 'doctors,' said the Emperor, 'have laid their heads together to give Surrentinum a testimonial – and I must say it's excellent vinegar!' (XIV. 64). The anecdotes about Greek artists

---

[1] XXIX. 14.
[2] *Praef.* 6: 'uolgo scripta sunt'; 12–13: '(*sc.* hi libelli) nec ingenii sunt capaces, . . . neque admittunt excessus aut orationes sermonesue . . . sterilis materia, rerum natura, hoc est uita, narratur. . . . '
[3] X. 9: 'tendente . . . abigente . . . cadente . . . ostendente . . . emergente.'
[4] *Ep.* IX. xxxiii.

have the merit of retelling the competition of Zeuxis's picture of grapes *versus* Parrhasius's picture of a curtain (XXXV. 65), and the equally famous incident of the cobbler who, as a conceited art-critic, proved that he ought to have stuck to his last (*ne supra crepidam sutor*, XXXV. 85).

Seneca's brevity, acting on a sarcastic vein in Pliny, sent him in expression half-way on to Tacitus. With less toilsome accumulation to face and more leisure for reflection, he might have developed a pretty wit: as things are, the mass of his work is so huge that he does not always get credit for his ingenuity. This pre-Tacitean irony colours his implication that some emperors had divinity thrust upon them, when in reference to 'that god Augustus' he gravely adds the aside, 'and I can't say whether he simply got heavenly honours or deserved them' (VII. 150); and there must be a spice of mischievous raillery when in Book XXI he applies the phrase 'God's letters' to Augustus's epistles complaining about his daughter Julia's nocturnal revelries. Sometimes, the jest may be at the expense of idolatry: 'once on a time wood served for images of the gods, for as yet nobody had discovered the value of beasts' carcases, but nowadays by divine concession to luxury, the ivory (of elephants) makes gods' heads and table-legs!' (XII. 5). Or it may be at the expense of civilisation: he contrasts the honesty in Arabian forests – where the trees tapped for liquid incense need no watch set upon them; but in the perfume establishments of Alexandria 'no supervision can sufficiently guard the workshop and the workman has his pants sealed up' (XII. 59). Much of his mockery, like Martial's, is expended on medicine. 'A tiny ulcer must have a drug from the Persian Gulf' (*ulcerique paruo medicina a Rubro Mari imputatur*, XXIV. 5). 'In matters affecting health, people are less trustful if they understand' (XXIX. 17: that is why a mysterious Greek practitioner is appreciated). 'Physicians learn at our risk and conduct experiments through deaths' (*ibid.* 18). 'It's not modesty but competition that brings medical fees down' (*neque enim pudor sed aemuli pretia summittunt, ibid.* 21): 'the hot baths prescribed for digestion so reduce the strength that the doctor's most obedient patients are carried to their graves!' (*ibid.* 26). Apropos of the wrangling among physicians over invalids and the epitaph on the man who 'died of a crowd of doctors' (*turba se medicorum perisse*), Pliny remarks: 'It's an open secret that the most loquacious among these Greek doctors becomes straightaway the arbiter of a Roman life or death': the fact is 'Greek talent is the breeze that drives us Romans' (*ingeniorum Graeciae flatu impellimur*, XXIX. 11).

Some of the above are general enough in application to approach the semi-proverbial *sententia*, which gains in force if scathing and disdainful, like 'When all hope is away, it is high time to pray' (*tum praecipuus uotorum locus est cum spei nullus est*, VIII. 57); 'Absolutely nothing pleases man as it pleases nature' (*nihil utique homini sic quomodo rerum naturae placet*, XIX. 55); and 'It is fitting that even luxury must be protected against faked gems' (*quando etiam luxuriam aduersus fraudes muniri deceat*, XXXVII. 198). Pliny displays aptness of personification in such conceptions as 'nature at play' amidst the variety of her shells (*magna ludentis Naturae uarietas*, IX. 102), or the Nile-water 'filling the rôle of farmer' (*Nilus coloni uice fungens*, XVIII. 167). He gives also many pithy summaries of a situation. *Latifundia perdidere Italiam* (XVIII. 35), on the ruin of agriculture, is often quoted: by way of contrast, he lays it down that 'cultivation consists in labour, not outlay' (if the reading is *opera non impensa cultura constat*) – 'that is why our ancestors said "The master's eye is the most fertilising thing"' (XVIII. 43). Other epigrams touch neatly on the dangerous pursuit after riches, 'We mine for wealth in the depths of hell' (*in sede manium opes quaerimus*, XXXIII. 2); on the deterioration caused by luxury, 'The life of pleasure began, real life stopped' (*uoluptas uiuere coepit, uita ipsa desiit*, XIV. 6); and on the drawbacks entailed by the Empire on Rome in the loss of her ancient customs, 'Our victory has meant moral defeat: we are dependents of the foreigner' (*uincendo uicti sumus: paremus externis*, XXIV. 5).

Certain longer passages, where he indulges in 'fine writing,' exemplify his fanciful style and hankering after point. Here is an encomium upon Italy introduced with an apology for his brief treatment of Italian geography:

'Neither am I ignorant that it might be taken, and that justly, for a sign of an unthankful and a lazy mind, if one should speak merely in passing, after this cursory manner, of a land which is at once foster-child and parent of all lands. Divine grace has chosen Italy to make heaven itself more glorious, to unite scattered empires, to civilise manners, to draw together by interchange of speech the discordant and savage tongues of so many nations, to give to humanity humane culture, and in a word to become for all peoples in the whole world their one and only country. . . . The city of Rome that stands alone therein – how worthy a face upon so charming a neck! – by what means ought she to be set forth?'

He proceeds to praise the climate, fertility and trade of the peninsula, 'An open bosom for the commerce of the world from all parts, herself as it were eagerly running out into the sea to help mankind. The very Greeks – a stock most unrestrained in self-laudation– have delivered judgement on Italy by giving to what is but a small part of her the name of "Great Greece."'[1]

A parallel passage near the close of the work comes near to being a sort of peroration:

'Now that we have fully treated all the works of nature, it is fitting to draw some distinction among things themselves and among countries. Over all the globe, then, everywhere beneath the dome of heaven, the

[1] III. 39 *sqq.*

most beautiful land, the one that holds for products the highest rank
in nature, is Italy – queen and second mother for the world (*rectrix
parensque mundi altera*),[1] and there follows a summary of her pre-
eminence in men and women, soldiers and slaves, arts and talents,
position and healthiness, water-supply and fertility.

His rhetoric may be elaborate, like his apostrophe to Cicero (VII.
116–117) and the passage on the question 'What did Dame-Nature
mean by making some honeys poisonous?' (XXI. 78); or it may consist
in short swallow-flights of sentiment like his regret over decay in
bronze-work (XXXIV. 5–6), his pleasure over the power of art to draw
the eyes of the Senate (XXXV. 28), and his allusion to the fall of the
Carthaginian Hercules into dishonour (XXXVI. 39). All this betrays
artifice designed to counterbalance the commonplace technicalities
forced upon him by agriculture, medicine and mining. Another side of
this desire to escape from his subject-matter appears in the poetic ingredients of his vocabulary – forms such as *senecta* and *iuuenta* shared
with poets and the later prose-writers, or a world like *gemmans* employed
in the poetical sense of 'sparkling.'[2] When Pliny wrote *sortis humanae
uolumina* (VII. 147), meaning 'revolutions or reversals of human fortune,' he gave a metaphorical turn to the poetic use of *uolumen* in the
sense of 'whirl' or 'eddy.' A Livian word like *sugillatio* (VII. 150;
XXXII. 74) is also characteristic: it may have come direct from Livy,
who in many respects is a forerunner of Silver Latin, or Pliny may have
got it through Valerius Maximus. Further symptoms are noticeable in
personifications and use of abstract nouns for concrete: *leonum feritas
inter se non dimicat* (VII. 5, for *leones feri*), *uniuersa mortalitas* (VII.
147, for *cuncti mortales*, *cf. mortalitati*, XXXIV. 141), *potestatum* (IX.
26 'of men in power'), *seruitus* (XIV. 5, 'slaves'), *seruitia* (XXXIII. 23,
'slaves'), *ministeriorum* (XXXI. 7, for *ministrorum*).

Pliny's frequent curtness does not make for limpidity. Too often he
writes as one in a hurry, with the result that both expression and structure suffer. The ordinary Plinian sentence, in its badly fitted series of
condensed clauses and phrases, forms a great contrast to the finished
Ciceronian period; it loses proportionately in rhythm, logic and clearness. Any schoolboy will detect the inelegantly loose employment of the
present participle in writing *inde eductum custodia bibere iussit illico
exspirantem* (XXI. 12) to convey the fact that 'She [Cleopatra] had a
prisoner brought from custody, whereupon she ordered him to drink,
and he died on the spot.' Nowhere, however, is Pliny more exasperating
than in his maltreatment of the ablative case. He uses ablatives in a
slack sense, accumulates them cumbrously, introduces contiguous

[1] XXXVII. 201.
[2] *Senecta* and *iuuenta* are not entirely confined to poets and later prose-writers;
senecta appears in Varro *De L.L.*, and both words are used by Livy – but he is a
herald of the Silver Age. Besides Pliny, Columella is another Silver Age author
to use *gemmans* for 'sparkling' in prose.

ablatives in confusingly different meanings, plasters a heap of ablatives absolute on to a sentence, or awkwardly suspends a gerund to the close (*e.g. prodendo*, XII. 17). Thus *tenui gutta ploratu lanis* (XII. 116) is intended to mean 'after exuding in thin drops on to linen';[1] and the lumbering collocation *adhibetur et ars iecori feminarum, sicut anserum, inuentum M. Apicii, fico arida saginatis a(c) satie(tate) necatis repente mulsi potu dato* (VIII. 209) refers to the mode of securing sow-liver as well as goose-liver – 'the sows being stuffed with dry figs, and then, when fattened, suddenly killed after having honeyed wine given to them to drink.' Fortunately the world has not judged Pliny by his style.

Himself a pre-eminent epitomator and excerptor, Pliny in turn fell into the hands of the epitomators and excerptors of the third and fourth centuries. Their interest lay chiefly in his geographical and medical portions.[2] The *Collectanea rerum memorabilium* by Solinus in the third century shows much of his influence acting either directly or indirectly;[3] and the so-called *Medicina Plinii* of the next century drew copiously on his medical books, as the third-century poem in 1115 hexameters by Serenus Sammonicus had also done. Abridgement brought upon many ancient originals the fate of disappearance; but this did not befall the *Natural History*. From Symmachus in the fourth century we learn that it was widely read; certainly it was used by Martianus Capella and Isidorus of Seville. In the surviving MSS. we have about a couple of hundred witnesses to its popularity in the Middle Ages. Bede in the eighth century possessed a copy,[4] and an astronomical work in an Anglo-Saxon monastery drew material from at least two of the books.[5] At the end of that century Alcuin applied to Charlemagne for part of the text: a poem by Alcuin includes Pliny among the volumes of the library at York; and the Irish monk Dicuil made extracts from Pliny for his *De mensura orbis terrae*. In the twelfth century Robert of Cricklade (in North Wilts), Prior of St. Frideswide at Oxford, dedicated to Henry II of England his elaborate *Defloratio* in nine books excerpted from the *Natural History*.[6]

Writers of every period, in fact, profited by the diligence of a compiler who took advantage of all moments to construct a main conduit whereby the science of the ancient world might pass on to later times. But it is natural that, while during less enlightened centuries he was accepted as

[1] Most editions now transfer *lanis* to the following sentence, thus lessening the difficulty.
[2] Galdi, *L'Epitome n. lett. lat.* pp. 157–174.
[3] The dispute concerning the relation of Solinus to Pliny as a source is discussed by Galdi, *op. cit.* pp. 159–166.
[4] H. Welzhofer, *Bedas Citate aus der N.H.*, in *Abhandln. . . . W. v. Christ . . . dargebracht*, Mun. 1981, pp. 25–41.
[5] R. Rück, *Auszüge aus d. Naturg. des P. in einem astronomisch-komputist. Sammelwerke des 8ten Jahrhts.* Mun. 1888.
[6] Rück, *Das Excerpt der N.H. des P. von Robt. v. Cricklade*, Mun. 1902; *Die Geographie u. Ethnographie der N.H. des P. im Auszüge des R. v. Cricklade*, Mun. 1903 (with conspectus of Pliny's 'Fortleben' prefixed).

an authority, the modern spirit of research should demand a fresh orientation towards his work judged as science. It is significant that 'a large part of Pliny's work has gradually passed into folk-keeping, so that through its agency the gipsy fortune-teller of today is still reciting garbled versions of the formulae of Aristotle and Hippocrates of two and a half millennia ago.'[1] That, however, is only one phase of his survival. On the permanence of his historical value stress has already been laid. It is under this aspect that the gigantic encyclopaedia best justifies the author's unremitting pains and a reader's interest today.

FLAVIAN HISTORY

As Pliny was a historian, it is in place to give here the brief chronicle of Flavian history. Primarily a business-like emperor, Vespasian himself wrote memoirs. Cluvius Rufus[2] connects the Claudian and Flavian epochs. Of consular rank when Caligula was assassinated in 41, he was governor of Spain in 69, and in his later years under Vespasian composed his work on Nero's reign which Tacitus used. Another recent historian used by Tacitus was Fabius Rusticus[3] who seems to have been alive as late as A.D. 108. Vipstanus Messalla, an orator like Quintilian with a preference for the old style, was a friend of Tacitus's youth and author of historical studies.[4]

Under Domitian, history could not but suffer blight. The only names that call for mention are those of Vibius Maximus, destined to become prefect of Egypt in A.D. 104, and author of a universal history in which Statius saw qualities recalling Sallust and Livy;[5] and the two Stoics Arulenus Rusticus and Herennius Senecio, composers of eulogies upon Paetus Thrasea and Helvidius Priscus respectively, which, with their philosophical independence, cost them their lives.[6] These were days when sentence of death was passed on Hermogenes of Tarsus because his history offended the Emperor, and on Mettius Pompusianus because he was interested enough in Livy to keep a volume of speeches by kings and generals extracted from his pages.[7]

[1] C. Singer, *Greek Biology and Gk. Medicine*, Oxf. 1922, p. 63.
[2] Tac. *H.* I. viii, IV. xliii; *Ann.* XIII. xx, XIV. ii; Suet. *Nero* xxi; Dio lxiii. 14.
[3] Tac. *Agr.* x; *Ann.* XIII. xx, XIV. ii, XV. lxi.
[4] Tac. *Dial.* xv. i, xxviii. 1–6, xxxii; *H.* III. ix, xxv, xxviii; IV. xlii.
[5] Stat. *Sil.* IV. vii. 53 *sqq.*
[6] Tac. *Agr.* ii; Suet. *Dom.* x; Dio lxvii. 13.
[7] Suet. *Dom.* x.

Chapter II

QUINTILIAN: DECLAMATIONS AND ORATORS

Spanish birth and Roman influences – Immediate predecessors, Africanus, Domitius Afer, Nonianus, Trachalus, Vibius Crispus and Julius Secundus – A professorial chair – Pathos of bereavements – Quintilian's pupils – Lost works – Date of the *Institutio Oratoria* – Its scheme – Four prominent books – Importance of the child – Fundamentals – Transition from Grammar to Rhetoric – On oratory without training – Hard work essential – Moral and intellectual qualities involved – Subject-matter and arrangement in a speech – Attitude to technicalities – Practical application of oratory to law – Virtues of style – Mechanism of adornment – The best authors – Quintilian as critic – On delivery – Parallels with painting and sculpture – Attic, Asian, Rhodian styles – Latin compared with Greek – Eloquence and everyday language – *Sententiae* spoken and written – Another division of styles in oratory – The complete orator – Sources – Common sense – Aspects of Quintilian's achievement – His style – Reputation through the centuries.

The two sets of declamations under Quintilian's name – Characteristics – Persistence of rhetorical exercises – Rhetoricians and orators of the day.

QUINTILIAN

IN M. Fabius Quintilianus we meet the premier teacher of imperial rhetoric and the greatest Latin authority upon education. The epigrammatist justifiably invoked him as

> Quintilian, sovran guide of wayward youth,
> Quintilian, glory of the Roman gown![1]

Belonging to Calagurris in Spain,[2] he spent some part, perhaps a great part, of his early life in Rome, where his father may have been a rhetor.[3] Quintilian recalls the trial of Cossutianus Capito[4] in A.D. 57 as an event

---

[1] Martial, II. xc. 1–2:
> 'Quintiliane, uagae moderator summe iuuentae,
> Gloria Romanae, Quintiliane, togae.'

[2] Hieron. *Chron. Euseb.* ad ann. Abr. 2104 = A.D. 88, 'Quintilianus ex Hispania Calagurritanus'; Auson. *Prof. Burdig.* I. 7.

[3] *I. Or.* IX. iii. 73. It is doubtful whether this is the Quintilianus of Seneca's *Contr.* X. *praef.* 2; *ibid.* iv. 19.

[4] *I. Or.* VI. i. 14 (*cf.* Tac. *Ann.* XIII. xxxiii).

of his youth (*nobis adulescentibus*): he mentions also his youthful attendance on the aged speaker Domitius Afer,[1] who died a year or more later. The conjectural date, then, for his birth would be about A.D. 35. If we accept the evidence of the scholiast on Juvenal,[2] the distinguished grammarian Palaemon was one of Quintilian's teachers; and the common impression has been that his education was mainly in Rome. He had studied observantly the methods adopted by speakers of the previous generation, and his own criticisms indicate some of the qualities that acted upon him. Among these predecessors he ranked Domitius Afer and Julius Africanus high.[3] The former was his old master, for whom, although a detestable informer under Tiberius, he entertained a deep respect. He liked his *bons mots* and his ripeness (*maturitatem*): he recalls his treatise *On Witnesses* and a speech that circulated in his boyhood.[4] Africanus had a vehement style. Careful to a fault in choice of words, somewhat tedious in phraseology and lavish in metaphor, he must have at times been guilty of irrelevance or obscurity. Of one speech of his, we learn from the younger Pliny, it was remarked 'Very fine, indeed; but what's the point of it?' (*Bene mehercule, bene; sed quo tam bene?*)[5] Among others who exerted influence on Quintilian was Servilius Nonianus, to whose able though discursive histories he had listened.[6] Three recent orators he particularly mentions together.[7] They are Galerius Trachalus, whose lofty style and lucidity appeared to more advantage when heard than when read; for, says Quintilian, 'he was blest with a voice such as I never heard in anyone else and a delivery that would have done credit to the stage' (*pronuntiatio uel scenis suffectura*);[8] Vibius Crispus, the notoriously successful informer whose pleasant style was apparently better suited to private than to public cases;[9] and Julius Secundus, like Marcus Aper one of the figures in Tacitus's *Dialogus*, and prevented only by his premature demise from developing into a great orator.[10]

While, however, rhetoric pervaded the atmosphere of Rome, we have no means of determining how much Quintilian owed in training to his own cultured home-province of Spain or whether he actually taught there. At some time or other he had gone back to Spain; for in 68 Galba brought him to Rome.[11] He then entered on his career of teaching as a professor, holding what may be termed an imperially subsidised

[1] *I. Or.* V. vii. 7, XII xi. 3.
[2] Juv. VI. 452–453. F. H. Colson, ed. of Quint. I, Introd. p. x, suspects the scholiast.
[3] *I. Or.* X. i. 118.
[4] V. vii. 7; VI. iii. 27 and 42; X. i. 23 and 118; XII. x. 11.
[5] XII. x. 11; X. i. 118; Plin. *Ep.* VII. vi. 11.
[6] *I. Or.* X. i. 102.
[7] X. i. 119–120.
[8] X. i. 119, XII. v. 5 and x. 11.
[9] *I. Or.* X. i. 119, XII. x. 11; Tac. *Ann.* XIV. xxviii; *Hist.* II. x, IV. xli and xliii; *Dial.* viii and xiii.
[10] *I. Or.* X. i. 120, iii. 12.
[11] Hieron. *Chron. Euseb.* ann. Abr. 2084 = A.D. 68.

chair of rhetoric.[1] His lectures earned him reputation, honours and wealth, and pupils surreptitiously pirated his discourses. After retirement from public teaching, he devoted the evening of life to his work on the principles of oratory, dedicated to Victorius, or Vitorius, Marcellus. Domitian entrusted to him the tutorship of his two grand-nephews, as we learn from the proem to his fourth book, where he combines a perhaps diplomatically unavoidable flattery of the emperor with the explanation that this mark of confidence in his educational power had stimulated him to provide more than a manual on rhetoric for the son of Marcellus and his own son. Before he had gone quite half-way through his literary task the author suffered the pangs of severe bereavement.

Striking the most personal note in his work, the proem to the sixth book turns from technicalities to the broken hopes of a sorrowing father. Addressed to Marcellus as the real begetter of the treatise, it tells how the author had counted on bequeathing the work to be the richest of inheritances for his son, then a promising lad of nine, but death had intervened. In a fit of human petulance he upbraids the gods for causing him to outlive all his dear ones. He had already lost his young wife in her nineteenth year, then one boy of five, and now the surviving boy – a clever child on whose accomplishments in Greek and Latin and patience during illness he dwells tenderly, so that amidst his apostrophes of grief and Stoic reflections we are drawn nearer to him than anywhere else in his writings. In spite of a few epigrammatic antitheses, true to the rhetoric of the age, one cannot but be touched when he begs indulgence if mourning should make his energy flag, finds his best security in the thought that fortune has left herself no further chance of afflicting him, and bespeaks a kind attitude to labours that are not selfish but altruistic in aim. 'This work, alas, like the acquisitions of my fortune, I shall leave for others than those for whom I designed it.'[2]

The first ten chapters of the second book enable us to picture the sort of exercises prescribed by Quintilian in his apparently rather select academy. These were written themes to be criticised; reading lessons in historians and orators, with exposition and questioning; choice passages for committal to memory; courses on the theory of rhetoric – all leading to the supreme test of the declamation. A rhetorical instructor evidently led a busy life. Help had to be given to pupils in laying out a scheme of treatment, or marshalling arguments; the prepared speech had to be listened to and criticised; models for comparison had to be composed by the master. In addition, Quintilian took engagements outside school: he gave public exhibitions of his skill,[3] and he accepted

---

[1] *Ibid.* ann. Abr., 2104=A.D. 88: 'Quintilianus . . . primus Romae publicam scholam et salarium e fisco accepit et claruit.' Jerome's date is too late; for Suet. *Vesp.* 18 shows that Vespasian, who died A.D. 79, first gave the annual grant to *rhetores.*

[2] VI. *pr.* 16.   [3] XI. ii. 39.

briefs.[1] Many, therefore, who were not formally pupils came under his influence. The younger Pliny mentions him as his teacher.[2] On the other hand, there is no proof that Tacitus or Juvenal attended his school. It is not impossible that the former, who began his literary career with a flavour of Ciceronianism, had, like his friend Pliny, studied under Quintilian; and passages in Juvenal,[3] which look like reminiscences of Quintilian, may imply acquaintance with the *Institutes of Oratory* as a book or with its author as an instructor. But here positive statement is not defensible. Nor can a date be assigned for his death: it is usually placed before A.D. 100.

Of his lost works the most valuable would have been his investigation into decadence in oratory, *De Causis Corruptae Eloquentiae*.[4] This was a subject sure to engage the attention of criticism. Petronius, in his romance, had put his finger on the weak spots in declamations, and Tacitus handled the question in the *Dialogus*. Quintilian's attitude, we can infer, was that of the expert who recognised the evil effects of unpractical exercises divorced from the concerns of ordinary life and marred by artificial figures of speech.[5] To Tacitus's genius the same problem presented itself in its historical setting: political developments at Rome were no longer, he realised, such as to foster the ancient greatness in oratory. Among Quintilian's orations there was only one which he published himself – an early effort defending Naevius Arpinianus and admittedly issued from ambitious motives.[6] But there were others which admirers had taken down imperfectly in shorthand and circulated under his name with a minimum of the real Quintilian in them (*minimam partem mei habent*). We cannot tell whether such collections included the two other cases which he definitely specifies – his speech for Queen Berenice and that for a widow alleged to have forged a will.[7] There was, besides, a pair of unauthorised publications of his lectures based on notes taken by enthusiastic students – the one on a two days' discourse; the other on a longer course.[8] These appeared under Quintilian's name, but, as they are stated to be *libri artis rhetoricae*, they can hardly be identified with either collection of *Declamationes* which used to be ascribed to Quintilian and which fall to be noticed later.

His single extant work, the *Institutio Oratoria*, in which he gathered up an educational experience of twenty years, was undertaken only

[1] IV. i. 19 ('pro regina Berenice'), IV. ii. 86, VII. ii. 5 and 24, IX. ii. 74 (where a ticklish case is cited from his own experience).
[2] *Ep.* II. xiv. 9: 'ita certe ex Quintiliano praeceptore meo audisse memini.'
[3] *Cf. I. Or.* I. ii. 4 *sqq.* with *Sat.* XIV. 31 *sqq.* In X. 122 Juvenal cites as his example of Cicero's bad verse one of the well-known lines quoted in *I. Or.* XI. i. 24. When, however, Juvenal was caned at school (I. 15), his master was presumably not Quintilian, who did not believe in corporal punishment (*I. Or.* I. iii. 13).
[4] A. Reuter, *De Qi. libro qui fuit de causis corrupt. eloq.*, Gött. 1887.
[5] *I. Or.* VI. *pr.* 3, VIII. iii. 76, II. iv. 42 ('alio quoque libro'), II. x. 3–5, V. xii. 17–23, VIII. iii. 57–58 ('corrupta oratio').
[6] VII. ii. 24.   [7] IV. i. 19, IX. ii. 73–74.   [8] I. *pr.* 7.

after prolonged resistance to requests made to him in his newly won
leisure: it took over two years to write, and even then, conscious of
Horace's precept against hurried workmanship, he delayed publication,
as he explains to his publisher Trypho, from a sense that the two years
had been given more to collection of material than to style.[1] If, as is
usually thought, the twenty years of teaching mean years spent in Rome
after his return in 68, then his retirement happened in 88, and the
earliest date for the issue of the treatise would be four or five years
afterwards, 92 or 93.[2] In the other direction, the latest date must fall
before Domitian's death in 96.

The author's outline of his scheme in the twelve books is as follows.[3]
Book I treats preliminary education from infancy; II, the initial
training under a professor of rhetoric. This leads to a definition of
rhetoric in which the essential divisions are *inuentio* (getting the right
subject-matter) and *elocutio* (use of the right style). Five books (III–VII)
are assigned to *inuentio* with the allied subject of *dispositio* (arrangement),
and then four (VIII–XI) to *elocutio* with *memoria* (memorising of a
speech) and *pronuntiatio* (delivery). XII, as a culmination to the work,
draws the picture of the finished orator.

The books that stand out distinctively are the first, in which Quintilian's greatness as an educator is apparent – just where he would have
wished it to appear – at the earlier stages of education; the second, in
which he exhibits his method of teaching rhetoric; the tenth, in which
his list of authors suitable for study is accompanied by brief literary
judgements, many of them since grown familiar and famous; and the
twelfth, which conveys his final conception of the trained speaker. But all
the books possess value far beyond what might be looked for in a treatise
on oratorical instruction. This is largely due to the width of the author's
purview. To educate a speaker was to educate a Roman gentleman;
and capable speaking was expected of all in public life. The training too
was in much more than in speaking. It had to build up character, and to
embrace the liberal arts.

Quintilian's thoroughness impresses one from the outset. This is
what gives to the first book its permanent appeal. In education the initial
steps are of vital importance; for early influences leave an indelible
imprint.[4] No detail, therefore, is overlooked that might count – the
speech of a child's nurse, parental example, manners of slaves, ways of
learning the letters, attention to syllables, or practice in saying hard

[1] See introd. epistle to Trypho, and I. *pr.* 1.
[2] Colson, *op. cit.* p. xvi, suggests an earlier date, A.D. 86, as a possibility, on the
ground that twenty years of teaching might include an unknown period in
Spain.
[3] I. *pr.* 21–22.
[4] J. Overbeck, 'Die Entdeckung d. Kindes im 1. Jahrht. n. Chr.' (*Neue Jb.
K. A.* liv, 1924), establishes, from literary and medical sources, the intelligent
interest taken at this period in children and their upbringing. Stoicism contributed to it.

316 LITERATURE OF THE FLAVIAN PERIOD

words. The last contributes to clear enunciation – so much neglected in English education that we are fast becoming a nation of bad readers. The principle of the kindergarten is foreshadowed in the dictum that mental work ought at the start to wear the shape of amusement. Quintilian offers sound reasons for preferring school to the home as an educational instrument: he believes in healthy emulation among boys and in the bond of initiation into common pursuits. 'Ambition,' he remarks, 'may be a vice, but it is often the root of virtues' (I. ii. 22). The best teacher must be secured even for the rudiments, but the standard should never be beyond the pupil's capacity – the vessel must not be overfilled. One section is concerned with testing intelligence and temperament, to which instruction is to be adapted. Greek is prescribed from the beginning of the school-course, as well as the use of standard authors, even though the pupil may not appreciate them fully till later in life. Wider than in modern times, 'Grammar,' we have seen,[1] embraces both the correct use of language and the study of literature. Linguistic foundations cannot be dispensed with: 'without them the superstructure will collapse' (*quidquid superstruxeris corruet*, I. iv. 5). The warning about the danger of showy haste is as necessary now as in the first century. 'This advice' (to study grammar), he says, 'would be superfluous, were it not that most teachers, in their pretentious hurry (*ambitiosa festinatione*), begin with what should come later, and, through a preference for parading their pupils' attainments in regard to the more brilliant parts of their subject, actually hinder their progress by the short cut' (I. iv. 22).

When, after careful grounding in language, the young scholar reaches literature – where Homer and Virgil make the best reading-books – it will be found that, as honey is drawn from various blooms, so eloquence needs many arts for its support. There must be geometry and at least some philosophy; besides, ancient poetry could not be understood without some knowledge of music and astronomy. Before the book closes, a fine plea is made for breadth of training, and for the love of accomplishments for their own sake. Concurrent teaching of varied subjects is advocated, because change of study stimulates mental activity, and there is a tendency to underestimate the power of boys to bear the strain. For many studies there will never be more free time than in boyhood: we are apt to forget this and 'shield laziness under the excuse of difficulty' (*difficultatis patrocinia praeteximus segnitiae*, I. xii. 16). Protesting against mercenary estimates of a subject, Quintilian says, 'I don't want to have a reader who is going to count up how his training is to pay him' (I. xii. 17).

The age for beginning the higher study of rhetoric, in contradistinction to grammar, must depend not on years but on attainment (II. i. 7). As the type of exercise in vogue has been indicated in the

[1] See chap. on 'Roman Education under the Empire,' esp. pp. 23–24.

chapter on Roman education and in the sketch of Quintilian's academy, it need not detain us. But attention may be drawn to the sanity of the pronouncements on the need for ability, character, good temper and patience in a teacher; on the mischief done to pupils by excessive applause or excessive severity; on the promise indicated by exuberance of style; on the correction of written work; on test-questions to make pupils think for themselves; on the discussion of blemishes and excellences in speeches chosen for study; on the deleterious influence of the proud parent; on the affection due from pupils to teachers who are 'the parents of the mind' (*parentes mentium*, II. ix. 1). Regarding declamations it is worth observing that Quintilian, while he recognises their weaknesses and suggests improvements (II. x. 9), will not go the length of forbidding the imaginative type of theme.

There is a passage that implicitly states the case for such a work as the *Institutio Oratoria*, by answering the question why the untrained in speaking are sometimes thought more effective than the trained:

'An untrained speaker (*ineruditus*) employs abuse too openly and too often, even to the peril of the party whose case he has taken up, and to his own peril as well. At the same time, such a line gains a reputation, for people like very much to hear things said that they would never have consented to say themselves. A speaker of this sort still less escapes the other peril that lies in style: he makes frantic efforts (*conatur perdite*), with the occasional result that, while invariably casting about for the extravagant (*nimium*), he may chance on a fine effect (*aliquid grande*); but it is of rare occurrence and does not compensate for undoubted faults. For this reason, the uninstructed sometimes appear to have the fuller flow, because they say everything: trained speakers feel the need of both selection and restraint (*et electio et modus*). There is the further point that untrained speakers abandon the task of proving what they have asserted! By this means they avoid what our decadent law-courts (*corrupta iudicia*) consider dryness of question and argument; and they seek solely the kind of thing calculated to gratify the ear of the court with spurious delights. Besides, their very epigrams (*sententiae*), which they make their one great aim, are the more striking because the whole context is poor and mean – it is the case of flashes that show brighter not in shadow, as Cicero has it, but in downright darkness. So then one many call them geniuses to one's heart's content, provided it remains clear that such praise would be an insult to a really eloquent man.'[1]

So much for the justification of his task. Full success, he is convinced, is the fruit of hard work devoted to a difficult subject of wide ramifications; and he can only congratulate, he remarks ironically, those persons who are eloquent without any trouble or system or study (*sine labore, sine ratione, sine disciplina*). The leisure secured by his retirement

---

[1] II. xii. 4–7: 'maledicit . . . laudari disertum.'

from teaching and pleading while his services were still in demand (*dum desideraremur*) will enable him to formulate principles likely to help genuine students.[1] To be sure, an absolutely fixed system is impracticable: rhetoric would be a simple matter, if even a division of it were capable of being summarised in one brief instruction.[2] But, subject to certain rights of deviation, rules there must be:

> It is upon great labour, continual study, varied practice, repeated experiments, profound sagacity and ready resource that the art of speaking depends. But it is also assisted by these rules, provided they point out the straight road instead of one fixed wheel-rut (*orbitam*); for if anyone believes it a sin to deviate from it, he needs must submit to the slow progress of a tight-rope walker! So we often quit the main military road, allured by a short cut. . . . The orator's task is of wide extent and variety, fresh almost every day, and on it the last word will never have been said.[3]

So Quintilian addresses himself to the details of his work with a dignified consciousness of its utility and indeed of its divine call – for speech, the God-given endowment which distinguishes man from other beings, undeniably deserves assiduous cultivation.[4] Defined as *bene dicendi scientia*, rhetoric, in addition to natural ability and expert training, demands a moral basis. A good character is insisted upon over and over again as an essential qualification of the orator, who is defined in Cato's familiar words as *uir bonus dicendi peritus*.[5] Without sound morality the glib speaker endangers both the community and his own soul. Equally indispensable to a great orator is wide knowledge. As shown in the chapter on Roman education, Cicero actually recommended *omnium rerum magnarum atque artium scientiam*, while Quintilian's requirements are more moderate – *sed mihi satis est eius esse oratorem rei de qua dicet non inscium*,[6] *i.e.* he must study the subject on which he is to speak. This explains why during schooldays, though the pupil's individual bent is to be taken into account, yet some breadth of training should be compulsory for all. It will be observed that this raises the question of the educational profit of training in subjects which a student may not like. We have seen that acquaintance with subjects like music, geometry, astronomy, outside the professional training was recommended at an earlier stage: and the importance of ethics, physics, dialectic, law and history could not be overlooked.[7] Purely vocational specialisation for an orator would defeat itself.

---

[1] II. xii. 12.   [2] II. xiii. 2.   [3] II. xiii. 15–17.

[4] II. xvi. 12–19: 'deus ille, parens rerum fabricatorque mundi nullo magis hominem separauit . . . quam dicendi facultate.'

[5] I. *pr.* 9–10, II. xv. 1, XII. i. 1. In the teacher of oratory also moral qualities are required, II. ii.

[6] II. xxi. 14. Quintilian quotes the Ciceronian recommendation from *De Or.* I. vi. 20.

[7] I. *pr.* 16, XII. ii. 10, XII. iii and iv.

At the outset of the five books allotted to matter and arrangement (III–VII), Quintilian, conscious that technicalities are unavoidable, gives warning that there will be 'much wormwood and little honey' (*parum mellis et absinthii multum*). To his credit, he is not so dry as he promised to be. Certainly we are no longer interested in deciding into how many divisions the *status* of a case should fall. On the other hand, it would be too much to expect him entirely to renounce or even denounce the *multa in nominibus differentia* (III. vi. 47) as futile verbiage; for that would be opposed to the loyal spirit which led him to record, with merciful reductions, the terminological exactitudes used by generations of predecessors. We may, then, rest content in the confidence that he must have writhed under a boredom which he could not end. Technicalities notwithstanding, there is much of value. We would not be without his sketch of Greek and Roman writers on rhetoric,[1] which marks his interest in the past of his subject and constitutes an ancient bibliography on it as well as some indication of his sources. It is good to be told that of the two schools Apollodoreans and Theodoreans, the former represented an older type of oratory and were specially keen on *narratio*, the statement of a case; also, that Apollodorus taught Augustus, whereas Theodorus taught Tiberius. Again, when, after adopting the ancient tripartite division of oratory into laudatory, deliberative, and judicial, Quintilian adduces among deliberative exercises a technical term like *prosopopoeia*,[2] his remarks have the refreshing merit of showing his sound educational preference for a difficult thing. *Prosopopoeia* was a dramatic exercise in character – a declamation where the speaker assumed the personality of the supposed deliberator; and Quintilian holds it to be the most useful of exercises for the excellent reason that it involves double the amount of work and develops the powers of future poets and historians.

Another testimony to his concern for the practical application of oratory is found in the predominance of its judicial aspects. In none of the parts of a speech, *prooemium* or *exordium*, *narratio*, *probatio*, *refutatio*, *peroratio*, do we ever seem far from the law-courts, so that interesting and sometimes entertaining light is thrown on criminal and civil procedure. Illustrations are drawn from the handling of arguments in Cicero's speeches; and various problems are threshed out, such as the conciliation of a judge, the countering of an opponent's pleas, or the admissibility of more than one answer to a charge. We are reminded of risks in a digression (*egressio*) which is sandwiched between the statement of a case and the enumeration of points to be dealt with (*propositio*). We recognise the virtues of a *narratio* when told that it must above all be understood, remembered, believed. Further, we learn the autobiographical fact that Quintilian was an adept at *narratio*, with the consequence that, in lawsuits where the pleading was shared among

---

[1] III. i. 8–21.   [2] III. viii. 49.

several advocates, he was usually asked to present the case – a circumstance which he mentions with a justifiable Apollodorean pride.

This legal atmosphere prevails throughout the fifth book in the treatment of proof, oaths, witnesses and rebutting arguments; and again through the sixth on perorations, sway of emotions, and the *altercatio*. Fortunately other matters are touched on. In one passage[1] he denounces the absence of solid reasoning – a want of virility to his mind – which weakened declamations composed merely to attract notice. They are like foils with the button on (*praepilatis*), and have no sinews (*neruis carent*). Among the emotions he examines laughter – a perennial problem for the psychologist – and on it is prudent enough to confine himself to a single chapter, recognising the merits of the facetious and illustrating various types of pleasantry more or less funny. The attempted classification of jokes foreshadows no solution of the origin of laughter on the basis of psycho-analysis or otherwise: he is frankly puzzled: 'a joke is appreciated not by the reason but by a mental impulse perhaps inexplicable.'[2] The seventh book – on arrangement – largely reflects the management of actual lawsuits. Here the process of thinking out points in a case recalls often to the author his own practice. There is one most instructive example of the different lines on which the same academic case may be argued.[3]

With four books to write on style (*elocutio*) and delivery (*pronuntiatio*), Quintilian declares that difficult portions of his work are still ahead. Good style is not compassed by taking thought: as he mischievously remarks, 'it has happened that some most painstaking authors of manuals have themselves been very far away from eloquence.'[4] Mere attention to words (*cura uerborum*, VIII. *pr.* 18) is not enough, for real style is not a matter of showiness. Solicitude over verbal niceties quenches the ardour of imagination.[5] Yet the right sort of labour earns its reward: 'no appropriate word will be lost by the man who first of all has learned the principles of eloquence, and by prolonged and judicious reading has acquired a plentiful stock of words, and applied thereto skill in arrangement; and who, besides, has strengthened all by abundant practice, so as to have it constantly at hand and before his eyes. . . . When our words are sound Latin, significant, elegant and appropriately arranged, why need we trouble further?'[6]

One of the positive virtues in style is its due embellishment (*ornatus*); for the attainment of correctness and perspicuity is but to have avoided faults.[7] Such adornment should be virile, noble and chaste: it must not court an effeminate flightiness or artificial showiness: it ought to be radiant, as it were, with healthy blood and vigour. And so *ornatus* leads him to its mechanism in 'tropes' (including metaphor, metonymy,

[1] V. xii. 17–23.   [2] VI. iii. 6.   [3] VII. i. 42–62.
[4] VIII. *pr.* 3.   [5] VIII. *pr.* 27.   [6] *Ibid.* 28 and 31.
[7] VIII. iii. 1.

irony, hyperbole) which he distinguishes from the 'figures'of Book IX. These figures depend either on the thought (like interrogation, personi-fication, apostrophe) or on language (climax, paronomasia, antitheton or balance).

The chapter on the cultivation of style (*de compositione*, IX. iv) is of vital importance for the student of Latin. It deals with charm in style, with the compact and the loose type of prose (*uincta* or *contexta*, and *soluta*),[1] order of words, jarring of consonants, final -*m*, jerkiness pro-duced by a run of monosyllables, and prose-rhythm. It is an appro-priate echo that the book should end with the Ciceronian *clausula* 'esse uideantur.'

The long opening chapter of Book X contains Quintilian's list of the best authors for study, first Greek and then Latin, in the provinces of poetry, drama, history, oratory and philosophy. When he comes to Roman writers, he adds satire, and makes the well-known claim, *satura quidem tota nostra est*, which, though fully defensible in one sense needs in another as much qualification as Horace's statement that Lucilius depends entirely on old Attic comedy. In estimating Quintilian's judgements, it should be remembered that they are primarily made from an oratorical standpoint. The chapter is not a piece of pure literary criticism. There is in it, as regards the Greeks, a good deal of traditional appreciation according to Alexandrian and Pergamene canons, and in many of the brief findings we feel that Quintilian has missed saying the right thing. Again, his attitude to history shows the limitations of his period. Here he is not advanced enough to conceive of history as a science as well as an art. Influenced by the prevailing tendency to com-pose history on rhetorical lines with purple patches and poetic descrip-tions, he holds it to be *proxima poetis* and in a sense 'poetry free from the shackles of metre' (*carmen solutum*, X. i. 31). Nor is there any dream of a philosophy of history; there is no testimony to its power of guidance in the hands of the greatest masters; and when he avers that, in contrast with forensic oratory, it has nothing to do with proof, he ignores the part played in historical investigation by the weigh-ing of documents and evidence. All the same, on the purely stylistic aspect of history, he has said memorable things, like *densus et breuis et semper instans sibi Thucydides, dulcis et candidus et fusus Herodotus*,[2] or his ascription of *lactea ubertas* to Livy[3] and of *breuitas* as well as *im-mortalis uelocitas* to Sallust.[4]

The traditional element in his criticisms, particularly on Greek literature, lessens his claim to originality. Broadly similar to Dionysius of Halicarnassus in order of treatment, he probably used both his work

---

[1] From another standpoint oratorical prose may be 'simple' or 'grand' or 'intermediate,' X. i. 44: *Cf.* XII. x. 58–61 and 63.
[2] X. i. 73.
[3] *Ibid.* 32 (*cf.* 101 for more on Livy).
[4] *Ibid.* 32 and 102.

M

Περὶ μιμήσεως and some of its sources.[1] Though he does not name him in Book X, he does so elsewhere more than once. But it should be remembered that he had open access to an extensive *corpus* of Greek criticism with its canonical lists of authors arranged in different branches of literature. Such literary canonisation received the sanction of renowned authorities like Aristophanes of Byzantium and his follower Aristarchus; and similar lists issued from Pergamum. The stiffness of treatment and fixed habit of comparison which are the outcome of this inheritance leave their mark upon Quintilian: he is too starched in his grouping and too fond of finding for Greek writers a supposed analogue among the Romans. In respect of Latin literature, he is freer to employ his own reading and his own judgement. Though he had at least three well-known predecessors in the field of Latin criticism – Varro, Cicero and Horace – who were available, still here he speaks more clearly for himself.[2] There is no mistaking either his genuine predilection for Cicero,[3] whom he only occasionally criticises and then apologetically, or his almost consequential dislike of Seneca as master of a newfangled but unhealthily attractive style in prose.[4]

Neat though many of the verdicts on Roman writers be, they are, except in fuller critiques like those on Cicero and Seneca, too perilously adapted for unintelligent repetition by label-lovers. What purports to be criticism in a nutshell contains so small a fraction of the whole truth as to be virtually false or positively useless. It takes us, for instance, but a little way to find Lucretius put alongside of Macer for graceful handling of material, with the qualification that the latter is 'tame' (*humilis*) while the former is 'hard reading' (*difficilis*); and, while among elegiac poets Tibullus may properly be singled out for smooth finish, it is extraordinarily unsatisfying to read the added words 'there are some who prefer Propertius.' Equal disappointment is felt on realising that Catullus is regarded as a bitter lampoonist rather than a lyric poet. Yet within his limits Quintilian has given us much to be grateful for. It is illuminating to read the comparison of Ennius to the venerable oaks of the forest; or the opinions that Julius Caesar, granted more time for forensic oratory, would have rivalled Cicero; that Ovid was too much in love with his own genius; and that Lucan for all his fire, impetuosity and epigrams, must be frankly reckoned a model for orators instead of

[1] J. D. D. Claussen, 'Quaest. Quintilianeae' (*Fleck. Jb.* Supplbd. vi, 1872); H. Usener, *Dion. Hal. libri de imitat. rel.* etc., Bonn 1889. Usener denies Q.'s dependence on Dionys., but see W. Peterson, ed. Bk. X, Intr. pp. xxx ff.; W. Heydenreich, *De Quintiliani Inst. Or. libro X, de Dionysii de imitatione libro II*, etc., Erlangen 1900.
[2] H. Nettleship, 'Lit. Criticism in Lat. Antiquity' in *J.Ph.* xviii, pp. 225 ff. (rp. in *L. and E.* ii. 44 ff.); C. N. Cole, 'Q.'s Quotatns. fr. Lat. poets,' *C.R.* xx (1906) p. 47.
[3] X. i. 105–112. The test of real progress, he says, lies in the student's enjoyment of Cicero: 'ille se profecisse sciat cui Cicero ualde placebit.'
[4] X. i. 125–131. S. Rocheblave, *De Q. Senecae iudice*, Par. 1890, defends Seneca against Q.'s antagonism.

poets. It is of service also to have testimony to the excellence of lost plays like Varius's *Thyestes* and Ovid's *Medea*. Quintilian's view was that Latin tragedies might rival Greek, but that in comedy Rome was crippled.[1]

The treatment of *memoria* in Book XI gives an opportunity for the record of some wonderful powers of memory. *Pronuntiatio* (or delivery), which follows, is, we are told, termed 'action' by most authorities, 'but it appears to derive the one name from the voice, the other from gesture.' On this appeal to ear and eye, Quintilian lays great stress: 'personally, I should be inclined to declare that language of but moderate quality, if recommended by forcible delivery, will produce a more powerful effect than the most excellent language, if deprived of that advantage.' He contemplates in language a standard of correct, clear, elegant Latin pronunciation free from anything rustic or foreign,[2] and in gesture a convincing fitness to the thought. 'If gestures and looks are at odds with our speech, if we utter melancholy words with a cheerful air, if we assert anything in a tone of denial, it is not merely impressiveness that is lacking to our words, but credibility as well.' Besides, there must be restraint: to prance about while speaking is to 'overdo the business' – the bad habit of the professor who was jocularly asked how many miles he had declaimed![3]

It is in the last book that the moral dignity of Quintilian's conception is best revealed. In the definition of an orator as 'the good man skilled in speaking,' the indispensable requisite is put first: whatever academic labour may be involved in gaining the prescribed skill, he must before everything be good. 'This is of moment,' he insists with a Roman *grauitas*, 'because, should the oratorical power furnish the equipment of wickedness, then nothing would be more ruinous than eloquence alike to national and to private interests.' He might be expected to share Hecuba's contempt for Odysseus as the glib orator, prepared to sacrifice every consideration to please the majority.[4] This stress on morality is so emphatic that his occasional concessions regarding a speaker's avowal of the truth almost wear the guise of Macchiavellian lapses.[5]

The tenth chapter of Book XII is full of value. Brief parallel surveys of Greek painting and sculpture faintly raise the hope that an attempt might be made, as in Lessing's *Laocoon*, to demarcate the provinces of painting and literature. What in fact they lead up to is an instructive glance at dominant qualities in different Roman orators, and at the change in prevalent opinion about Cicero's speeches. Once upon a time censured by hostile critics as florid and exuberant, they had come in

---

[1] X. i. 98–99.
[2] XI. iii. 30: 'in quo nulla neque rusticitas neque peregrinitas resonet.'
[3] XI. iii. 126: 'quot milia passuum declamasset.'
[4] Eurip. *Hec.* 254 *sqq.*
[5] *E.g.* II. xvii. 19 (false argument comparable to a military ruse); *ibid.* 36 (strict veracity may be postponed to public utility).

Quintilian's day to be thought meagre and dry. Thereupon we get the famous division of oratory into three traditional styles – the restrained Attic, the inflated Asian and the intermediate Rhodian. With the grammarian Santra's explanation of Asianism as due to the circumlocutions used by imperfect speakers of Greek on the Asiatic coast, he cannot agree. More plausibly he refers differences in oratory to national and racial differences in speaker and hearer. 'Attic' one may cheerfully pronounce the best style; but there is Attic and then again Attic. In an admirable passage he picks out types of Attic orators, among them Demosthenes and Pericles, to remind us how distinct in quality they were.

But now, as to what vitally concerns him, Latin eloquence (*Latina facundia*) he feels it cannot be properly discussed except from a comparative standpoint. How does the Latin language appear when placed side by side with Greek? Here two thoughts may present themselves to the reader, first, that Quintilian possessed the great advantage which Aristotle as a critic did not possess, and the later author of the Περὶ ὕψους did not use to any extent, of having the best of both Greek and Roman literature on which to form a judgement, and, second, that some authorities have tended to overstate Quintilian's homage to Greek. On the latter point it may be said that this passage shows the Roman critic endeavouring to hold the balance evenly between a well-grounded traditional reverence for Greek and a patriotic confidence in the virility of Latin. No modern can hope to estimate either Greek or Latin sounds exactly with Roman ears, or to appreciate fully the counts on which he finds Greek more pleasant than Latin. He dislikes, for example, the letter *f*, particularly in the combination *fr*: he prefers the ringing final *-v* of Greek to the 'lowing sound' of the Latin *-m*. It is, however, easier to follow his complaint about the *paupertas* which involved Latin in repetitions unneeded by Greeks, and he is entitled to note the rich variety of Greek dialects. Yet he is not dismayed:

> He who is to demand from the Latins the acknowledged grace of Attic speech must give me the same sweetness in utterance and equal supply of words. . . . The less help our language gives, the more we must battle in the production of thought. Sublime and varied conceptions must be brought forth. All the emotions should be stirred, and our speech illumined with the gleam of metaphor. We cannot be so graceful as the Greek: let us be more vigorous. We are defeated in subtlety: let us prevail in weight.[1]

A curious anticipation of the Wordsworthian doctrine of poetic diction in the preface to the *Lyrical Ballads* appears in the contention next examined – that there is no natural eloquence except in the language of ordinary life.[2] Quintilian furnishes a sensible answer in his

---

[1] XII. x. 35–36.   [2] *Ibid.* 40.

insistence on the fundamental difference between the common language
and the speech of an eloquent man. If the theory were correct, then the
orator's sole task would be to apply plain words appropriately, whereas
his duty is the wider one of delighting, touching, influencing hearers,
and for such aims he must employ other aids – aids that are also granted
to man by nature. Exercise is as needful and natural for the orator as for
an athlete; and so in all nations one man is recognised as more eloquent
than another.

Passing to the striking thoughts (*sententiae*) characteristic rather of
Latin than of Greek oratory, Quintilian holds they are admittedly serviceable within limits – if they bear on the case, are not overdone, and
contribute to a speaker's success.[1] They have the merit of being impressive in a single hit (*uno ictu*), memorable for brevity, and effective by
their charm (*ipsa breuitate magis haerent et delectatione persuadent*). Now
are these ingenious flashes of epigram permissible in a spoken but not in
a written oration? On this question, while he owns that the spoken
speech may have to be somewhat cut to fit it for permanent book-form,
Quintilian yet makes the significant declaration that ultimately an
identical law of criticism must rule: 'I consider it one and the same
thing to speak well and to write well.'[2] The broad validity of this is not
impaired by special circumstances like the necessity for addressing a
popular jury or adapting one's pronunciation to suit an illiterate witness.

Thereupon another threefold division of styles is given without any
explicit attempt to relate it to the previous geographical triad. The three
types are the plain (ἰσχνόν), to instruct; the grand (ἁδρόν), to move;
and the intermediate or flowery (ἀνθηρόν), to charm.[3] We are quickly
assured that the three have many subdivisions and gradations of shade,
and that eloquence cannot be confined rigidly by classification. All
varieties have their uses: besides, an orator is not always equal to himself. One thing is clear – it is a mistake to believe that a corrupt and
flamboyant type is sure to be popular.[4] In any case, the true orator will
achieve his supreme effects with the ease that comes to the successful
climber above the zone of difficulty, and he will respect that sense of due
restraint (*modus*) without which nothing is praiseworthy or beneficial.[5]
Similar judgement (*ratio*) is applicable to all aspects of oratory, where,
as in Aristotelian ethics, virtue lies in the mean (*utriusque ultimum
uitium est*).[6]

Towards the end, he not unnaturally thinks of the judgements which
his work may encounter. To the best of his ability, he has put his knowledge at the service of those desirous to learn: 'and it is enough for an
honest man to have taught what he knew.'[7] But he anticipates criticism
on his exacting demand that the same individual shall combine the

[1] *Ibid.* 48. [2] *Ibid.* 51. [3] *Ibid.* 58–61.
[4] *Ibid.* 73. [5] *Ibid.* 79. [6] *Ibid.* 80.
[7] XII. xi. 8: 'id uiro bono satis est docuisse quod sciret.'

highest ethical qualities with the highest intellectual proficiency based on extensive academic study – a sort of Admirable Crichton in oratory. If it be objected that his conception is too ideal, that it implies too much work, and that there is no time for a training so elaborate, then the answer to each count is ready: 'Let those who incline to despair reflect how great is the ability of the human mind, and how capable of realising its aims . . .[1] Next let them think how noble is the object, and that no toil should be shirked with such a reward in view'; then in a Senecan tone he adds, 'it is we ourselves that make our time short; for how little do we devote to study! The empty ceremonial call filches some hours, leisure squandered on gossip other hours, public shows and conviviality others still.'[2] He is conscious of an aim transcending all this as he continues: 'let us pursue wholeheartedly the true majesty of eloquence, than which the immortal gods have granted nothing better to mankind, and deprived of which all things remain dumb, lacking illumination for the present as well as remembrance among posterity: let us unceasingly strive after the highest, for so doing we shall either attain the summit or at the least behold many below ourselves.'[3]

Quintilian's eclectic erudition was drawn from wide reading in Greek and Latin. A full list of its sources would almost amount to a catalogue of rhetorical literature.[4] He was conversant with Greek theories, old and new, on his subject. Both Aristotelianism and Stoicism exerted influence upon him; Chrysippus[5] contributed important elements to his educational doctrine; and there is ground for believing that he studied the critical works of learned Greeks who had lived in Rome under Augustus, like Caecilius Calactinus (*i.e.* from Cale Acte in Sicily) and Dionysius of Halicarnassus. Among his Latin authorities on rhetoric Cornificius (by many identified with the *Auctor ad Herennium*), Cicero and Celsus were notable; while grammatical material was borrowed from Verrius Flaccus, Remmius Palaemon, and the elder Pliny. Quintilian possessed besides, as his quotations, allusions and criticisms show, an indispensable acquaintance with the best poetry and oratory composed in Latin.[6]

Perhaps more than his learning, already glanced at, it is Quintilian's prevailing sanity that impresses us. His common sense is apparent in his refusal to lose himself, despite an intricate subject, amidst a maze of rules, definitions or subdivisions; in his consequently drastic reduction of the technicalities infesting the ordinary *artes* or handbooks; in his repeated reminders that actual oratory gave birth to the rules, not the

---

[1] XII. xi. 10.   [2] XII. xi. 17.   [3] XII. xi. 30.
[4] His *prooemium de scriptoribus artis rhetoricae* (III. i), as indicated, is a kind of ancient bibliography for rhetoric. For modern works on his sources, see S.H. § 484. A few are mentioned, *infra*, Bibl. *re* p. 311.
[5] I. i. 4 and 16, etc.
[6] It has been calculated that he refers to over 450 passages of Cicero and nearly a third as many Virgilian passages.

rules to oratory, and therefore that mere adherence to rules will never make a great speaker; in his admonition that rules cannot fit all occasions, but that circumstances alter cases; in the instructive citations of his own practical experience; in his recognition that weighty responsibility in a law-court is very different from the fictitious cases of the schools, with the corollary that practice without learning is better than learning without practice;[1] and in the broadminded pronouncements that one's chief model should not be one's sole model,[2] and that the moderns are not entirely to be ignored.[3] With a similar eye for the practical, believer though he was in ideals, he condemns the foolishness of aiming at an unattainable perfection, and tells an illustrative anecdote. Julius Secundus, when a young student, was once found by his uncle in despair over the exordium of a speech on which he could not make a satisfactory start in spite of three days' work: his uncle, an experienced speaker, rallied him smilingly into a sensible view by the pertinent question: 'You don't want, do you, to speak better than you can?'[4] Quintilian would not have progress in a great subject hindered by fantastic hypercriticism: *dicendum pro facultate*.

So much common sense and such preoccupation with the making of an orator may forbid us to expect anything startling in his criticisms. Practical in restrospect and outlook, he could not fail to value literature mainly by standards of utility. He does not turn his eye upon sheer beauty of words as the author of the Περὶ ὕψους does;[5] nor has he any *flair* for romance that might have made him appreciative of the tale of *Cupid and Psyche* or the *Peruigilium Veneris*, had they appeared in his day. It is not without significance that the grim wrestlings in Lucretius's soul or in Catullus's heart appear never to have affected him. The frenzy of despair and the fires of love are not such stuff as sound oratory is made of; and in any case it may be that he shares Horace's antagonism to Catullus and Propertius, who had the temerity to exalt love into an absorbing passion and who could never have taken the Augustan official view of marriage as a civic duty. But Quintilian has admirable qualities which find parallels in our own Age of Reason during the eighteenth century. In contrast to the manifold affectations of his day, he shows a noticeable severity of taste. He seeks on all occasions to discern clearly and think directly, because he has a zest for truth; he uses learning without flaunting it, while his maturity of judgement is saved from becoming oppressive by grace of expression and occasional gleams of humour. The kindliness of his heart, his sympathy with learners, and his steady resolve to help education forward are winning traits that make the *Institutio* something far higher than a manual of rhetoric.

---

[1] XII. vi. 4: 'plusque, si separes, usus sine doctrina quam citra usum doctrina ualet.'
[2] X. ii. 24: 'non qui maxime imitandus et solus imitandus est.'
[3] XII. x. 45.   [4] X. iii. 13–14.
[5] *E.g.* xxx: φῶς γὰρ τῷ ὄντι ἴδιον τοῦ νοῦ τὰ καλὰ ὀνόματα.

It had been his ambition to produce an up-to-date handbook on an orator's training that might be deemed equally classic with the rhetorical works of Cicero. To this object he devoted the fruits of his reading, teaching, and thinking, so that on the technique of the past conjoined with his personal experience he was enabled to rear with admirable discernment a coherent system from which the aspirant after oratorical triumphs might realise the extent and pertinacity of effort involved. Within the field of rhetoric, no ancient writer has rivalled him in varied fullness of achievement. He not merely gave us an excellent treatment of grammar in its literary aspects, of rhetorical technicalities, of idiomatic and euphonious prose, of the contrasted virtues and styles perennial in speaking and the avenues towards success; he not merely left us an incidental sketch of select Greek and Latin authors; but even outside the realm of composition and criticism he proved himself to be one of the great educators.[1] Though there may be no inkling of modern psychological pedagogy or of recently devised intelligence-tests, yet many of the eternal principles of a sound education are to be found in him stated for all time with convincing authority. The fact that many of his pronouncements retain their applicability amidst modern problems of teaching is, like the constant citation of his critical dicta, among the proofs of his permanent value.[2]

Quintilian's personal preferences in style can be gauged from the two cautions prescribed for young students, the one against an uncouth archaism, the other against the allurements of modern affectation (*ne recentis huius lasciuiae flosculis capti uoluptate praua deleniantur*).[3] Admirer though he was of the Latinity of the Golden Age, and, in particular, a confessed follower of Cicero, abjuring all such artificial glitter as he associated with Seneca's compositions, he was yet sufficiently a product of his own age to betray in his prose the new literary tendencies. That was inevitable. The most potent will could not avail to reimpose on writers a Ciceronian Latin unchanged after a lapse of nearly a century and a half. Quintilian, then, while he soberly avoids meretricious tinsel, is himself a proof of the alteration in the language since the close of the republic. The examination of single words, idioms, sentence-structure, and of literary ornament half-shyly used, must definitely place him in the Silver Age. There are words like *amaritudo*, *consummatus*, *formator*, *professor* which he shares with several post-Augustan prose-writers; some like *insenesco* and *secessus* that have come from Augustan poets into subsequent prose; others of which we do not

---

[1] See S. S. Laurie, *Hist. Survey of Pre-Christian Educn.*, Lond. 1895. Colson, *op. cit.* Introd., gives an account of Q.'s relation to the education of his times, his own educational principles, his scheme for teaching the mother-tongue and a brief comparison with (pseudo-)Plutarch's *De Liberis Educandis* and Tacitus's *Dialogus*.
[2] Th. Froment, *Quid e Qi. orat. inst. ad liberos ingenue nunc educandos excerpi possit*, Par. 1874; H. A. Strong, *Q. the Roman Schoolmaster (Some of his probable views on mod. educn.)*, Univ. Press, Liverp. 1908. [3] II. v. 21-22.

know in Latin before him, like *adnotatio, circulatorius, destructio*.[1]
He has his own dash of the poetic tinge that now coloured prose –
simple verbs for compounds (*finire* for *definire*, *solari* for *consolari*),
abstracts for concretes, and adjectives employed as substantives.[2] Signs
of Silver Latin are noticeable in the sense he gives to adverbs like *alioqui*
and *olim*, or to prepositions like *circa* and *citra*. Equally symptomatic is
the fondness for augmentatives in *prae-*, like *praedurus, praedulcis,
praetenuis*, and the extreme rarity of the intensive *per-* compounds
familiar in Cicero.[3] So, too, with syntax, in such constructions of the
infinitive as *legi dignus* or *qui . . . meruit credi secundus*. The change is,
however, more than one in vocabulary and syntax. The usual ring of the
sentence is different from the Ciceronian.[4] The old amplitude of period
is rarely present: it is replaced by a frequent looseness of structure
whereby causal and adjectival clauses are tacked on to the sentence in
a semi-detached fashion which operates against the harmony and
euphony of the whole. Consequently, in spite of express preference for
the ancient style of oratory,[5] there is no longer the same fullness or
symmetry in Quintilian's modified Ciceronianism. It was Filelfo, in the
fifteenth century, who suggested that one might detect in Quintilian a
smack of Spain (*sapit Hispanitatem*) and departure from good Latin
(*barbariem quandam*); but it is as hard to isolate any characteristic
Spanish colour or atmosphere or humour in him as it is to recognise the
Patavinity of Livy. His style is, at least, free from that smart artificiality
which offended him in the oratory of his day; for he stigmatises it as a
great contemporary fault to court praise by studied effects under which
the artifice lay transparent. 'People consider that the art is lost, unless
it is obvious; whereas it ceases to be art, if it is obvious.'[6] Ovid in
another connexion had said much the same, *si latet ars prodest* (*A.A.*,
ii. 313), and as a maxim of literary and aesthetic sobriety the thought
reappears in the later proverb, *ars est celare artem*. A pervading restraint
recommends Quintilian to the confidence of readers, and has contributed
to form a prose which, without Aristotelian profundity or Ciceronian
brilliance, is worthily adapted to the ripeness of experience that everywhere seems to speak through it. So it comes that after Seneca's clever
restlessness one has a sense of calm in Quintilian.

[1] Fuller lists are given by Peterson, ed. of Bk. X, p. xli ff.
[2] P. Hirt, *Ueber d. Substantivierung des Adject. bei Q.*, Berl. 1890.
[3] 'Pas un seul augmentatif en *per-*,' L. Laurand, *Manuel des études gr. et lat.*, Par.
1918, p. 606. But *perexiguus* occurs at XI. ii. 27.
[4] Q.'s *clausulae* have been examined by J. Gladisch, *De Clausulis Quinti-
lianeis*, Bresl. 1909, and De Groot, *Prosarhythmus*. Their statistics are arrived
at by different methods, but both indicate considerable contrast (though apparently not the same amount of contrast) between Cic. and Q.
[5] *E.g.* IV. ii. 122.
[6] IV. ii. 127: 'perire artem putamus nisi appareat, cum desinat ars esse si
apparet.'

M*

What were the vicissitudes of Quintilian's reputation? Martial's apostrophe, already cited, was a proclamation of his educational supremacy, as, in a left-handed way, was the fathering of spurious *Declamations* upon him. The *Dialogus* of Tacitus owed its inception probably to Quintilian's inquiry into decadence in oratory. Published to meet an express demand, his *Institutio* must have enjoyed for a time a vogue which is reflected in the attitude of Juvenal and Suetonius. From Suetonius descended the information entered in Jerome's *Chronicle* of the fourth century: besides, Jerome's letters imply acquaintance with Quintilian's writings. But the Frontonian archaisers of the second century had checked the pro-Ciceronian authority of Quintilian, and in fact we have for 300 years no evidence proving direct knowledge of his work.[1] In the fourth century Quintilian appears to be known, except to Jerome and possibly Lactantius, solely through the *Declamations*. After Jerome, in spite of the fact that Cassiodorus and Isidorus recognise his rhetorical eminence, there are great intervals in time during which no mention of Quintilian can be traced. One of these long silences was broken in the ninth century when Servatus Lupus wrote to the Abbot of York asking for a copy of the twelve books of the *Institutio* – a request which he also preferred to the Pope with the explanation that he possessed only incomplete copies of Quintilian and of the *De Oratore*.[2] Silence falls again for a couple of centuries until, in the twelfth, the testimony of John of Salisbury proves that some of Quintilian's methods were in use at the school of Chartres; nor is that the solitary evidence for monastic acquaintance with his work at this period.[3] Next century, the encyclopaedist Vincent of Beauvais knew his text at first hand; and then Petrarch's enthusiastic handling of a manuscript of the *Institutio*, 'discerptus et lacer' though it was,[4] brings us to the verge of the Renaissance.

A strong reinforcement in the posthumous influence of Quintilian came with the rediscovery of a complete text by Poggio at St. Gall in 1416. Five years earlier, in 1411, Guarino had translated into Latin the treatise of disputed authenticity Περὶ παίδων ἀγωγῆς which is included among Plutarch's writings and which is affected by a great deal of Quintilian's educational theory.[5] The two events united to confirm the

---

[1] Colson, Bk. I, Introd., traces through the centuries the evidence for knowledge of either the *Institutio* or its author.

[2] To this century belongs the 'Liber Glossarum,' that portentous medieval collection of glosses, which was perhaps compiled by Adelhard, abbot of Corbie. Three scraps from Q.'s ninth book are quoted in the medieval glossaries to exemplify the use of *pugnaciter, caesim* and *austera*, but there is no proof whether these come direct from the text or through some intermediary. See J. F. Mountford, *Quotations fr. class. authors in medieval Latin glossaries* (Cornell publn.), New Yk. and Lond., 1925, pp. 85–86.

[3] Colson, *op. cit.* li.

[4] It survives as Parisinus 7720.

[5] W. H. S. Jones, 'Quint., Plutarch and the Early Humanists,' *C.R.* xxi (1907) pp. 33 ff.

hold of Quintilian over humanism at the Revival of Learning. In the general purpose of the humanist educator – the production not of a pedantic recluse but of an all-round man and fully equipped citizen – there was great similarity to the aims of the *Institutio*. For the attainment of Quintilian's ideal no less than for that of the Renaissance, it was requisite to develop natural gifts by training, to form character by the lessons of standard literature, and to ensure an attractive dignity of bearing in social relations. The modern might be expected to find more ways of employing leisure nobly than a Roman gentleman of the Empire, to have more freedom of personal grace, and to show, if less oratorical cleverness, then perhaps more skill in conversation – but the fundamental basis for both systems was the same, and this explains why Quintilian was so warmly taken to the hearts of the humanists. His influence was enormous on educators like Vittorino da Feltre, Aeneas Silvius Piccolomini (Pius II), Guarino, Agricola, Bebel, Vives and Melanchthon. Nowhere did it work more clearly than on Erasmus himself. In England Quintilian's authority can be traced decidedly as far back as Elyot's *Governour* of 1531. Ascham was much less impressed; whereas extensive borrowings from Quintilian went to the making of Ben Jonson's *Discoveries*. Later, among great figures in our literature, Pope stands out as the one who had most understanding of 'grave Quintilian's copious works,' where 'the justest rules and clearest methods' are 'all ranged in order and disposed with grace.'[1] Apart from inevitable references in the comparatively modern treatises on rhetoric by Blair, Campbell and Whately, it must be recognised that Quintilian has scarcely attracted in Britain his due share of attention – but then we are not a rhetorical nation.

DECLAMATIONS AND ORATORS

Two sets of *Declamationes* have come down under Quintilian's name in separate MSS, the one consisting of nineteen fairly elaborate productions, the other of 145 shorter and sketchy ones from a collection originally numbering 388; for time has mercifully relieved us of the first 243. The ascription to Quintilian does not now convince many scholars of the authenticity of either collection. There has not, however, always been equal distrust. The Oxford editors of the longer declamations in the seventeenth century published them as specimens of his method, anticipating in the preface gratitude for omitting 'the sorry remains and unsightly ruins' (*miseras reliquias et informia rudera*) of the 388 shorter ones. On the other hand, these same remnants were claimed for Quintilian by Aerodius in the sixteenth century and by Ritter in recent times.[2]

---

[1] *Essay on Criticism*, ll. 669–694; *cf*. Pope's own notes.
[2] Against Ritter's belief in their authenticity may be put the works of Trabandt and Fleiter cited in Bibl., *infra*, *re* p. 311.

In neither collection is the Latin notably irregular. There are in the nineteen longer declamations no very glaring deviations from classical diction to make belief in Quintilian's authorship *prima facie* absurd on bare linguistic grounds. Yet features in the form of argument and the over-frequent recourse to *sententiae* of doubtful relevance point to a later date for some of them at least. Ritter thinks four authors[1] are represented; and Reitzenstein thinks even more, in which he is supported by Golz after an examination of the *clausulae*.[2] Few may accept in detail the groups arrived at by tests partly subjective and partly numerical; but it is likely enough that some are nearer in time to Quintilian than others and may actually represent themes used in his school. A plausible guess is that we have here a collection made and perhaps amplified by a contemporary of Gellius or Apuleius.[3]

As early as the third century A.D., there was current a collection of declamations referred to Quintilian but recognised as containing spurious specimens.[4] Jerome and Servius in the fourth century, and later Isidorus, quote from the longer declamations; Jerome, indeed, like Lactantius, quotes other declamations now lost. The belief of antiquity, therefore, that some of the declamations came down from Quintilian was unquestioning. But here, where there is so much triviality, so much of what he himself condemned in oratory, our hardest task is to believe either collection worthy of the great teacher. Ritter, however, has championed the authenticity of the shorter pieces, claiming that as legal speeches by Quintilian were brought out without his permission, so it is possible that these scholastic speeches were issued in an unauthorised way. Of two works in the province of rhetoric mentioned by Quintilian as having been published by enthusiastic pupils from notes, Ritter identifies the second with the shorter declamations; but, as this second work is stated to have been taken down in a comparatively few days, it is not easy to think it the same as the long series of what was once 388 school-themes, or to think it could be appropriately mentioned as an *ars rhetorica*.[5]

It remains to glance at the collections themselves. The 'learned and ingenious hand' who made the English version of the nineteen specimens in 1686 regarded them as an 'exercitation or praxis upon Quintilian's XII Books,' naïvely pronouncing them to be 'the cream and

[1] C. Ritter, *Quintilianische Declam.*, 1881; groups (1) I; (2) X; (3) II, IV, V, VII, VIII, XI, XIV–XIX; (4) a group which may show the influence of Quintilian or a pupil, III, VI, IX, XII, XIII.

[2] R. Reitzenstein, 'Zu Qs. grossen Decl.' *Hermes* xliii (1908) 104 ff., and *Studien zu Qs. grösseren Decl.* Strasb. 1909. G. Golz, *Der rhythmische Satzschluss in d. gröss. pseudo-Quintilianischen Decl.*, Kiel 1913; esp. pp. 61 ff.

[3] C. Hammer, *Beitr. zu den 19 gröss. quintil. Dekl.* Mun. 1893, p. 44. R. Ellis, Notes on the 19 Larger Decl.,' in *Hermathena* 1909, pp. 328 ff., alludes to these almost forgotten exercises as 'dating perhaps from the second, perhaps from the fourth century A.D.' The latter alternative seems too late.

[4] S.H.A. *Trig. Tyr.* iv. 2; Auson. *Prof. Burdig.* i. 15–16.

[5] *I. Or.* I. *pr.* 7.

QUINTILIAN

product of the most promising wits (in the schools) culled out and
polished by the second hand of the master.' Some turn upon immorality
or crime: some have a public bearing: more often, with features akin to
the Greek comedy of manners or a modern novel, their interest is social
or domestic. A few could be served up as romances like *The Philtre of
Loathing* (XIV, XV), or as spiritualistic cases for investigation by the
Psychical Research Society, like *The Spell-bound Tomb* (X), in which a
mother, hitherto comforted by visions of her dead son, is aggrieved
because a magician, at her husband's instigation, has by enchantment cut
off communication with the ghost. A detective story might be made out
of *The Wall with Handprints of Blood* (I); and then we have the usual
quota of pirates. A half-romantic theme like a wizard's prophecy may
be entangled with two imaginary laws which create a dilemma for debate.
Thus, the fourth case concerns a brave young soldier whose horoscope,
read by an astrologer long ago, had foretold that he would win distinction
in battle but would one day kill his father. Now, there are supposed to
be in this state two laws; (i) 'A warrior who has served his country
nobly may choose his reward'; (ii) 'A citizen who meditates suicide
must render satisfactory reasons for his resolve in open senate, under the
penalty (so dreadful to the ancients) of having his body refused burial.'
Here is the crux. The wizard's prophecy about his valour has come true:
he cannot face the likelihood of committing parricide which has by the
power of suggestion become an obsession. The only way out, therefore,
is to kill himself; but to secure burial he must gain the senate's approval.
This, then, is the reward which he will ask – leave to put himself to death:

'I, who am willing to die that I may not commit parricide, do not
see but I must commit it if I continue to live. . . . As for my father,
who would keep me alive against my will, I do not wonder at him,
because he is still overjoyed at the fresh acquist of my martial glory
(*adhuc recenti gloriae nostrae gaudio stupet*). . . . He cannot see the
parricide through the champion.'

The situation is not one which could ever trouble the student in
actual life, but, like many other exercises, it served to evoke ingenuity
in pleading. We seem to see literature in the making, when we chance
upon a miniature study in the workings of fate that might form the
basis of a Greek tragedy:

'My father was so far from being deterred by the prediction of his
own danger that he himself, I say (alack for the melancholy force of
fate – *proh tristis necessitas!*), girt on my arms and equipped me for
battle with his own hands, as if assured of the astrologer's veracity
(*tanquam mathematico iam credidisset*). . . . And now he will not have
me die, though there is nothing left for me to do but to murder him.
O Death, who art commendable for the valiant, desirable for the
wretched, and not to be rejected even by the happy! How much have
I courted thee in war! (*quantum te quaesiuimus in bello!*)'

He relates how he bore a charmed life amidst the deadliest dangers: as no foe could slay him, he now must beg permission to kill himself:

> 'Titles, statues, dignities – reserve them for those who must live: guarantee me but my father's safety, my own innocence, and the respect of history (*temporum pudorem*). . . . I trust the House will not consider that my father's appearing against me (*contradictione*) debars me of my reward.'

The pleader contends that in any case it is better to die young in the midst of one's fame than to endure the decrepitude of old age; but, in his special case, he is destined by his horoscope to die as a felon, if the fortune-teller spoke truth. Then comes a fresh turn. His valour in battle after all could only have been downright frenzy:

> 'I was not myself when I fought so gallantly; and I shall commit parricide too when I am not myself. . . . God forbid that I should tarry till the issue decide the conflict betwixt the wizard's response and myself. I had rather defeat the astrologer than find fault with his predictions (*mathematicum uincere malo quam reprehendere*).'

This, then, is the paradoxical *impasse*: he can baulk his destiny only by death. If he is allowed to die now, his father, who admittedly loves him, will be able to shower affection upon his body, and (in the peroration)

> 'when you have had enough of farewell embraces, then and not till then is it right to lift up your hands towards heaven and cry out, "Wizard, thou art a liar!' (*mathematice, mentitus es*).'

It is wonderful with what variety of argument or reflection upon life and death, astrology and the power of prediction, such a theme can be elaborated. Similar dexterity, worthy of more solid cases, pervades most of the orations. It scarcely matters whether we have a lawsuit to compensate a poor man's loss of bees through poison sprinkled on his rich neighbour's flowers, or a strange malady of sleepy sickness attacking twins, of whom the doctor undertakes to cure one if he is allowed to put the other to death and hold a *post-mortem*!

The shorter declamations (and some are fortunately quite short) are more profitably represented in specimens than in their wearisome total. The problems are such as arise out of cases of outrage, divorce, adultery, murder of or by outlaws, tyrannicide, military desertion, shipwreck, prodigality of sons, harshness of fathers, or (like later Italian *novelle*) marriage between a son and a daughter of hostile families. Handling the type of theme already worn threadbare in Augustan days, they cannot be considered uniformly entertaining. Yet there are exceptions, and all is not monotony. One may even be grateful for absurd instances with outlines that might serve for wildly impossible tales; and, dipping further into the collection, one cannot deny that it has some variety. We may light upon the Gilbertian situation of a Cynic youth with a professed contempt for the good things of life objecting to dis-inheritance by his father; or a sober question of legacies to relatives or freedmen; or a semi-economic discussion on a proposed equalisation of property, with such pertinent queries as whether it is to be once and for all, or whether the equalising process is to be carried out as often as someone, for any reason whatever, is found to have less than his fellows. Favourite themes are dilemmas due to conflict between two laws: *e.g.* If a man exiled for treason has come so gallantly to the aid of his country in wartime that she gratefully recalls him, can he have his original con-viction reviewed in spite of a law that the same case must not be heard twice? Or, again, if an exile has illegally come home before his time has expired, is he entitled to plead a law permitting an injured husband to inflict on his wife and her paramour the fate that befell Paolo and Fran-cesca? A common *motif* is that of an outraged woman. There is a refine-ment of this theme in the case where the unfortunate lady seems at various crises to jump out of the frying-pan into the fire. Against her father's wish, she had exercised her option to marry the violator rather than have him put to death. For this compassion her father disowns her. When her father afterwards fell into poverty, filial affection impelled her to relieve his straits in spite of her husband's objection; and for this he divorces her! Many cases, however, are of a stereotyped character, with little to differentiate them from the elder Seneca's examples, ex-cept perhaps greater silliness.[1] In the case of the imported slave dressed by a dealer as a free citizen to cheat the Customs, one recognises a parallel to that given by Suetonius as an illustration of the *controuersia*.[2]

It is usual to find imaginary points of law freely and subtly raised, effective lines of argument being sketched in the *sermo* and the rhetorical handling in the *declamatio*. Sometimes we get more than one *sermo* and *declamatio*: sometimes a section is devoted to the law of the case before it is examined in equity: sometimes the *sermo* is absent, leaving the *declamatio*, as in the dispute among three sons, an orator, a physician, and a philosopher, claiming the property of their deceased father, whose will constituted as his heir the son who should be proved to have best served the state. The general method may be exemplified in *The Digging up of the Parricide's Bones*.[3] Two laws are here assumed that may con-flict: (i) 'Let a parricide's body be cast out unburied'; (ii) 'Let the vio-lation of a grave be actionable.' The statement of the case is in brief as follows: a father on his death-bed, declaring that his two sons have poisoned him, enjoins on his daughter the duty of vengeance. She

---

[1] *E.g.* the charge of attempted parricide brought against a son found mixing poison in No. ccclxxvii may be compared with Sen. *Cont.* VII. iii, and No. xvii of the longer declamations.

[2] cccxl; *cf*. Suet. *De Rhet.* i. The case is stated in the chapter on Roman education, p. 28 *supra*.

[3] *Ossa eruta parricidae*, ccxcix.

accuses them both. Before the trial one commits suicide and is buried in the family tomb. The other, when tried, is found guilty, put to death, and his body left to rot. The daughter, presuming the guilt of the suicide, has his corpse exhumed and cast forth. She is charged with illegal violation of a grave. In the *sermo*, among questions suggested for discussion are these: is it illegal to disinter a buried person in any circumstances? More particularly, is it legal for one who could have prevented the burial in the first instance? Does the law, in forbidding burial of a parricide, forbid burial only of persons duly convicted? From the *declamatio* a few sentences may indicate the rhetorical line of defence:

'So then [had he not been exhumed] the dead parricide would have been buried and laid in lasting rest beside his father [his victim]! . . . Is such treatment to be conceded to one whom the law would cut off from the light of heaven when alive and from the earth when dead? . . . Must not a dutiful daughter listen to the troubled ghost of her father, unable to bear contact with a guilty son?'

Tediously unreal though the declamations are, they have a genuine importance in the history of ancient education and eloquence. They link the exercises of the Golden Age, as recorded by the elder Seneca, with those of several succeeding centuries. Deserving to die of their own dullness, they yet had surprising vitality, so that when we turn to the Greek declamations of the sophist Libanius, whose works help to make the century of Gregory Nazianzenus, Basil the Great and Julian the Apostate live again for us, we find the time-honoured themes still under treatment in the Eastern empire. The gibe of Gibbon that Libanius lived too much in the times of the Trojan War and in Athenian history might lead one to overlook other themes of his, of equal artificiality but of more social interest, in which preternaturally embittered fathers, unscrupulous stepmothers and disinherited sons play much the same part as they do in the Latin exercises that passed under Quintilian's name.[1]

Quintilian himself passed on what he found valuable in the rhetorical lore of writers like Rutilius Lupus and Celsus. He mentions together[2] the senior rhetorical authors of his own day, Verginius Flavus, Pliny (the elder), and Tutilius, thus looking back in the case of the first-named to the Neronian age; for Verginius, as has been noted, taught Persius. Tutilius is named by Martial,[3] when he counsels a parent to avoid for his boy's instructors all grammarians and rhetors, and so 'leave Tutilius alone in his glory.' It is unfortunate for the completeness of our record that Quintilian expressly omits mention of authors alive when he wrote the *Institutio*.[4] Princeps was a rhetorician whom

---

[1] *Cf.* Liban. *Decl.* xlix with the first of the nineteen longer declamations.
[2] *I. Or.* III. i. 21.
[3] Mart. V. lvi. 6: 'famae Tutilium suae relinquat.'
[4] *I. Or.* III. i. 21: 'parco nominibus uiuentium.'

Suetonius could remember as giving on alternate days exhibitions of declamation and disputation. Julius Tiro is mentioned just after Quintilian himself in Suetonius's list of rhetoricians, and Julius Gabinianus, who figures in the same list, won a great name as a teacher in Gaul during the Flavian period.[1] M. Aquilius Regulus, the younger Pliny's bugbear, wrote books including a biographical lament on his dead son, but unscrupulously applied his oratorical gifts in delation, as did the hated Baebius Massa, Mettius Carus and Palfurius Sura. At the bar there were many able speakers less famous than Tacitus and Pliny themselves, such as Herennius Senecio, who was with Pliny in the impeachment of Baebius Massa; Vitorius Marcellus to whom Quintilian dedicated his *Institutio* and to whom Statius addressed *Siluae* IV. iv;[2] the African Septimius Severus, an ancestor of the emperor of that name, and known to Statius[3] and Martial; Satrius Rufus whom Pliny characterises as content with contemporary style without seeking to rival Cicero (which Pliny himself tried to do); Valerius Licinianus, a native of Bilbilis, admired as a sort of Cicero by his fellow-Spaniard Martial, exiled under Domitian, but allowed by Nerva to settle as a professor of oratory in Sicily; and one of Martial's patrons, the Spaniard Licinius Sura, who later composed speeches for Trajan.

[1] Hieron. *Chron. Euseb.* ad ann. Abr. 2092 = A.D. 76; *cf.* Tac. *Dial.* xxvi. 11.
[2] *Cf. supra,* p. 313 and *infra,* p. 391.
[3] *Cf. infra,* p. 391.

Chapter III

FRONTINUS AND TECHNICAL WRITERS

Career of Frontinus – A general's prose anthology of *Stratagems*
– Authenticity of the fourth book – Frontinus's treatment of sources
– The water-commissioner's account of *The Aqueducts* – His
scheme – Belief in honest work – Glimpses of his character –
Latinity.
Professional writers of the Flavian age.

FRONTINUS

THE works of Sextus Julius Frontinus originated largely in
posts which he held during his public career. No one could have
shown more of that thorough devotion to the details of official
duty with which many of the best-born Romans ensured the greatness
of the Empire. Frontinus was of good family, and his friend Martial
alludes to a poetic vein discoverable in him during leisure hours at the
coast.[1] Since, however, his books are practical rather than literary, it
looks as if the energetic general and water-commissioner found scant
time for any play of fancy. On New Year's Day A.D. 70 we meet him[2] at a
sitting of the senate, which he had summoned as city praetor, prepared
presently to hand over his office to the young prince Domitian. His
birth-date, then, may be guessed as about 40. In Britain his name is of
historic interest; for as governor (75–78) he proved a worthy successor
to the vigorous Cerialis, whose successes against the Brigantes of the
North he equalled by victories over the Silures in the difficult territories of
South Wales.[3] It is possible that the Roman road from Bath to the Bristol
Channel and beyond it westwards by Caerwent and Caerleon was engineered under his orders even if it was not yet called the Via Julia.[4] He was
succeeded by Agricola in 78; but presumably saw further military service with Domitian in Germany against the Chatti in 83, since he makes
specific allusions to the emperor's tactics.[5] Some time afterwards,
we know from internal evidence,[6] he was at work on a collection of

[1] *Epig.* X. lviii. 5–6: 'Doctas tecum celebrare uacabat Pieridas.'
[2] Tac. *H.* IV. xxxix.
[3] Tac. *Agr.* xvii: 'sustinuit molem Iulius Frontinus.'
[4] The name Via Julia maritima was unwarrantably given to this road by
Charles Bertram in the eighteenth century.
[5] *Strat.* I. i. 8, I. iii. 10, II. iii. 23, II. xi. 7.
[6] Domitian's cognomen 'Germanicus' is mentioned, *Strat.* II. xi. 7; he got
it in A.D. 84.

stratagems in continuation of an earlier tactical manual, and at its outset
he claims to be the solitary author to treat military science systematic-
ally.[1] It was in 97 that Nerva, aware of much slackness and corruption
in the administration of the water-supply for Rome, showed confidence
in the ability and integrity of Frontinus by appointing him superin-
tendent of the aqueducts (*curator aquarum*).

To the new commissioner's determination never to rely upon subordinates for advice but to learn for himself everything of moment affecting his task[2] we owe his immediate start upon the historical, topographical
and statistical record which we possess in the *De Aquis*. Consul for a
third time in the year 100, he held the position of augur until 103, the
date of a letter by the younger Pliny[3] acknowledging a correspondent's
congratulations on his own nomination by the emperor to the college
of augurs in succession to Frontinus. We may therefore infer that he
died in that year.

If all his writings had survived, they would have added still more to
the technical and professional effect of those we have. He composed a
work on land-surveying and land-laws, but of this gromatic treatise
only excerpts have come down.[4] His theoretical treatise on military
science (*De re militari*) is lost; but in the extant *Strategematon Libri Tres*
we have a sequel for the use of officers,[5] illustrating principles of war
by stratagems chosen from Greek and Roman history. They are grouped
as those for use (Book I) before battle, (Book II) during battle and after;
(Book III) at sieges; and are again subdivided into sections headed 'on
concealing one's plans,' 'on finding out the enemy's plans,' 'on escaping from difficult positions,' and so on.

A fourth book, containing anecdotes of another sort, has come down
with *The Stratagems* and constitutes a problem. The preface acknowledges that the recorded instances illustrate military management rather
than stratagems (*exempla potius strategicon quam strategemata*). They
are treated in categories such as 'discipline,' 'restraint,' 'justice,'
'determination,' so that the ethical aspect forms a contrast to the three
preceding books. The authenticity of this supplementary book was
assailed in the latter half of the nineteenth century by Wachsmuth,
Wölfflin, and Gundermann.[6] Thereafter, despite defences by Fritze,
Esternaux and Kortz,[7] the majority of scholars regarded it as spurious,
until in 1938 Bendz published his *Die Echtheitsfrage des vierten*

---

[1] *Strat.* I, *init.*: 'cum ad instruendam rei militaris scientiam unus ex numero
studiosorum eius accesserim. . . .'
[2] *De Aq. praef.* 1: 'nosse quod suscepi'; 2: 'indecorum . . . delegatum officium
ex adiutorum agere praeceptis.'
[3] *Ep.* IV. viii.
[4] See Lachmann's *Gromatici Veteres*, 1848; C. Thulin, *Corp. Agrimensorum R.*
Vol. I. i (Teub.) 1913.
[5] *Strat.* I. *praef.*: 'cum hoc opus, sicut cetera, usus potius aliorum quam
meae commendationis causa aggressus sim.'
[6] See Bibl.   [7] See Bibl.

Buches der Frontinschen Strategemata. Since then Book IV has been generally accepted as genuine. The case for rejection was certainly formidable. Whereas the three books on stratagems bear marks of common authorship with the *De Aquis*,[1] there are considerations that tend to isolate the fourth book. These include differences in thought and treatment, in build of sentence, in turn of expression and use of words.[2] The assailants of Book IV were divided about its date. Wachsmuth and Wölfflin put it in the fourth or fifth century. Its Latinity is against that. Expressions such as *de uariis consiliis* quoted to support a late date are not decisive. Wölfflin found a number of resemblances[3] between the Latin of I–III and that of IV, which he tried to explain away as deliberate imitation on the part of the spurious author. Representative words in Book IV bear the same general post-Augustan stamp, usually with a Livian association, like *praecessisse* (IV. ii. 1, 'be before others' in getting a bridge built), *acclinauerat* (IV. ii. 5, 'leaned against'), *ampliaretur* (IV. iii. 12, 'be increased,' an extension from the legal sense of adjournment). As a significant parallel to *inrequietum* in the unchallenged part of Frontinus, we have an Ovidian word in *obmurmurare* (IV. vi. 2). The whole linguistic evidence runs counter to any violent separation of the books in time of composition.

Gundermann passed a more discriminating judgement upon the Latin of Book IV by referring it to a date close to Frontinus's own, early in the second century. Schanz's hypothesis claims that the author was contemporary with Frontinus and that he recorded an actual experience

[1] Wölfflin (*op. cit.* in bibl.) points out resemblances in thought despite the difference of subject; and the occurrence of significant similarities like *conuolnerare*, *Str.* II. v. 31, *Aq.* 27 and 115; *depressus=humilis*, *Str.* I. v. 24, *Aq.* 65; *adiutorium=auxilium*, *Str.* II. v. 11, *Aq.* 14 and 67.

[2] *E.g.* Bk. IV abandons certain principles of subdivision followed in I–III (but that is natural considering its less specially military character). Book IV draws its examples from Valerius Maximus much more largely than do Bks. I–III and sometimes copies V.M. almost verbatim. Bk. IV is said to be less conscientious as to its facts. 'Scipio Africanus' in I–III means Africanus Maior, in IV Africanus Minor. With place names, I–III use *apud* 26 times and *ad* 12 times, IV uses *apud* not at all and *ad* 8 times. *Traditur* impersonal appears never in I–III, twice in IV. Expressions such as *fertur, dicitur, memoriae proditum est,* showing a reliance on tradition, occur more times in IV than in the whole of I–III. *Ob hoc, ob id, et ideo, itaque* appear respectively 9, 6, 3, and 6 times in I–III but never in IV. *Atque ita,* a favourite in I–III, is absent in IV. Wölfflin instances also as a fault peculiar to IV an unnecessary use of *suus* with *frater, filius,* etc. (There is little in this; in IV. i. 32 *suum* is properly added to *fratrem* for emphasis; but *filium* in 40 and *fratrem* in 41 have no *suum*.) Sometimes a stratagem-example already used recurs later with minor changes. In all but one of these duplicates the recurrence is in Bk. IV. The sceptics assume interpolation; sometimes, they say, the author of I–III borrowed from IV, sometimes an editor inserted in I–III material from IV. And for the duplicate of which IV cannot be guilty (I. i. 11 and I. v. 13) critics are divided as to which passage is original and which repeated by an editor.

[3] *E.g.,* 'adiutorium' IV. vii. 31; *cf.* II. v. 11; 'foret' IV. vi. 3, vii. 9; *cf.* 'forent' III. xvi. 3; 'notabilis' IV. iii 13 ('notabiliter' IV. i. 1.); *cf.* III. viii. 2; 'subinde' IV. i. 1, vii. 13; and often in the earlier books.

of his own in the surrender of the Lingones in A.D. 70 to himself.[1] It is difficult to believe in this unknown officer, who for this one occasion betrays his personal experience and in several other places relies upon Frontinus's instances. The hypothesis in any case has to assume that a third person combined this book with the genuine three, and, to effect a plausible deception, not only wrote a fictitious preface for the later book, but also foisted a passage ostensibly by Frontinus into the original introduction to the earlier work.[2]

However, if one takes the preface to Book IV at its face value, the book is a supplement, perhaps an afterthought. If one further assumes that it was hastily put together,[3] then most of the difficulties disappear and there is no reason why it should not have been written by Frontinus himself. This is Bendz's conclusion. After an exhaustive study of all the relevant features of both parts of the *Strategemata*, he finds that many of the divergences are not so sharp as the sceptics make out, and that other differences are explained by the special character of Book IV and the conditions in which it was composed. Moreover be adduces stylistic and 'prosarhythmic' arguments in favour of unity. The practice of alliteration in Book IV is similar to that followed in the earlier books, and the *clausulae* are more in favour of genuineness than against it.

Any collection of anecdotes pure and simple, even in the lightest vein, is apt to pall: so one tires of the concentrated essence of stratagem in campaign or siege administered in tabloid doses without comment. While Macaulay can thrill in relating 'how well Horatius kept the bridge,' Frontinus's bald account is Livy with all the *lactea ubertas* squeezed out.[4] Here and there, however, points of interest arise. Some of his examples of Machiavellian diplomacy or astute *ruses de guerre* prove that everything may be held fair in war. When we read about a screen of prisoners (*captiuos lateri euntium praetexuit*, I. iv. 1: cf. 2), or about poisoning an enemy's water-supply (*aquam helleboro corruptam*, III. vii. 6), we recognise that unchivalrous devilry in military operations is not a peculiarity of any one period; while an instance of premeditated disregard of a covenant (III. iv. 6) anticipates the doctrine that treaty obligations must yield to military necessity. If such examples are abreast of modern ruthlessness, the author himself appears hopelessly antiquated in his naïve confession that he sees no prospect of improving engines of war.[5]

[1] *Philol.* xlviii (1889), p. 647. See *Str.* IV. iii. 14: 'Lingonum opulentissima ciuitas . . . septuaginta milia armatorum tradidit mihi.'
[2] *Str.* I. *praef.* par. 4 is designed to account for the existence of a fourth book on a commander's conduct of affairs in general as a pendant to the specially military stratagems of I–III. The assailants of Bk. IV of course regard this paragraph as spurious.
[3] The duplicates (*cf.* p. 340, n. 2) could be taken as evidence of haste, as indeed could many features of Bk. IV usually adduced against its authenticity.
[4] *Cf.* Livy II. x, with *Strat.* II. xiii. 5.
[5] *Strat.* III. *praef.*: 'machinamentis quorum expleta iampridem inuentione nullam uideo ultra artium materiam.'

Frontinus took the majority of his examples from Greek and Roman history before the Empire. Occasionally we find something later, like an allusion to the *Variana clades* of A.D. 9, or to Corbulo's fighting in Armenia during Nero's reign, or to Domitian's campaigns; but his main sources are Caesar, Sallust and Livy. No stress need be laid on the two passages where Livy is cited by name (II. v. 31 and 34); for both are possibly interpolations. On the whole, Frontinus is free in his rehandling of originals, as may be seen if one compares passages in Livy with his adaptations.[1] If, further, one compares passages in Livy with the adaptations by both Valerius Maximus and Frontinus,[2] one will find that the latter does not show, except in Book IV,[3] any slavish dependence upon Valerius. Sometimes indeed Frontinus is free to the extent of carelessness and inaccuracy. He is capable of confusing occasions and individuals. Thus he misrepresents Livy's Diodorus as Diodotus (III. xvi. 5); turns a device used by Cincinnatus against the Volscians into one by Capitolinus against the Falisci (II. viii. 3); alters to Cimbrians Livy's Celtiberians (II. v. 8), having in the preceding section (II. v. 7) called Viriathus 'dux Celtiberorum,' though he is 'dux Lusitanorum' elsewhere (II. xiii. 4). The trick ascribed to Manlius as a means of encouraging his men against the Etruscans (II. vii. 11) appears, on comparison with Livy and Dionysius, to involve a mistake between two colleagues. In such cases Frontinus's memory may have played him false amidst the multitude of names with which he had to deal.

The *Strategemata* belongs to Domitian's reign. The more famous treatise *De Aquis Vrbis Romae*, in two books, was begun under Nerva, but not finished until Trajan had succeeded him.[4] Only those without historical sense will dismiss as totally unreadable his description of aqueducts once vital in their utility and still in ruin imposingly picturesque. Undertaken in the conscientious spirit of mastering his business and instructing successors,[5] the author's labour was lightened by bel ef in the value of his duties; for, in his eyes, the maintenance of the aqueducts gave 'a signal testimony to the greatness of the Roman Empire' (*cum magnitudinis Romani imperii uel praecipuum sit indicium,*

[1] Perhaps one of his closest copies is *Str.* I. v. 16, based on Livy XXXV. xi. Here, Livy's 'Caudinae cladis memoria . . . obuersabatur' becomes 'obuersaretur Caudinae cladis exemplum'; 'per ludibrium spectaculo esse' is repeated word for word; and 'subditis calcaribus per medias stationes hostium erupere' becomes 'additis calcaribus per intermissas hostium stationes eruperunt.'
[2] *E.g.* Livy I. xxvii; Val. Max. VII. iv. 1; *Str.* II. vii. 1. Here Frontinus seems independent of Val. Max., though, like him, he happens to introduce the word *fiducia*.
[3] In *Str.* IV. i. 31 a dozen consecutive words (but for a change of an adjective to a noun) are identical with Val. Max. II. vii. 4. As indicated above (p. 340 n. 2) the increased dependence on Val. Max. in *Str.* IV was an argument against the authenticity of the book. It can equally well be an indication of the haste in which it was compiled.
[4] *De Aq. praef.* 1: 'Nerua Augusto'; 93: 'Traianum Augustum'; 118: 'diuus Nerua.' F. Krohn (Teubner ed. 1922) defends in his preface the title *De Aquaeductu Vrbis Romae.*
[5] *Praef.* 2.

119). He had to contemplate a state of things very different from the old times when for 441 years Rome had been content with water from the Tiber, wells, or springs. Springs, he allows, may have healing virtues, and are still the objects of veneration (*fontium memoria cum sanctitate adhuc exstat et colitur*, 4); but his concern is now a practical one, directed upon nine or ten majestic conduits bringing water for miles over stone arches into the city.

His scheme embraced an account of the builders of the aqueducts, dates of construction, direction, length of channels, elevations, measurements of pipe-capacity and of volume at intake and delivery, as well as a list of curators up to his own day. Statistical details of wastage and of the amounts of water distributed by the several aqueducts in the several wards are certain – and the author knows it – to be complicated as well as dull (*non ieiunam tantum sed etiam perplexam*, 77); but he prescribes a cure in judicious skipping (*licebit transire leuiora*). We soon weary of the *quinaria*, the official unit of measurement, which Di Fenizio has calculated to have equalled 0·48 litre per second or 41·5 cubic metres per 24 hours. Yet even a cursory perusal yields instructive items. We read about the limpid drinking water that came from the Marcia; about unnecessary blending with turbid waters which spoiled the best; about fraudulent tapping of the supply; about the system of repairs; and topographical facts which illuminate features of the landscape near Rome today. A good deal is not literature but archaeology or engineering. All the same, it is a human document presenting an unvarnished picture of scrupulous and observant fidelity in the control of an essential public service, where there had been slackness and dishonesty. Through its unpretentious style shines a personality with a true conception of civic virtue, determined to aid Nerva and Trajan in undoing the abuses of the previous reign. For a man of culture it must have entailed some self-sacrifice to settle down upon the dry *minutiae* of the water-supply. Still, he was rewarded by a satisfaction in work well done which justified his proud reflection that his reforms had, under imperial auspices, made Rome a salubrious city:

> The Queen and Mistress of the globe realises from day to day the care bestowed by our devoted emperor Nerva, her ruler; still more will the health of this same eternal city realise it in the increase of reservoirs, water-works and -establishments; and tanks. No less benefit is distributed among individual consumers owing to the increase in the emperor's private grants: those also who nervously used to draw an illegal water-supply are now relieved from anxiety and enjoy it by imperial bounty. Not even waste-water is lost: the look of the city is clean and improved: what we breathe is purer: and, as regards the unwholesome atmosphere, the causes which gave to the air of Rome its bad name with the ancients have been removed.[1]

[1] *De Aq.* 88: 'Sentit hanc curam imperatoris piissimi Neruae principis sui regina et domina orbis in dies, et magis sentiet salubritas eiusdem aucto

The old-fashioned practical Roman of limited outlook speaks through the disdainful self-complacency of his exclamation:

With such a number of indispensable structures for all these waters you are welcome to compare the idle Pyramids or all the futile, though renowned, works by Greeks.[1]

This, however, is a note of national *hauteur*. As an individual he was the reverse of boastful, and his modesty is illustrated in Pliny's story about his forbidding any monument to be erected to himself, because, as he pithily put it, 'Our memory will last if deserved by our life' (*memoria nostri durabit si uita meruimus*).[2]

The composition of the *De Aquis* involved, besides personal observation and inquiries, research among records and business documents. Part of its material is based on reports from surveyors and engineers. Senatorial decrees affecting the aqueducts are recited.[3] Among Roman writers quoted are Fenestella, Ateius Capito and Caelius Rufus.[4] It was characteristic of the man that his style should be straightforward in its freedom from artifice. He liked parade in composition as little as he did in the performance of duty. Dispensing with the attendants decreed to a water-commissioner on official business outside Rome, he declares: 'for myself, when on my rounds inspecting the conduits, my own honesty and the authority given by his Majesty will serve for lictors' (101). So, too, he wisely refrained from pomp or epigram on such a subject as the water-supply. Very occasionally there is a sly hit, like that at the honesty required from masons on the wall 'in accord with a law more honoured in the breach than in the observance' (*secundum legem notam omnibus sed a paucis obseruatam*, 123). But his belief, as we have learned from Pliny, that a man's surest memorial is a worthy life makes a complete *apologia* for the absence of literary refinements.

His Latinity has been glanced at in connexion with the problem of *Strategemata* IV. The 'Silver' mark is at least suggested in such usages as *citra* meaning 'without,' *circa* meaning 'concerning,' *quamquam* with subjunctive or participle, and future participles with a notion of purpose.[5]

---

castellorum, operum, munerum et lacuum numero. Nec minus ad priuatos commodum ex incremento beneficiorum eius diffunditur; illi quoque qui timidi inlicitam aquam ducebant, securi nunc ex beneficiis fruuntur. Ne pereuntes quidem aquae otiosae sunt: alia munditiarum facies, purior spiritus, et causae grauioris caeli, quibus apud ueteres urbis infamis aer fuit, sunt remotae.'

[1] *De Aq.* 16: 'Tot aquarum tam multis necessariis molibus pyramidas uidelicet otiosas compares aut cetera inertia sed fama celebrata opera Graecorum.'

[2] Plin. *Ep.* IX. xix. 6.

[3] *De Aq.* 100–101, 104, 106, 108.

[4] *De Aq.* 7, 76, 97. Vitruvius, the architect, is mentioned twice in 25.

[5] *E.g.*, 'Citra uexationem,' *Str.* I. viii. 9; 'circa praedam occupatos,' I. vi. 3; 'circa gratulationem morantis,' II. ix. 8; 'quamquam dissimularent,' I. ii. 9; 'instructuris,' II. *praef.* 1; 'traditurus,' III. *praef.* Circa had been used for 'concerning' in Hor. *A.P.* 132 and Livy, XXXVI. vii. 1, and *quamquam* with the subjunctive in Nepos (*e.g. Att.* xiii. 6), and Livy (*e.g.* XXXVI. xxxiv. 6), and future participles for purpose a number of times in Livy.

A reader can tell his whereabouts in the history of the language, when three lines in the preface to Book III give him *hucusque*, *prae-locutione*, and *attentione* (used absolutely, as in Quintilian). Many such typically post-Augustan words as *sequelae* (II. iv. 8) occur, or at least words, as we should expect remembering the main source of the *Strategemata*, that are Livian but otherwise mainly post-Augustan, like *exasperatus* (II. i. 11), *praeualere* (II. i. 8) and *subinde* (I. iii. 10, iv. 13; II. iii. 23, ix. 1; III. ix. 7). There are poetic epithets like *inrequietum* (II. ix. 1) which prose took over from Ovid, and there are phrases like *profunda siluarum* (I. iii. 10) that have a Tacitean ring. *Annuntiare* (= *nuntiare*, I. ix. 2), common to Frontinus with Curtius, Seneca Philosophus, the elder Pliny, Suetonius and Apuleius, is one of the words which passed through the *sermo cotidianus* and ecclesiastical Latin into the Italian *annunziare* and the French *annoncer*.

We have had occasion to point out resemblances between the *Strategemata* and the *De Aquis* in their Latin. The latter is nowhere more obviously post-Augustan, or non-Ciceronian, than in its employment of the superlative *püissimus* (*De Aq.* 88). Used by Mark Antony and condemned by Cicero as impossible,[1] it was accepted by Curtius, Seneca, Tacitus and Florus.

TECHNICAL WRITERS

In the professional writing of the Flavian age, law and grammar may be included. Under Vespasian, the Sabinian school of jurists was represented by Caelius Sabinus, and the Proculian by Pegasus. Other legal writers were Urseius Ferox, Plautius, and Juventius Celsus the elder. The younger Juventius belongs, with Neratius Priscus, to later Flavian days and still more to Trajan's reign. One of the juridical writers of Domitian's time was Aufidius Chius, mentioned by Martial. Among refined literary critics of the day was Apollinaris, also in Martial, whose Claranus, however, perhaps belonged to an earlier period. Possibly, but not certainly, we may place here Largius or Larcius Licinus, whose *Ciceromastix* is significant of a literary quarrel; and Aemilius Asper, the erudite grammarian, who left his mark on ancient scholarship by his commentaries upon Terence, Sallust and Virgil.

[1] *Phil.* XIII. xix. 43: 'uerbum omnino nullum in lingua Latina.'

Chapter IV

VALERIUS FLACCUS

What is known of the life of Valerius Flaccus – Romance in his
theme – Predecessors – The story of the *Argonautica* – Apollonius of Rhodes and Valerius – How was the epic designed to
end? – The Roman element – Comparative lack of vogue –
Features of his language – Metre – Qualities of style.

C. VALERIUS FLACCUS belongs, at least in part, to the time of
Vespasian. If we accept 'Balbus Setinus' or 'Setinus Balbus,' the
additions to his name in *subscriptiones* of the Vatican MS., then
he may have been a native of Setia, but whether that was the Setia in
Campania or one of two Setias in Spain it is impossible to determine.
No special Spanish qualities are discoverable in him, and he was
Roman enough to serve on the committee of fifteen for sacrifices.[1]
Almost at the outset of his *Argonautica*, in invoking the emperor, he
refers to Vespasian's service in British seas, to the recent capture of Jerusalem by Titus in A.D. 70, and to the supposed likelihood that Vespasian's younger 'offspring' (*proles*), Domitian, might celebrate his
brother's exploits:

> O thou yet more renowned for opening
> The ocean, since the Caledonian wave
> (That erst disdained our Trojan-blooded race)
> Hath yielded to thy sails, O sire revered,
> Raise me above the herd, and cloudy earth.
> Show favour to a bard who sings the fame
> Of heroes of old days and deathless deeds.
> Thine offspring shall unfold (for he hath skill)
> Judaea's fall, and how his brother, smirched
> With Salem's dust, launched firebrands everywhere,
> War-maddened all along the towered walls.[2]

Beginning his epic, therefore, soon after 70, he made slow progress;
for in the third and fourth books[3] he alludes to the eruption of Vesuvius in 79, and apparently he never completed the eighth book. Quintilian, writing in the early nineties of the century, is the only classical

[1]*Arg.* I. 5 *sqq.*; *cf.* III. 417 *sqq.*, VIII. 239 *sqq.*
[2] I. 7. *sqq.*   [3] III. 208, IV. 507.

writer who mentions him. His words of regret over his recent death (*multum in Valerio Flacco nuper amisimus*, X. i. 90) suggest that Valerius died about A.D. 90.

In the Quest of the Golden Fleece Valerius had a subject which no one could make entirely dull. The tale of the earliest of ships,[1] the Argo, of its hazards by sea and land, of the love between Jason and the outlandish princess Medea, and of the perilous winning of the dragon-guarded treasure contains the same inherent romance as that which colours adventures upon the Spanish Main, so that Hérédia's line in *Les Conquérants* might equally well have been written of Jason's crew,

Ils allaient conquérir le fabuleux métal.

Here too were voyagers for whom, under the perpetual imminence of the unknown, each night brought hopes and dreams of heroic morrows. This is the stuff of which epics can be made. Valerius, luckier in choosing such a theme than Lucan and Silius were in drawing upon history, could hardly fail, notwithstanding the trammels of his episodes, to catch and convey some gleams of its pure roseate charm. The story of Statius's *Thebaid* stirs in the bosom little perceptible emotion; but it is otherwise with the fortunes of the Argonauts. A primeval glamour plays round a legend which may be older than the tale of Troy: and we can be sure that it is older than the composition of one of the Homeric poems as we have it, for in the *Odyssey* Jason's fabled ship is mentioned as in all men's minds.[2]

In a story so old, Valerius had many predecessors. He was not even the first Roman poet to handle it. Varro of Atax had based a work on the *Argonautica* of Apollonius of Rhodes, and a reference in Probus[3] to Varro makes it likely that his poem was accompanied with a commentary whence Valerius might have derived material. Ancient Greek writers on the myth, Herodotus, the Attic tragedians, Apollodorus and Diodorus seem to have furnished Valerius with subject-matter, but whether directly, or indirectly through *scholia* on his chief source, Apollonius, it is hard to say.[4] Later Greek writers also contributed their portion; and his geographical learning, as in the catalogue of peoples in Book VI, came more probably from Eratosthenes than from the elder Pliny. To his material sources Valerius added inventions of his own, and treated the whole in a style upon which the influences of Virgil and of Ovid are unmistakable.

The hexameters of the eight books reach a total of 5,593, and Book I

[1] Valerius is not consistent about the Argo as first of ships. However strange its building may be considered in the Thessaly of Bk. I, the Lemnians of Bk. II are supposed to have sailed back in ships from Thrace (II. 108–111), and Hypsipyle sent her father off secretly in an old ship (II. 285–287).

[2] *Odys.* xii. 70: Ἀργὼ πᾶσι μέλουσα.

[3] Prob. ad *Georg.* II. 126: 'Media . . . a Medo, filio Medeae et Aegei, ut existimat Varro qui iv libros de Argonautis edidit.'

[4] W. C. Summers, *A Study of the Argonautica*, Camb. 1894, pp. 15 ff.

is the longest (851). Greek though the theme be, the poet's aspiration is that his 'utterances may fill the cities of Latium' (l. 21). The narrative opens with the jealousy felt by Pelias, king of Thessaly, towards Jason, the son of his brother Aeson, and his crafty plan to despatch his nephew on the dangerous Quest of the Golden Fleece under the pretext of revenge on Aeetes of Colchis for the murder of Phrixus. Jason feels the lure of glory, prays for the favour of Juno, and at Minerva's command builds, decorates and solemnly launches the Argo. Heroes flock to man her – Hercules brings the youth Hylas, and Chiron his ward Achilles. Sunset comes and

> Dotted along the crescent bay are lights
> That show not lands as yet to mariners,[1]

because there are no mariners! Orpheus whiles away the hours of night with a relevant ballad on the drowning of Helle by falling into the sea from the back of the golden ram, and on the escape of Phrixus, her brother. When the Dawn-goddess comes, 'setting the sea a-shimmer with the morning sun,'[2] it is to display the adventurers in readiness for their start, which takes place after Jason's parents, Aeson and Alcimede, have given utterance to their grief at the parting. A catalogue of the crew is added in about 130 lines (352–483). Their number is fifty, including Acastus, Pelias's son, who joins stealthily at the moment of sailing. It is one of Valerius's many departures from Apollonius that he more subtly represents Jason as inducing his cousin to share the dangerous voyage, whereas Apollonius makes him join voluntarily. Another difference is his introduction of the catalogue at a considerably later point than in Apollonius – an improvement, because he has first roused the human interest in the heroes. To the signal of three trumpet-blasts the galley sets forth, Telamon stroking on port-side and Hercules on starboard, with Orpheus to give time to the rowers, Argus in charge of ship-repairs, and Tiphys as pilot. The sailing has not passed unnoticed in heaven. The Sun-god, sire of Aeetes, whose domain is threatened, complains to Jove, Mars supporting the complaint, while Juno and Pallas oppose it. It is the old celestial machinery conventional in epic. As in Virgil, Jove replies, unfolding destiny with a Roman note prophetic of other empires,[3] and, again as in Virgil, the hero's ship is menaced by a storm which Neptune calms. Meanwhile, Pelias's impotent grief over the secret departure of his son in the Argo is vigorously described. He can strike at Jason through his parents, as he declares in Latin reminiscent of Virgil:

[1] I. 275–276:
  '. . . Sparguntur litore curuo
  Lumina nondum ullis terras monstrantia nautis.'
[2] I. 311: 'Alma nouo crispans pelagus Tithonia Phoebo.'
[3] I. 558–560.

Here too, thou robber, thou canst suffer wounds:
Here there be tears and thy beloved sire.[1]

But the old folk resolve to forestall the cruelty of the king, and drain a
cup of bull's blood. The death of Aeson and his consort is the occasion
for a picture of the underworld strongly marked by Virgilian influence. Both in ideas and language the last twenty lines of the book recall
Aeneid VI: *e.g.* the new adaptation of the Twin Gates; the joys of light,
dance and song in the abodes of bliss; and the type of life on earth that
is a passport to happiness.[2]

The feeling that the Argonauts were 'the first that ever burst' into
a silent sea is skilfully suggested early in Book II by the description of
sundown:

> The sunset hour had doubled every fear,
> When now they saw heaven's face revolve, while hills
> And plains were wrested from their eyes, and round
> Lay darkness heavy. E'en the peace of things –
> The great world's silences – affrighted them,
> And stars, and sky begemmed with streaming locks.
> Then, as one who in land unknown is lost,
> Still wandering on his journey through the night,
> Finds ne'er a rest for eye or ear, but all
> Around the blackness of the earth, and trees,
> That seem to meet him blacker for their shade,
> Deepen his dread of night – not otherwise
> The heroes felt alarm.[3]

Guided by the stars, they make Lemnos; whereupon a digression relates
how it came that Vulcan loved and Venus hated the island. Digression
though it be, it is a well-told tale (which in turn influenced Statius) concerning the murder by the Lemnian women of their husbands returning
from war, and Hypsipyle's rescue of her royal father in an old ship.
Her love for Jason is a copy in miniature of Dido's for Aeneas. Jason,
like the Trojan prince, has to be reminded of his mission; and there is
grief in Lemnos when the Argonauts leave. The book contains a further

---

[1] I. 723–724:
> 'Sunt hic etiam tua uulnera, praedo,
> Sunt lacrimae carusque parens.'

[2] *Cf. Arg.* I. 833–851 with *Aen.* VI. 638–641 and 660–664. Many words are
ntentional echoes, *amoena, deueniant, campos, sol.*

[3] II. 38–47:
> 'Auxerat hora metus, iam se uertentis Olympi
> Vt faciem raptosque simul montesque locosque
> Ex oculis circumque graues uidere tenebras.
> Ipsa quies rerum mundique silentia terrent
> Astraque et effusis stellatus crinibus aether.
> Ac uelut ignota captus regione uiarum
> Noctiuagum qui carpit iter non aure quiescit,
> Non oculis, noctisque metus niger auget utrimque
> Campus et occurrens umbris maioribus arbor,
> Haud aliter trepidare uiri.'

incident – the rescue by Hercules and Telamon of the daughter of Laomedon from the sea-monster, and the scheming of the mean-souled Laomedon to avoid giving the rescuer the promised reward of white horses. Putting to sea again, they pass the narrows between Europe and Asia and are welcomed by King Cyzicus in his town.

Most of Book III is occupied with two incidents – the fight against Cyzicus and the capture of Hylas by a water-nymph. The former is a fatality due to a mistake pathetic in intention but in essence incredibly grotesque. The Argonauts have sailed away laden with farewell gifts from Cyzicus. Now, the goddess Cybele nurses a grudge against the royal house for the slaughter of one of her sacred lions during a hunt. It is, therefore, brought about that Tiphys, the steersman, is sunk in deep slumber and that the Argo drifts back to Cyzicus's city, where in the dark enemies are fancied to be at hand. The battle thus begun in error lasts, we are expected to believe, through much of the night, and the Homeric slaughter wrought by the Argonauts is told with a realism considerably overdone: bones and jaws resound beneath the blows, and the land is white with scattered brains! (*sparsusque cerebro albet ager*, 166–167). The mighty boon (*donum ingens*) of being killed by Hercules leads one victim to the knowledge that a dreadful blunder has been made, and, after the king has fallen by Jason's spear, Jupiter intervenes. With the dawn Tiphys realises that they have been fighting against a friendly state: it is a tragic recognition, like a frenzied Bacchanal's return to her senses. Jason is filled with grief over his host of yesterday and arranges for elaborate funeral honours. This affords an opening for an exposition of the philosophy of the soul and of conscience by the soothsayer Mopsus, who ordains ceremonies of expiation. Artificial scapegoats are employed, upon which, by a curious ritual magic, the anger of the hell-powers is to be diverted, and so the Argonauts row away light-hearted. The rebound from sorrow to happiness is reflected in the jocular rivalry among the oarsmen and by the humorous description of the 'crab' caught by Hercules which smashes his oar and sends him floundering back on several others. Fresh trouble, however, comes with another landing: and some pretty description marks the story of how Hylas in hot pursuit of a stag stoops to drink at a brook and is drawn into it by a water-nymph. A series of similes illustrates the restless anxiety of Hercules as he leaves his comrades and searches for the missing youth:

> 'Hylas' again and 'Hylas' yet again
> He shouts through distant wilds. But naught replies
> Save woods and wandering echo's rivalry.[1]

The Argonauts become impatient over the prolonged absence of Hercules, and debate (with traces of the rhetoric in a *controuersia*) whether

[1] III. 596–597:
'Rursus Hylan et rursus Hylan per longa reclamat
Auia: responsant siluae et uaga certat imago.'

they should sail without him. In the end, after Jason, with reluctance, has loosed the cable, his men grieve to miss the lion's skin and see the empty bench:

> As the ship goes, all yet shout 'Hercules'
> And 'Hylas' all – names lost amidst the waves.[1]

In Book IV the chief incidents are the appearance of Hylas in a vision to recount his fate to Hercules, who does not rejoin the Argonauts; the arrival of the Argo at the land of the Bebryces, whose arrogant boxer-king, Amycus, is humbled by Pollux; Orpheus's song of Io's transformation into a heifer, in reference to the legendary name of the Bosphoros; the freeing of blind old Phineus from the torment of the Harpies, and his foretelling of the main stages of the Argonauts' adventures; the narrow escape of the Argo from the Clashing Rocks ('how,' reflects Jason, 'could they on their return voyage ever thread their way through again?' – a hint of the poet's intention to bring them back by a different route); and the attainment of the Euxine, where a dull and unpoetic description is inserted. Their welcome from the prince of the Mariandyni is all the warmer because, like them, he loathed King Amycus: as Valerius remarks in one of his comparatively few *sententiae*,

> Sure bond it is to face the selfsame foe.[2]

At the beginning of Book V death has thinned the number of the Argonauts, and fresh comrades join who relate their exploits in following the arms of Hercules against the Amazons. By night the noise of the Chalybes can be heard at work on implements of war – evil inventions which had brought into activity the Hates, the Angers and the avenging Fury. Caucasus is next sighted – the scene of Prometheus's torment, and it so chances that Hercules has arrived to free the Titan that very day. Next comes the first sight of the Colchian land, with a fresh invocation to mark a new portion of the epic. Their hardest task is now before the Argonauts, and Jason reminds them that nothing must prevent their bringing back the Fleece:

> Necessity should never know a qualm
> (*rebus semper pudor absit in artis*).

Medea, King Aeetes's daughter, after a night of ominous dreams, is early astir with her handmaidens. She is likened to Proserpine:

> As o'er Hymettus' flowery ridge in spring
> Proserpina once led the dance, or 'neath
> Sicilian crag, by Pallas stepping close,
> Yet linked to loved Diana, and more tall
> Than any, with no rival in her train,
> Till that day when she blenched and at the sight
> Of Hell had all her comeliness dispelled.[3]

---

[1] III. 724–725.
[2] IV. 744: 'Certa fides animis idem quibus incidit hostis.'   [3] V. 343–347.

Valerius describes her, when she first sees the strangers, as a shy girl with nothing in her manner to suggest the sorceress. She depends for reassurance on her old nurse, who recognises the aliens as Greeks. The mutual impressions of hero and heroine follow: she, reduced to silence, draws back a few steps, but has eyes for him alone; he concentrates attention on her as a princess among the foreign women. Answering his courteous appeal, Medea declares herself daughter of Aeetes and instructs him about his way. So Jason proceeds shrouded in a mist of invisibility to the audience-chamber of the king in the Sun-god's temple. In all this there is a contamination of epic sources, and a modelling of incidents upon earlier poems. The meeting of Jason and Medea is based partly on Odysseus's meeting with Nausicaa in Homer, partly on Aeneas's meeting with Venus under the guise of a huntress in the *Aeneid*. Jason, like Aeneas, proceeds in a miraculous cloud of concealment. The first interview with royalty in the *Argonautica*, as in the *Aeneid*, takes place in a temple. Just as there were tableaux on the walls from the Trojan war to interest the hero of the *Aeneid*, so for Jason there are provided, thanks to the prophetic skill of Vulcan, pictures of the Golden Fleece and the coming expedition of the Argonauts. This parallelism is one of the cramping conditions of ancient epic, and when it passes the bounds of the pleasantly reminiscential the reader feels that the poet has sacrificed his individuality to standard authority.

Jason's claim to possess the Fleece angers Aeetes, but he dissembles and promises it as recompense if the Argonauts will help him against the menace of his brother Perses. It is a promise which causes commotion among the gods.

Much of the fighting against Perses and his catalogued allies in Book VI is wearisome. It is one of the innovations made on the story by Valerius, but we do not follow Jason on the battlefield with the love-lit gaze of Medea, when Juno, disguised as Medea's sister, has led her to the town walls to watch the conflict. There is a note of pity for this girl ignorant of coming ill and the victim of a scheming goddess:

> So gleams the lily white, pre-eminent
> Amid the hues of spring; but short her life:
> Her glory hath brief flourishing – e'en now
> The dark wings of the South o'ershadow her.[1]

Jason performs deeds of prowess and Perses is defeated. With nightfall the din of battle dies away.

If Book VI has dull stretches, the last two books are the most attractive and possess great human interest. This is notably true of Book VII; for it traces the growth of Medea's passion for Jason, the mental conflict between loyalty to her father and love for a stranger, and the avowal of their affection by the lovers in the temple of Diana. The

[1] VI. 493–495.

speeches, though coloured inevitably with some rhetoric and some
Virgilian echoes, show real emotion.

Aeetes disdainfully breaks his promise and makes a new proposal –
Jason must yoke to the plough the fire-breathing bulls, sow the dragons'
teeth and face the crop of warriors that will arise. His perfidy meets
with a spirited reply from Jason:

> Not this the recompense, Aeetes, nor
> The hope you offered to the Argonauts,
> When first we donned our armour for your walls.
> What means this change of faith? What craft is planned
> By your commands? Another Pelias,
> Another ocean here I see! Nay, come,
> Ye princes all, combine to hunt my life
> With hate and hests. But ne'er shall my right hand
> Or hope desert me. 'Tis my wont to bow
> To orders, not to quail before the hard.
> One boon I pray for – whether yonder crop
> Whelms me with its own spear-growth, or the fire
> To-morrow swallows me with threatening maw –
> Send hence to Pelias' cruel ears the news
> That here died *men*, and that, had *you* kept faith,
> Jason could have regained his country safe.[1]

Alarmed for the hero, the lovesick princess wanders distraught in the
palace; and still more passion is breathed into her soul by Venus under
the form of Circe, daughter of the Sun. Her inward struggle is vividly
represented – which shall she favour, father or alien? She is trapped
(*prensa*). Would that earth could swallow her, and so she might escape
accursed suggestions. Now she will, now she will not, betray her father;
but at last, overcoming scruples, she turns to her most potent drugs to
aid Jason. Possessed of these magical charms, she passes out into the
night, and, after a final hesitation, through the city gates. Here Medea
is a dual personality, now a timid maiden with a sense of modesty and a
regard for duty, now an astonishingly powerful enchantress capable of
controlling the passage of Night and the heavenly bodies. In Diana's
temple she and Jason confront each other. Jason breaks silence:

> Pray, maiden, act not like thy cursèd sire;
> Unkindness fits no countenance like thine.[2]

Protesting against the king's ingratitude and perfidy, he declares his
unalterable resolution:

> Ne'er shall I quit this land without the Fleece:
> Thou shalt not first behold me fail my race.[3]

Scarce lifting her eyes, the Colchian princess half resentfully, half

[1] VII. 89 *sqq.*   [2] VII. 415–416.   [3] VII. 429–430.

N

scornfully, asks Jason why he ever came to her land; why he, a Thessalian foreigner, should look for aid from her. Her final entreaty is that, finding help elsewhere, he should let her go back to her father innocent as yet of treachery. But Jason snatches the proffered charms with avidity; henceforth irrevocably she is the guilty betrayer of her father. Round her lover she must put a sevenfold spell, and instruct him how to face the dread crop of warriors:

> Be mindful, pray, of me: Medea's self
> Shall ever in return remember thee.[1]

She calls him *hospes* and he calls her *coniunx*, a contrast designed to recall Dido and Aeneas;[2] and when Jason imprecates fire and destruction upon himself if he should forget Medea's sacrifice of royalty and home, the tragedy of their broken love (though Valerius never completed the tale) is foreshadowed. The lists are made ready for his ordeal against the fire-breathing bulls and the warriors who will spring from the furrows; and Jason, with the aid of Medea's magic and counsel, proves victorious.

Book VIII: Only one course is now open to Medea. In terror at her own acts and afraid of her father, she bids farewell to the palace and joins her lover in the forest. There is still the Fleece to win. To enable Jason to carry it off, she charms the guardian Dragon to sleep, though, as she bends over the prostrate beast which hitherto she has fed, she cannot but utter her sorrow for it when it wakes to realise the theft. But now there is need for despatch; and the supporting tree yields up the Fleece to the hero, while melancholy gloom gathers in the place; but elsewhere the land is lit up by the brilliant gold as he bears it away. Cheers rise from his men: the Argo draws near to meet him; and he hastens aboard with Medea.

Meanwhile dismay invades the palace on the discovery of her flight. Her mother, who has hitherto played no part, comes into the story with a rhetorical apostrophe to her fugitive daughter – she would fain scratch the face of the robber; she would have Fleece or any other sacred thing taken, if only Medea were given back; and details (*singula*) now too late recur to the queen's mind that should have betrayed Medea's love for the Thessalian; that was why she had no appetite (*nullae dapes*)! The scene changes: the lonely princess is at sea, the one woman among foreigners, uncertain whether the man for whom she has sacrificed so much will make her his bride. This anxiety ends, however, with their marriage in the island of Peuce. But the festivities are disturbed by the arrival of Medea's brother Absyrtus with a fleet which Valerius wishes his readers to believe was very suddenly built. The Argonauts grumble over the prospect of attack from their Colchian pursuers, and would

---

[1] VII. 477, a highly alliterative line:
　　'Sis memor, oro, mei, contra memor ipsa manebo.'
[2] *Aen.* IV. 323–324.

restore the girl if they might keep the Fleece. Jason does not hold out
boldly against his men's advice, but, with groans and qualms about his
plighted troth, meditates treachery to his bride. So, within less than one
hundred lines of the abrupt close, Valerius brings out the worst in
Jason's character. Divining his cowardice, Medea remonstrates with
argument and question and irony. Is she a captive on the vessel?
May she not hear the plans proposed?

> Most faithful husband mine, I know no fear;
> Yet pity me and keep thy marriage vows
> At least as far as some Thessalian port –
> Then cast me off in thine own house! Thou knowest
> 'Twas thou, and not thy crew, swore faith to me.
> Perchance they may have right to give me up;
> But thou hast not the same prerogative,
> And I must drag thee back with me; for I,
> The guilty maid, am not their only quest:
> All on this ship alike are fugitives.[1]

Is he afraid, she asks, of her brother's ships? Still even against a greater
fleet she deserves to be defended.

> Would God my love had not dared all for thee,
> But felt a scruple! Nay, bethink thee now
> Of fresh commands. Alack, is cruelty
> So tongue-tied? Can this shamefast mien of thine
> Bode aught but harm? I ask thee, who wert once
> Mine own loved Jason – is it right that I,
> That I, with suppliant breath, should pray to thee?[2]

A night of agony over Jason's pusillanimous ingratitude has wrought a
change on the beautiful girl:

> She comes not now the glory of her race
> Nor the illustrious grandchild of the Sun,
> Nor yet the flower of youthful savagedom,
> As once when from the tree Chaonian
> She bore the radiant Fleece in joy and 'mid
> The mighty names of Greece on Pallas' prow
> Stood forth a Maid that seemed the Goddess' peer.[3]

Swayed two ways, Jason tries to say soothing words to Medea, and the
epic breaks off leaving its hero discredited. The poet has, however, en-
listed our sympathies for Medea, as Virgil has done for Dido.

Even the sketch just given serves to show that Valerius was not a
slavish imitator of Apollonius of Rhodes. Certainly he owed him much
in episodes, similes and ideas. But under each of these three heads he
also shows independence. Episodes are amplified, abbreviated, or transferred, and original episodes are introduced; if some similes are copied,

[1] VIII. 419 *sqq.*   [2] VIII. 439 *sqq.*   [3] VIII. 458 *sqq.*

fresh ones are invented; and, if there is a certain amount of close rendering of the Greek text, there is, besides, a great proportion of the poem
which is due not merely to borrowings from Homer and the Latin of
Virgil, Ovid, Lucan, and Seneca's tragedies, but to Valerius's own
genius. Thus, while it is instructive to estimate his debt to Apollonius,
it is equally instructive to remember the contrasts between them, and
competent critics have studied this question.[1] Broadly, in construction
and probability of narrative he excels his Greek forerunner; but Valerius
is most distinctively himself when he displays his gift of description
(which is, on the whole, free from the flagrant vices of rhetoric and sometimes reaches a high level of beauty) and when he applies his psychological ability to the character of Medea. One cannot fail to see that in
his unfolding of her love he is not tied to the Apollonian account: one
notes the influence of Virgil's Dido: one suspects Ovid's influence as
well; but there is no reason to deny to an artist like Valerius his own
large share in elaborating his heroine's passion.

It is, on several grounds, likely that the incompleteness of the epic
was caused by the author's death rather than by the ravages of time.[2]
Some of the charges of inconsistency and disconnectedness brought
against Valerius by critics might have been averted, it is contended, had
he lived to revise his epic. All the same, it must be remembered that
Valerius took years over his work and might never have removed such
blemishes. As Summers points out, Statius's echoes of Valerius's
language suggest familiarity with his poem; but of about a score of allusions which Statius makes to the Argonautic legend none bears on the
return voyage of the heroes, and this is just the portion which is missing
in Valerius. An interesting problem turns on the author's design for
finishing his epic. One may conjecture that he contemplated four more
books to equate the number with Virgil's twelve; and it is a plausible
guess that he would have, in his closing books, evinced still more independence of his Greek model. Since he elects to place Jason's marriage
in Peuce, he presumably would have dropped the visit to Phaeacia.
There is another feature which, while it illustrates his individuality,
at the same time lends colour to the belief that he meant to bring his
heroes into connexion with Italy.[3] This feature is the frequency of the
allusions to Rome and her customs which the poet engrafts upon this
epic of early Greek mariners. Surprise is scarcely felt that at the beginning we should find his autobiographic hint about the Sibyl's tripod in
his house, or his references to recent Roman history in his invocation
to Vespasian, or his desire that his poem should be famed in Latin-
speaking cities.[4] But the recurrent Roman note in the course of the

[1] Summers, *op. cit.* pp. 18–26; Butler, *Post-Aug. P.* pp. 182–188.
[2] K. Schenkl, 'Studien zu d. Arg. des V.F.' in *Sitzb. Wien*, 1871, pp. 279 ff.;
Summers, *op. cit.* pp. 2–3; *cf.* p. 6.
[3] Summers, *op. cit.* p. 7.   [4] I. 5–6, 7–17, 20–21.

narrative is more significant. Jove is made to foreshadow the coming of
empires which must include Rome; Hypsipyle's renown is to last as
long as Roman chronicles; and allusions are made to Jupiter of the
Alban mount and to the connexion of Rome with Troy.[1] In the sixth
book there is an anticipation of the military emblems of Rome; a likening of the battle between Perses and Aeetes to internecine strife between Roman legions; and illustrations are drawn from shipwrecks on
the Latian coast and from hunting in Umbria.[2] In the next book Jason
is said to be as much dismayed by Aeetes's refusal to keep his promise
as a Tuscan pilot looking for the Tiber mouth but blown upon the quicksands off Africa; and Venus, disguised as Circe daughter of the Sun,
pretends to be consort of the Italian Picus and 'queen of the Tuscan
main.'[3] These and other instances incline one to believe that Valerius
was leading up to a sort of Italianisation of his Greek theme in its later
phases, in which case he would have been at once more national and
more Virgilian. For, just as the later half of the *Aeneid* has its scenes laid
in Italy, so Valerius may have decided to imitate Virgil in bringing his
Argonauts back by a route more familiar to a Roman reader than that
by which they ventured out to Colchis. If the adventurers, by some
river supposed to have outlets in both the Black Sea and the circumfluent
Ocean, were eventually to reach the North Sea and so sail homewards
past Britain and Gaul and into the Mediterranean, this would have
fittingly accorded with the address to Vespasian in the opening book;
and poetic justice might have been done by prolonging the epic to
include the death of Pelias, the wicked uncle who had sent Jason on
the adventure hoping he would lose his life in the course of it.

The fact that there is only one classical mention of Valerius (that by
Quintilian recognising his death as a loss to literature) does not suggest
that he had a wide vogue. Yet his influence is traceable in Statius and
Silius;[4] and Juvenal may be thinking of him in his gibe at the conveyance of 'the gold of the stolen fleecelet.'[5] After age-long oblivion,
attention was once more directed to his poem by Poggio's discovery at
St. Gall in 1417 of a manuscript containing *Argonautica* I – IV. 317. In
spite of considerable poetic quality Valerius is not a readily quotable
author. There is little criticism of life in him – little even in the way of
the *sententia*: so readers have not found much to lay hold on, and his
influence has been lessened. Thus, in estimating the classical sources of a
work like William Morris's *Life and Death of Jason* it is the relation to
Apollonius rather than that to Valerius that one makes prominent.

The language[6] of Valerius is an interesting complex. As in the treatment of his epic theme he was both borrower and innovator, so with his

---

[1] I. 559, II. 245, 304, 574.
[2] VI. 53–56, 402 *sqq.*; 410, 420.   [3] VII. 83–86, 232–234.
[4] Summers, *op. cit.* pp. 8–12.   [5] Juv. I. 10–11.
[6] See Gebbing's pamphlets in Bibl. *re* p. 346; and Summers, *op. cit.* esp. pp.
42–49.

style. Deeply influenced by Virgil and other predecessors, he yet strikes into fresh paths of expression: he even coins words. Among the compounds (many of them dactylic) which he loves, he revives old epithets like *auriger, omnituens*; uses rare ones, like *astrifer, gemmifer, luctifer* (in Seneca also); notably shares some with Ovid like *piniger, reparabilis, turifer*; and others, like *monstrifer* and *monstrificus*, with the elder Pliny. The adjectives *flammiger* and *undisonus* recur in Statius; *astrifer*, used already by Lucan, recurs in Statius and Martial; *flammifer* (which is Ennian, Ovidian and Senecan), *auricomus* (Virgilian), *securiger* (Ovidian and Sen can), and others, recur in Silius. But he has adjectives that are entirely his, *aegisonus, arcipotens, implorabilis, intemerandus, soligena*, just as he has ἅπαξ εἰρημένα among his verbs like *protono, superincendo*, and among his nouns like *lustramen, ouatus* ('rejoicing'), *memoratrix, mugitor*, the last term being used in one of his references to volcanic activity:

> As bellower Vesuvius pants, when he
> In wrath awakes the panic-stricken towns.[1]

There are also forcible applications of words in new connexions, or extensions of meaning: *e.g. Medea adnuitur thalamis* (V. 258), 'Medea is granted to the marriage-couch'; *inuasit habenis murmur* (VII. 605), 'attacked the horse's *neighing* with the reins,' *i.e.*, 'set bit and bridle to its mouth'; *ueteris sub nocte cupressi* (I. 774), 'beneath the night-like shadow of an old cypress-tree,' resembling the phrase *noctem implicat* (VII. 598) of entangling a bull in a *cloud of darkness*, or Juvenal's *tenebrae* for 'a dingy hovel.' *Fragor* expresses vigorously news that comes in a crash:

> A startling rumour spreads it thro' the town –
> 'The King is summoning a thousand hands!'
> > (*regemque fragor per moenia differt*
> > *mille ciere manus*, I. 753–754).

The mixture of convention and boldness in Valerius makes him an intensely interesting linguistic study.

Despite his profound debt to Virgil, and traces of lines with a still more archaic flavour, the technique of Valerius's verse is predominantly Ovidian. He recalls Ovid in dactylic movement, in lack of varied pauses, and in smooth versification. This smoothness of post-Ovidian poetry, which was based on a comparative avoidance of elision, missed that subtle entanglement of word with word which Virgil artistically employed to counteract some of the heaviness of the Latin language. Valerius has not the technical skill of Statius in hexameters: he is often monotonous in rhythm, in repetitions of words within a few lines, and in over-symmetric arrangement. Yet he is less monotonous than Lucan,

---

[1] III. 208–209:
> 'ut mugitor anhelat
> Vesuius, attonitas acer cum suscitat urbes.'

although when the test is intellect Valerius is unquestionably Lucan's
inferior. It is easy to illustrate some phases of his monotony: in Book
VIII, a short one of 467 lines, one can count at least 35 dactylic verbs
(*implicat, prosilit*, etc.) forming the first foot of the line, without counting other dactylic words like *uellera* (at least four times), *immemor*
(at least twice). Some of his endings too are monotonous: *e.g. proles*
four times in less than ninety lines in Book IV,[1] although we may accept
this as an echo of ancient epic phraseology. It is also convention which
prompts his alliterative effects such as these in his later books:[2]

> *impingit pecorique pauor qualesue profundum*
> *per chaos occurrunt caecae sine uocibus umbrae* (VII. 401–402)

or

> *iam magis atque magis mentem super alta ferebat* (*ibid.* 473)

or

> *fata domus luctumque ferens fraudemque fugamque* (VIII. 135)

More subtle is the onomatopoeic effect which he achieves in describing
the gloomy sea-cave

> That knows nor daylight's gifts nor starry flame,
> Ill-starred abode that rocks to ocean's boom
> (*non quae dona die, non quae trahat aetheris ignem,*
> *infelix domus et sonitu tremibunda profundi*, IV. 179–180).

To the credit of his common sense, he is less rhetorical than either
Lucan or Statius. He rants less. He indulges in fewer epigrams. In
eight books his *sententiae* do not exceed a dozen.[3] Doubtless, his similes
are too numerous,[4] but they are, as a rule, brief. Unfortunately, though
some have beauty, others are in bad taste, like the comparison of the
love-sick Medea to a dog going mad; and others are far-fetched, like
the comparison of the flight of the Harpies to the rain of ashes from
Vesuvius in eruption.[5] He has his lapses into absurdities, hyperbole
and artificiality. In the battle of Book VI there are extravagant details
which recall Lucan; and the danger of mythology can be seen when
Jason, instead of the simple question, 'Where is Hercules?' asks,
'Where is he who was equal to the monsters sent by his stepmother?'[6]
Such mythological allusions play their part along with inverted order of
words and compact forms of expression in producing an effect sometimes
far from clear: even though he is relatively free from laboured conceits,

---

[1] IV. 462, 501, 542, 549.
[2] Summers, *op. cit.* p. 54, gives a list of alliterations from the first four books.
[3] Summers, *op. cit.* p. 62, gives references to ten; *e.g.*, IV. 158: 'melior uulgi
nam saepe uoluntas' ('a people's heart is often better than their king's').
[4] *E.g.* Similes become especially frequent in the description of the fighting in
Bk. III, and in Hercules's alarm over the absence of Hylas (III. 577, 581, 587).
Among natural and pathetic similes is that from children praying that their father
seriously ill may be spared (V. 22–24).
[5] VII. 124 *sqq.*; IV. 507.
[6] V. 43: 'ubi monstriferae par ille nouercae?'

he falls far short of Virgil's classic lucidity. There is undoubtedly in Valerius descriptive power, varied incident, vivid narrative, and the perennial attraction of the way of a man with a maid. Except for this last psychological interest his merits are mainly related to the objective and concrete with little to suggest that he had reflected profoundly on life or had any guidance or solace to offer to humanity.

Chapter V

SILIUS ITALICUS

Life – An ancient Southey – Evidence for date of the *Punica* –
Scheme of the seventeen books – Weaknesses – Certain merits
– Stoic notes – *Sententiae* – Imitations and innovations – Virgilian
echoes.

F EW literary figures of the first century are so well known bio-
graphically as Ti. Catius Silius Italicus. The information comes
mainly from a letter by the younger Pliny (III. vii), who, writing
in A.D. 101 about the recent death of Silius, took the opportunity to
sketch his career. Other facts of his life are learned from Martial and
Tacitus.[1] He is called Silius Italicus in MSS., in Pliny and in Tacitus;
Martial calls him either Silius or Italicus; his full name we know from
an inscription.[2] It is argued that, if 'Italicus' implied birth at Italica in
Spain, Martial would have expressly claimed him for a countryman.
Pliny's evidence that he was over seventy-five when he died enables us
to date his birth as A.D. 25 or 26. Under Nero he had got an evil name
as an informer. He was the last Neronian consul (A.D. 68), and, in the
struggle for the succession, a supporter of Vitellius, whom Cluvius
Rufus and he attended at his interview with Flavius Sabinus in the
Capitol. The reputation which he gained as proconsul of Asia in Vespasian's time and his subsequent life of literary retirement did something to wipe out the stain of his ill-employed activity in Nero's days.
Leisure hours in intervals of writing were devoted to the reception of a
circle of visitors and to learned discussions, presumably philosophical.
His readings from his own works were planned to be practical tests of
his friends' critical judgement. In the later part of his life he left Rome
for the quiet of Campania, from which not even the accession of the
new emperor, Trajan, in A.D. 98, could lure him back. A connoisseur
($\phi\iota\lambda\delta\kappa\alpha\lambda$os, as Pliny says), he could not resist the temptation to buy fine
country houses, in this respect becoming even more extravagant than
his friend Pliny. He surrounded himself with books, statues and busts,
above all venerating the portrait of Virgil, the anniversary of whose

[1] Tac. *Hist.* III. lxv; Mart. VII. lxiii, VIII. lxvi, IX. lxxxvi, XI. xlviii and l,
XII. lxvii. 5.
[2] From the *fasti sodalium Augustalium Claudialium* (*C.I.L.* VI. 1984; or
(with omissions) Dessau, *I.L.S.* 5025).

birth he observed more scrupulously than his own. Virgil's tomb at Naples was to him a holy place (*adire ut templum solebat*). Before he attempted an epic, he had made some name in oratory, especially as a pleader in court.[1] His death on his Neapolitan estate was due to voluntary starvation. A tumour from which he was suffering was pronounced incurable, and he decided to refrain from food. It was a Stoical resolution; and he had, in fact, relations with the Stoic philosopher Epictetus.[2] Of two sons one predeceased him, the other reached the consulship and survived his father. Among additional facts derived from Martial we learn that one of his villas had been Cicero's, that Virgil's grave was on one of his properties, and that he began his *Punica* after his consulship. The ascription to him of the epitome known as the *Ilias Latina* or *Homerus Latinus* is mentioned elsewhere.

A diligent but usually uninspired writer, fitly described by Pliny as having composed with more pains than genius (*maiore cura quam ingenio*), Silius must have resembled Southey in his methodically calculated production of verse; and his *Punica* may be said to occupy in Latin literature a position not unlike that of *Madoc* in English. By A.D. 88, the date of Martial's fourth book, the plan of Silius's epic was apparently known and friends were acquainted with parts of it.[3] By the end of 92[4] some at least of the *Punica*, wildly praised by Martial as immortal, was in book form; but the reference to Domitian's war in Silius (III. 607). cannot have been written before that same year, as the Sarmatian campaign was fought in A.D. 92–93. Since XIV. 686 refers to Nerva (96–98), we may assign the latest books to the beginning of Trajan's reign. It has been contended that so comparatively early a part of the work as Book VII must have followed the death of Domitian (96), on the ground that the introduction of Minerva there as hostile to Rome would have been unsuitable during the life of an emperor attached to the cult of that goddess.[5]

Silius's narrative of the Second Punic War is told in over 12,200 hexameters distributed among seventeen books. Of the three conflicts between Rome and Carthage the author realises, at the outset of his task (I. 12–14), that this middle one demanded the greatest efforts from the combatants, and that the victors themselves were imperilled. Book I relates how in Dido's city Juno pits against fate the war-loving and indomitable leader Hannibal, who resolves to strike a blow at Rome from Spain by besieging Saguntum. The Saguntine danger is laid before Rome; then in Book II Rome is embroiled with Carthage; and Saguntum, after

[1] Mart. VII. lxiii. 5–8; cf. IX. lxxxvi. 2: 'Ausonio non semel ore potens.'
[2] Epict. *Diss.* III. viii. 7.   [3] Mart. IV. xiv. 1–5.
[4] Mart. VII. lxiii. 1–2:
  'Perpetui numquam moritura uolumina Sili
    Qui legis.'
Martial's seventh book belongs to the end of 92.
[5] E. Bickel, *Rh.M.* lxvi (1911) p. 505.

a heroic defence, is taken by Hannibal. During the fighting, Queen Asbyte, the Camilla of the Carthaginian side, falls, and the flight of the enemy before Hannibal as he seeks to avenge her is likened, in a typical simile, to the homeward flocking of birds or the swarming of bees to their hive:

> As thro' the gloaming late the evening star
> Drives on light wing the birds from quest of food
> Home to their nest, or as on Mount Hymet
> By Athens swarms of bees among the flowers
> Are summoned at the threat of watery cloud
> To their sweet waxen toil, and honey-fraught
> Haste to the grotto of their fragrant hive,
> And massed in flying throng the threshold fill
> With murmur hoarse.[1]

Early in Book III there are digressions for the sake of descriptive writing. Neither the labours of Hercules on the portals of the temple where Hannibal seeks responses, nor the marvels (*mira*) of the inrushing tide are subjects possessing artistic necessity. The episode of the parting of Hannibal from his wife and child on the seashore is at once more natural and more relevant: it portrays her disappointment that she may not share his dangers; it also portrays his realisation, as her ship waits, that the stirrings of ambition must tear him from her:

> How differs unrecorded life from death![2]

After such human motives it is weak to have intruded Jupiter's designs for trying the Romans by peril and his despatch of Mercury to hasten Hannibal's plans for the invasion of Italy. The catalogue of the Carthaginians and the crossing of Pyrenees, Rhone and Alps, with incidental episodes and risks, occupy the rest of the book. Opening with alarm in Italy, the next book narrates the fighting at the Ticinus and the Trebia. Warriors on the field after epic fashion are invoked in the second person and perform prodigies of valour, while the unreality is increased by bringing Hannibal on the scene attended by Panic, Terror and Rage. The disaster caused by the Carthaginian elephants at the Trebia suggests the reflection:

> The test of manhood is adversity,
> And up Mount Difficult through jeopardy
> Strides Valour undismayed to Fame.[3]

---

[1] *Pun.* II. 215:
'Sicut agit leuibus per sera crepuscula pennis
E pastu uolucres ad nota cubilia Vesper;
Aut, ubi Cecropius formidine nubis aquosae
Sparsa super flores examina tollit Hymettos,
Ad dulces ceras et odori corticis antra
Mellis apes grauidae properant, densoque uolatu
Raucum connexae glomerant ad limina murmur.'

[2] III. 145: 'Quantum etenim distant a morte silentia uitae!'

[3] IV. 603–604.

Amidst the rigours of the Apennines Hannibal has lost an eye, when senators arrive from Carthage to claim in sacrifice his son. The demand had been debated at home, supported by Hanno because of an old grudge, but bitterly opposed by Hannibal's wife Imilce, whose creed concerning sacrifice is thus avowed:

> What piety is sprinkling shrines with gore?
> Chief cause, alas! of guilt in feeble man
> Is not to know God's nature. Go and pray
> Aright with holy incense and avert
> The barbarous ritual of butchery;
> For God is kind and kindred unto man
> (*Mite et cognatum est homini Deus*).[1]

Book V is on Lake Trasimene, opening in legend and the mists of dawn, and then advancing, through Homeric armings and challenges, to the death of the consul Flaminius and to Hannibal's chivalrous admiration for the bravery of his fallen enemies:

> The brows still threaten and their looks are wrath.
> I fear a land so pregnant with a brood
> Of high-souled heroes may from Destiny
> Win power imperial and by very woes
> Yet subjugate the world.[2]

Book VI is largely devoted to the story of Regulus taken from the first Punic War. His son, Serranus, severely wounded, reaches the door of Marus, one of his father's old soldiers, who preaches endurance amidst the reverses of Rome:

> In the ancestral way, most valiant Sir,
> Bear present hardship and our fortune's swerve:
> So by Heaven's law adown life's sloping path
> Headlong thro' chequered hazards rolls Time's wheel
> (*Per uarios praeceps casus rota uoluitur aeui*).[3]

The old man's tale of Regulus is partly legendary, partly historical: it begins with dragon-fighting, and proceeds, not without rhetoric, to relate how Regulus kept his *parole* when the Carthaginian senate sent him to Rome in the vain hope that he would advocate an exchange of prisoners. There must always be a moral greatness in this story of self-abnegation and Stoic austerity:

> Squalor and starveling meals and restless couch
> And strife with crowding ills he reckoned more

---

[1] IV. 791–795.
[2] V. 673–676.

> 'Fronte minae durant, et stant in uultibus irae.
> Et uereor ne quae tanta creat indole tellus
> Magnanimos fecunda uiros, huic fata dicarint
> Imperium, atque ipsis deuincat cladibus orbem.'

[3] VI. 118 *sqq.*

> Than vanquishing a foe; nor counted it
> So noble to escape adversity
> By care as by endurance to prevail.[1]

And yet Silius's long-drawn narrative has not the moving force of Horace's brief treatment of the same episode in the third book of the *Odes*. The digression ends at line 552, where Silius returns to his true subject – panic in the city and Jupiter's prompting of the Romans to entrust all to Fabius.

The saving of Rome by Fabius's delaying tactics is the theme of Book VII. The digressions include the legend of the 300 Fabii told to Hannibal by a prisoner, a story of Bacchus occasioned by the Carthaginian inroad on the Falernian vineyards, and, at the approach of the Carthaginian fleet, the introduction of Nereids with the Virgilian cave of Proteus. The delays are not confined to the inaction of Fabius: Proteus is asked to prophesy, but first he must hark back to the Judgement of Paris. There is, however, a foil to Fabius's caution in the impetuous Minucius, who is magnanimously rescued from the consequences of his foolhardiness by his colleague.

Book VIII forms a prelude to the battle of Cannae, as related in the two following books. The unreal device of Juno's despatch of the nymph Anna to encourage Hannibal leads us back to the Dido story for a time.[2] Then the narrative is resumed. The consuls of 216 have entered office, and Aemilius Paulus dreads the abyss to which the arrogance of his colleague Varro may lead. His arguments are stated in the debating manner of the schools,[3] making brief ironical points one after another – 'the impetuous consul fears that he might leave Rome's ruin for another man's consulate; it might be well to summon a consul from Carthage, for even a Carthaginian would not be so dangerous!' The catalogue of Italian warriors, extending to over 260 lines, gives a chance of introducing famous names. There is, for example, a Tullius, descended from King Tullus, and destined, as ancestor of Cicero, to give in later days a noble citizen to Ausonia: next follows a eulogy on the orator:

> Beyond the Ganges heard and furthest Ind,
> His voice will fill the earth, and frenzied war
> Will bow before his lightning tongue, nor can
> Descendants hope for equal fame in speech.[4]

So too there is a Scaevola, a Sulla, Nero the Sabine, a Piso, a Galba, a Brutus and others. Among the men of North Italy those are not forgotten who come from Virgil's birthplace,

---

[1] VI. 373 *sqq.*
[2] VIII. 144–223 belong to this digression, and first appeared in the Aldine ed., 1523, supplying a lacuna in earlier edns. Their genuineness is effectively defended by Heitland, *J.Ph.* xxiv (1896).
[3] VIII. 327–348. [4] VIII. 408–411.

The home of Muses, Mantua, upraised
By song Aonian to the stars, and peer
Of Homer's minstrelsy.[1]

In the description of the battle of Cannae, Silius's aim is not historical accuracy, but epic embellishment. His true model, therefore, is not such brief narratives as those in Polybius (III. 115–116) or Livy (XXII 47–49), but the manner of the *Iliad* and the *Aeneid*, so that the account is expanded to fill nearly two books, IX and X; and is diversified by similes, divine interferences, Homeric slaughter, and episodes like the unwitting slaying of a father by a son. Though it be mythological, there is a grim suggestiveness in Charon's rejoicing in the expectation of receiving the dead:

Glad on the pallid mere the Ferryman
Now cleared the thwarts for ghosts that were to come;[2]

and the poet has a conception of Roman greatness in adversity:

Would that hereafter, Roman, thou mayst face
Fair fortune nobly as thou didst defeat.
Be this thy last disaster! May Heaven consent
Never to try if Trojan progeny
Can bear a war so dread! I pray thee, Rome,
That tremblest for thy destiny, to dry
Thy tears and to adore thy wounds that must
Bring thee renown unto eternity.
Greater at no time shalt thou ever be:
For soon the slippery pathway of success
Shall make thee hold misfortune but a name.[3]

There is nobility in Hannibal's character as drawn by Silius, when he decrees funeral honours to the fallen consul Paulus and muses over his body:

How great thou liest in death! For me thou art
More cause of triumph than those thousands slain.
When fate shall call, such death be Hannibal's,
If Carthage be but safe;[4]

and, later, in his address of almost envious farewell:

Go, glory of Ausonia, where needs
Must go the souls for valiant action crowned.
Thy fame is won by death illustrious.
For me, my toils are yet in Fortune's hands:
I may not know the hazards that shall be.[5]

The sorrow-stricken capital is encouraged by Fabius, who calms the wrath of the people against Varro, so that the latter on his return to Rome is thanked because he did not despair of the republic, though Silius

---

[1] VIII. 593 *sqq.*   [2] IX. 250–251.
[3] IX. 346–353.   [4] X. 521 *sqq.*   [5] X. 572 *sqq.*

unhappily uses the stilted expression, 'he did not despair for the city of Laomedon's descendants.'[1] Indeed some twenty lines towards the close of the tenth book are full of indirect and far-fetched expressions.

Book XI brings Hannibal to Capua, where luxury begins its demoralising work. The banquet has an obvious Virgilian basis. At Carthage the news of victory and the heap of rings from the fallen Romans fail to induce Hanno to join in the general plaudits for Hannibal. Instead, he advocates making terms with Rome, pleads war-weariness, and extols peace:

> Peace is the best of blessings given to men
> To know: and Peace alone is better than
> Uncounted triumphs: Peace hath power to keep
> Our safety and make equal citizens.[2]

In Book XII, with the coming of spring, Hannibal stirs forth from Capua, like a serpent after hibernating. Henceforward his luck wanes, for the Romans win their first victory in the war. Among those celebrated for bravery is Ennius, whose poetry is eulogised. Hannibal appears outside Rome and rides round the walls to reconnoitre; but Jupiter checks his plans by raising storm after storm. It is a ludicrous see-saw of good and bad weather.

Book XIII, the longest book (895 lines), contains, besides digressions, the recapture of Capua, and its rescue by Pan from burning though not from pillage. Sent to inspire mercy, Pan is minutely described – horned and horny-hoofed, peak-eared, bearded and tailed, nimble and sportive, carrying a shepherd's staff, altogether a strangely incongruous figure in the midst of historical events. In Spain, the two Scipios – father and uncle to the younger Scipio, afterwards Africanus – meet their death; and this leads to a long passage founded on Aeneas's visit to the Underworld in *Aeneid* VI. Scipio, as the ultimate victor, is a kind of hero for Silius. As in the *Odyssey*, sacrifice and the blood-trench are indispensable preliminaries to holding converse with departed spirits; but the interview with the shade of Appius Claudius becomes ridiculous when Scipio lectures the ghost on different ways of disposing of the dead. The Sibyl is asked to unfold the mysteries of the Underworld and of the different souls admitted through the Ten Gates. The infernal rivers, the personified evils of human life, and the monsters of mythology burden the description, and thereafter the wraiths of Scipio's father and mother appear. Not only do the shades of Aemilius Paulus and of others killed at Cannae drink of the blood and speak, but Romans of ancient times appear, as well as Hamilcar, Alexander the Great, and the god-like ghost of Homer. Among souls of the great not yet incarnate are those of Pompey and Julius Caesar. When the Sibyl has foretold the eclipse of Hannibal's career, Scipio returns to his men rejoicing.

[1] X. 629.   [2] XI. 592–595.

In Book XIV the Muses are invoked to turn to Sicily, where Marcellus captures Syracuse after a defence prolonged by theme chanical ingenuity of the famous Greek mathematician Archimedes (who is referred to,[1] but, owing to hexametric exigencies, not named). In Book XV the Roman Senate anxiously consider the question of finding a general to succeed the two Scipios killed in Spain: and at this juncture Silius introduces the young Scipio confronted with the figures of Virtue and Pleasure after the model of the fabled Choice of Hercules. Gaily attired, Pleasure is one whose

> frolic eyes
> With wayward movement darted flame on flame.[2]

Her alluring promises, coloured with an Epicurean idea of bliss,[3] contrast with the appeal directed by Virtue to the celestial element ennobling man. Virtue's offer is 'not purple or scents but victory over the enemy'; and, on Scipio's acceptance, Pleasure retires displeased, but satirically prophesying that one day her hour will come in Rome. So Scipio mounts the *rostra* asking for control of the war. He afterwards justifies his selection by the capture of Nova Carthago in Spain. The book is crowded with other incidents such as the alliance of Philip of Macedon with Carthage, the funeral honours paid by Hannibal to Marcellus (killed in battle near Venusia), and the defeat by Claudius Nero of Hannibal's brother Hasdrubal at the Metaurus on his way to join Hannibal. Book XVI recounts Scipio's operations in Africa and Spain, and his games to honour the dead – chariot-race, foot-race, sword-fight, javelin competition, in which traditional epic elements are discernible. His request in Rome to be allowed to transfer the war to Africa, though hotly opposed by Fabius, is granted by the Senate: so in Book XVII he crosses to Africa and is thus the means of forcing Hannibal to quit Italy, to his poignant sorrow.[4] After a display of Homeric prowess by Scipio and deceits practised by Juno on Hannibal, the decisive victory of Zama is won. Hannibal may be overwhelmed, he reflects, but Jupiter himself can never blot out the memory of Cannae, nor will the nations pass over his deeds in silence. He will live still to be a menace to Rome.[5] Scipio recrosses the sea to hold his triumph, with Syphax and Hanno as notable captives, and the work closes with an apostrophe to him as the unvanquished sire, in merit comparable with Quirinus or Camillus, and truly claimed in Rome to be an offspring of the gods.

[1] XIV. 341 *sqq.*
[2] XV. 26–27:
> 'lasciuaque crebras
> Ancipiti motu iaciebant lumina flammas.'
[3] *E.g.* esp. XV. 53–67.
[4] XVII. 213–217, an imitation of Lucan's description of Pompey's farewell to Italy, *Phars.* III. 3–5.
[5] XVII. 608–612.

Even a summary betrays many of Silius's weaknesses. His theme, the struggle of two peoples for world-supremacy, as derived from Livy, was a great one; and yet his quest after poetic embroidery divorced it from reality.[1] He makes gods interfere where a historian would investigate causes and motives: he relates battles, not as matters of strategy, but as conglomerates of individual combats. Military history is, therefore, not to be demanded from him; but a more penetrating genius, even though he might in epic spirit, like Silius, have concentrated largely on occurrences affecting the heroic figure of Hannibal, would still have placed in true perspective the evolution of the conflict. As it is, one would never grasp from Silius the significance of events like the siege of Syracuse and the younger Scipio's Spanish campaign; nor would one learn what the defeat of Carthage meant for the world. Traces there are, it is true, of the imperial note, but Silius does not convey through his poem a sense of the greatness of Rome as his master Virgil did. Author and reader are alike oppressed by the outworn conventions of invocations, apostrophes, similes,[2] lineages and colloquies of antagonists who fight in the Homeric fashion, intervention of mythological deities, unilluminating geography, and lack-lustre catalogues of names, in using which Silius has no Virgilian or Miltonic gift of making beautiful music.[3] All this goes to constitute the head and front of his offending – he is, taken altogether, dull and uninspiring. Hardly any of his characters live. Hannibal may be said to live at times, Scipio scarcely at any time: and interminable *longueurs*, verging on the dismal, force one in the end to wonder what imaginable constraint other than editorial necessity should ever drag one to a second perusal of these seventeen ponderous books.

Yet, even so, Silius has merit. He can be rhetorical, but he is not so insistently in search of striking points as the other epic-writers of his century. A curious nemesis overtakes him when he imitates; for some of his least natural effects arise from his enslavement to the example of Homer, Virgil and Lucan. It is particularly to the baleful influence of Lucan that one must ascribe his misdirected attempts at realism. One wishes that Silius, over his slain warriors, had felt a portion of the Virgilian pity; but instead he overdoes his descriptions. The last notes of a bugler, mortally hurt at the Ticinus, pass lingeringly through his

[1] On the oratorical side also Silius departs from Livy's themes without any intention of making his speeches historical in effect. See R. B. Steele, 'The Method of Silius Italicus,' *C.P.* xvii (1922) p. 319 ff.
[2] The conventionality of the similes is emphasised by their frequency, and their effectiveness proportionally lessened. At least 15 occur in Bk. VII, 13 in Bk. X, 11 in Bk. XVII. They are sometimes elaborated to 6 or 7 lines, sometimes restricted to a few words, *e.g.*, 'ut torrens,' XV. 712, the first of 5 similes in 3 lines.
[3] It was unfortunate for Silius that his employment of proper names and the position assigned to them in his metrical structure followed Lucan's manner rather than Virgil's.

instrument after his lips are already mute in death; the final breath of a
gigantic soldier stirs the dust on the plain; a head is struck off, but the
body runs on from its own impetus; or a victim's murmured appeals
continue after his head is severed.[1] Lucanesque reminiscences over-
paint the naval engagement off Syracuse in Book XIV – a man is cut in
two by a prow; oars splash blood; hands grasping an enemy ship are
hacked off and carried away still clinging; open wounds admit the sea.[2]
In similarly exaggerative manner he makes corpses bridge a river,[3]
and copies more than once Lucan's idea of the wounded having no
room to fall.[4] Yet there are not nearly so many of these excesses as in
Lucan; and there are comparatively few strained conceits, like the
topsy-turvy one, which he approves sufficiently to repeat, of fighters
avenging their deaths in advance by abundant slaughter.[5] More often
he is straightforward and non-rhetorical, with touches of natural description, as of the river Ticinus crystal-clear and gliding softly between
shady banks to the notes of birds;[6] with an occasional eye for colour, as
where he marks the rosy dawn over the blue waters, the glint of the
Roman arms at Cannae, or the Carthaginian priest's robe of blue on
which precious stones glitter;[7] or, again, with a gleam of romance to
light up the catalogue of Hannibal's host, when from the far western
gardens of the Hesperides came a leader,

> Who in that faëry woodland by the sea
> Beheld the golden fruitage 'mid the leaves.[8]

Traces of Stoic thought in Silius may be in part prompted by the
Stoicism recurrent in Lucan's epic, but may conceivably be due to its
contemporary prevalence. Among instances may be cited the unflinching constancy of the slave tortured by the Carthaginian whose 'mind
remains untouched, surmounting pain with smiles'; Decius's claim that
nature has granted no such boon to man as the open doorway out of life;
the rivalry between Pleasure and Virtue for control over Scipio; and the
fortitude with which Hannibal, when his brother's head is exhibited on a
spear,

> checked his tears
> And by endurance made disaster less.[9]

His *sententiae*, because not too numerous to be tedious, are the more

---

[1] IV. 173–174, V. 455–456, XIII. 246–248, XV. 470 ('absciso durabant mur-
mura collo').
[2] XIV. 550.   [3] XV. 767–768.
[4] *Phars*. II. 203; *Pun*. IV. 553, IX. 321.
[5] V. 210 *sqq*., VI. 300 ('praesumpta piacula').   [6] IV. 82–87.
[7] IV. 481, XI. 513–515, XV. 676–677.
[8] III. 285–286:
> 'qui sacratas in litore siluas
> Atque inter frondes reuirescere uiderat aurum.'
[9] I. 179; XI. 186–188; XV. 20–120, 819–820.

effective. Some of the most telling are 'The test of manhood is adversity' (IV. 603); 'Banish delay: short-lived is fortune's smile' (IV. 732); 'War must have craft: a leader's stout arm wins less fame' (V. 100); the cynical observation 'in happy days the altars seldom reek' (VII. 89); 'Anger against one's country is sin' (VII. 555, *succensere nefas patriae*); 'never doth love abandon hope' (VIII. 95, *non unquam spem ponit amor*); 'valour is her own most fair reward' (XIII. 663); and Alexander's counsel on celerity in fighting:

> Unhonoured is the craft of long-drawn war:
> Boldness must end campaigns: faint hardihood
> Ne'er raised itself above its jeopardy.[1]

In spite of his debt to Virgil and Lucan, Silius gives signs of originality in his language. Occasionally he ventures on bold expressions: 'a draught of Hannibal inflames' his soldiers (I. 345–346, *haustusque medullis Hannibal exagitat*); and, in reference to Capuan demoralisation, 'the yelps of vice (XI. 426, *uitia adlatrantia*)[2] shake a character so far unsmirched by prosperity.' He employs a large number of compound adjectives, especially in *-fer* and *-ger*. Some are Lucretian words transmitted through Virgil like *aestifer*, *saetiger*, *horrificus*. The adverb *regifice* he shares with Ennius. Many of his compounds had been used by Ovid and Lucan. Others cannot easily, if at all, be discovered elsewhere; *uiticola*, *austrifer*, *nubiuagus*, *pharetriger*, *sceptriger*, *criniger* (possibly in Lucan, unless he wrote *cirrigeros* in *Phars.* I. 463). *Diffulminat* seems to be Silius's own invention. It is to be expected that he should share several compounds with his contemporaries, *e.g. luctificus*, *securiger*, *gemmifer*, *uuifer*.[3] Whether the compounds shared with Statius are instances of the influence of Silius on that poet cannot be determined, but Statius certainly borrowed the gold-digger of Dalmatia from Silius's 'greedy Asturian.'[4] Silius's use of *sonipes*, *quadrupes* and *cornipes* for *equus* (which he does not however entirely renounce) becomes wearisome.

Apart from Virgilian influence on incidents like the cave of Proteus (VII. 419 *sqq.*), tree-felling for funeral pyres (X. 527 *sqq.*), the banquet

[1] XIII. 772–774.
[2] *Cf.* VIII. 290–291: 'nigro adlatrauerat ore uictorem inuidia.'
[3] *Luctificus*, used earlier by Cicero and Virgil, he shares with Sen. Trag., Lucan, Val. Fl. and Statius. *Securiger*, used earlier by Ovid, he shares with Sen. Trag. and Val. Fl. *Gemmifer*, used earlier by Propertius, he shares with Sen. Trag., Pliny *N.H.*, Val. Fl. and Statius. *Uuifer* he shares with Statius.
[4] *Pun.* I. 231–233:

> 'Astur auarus
> Visceribus lacerae telluris mergitur imis,
> Et redit infelix effosso concolor auro';

Siluae IV. vii. 14–16:

> 'Dalmatae montes, ubi Dite uiso
> Pallidus fossor redit erutoque
>   Concolor auro.'

at Capua (XI. 267 *sqq.*), the Sibyl's exposition of the lower world in Book XIII, and the funeral games of Book XVI (down to the detail of fouling transferred from the foot-race of the *Aeneid* to a chariot-race), there are frequent reminiscences of Virgil's language in such phrases as *quaerentia lumina caelum* (VI. 11) or *ille quidem cruda mente et uiridissimus irae* (V. 569). Still more old-fashioned echoes are his *ac tuba terrificis fregit stridoribus auras* (V. 189);[1] *ensis contunditur ense, pes pede uirque uiro teritur* (IX. 324–325);[2] and the ancient legal form *capital* as a substantive meaning a capital crime (XIII. 155). Silius did not write in a style so elaborate as that of Valerius Flaccus or Statius, and he did not try to be so clever as Lucan; but he is composite enough to be acquitted of bald simplicity. His hexameters are often highly alliterative, some lines having alliteration on three different consonants. There is much also which proves the metrical influence of Ovid, though Silius is less dactylic and moves less lightly than any of the epic poets of his time.

[1] *Cf.* Ennius's 'At tuba terribili sonitu taratantara dixit,' and Virgil, *Aen.* IX. 503:
   'At tuba terribilem sonitum procul aere canoro
   Increpuit.'

[2] *Cf. Iliad* XVI. 215: ἀσπὶς ἄρ' ἀσπίδ' ἔρειδε, κόρυς κόρυν, ἀνέρα δ' ἀνήρ: Ennius, 'hic pede pes premitur, hic armis arma teruntur'; Furius Antias (*c.* 100 B.C.) ap. Macrob. *Sat.* VI. iii. 5: 'pressatur pede pes, mucro mucrone, uiro uir'; Virg. *Aen.* X. 361: 'haeret pede pes densusque uiro uir'; and Statius, perhaps reminded by Silius, takes over this conventional trick, *Theb.* VIII. 399: 'ense minax ensis, pede pes, et cuspide cuspis.' The half-dozen lines in Silius (IX. 321 *sqq.*) make a good example of a mosaic of archaisms; Lucan is imitated in 'nec . . . artatis cecidisse licet'; the rare *flictu* is Pacuvian and Virgilian; *fatiscit* echoes Virgil; and the alliteration introduced is designedly quaint.

Chapter VI

STATIUS

Statius and his father – Dates of publication – Lost works –
Friends – His times – The *Thebaid* and its twelve books – Mytho-
logy – Sources – Influence of Antimachus and Virgil – *Achilleid* –
His epic fame – *Siluae* – Qualities of his occasional poems – Style
– Artificiality and conceits – Compounds and similes – Metre.

P. PAPINIUS STATIUS, a Neapolitan whose miscellaneous
poems reflect many aspects of Rome in the Flavian age, is, even
if judged solely by his posthumous influence, a considerable figure
in the annals of epic. For his life our main source of information lies
in his own *Siluae*. The date of his birth is a matter of inference, and the
tendency is now to place it earlier than once was common. A passage
formerly taken to mean that he was on the threshold of life at his father's
death does not really bear that sense,[1] and, while a reference to his own
old age (*senium*)[2] in the *Siluae* need not be literally pressed, it is most
likely that these poems were written in mature years. For several reasons
his birth-date cannot be put later than A.D. 45. His native town was
Naples (*mea Parthenope, Silv.* I. ii. 260–261), a meeting-place of Greek
and Roman culture, where his father, a man of good family, was a celebrated teacher. The lament (*epicedion*) on his death (*Silv.* V. iii) tells
how his father possessed poetic skill, had won victorious contests in
poetry, kept a popular school, turned out pupils successful in after life,
trained his son's taste, and encouraged the epic on Thebes. The elder
Statius's affection for his wife, the poet's mother, was only one of many
endearing qualities which explain the depth of the son's grief in bereavement. Before his father's death Statius had begun to make a mark. He

---

[1] *Silv.* V. iii. 72–74:
> 'mihi limine primo
> fatorum et uiridi, genitor, ceu raptus ab aeuo
> Tartara dura subis.'

'To me, father, it seems as though on the first threshold of thy fate and in a
hale youth thou hadst been torn away to enter the pitiless Underworld' (D. A.
Slater's trans.).

The *limen primum fatorum* is not Statius's but his father's. The poet regards his
father, although a man of 65, as having been snatched away from vigorous
manhood by an untimely death.

[2] *Silv.* IV. iv. 69–70: 'nos facta aliena canendo vergimur in senium.'

had won the prize for poetry at the Neapolitan *Augustalia*. At Rome he made money by such a libretto as that on *Agaue* supplied to the actor Paris,[1] and his *recitationes* from his works attracted good audiences.[2] Statius senior certainly did not die till after the eruption of Vesuvius in A.D. 79, because a passage in the *Siluae* (V. iii. 205) shows that he contemplated a poem on it, as he had already narrated in verse the destruction in 69 of the temples on the Capitol. The passage reads as if he did not long survive the eruption; and yet, since he encouraged his son's work on the *Thebaid* (*Silv.* V. iii. 233), he must have lived an appreciable time beyond its inception in A.D. 80. However that may be, he was no longer alive[3] at the time of Statius's memorable triumph in the Alban competition instituted by Domitian, and the probable date of this success with a poem on the emperor's exploits is 90.[4]

Meanwhile, although he had given recitations, none of Statius's extant work had been published; but he had long been elaborating his epic on the seven champions against Thebes. That poem, the *Thebaid*, was issued in twelve books shortly before[5] the publication of the first book of the *Siluae*, which can be dated A.D. 92. Certain passages,[6] it is true, in the *Siluae* refer to the author as still at work on the *Thebaid*; but they must be assumed to have been written, though not published, before 92. The poet's farewell to a task of twelve years bears interesting testimony to his speculation on its claim to lasting renown, his complimentary attitude to Domitian, his knowledge that his own writings were being already studied, and above all his worshipful reverence for Virgil, the inspirer of his epic style:

> Shalt thou, my lay of Thebes, my wakeful toil
> For twice six years, shalt thou far off endure,
> And, when thy maker is no more, be read?
> E'en now, be sure, fame hath made fair the way
> For thee, and seeks to show thy novelty
> To men unborn. E'en now our noble Prince
> Grants thee acquaintance; now Italian youths
> Learn thee by heart amain. Live on, I pray!
> Yet vie not thou with Virgil's god-sent strain –
> Follow afar: his every step adore.[7]

---

[1] Juv. VII. 86. This must have been before Paris's loss of Domitian's favour in 83.

[2] Juv. VII. 82.   [3] *Silv.* V. iii. 227.   [4] S.H. § 406 n.11.

[5] *Silv.* I. *praef.*: 'adhuc pro Thebaide mea, quamuis me reliquerit, timeo.' The words in *Silv.* IV. iv. 89, 'Thebais optato collegit carbasa portu' (published in A.D. 95), apparently refer to the attainment of fame by the *Thebaid* some time after publication.

[6] *Silv.* I. v. 8; III. ii. 40 and 142; III. v. 35–36.

[7] *Theb.* XII. 810 *sqq*:

> 'Durabisne procul dominoque legere superstes,
> O mihi bissenos multum uigilata per annos
> Thebaï? . . .'

Cf. Silv. IV. vii. 26: 'Thebais multa cruciata lima.'

Attracted from the subject of Thebes to 'the tale of Troy divine,' he was yet to attempt another epic; but, for an interval, he was free to collect some of his miscellaneous poems, and the first book of the *Siluae* was issued in the same year, as is inferred from its prefatory reference to the death of the city prefect Rutilius Gallicus, whose recovery from illness is the theme of the fourth poem. This book, dedicated to the poet Stella, whose marriage is celebrated in the second poem, was followed during the poet's lifetime by II, III and IV, all addressed to different friends. Book IV can be definitely dated, as its opening piece celebrates Domitian's seventeenth consulate: the book is assigned to the summer of A.D. 95. It is a fair surmise that Book II had been published in 93 and Book III in 94. Book V may have been post-humously issued; for its preface to Abascantus bears solely on the first poem, and the fifth is incomplete.

Statius writes as if his attempted epic on Achilles had to yield place to the idea of an Italian subject – the wars of Domitian.[1] He had begun his *Achilleid* in 95,[2] and although it had not gone far beyond a single book, he gave public readings from it.[3] But the final interruption came with his death. The presumption is that Statius did not outlive Domitian, whose assassination occurred in 96.

The lost works of Statius are the pantomime *Agaue* from the tragic Theban story of Pentheus; the epic on the German campaign of Domitian, of which four hexameters survive;[4] and an epistle concerning the *Thebaid* sent to Vibius Maximus, the recipient of Statius's Sapphics (*Silv.* IV. vii), and an epitomator of Livy.[5] From the ode to him and the allusion in the preface to *Siluae* IV, we realise that Statius admired his literary power and felt gratitude for his inspiring encouragement while the *Thebaid* was being written.

Statius's love for his native Naples is obvious in his works. It was thither that he repaired towards the end of his life, mortified by his defeat in the Capitoline contest of 94, though sustained by the sympathy of his wife Claudia. But he had lived much in Rome and at the Alban villa which he owed to the emperor. His circle of friends was representative of the age. It included Domitian himself, whom he flattered far more than was justified by the grant of a special water-supply or by invitations to dinner. It included also men prominent in public life like the prefect Rutilius, imperial secretaries like Abascantus or sons of secretaries like Claudius Etruscus, men who combined literary tastes with national service, like the poet Arruntius Stella who rose to the

---

[1] *Silv.* IV. iv. 94–96.
[2] *Ibid.* IV. vii. 23–24: 'primis meus ecce metis haeret Achilles'; V. v. 36–37: 'pudeat Thebasque nouumque Aeaciden.'
[3] V. ii. 162–163.
[4] Postgate's *C.P.L.* p. 430; or at end of Garrod's ed. of *Theb.* and *Ach.* (*O.C.T.*) 1906; or in A. Klotz's ed. of *Siluae* (Teub.).
[5] As a Livian epitomator he is discussed by M. Galdi, *L'Epitome n. lett. lat.* pp. 40–43.

consulship, and the historian Vibius Maximus who under Trajan became governor of Egypt. It is plain that Statius and Martial belonged to the same social grade; for Etruscus, Stella, and Lucan's widow Polla appear in the works of both; and among other friends in common were Atedius Melior and Novius Vindex. But neither poet names the other, and the silence may be due to dislike.

The age was a tranquil one, favourable to aesthetic refinement rather than powerful creation; and Statius is its perfect counterpart in his quiet learning, power of polished expression, appreciation of beautiful scenes and beautiful works of art. We can discern his warmth of heart in the love he bears his father and his wife, and in his sorrow over the death of the little boy whom he adopted; for his marriage to Claudia, a widow with a daughter, proved childless. Very appropriately in a poem addressed to Vitorius Marcellus he contrasts that busy man of affairs with himself, a poet idly touching his lyre, but filled with a scholar's veneration for Virgil:

> Thy talents are alive; thy spirit, girt
> For mighty tasks, can face both foul and fair.
> But I, a singer whiling easeful hours,
> Quest after reputation's airy joys:
> And, lo! I woo the dreamful happy shore,
> Where, newly landed in Ausonia,
> Parthenope found haven; there I touch
> With idle thumb my slender-stringèd lyre,
> And seated by the marge of Virgil's shrine
> Take heart to hymn my mighty master's grave.[1]

We may rest assured that, while courtier-like he felt compelled to feign a celestial rapture in being a guest at Domitian's table[2] and to suggest that it outshone the Homeric banquet of King Alcinous or the Virgilian banquet of Queen Dido, still his secret preference must have been for some such feast of reason and flow of soul as he was safe to find when he dined with his poet-friend Vindex.[3] At the board of that cultured connoisseur, gifted with unerring judgement of art-treasures, the menu – unlike that of Trimalchio in Petronius – did not consist of freakish whets to the appetite (*ludibria uentris*), but was in keeping with the literary talk and cheery jests which made a midwinter night fly[4] – a night to mark with pearls (*nox et Erythraeae Thetidis signanda lapillis*).

[1] *Silv.* IV. iv. 48–55:
> 'sed uiget ingenium et magnos accinctus in usus
> fert animus quascumque uices. . . .'
[2] *Silv.* IV. ii.
[3] *Silv.* IV. vi.
[4] *Silv.* IV. vi. 12–14:
> 'nobis uerus amor medioque Helicone petitus
> sermo hilaresque ioci brumalem absumere noctem
> suaserunt.'

In these social surroundings we can best understand the personality of Statius.

One might feel a temptation to dismiss the *Thebaid* with a summary as brief as the twelve bald hexameters in the *Codex Toletanus*; but that would convey a beggarly impression of a narrative nearly 10,000[1] lines long, in which, despite dull tracts, there are vigorous incidents and great moments. If Statius had studied the construction and proportions of his story more exactly, if he had condensed some and rigidly excised others of his episodes, the *Thebaid* would have gained in unity and attractiveness, while his readers and his reputation might have been increased by the reappearance as separate poems of the best among the banished portions. The following analysis may serve to confirm this.

Book I. Statius makes a dull start with frigid professions of ignorance as to where in the Theban story he should begin, and with equally frigid flattery of Domitian. The requisite note of gloom is struck in the fiendish prayer of the self-blinded Oedipus to the Fury Tisiphone that she should estrange his sons Eteocles and Polynices, and ensure discord through Eteocles's refusal to keep his promise of letting his brother reign for a year in his stead at Thebes. Sharing none of Lucan's objections to divine interference in epic action, the poet describes a council of Gods attended by Demigods, Rivers and Winds at which ruinous war between Thebes and Argos is ordained. Polynices, the prince exiled from Thebes, reaches Argos and during a terrific storm fights with another stranger to the land, Tydeus, for shelter by the palace door. The two combatants are received by King Adrastus, become fast friends, and are recognised by their host as the Lion (Polynices) and the Boar (Tydeus), destined to be his sons-in-law. At a royal banquet they see the two princesses, their future brides:

> The face of men was new to them and set
> Them blushing; and together red and white
> Coursed o'er their glowing cheeks; their modest eyes
> Turned to their venerable sire once more.[2]

The king's tale of the dealings of Apollo with Argos owing to the death of the god's child is a digression.

Book II. The woes of an accursed house work even beyond the grave. The ghost of Laius, father of Oedipus, escapes – to the envy of the other dead – from the lower world for the purpose of hardening Eteocles against his brother. Meanwhile at Argos there are wedding festivities, but also bad omens, when Argia is married to Polynices and Deipyle to

---

[1] The exact total is 9741 hexameters.
[2] *Theb.* I. 536 *sqq.*:
> 'Noua deinde pudori
> Visa uirum facies: pariter pallorque ruborque
> Purpureas hausere genas oculique uerentes
> Ad sanctum rediere patrem.'

Tydeus. The story of the fatal necklace of Harmonia worn by Argia is told incidentally. After twelve days of rejoicing, Polynices turns to his claims on Thebes:

> Grief and mad anger gnawed his mind, and that
> Than which no heavier burden vexes men –
> Hope long deferred.[1]

Tydeus undertakes a mission to Thebes to require from Eteocles observance of his pact; but Eteocles refuses and plots to waylay the envoy on his way back by ordering an ambush of fifty men to await him. Tydeus's fight against his foes in the pass is one of the most spirited and saga-like passages of the *Thebaid*. His challenge to the lurking assassins is given in ringing tones:

> 'Step forth and face me. Out! To open ground!
> Why dread to dare? What cowardice is this?
> 'Tis I alone, alone, that offer fight.'[2]

At the stone of the Sphinx he baffles their onset, slaying one after another:

> Alarmed they miss their fellows, then they count.
> Their murder-lust is changed amid their grief
> Over the thinning of so strong a band (*rarescere turbam*).[3]

One survivor is spared to take back the tidings to the treacherous king Book III. At the news there is sorrow in Thebes. To stir up Argos, Jupiter despatches Mars and overawes the gods into compliance with his will. The hush produced by his threats is likened to a windless calm in summer-time:

> As when the ocean is becalmed amid
> Long surcease of the gales, and every shore
> Reposeth in an unresisting sleep,
> When drowsy summer fans the woodland leaves
> And clouds with scarce a breath; then do the pools
> And murmuring meres abate their height, and streams
> Are hushed, for burning suns have parched them dry.[4]

Exultant in his chariot, Mars is met and reproached by Venus in vain. Tydeus, battle-worn and wounded, presents himself at the council of King Adrastus in Argos and relates his adventure. The debate is 'war or no war?' The seer Amphiaraus, when consulted, foresees disaster, and, though reluctant to reveal the worst, opposes the impetuosity of Capaneus. The seer's speech when induced to break his silence is a

[1] II. 319 *sqq.*:
> 'Exedere animum dolor iraque demens
> Et qua non grauior mortalibus addita curis,
> Spes ubi longa uenit.'

[2] II. 547 *sqq.*　　　　[4] III. 255 *sqq.*　　　　[3] II. 611-612.

forcible effort. Argia pleads for hostilities. Her speech has an effective
close in human feeling: she would have her royal father consent to the
war which is the heart's desire of her husband; but she knows that, when
the parting comes and the bugles sound for the men who march away,
she would wish it otherwise.

Book IV. King Adrastus decides on war in the third spring after
Polynices left Thebes. The leaders are Adrastus, Polynices, Tydeus,
Hippomedon, Capaneus, Amphiaraus and Parthenopaeus. The description of the forces of these seven warriors against Thebes forms a
dull catalogue of blended geography and mythology. At Thebes the
dejected king consults the prophet Teiresias, who advocates recourse
to the oracles of the dead in a forest of gloom comparable to Lucan's
eerie forest near Massilia. Statius conveys an appropriate sense of
weirdness in his description:

> At noontide yet and in the lonely night
> Thro' shadowland the damnèd ground exhales
> Appalling battle-fumes: black figures rise –
> The Earthborn dead – to urge their ghostly war.
> The peasant flees his half-ploughed field unnerved,
> And cattle come back to the steading mad.[1]

From the sadness of the Argolic ghosts whom he evokes Teiresias infers
an ultimate Theban victory. Bacchus, aiding Thebes, hinders the
Argives' march by a miraculous drought:

> It was the hour whereat the panting day (*anhela dies*)
> Raiseth the sun high as the mid-world peak,
> When o'er the gaping fields a sluggard haze (*tardus uapor*)
> Broods, and each forest lets the sunlight in.[2]

And amidst this anguish of the solstice they are guided to the one spring
remaining in the land by Hypsipyle, once of Lemnos and now a nurse
to a king's child Opheltes or Archemorus. Suspecting no danger, she
leaves the child, in order to show them the water more quickly.

Book V. King Adrastus is desirous of knowing who this benefactress
is, and nearly 500 lines are devoted to the fortunes, past and present,
of Hypsipyle. She relates the crime of the Lemnian women in murdering their menfolk, the consequences to herself of having surreptitiously
saved her father, and the visit of Jason in the Argo. Statius here tres-
passes on the subject of Valerius Flaccus's *Argonautica*; and it may be
noted that while in the *Thebaid* Hypsipyle states that she was forced into
a union with Jason, Valerius represents her as attracted into an amour
by Jason's looks.

The child Archemorus has been all this time left unattended, and
another digression describes the venomous serpent which attacks him.

[1] IV. 438 *sqq.*   [2] IV. 680 *sqq.*

Cries 'like half-completed words in dreams' (*qualia non totas peragunt insomnia uoces*) are heard, and on her return the errant nurse finds the child dead. Against the furious anger of its father she is protected by the grateful Argives.

Book VI. The epic interest is considerably less in a book concerned first with the building of a funeral pyre and cremation of the child, and then with an elaborate account of the games in its honour – chariot-race, foot-race ('running,' remarks the poet, 'is a useful accomplishment in war, if success fails one'!), quoits, boxing and wrestling.

Book VII. Jupiter is vexed that the Argives should delay the war by holding games – and in mid-epic readers may sympathise with Jupiter's feeling. A further intervention is made by Mars and Bacchus. Eteocles hears of the Argive advance, and there follows a catalogue of the host, as pointed out by old Phorbas to Antigone (sister of the arch-opponents) while they look forth from a tower in Thebes. Jocasta, mother of the rivals, comes forth

> In all the mighty majesty of woe
> (*egreditur magna cum maiestate malorum*)[1]

to carry the olive branch (*ramum oleae*) into Polynices's camp and make an appeal for peace. Polynices is touched; but, while he is wavering, Tydeus intervenes, bitterly recalling the treachery to which he had been subjected by Eteocles. The overtures fail: the Fury rouses the old passion for blood: fighting begins. A Theban warrior longs to slay Amphiaraus, counting other victims trivial in comparison. He hurls his spear; but another doom has been appointed for Amphiaraus: his father, the god Apollo, diverts the fatal weapon to his charioteer, and takes the dead driver's place, spreading death everywhere as the chariot careers on its dread path among bleeding corpses and dying men. Then by a solemn intuition Amphiaraus realises the presence of Apollo and his own nearness to the brink of the other world:

> 'Long since, Cirrhaean sire, my quivering car
> Told me 'twas thou that by my fated team
> Didst sit (why honour human frailty thus?)
> How long wilt thou delay th' approaching ghosts?
> I hear e'en now the Stygian torrent's rush,
> Pluto's black rivers and the triple bark
> Of hellish watch-hound. Take my laurel crown,
> Take now thine honours girt about my head:
> To carry these to hell were sacrilege.
> With my last words – if aught of thanks thou ow'st
> Unto thy prophet passing hence – to thee,
> Phoebus, I trust a home betrayed, and doom
> Of wife accurst, and generous wrath of son.'
> – Down leaped Apollo sad, but hid his tears.[2]

[1] VII. 478.   [2] VII. 779 *sqq.*

Then came the mysterious passing, as the ground opened beneath the doomed man:

> Sheer yawned the earth below with jaws profound.
> Dread seized in turn on stars and shadowland.
> Him did that cavern measureless drink down,
> Engulfing steeds that made as if to cross.
> He loosed not grip of weapon or of rein,
> But, as he was, drove straight for Tartarus,
> And, ever lower fallen, gazed at heaven,
> Groaning to see the land close over him,
> Until a lighter shock conjoined again
> The parted fields and blocked daylight from Hell.[1]

Book VIII. Excitement reigns in the lower world over the sudden descent of Amphiaraus; and the querulous utterances of Pluto, almost Lucianesque in their scoffing spirit, have a wholly different ring from the consistent solemnity of Virgil in *Aeneid* VI. The Argives are inwardly shaken and fall back: so there is joy in Thebes. Adrastus summons a council to choose a successor to the prophet Amphiaraus. The battle is renewed on the Theban side by a sally, and a narrative of wounds and death ensues. The daughters of Oedipus, Antigone and Ismene, a pair of contrasting characters (*par aliud morum*), lament the sorrows of their house with divided sympathies in the conflict:

> Both ways their fears incline: whom would they wish
> The vanquished, whom the victor in the war?
> The exile wins their preference unowned
> (*tacite praeponderat exsul*).[2]

Real pathos marks the end of Ismene's lover, Atys, the warrior brought home dying, with her name the only word on his chill lips.[3] Tydeus works havoc among the enemy, and sends whirling through the air helmets with heads inside (*galeasque rotat per nubila plenas*, 699). He and Melanippus mortally wound each other, and the book closes with the horrible spectacle of Tydeus gnawing the head of his adversary.

Book IX is mainly concerned with the valour of two heroes, Hippomedon and the young Arcadian Parthenopaeus, whose parting from his mother Atalanta formed a brief episode in Book IV. Stoutly defending the dead Tydeus, Hippomedon is tempted away by Tisiphone's lying message that Adrastus is taken prisoner, and on returning discovers that the foes have secured his friend's body. During Hippomedon's subsequent deeds of prowess, he is opposed by the River-god Ismenus and is saved from drowning only to succumb on the bank under a rain of darts. Parthenopaeus signalises himself by feats of archery. He is in the end, at the instigation of Mars, slain by Dryas, who is in turn slain by an invisible hand, deemed to be that of Diana herself. The book concludes with the dying behests of Parthenopaeus.

[1] VII. 816 *sqq.*   [2] VIII. 614 *sqq.*   [3] VIII. 643.

Book X. Theban troops, inspirited by Eteocles's harangue, plan to surround the Argives and prevent a retreat; but are themselves overcome by a divinely contrived sleep and surprised by the Argives, who break their lines and do much slaughter. At daybreak a fierce attack is delivered on Thebes, when Menoeceus, son of Jocasta's brother Creon, devotes himself for his city, plunging to death from a rampart-tower. Capaneus, defiantly scaling the town walls, is struck dead by Jupiter's thunderbolt.

Book XI. Goaded by Tisiphone, Polynices challenges Eteocles to single combat, and the latter, over-persuaded by Creon to face his brother, will not listen to the entreaties of his mother Jocasta. Polynices similarly rejects his sister Antigone's appeals. Heaven, earth and hell are revolted by this detestably unnatural duel. The horrified Adrastus endeavours in vain to part the brothers and retires to Argos. The agonised intervention of Pietas descending from the skies is foiled by the malignant Fury.

Thus, at last, half-way through the eleventh book, Statius makes the two protagonists meet, with the result that the compression of the last eleven hundred lines produces a much balder effect than that of the more spacious books which precede. Both combatants die, Polynices being mortally wounded as he stoops to strip his rival. Creon, assuming the crown, decrees that no invader is to be buried. Led by Antigone, Oedipus laments over the bodies of his sons, and meditates suicide, which his daughter prevents. Jocasta stabs herself, and is tended by Ismene. Then Antigone's intercession obtains a mitigation of Creon's arrogant sentence of exile launched upon Oedipus. The remnants of the invading army disperse to Adrastus's dominions.

Book XII opens with funeral honours for the Theban dead. A report of Creon's decree withholding burial from his fallen foes is brought to the wives of the six[1] slain leaders on their way from Argos to recover the bodies of their dead. Except Argia, Polynices's widow, all the women go to implore aid from Theseus, king of Athens. Argia, arriving outside Thebes, burns the body of her husband on Eteocles's pyre, where there are signs to show that fratricidal hatred had survived death; she is met and helped by Antigone. The two are detected, haled before Creon, proudly own their act and are sentenced to death. Athens meanwhile consents to help the Argive war-widows. Very significantly the altar of mercy in Athens is described, as a symbolic contrast to the harshness of Creon at Thebes. The passage is remarkable for the colour it gave to the notion of after times that the poet was a Christian:

> There stood an altar at the city's heart
> Reared to no God of Power: Mercy mild
> Made it her shrine, and human misery
> Had hallowed it. It never lacked for prayers

[1] Adrastus is the only one of the seven leaders to survive.

Renewed, nor e'er repelled a suppliant.
There whoso asks is heard, and day and night
The way is open, and the offering
The Holy One requireth is a cry.
The worship costs but little: incense-flame
And victim's blood find no acceptance there.
That altar sweats with tears.[1]

So the Athenians approach Thebes and win the victory, Creon dying at the hands of Theseus. The obsequies of the fallen and the *envoi* (already translated) complete the work.

To appreciate an allusive epic like the *Thebaid* the reader needs equipment in the myths of Thebes: he must know more than the story of Oedipus, the fated king, his house, and the 'Seven Against Thebes': he must remember the outlines of legends about Amphion, about Cadmus son of Agenor, about Dirce, and he must be expert enough to grasp why Statius calls Thebes by varying epithets like 'Aonian' (I. 34), 'Echionian' (I. 169, II. 90), 'Ogygian' (I. 173, 328, II. 85), or 'Sidonian' (III. 656), and why Polynices is the 'Ismenian hero' (I. 673), and why the Argives are *Inacha pubes* (I. 619). The well-springs of all such mythological lore lay far back in the ancient Greek Cyclic story of Thebes; in the tragedies of Aeschylus, Sophocles and Euripides;[2] and in Statius's main source for material, Antimachus, who, before the days of the Alexandrian poets, but anticipating their erudition, composed a massive epic in his *Thebais*. He wrote rather for the leisured and the learned than for the ordinary reader. Alexandrian critics put him second among epic authors: and Hadrian is said to have preferred him to Homer. But he used his spacious limits unrestrained by any canons of unity. Not content to end the forbidding tale of fratricidal strife on the more human, more really tragic note of Antigone's devotion to her slain brother, he involved himself in two additional sequels, the war with Athens and the revenge of Argos. Statius showed more wisdom in writing fewer books on the theme, in condensing the war with Athens, and in omitting the triumphant return during the next generation of the Argive avengers, the Epigoni. When he is criticised, as he deserves to be, for his digressions, it is fair to remember the almost overpowering literary legacy which he inherited. There are

---

[1] *Th.* XII. 481 *sqq.*:

> Vrbe fuit media nulli concessa potentum
> Ara deum: mitis posuit Clementia sedem,
> Et miseri fecere sacram; sine supplice numquam
> Illa nouo, nulla damnauit uota repulsa.
> Auditi quicumque rogant, noctesque diesque
> Ire datum et solis numen placare querellis.
> Parca superstitio: non turea flamma, nec altus
> Accipitur sanguis: lacrimis altaria sudant.

[2] Statius's use of Euripides has been considered by A. Reussner, *De Statio et Euripide*, diss., Halle, 1921.

signs that he also consulted Seneca's *Phoenissae* and *Oedipus*; but in Latin his master was Virgil, although Ovid and Lucan[1] also went to his making. The Virgilian influence is manifest both in his language and in the construction of his incidents. Sometimes actual phrases are copied as in *magnanimosque duces* (*Th.* III. 55); *procumbunt piceae* (*Th.* VI. 100, to remind readers, as if by a traditional phrase, that the whole passage is based on the felling of the wood in *Aen.* VI. 179 *sqq.*); *pede pes* (*Th.* VIII. 399, repeating the Ennian words borrowed by Furius of Antium as well as by Virgil, *Aen.* X. 361, and in structure going back to Homer himself).[2] The *Siluae* present the same features in phrases like *urbis opus* (*Silv.* II. ii. 31) and *qualis eras!* (II. vi. 34). Or, again, a different turn may be given to the original expression, as Virgil's *Quis fallere possit amantem?* becomes *nil transit amantes* (*Th.* II. 335), or his *forsan et haec meminisse iuuabit* is elaborated into

> *forsan et has uenturus amor praemiserit iras*
> *ut meminisse iuuet* (*Th.* I. 472–473).

Elsewhere Statius gives us a blend of verbal and material reminiscence, as when he implores his father's spirit to revisit and counsel him in dreams issuing from 'the Gate of Horn' rather than from 'the Ivory Gate' (*Silv.* V. iii *sub fin.*; *Aen.* VI *sub fin.*). His debt to Virgil for incident is also heavy – too heavy, in truth, for genuine originality. It was not merely that he took over through Virgil the convention of supernatural interferences, as also of copious decorative similes, and outdid all his predecessors in these: he went further and allowed his imitation to become too obsequious in a parallelism of incidents. Because Evander told the story of Hercules and Cacus in the *Aeneid*, we must, before the first book of the *Thebaid* is completed, have Adrastus's digressive tale about Coroebus's resolve to rid his country of a punitive monster sent by Apollo; because there were funeral games in Virgil, we must have almost a whole book devoted to the rites and contests in memory of the child Archemorus; and because *Aeneid* IX celebrated the bold night-raid by Nisus and Euryalus, we must have a corresponding pair, Hopleus and Dymas, in the tenth book of the *Thebaid*, intercepted during their quest for the bodies of Tydeus and Parthenopaeus.

The other epic effort by Statius was his *Achilleid*, cut short by death when little over 1,100 lines were written. What dimensions this tale of Troy might have reached we can only guess: it certainly was to cover a wider field than a 'Wrath of Achilles'; for the author, immediately after his invocation, declares that his design is to relate more than the *Iliad* contains – not to end with the fate of Hector, as Homer did, but

---

[1] One finds chains of phraseology like Ovid, *Met.* XV. 529: 'unumque erat omnia uolnus,' Luc. *Phars.* IX. 814: 'totum est pro uolnere corpus,' Stat. *Theb.* V. 598: 'totumque in uolnere corpus.'

[2] Silius (IX. 32) has 'pes pede uirque uiro teritur,' *cf.* p. 372 and note.

to escort the young hero throughout the Trojan war.[1] This then, is a second laurel wreath which he asks Apollo to plait for him, inasmuch as he announces himself no stranger to the Muses but known for his poem on Thebes.[2] True to his more extended view of Achilles's life, Statius begins early in it with the fears of the hero's mother Thetis that danger threatens her son from the elopement of Helen with Paris. So, with the purpose of transferring Achilles to a safe hiding-place, she visits the cave of the Centaur Chiron under Mount Pelion where the youth is being brought up. Her son is absent: Chiron tells his mother he has remarked a change in him:

> Once he was wont to bear rebuke and hear
> Commands with zeal, nor far desert the cave;
> Now Ossa holds him not nor Pelion's
> Towering mass, nor snows of Thessaly.[3]

Just at that moment, radiant after an adventure on which he has killed a lioness, he returns,

> Yet, spite of war and toilsome energy,
> Comely to look upon: there floated o'er
> Fair lineaments a rosy fire: his hair
> Outshone the gleam of yellow gold, and time
> Had not yet changed his earliest youthful down.
> Eyes with a quiet flash were his, and you
> Could see his mother written on his face.[4]

She decides that he must be concealed in the island of Scyros, and a pleasant picture of mingled nature and fancy is given us of his half-miraculous transference thither. Achilles, sunk in the profound sleep that falls on the young (*qui pueris sopor*), is borne by his goddess-mother down to the quiet seashore (*iussa tacere litora*). The way lies clear in a moonlit world. Their escort, the Centaur, seeks to hide his moist eyes (*udaque celat lumina*), when suddenly a dolphin team hurries mother and son off across the waters, and he can with effort (*erecto prospectat equo!*) just see them pass from sight where the white foam lingers behind their course. Then gloom descends on Thessaly; for the heights of Pholoë lament the youth that will never return, and cloud-capped Othrys sighs, and the river Spercheos wastes with pining – a frigid sort of 'pathetic fallacy' like the legendary sorrow of nature for Balder dead. It is a more natural touch to say that the cave where the old Centaur taught Achilles music is now mute, or even to fancy that the woodland Fauns miss his boyish melodies, but the grotesque is reached in the mourning of the nymphs for the lost opportunity of marrying Achilles! This and the too matter-of-fact reference to the Centaur on his hind legs (*erecto equo*) are among the not infrequent instances where mythology betrayed

---

[1] *Ach.* 7: 'tota iuuenem deducere Troia.'
[2] *Ach.* 8–13.   [3] *Ach.* 149–152.   [4] *Ach.* 160–165.

O

Statius into absurdity. Nearly all the rest of the existing fragment, which might borrow Robert Bridges' title 'Achilles in Scyros,' relates his reception in women's attire at court there, his passion for one of the princesses, the detection of his disguise by Ulysses, and his departure for Troy.

The *Achilleid* has much the same qualities as the *Thebaid*. There are still echoes of Virgil, mythological erudition, and ornamental similes. The subject, however, is a more attractive one than that of the *Thebaid*, and it is unfortunate that the incompleteness of the *Achilleid* makes elaborate comparison between them nugatory.

Probably Statius and his contemporaries felt that his fame would be founded on his epic work, and it was for his *Thebaid* that he was valued in the Middle Ages. In Dante he plays an elevated part, and is often quoted. Chaucer, who mentions him with enthusiasm several times, calls him 'Stace of Thebes' in *The Knightes Tale*, and in the *Hous of Fame*, repeating Dante's confusion[1] of him with a rhetorician of Toulouse,

> The Tholosan that highte Stace,
> That bar of Thebes up the fame
> Upon his shuldres, and the name
> Also of cruel Achilles.

Here, then, as in *Troilus and Criseyde*, where he tells his 'litel book' to go

> And kis the steppes, whereas thou seest pace
> Virgile, Ovyde, Omer, Lucan and Stace,

it is among the great narrative poets that Chaucer places Statius. His hold upon the Middle Ages[2] is not altogether easy to explain. Was it the tradition that he became a Christian which threw a halo round him in the eyes of medieval Catholicism, and did that tradition in turn grow out of his worshipful attitude to Virgil and the tenderness of feeling which found one of its most remarkable expressions in his description of the Shrine of Mercy at Athens? Modern criticism, however, is not likely to forget that he was also the author of the miscellaneous *Siluae*, which after centuries of oblivion were restored to notice, when Poggio on his travels in 1417 or 1418 found them in a manuscript along with Manilius and Silius and had a copy made to be sent back to Italy.[3]

The thirty-two poems in the five books of the miscellany entitled the *Siluae* are mostly in hexameter verse, though there are four in hendecasyllables[4] and one set each of Alcaics and Sapphics.[5] The number of

---

[1] *Purgat.* xxi. 89: 'Tolosano.' *Cf.* B. A. Wise, *Infl. of S. upon Chaucer*, Balt. 1911.
[2] See A. Graf, *Roma nella memoria e nelle immagionazioni del medio evo*, Tur. 1882, ch. xvii.
[3] A. C. Clark, 'The Literary Discoveries of Poggio,' *C.R.* xiii (1899) pp. 119–130; Phillimore, *Siluae (O.C.T.)* ed. 2, 1920, *praef.*
[4] I. vi; II. vii; IV. iii and ix.   [5] IV. v and vii.

lines in each book is between 700 and 800. In the fifth book, the longest
poem of all, 293 lines on the poet's father, is in juxtaposition to the
shortest, the 19 lines to Sleep. The variety of the poems is the outcome
of their origin: they fit some passing event; pay a compliment to the
emperor or a friend; describe a country house or work of art; frame an
elegy on the poet's father, a slave, a lion or a parrot; indite an invocation
to Sleep; or celebrate the dead poet Lucan's birthday. In other words,
they are occasional verses, being, the author tells us in one of his five
prefaces,[1] rapidly composed, so that they illustrate Quintilian's description of what is meant by a *silua* in literature.[2] Statius had long hesitated
about issuing in collected form poems which were composed separately,
but considered that the author of the *Thebaid* might be pardoned for
this venture, on the analogy of great poets who wrote light verses as
Virgil did the *Culex*.[3] All students of the archaeology and social history
of the Flavian age have reason to applaud the poet's decision to give
them to the world; and as literature there is nothing quite like them in
Latin. They are not to be judged as claiming high inspiration, but as
pieces in which the recurrent artificiality is time after time illuminated
by the play of a pretty fancy and the grace of clever expression. Nor is
the artificiality wholly inconsistent with sincerity of feeling. A survey of
the poems may illustrate their qualities.

Book I. Statius is not at his best in the opening poem, on the equestrian statue of Domitian, where he strikes an exaggerated note in suggesting that the work has come down complete from heaven, that the
rider is a greater than Julius, and that the burden of divinity makes
Earth pant beneath the statue. The long epithalamium which follows,
on Stella's marriage to Violentilla, who was a Neapolitan like Statius, is
pleasanter, though modern tastes wearies of its Venus, Cupids, Apollo
and Bacchus. More concrete and engaging is the third poem, on a visit
to Vopiscus's cool retreat at Tivoli where the natural beauty of the
scenery makes a genuine impression on the poet,[4] and compensates for
the attendant artificialities. Then the recovery of Rutilius Gallicus is
celebrated in polished lines, which, however they suited the first century,
read rather frigidly when they introduce a rescue by Apollo and Aesculapius. Statius holds us more in describing his friend's considerate
conduct as a judge[5] and his premature breakdown owing to the strain
of official duty. The lines appear to argue in their author maturity of
years, and bear on the question of his birth-date: to him in this poem
sixty is not old age:

---

[1] *Silv.* I. *praef.* Statius says none of these pieces occupied over a couple of
days, 'nullum enim ex illis biduo longius tractum'; *cf.* his references to 'gratiam
celeritatis' and in II, *praef.*: 'stili facilitatem'; III. *praef.*: 'libellorum istorum
temeritatem' and 'audaciam stili nostri.'

[2] *Inst. Or.* X. iii. 17: 'primo decurrere per materiam stilo quam uelocissimo
uolunt et sequentes calorem atque impetum ex tempore scribunt: hanc *siluam*
uocant.'

[3] *Silv.* I. *praef.*   [4] *Silv.* I. iii. 13–23.   [5] *Ibid.* I. iv. 43–49.

'Twas not the fault of years (for they had scarce
O'ertaken twice six lustres) but the toil
Incessant and the vigorous mind's control
Over the body, all the watchful care
For his own emperor – a task beloved.
So stole upon the core of that tired frame
Ensnaring ease, slow disregard of life.[1]

In the fifth poem his sportive theme is the decoration of Claudius
Etruscus's baths and his task to celebrate not Greek springs but the Latin
waters of the aqueducts Virgo and Marcia. Having struck this Roman
note, however, he returns to Greek mythology: it is our Lady of Cy-
thera, Venus, and her husband the Fire-god, who with the aid of the
Loves' torches are responsible for heating the bath furnaces! Everything there is costly (*nil ibi plebeium*); for Statius had aristocratic tastes:
the water is fit to be Cytherea's birthplace, Narcissus's mirror, Diana's
bath! And after these mythological conceits comes the prosaic assurance that not even a visitor from the seaside would despise those bath-
ing facilities.[2] The book closes with the praises of the emperor's carnival,
memorable for a fair-weather rain of delicacies and fruits, a lavish
bounty surpassing the Golden Age, Domitian's condescension in sharing the feast, spectacular features like women combatants and dwarf
warriors, and the cosmopolitan crowd at the theatre – buxom Lydian
damsels clapping their hands, the jingling musicians of Cadiz, noisy
Syrians, and those who barter common sulphur for broken glass.

The consolatory poem sent to Melior on the death of a slave-boy
adopted by him has touches of real feeling, and is less over-loaded with
mythology. Closeness of blood, he argues in excuse for the adoptive
father's frantic grief, does not always make the strongest tie:

Sons we beget perforce – adopt at will.[3]

But there is comfort in regarding death as freedom from anxiety:

We all must go, must go; and Aeacus
Shaketh the urn amid the boundless shades (*umbris*, v.l. *ulnis*).
Yet he we mourn is happy in th' escape
From men and gods and hazards unforeseen
And life's dark instability; for him
Fate may not touch. He never asked nor feared
Nor yet deserved (*meruit*, v.l. *renuit*) to die; but we, a crowd
Distressed and wretched, know not whence may come
Our final day or what shall end our time.[4]

[1] *Silv*. I. iv. 52:
'Non illud culpa senectae
(Quippe ea bissenis uixdum orsa excedere lustris),
Sed labor intendens animique in membra uigentis
Imperium uigilesque suo pro Caesare curae,
Dulce opus. Hinc fessos penitus subrepsit in artus
Insidiosa quies et pigra obliuio uitae.'
[2] *Ibid*. v. 60–62.   [3] II. i. 87–88.   [4] *Ibid*. 218–225: 'ibimus omnes,' etc.

The poem on the mansion of Pollius and Polla at Sorrento shows how the effects of nature and of art compete in the poet's mind. To adjudicate between the charms of a crescent bay outside and the architectural amenities of the villa itself is embarrassing.[1] Characteristically he divides his praises among aesthetic treasures and the view from different rooms, with his eye now on Naples in the distance, now on the variety of marbles around him. He draws from nature in his picture of the seaside villa in the gloaming,

> When day is wearied and the shadow falls
> Upon the water from the hill at dusk,
> And mirrored mansions float upon the bay;[2]

or he indulges in a purely fanciful picture:

> Oft when the grape is ripe with autumn-down,
> A sea-nymph climbs the cliff, who, canopied
> 'Neath the dark night, with full-grown tendril clears
> Of brine her dripping eyes, and from the slopes
> Snatches the clusters sweet. The spindrift oft
> Splashes the vintage from the neighbouring waves.
> The Satyrs seaward dive and 'mid the surf
> The Hill-gods long to seize the naked nymph.[3]

Three short pieces follow, each touching on a possession of Atedius Melior – his plane-tree by the garden pool concerning which Statius daintily relates the legend of a nymph's escape from Pan; his parrot for whose sudden death a train of mourning birds is invited to chant a dirge; and his tame lion slain in the amphitheatre to the just indignation of his fellow-lions, but with the consolation of having roused the emotion of people, senate and emperor! Of the dead slave of Flavius Ursus, commemorated in the next poem, he affirms that his fine qualities of soul justify the free display of grief which Statius in such consolations takes pains to emphasise. The book closes with the *Genethliacon Lucani*, which in neat hendecasyllabics congratulates Spain, land of the west, on its gift of Lucan to the world, and extravagantly claims that Homer and Virgil are out-rivalled by him. But we are grateful for the light thrown by the Muse's prophecy on the subjects of Lucan's writings. Nor are the exclamatory lines[4] on a young life cut short unnatural:

> Ah! Fates too cruel and severe!
> Ah! Brief the span of high career!

[1] II. ii. 44 *sqq.*
[2] *Ibid.* 48–49:

> 'Cum iam fessa dies et in aequora montis opaci
> Vmbra cadit uitreoque natant praetoria ponto.'

[3] *Ibid.* 100–106: 'Saepe per autumnum iam pubescente Lyaeo,' etc.
[4] *Ibid.* II. vii. 89 *sqq.*:

> 'O saeuae nimium grauesque Parcae!
> O numquam data longa fata summis!

> Why round the peak must perils rage?
> Why may not greatness reach old age?

Book III opens with a record of the dedication of a temple to Hercules by Pollius Felix at Sorrento on a spot where the old narrow shrine once gave shelter to a picnic party surprised on a hot summer day by tempest. The poet thinks the spacious building has improved what was

> A barren sandy shore but yesterday,
> A hillside which the sea-foam splashed upon,
> Cliffs rough with briar, ground that foothold grudged.[1]

The second piece is a send-off (*propempticon*) to the author's patron Maecius Celer about to sail for Egypt, where, the poem reminds us, the grain ships come from. Echoing Horace, Statius says his patron takes with him the better half of his soul (*animae partem . . . maiorem*), and he dwells on the pain of parting. The gradually disappearing vessel is pictured:

> The barque speeds o'er the wandering tides in flight,
> Faint by degrees, defeating eyes that strain
> Afar, and clasps within its slender boards
> Legions of fears.[2]

His self-recrimination over failure to go abroad with his patron scarcely rings true, especially when supported with mythological instances; but the imagined reunion on the traveller's return and the anticipation of the story of intervening years make a natural conclusion. The third poem is another consolation: it is addressed to Claudius Etruscus on his father's death. The poet too, he says, had mourned a father.[3] The deceased, though of servile origin, was ennobled by service, and obedience is a law of nature. The sketch of his career is interesting. Originally a slave of Tiberius, he attended Caligula as a keeper might a wild beast; he had high responsibilities under Claudius and Nero, probably being manumitted by the former; and his preferment in the civil service to the treasury was a tribute to his ability in dealing with estimates. All this is cleverly told in well-turned verses; and a pleasant account is given of his married life. Unfortunately, artificiality is not absent. The conceit of fluttering Cupids dropping wing-feathers on a funeral pyre or supplying discarded arrow-cases to make fuel for the cremation is supremely ridiculous; and when the grief of Etruscus for the loss of his father is compared with the grief of Theseus in like case, we feel the

---

> Cur plus, ardua, casibus patetis?
> Cur saeua uice magna non senescunt?'

[1] III. i. 12–14.
[2] *Ibid.* ii. 78–80:

> 'Fugit ecce uagas ratis acta per undas
> Paulatim minor et longe seruantia uincit
> Lumina tot gracili ligno complexa timores.'

[3] *Ibid.* iii. 39–40.

mythological parallel detracts from the simplicity befitting a deep sorrow. The fourth poem, one of the least pleasing, turns on the dedication to Aesculapius of the locks of Earinus, one of the emperor's eunuchs. The fifth, on the other hand, has charm in its playful remonstrance with his wife on her alleged reluctance to accompany her husband when he has decided to quit Rome for the Bay of Naples. Could she refuse, after sharing loyally his hours of triumph and defeat, after full knowledge of his literary toil on the *Thebaid*, after nursing him back from the point of death? Facetiously he assures her that her daughter can find suitors elsewhere than in Rome: the district of his choice has not been completely devastated by the fires of Vesuvius! This home to which he invites her is 'his own, his native land' (*natale solum*), blest with temperate climate and with peace. He ends this persiflage with a reminder of the legendary and literary associations of the Bay of Naples.

The first three poems of Book IV are overburdened with the praises of Domitian, and celebrate respectively his Majesty's seventeenth consulship, his hospitality in the banqueting-hall, and his greatness as a road-maker. There follows a poetical epistle counselling Vitorius Marcellus (to whom Quintilian dedicated his *Institutio*) to take a holiday:

> Timely repose incites and nurtures strength,
> And manhood after rest grows manlier.[1]

The one Alcaic lyric of the *Siluae* is a spring-ode to Septimius Severus, a native of North Africa.[2] After it stands the hexametric poem which proves the value attached by Statius to the literary and artistic accompaniments of a dinner-party. Then Sapphics are addressed to Vibius Maximus abroad:

> When will sweet Latium once more welcome you
> From the Dalmatian hills, where, having sought
> In hell, the miner comes back pale, in hue
> Like gold up-brought.[3]

But there is a child at home to greet Vibius: let the child learn from his father the historical skill wherewith he traces the antiquity of the world, recalling the style of terse Sallust and of 'the nurseling of Timavus' (Livy). The eighth poem conveys congratulations to Julius Menecrates on the birth of a third child, so that, as the poet is quick to point out, the emperor's previous concession of the *ius trium liberorum* had merely anticipated Lucina's actual gift. The final piece, addressed in a bantering spirit to a friend on his return-present of a mouldy old book, submits a humorous list of possible cheap things to give away.

---

[1] IV. iv. 33-34:
'Vires instigat alitque
Tempestiua quies, maior post otia uirtus.'
[2] An ancestor of the Emperor Septimius Severus. *Cf. supra*, p. 337.
[3] *Ibid.* vii. 13-16.

Book V begins with the commemorative poem consoling Abascantus in his continued grief over the loss of his wife Priscilla, a dear friend of Statius's wife. Their loyal union is beautifully drawn and makes one of several engaging pictures in Statius of married happiness. Priscilla felt rapturous joy over her husband's attainment to high office in the state, but the raptures did not turn her head:

> Luck never sapped thy calm: thine honest heart
> Swelled not with bliss, but kept the even way.
> High fortune left thee modest as before.[1]

She attended to her careworn husband's wants with the regularity, solicitude, and simplicity to be found in a rural home:

> As thrifty husbandman's Apulian wife
> Or house-dame sun-browned in the Sabine glare,
> Knows, when the stars peep out, the hour has come
> That ends his work, and plies her bustling toil
> O'er bed and board, and hearkens for the sound
> Of the returning plough.[2]

The doom that assailed this favoured home is the prevailing theme in the second half of the poem. The succeeding piece is on a youth of sixteen, Crispinus, going out to face the work of the world, with the inspiring memory of a father's distinguished services. The next, a long 'In Memoriam' on Statius's own father, has been extensively drawn upon in connexion with his life. Like prose *Consolationes*, such an *epicedion* shows conventional features in structure and thought. It is followed by the briefest and most poetic of the *Siluae*. Mackail says 'one might almost call it a sonnet,'[3] and, if certain mythological lines are dropped, it can be reduced to the requisite proportions:

> What crime, O Sleep, thou God of calm confessed
> Brings my young heart alone to lack thy boon?
> Wild things of earth or air in slumber swoon:
> The tree-tops droop the head in mimic rest:
> Loud streams are hushed: the rough sea smooths his breast:
> Fierce waves find peace upon the strand full soon.
> But stars of eve and seventh returning moon
> Behold me ever in pale woe depressed.
> Dawn passing leaves me in her ruth bedewed:
> E'en now some lover, clasping hand in hand
> His love by night, repels thee, Sleep, with zeal.

---

[1] V. i. 117–119.
[2] *Ibid.* 122–126:
> 'Velut Apula coniunx
> Agricolae parci uel sole infecta Sabino,
> Quae uidet emeriti iam prospectantibus astris
> Tempus adesse uiri, propere mensasque torosque
> Instruit exspectatque sonum redeuntis aratri,'
[3] *Latin Lit.* p. 189.

Leave him – not on my eyes full-winged to brood,
As joy might crave. Nay, touch me with thy wand:
Enough if, o'er me poised, thou lightly steal.[1]

In the final poem of the miscellany is a lament on the death of the poet's adopted son which marks the tenderness of his heart. 'I,' he says, 'who once could offer balm to the bereaved now crave the healing hand: and who art thou that censurest my lament?'

> Better detain the flood that breaks its bank,
> Or counter ravening flame than try to bar
> A broken heart from grief.[2]

There are some books – and shall we not include the *Siluae* or still more the *Thebaid*? – of which the reader feels that it were best not too earnestly to plod through them, but when one chances upon the wearisome to leave it as one found it, perhaps preferring my Lord of Montaigne's method 'of running over by divers glances, sodaine glimpses and reiterated reprisings.' To come from a simple and direct kind of poetry to Statius is like passing out of the open breeze into a conservatory of flowers, where many are beautiful but many raise the conviction that they are forced. He had inherited the Alexandrian and Catullan fondness for picture-drawing; and it is a natural result that descriptions emanating from an art-admirer like Statius should be influenced by his recollection of paintings and statues. At the same time this influence removed him one degree further from nature and led to that over-elaboration, which, by leaving little to the reader's imagination, loses the charm of vague suggestiveness.[3] It is a learned and allusive style, apt to be far-fetched in fancy and excessive in eulogy. The *Siluae*, in particular, have the elegance of the eighteenth century. They imply a cultured leisure fertile in refined improvisations. The elegance bears a resemblance to that of Pope and Thomson, and the scenery to that of Watteau's *Fêtes Champêtres*. Some of the missives have a tone that would have suited the boudoir of a French *marquise* or the library of a noble patron of letters in the time of Queen Anne or the early Georges. Nor is it surprising that the *Thebaid* should have made an appeal, if only a transient one, to Gray, whose works contained a fragment of his early translation into heroic couplets of part of its sixth book.

Statius's artificiality is largely apparent in his enslavement to an unreal mythology, but partly also in his liking for literary conceits,

---

[1] From 'Sonnets from the Antique,' by J. Wight Duff in Quatercentenary number of *Alma Mater* (Aberdeen Univ. Mag.) Sept. 1906.
[2] V. v. 62–64:
> 'Potius fugientia ripas
> Flumina detineas rapidis aut ignibus obstes
> Quam miseros lugere uetes.'
[3] See T. S. Duncan, *Influence of Art on Description in Poetry of S.*, diss., Balt. 1914.

O*

which may or may not be mythological. Modern readers are mildly amused at the feather-dropping Cupids (*Silv.* III. iii), or at Leander's fire of love fit to warm the sea but not equal to Stella's love for Violentilla (I. ii), or at the descent from the sky of Domitian's celestial kindred to embrace his equestrian statue:

> Thus one neck shall find room for all the stars! (I. i. 98).

In great part the artificiality was traditional. Thus, when Statius addresses elegiac poets as 'Ye who defraud the renowned verse of its final stride,' he is intentionally aping Ovid's conceit of making Cupid responsible for the change of the heroic hexameter to the pentameter.[1] Often the attempt to make a myth realistic merely succeeds (as with Lucan) in achieving the grotesque: *e.g.* when the ghost of Laius mortally wounded years before is imagined to drop blood on the sleeping Eteocles in *Thebaid* II, or when the deaths of Niobe's fourteen children are arithmetically related to the seven gates of Thebes:

> Two funerals thronged each massive city-gate.[2]

Sometimes the artificiality lies more in the phrasing. It is fairly obvious that 'the bridler of fiery-footed steeds'[3] must be the Sun-god; that, if Hercules is 'soaked plentifully with his brother,' the reference is to the grape juice of Bacchus;[4] and that, when in years a boy 'equalled the sum of Hercules's labours,' he ought to be twelve.[5] Rather more remote is the epithet 'Ledaean' applied to a swan-plume because of Leda's metamorphosis, or the author's mode of suggesting that a cool mansion is free from the scorching summer sun of the Olympic games:

> The house seethes not with heat of Pisa's year.[6]

Again, the artificiality may depend on no allusion, but on a curiously strained form of expression. 'He slants (*obliquat*) his entreaties' is used of entreaties addressed to bystanders; 'they hold exchange of breasts' means embracing; 'she reduced the glades to peace with her horn' means that Atalanta, when hunting, killed the wild beasts therein; and 'the liquid fodder of eastern mid-winter' is a Statian expression for rains that feed the Nile.[7] It is easy to laugh at such lapses from the straightforward and to complain of Statius's artificiality and prolixity: it is easier still, and perhaps commoner, to decry him without reading

---

[1] *Silv.* I. ii. 250–251: 'qui nobile gressu extremo fraudatis opus'; *cf.* Ov. *Am.* I. i. 3–4: 'risisse Cupido dicitur atque unum surripuisse pedem.'
[2] *Th.* III. 198: 'bina per ingentes stipabant funera portas.'
[3] *Th.* I. 27: 'ignipedum frenator equorum.'
[4] *Silv.* III. i. 41: 'multo fratre madentem.'
[5] *Silv.* II. i. 124.
[6] *Silv.* I. iii. 8: 'Pisaeumque domus non aestuat annum.'
[7] *Th.* III. 382: 'obliquatque preces'; *Th.* V. 722: 'alternaque pectora mutant'; *Th.* IV. 248 *sqq.*: 'saltus . . . pacabat cornu'; *Th.* IV. 706: 'Eoae liquentia pabula brumae.'

him. But neither carping nor neglect is the right attitude towards a great influence in literature. More profit is derivable from remembering that he can show, as an epic writer, vigour in narrative and speech, and, as an occasional poet, a real taste for landscape and colour,[1] besides letting his fancy at times go free. Nor should strained compliments, strained consolations, strained mythology wholly obliterate that depth of affection which is nowhere more manifest than in the last book of the *Siluae*.

If he is more Virgilian than Lucan, Statius is less obtrusively rhetorical. There is less of the *sententia*, less epigram, less antithesis, and more of a quiet scholarly elaboration of the traditional epic manner. Thus it is rarer to find in him than in Lucan semi-proverbial phrases of a quotable cast, like 'Panic believes every thing' (*nil falsum trepidis*, *Th.* VII. 131), or 'Hope deferred maketh the heart sick' (*spes anxia mentem extrahit et longo consumit gaudia uoto*, *Th.* I. 322: *cf.* II. 320–321). His elaboration tends to war against pithiness, but some phrases and lines are readily recalled: *e.g. Cur oculis sordet uicina uoluptas?* (*Silv.* I. iii. 98, virtually 'why does distance lend enchantment to the view?'); *calcabam necopinus opes* (*Silv.* I. iii. 53, 'I trod on wealth and knew it not') of a rich mosaic floor; or, from the simile of Pluto's entrance upon his sovereignty over the lower world, words that would fit Milton's Satan, *palluit amisso ueniens in Tartara caelo* (*Th.* XI. 446, 'blenched as he came to Hell when Heaven was lost.').

What we must expect in a style so elaborate is an avoidance of the more simple and concrete modes of expressing ideas and a preference for abstractions, personifications, metaphors, as well as erudition. The lion that, even when mortally wounded, dies fighting to the last is referred to in these abstract terms: 'as he fell, his valour returns from the midst of death and not at once did all his threats present their backs,' *i.e.* turn to flight.[2] Statius makes great use of compound adjectives (*e.g. uuifer, oliuifer, rorifer, laborifer, fumifer, flammiger, saetiger, noctiuagus, montiuagus, fluctiuagus, anguicomus*), also of one of the traditional decorations in epic – the simile. There are well over thirty similes in *Thebaid* VI in connexion with the games, and well over twenty in many of the other books. They are elaborated often to the extent of six lines, sometimes to eight, and show considerable variety. Many that illustrate violent action introduce such animals as lions, tigresses, wolves, bears, boars, bulls; others picture birds in flight like cranes, or twittering like swallows: a snowstorm, a hunter, a passing ship, a ruined nest, a Spanish gold miner underground, an avalanche (which the old Delphin edition illustrates from Rhaetia), or a cow grieving for a lost calf (a passage that

---

[1] He has an eye for colour in marble, woods, a parrot, a peacock, etc., and an evident liking for *uiridis* both in its literal and in its metaphorical sense.
[2] *Silv.* II. v. 17–19:
                 'Virtusque cadenti
A media iam morte redit nec protinus omnes
Terga dedere minae.'

recalls a similar situation in Lucretius). King Adrastus is likened to a victorious bull, and Hippomedon to a Centaur; runners are compared cumulatively to race-horses, arrows, and stags escaping from a lion; and a falling quoit to the moon brought down from heaven by magic. The hexameters of Statius exhibit less montony than do those of Ovid, Lucan, or Valerius Flaccus. He secures this greater variety by dexterity in the use of pauses. His metrical movements are composed with skill, and often are felicitously appropriate to the sense, as in the passage on Night and Sleep in *Thebaid* I, where he brings into juxtaposition a line with five spondees and one with five dactyls, then has a quick line of four dactyls, returns to a slow movement of five spondees, and closes on one where the feet are exactly balanced:

> Titanis late, mundo subuecta silenti,
> Rorifera gelidum tenuauerat aera biga;
> Iam pecudes uolucresque tacent, iam Somnus amaris
> Inrepsit curis pronusque ex aethere nutat
> Grata laboratae referens obliuia uitae.[1]

Computations[2] have been made which show that, while Statius is more dactylic than Virgil, he is less so than Ovid and Valerius. He has fewer elisions than Virgil. Altogether his line falls short of supreme epic dignity. In the *Siluae* his hendecasyllabics, like Martial's but unlike some of Catullus's, regularly begin with a spondee. His two imitations of Horatian lyric metres display small inspiration. But in the *Siluae* his hexameters appear to most advantage, attaining a facility suitable to the lighter and more sportive subjects in the collection. Here, then, Statius is in matter and form most truly himself. He portrays in the main the surface of life, and is acquainted with its amenities and even its pathos; but he does not penetrate into its meaning.

[1] *Th.* I. 337–341.
[2] Butler, *Post-Aug. P.* p. 123, cites statistics from Drobisch, *Versuch üb. die Formen des lat. Hex.* 140.

Chapter VII

MARTIAL AND MINOR FLAVIAN POETRY

Martial's career – Poetry and patronage – Order of his books –
Numeration and fresh editions by the author – His personality –
Relation of literary trifles to real life – Distaste for epic – Varied
assortment of Flavian types – Contemporary Rome envisaged –
The humorous and incongruous – Martial's friends – The epigram before him – His impress on it – Verse-forms and sources –
Comparative absence of rhetoric – Simplicity, wit, polish combined – Pointed end in an epigram – Confidence in popularity and
immortality – Sense of wasted time – Double nemesis of his two
great faults – Adulation and coarseness – The sentimental side –
Poems on the dead – On friendship – On natural scenery – Quotability – His influence.

Minor Flavian poetry – Maternus's post-Neronian plays – Saleius
Bassus – Poets under Domitian – Lyrics by Spurinna – Epics by
Cerialis and Codrus – Erotic poems by Verginius Rufus, Arrun-
tius Stella and Sulpicia – Satires by Turnus – Tragedies by
Scaeva Memor and Canius Rufus.

MARTIAL

M VALERIUS MARTIALIS was a native of Bilbilis in Spain.
In his tenth book, which belongs to A.D. 95–98, he celebrates
his fifty-seventh anniversary,[1] so that his birth fell between 38
and 41. His cognomen was due to his having been born on the first of
March.[2] While he claimed descent from Iberians and Celts,[3] his name
indicated Roman citizenship. His parents, Fronto and Flaccilla,[4] secured for him a literary education to which he owed an incalculable debt,
although in a fit of cynical depression in his fifties he says:

> My foolish parents taught me poetry,
> But what were dominies and dons to me?[5]

Already intellectually well-equipped when over twenty, he left Spain

---

[1] X. xxiv.
[2] IV. lii. 3. Why the surname *Coquus* was added in the Middle Ages remains a
mystery.
[3] X. lxv. 3–4.   [4] V. xxxiv.
[5] IX. lxxiii. 7–8:
> 'At me litterulas stulti docuere parentes:
> Quid cum grammaticis rhetoribusque mihi?'

in A.D. 64 to find a wider scope for his abilities in Rome, which had grown so cosmopolitan that its population struck his fellow-Spaniard Seneca as made up more of foreigners than of citizens.[1] This first immigrant – a young 'compatriot of the Tagus' with bristling Spanish hair, as he describes himself[2] – had before him a reasonable prospect of success as a lawyer or a speaker; but he did not choose to employ his training in oratory. What attracted him was verse-writing, with the patronage which verse might win. The common link with Spain explains why Seneca and Lucan were his earliest patrons; but the introduction to society in the capital begun under such auspices was followed next year by the ruinous implication of both patrons in the Pisonian conspiracy against Nero. The career to which he had turned, or drifted, was sure to be one of vicissitude and disillusion; and Martial had frequent cause to recognise that only the few among clever poets or obsequious clients could scrape a living, while the rest starved (*pallet cetera turba fame*).[3]

We read of juvenile productions which an enthusiastic bookseller would not let die;[4] but virtually Martial's life is a blank for the first sixteen years of his residence in Rome (A.D. 64–80). What his works make certain is that he gained an intimate acquaintance with all grades of society, the highest and the lowest. Some honours came his way, of a kind that indicate his possession of more influence than money. He became a *tribunus militum*, perhaps without seeing military service; he was confirmed in the accompanying title of *eques* without possessing the means to support the position;[5] and he had obtained from two princes the *ius trium liberorum*[6] without being a father – in fact, the tone of his work throughout argues the bachelor.[7] It is doubtful if his plot of farmland at Nomentum was in his hands early enough to have been a gift from Seneca, as has been guessed; but whether it came from him, or from Lucan's widow Polla, or from someone else, it must have often afforded a welcome change after his third-floor back-room in the sweltering city.[8] Later, he had a small house of his own on the Quirinal.[9] Neither from Caesar, however, nor from grandee did Martial ever obtain as much as he expected and craved. As it was, he survived by adroitness in courting the favour of well-to-do citizens so as to earn personal

[1] *Ad Helv.* vi.
[2] X. lxv. 4–7: 'Tagique ciuis. . . . Hispanis ego contumax capillis.'
[3] III. xxxviii. 12.   [4] I. cxiii.   [5] *Trib. mil.*, III. xcv. 9; *eques*, V. xiii. 1–2.
[6] II. xci, xcii; III. xcv. 5, where 'Caesar uterque' may imply conferment of the *ius* by Titus on the recommendation of his brother Domitian, or Domitian's confirmation of a concession promised by Titus. Schanz mentions Lieben's view that the 'two Caesars' were Vespasian and Titus: S.H. § 412.
[7] 'Valebis uxor,' II. xcii. 3, means 'farewell to you, the wife of my imagination' or 'farewell to the idea of a wife.' The wife addressed in an indecent manner in another epigram could not conceivably have been his own.
[8] For Nomentum, II. xxxviii; XII. lvii; XIII. xlii, cxix; 'scalis habito tribus sed altis,' I. cxvii. 7.
[9] IX. xviii. 2, xcvii. 7–8.

presents or the dole of the *sportula*. If he was temperamentally unfit to do anything but write verse, it is hard to see what other opening there was, apart from a way of life indistinguishable from sponging. For the surmise that he practised at the bar there is no justification either in the advice he quotes from a person whom he asked for a loan, 'if you want to be rich, plead cases,' or in the poem he addressed to Quintilian.[1] In spite of the fact that his verses had a sale, there was no such reading public as could ensure returns adequate for his maintenance: so pique at times made him argue that, if money-making is the supreme object, parents ought not to spend on education: much better make a boy something practical, a musician, an auctioneer, or an architect.[2] For himself, he felt obliged to live, whatever scoffers might say about the necessity; and consequently had to capture patrons to be the props of his subsistence and, as he believed, the indispensable conditions of poetic production (*sint Maecenates, non derunt, Flacce, Marones*, VIII, lvi. 5).

His first publication known to us was the *Liber Spectaculorum* of A.D. 80 which commemorated the opening by Titus of the Flavian Amphitheatre familiar now as the Colosseum. Though anything but inspired, the surviving thirty-three poems of this group throw interesting light on the contests of the arena. Some four years later appeared the collections, almost entirely of couplets, which are usually printed in defiance of chronology, as Books XIII and XIV of the *Epigrams*. They owed their occasion to the *Saturnalia* in December, when gifts might be sent to guests (*Xenia*) or taken home from the festive board (*Apophoreta*). The 127 pieces of the one, and 223 of the other were nearly all meant as suitable mottoes for such presents. Luckily Martial was capable of cleverer work. Epigrams of his had appeared before 86 when he published, perhaps together, the first two books of those which made his fame. Allusions enable us to date his volumes with fair closeness, and, while there are a few complications due to revised editions and collected issues, it is broadly true that from 86 until his return to Spain in 98 he brought out a new book about once a year. Taken together, his poems, few of them other than quite short, constitute one of the most extraordinary galleries of literary pictures, vignettes, miniatures, portraits, caricatures, sometimes almost thumbnail sketches, that have ever made a past society live again in the mind's eye. While grace in the sight of the emperor commended him to those in high places, including the worst creatures at court like the notorious Crispinus and Paris, there were many at the other end of the social scale, needy and seedy outcasts, to whom Martial's Bohemian indigence introduced him. He observed all. He is one of the great spectators in literature. But the vanity of the whole spectacle recurrently depressed him. Unremunerative attendance at the receptions of the great as well as disgust at loathsome vices which he exposes, contributed towards his tedium. Once weariness

---

[1] II. xxx. 5; II. xc.   [2] V. lvi.

drove him to Cisalpine Gaul, whence he issued an edition of Book III.[1] In the very next book[2] he is hankering after Venetia as a retreat for his old age. Yet years passed before he could tear himself away from Rome where, despite its drawbacks, he knew all the literary men of the day. At last in 98 the sense of monotony told. The ordinary expenses of life seemed as hard to meet as ever, and the old scenes in Spain, never wholly forgotten during more than the third of a century, came back now with alluring insistence to his mind:

> While four-and-thirty harvests passed away,
> Others gave Ceres rustic cakes at home;
> But I, inhabiting fair sovran Rome,
> Have turned in Italy from dark to grey.[3]

Perhaps too some occult warfare in his soul between spirit and sense made him realise, as never before, the emptiness of the life around. At any rate the Flavian régime had suited him best; for under Nerva and Trajan a new age had dawned, when sycophantic blandishments were futile and *rustica ueritas* had been restored (X. lxxii). His well-to-do friend, the younger Pliny, found money for the impecunious poet's journey to Spain. There, settled at Bilbilis on land granted to him by a patroness Marcella, he could indulge to the full that yearning for a quiet retreat which he revealed in lines addressed to the great satirist of the time:

> Mayhap, my Juvenal, your feet
> Stray down some noisy Roman street, . . .
> While after many years of Rome
> I have regained my Spanish home.
> Bilbilis, rich in steel and gold,
> Makes me a rustic as of old. . . .
> Outrageous lengths of sleep I take
> And oft refuse at nine to wake.
> I pay myself nor more nor less
> For thirty years of wakefulness.[4]

Missing the stimulus of the capital, he let three years elapse before his twelfth and last book was sent out from Spain in 102. He did not long survive its publication; for Pliny in a letter belonging to A.D. 104 mentions his death, adding the criticism that he was a man of talent, subtlety and vigour, whose writing was characterised by abundance of wit and pungency, but no less frankness.[5]

The form in which Martial's works have come down calls for brief remark. Imperfect though the book of *Spectacula* is, the missing portions

---

[1] The 'liber prior' of III. i. 3 was either a previous edition of III or a combined edition of epigrams afterwards separated into Books I and II, as Friedländer thought (ed. 1886 *ad loc.*).

[2] IV. xxv.   [3] X. ciii. 7–10.   [4] XII. xviii. 1–2, 7–9, 13–16.

[5] Plin. *Ep.* III. xxi: 'erat homo ingeniosus acutus acer, et qui plurimum in scribendo et salis haberet et fellis nec candoris minus.'

are perhaps a greater loss to archaeology than to literature. In the *Xenia* and *Apophoreta*, unlike the later books, short headings (*lemmata*) are given to which the reader is facetiously told he may, if he likes, confine himself; and the presents of the *Apophoreta* are arranged in pairs, expensive and less expensive. As regards the existing division into books, the numeration was Martial's own,[1] though some books, as we have them, are not exactly as originally issued. For instance it is inconceivable that his first book was from the beginning entitled 'Liber Primus,' with the implication that he was certain of success enough to justify future issues, still less is it conceivable that in the original issue of his first book he could have been described as *toto notus in orbe Martialis*. His preface to Book II, which defends the innovation of an introductory prose epistle, reads as if it were written before the preface to Book I; and this latter preface, by speaking of 'little books' (*libelli*) in the plural, suggests that it could not have been added till more than one book of epigrams had appeared – probably when a collected edition of I–VII was issued. Among the later books, X and XI, originally belonging to A.D. 95 and 96 respectively, had an Anthology made from them in 97; and a second edition of X came out in 98.[2] Interesting prose prefaces are given to Books I, II, VIII and XII, while a few lines of prose at the opening of IX introduce verses for the poet's bust in Stertinius's library. The preface to I offers an apology for the coarse outspokenness in the epigrams, with a significant list of literary predecessors; that to Book II is, as mentioned, an apology for an introductory epistle, in answer to the objection *epigrammata curione non egent*; that to VIII professes that there has been less indulgence here than elsewhere in the licence of the mime; and the last preface is an apology for slackness in publishing, since Martial's retreat to Spain has deprived him of his stimulating Roman environment.

Martial, in his epigrams, reveals himself, and, even more, the company he kept. With him we enjoy the luxury of an intimacy unusual among writers of the Silver Age. Seneca, it may be said, opens his philosophic heart, yet he does not make – it is hardly imaginable that under Nero he should make – a complete self-revelation. Juvenal's outspokenness is that of indignant censure rather than of personal confession. But Martial is naked and unashamed: he does not hide his thoughts, and even those quick flashes in which he divines the thoughts of others still further illuminate his own. Thus his personality is reflected in his themes, and is inseparable from the things he described and the men he loved or hated. A spectator of life, he was yet no detached

---

[1] II. xciii refers to Books I and II. The author in V. ii calls the book his fifth, and refers to the preceding four. The arrangement (to date) in seven books is mentioned VII. xvii. 6.

[2] Friedländer's chronology is generally accepted with slight modifications. It is not seriously upset by A. Dau, *De Mart. libellorum ratione temporibusque*, Rost. 1887. *C*. S.H. § 413.

spectator, but in a sense a part of his own observations, so that his resolve
to reflect his surroundings leaves him at the same time essentially autobiographic. We become familiar, then, with his poverty, his mendi-
cancy, his contempt for shams, his confidence in his literary powers, his
pride in Spain, his determination to pander to readers by spicy attacks
on the uncleanest vices. At times he seems a sort of Villon, never so
much of a gallows-bird as the French poet, nor ever master of so deep
a note of anguish, but yet like him in Bohemian neediness and in direct
vigour of style.

In the last resort, the key to his personality, to his style, to his reputation, to everything that matters respecting Martial, is to be found in this
attitude towards life. Life afforded the inexhaustible material whence
he recognised it was his special *métier* to draw. His brief poems – some
of them butterfly flights as brief as Japanese *tankas* – might be trivialities, but they at least sprang from the actual. There is a sort of double
antinomy in him. On the one hand, he often calls his verses *nugae* or
ioci, as if he made no higher claim for them than the knack of amusing;
yet he is insistent that they are not mere flippancies:

> He misses what is meant by epigram
> Who thinks it only frivolous flim-flam.[1]

On the other hand, he explains elsewhere[2] that he could write seriously,
but prefers to write entertainingly – the secret of his vogue. At the
same time, he cannot make a living out of pleasantries: instead, he gets
praise and starves:[3] so he jocularly even threatens to turn lawyer! In
fact, however, though he said, and showed, that he could write seriously,
he seldom chose to. The sportive, the flippant, the ludicrous, and often
the indecent, appealed to him irresistibly; for the truth is that he wrote,
like all literary artists, because it was his pleasure:

> For all their compliments, do verses pay?
> They mayn't, yet these same poems make me gay.[4]

But he would not have been human, he would certainly not have been
Martial, if he had not expected an adequate return from verses that
entertained or flattered; and occasionally his tone appears to meditate a
sort of literary strike – *pas d'argent, pas de poésie*:

> A man on whom my poetry
> Pronounced a handsome eulogy
> Pretends that he owes naught to me –
> I call this downright trickery![5]

---

[1] IV. xlix. 1–2:

> 'Nescit, crede mihi, quid sint epigrammata, Flacce,
> Qui tantum lusus illa iocosque uocat.'

[2] V. xvi. 1.   [3] V. xvi. 13–14.   [4] V. xv. 5–6.
[5] V. xxxvi:

> 'Laudatus nostro quidam, Faustine, libello,
> Dissimulat quasi nil debeat: inposuit.'

No writer ever more clearly recognised his field. In the third poem of Book VIII he pretends to hesitate over multiplying epigrams – five books, six, seven are already out and the whole collection is thumbed everywhere (*teritur noster ubique liber*): there should be some stint and limit (*sit pudor et finis*). Here the rebuke from the Comic Muse Thalia is significant: 'Abandon your charming trifles! But what better thing is an idle singer (*desidiosus*) to do? Not tragic drama surely? Not epic? No, Martial's function is to hold the mirror up to the manners of the day':

> Nay, dye your Roman booklets smart with wit
> That Life may read and know the portraits fit.[1]

The claim is also well illustrated in his objection to mythological twaddle – an objection sufficient to account for a radical lack of sympathy with Statius, the only prominent poet of the time whom he does not name:

> What profit empty myths in sorry lays?
> Read this of which Life says 'It is my own.'
> No Centaurs here, Harpies, or Gorgon face
> You'll find: my pages smack of man alone.[2]

This confident acceptance of life as his great exemplar explains the variety and truth of Martial's pictures. He knew that he could portray his fellows with a sure hand; and his conviction that his forte lay in light verse reflecting manners and morals gave him an assurance that his work had force enough to last. It is essentially Flavian Rome that he drew; for, though his writing continued under Nerva and the first few years of Trajan's reign, nine books of epigrams had come out under Domitian. The repression of the Reign of Terror, which for Tacitus meant fifteen years of silence, did not affect the sort of verse which Martial composed. It was spicy, but not at the expense of the emperor or the imperial system. All contemporary types appear in Martial's pages (*hominem pagina nostra sapit*). They range from Domitian himself, haloed beyond recognition, down to the vilest of characters to whom Martial owed no flattery and of whom to tell the truth was to produce a shudder. Since fun comes easiest at the expense of human weakness, there is a predominance of types in some way objectionable. Hence a multitudinous array of spongers, dinner-hunters, fortune-hunters, bores, coxcombs, charlatans, topers, freaks, stingy hosts, and incorrigible reprobates. But if there are false friends there are also

[1] VIII. iii. 19–20:
> 'At tu Romanos lepido sale tingue libellos:
> Adgnoscat mores uita legatque suos.'

[2] X. iv. 7–10:
> 'Quid te uana iuuant miserae ludibria chartae?
> Hoc lege, quod possit dicere uita "meum est."
> Non hic Centauros, non Gorgonas Harpyiasque
> Inuenies: hominem pagina nostra sapit.'

firm ones, there are faithful slaves as well as faithless, moral wives as well as immoral, and genuine poets as well as poetasters. The eye for detail is remarkable: nothing is too slight for mention: the hawker of sulphur and the purchaser of broken glass are not overlooked any more than a wealthy *connoisseur* of artistic treasures. Such pieces as the neat summary of how the hours in a Roman day were spent convince one that Martial saw things as they were, whereas Juvenal, though possessed of an unchallenged sense of picturesque realism, tended to overlay his subject with violent exaggeration or with a thesis-like treatment in the manner of the rhetorical schools.

Thus to turn over Martial's leaves in the most casual way transports one to ancient Rome. There we find the Stoic heroine and hero, Arria and Paetus, face to face with death; and intimates of the author who have to be admonished about using life aright, or welcomed home, or reminded of the enjoyable ideals of the unambitious, or urged, on the principle of Satan reproving sin, to decide on a profession (*dum quid sis dubitas iam potes esse nihil*). We can enter a private library; we can join in the despatch of marriage greetings, or condolences under bereavement or congratulations to a lucky person on the prospect of a long holiday which will send him back sun-burnt to the pale dwellers in town. We can see artistic triumphs in a handsomely enchased wine-bowl, or an antique bronze statuette. Again, we may listen to the author's petition for the *ius trium liberorum*, his request for a supply of domestic water from the Aqua Marcia, or his many growls over the burdensome duty of calling on patrons, over paltry presents (some folk, he observes, send less and less each December!) and over the failure of patrons to maintain him fittingly; he is, he complains, not so well sheltered as his patron's orchard-trees:

> I've got a room where window-draughts do play –
> One where the very North Wind wouldn't stay![1]

But it is not solely for town life that he has an eye. We note the almost Dutch detail in some of his sketches of rustic scenes. Especially out on Faustinus's estate with its steading, the corn in heaps, the wine in casks, the barn-yard fowls, the labourers' work, the rural fare, he appears to reveal in 'the genuine country, uncivilised' (*rure uero barbaroque*).[2] He envisages for us a real farm in Spain free from the formal dress of Rome, and provided with shade against the summer heat, and against the winter cold with a wood fire surrounded by grubby youngsters.[3]

True to the author's promise, there are many figures that amuse – the dry-as-dust antiquary spoiling his wine-parties by tedious rigmaroles about the pedigree of his silver goblets, the prosy pleader in court who

---

[1] VIII. xiv. 5–6.   [2] III. lviii.
[3] I. xlix. 27–28: 'focum infante cinctum sordido'; *cf.* II. xc. 7–8; XII. xviii. 19–21.

needs hours to make a few legal points, the counsel who sagaciously
blushes in preference to stating his client's full case, the guest who arrives
too late for breakfast but too early for lunch, and the too prolific poet
who finds no time to revise his hasty compositions:

> You write two hundred lines 'twixt each sunrise,
> But never read them, silly! – yet how wise![1]

The element of humour in Martial was largely due to a keen sense of the
incongruous. He could not help chuckling at the notion of keeping about
eight birthdays each year to secure presents, or at the huge Gaul who
sprained his ankle and was glad to be carried home on a pauper's bier,
or at the nuisance who rummages a shop for *objets d'art* and gives endless trouble without buying enough to compensate for it.[2] Again there
is the decidedly plain lady who takes care to frequent the company of
ladies still plainer so as to appear a beauty by comparison:

> Your friends, Fabulla, either are
> Old crones or beldames uglier far:
> These frumps you trot around with you
> To parties, plays, and galleries too:
> And so, my dear, such hags among
> You look quite pretty and quite young![3]

Ailments and the medical profession are the subjects of many jests.
There was the rebellious client who pretended to have gout in order to
avoid calling on his patron, but who, after hobbling about swathed in
wrappings, finally got the genuine disease; there was the patient who
died because he dreamt of his medical man overnight; there was the ex-
physician who turned undertaker and therefore had undertaken the
same undertaking for the sick as before; and there was the doctor who
on his clinical rounds gave a sufferer fever:

> When I was ill, you came to me,
> Doctor, and with great urgency
> A hundred students brought with you
> A most instructive case to view.
> The hundred finger'd me with hands
> Chill'd by the blasts of northern lands:
> Fever at outset had I none –
> I have it, Sir, now you have done.[4]

Such alert perception of the incongruous made him scoff at shams –
the cupboard love that acts friendship with a view to hospitable invitations, the lady whose artificial aids to beauty leave her with no face of
her own, the hypocrisy of pretended philosophers who were at heart
dissolute reprobates.[5]

---

[1] VIII. xx.   [2] IX. lix. 22: 'asse duos calices emit et ipse tulit.'
[3] VIII. lxxix.   [4] V. ix.   [5] IX. xiv, xxvii, xxxvii.

Ability to see the ludicrous side of things is always an entertaining social recommendation. With the literary circles of the day Martial was on familiar terms. He sends lines to Lucan's widow on an anniversary of the poet's birth, he records Caesonius's fidelity to Seneca in exile, and shows patriotic pride in mentioning the Spanish birthplace of the Senecan family.[1] Quintilian, Arruntius Stella, a writer of polished verse, and a poet Flaccus[2] were among his friends. Despatching poetry to the younger Pliny, he good-humouredly quizzes him on his serious work at the bar: the judicious moment of festive relaxation 'when rose-leaves reign, when locks are scent-bedew'd' must be chosen for the presentation of Martial's trivialities.[3] With Silius Italicus he was well acquainted: would that epic poet, 'pride of the Castalian sisterhood,' he asks, deign to spare some leisure for the sportive trifles which he begs to forward? Just so, he suggests anachronistically, might Catullus have sent his *Sparrow* to Virgil![4] He also shows interest in Silius's activities and expresses sympathy for him in bereavement.[5] But no one, he felt, could embroil him with so true a friend as Juvenal, to whom he wrote after his retirement to Spain and whose distaste for long-winded epics he plainly shared.[6] As regards Statius, who often wrote about the same things and people as Martial did, their mutual silence must have been due to incompatibility of temperament. Martial's circle included also the orator Aquilius Regulus, whom Pliny could not bear; Antonius Primus from Toulouse, who helped as a commander to secure the Empire for Vespasian; Julius Martialis, a close intimate; Q. Ovidius, a country neighbour at Nomentum; wealthy knights like Atedius Melior and Claudius Etruscus; but also many people less prominent like the centurions Varus and Pudens. While he gives the real names of friends, it is to his credit that he uses disguised names for the victims of his satire. Disclaiming any intention of hurting (*ludimus innocui*), he declares that his concern is to attack not persons but vice (*parcere personis, dicere de uitiis*).[7] Consequently, resentful at having scurrilous verses fathered on him, he draws a lurid picture of the punishment which ought to befall a slanderous poet.[8] The systematic backbiter, he agrees, may be called malign; but, with a fine touch of human feeling, he adds:

> I think he needs our pity who likes none.[9]

The epigram in Martial is to be distinguished from, even if related to,

---

[1] VII. xxi, xxii, xxiii, xliv, xlv; I. lxi. 7–8.
[2] Probably not the author of the *Argonautica*.   [3] X. xix.
[4] IV. xiv. By *Passerem* (l. 14) he means a collection of Catullan poems with no. ii ('Passer, deliciae' etc.) standing first. See A. L. Wheeler, *Catullus and the Traditions of Anc. Poetry*, Berkeley (Calif.) 1934, p. 19 ff.
[5] VII. lxiii; IX. lxxxvi; XI. xlviii.
[6] VII. xxiv, xci; XII. xviii; *cf.* Juv. I. 7–14 with Mart. X. iv. 7–10.
[7] VII. xii. 9; X. xxxiii. 10.
[8] X. iii, v.   [9] V. xxviii. 9: 'ego esse miserum credo cui placet nemo.'

the epigrammatic in contemporary rhetoric, whether prose or verse. In Martial it is a short independent verse composition, not one of a series of glittering ornaments in a continuous poem, history, or oration; that is, it constitutes a miniature unity; and there is a notable freedom from the forced conceit with which the epigrammatic is often allied in writers like Lucan. The epigram reached Rome from Greece in the form of a brief poem originally inscriptional in character, as its name implies. But the Greek ἐπίγραμμα itself had gone through a wide evolution since Simonides of Ceos employed it for the tomb of the Spartans who fell at Thermopylae. Beyond its use for epitaph, memorial, dedication, or gift, the elegiac metre in particular had been devoted, with its Greek quality of delicate and finished charm, to occasions which in modern times would be considered essentially lyrical. The impression made by a passing event or inward experience found utterance in a brief poem: the poem might convey the feeling produced by a landscape, a book, a storm, an artistic work, a misfortune, a mental disturbance, a friendship, an affair of the heart. In contrast therewith, the Roman tendency, on taking over from the Greeks this ill-defined branch of lyric, was to sacrifice the poetic flavour to point, and most of all to the point that stings. Hence, losing much of the lyric charm of the Greek, the epigram was largely transferred to the service of satiric purposes. Catullus, though certainly not wanting in true lyric quality, gave to the elegiac that bent towards invective which was more definitely associated with the abusive iambic. In this latter field, it is noticeable that Diomedes,[1] describing the bitter iambic, names, along with the Greeks Archilochus and Hipponax, the Latin writers Lucilius, Catullus, Horace and Bibaculus. Now Martial owns his obligations and traces his freedom of speech (*lasciuam uerborum ueritatem*)[2] to Catullus, Domitius Marsus, Albinovanus Pedo, and Lentulus Gaetulicus of Caligula's reign. Roman *dilettanti* of the Empire liked composing such verses, and it is among the freaks of time that, though many authors like Marsus, Pedo, Gaetulicus, Seneca and Petronius wrote epigrams, too little has survived in this *genre*, outside Martial's collection, to afford a criterion of their individual contribution. Clearly, however, the march of literature had worked changes that could not fail to affect Martial. By his days, satire and rhetoric had both played a great part. He is but following the traditions of the epigram in maintaining its essential elements of concise expression and unity of idea; but he owes a debt to satire for his width of range (Juvenal's *farrago libelli*), his dramatic vigour, his scraps of dialogue, his reflective pieces, his mordant wit and irony. So too, although he is not enslaved by rhetorical artifice, he knows how to make use of rhetorical point, as the culmination – usually a stinging culmination – up to which the rounded whole of a short poem should lead. His satiric epigrams, then, mark the close of the evolution of this partly lyric

[1] Keil, *G.L.* I. p. 485.   [2] I. *praef.*

type.[1] Hence Martial's individual impress on the epigram is permanent. With him it reached that fixity of form which it has retained up to modern times.

In a total of 1,561 epigrams in the *Spectacula* and fourteen other books, 1,235 are in elegiac metre, 238 in hendecasyllabic, and 77 in choliambic or scazon. There are, besides, a few in hexameter and iambic verse. The elegiac distich is common, and is almost the only form among the 350 pieces of the *Xenia* and *Apophoreta*. Often, however, his elegiac poems run to ten or a dozen lines, occasionally to twice that length. When the delights of Faustinus's farm tempt him to write 51 scazons, or when a dinner menu needs 32 hendecasyllabics, one hesitates whether to call these epigrams at all. Vigorous and correct in versification, his metres are in felicitous accord with the theme and spirit of his various pieces. With great skill he can employ the elegiac to express tender sentiment or weighty compliment, the hendecasyllabic for sportive and ironic occasions, and the scazon for trenchant invective. But, if the mood takes him, he can equally adapt the elegiac to satiric, and both hendecasyllabics and scazons to descriptive purposes. Martial's favourite verse-form, the elegiac, is based, though not pedantically so, on Ovid: lines and phrases are occasionally taken from him, but Martial does not strictly adhere to the Ovidian ending of the pentameter on a disyllable. Typical endings such as *hospitibus, ingenio, undecies, amicitiae* show that here, as elsewhere, he is under the influence of Catullus. It is upon Catullus principally that his hendecasyllabics and choliambics are founded, with the notable difference that Martial, departing from the Catullan freedom in the opening foot of the hendecasyllabic, restricts himself to a spondee. In style and metre we can trace some echoes of Virgil, Horace, and the *Priapea*; and, to a less degree, of Tibullus and Propertius. Nor was the pointed manner of his early patrons Seneca and Lucan without effect on him,[2] Greek authors too have their share in his sources, but, on the whole, he is remarkably independent of models. Sometimes he appears to do little more than continue the kind of popular tradition found in the smarter *graffiti* at Pompeii. This, for example, is not unlike his manner:

> I wonder, wall, that you have not gone smash –
> You've had to bear so many scribblers' trash.[3]

Low life and the commonest objects came under his survey and saved him from bookish pedantry. The workaday spoken Latin of the *caballus* type, and words which many Romans would have shrunk from uttering (as we know from Cicero), enter into his pages, alongside of language

[1] *Cf.* C. W. Mendell, 'M. and the Satiric Epigram,' *C.P.* xvii (1922) p. 1 ff.
[2] *Cf.* G. Friedrich, 'Zu Seneca und M.' *Herm.* xlv (1910) 583–594.
[3]   'Admiror, paries, te non cecidisse ruinis,
          Qui tot scriptorum taedia sustineas.'

sanctioned by exalted literary usage. This range of vocabulary is proportionate to the width of his outlook, which contemplated, perhaps occasionally with too heartless an indifference, the ugly as well as the beautiful. His unabashed persistence in observation and his conscious power of natural portrayal left him free to use at will, or not to use, the literary predecessors whom he had studied. On subjects drawn direct from life he writes with a finished neatness of expression and a freshness that reads like improvisation. Over and over again, his natural themes appear to fall into natural phrases. It is a straightforwardness that gives him, for all his debt to patterns, the unmistakable ring of originality. In literature there is only one Martial.

Rhetoric is in the main absent from one who, primarily interested in man, wrote as a realist. His most representative work is simple, with little of that Spanish note of excess which one detects or suspects in several of his compatriots, from the violent Porcius Latro onwards, not excepting Lucan and at times Seneca himself. Martial feels no attraction to mythology, though a court-poem might involve a few learned allusions. He is content that elevated epics should be praised, admired, even adored, so long as his own verses are read. Hence the fundamental contrast, and therefore presumably the antipathy, to Statius[1] already mentioned. Hence too the justification for Martial's pronouncement: 'all turgid rhetoric (*omnis uesica*) is foreign to my writings: my muse swells not in wild tragic robe.'[2] Conformably thereto, he has a genial way of disarming criticism by making no high claims:

> Here are excellent bits, you will find,
> And bits of a so-and-so kind:
>   Still more than the latter
>   Are bad bits – no matter!
> All sorts in a book are combined.[3]

In another piece he admits that, while tossing off epigrams may appear simple, the crux lies in making a book; and, again, the criticism that a book of his shows marked inequalities is answered by the contention that this is in its favour, because a bad book is of uniform quality![4] No author ever passed a more honest criticism on his work. It is just this unevenness that makes Martial a successful surprise. Alongside of plain-speaking – the plainest of the plain – the reader may chance upon poems which prove in him an exquisite sense of beauty. If the seaside or a pretty name engages his fancy, he rises to a style in keeping with the subject. There are no finer scazons in Latin than those he wrote on 'the sweet strand of genial Formiae' to rival the Catullan scazons on Sirmio:

---

[1] While Statius is never mentioned, it is likely that there are indirect glances at him; *e.g.* IV. xlix; VIII. iii; IX. l; X. iv; XIV. i. 11.
[2] IV. xlix. 7–8.
[3] I. xvi.   [4] VII. lxxxv, xc.

Here Thetis' face is ruffled by
A gentle wind: the waters lie
Not in dead calm, but o'er the main
A peaceful liveliness doth reign,
Bearing gay yachts before a breeze
Cool as the air that floats with ease
From purple fan of damozel
Who would the summer heat dispel.[1]

So the liquid consonants of the admired 'Springtide Lad' (*Earinos*)
seem to run over into his enthusiastic hendecasyllabics on

A name with violets and roses born,
Name that the loveliest time of year hath worn,
Fragrant of Hybla and of Attic thyme
Or of the nest where dwells the bird sublime,
A name sweet heavenly nectar to outvie,
One that fair Attis would be callèd by,
Or he that blends the cup for Jove on high,
Which, uttered once in the Parrhasian Hall,
Would make the Powers of Love sing madrigal.[2]

So beauty of idea is combined with neatness when he sends a rose-
wreath to a friend:

Go, happy rose, with thy soft chaplet bind
My own Apollinaris' locks; and see
One far-off day, when they are white, thou wind
Rose leaves around them: so may Love love thee![3]

There the pedigree of the opening movement in Waller's 'Go, lovely
rose' and Herrick's 'Go, happy rose' is evident. Much, indeed, that
might be called Herrickian comes from brief pieces like

Polla, why send me wreaths of blooms new-born?
I'd rather handle roses *you* had worn.[4]

This neatness in expression underlies the characteristic suspense of

[1] X. xxx. 11-15:
'Hic summa leni stringitur Thetis uento;
Nec languet aequor: uiua sed quies ponti
Pictam phaselon adiuuante fert aura;
Sicut puellae non amantis aestatem,
Mota salubre purpura uenit frigus.'

[2] IX. xii. 1-9:
'Nomen cum uiolis rosisque natum,
Quo pars optima nominatur anni . . .
Respondent Veneres Cupidinesque.'

[3] VII. lxxxix:
'I felix rosa, mollibusque sertis
Nostri cinge comas Apollinaris:
Quas tu nectere candidas, sed olim,
Sic te semper amet Venus, memento.'

[4] XI. lxxxix.

point until the concluding line, phrase, or even word of an epigram –
the typical manner of Martial familiar to us from imitations in neo-
Latin writers, in writers of our own eighteenth century and in Byron,
on the bee-like principle that

> The body should always be little and sweet
> And the sting should be left to the tail.

Very often, whether the piece is a brief couplet or a more extended set
of elegiac, choliambic, or hendecasyllabic verses, the surprise and the bite
come at the end. The epigram thus constitutes an artistic 'period.' Such
is the force of the sharp *tussit* of I. x: 'What is the inducement that lures
Gemellus to propose marriage to Maronilla? Why does he long, plead,
implore, send presents? Is she pretty? Nay, none so ugly! What is the
bait and charm then? Why, her churchyard cough!' – an ugly but
effective close on the attraction of a consumptive heiress for a fortune-
hunter.[1] So he retorts on a person whose absence would be a good rid-
dance:

> You ask me, Linus, what my field
> Out at Nomentum is to yield:
> Well, this it yields to me: the view,
> My Linus, has no sign of *you*.[2]

He makes fun of unwelcome kisses:

> With half your lips, my Postumus, you kiss.
> Thanks: you may take a half away from this;
> But would you give me joy beyond compare?
> Then keep the other half of that half-share.[3]

Again, less briefly than, but to the same effect as, Mr. Punch's advice to
those about to marry, he writes on a debtor's going to law to dispute a
claim:

> The judge expects a fee from you,
> Your lawyer looks for payment too –
> Best pay your creditor his due![4]

From the idea of uniting in wedlock a much widowed widow with an
equally bereaved widower he extracts grim fun:

> Fabius buries all his wives:
> Chrestilla ends her husbands' lives.
> The torch, which from the marriage-bed
> They brandish, soon attends the dead.
> O Venus, link this conquering pair!
> Their match will meet with issue fair,

[1] *Cf.* with I. x. 4 such endings as II. xi. 10: 'domi cenat'; II. xxix. 10:
'splenia tolle, leges.'   [2] II. xxxviii.   [3] II. x.
[4] II. xiii:

> 'Et iudex petit, et petit patronus:
> Soluas, censeo, Sexte, creditori.'

> Whereby for such a dangerous *two*
> A single funeral will do.[1]

He introduces us smilingly to a Roman hairdresser:

> There once was a barber called Smart
> Who plied his tonsorial art
> Over Wolfaway's face;
> But in spite of his pace
> A new beard was ready to start.[2]

He jeers at the systematic diner-out:

> Philo declares he never dines at home,
> And that is no exaggeration:
> He has no place whereat to dine in Rome,
> Unless he hooks an invitation.[3]

This last is a frequently imitated form in which the apparent confirmation of the first statement leaves the final state of the victim worse than the first. A similar effect is got by an apparent contradiction of the original statement:

> 'Tis said Acerra reeks of last night's wine:
> 'Tis false: he always drinks till morning-shine.[4]

Just as elsewhere we trace the legacy of Martial in some of the gallantry of Cavalier poets, and as his 'Non amo te, Sabidi' descends to 'I do not like thee, Dr. Fell,' so this corrective form of epigram is the prototype of such quips as Samuel Rogers's:

> Ward has no heart, they say; but I deny it:
> He *has* a heart – and gets his speeches by it.

An engaging blend of modesty and confidence is an ingredient in the variety of Martial. At times, by way of pose, he may wish to give the impression that, like Byron, he 'rattles on exactly as he'd talk' and that his verses are of little consequence:[5] at other times, he is both proud of his popularity and confident of his permanent place in literature. The emperor read him (II. xci): so did ministers of state and men of letters (VI. lxiv. 8–10): everybody at Rome did, in fact (VI. lx). He was pointed out (*monstramur digito*, IX. xcvii. 4), and people whispered 'There he is!' (V. xiii. 3). Such a vogue had he that it was possible to find a nuisance of a person who could repeat Martial by heart and decline to stop! (VII. li). In mock-heroic strain he declares:

> Lo! I the man for trifles unsurpassed:
> You mayn't admire me, but I hold you fast.

---

[1] VIII. xliii.
[2] VII. lxxxiii:
> 'Eutrapelus tonsor dum circuit ora Luperci
> Expingitque genas, altera barba subit.'
[3] V. xlvii.   [4] I. xxviii.   [5] I. xvi; VII. lxxxi.

> Great themes are for great bards: enough to see
> You oft re-reading my light poetry.[1]

His naughty jests (*nequitiae*, VI. lxxxii. 5) were known to everyone who
had not a Dutchman's ear: no wonder, then, that his circle of readers
should be as wide as the world (I. i. 2; V. xiii. 3; VIII. lxi. 3). He was
flattered to realise that he was a favourite in Vienne (VII. lxxxviii):
his poems might be despatched to one person, but would be read by all
(*uni mitteris, omnibus legeris*, VII. xcvii. 13). Away among the Goths a
centurion thumbed his Martial (*a rigido teritur centurione liber*), and
Britain learned to repeat his verses (XI. iii. 3–5). His books went
through different editions; they were on sale by Secundus in parchment
binding (I. ii. 3, 7–8), suitable for travellers; or at Atrectus's shop, smart
in purple (I. cxvii. 13–17); or at the establishment of Trypho (IV. lxxii),
who was Quintilian's publisher. Furthermore, his juvenile verses could
be had in collected form (I. cxiii), and plagiarists stole from his works.
Yet even a 'best seller' in ancient Rome could not ensure handsome
returns: Martial significantly takes satisfaction in the thought that anyone can make money, but not everyone can be a poet (V. xiii. 9–10);
for he has a fine consciousness that a book, to live, must possess an
indwelling spirit (VI. lxi. 10). No doubt crosses his mind about his own
literary survival (X. ii. 7–12), or about the immortality which mention
by him can confer (V. xv. 3–4). Nobodies, therefore, must not expect
to have their names perpetuated in his verse (V. lx. 6–7).

Alongside of this confidence, however, there rings out a note of
impatient fretfulness. Weariness of the bustle in the Vanity Fair of Rome
brought to this merry companion his intervals of heart-searching. Surrender day by day to the solicitations of purely trivial circumstance produced a natural revulsion against such waste of time. Led by a too facile
compliance into insipid society, he awakes upon occasion to a sense of
paltry achievement and lost opportunity. Etiquette, he felt, wars with
poetry:

> I walk you out: I see you home:
>   I listen, sir, to all your chatter.
> Your words and deeds I praise through Rome –
>   D'you think it really doesn't matter?
> Yet all this time I might instead
> Have fashioned poems in my head. . . .
> Tell me, Labullus, is this right?
> Can any call it honour bright
> That just to swell *your* client-crew
> The books *I* write should be too few?
> About a month has gone so fleet
> I've hardly filled a single sheet.
>   In this the poet is the sinner
>   If he won't stay at home to dinner.[2]

[1] IX. *praef.* 5–8: 'Ille ego sum. . . .'   [2] XI. xxiv.

The same fretful malady of the age troubled him when he wrote to his namesake Julius Martialis on making the best of time:

> Defer not joys thou mayst not win from fate:
> Judge only what is past to be thine own.
> Cares with a linkèd chain of sorrow wait.
> Mirth tarries not; but soon on wing is flown.
> With both hands hold it – clasped in full embrace,
> Still from thy breast it oft will glide away!
> To say 'I mean to live' is folly's place:
> To-morrow's life comes late; live, then, to-day.[1]

The same friend is reminded that social duties may hamper one in living one's own life:

> If you and I, dear Martial, might
> Enjoy our days in Care's despite,
> And could control each leisure hour,
> Both free to cull life's real flower,
> Then we should never know the halls
> Of patrons, or law's wearying calls,
> Or troublous court or family pride;
> But we should chat or read or ride,
> Play games or stroll in porch or shade,
> Visit the hot baths or 'the Maid.'
> Such haunts should lure us constantly:
> Such should engage our energy.
> *Now* neither lives his life, but he
> Marks precious days that pass and flee.
> These days are lost, but their amount
> Is surely set to our account.
> Knowledge the clue to life can give:
> Then wherefore hesitate to live?[2]

[1] I. xv. 5–12:
> 'Non bene distuleris, uideas quae posse negari,
> Et solum hoc ducas, quod fuit, esse tuum.
> Exspectant curaeque catenatique labores;
> Gaudia non remanent, sed fugitiua uolant.
> Haec utraque manu complexuque adsere toto:
> Saepe fluunt imo sic quoque lapsa sinu.
> Non est, crede mihi, sapientis dicere 'Viuam';
> Sera nimis uita est crastina: uiue hodie.'

[2] V. xx.
> 'Si tecum mihi, care Martialis,
> Securis liceat frui diebus,
> Si disponere tempus otiosum
> Et uerae pariter uacare uitae,
> Nec nos atria nec domos potentum
> Nec litis tetricas forumque triste
> Nossemus nec imagines superbas;
> Sed gestatio, fabulae, libelli,
> Campus, porticus, umbra, Virgo, thermae,
> Haec essent loca semper, hi labores.
> Nunc uiuit necuter sibi, bonosque

Yet in spite of this discontent over a partially spoiled life, it may be doubted whether Martial was capable of more than he accomplished. He could only be himself. While he ought not to be called entirely shallow, he lacked the profundity which might have made him other than a laureate of the occasional.

The two glaring faults in Martial, servility and obscenity, brought each their own nemesis: where he is most flattering he is least simple, and where he is most indecent he is least witty. Both defects sprang from his circumstances. Never wealthy, he found in adroit dedications a more likely source of profit than in book-sales. Subservience towards patrons, on whose uncertain favours he had to rely, was inevitable. Hence adulation of the emperor, cringing to exalted personages, and continual clamour for bounty. He flattered Domitian because there was no choice. In touch with court, he could not logically keep out of his verse the official title of 'Lord and God' assumed by the emperor: not belonging to the political opposition, he had no doubt a genuine belief in the imperial system; and, as the most fulsome compliments were acceptable, he resorted to mendacious homage. It is not merely that it appears historically ludicrous in Martial to apply to Domitian the epithet of chaste (*pudicus*) or to commend one of his own volumes as fit to be read without a blush by that permanently red-faced prince; but it is also, as already suggested, noticeable that he pays a literary penalty for his moral weakness herein by deviating from his usual straightforwardness of style. In the midst of his extremest sycophancy, he becomes artificial owing to the intrusion of over-ingenious conceits. Thus, it is grotesque to assert[1] that Rome envies the barbarians with whom Domitian has been warring in person, because they were lucky enough to see the emperor's face, whereas the poor capital had to be content with the laurel-wreathed despatch of victory. And no one can take seriously the far-fetched absurdity of his congratulations to the enemy on seeing Domitian's face at close quarters and in that countenance finding material for both terror and rejoicing. Similar extravagance marks his welcome on his Majesty's return from Dacia.

> Come, Caesar, e'en by night – let stars delay;
> If thou but come, thy folk will find it day.[2]

His argument, also, in favour of making requests to the divine emperor is far too clever; 'it is not the sculptor of an image who makes a god; it is the man who prays.'[3]

Martial's indecency palls no less than his adulation. We are not amused. The foulest epigrams force on the reader a resilient disgust as if

---

Soles effugere atque abire sentit,
Qui nobis pereunt et imputantur.
Quisquam, uiuere cum sciat, moratur?'

[1] VII. v.   [2] VIII. xxi. 11–12.   [3] VIII. xxiv. 5–6.

from some sickening contagion; and repeated shocks end in boredom. Conceivably it was a salutary instinct that prompted the quaint idea of a Delphin editor to remove from their original place in the text all the unsavoury epigrams into a *musée secret* at the end of the volume, in which might be taken one nauseating draught of concentrated impropriety. They number more than 150 or over ten per cent of the whole. Many open out vistas down by-lanes of hideous vice. It might be argued that even the foulest practices of sexual inverts had to be included in a complete picture of pagan Rome; and that there was much to which an avowed realist could not shut his eyes. Perhaps just because in their naked *Romana simplicitas* the worst epigrams are so repulsive, they might, though filthier, be considered less pernicious than Ovid, or than a sex-encumbered modern novel, which often lacks Martial's truth to life. Here we have a repellent rather than an erotic obscenity. The author realises that some apology is needed for overstepping the limits of propriety. His poems are not for the prim and prudish, who are in set terms warned away with the mischievous suggestion that the warning will only whet their curiosity.[1] Certain of his books he can recommend as respectable:[2] in general, however, he does not address children but the seasoned onlookers at the Floralia and folk of easy morality.[3] So the freedom of Book XI is defended by the licence of the Saturnalia.[4] The fundamental excuse offered is one which not a few Roman writers were at pains to make by way of protest against any assumption that he who composes foul verses must himself be foul. Martial's declaration 'our page is wanton but our life is clean'[5] is couched in terms similar to those used by Catullus and Ovid, and practically repeated by Pliny, Apuleius and Ausonius.[6] The attitude suggests that the author had no objection to giving readers the particular spice they wanted: sometimes a fine poem is marred by a gross jest reserved as a surprise.[7] Beside so much nauseating coarseness, the claim of *ludimus innocui* (VII. xii. 9) may sound ironical; yet this can be said by way of comment, if not of palliation – he is not a slanderer, for in general real names are avoided. If victims were foully satirised, it was left to themselves or others to fit the cap. He resents the impudent dishonesty of a verse-writer who 'vomits viperous venom' under Martial's name.[8]

His character is too complex to be satisfactorily analysed on psychological principles. Whether one thinks of a superman as well as a subterman within the same self, or thinks of the surprising contradictions in him as liberated at different crises from the oubliettes of a chequered

---

[1] III. lxviii. 4, 'exuimur'; *cf.* 11–12.
[2] V. ii; VIII. i.   [3] I. *praef.*; III. lxix.   [4] XI. ii.
[5] I. iv. 8: 'lasciua est nobis pagina, uita proba.'
[6] Cat. xvi. 5; Ovid, *Tr.* ii. 354; Plin. *Ep.* VII. ix; Apul. *Apol.* 11; Auson. *Eidyll.* 360 ff. (= Bk. xvii – *Cento Nuptialis* – 132 ff.).
[7] *E.g.* VII. xiv.
[8] VII. xii. 7. *Cf.* his desire to have it known that poems steeped in black poison are not his, VII. lxxii. 13–16.

experience, the diversity of his genius remains beyond full explanation. If one side belonged to a realm where ethics and ideals seemed contraband, he presented another side in which sentiment under various aspects prevailed. Wrapped up with the sentiment on this more kindly and genial side there is admittedly some conventionality: the Greek tradition may act in one place, and the Latin tradition through poets like Catullus in another. A certain amount of sentiment may be due to the growth of more humane feelings in his age, as is traceable in Seneca. Yet a large portion must be ascribed to Martial's own disposition. These phases of sentiment are most observable in his attitude to the dead, his genius for friendship, and his love of nature.

His best known epitaph, that on a little girl Erotion, bespeaks for her spirit in the land of shades the sheltering protection of his own parents Fronto and Flaccilla, who had gone before. It ends.

> Soft be the turf that shrouds her! Tenderly
> Rest on her, earth; for she trod light on thee.[1]

This conclusion, suggestive of the 'sit terra tibi leuis' in sepulchral inscriptions, was twisted to malicious effect by Martial himself on a disreputable person:

> Light may earth's crumbling sand be laid on thee
> That dogs may dig thy bones up easily![2]

Long afterwards it was parodied in reference to the massive buildings of the architect Vanbrugh:

> Lie heavy on him, earth! for he
> Laid many heavy loads on thee.

A slave-boy is thus commemorated:

> Dear Alcimus, Death robbed thy lord of thee
>   When young, and lightly now Labican soil
> Veils thee in turf: take for thy tomb to be
>   No tottering mass of Parian stone which toil
> Vainly erects to moulder o'er the dead.
>   Rather let pliant box thy grave entwine;
> Let the vine-tendril grateful shadow shed
>   O'er the green grass bedew'd with tears of mine.
> Sweet youth, accept the tokens of my grief:
>   Here doth my tribute last as long as Time.
> When Lachesis *my* final thread shall weave,
>   I crave such plants above my bones may climb.[3]

---

[1] V. xxxiv. 9–10:
> 'Mollia non rigidus caespes tegat ossa nec illi,
>   Terra, grauis fueris: non fuit illa tibi.'

[2] IX. xxix. 11–12;
> 'Sit tibi terra leuis mollique tegaris harena
>   Ne tua non possint eruere ossa canes.'

[3] I. lxxxviii.

P

In the following dirge on a youth from North Italy who has died in Asia
Minor there is a manifest sense both of the poet's personal loss and of
the blow to the bereaved father.

> My Sixth Book, Rufus, thou canst never greet:
> It may not look, friend, to be read by thee.
> Thine ill-starred sojourn in the cursèd East
> Restores but bones and ashes to thy sire.
> Widow'd of Rufus, come, Bologna, weep:
> Ring out lament thro' all Aemilia!
> How great a love, how young a life is lost!
> (*Heu qualis pietas, heu quam breuis occidit aetas!*)
> He had but seen a fifth Olympiad.
> Ah, Rufus, wont with mindful heart to quote
> My trifles and recite my jests in full,
> Accept thy sorrowing friend's brief tear-stained song
> And deem this incense offered from afar.
> (*Accipe cum fletu maesti breue carmen amici*
> *   Atque haec absentis tura fuisse puta.*)[1]

Kindly affection towards associates came easily to Martial. Q. Ovidius's
birthday and his own he considers

> Days that all others in the year transcend:
> One gave me birth: the other, more – a friend.[2]

Enthusiasm animates his admiration for Decianus:

> If there be one to rank with those few friends
> Whom antique faith and age-long fame attends;
> If, steeped in Latin or Athenian lore,
> There be a good man truthful at the core;
> If one who guards the right and loves what's fair,
> Who could not utter an unworthy prayer,
> If one whose prop is magnanimity,
> I swear, my Decianus, thou art he.[3]

Again, in a brief review of an intimacy of thirty-four years with Julius
Martialis, he finds it has contributed on the whole to happiness, but
pathetically fights against the notion of making friendship too warm,
lest its loss prove overwhelming:

> Good comrades, Julius, have we been
> And four-and-thirty harvests seen:
> We've had the sweet mixed with the sour,
> Yet oftener came the happy hour.
> If for each day a pebble stood,
> And either black or white were hued,
> Then, ranged in masses separate,
> The brighter ones would dominate.

---

[1] VI. lxxxv.   [2] IX. lii.   [3] I. xxxix.

> If thou wouldst shun some heartaches sore
> And ward off gloom that gnaws thy core,
> Grapple none closely to thy heart –
> If less thy joy, then less thy smart.[1]

Martial's appreciation of the country was inspired by something deeper than the relief felt by a jaded town-dweller. His ideals may not have been mightily exalted, but he had the poet's eye for landscape and colour, and therewith a gift of fancy. Nowhere does he seem more poetic in his attitude towards external nature than in his lines on Vesuvius visited some years after the terrible eruption of A.D. 79. The poem has the interest of treating volcanic soil, which made both a practical and an imaginative appeal to the Romans.[2] The poet's recollection of the old fertile greenery and cool shadows of the vines (*hic est pampineis uiridis modo Vesbius umbris*) contrasts with the bare desolation of the land now buried beneath the mournful ashes of the volcano (*cuncta iacent flammis et tristi mersa fauilla*). Then an exquisite touch of romantic imagination pictures the vine-slopes as once haunted by the Wine-god, near the dancing-places of the Satyrs (moderns might fancy them as gnomes and elves) – a region where Pompeii enjoyed the patronage of the Queen of Love and Herculaneum was called after the renowned demigod:

> This is Vesuvius where but late 'mid vines
> Green shadows played, and noble clusters filled
> The brimming vats. This is the very ridge
> More dear to Bacchus e'en than Nysa's heights.
> On this same mount the Satyrs yesteryear
> Did foot their frolic dance: here Venus found
> A sweeter home than Lacedaemon gave.
> A city here bore Hercules' great name:
> Now all lies whelm'd in fire and ashes dread,
> And Heaven might well repent such fatal power.[3]

So the poem ends in a tone of heartfelt sorrow over beauty destroyed, while other pieces are full of a healthy delight in fresh air and country scenes. A plane-tree might set his fancy roaming into fairyland:

> Oft 'neath this tree the tipsy fauns have played,
> And the late pipe hath scared a silent home.

[1] XII. xxxiv.
[2] W. Warde Fowler, *Presidential Address to Class. Assoc.*, 1920, pointed out that, while volcanic soil influenced drainage schemes, it also set the Romans adventuring on the search for portents.
[3] IV. xliv: 'Licuisse' in the closing couplet,

> 'Cuncta iacent flammis et tristi mersa fauilla:
> Nec superi uellent hoc licuisse sibi'

is surprisingly taken to refer to auction-bidding by W. J. Courthope, *Selectns. fr. Martial Translated*, Lond. 1914:

> 'Now for the place 'neath these sad ashes hid,
> If up for sale, what single god would bid?'

Fleeing the midnight Pan o'er lonely mead
Oft 'neath its leaves the woodland Dryad lurked.[1]

Nature could bring him lively sensations of sight and smell, so that he
scents the fragrance from the myrtle, from the vine flowering white in
its first clusters, and from the grass newly nibbled by the sheep.[2] Such
images for the moment at least shut out the revolting vices of the city.
His own career in restrospect, when he left Rome for ever, contained
much to dissatisfy him. But though he had fallen short of the noblest
ideals, his experience enabled him to appraise aright the value of a good
conscience in a review of bygone years. To this thought he has given
admirable expression:

Good men make life a twofold span to last:
Twice doth he live who can enjoy his past.[3]

The pith of style which contributed to Martial's vogue in his own day
has always kept his poems alive; for quotability favours the preservation of literary work. Among his memorable sayings, in addition to the
couplet just quoted, are 'To live is not a life – one must live well' (non
est uiuere sed ualere uita, VI. lxx. 15); 'Tomorrow's life comes late –
live then today' (sera nimis uita est crastina, uiue hodie, I. xv. 12);
'Accept the lot thou hast – prefer naught else' (quod sis esse uelis nihilque
malis, X. xlvii. 12); 'He hath no home whose home is everywhere'
(quisquis ubique habitat, Maxime, nusquam habitat, VII. lxxiii. 6), which
suggests his curt apostrophe to the owner of a spacious but comfortless
mansion, 'How well you are – not housed!' (quam bene non habitas!
XII. 1. 8). His dislike of shams appears in 'There is a gulf 'twixt goodness and pretence' (refert sis bonus an uelis uideri, VIII. xxxviii. 7).
Many sundials have repeated his reflection on the flight of 'sunny days
that are lost but set to our account' (soles . . . qui nobis pereunt et imputantur, V. xx. 12–13); and there is educational wisdom in the hint 'Boys
who keep fit in summer learn enough' (aestate pueri si ualent satis dis-
cunt, X. lxii. 12). For literary production he values patronage: 'Give us
but patrons – Virgils will not fail' (sint Maecenates, non derunt, Flacce,
Marones, VIII. lvi. 5); but he goes deeper when he says 'To live, a book
must have a soul within' (uicturus genium debet habere liber, VI. lxi. 10),
which is in keeping with ''Tis not a reader your books need but Apollo'
(non lectore tuis opus est sed Apolline libris, X. xxi. 3). On the risk of publishing too many books he reminds himself 'The rare delights: so early
fruits please best' (rara iuuant: primis sic maior gratia pomis, IV. xxix. 3).

Martial's influence began to act on Juvenal,[4] and remained operative
throughout antiquity. Fathers of the Church showed knowledge of him,

---

[1] IX. lxi. 11–14.   [2] III. lxv. 3–5.
[3] X. xxiii. 7–8:
        'Ampliat aetatis spatium sibi uir bonus: hoc est
            Viuere bis, uita posse priore frui.'
[4] Cf. Mart., I. xx. 4; Juv. V. 147.

and grammarians found illustrative material in his words and phrases. During the Renaissance he was much studied and edited. His hendecasyllabics were constantly imitated by the neo-Latin poets of Italy and France for satiric purposes. None followed more keenly in his steps than the Hungarian Janus Pannonius (1434–1472), who, besides modelling his epigrams in freedom of utterance upon Martial's elegiacs and hendecasyllabics, enthusiastically praised him as a 'father of sportive poetry and of wit' (*ludorum pater et pater leporum*)[1] to be invoked in preference to Apollo and the Muses. Alongside there also flows (what is present in Martial himself) the stream of Catullan influence observable in the easy though occasionally solecistic *Basia* of the *Pancharis* by Jean Bonnefons (Bonefonius) printed in Paris in 1587.

Then the influence passed over from Latin into the epigrammatic writing of all modern literatures. Even the couplets of the *Xenia* bore fruit; for from them sprang the sarcastic *Xenien* in which Goethe and Schiller confronted dullness and satirised their literary enemies. Although in quite recent times the epigram may have been less cultivated, in his own field Martial remains, as a pattern, supreme.

MINOR FLAVIAN POETS

The minor and lost poetry of the Flavian era reaches a considerable amount. Vespasian, though an enemy to philosophers, gave financial encouragement to rhetors and poets. Both his sons, Titus and Domitian, wrote poems; but the latter, after his accession, did little for poetry, unless we put to his credit the continuance of Capitoline and Alban competitions which ministered to his pride by eliciting laudatory verse. Curiatius Maternus, best known from Tacitus's *Dialogus*, has been included among poets of the Neronian age, when his career as dramatist began. His tragedy of *Thyestes*, however, and his *praetextae* entitled *Domitius* and *Cato* belong to Vespasian's reign. The epic poetry of Saleius Bassus may have been, like that of Valerius Flaccus, based on mythology. Statius's father was more attracted by current themes.

Under Domitian, dilettanti might keep the path of safety, if they confined themselves to such compositions as erotic poems, conventional epic, eulogies and colourless occasional verse for recitation before friends, or for public competitions or for private exchange with other literary men. The authors were the kind of persons whom we meet in Statius, Martial or the younger Pliny. A considerable list could be drawn up from these three sources; but it may suffice to select, in lyric, Vestricius Spurinna,[2] a military commander on Otho's side; in epic, Julius Cerialis

---

[1] *Poemata*, Utr. 1784, p. 563.
[2] Plin. *Ep.* II. vii. 1; III. 1. Four mutilated choriambic odes, ascribed by some to Spurinna, are convincingly rejected as forgeries: for text, Baehrens, *P.L.M.* V. 408. *Cf.* J. Held, *Ueber d. Werth d. Briefsammlung des jüng. Plinius in Bezug auf Gesch. d. röm. Lit.*, 1833.

and the Codrus or Cordus whose *Theseid* is mentioned in Juvenal's second line; in erotic verse, Verginius Rufus, an elderly friend of Pliny's; Arruntius Stella, consul in 101, author of passionate poems on Violentilla, whom he afterwards married; and Calenus's wife, Sulpicia, to whom the later so-called satire of Sulpicia in seventy hexameters should not be ascribed.[1] Turnus succeeded in writing satire and yet surviving at the court of Domitian.[2] His brother Scaeva or Scaev(i)us Memor, we have seen, wrote tragedies, as did Canius Rufus, along with others mentioned by Martial and Juvenal. There are also traces of lost *palliatae* and *togatae*. Neither these, however, nor productions like the *Agaue* by Statius prove that there was any real renascence of drama. It had fallen on evil days.

[1] *Sulpiciae Fabella*, ed. Unger, Halle 1887. Contained also in O. Jahn's 1868 and subsequent edd. of Persius and Juvenal and in Baehrens, *P.L.M.* V. 93. Both Calenus's wife and the ‘Sulpicia’ of the satire should be distinguished from the Sulpicia of the *Corpus Tibullianum*.
[2] Valla's schol. on Juv. I. 20; Mart. XI. x.

PART IV

Literature under Nerva and Trajan

A.D. 96–117

Chapter I

PLINY THE YOUNGER AND MINOR CONTEMPORARIES

Early life – Problems in chronology – Later career – Poems – Orations – The *Panegyricus* – The amplified speech – Flattering picture of an ideal prince – *Epistulae* – Roman success in letter-writing – The essay-like epistle – Contrast with Cicero's letters – Plinian parallels in eighteenth century – Correspondence with Trajan – Pliny's gentlemanliness – Passion for literary pursuits – Naïve vanity – Religion and politics – Composite style – Neologisms – Influence.
Pliny's literary circle and minor contemporaries – Verse – History and Oratory – Jurisprudence – Scholarship – Gromatics.

PLINY THE YOUNGER

THE Latin name of the younger Pliny after his adoption under his maternal uncle's will in A.D. 79 was C. Plinius Caecilius Secundus. Previously he had been called P. Caecilius Secundus, and was one of the sons of L. Caecilius Cilo, a man of substance belonging to the old northern family of the Caecilii at Comum (Como). Pliny thus retained his gentile name instead of changing it to Caecilianus according to the republican mode. He was born at Comum,[1] in either 61 or 62; for he says he was in his eighteenth year when his famous uncle lost his life in the eruption of Vesuvius, August 24th, A.D. 79.[2] His father's early death left him under the guardianship of the distinguished general Verginius Rufus, who twice refused the imperial purple: to him and to his uncle he owed guidance in his studies. There was no public teacher at Comum (a disadvantage which Pliny sought to remedy in later years), so that his education in the north must have been conducted either privately or at Milan. In time, however, he went to Rome and studied under Nicetes Sacerdos and Quintilian.[3] The elder Pliny's example and precepts kept his nephew assiduously employed: even a walk was frowned upon, and on the occasion of the fatal eruption the youth was engaged on a literary exercise set him by his uncle, and was also working on Livy.[4] Such teaching and his own diligence led to

---

[1] 'patria mea,' *Ep*. IV. xxx. 1.   [2] VI. xx. 5.
[3] VI. vi. 3; II. xiv. 9–10.   [4] III. v. 16; VI. xvi. 7, xx. 5.

his early appearance as a pleader; for he argued his first case in his nineteenth year.[1] This was in Titus's reign; thereafter, under Domitian, he filled a round of offices and built up a reputation by speaking, sometimes in the Senate, but mostly in what he calls his special 'arena,' the centumviral court for the trial of lawsuits about disputed properties or successions.[2] The literary works, however, by which he is known belong almost entirely to the time of Nerva and Trajan, and are therefore post-Flavian.

Except Cicero, no Latin author is so well-known to us. We have a full self-revelation in his letters, while a few inscriptions record his *cursus honorum*.[3] Yet, clearly though his personality stands out, teasing puzzles remain, affecting his life and works. For these problems brief mention must suffice. Ever since Mommsen published his elaborate article 'Zur Lebensgeschichte der jüngeren Plinius' in *Hermes* in 1869,[4] discussion has continued on the dates when Pliny held certain of his offices and on the interconnected question of the dates when the different books of the epistles were written and issued. Though finality has not been reached, some of Mommsen's pronouncements have been controverted, and doubts thrown upon his basic conception that Pliny is misleading his readers, with a view to produce a false impression of fine carelessness, when he declares that the letters are not in chronological order. Mommsen used his findings on the chronology of the letters as a foundation for his account of Pliny's life. It is impossible here to enter into the arguments with which critics have assailed him or each other.[5] After all, however important such details are in the interests of historical accuracy, it does, from the standpoint of pure literature, make little difference, if, for example, Mommsen was wrong (led wrong perhaps by implications in his own theory)[6] as to Pliny's tenure of office at the *aerarium Saturni*, or if he was right in assigning Pliny's praetorship to 93.[7]

[1] V. viii. 8.

[2] VI. xii. 2: 'in harena mea, hoc est apud centumuiros.'

[3] *C.I.L.* V. 5262 (=Dessau, *I.L.S.* 2927), 5263, 5264, 5667. V. 5279 (=Dessau, *I.L.S.* 6728), records appointment of three trustees (one of them the younger Pliny) to administer a fund left by his father Cilo to provide oil at the Neptunalia for athletes and bathers at Como.

[4] =*Gesamm. Schr.* iv. 366.

[5] Merrill's complete ed. of the *Epistulae*, Lpz. 1922, gives a list of the principal *Abhandlungen* on the subject by Stobbe, Gemoll, C. Peter, Asbach, Schultz and H. Peter. Schanz (S.H. § 447), gives a useful summary of their conclusions; and the reports on Plinian literature in Bursian's *Jahresberichte* reveal still more extensive activity. *Cf.* Merrill, *Sel. Lett.*, London 1903, p. xxxvii ff.

[6] E. T. Merrill, whose authority on Plinian matters is deservedly great, undermines Mommsen's position here: 'On Date of Pliny's Prefecture of Treasury of Saturn,' *A.J.P.* xxiii (1902) p. 400 ff.

[7] W. A. Bährens, 'Prätur des jüng. Pl.,' *Herm.* lviii (1923) p. 109 ff., agrees that Otto's instructive paper on Pliny's *Lebengeschichte* in *Sitzb. Mun.* 1919 corrected several of Mommsen's results, but rejects Otto's date of A.D. 95: 'Plinius war, wie schon Mommsen meinte, in Jahre 93 Praetor.' Otto replied in *Sitzb. Mun.* 1923. Allain, *Pline le jeune*, I. 288, gives 94.

Nor is there any stagnation in Plinian textual criticism, as the issue of editions in this century proves;[1] and, though a literary history is not directly concerned with an author's MSS., it is difficult to forget that the sole written copy on which Pliny's correspondence with Trajan rests has long since been lost, and that the establishment of the text in the other books of letters – not an easy matter – depends on a right assessment of three distinct families of MSS.[2]

Fortunately, the essential facts of Pliny's life are beyond dispute. He went through the two preliminary stages of a civil career by performing in the 'vigintivirate' the duties of assisting the praetor as *decemuir stlitibus iudicandis* and by serving in garrison abroad as military tribune in Syria. After his return to Rome, he received the compliment of being appointed *seuir* of the *equites*; he held the quaestorship 89–90, tribunate of the people 91–92, and praetorship in 93. An imperial dispensation abolished for him the usual interval between tribunate and praetorship. He was, then, praetor in a year signalised by Domitian's determined endeavour to quell what he considered a 'Stoic Opposition.' How far Pliny did or could help his Stoic friends cannot be determined. He is at some pains at a later date to declare that he supported the philosopher Artemidorus with money and a personal call of sympathy outside Rome, and to indicate that he was himself the subject of a secret information;[3] but Pliny had a hazardous position to fill, especially in 93, as a magistrate, as a recipient of the emperor's favour, and as a temperamental objector to anything like martyrdom. Further confidence was shown in 94, when Domitian made him one of the three prefects of the military treasury. Discretion and the right sort of silence brought him safely to Nerva's reign, when his business experience recommended him for nomination early in A.D. 98 to the prefecture of the *aerarium Saturni*. Nerva died before the end of January; but Pliny was confirmed in his prefecture by Trajan, who, two years later, in September, 100, promoted him to a suffect consulship. It was on assuming the chair in the Senate that Pliny pronounced before the emperor the *Panegyric* which was the spoken basis of the over-elaborated oration that survived. A break in magisterial duties ended a few years later, when Trajan granted him a seat in the college of augurs in succession to a revered friend, Julius Frontinus: next came his commission on the Tiber

---

[1] *E.g.* Kukula, ed. 1912, noticed J. Wight Duff, *C.R.* xxviii (1914) pp. 134–137; E. T. Merrill, 1922, noticed J. P. Postgate, *C.R.* xxxvii (1923) pp. 35–36. *Cf.* Bibl.

[2] E. K. Rand, who with E. A. Lowe published (Washington 1922) the facsimile of the uncial remains of the *Letters* now in the Pierpont Morgan Library, N. Yk., has indicated a new method of approach through the Aldine edition, in the belief that these fragments form part of the lost Codex Parisinus which Aldus used for his ed. of 1508 (*Harv. Stud. in Cl. Phil.* xxxiv, 1923). Merrill did not accept this identification or the 6th cent. date suggested for the uncials (*C.P.* 1923).

[3] III. xi; VII. xxvii. 14.

Conservancy Board, involving superintendence of the banks and channel of the river and the drainage of the city. When Trajan, therefore, had taken over from the Senate the badly managed province of Bithynia, he paid a well-deserved compliment to Pliny's executive and financial ability by letting his choice fall upon him as his special and personal representative. The emperor knew him intimately, and on one occasion summoned him as an assessor in trials heard by his Majesty at Centum Cellae (Civita Vecchia), some forty-seven miles distant from Rome.[1] The evidence on the whole points to A.D. 111–113 as the period of two years during which Pliny was governor in Bithynia.[2] It may have been only in his second year of office that he found time to extend his movements beyond Bithynia proper, and to visit the eastern or Pontic part of his province.[3] Presumably he died in harness: at least the correspondence comes to an abrupt close. In the last letter of his which we have, he mentions having sent his wife back to Italy post-haste on account of her grandfather's death, and the emperor's reply ends the collection.[4] It is not wholly unfitting that this mainly official book should conclude with a domestic touch. Pliny was deeply attached to his third wife, Calpurnia: what he writes of her shows how much he appreciated her interest in his work: what he writes to her when they are separated shows that a love letter was within his capacity.[5]

Pliny's marriages brought him no children, but Trajan conferred upon him the *ius trium liberorum* in 98. Generous to friends, he showed munificence to his native town during his lifetime by presenting and endowing a library, devoting a sum to the support of freeborn boys and girls, and promising to pay one-third of the salary for a professor of rhetoric. The longest of the inscriptions[6] concerning him proves his bequests for baths, for the maintenance of a hundred freedmen, and on their death for banqueting the townsfolk.

Of poetry we should scarcely have suspected him, but that he pleads guilty, and is manifestly anxious to be thought capable of composing the lightest of light verse. Pliny endeavouring to be naughty or even frivolous is difficult to conceive. However, he had tried his hand at a variety of forms; at a Greek tragedy, when he was fourteen, and later at Latin elegiac, epic and hendecasyllabic verse.[7] An epigram by Cicero on Tiro tempted him once to use his midday siesta for poetic composition; and the thirteen hexameters which resulted show that he had much

---

[1] VI. xxxi.
[2] E. G. Hardy, ed. of *Epist. ad Traian.* Introd. p. 24 ff. and footnote to Letter xv, pp. 105–106.
[3] Such is U. Wilcken's view, *Herm.* xlix (1914), in opposition to Mommsen, who placed Pliny's visit to the eastern parts of the province in the latter half of his first year. Wilcken thinks that in late autumn of 112 Pliny took ship to Sinope, and that after this he wrote from Amisus the famous letter touching the trial of Christians.
[4] X. cxx and cxxi.
[5] IV. xix; VI. iv, vii; VII. v.
[6] *C.I.L.* V. 5262 = Dessau, *I.L.S.* 2927.
[7] VII. iv. 2–3.

better have slept.[1] The eight elegiacs of versified advice preserved elsewhere as one of his sportive trifles (*lusus*) are mediocre.[2] Yet he is proud to have issued a volume of hendecasyllabic poems, which, he says, are read, sung to music, and actually lure Greeks to study Latin. 'I simply pray,' is his complacent remark, 'that future ages may endorse the mistake or the appreciation of my contemporaries.'[3] But the ages have not spared the book.

Pliny felt still more pride in his oratory as a basis of fame. Much of his speaking must have been too strictly legal for preservation; but there were occasions in and outside Rome which made his eloquence in his own eyes worthy of permanent record. With some speeches he took enormous pains after delivery: they would be carefully revised, retried upon a small circle of friends, sent in whole or in part to correspondents for criticism, delivered afresh before a large invited audience, and, after final emendation, possibly published.[4] 'I reflect,' he remarks, 'what a serious matter it is to put something into the hands of the public.'[5] He was perfectly conscious of the risk that such a redelivered speech ran of losing its fire, and yet he wonders why he should be criticised for his practice of serving up speeches at a formal *recitatio*.[6] We know of at least seven speeches of his that reached book-form, though they have not reached us. These include his address at the dedication of the library at Comum; pleadings in defence of Julius Bassus and Rufus Varenus on the two occasions when Pliny acted as counsel against the Bithynians, whom he was one day to govern; a speech for Attia Viriola to show cause why she should not be disinherited; and an attack in the Senate, after Domitian's death, upon Publicius Certus as responsible for the conviction of the younger Helvidius. This last oration[7] gave Pliny a safe opportunity of eulogising a Stoic family, and brought him from a friend the compliment, joyfully accepted, of comparing it to Demosthenes's speech *Against Meidias*. 'In fact,' replies Pliny, 'I had that speech in my hands when I composed mine – not to rival it (that would be outrageous or almost insane), but still to imitate and follow as far as difference of genius – a very great and a very small one – or the dissimilarity of the case would permit.'[8] Among other speeches, which may or may not have circulated afterwards, were those he delivered on the two occasions when, as advocate for the Baetic provincials, he

[1] *Ibid.* 4–6.
[2] VII. ix. 10–14.
[3] VII. iv. 10: 'unum precor ut posteri quoque aut errent similiter aut iudicent.' His 'libelli,' which were on sale at Lyon, may have contained poetry, IX. xi.
[4] VII. xvii. 7.
[5] *Ibid.* 15. For Pliny's public speaking see V. Cucheval, *Hist. de l'éloquence romaine . . . mort de Cicéron . . . à . . . Hadrien*, Paris 1893, II, chaps. xxiii and xxiv.
[6] II. xix. 2: 'neque me praeterit actiones quae recitantur impetum omnem . . . perdere'; VII. xvii. 2.
[7] IV. xxi. 3; IX. xiii.
[8] VII. xxx. 5.

prosecuted ex-governors of theirs, Baebius Massa and Caecilius Classi-
cus; his impeachment of the notorious Marius Priscus as counsel for the
Africans along with Tacitus in A.D. 100; and the defence of a group of
legatees charged in the criminal court with poisoning.

Nothing has, however, come down to represent his oratorical activity
except the re-edited form of the *Panegyricus* on Trajan, pronounced in
the Senate by Pliny on entering with Cornutus Tertullus upon the consulate in the later part of the year 100. One cannot hope to discern how
much of the original speech is embedded in what we now have. Soon
after its delivery, Pliny sent a copy to Voconius Romanus asking
for criticisms, and his letter[1] makes it clear that he was scrutinising his
own performance under various rhetorical heads. His contention
is that the well-known nature of the material (that is, Trajan's services
and qualities) must concentrate the attention unduly on style (*elocutio*),
whereas there are other points to consider like arrangement and transitions; also, just as in a picture, one demands high lights and shade.
No more illuminating introduction, however, to the *Panegyric* can be
found than in another letter mentioning an amplified form of the speech
which Pliny has been reading to a gathering of friends on three successive
days.[2] As they had assembled in spite of bad weather, their interest
was a compliment to literature, which, he says, was just reviving after
being nearly extinguished: 'it is not that there is more style than formerly, but people write with more liking because they have more liberty
(*liberius ideoque etiam libentius*).' Exuberance, he submits, must be
expected in such a composition: in fact, plain unadorned language
might appear out of place in a eulogy, though he hints at hopes that
literary taste will yet come to favour austere in preference to sugared
writing.[3] One most important point emerges bearing on the author's
design. Proper as it was that the fuller treatment in book-form (*eadem
illa spatiosius et uberius uolumine amplecti*) should do justice to the
excellence of the emperor, there was the further aim of drawing the
picture of a perfect prince. This is an implicit appeal to posterity. Yet it
only relatively makes the *Panegyric* more endurable: the praises remain
excessive, the figures strained, the prolixity wearisome. For us its chief
value lies in the historical light shed on the early part of a reign so
scantily documented as Trajan's is, apart from Pliny's speech and his
correspondence.[4]

The complimentary expression of thanks to which senators had
listened with secret chafing in Domitian's day was expanded by Pliny
into a *laudatio* in which he incorporated the two rhetorical prescriptions of detailed fact and psychological study. That is why the speech
divides itself broadly between Trajan's public acts and Trajan's personal

---

[1] III. xiii. [2] III. xviii. [3] *Ibid.* 10.
[4] Allain, *Pline le jeune*, ii. 582 and iv. 13, says Pliny is cited 293 times by De
la Berge (*Essai sur le règne de Trajan*), and is 'le véritable historien de Trajan.'

character. The exordium acknowledges a sense of the divine favour which has bestowed upon Rome such an emperor: it disclaims all intention of flattering; for abject obeisance, as if to a deity, is no longer necessary – Trajan is no tyrant, but a fellow-citizen. Then the keynote is struck. One reflects how highly endowed ought that person to be who controls the Empire by sea and land, in peace and war; but imagination can yield none worthier of such authority than the prince in whose presence the orator is speaking. Logically, then, he is the picture of an idea for future ages. Trajan's services before his recent arrival in Rome imply bravery, wide military experience, power of discipline and a loyal acceptance of his adoption by Nerva to be a colleague and successor. His triumphant entry into the city and at the same time his modest bearing form a fit prelude to a rehearsal of his public acts, such as liberality to the people, care of poor children, protection of commerce, solicitude for the corn supply that might well make Rome independent of 'haughty Egypt,' exhibition of manly games, abolition of espionage, repression of informers, discountenancing of treason-trials, stabilisation of finance, guaranteeing of wills, and a wise policy in building. The emperor devotes anxious thought to the provinces, and has a due regard for justice: in fine, he governs as the Creator does – a vicegerent on earth. His personal qualities are commended with allusions to the contrasted inhumanity of Domitian. So far is the emperor from self-assertion that he had long hesitated to accept a third consulship: so zealous is he that change of work is for him a form of relaxation. Unconscious humour lurks in the detailed picture of this indefatigable sportsman and handy seaman, unlike Domitian (*quantum dissimilis illi*) whom fear of the sea reduced to the condition of a victim led to the slaughter (*piaculum*). Next, his private life in the palace with wife and sister is touched on; then his affability to friends, and, with a glance at Claudius's court, his control over the freedmen of his household: 'You know that greatness in freedmen is the chief mark of littleness in a prince.'[1] Well does such an emperor deserve to be called *optimus*. After an apostrophe to his late Majesty, Nerva, the formal close comes in acknowledgements uttered to Trajan on behalf of Pliny himself and his colleague, and in deferential remarks to their fellow-senators.

Regarded under the aspect of an admonitory document for future princes, the *Panegyric* is less offensive to modern taste; because its words are not those of an obsequious toady but of a patriot insistent upon the services rendered by a wise emperor to his country. Its faults, too, such as affectation and long-windedness would certainly have been less present in the spoken form. As it now stands, it wearies the reader by its length, adulation and artifices. Trajan ceases to be interesting as a Sungod or an earthly Jupiter: he is more effective as a hard-working ruler.

[1] *Pan.* lxxxviii. 2: 'Scis enim praecipuum esse indicium non magni principis magnos libertos,'

The rhetorical element is also overdone: resort is too often had to anti-theses,[1] *sententiae*,[2] and a subtlety that degenerates into bad taste.[3] The specious *colores* of rhetoric betray themselves in over-ingenious turns: a mutiny, it is suggested, was the very thing wanted to prove Trajan a true *corrector emendatorque*; and his grey hairs were heaven-ordained to enhance his reverend appearance. What uncomplimentary rhetorical colour would have been given to grey hairs in Domitian's case may be imagined. Perhaps Trajan felt such elaborate praises as trying as he must have found some of the questions on detail included a dozen years later in Pliny's letters to him from Bithynia. Finally, the *Panegyric* contains much to illustrate the invasion of prose by the poetic: here the *egressio* on Egypt will provide apposite examples. As this epideictic performance, then, is our sole specimen of the author's oratory, we must beware of judging the lost speeches by it. In other speeches Pliny, though never an austere orator, may have indulged less in the rhetorical faults of his time.

Pliny's *Letters*, on which he prided himself less than on his poetry and speeches, constitute his real title to fame. The 247 letters of the nine books which precede the last book (containing 121 letters of official correspondence between Trajan and Pliny in A.D. 111–113) were written in the period from about A.D. 97 to about 109. Their chronology, it has been indicated, is a debated and still debatable matter; but there is a growing belief that the letters in the nine books were issued in groups, which one theory at least arranges symmetrically in triads.[4] Pliny did not adhere to strict chronological order; and his own statement to that effect is confirmed by several instances.[5] The collection in nine books may be assumed to have been complete before Pliny left Italy for his eastern province, and the so-called tenth book to have been published after Pliny's death by some friend or possibly by his widow.

To understand Pliny's significance as letter-writer it is necessary to observe what an *epistula* from his hand meant. We have nothing quite like it earlier: on the other hand, a long series of prose letters in later

---

[1] *Pan.* vii. 4: 'dignus alter eligi, alter eligere'; x. 6: '(*sc.* Nerua) tibi terras, te terris reliquit'; xvii. 4: 'non ideo uicisse uidearis ut triumphares, sed triumphare quia uiceris.'

[2] *Pan.* vii. 6: 'imperaturus omnibus eligi debet ex omnibus'; lxvi. 5: 'neque umquam deceptus est princeps nisi qui prius ipse decepit'; and paradoxes, xlix. 3: 'hoc inexpugnabile munimentum munimento non egere.'

[3] *Pan.* xxiv. 5: 'te ad sidera tollit humus ista communis et confusa principis uestigia.' (*I.e.* the use of his feet on common earth exalts the emperor to the sky!)

[4] H. Peter, *Der Brief in d. röm. Lit.*, Lpz. 1901, p. 107 ff., divides as follows: I–III, published A.D. 104; IV–VI, A.D. 108; VII–IX, a supplement, containing at least some letters of a date earlier than 108. For works on the chronology of the letters, see S.H. § 447.

[5] I. i. 1: 'Collegi non seruato temporis ordine, neque enim historiam componebam.' *E.g.* II. xx. is perhaps earliest of all. II. xi, on Priscus's trial, belongs to A.D. 100, but III. iv. to 98. IX. xxxiv mentions Pliny's idea of employing a reader; in VIII. i the idea has been acted on.

times and later literature bear a family resemblance to his. Classical
Greece presents in this field relatively slight remains. There are no indisputably genuine Greek letters to represent the best period, partly
because inside the small Hellenic communities it was pointless to write
to a man whom one might see in an hour or so, and partly because
external communication was hampered in many ways. As travel and
separation greatly predispose to letter-writing, it is natural to think that
the breadth of interest which furnishes the best epistolary equipment
came more easily to a Roman in the days of a world-empire: it is therefore natural to feel less surprise that, as the dialogue had become classic
in Greece, so the sort of halved dialogue which constitutes a good
letter became classic at Rome. Something in the Roman genius favoured
this literary form: it is not merely that there is no Greek analogy to the
three kinds of epistles written by Cicero, Seneca and Pliny, but in later
centuries Latin still holds the supremacy; for Julian the Apostate and
Synesius, Bishop of Cyrene, are not in letter-writing the equals of the
Gallic Bishop, Sidonius Apollinaris, or the statesman Cassiodor(i)us.

The letter, as published by Pliny, goes far beyond the scope of the
simplest private form written to make a request or give information.
This simplest form may be no more literature than an official letter is;
yet many letters, in the original sense, intended only for an individual
receiver may possess the charm of frankness and artlessness united with
just as much design as is needed for clear conveyance of the writer's
thoughts. One of the fascinations in Cicero's letters, especially those to
Atticus, is that he speaks to his friend as if to himself, uttering the first
thing that comes (*quidquid in buccam*, *Ad Att.* XII. i. 2); so that this
immediate committal of thought or experience to paper involves a disregard of academic rules and often a free borrowing of tone and expression from the *sermo cotidianus*. Wherever, in parts of the *Epistulae ad
Familiares*, there may cross Cicero's mind the possibility of publication,
he becomes at once less unconstrained and more formal. It makes all
the difference whether our letters are to be read by one or by many.
With the notion of a collective audience among contemporaries or posterity there begins the quest after artistry: then it is always possible that, on
redressing the balance, one may be compensated for the lost spontaneity
with new aesthetic effects. This more literary type is represented by
Pliny. With him the epistle has overstepped the rigid bounds of a letter:
it has become a *causerie* on paper, and the addressee is in a position comparable to that of the Pisones in Horace's versified epistle on poetry, or
Lucilius in Seneca's *Epistulae Morales*, or Madame de Sévigné's
daughter in her correspondence. The recipient really represents the
great public, while Pliny ranges at will anywhere through the width of
human life among themes likely to provide interesting material – a
senatorial debate, a trial, an illness, a death, a murder, a mysterious disappearance, floods on the Tiber, a volcanic disaster, ghost stories, a

book, a speech, a literary celebrity, questions of style, principles of education, advice about a tutor, social claims, a day in town, a day in the
country, scenery, a residence by the sea or in Tuscany or on the Lago di
Garda, an offer of a loan, a purchase of property, a mean host, a Corinthian bronze, the duty of forgiveness, greetings to friends or relatives,
congratulations, consolations. Elsewhere, in a light vein, he rallies a
poor correspondent, or an acquaintance who has forgotten to come to
dinner; regrets he has only got thanks to send for a present of thrushes:
acknowledges another gift with the information that, though his eyes
are troubling him, he can see it is a plump hen; tells another friend that
he is busy with the vintage, but will 'draw off' fresh verses for him;[1]
or again, much as Burns in one of his letters delightfully told three tales
about Alloway Kirk, so Pliny tells three anecdotes about Regulus with
the airy introduction: 'down with your copper and get a story worth
gold; no, three stories!'[2]

Expression must be manifold to keep pace in pliancy with every swift
turn of thought on such a variety of subjects. The general effect is that
of a miscellany of miniature studies or *feuilletons*,[3] in the sense that
Pliny's letters, essay-like, weigh some incident, experience, or idea in the
scale of the author's personal mood, or, if 'weighing' be too precise a
term, the author may be said to play lightly round his theme and put his
own spirit into it. This personal impress makes the letters as readable
as leaves from a well-written diary, so that they have, some of them, the
incidental, intimate, and literary interest which marks a work like the
Journal des Goncourt. Epistolary literature, even at its most artificial,
possesses the attraction of affording a sure insight into the nature of the
author. While it may be too much to declare, as Johnson did, that 'in a
man's letters, you know, madam, his soul likes naked,' still there must
always be in them a biography of the feelings: there will also often be –
and perhaps more interesting if undesigned – illumination thrown upon
the customs of the day. Since Pliny's letters do not belong to the kind
tossed off in fine careless freedom, one does not look to find in them the
rapid conversational and staccato notes of some of Cicero's, or the open
impetuosities of Byron; for Pliny's letters are more laboriously penned
with the thought of eventual publication and the hope of posthumous
fame: their sentiments and phrases are so cunningly disciplined and
marshalled that what they lose in unsophisticated charm they gain in
artistic grace. But with all this clever artificiality Pliny has much sound
matter to convey. Studied elegance is not necessarily inimical to sincerity, and his letters remain a true index to his personality and to the
life of his times. He realised the contrast between his own letters and

---

[1] I. xi, xv; V. ii; VII. xxi; IX. xvi.
[2] II. xx. 1: 'assem para et accipe auream fabulam, fabulas immo.'
[3] 'A suspicious feature may be noted: with hardly an exception each missive
is confined to a single subject.' R. Syme, *Tacitus*, Oxf. 1958, p. 96,

Cicero's. Their circumstances were different, and Cicero's fertile genius could readily find abundance of material in the stirring times that witnessed the death throes of the republic. Apologising, therefore, to a friend who has demanded full letters, Pliny pleads lack of thrilling subjects and fears that his epistles may become too academic (*scholasticae atque umbraticae*).[1] We may take it for certain that one reason why Cicero's letters so far outnumber Pliny's is that Pliny must have excluded from publication such of his letters as in substance could not lay claim to general interest or in form could not serve as patterns of style. It is noteworthy that there are no epistles of the literary type belonging to the period of his governorship, though it is conceivable that, but for his death, the world would have seen another issue of his open letters, adorned, as before, with that *bel esprit* which Europe has found so attractive.

This Plinian type of letter, where the underlying realities are retouched more or less lightly with literary refinements before publication, is one of the legacies of Rome to modern literature. Epistolography made no advance in the Middle Ages, but with the Renaissance the the recovery was well marked among scholars. When we turn to the eighteenth century, the palmiest age for letter-writing in English literature, it is impossible to avoid being struck with a similarity of spirit between Pliny's letters and those of Horace Walpole, Gray and Cowper. Despite Pliny's complaints about inroads on his time, and harder worker though he was than our chief letter-writers, he yet enjoyed the comfort and the leisure which seem indispensable to the production of the best literary epistles. Thoughtful, kindly, communicative, he was the very man to give human interest to his writing. Neither in Walpole, that caustic and voluminous man of the world, nor in Gray, largely a recluse with a fund of somewhat baffling restraint, do we discover the amiability which makes this pagan gentleman so winning. Perhaps Cowper, if we neglect his shy melancholy and quiet humour, presents most parallels to Pliny. Scholarly, sensible, well-mannered, free from ill-nature, artistic in expression, he had a turn for reflection which made much in his letters read as if the English would go straight into Plinian Latin. Certainly it is not without significance that one of the best English renderings of Pliny was that composed by Melmoth in the eighteenth century: it is too verbose, but even its generous verbosity suggests the spacious leisure of a period before the rush of modern life mortally wounded the art of letter-writing.

In contrast to the literary epistles, the correspondence with Trajan concerns the business of a provincial governor, some of it urgently demanding for settlement all the haste that the Roman imperial post by road and sea would allow. Here we find petitions for privileges on behalf of Pliny himself and others, reports on his struggles with the

[1] IX. ii. 2–3.

impaired finances of municipalities, knotty questions in civil or religious or criminal law, local difficulties in building a theatre or temple or aqueduct or baths, and repeated requests for a trained surveyor or architect from Rome. Most famous of all is the pair consisting of the letter from Pliny on prosecuting Christians and Trajan's answer. Historically the collection is most valuable, because it lifts the veil from the administration of a province in an abnormal condition; but much non-literary matter has, of necessity, to be introduced, and there is just that element of fussiness which good letters lack. One feels that the special commissioner refers too many minute points to Trajan, and deserves the reminder that some of his reported quandaries were exactly of the sort which he had been sent out to solve on the spot. Trajan's replies are business-like and brief, the findings of a fair-minded man: though they are friendly to his 'dear Secundus,' their very brevity sometimes implies that the governor is causing both the emperor and himself too much worry: once or twice, indeed, they verge on the snappy. That is one reason why it is incredible that they could have been the product of the imperial bureau in Rome – the personal touch is present. Reputations are not likely to be made by propounding theories that these replies came from an office instead of from the emperor, or by starting doubts about the authenticity of this correspondence in general or of the special letters touching the Christians whom Pliny had to judge in Bithynia.[1]

A personality so manifold deserves fuller examination than has been incidentally possible in a survey of his life and letters. If dignity, self-possession, broad-mindedness, considerateness, courtesy and generosity are qualities that constitute a gentleman, then Pliny was one. He knew how to ensure respect for the high magistracies which he held; he could keep his head in court so as to make the requisite retort to an unfair opponent; his wide experience of life taught him fairness in dealing with others; he was considerate to tenants and servants; treated superiors and inferiors with politeness, and performed notable acts of munificence. Although he devoted much energy to the preparation of cases on the court-roll,[2] his master-passion was literary study. Enthusiasm forces him to recommend it for others:

> Let this be your business, this your idleness; this your toil, and this your rest; in these pursuits let your vigilance, in these let your repose too be found.[3]

Amidst distracting avocations, he pined for retirement away from Rome where he could read and write:

> Shall I never break, if I mayn't untie, these cramping bonds?

[1] Cf. S.H. § 448.
[2] Mart. Epig. X. xx. 14–17, cited by Pliny, III. xxi. 5.
[3] I. iii. 3: 'Hoc sit negotium tuum, hoc otium. . . .'

Never, I suppose – for the old tasks have new tasks growing on them before the earlier ones are finished.[1]

So he writes from town:

What am I doing, you ask. What you wot of. I'm hard pressed with official duty; I've friends to attend to; sometimes I study, the thing to do which, not 'sometimes' but solely and continually, would be, I don't dare to say more virtuous, but surely more welcome.[2]

Even if he did get away to the lake-country for fishing and hunting, he liked to combine literary composition with his sport; and a saving grace let him see the humour of the situation when he tells Tacitus about waiting for the wild boar with writing material at hand.[3] What might easily have become mere bookishness was counteracted by duties, official and social, which involved intercourse with his fellow-men. As it happened, his career enabled him to discharge faithfully public and professional tasks, and yet in his leisure do good service to literature. Here his premier attention turned on oratory and poetry. While he knew and esteemed certain philosophers, he apparently shared some of Quintilian's suspicions about others; and while he once penned a handsome tribute to the divine majesty of history, he disavowed any purpose of competing in that field.[4] But, if he restricted his own output, he was catholic in his zeal for the production of all forms of literature. This appears in his enthusiasm for *recitationes*: it mattered little whether the reading were from history, comedy, poetry or oratory – Pliny was scrupulous in his attendance,[5] believing that private perusal was not enough to test a work without the *uiua uox*,[6] and offering sound reasons in defence of the practice as an aid to criticism.[7]

Similar zeal stimulates vigorous correspondence about the emendation of his speeches and verses, and repeated exhortations urging others to produce literary work.[8] His praises of contemporaries, though too lavish and partial, were in a measure due to the same genuine interest.[9] He may be extravagant in declaring that nothing so perfect had appeared of recent years as Augurinus's 'Poems in Little' (*Poematia*): here he seems naïvely to disclose the reason for his bias as personal liking or the poet's compliments to himself.[10] He may also have overstated the case

[1] II. viii. 2: 'Numquamne hos artissimos laqueos . . . abrumpam? . . .'
[2] VII. xv. 1: 'Requiris quid agam. Quae nosti. Distringor officio, amicis deserui, studeo interdum, quod non interdum sed solum semperque facere, non audeo dicere rectius, certe beatius erat.'
[3] I. vi. 1: 'Ridebis et licet rideas'; *cf*. IX. x.
[4] IX. xxvii; V. viii.
[5] I. xiii. 5: 'equidem prope nemini defui.'
[6] II. iii. 9.
[7] V. iii. 8; VII. xvii.
[8] I. iii. 4: 'effinge aliquid et excude quod sit perpetuo tuum'; V. x (to Suetonius); VIII. iv.
[9] IV. xx, xxvii; V. v, xvii; VII. xxviii; IX. xxii.
[10] IV. xxvii. 2.

in saying that Fannius's premature death robbed the world of an immortal work on Nero's victims.[1] Naturally some whisper reached him
in time that exception had been taken to his excessive commendations:
to which his answer, if not wholly valid, is at least candid:

You tell me that some people have condemned me in your hearing
for praising my friends at every opportunity beyond what is due. I
admit the impeachment (*agnosco crimen*) – welcome it, in fact. For
what is nobler than the fault of kindliness? After all, who are they
who know my friends better than I do? Yet suppose they do, why
grudge me a most delightful deception? For, supposing my friends
are not such as I declare they are, still I am happy in fancying them so.
Well, then, they'd better turn this maladroit activity of theirs (*sini-
stram diligentiam*) upon others: there's no lack of people who call it
'critical judgement' to pull their friends to pieces: they'll never per-
suade me into thinking that I love my friends too dearly.[2]

It is futile to argue that he was not severe enough, and might have
raised the literary standard by indulging, like Boileau, in outspoken
attacks.[3] What looks more likely is that the example and praise of a man
of Pliny's ability and reputation stirred contemporaries to do the utmost
of which they were capable. However that may be, the freedom from
envy implied in such praises must be set to his credit, and a good deal
should be forgiven to a benevolence which showed itself in many other
ways – in his charitable use of wealth, his willingness to help in misfortune, his ready emotion over the death of friend or slave.[4] None but a
considerate master would have chosen a room for study so as to avoid
any temptation to interfere with the festive rowdiness of his slaves when
celebrating the Saturnalia,[5] or have taken pains to arrange that his freedman Zosimus, who had been spitting blood, should go to the Riviera
and benefit by a prescription which medicine neglected for centuries
in the treatment of tuberculosis – excellent fresh air and properly
handled milk.[6] The tolerance which marked him as a governor made
him companionable for very diverse types of men – a brooder like
Tacitus or an airy mocker like Martial. It was rare for him to loathe
anyone as he did Regulus; for he recognised the inhumanity of being
too fierce a hater, and the virtue of forgiveness.[7] Temperate though rich,
Pliny followed a rule of life as commendable as the Stoic, yet without

---

[1] V. v. 4: 'immortale aliquid.' [2] VII. xxviii.
[3] L. Moy, *Qualem apud aetatis suae studiosos personam egerit C. Plin. Sec.*,
Paris 1876, p. 107: 'illi prosunt saeculo suo qui, sicut Bolaeus noster, publicam
quasi censuram agentes, parce laudant, uehementer reprehendunt.'
[4] *E.g.* I. xii; II. i. 10; III. xxi; V. v ('nuntius me graui dolore confudit');
V. xvi ('tristissimus haec tibi scribo'); and, for slaves, VIII. xvi, xix.
[5] II. xvii. 24.
[6] V. xix. 7: 'aera salubrem et lac eiusmodi curationibus accommodatissimum.'
[7] VIII. xxii. 2–3: 'ego optimum et emendatissimum existimo qui ceteris ita
ignoscit, tamquam ipse cotidie peccet . . .'; IX. xvii. 4: 'demus igitur alienis
oblectationibus ueniam ut nostris impetremus.'

Stoic rigidity; and if at times he appeared a little prim and priggish, let it be remembered how anxious he was at other times to show that he could unbend into frivolities.[1] His greatest weakness lies so patently on the surface that it amuses more than it offends. The passion for fame turned into an amiable vanity when he was convinced that the coveted fame had been attained. With a perfectly naïve egoism that disarms severe censure, he chronicles his own good deeds or desires a place in Tacitus's immortal works.[2] Can one wonder that he liked to have his name coupled with that of the historian?[3] He writes:

> I never experienced greater pleasure than from a talk with Cornelius Tacitus recently. He told me that he had sitting next him at last circus-games a Roman knight. After conversation on a wide range of learning, the latter asked, 'Are you from Italy or the provinces?' 'You know me,' was the reply, 'and from my literary works to be sure.' Whereupon the other asked, 'Are you Tacitus or Pliny?'[4]

The letter proceeds to recount another incident in which a stranger guessed Pliny's identity, and concludes: 'I'm not afraid to appear too boastful in quoting not my own but other people's opinion about me.' Still, it is his own golden opinion that he quotes about his speech for Attia Viriola as an inspired performance.[5] No wonder, then, that he should mention his delight when the judges in court could not help rising from their seats to show appreciation of his speaking,[6] or that he thought it a 'white pebble day' when he heard two young men (*egregium par*) pleading on opposite sides in the urban prefect's council, both exhibiting an excellent style which they had based on Pliny as their pattern (*exemplar*),[7] or that he should honestly confess that he enjoyed reading poetry which praised himself.[8]

But he was not without traits of modesty: he owned there was something beyond him in the virtues of a good philosopher, in the eminence of Cicero, and in the genius of Tacitus.[9] There is also something fine in his avowal that the attainment of glory is not all: it is the inner quality that counts, and to deserve success is no less honourable than to command it:

> Besides I have in mind how much finer a spirit it shows to set the rewards of honour in one's conscience rather than in men's applause. Glory should follow, not be sought after; and if by some chance or

---

[1] IV. xiv; V. iii; VII. iv.   [2] VII. xxxiii.
[3] VII. xx. 5–7.   [4] IX. xxiii. 2–3.
[5] VI. xxxiii. 1: 'accipe orationem meam, ut illa arma, diuinam (num superbius potui?), reuera ut inter meas pulchram.' According to Sid. Apoll. viii. 10, it eclipsed the *Panegyric*.
[6] IX. xxiii. 1–2: '. . . omnes repente quasi uicti coactique consurgerent laudarentque.'
[7] VI. xi.
[8] IX. viii. 1: 'omnia scripta tua pulcherrima existimo, maxime tamen illa de nobis'; cf. IX. xxxi.
[9] I. x. 3; IV. viii. 4–5; VIII. vii. 2: 'ne discipulus quidem debeam dici.'

other it does not follow, a deed is no less excellent for having failed to win glory.[1]

A natural piety, flecked with superstition in the matter of omens and dreams, prompted him to build temples in Italy and to hesitate in the East over disturbing a consecrated site.[2] However much he might feel officially opposed to the nonconformity of Christians in the observance of such public sacrifices as tested loyalty, against the principles of the Christian life he found nothing to say.[3] As to his own religious beliefs, he accepted a Divine Power as having vouchsafed Trajan to Rome, and recognised the obligation of prayer to the Providence sustaining the emperor.[4] On a bed of sickness, he knows the invalid discovers the vanity of worldly pursuits, and 'in that hour remembers there are gods, in that hour remembers he is man.[5] Sincerity of feeling enabled him, like Persius, to penetrate the inmost meaning of worship in the doctrine that 'the gods find pleasure not so much in exact petitions by their votaries as in innocency and holiness, and he who has brought to their shrines a clean and pure heart is found more acceptable than he who has brought a premeditated form of words.'[6]

His views on the Empire were those of acquiescence in the system of control by one ruler working for the general weal.[7] He had been able to keep to the path of prudence under a bad emperor, though even he claims to have been in danger from Domitian. After the dawn of better days, there came the raptures of the *Panegyric*, where the constitutional change is paradoxically summarised in his words to Trajan *iubes esse liberos: erimus.*[8] Admirers of the great past of Rome might take comfort in the fancy that a good *princeps* was a restorer of the olden times. Broadly, Pliny's political attitude is that difficulties in the state must be left to the higher powers to face: that is what an emperor is for.[9] On this principle he certainly acted when Bithynia was under his charge.

Interrogated on his style, Pliny might have called himself Ciceronian. For his letters he employs a rhythmic prose of a light type, decorating it with poetic quotations and allusions. If he cannot be said to be periodic in structure, he does largely follow the Ciceronian type of sentence-endings.[10] Yet in reality his prose was the resultant of different forces. It is true that he went back in his orations to Cicero as a master; but, in addition, he acknowledges his debt to Demosthenes in Greek and to Calvus in Latin. It is also true that, like his master Quintilian, he decries the oratory of the day,[11] and, like Quintilian again, holds that the best

---

[1] I. viii. 14.   [2] IV. i. 4–6; IX. xxxix; X. xlix and lxviii.
[3] X. xcvi. 7–8.   [4] *Pan.* i. 1 and 3; *Ep.* X. i, ii, xiii, xiv, xxxv, lii.
[5] VII. xxvi. 2: 'tunc deos, tunc hominem esse se meminit.'
[6] *Pan.* iii. 5; Pers. ii. 73–75.   [7] III. xx. 12.   [8] *Pan.* lxvi. 4.
[9] IV. xxv. 5: ἀλλὰ ταῦτα τῷ ὑπὲρ ἡμᾶς μελήσει.
[10] C. Hofacker, *De Clausulis C. Caec. Pl. Sec.*, Bonn 1903; F. Spatzek, *De Claus. Plinianis*, in *praef.* to Kukula's ed. (1912) p. vii.
[11] I. v. 12.

models (*optima quaeque*) should be imitated:[1] at the same time, it does
not follow that Pliny was unaffected by the rhetoric of his own era. On
the contrary, the reader soon discovers in the letters that he was an
offspring of the age in his studied use of the paraphernalia of rhetoric
such as antithesis, oxymoron, the emphatic anaphora,[2] and *sententiae*,
like 'many respect gossip, few conscience' (*multi famam, conscientiam
pauci uerentur*), or 'the favour of scoundrels is as untrustworthy as the
scoundrels themselves (*gratia malorum tam infida est quam ipsi*).[3] The
rhetorical ring due to artificial devices may be noted even in the English
dress of a representative letter to an official friend:

> Consider that you are sent to the province of Achaia, the true, the
> genuine Greece, where civilisation, literature, and even agriculture are
> believed to have originated. Consider that you are sent to regulate the
> affairs of free states; that is to say, men in the highest degree men,
> free men in the highest sense free, who have maintained the right
> which nature granted them by courage, by services, by friendliness,
> finally by compact and the sanctions of religion. . . . Let your feelings
> be those of reverence for their antiquity, their marvellous deeds,
> even for their myths. . . . Keep before your eyes that this is the land
> which sent us our legal code; the land which gave us laws, not after a
> victory, but at our own request. Remember it is Athens you approach,
> it is Lacedaemon you govern. To snatch from them the shadow that
> is left, the surviving name of freedom, would be harsh, cruel, bar-
> barous. . . . Recollect the past greatness of each state, but not so as to
> despise her for having lost it. Let there be no arrogance, no harshness.
> You need not fear contempt: can contempt be shown for the magi-
> strate invested with power and the insignia of office, unless he is a
> low, mean creature who has already a contempt for himself? Authority
> makes a poor test of its own force if it flouts others: it is a poor sort
> of homage that is won by terror: affection gives a far stronger guar-
> antee for holding what you want than fear does. For fear vanishes,
> if one quits the scene, while affection remains; and just as the former
> turns into hatred, so does the latter turn into respect.[4]

Yet Pliny was not a mere scholastic rhetorician: he was habitually versed
in business affairs and actual lawsuits: he had, therefore, to be more
practical in offence and defence than an academic professor had need
to be. In fact, he realises the weakness inherent in the rhetoric of the
schools when he draws a picture of the rhetor Isaeus as a simple-minded
teacher in contrast with the keen practised lawyer who necessarily
learns guile from close contact with the real disputes of men.[5] As to
his Ciceronianism, it is so modified that his style could not be mistaken

[1] I. v. 13.
[2] II. i. 12: 'Verginium cogito, Verginium uideo, Verginium iam uanis imaginibus . . . audio, adloquor, teneo.'   [3] III. xx. 8; I. v. 15.
[4] VIII. xxiv. 2–6. Somewhat similarly writes Cicero to his brother governing
the Greeks of Asia, Cic. *Ad Q.F.* I. i, esp. § 27.
[5] II. iii. 5: 'nos qui in foro uerisque litibus terimur, multum malitiae, quamuis
nolimus, addiscimus.'

for Cicero's. If he had been taught by Quintilian to eschew Seneca's brevity, he did not keep the rotundity of the Ciceronian manner. Rather he is a compromise between the two styles. In one of his eleven surviving letters to Tacitus, he raises an interesting question on the relative merits of the terse and the profuse.[1] True, at least, to theory, he favours the latter; and it may be imagined how illuminating it would have been to read the answer from the master of the condensed style. Pliny's own illustration of brevity has a delightfully vague freedom about it: Homer, though like Virgil he takes many lines to describe the armour of his hero, is brief, he maintains, because he accomplishes his literary design (*quia facit quod instituit*), and so Pliny's letter on his Tuscan villa must not be called big – it is the villa that is big! No single label indeed can fairly denote Pliny's style: if he could be so labelled, he would not have made such attractive reading. The great variety of his subjects met with corresponding variety of treatment from him, so that he is justified when he claims that in literature, as in life, the ideal effect is produced by a blend of the grave and the gay.[2]

In Pliny's choice of words alone there are characteristics, such as his liking for frequentative verbs, that mark him off from the Golden Age.[3] He is individual enough to invent words, *e.g.* the nouns *abactus, praelusio, renutus, socialitas, sinisteritas, arcessitor, reformator*, or to give fresh meanings to existing words, *e.g. descensio, egestio, nutatio, latitudo, gestator*. Again, he typically shares words with writers of the Silver Age, *e.g., cenatio*, 'dining-room' (Sen., Plin. Mai., Col., Petr., Mart., Suet.); *computatio*, 'account' (Colum., Sen., Plin. Mai., Quint., Front.); *captiuitas*, 'slavery' (Sen., Petr., Tac., Flor.); *diuersitas* 'difference' (Plin. Mai., Quint., Tac.). His locutions and syntax also present noteworthy features. One may find a Livian and poetic turn in *ne grauare* or *datum est facere*,[4] and a Virgilian base for constructions like *certus fugae* or *securus magnitudinis*. That Pliny based his Latin not strictly on Cicero but on the Latin of his own century is shown by much in the structure of the sentence, such as the general relinquishment of the period, and reduction of relative words; the new sense attached to conjunctions or abverbs like *alioqui, quatenus, quoque*; the use of participles in bold ways; much too in the use of moods,[5] like *quotiens intrasset* or *quocumque me contulissem* or *quamquam nouerim*.

---

[1] I. xx.

[2] VIII. xxi. 1: 'pulcherrimum et humanissimum existimo seueritatem comitatemque miscere.'

[3] J. P. Lagergren, *De vita et elocutione C. Pl.*, Ups. 1872, enters more exhaustively into Pliny's style than Oestling or Holstein did in their *opuscula*.

[4] Pliny uses the infinitive *e.g.* with certo, dignus, gaudeo (poetic and Silver prose); with sustineo, ualeo (poetic, Silver pr., Livy); w. permitto (poetic, Silver pr., rarely in Cic. and Livy). Lagergren's section on the infinitive (*op. cit.* pp. 162–166) is convenient. See also the works in the following note.

[5] For collected examples, E. Remy, *De Subjunct. et Infinitivo ap. Pl. minorem*, Louv. 1884. *Cf.* P. Menna, *De Infinitivi apud Pl. min. usu*, Rost. 1902.

Fronto's educational correspondence shows no knowledge of Pliny's epistles; but Tertullian's acquaintance with the two letters on the Christians is evident from his angry objections to them.[1] Macrobius[2] couples Pliny and Symmachus, the scholarly statesman of the late fourth century, as examples of the rich and luxuriant (*pingue et floridum*) style in oratory; but this does not convincingly prove that Symmachus's *Epistulae* were inspired by the Plinian collection. Cassiodor(i)us mentions Plinius Secundus as *orator et historicus cuius ingenii plurima opera exstant.*[3] It is natural to suppose that letter-writers in Latin should have used Pliny as a model, and that, as Pliny's books were sold at Lyon during his lifetime, they would still be remembered when Roman studies flourished in Gaul during the fifth century A.D. But it is doubtful whether there is absolute proof of his influence between Sidonius Apollinaris,[4] who was an admiring follower, and the tenth century.[5] In the Middle Ages the Fathers and Seneca eclipsed Pliny in favour, but from the time of Politian and Erasmus his influence was re-established, and his literary heirs have been many, especially in England and France.

MINOR CONTEMPORARIES

Pliny was so completely in touch with the literary movements of his day that a survey of his circle gives not only a restropect upon the Flavian age but an admirable introduction to literature under Trajan, and even, in the case of a slightly junior friend like Suetonius, carries us into Hadrian's reign. Pliny, we have seen, was fond of writing poetry and fond of poets. It is therefore appropriate here to review his minor contemporaries in general, whether they wrote verse or prose. Some of the chief Flavian authors, such as Silius Italicus, Martial and Frontinus, he knew well; and among his elderly friends was Vestricius Spurinna, already classed among minor Flavian lyric poets. With him may be named, as typical of culture at the time, the grandfather of the Emperor Antoninus Pius, Arrius Antoninus, whose Greek epigrams and mimes caused Pliny to fancy he was reading Callimachus or Herodas.[6] The information yielded by Pliny's letters about elegiac and lyric writers indicates a widespread passion for composing short poems; so that the Rome of Trajan may be pictured as a nest of gentlemen singing or trying to sing, and what Pliny called 'the crop of poets' accounts for his normally roseate view of the condition of literature. Two at least of his intimates, both of whom he pressed to publish, seem to have had an

---

[1] *Apol.* ii. [2] *Saturn.* V. i. [3] Cass. *Chron.* p. 387.
[4] Sid. Ap. iv. 22: 'ego Plinio ut discipulus adsurgo'; *cf.* i. 1, iv. 3, viii. 10.
[5] Merrill, ed. 1922, *praef.*, half allows the possibility ('nisi fortasse') that Einhart's 'mortalitatem magis quam uitam uidebam esse finitam' is based on Plin. II. i.10, as M. Manitius thinks, *Gesch. d. lat. Lit. des Mittelalters* (Müller's Hb. IX. ii), pt. i, Mun. 1911, p. 644.
[6] IV. iii. 3-4.

epic bent: these were Octavius Rufus[1] and Caninius Rufus.[2] Several
significant letters were addressed to the latter on literary events, such
as the death of Silius Italicus and the composition of a comedy by Vergilius Romanus. The story of a tame dolphin is communicated to him
as material for a poetic narrative; and Pliny approves of his intention
to write a poem in Greek on Trajan's Dacian War. Calpurnius Piso
took an old Greek title, καταστερισμοί,[3] for his elegiac poem, which
may have retold legends about the constellations in the spirit of Ovid's
Metamorphoses. Like several contemporaries, Pompeius Saturninus[4]
was an orator and historian as well as a poet. His lyrics and epigrams
after the manner of Catullus and Calvus evoke the utmost enthusiasm
from Pliny; and to him Pliny's speech at the inauguration of the Como
library went to be revised with his customary acumen (*qua soles lima*).
A very notable circumstance was that one day he read to Pliny certain
epistles which he said were by his wife. Pliny's comment is that he could
have believed he was listening to Plautus or Terence in prose,[5] though
he is not equally sure that such polished letters could have been written
by the lady. The importance of the incident lies in its testimony to the
growing practice of writing literary epistles of what we may call a
Plinian type. There seems to be here a hint, perhaps not sufficiently
grasped, that such letters were considered to contain, as Pliny's often
do, a poetic element; and this is confirmed by the instance of Voconius
Romanus, also an orator of ability, who was the author of letters that
gave an impression as if 'the Muses were speaking Latin.'[6] Another
imitator of Catullus and Calvus was Sentius or Serius Augurinus, the
youthful composer of *Poematia*, which were the best of their sort, we
are told, for years. Pliny cites from him a hendecasyllabic piece, which,
though it scarcely justifies the commendation in the letter, possessed
for the critic the merit of containing the line 'Pliny alone is as good as
predecessors for me.'[7] Passennus Paulus wrote Propertian elegies and
Horatian odes: the latter, says the complimentary Pliny, might well
suggest his descent from Horace, as in blood he was descended from
Propertius.[8] It was the opening of one of his lines, *Prisce iubes*, that gave
Javolenus Priscus at a *recitatio* the chance of pouncing upon it discon-
certingly with the rude interruption *Ego uero non iubeo*.[9] A most fascinating survival from the period, had fate allowed, would have been
the comic plays, some in Menander's style and others based on the old

---

[1] I. vii, esp. § 5; II. x.
[2] I. iii; II. viii; III. vii; VI. xxi; VIII. iv.
[3] V. xvii.
[4] I. viii; I. xvi.
[5] I. xvi. 6: 'Plautum uel Terentium metro solutum legi credidi.'
[6] II. xiii. 7: 'epistulas quidem scribit ut Musas ipsas Latine loqui credas.'
[7] IV. xxvii: 'unus Plinius est mihi priores.' Kukula had no right to alter the
traditional reading to 'his mihi prior sit' in his edition.
[8] VI. xv; IX. xxii.
[9] VI. xv. 2.

Attic comedy, by Vergilius Romanus.[1] The nature of the poems by Silius Proculus, which Pliny in one letter agrees to read, is unknown.[2]

On turning from poetry to prose (though, it will be remembered, some of those already mentioned were prose-writers as well as poets), we are met on the threshold by Pliny's most famous literary friend, Tacitus, the subject of a later chapter. The orator C. Fannius made some stir as a chronicler of Nero's victims: before his death three books of his work had appeared and became popular.[3] Titinius Capito chose for a historical theme 'The Ends of Illustrious Men' (*Exitus Inlustrium Virorum*), occupying himself also with a poetic treatment of the lives of the renowned.[4] He was a shining ornament of the age, a fosterer of learning, and restorer of what Pliny for the moment regards as a decadent literature.[5] Always willing to lend his house for *recitationes*, he was a regular attender at Pliny's readings, and a hero-worshipper who kept busts of the great republican champions at home. One of the three correspondents called Maximus in Pliny's letters directed against a certain Planta a polemic work, which Pliny desired to see published.[6] Writings by Sardus[7] so delighted Pliny by praising him that he read and reread them; and Atrius[8] is thanked for a book of his which he had not so far had time to read – the *liber* in question was possibly a speech. Julius Avitus is mentioned as having written much in a short life: since Pliny laments the loss of the whole by his premature death, the inference is that he never published his books.[9] A large number of contemporary orators, besides those just mentioned, appear in Pliny's pages; but they are too many to record here.

Jurisprudence under Trajan is represented by Neratius Priscus and Juventius Celsus on the Proculian side, and on the Sabinian side by Javolenus Priscus and probably Titius Aristo, one of Pliny's friends.

Grammatical and linguistic learning had several representatives. Urbanus, who is plausibly referred to this period, has his comments on Virgil quoted by Servius. Velius Longus was likewise a Virgilian scholar. A student of Ennius, Lucilius, Accius and other early Latin authors, he wrote on archaisms and derivations: as was natural, he used and quoted Varro and Verrius Flaccus. The date of Flavius Caper is not certain, but he also combined an interest in Virgil with studies of old Latin: a good deal of his lore passed into the works of Charisius and Priscian. Caesellius Vindex, who is cited in Aulus Gellius, compiled an alphabetic dictionary of *Antiquae Lectiones*, which seems to have had the alternative title of *Stromateis*.

One of several authors named Hyginus in Latin literature appeared at this period as a gromatic writer in a treatise, now fragmentary, on

---

[1] VI. xxi.   [2] III. xv.   [3] V. v.
[4] VIII. xii. 4; I. xvii. 3: 'clarissimi cuiusque uitam egregiis carminibus exornat.'
[5] VIII. xii. 1.   [6] IX. i.
[7] IX. xxxi.   [8] IX. xxxv.   [9] V. xxi. 3–6.

legal boundaries, *De Limitibus*. It has been disputed whether another work *De Limitibus Constituendis* is his or not. The *De Munitionibus Castrorum* ascribed to him must, from internal evidence, be placed much later. A manual of geometry for land-surveyors, which drew upon Euclid among other sources, was composed by the Balbus whom subsequent gromatics often cite. This same department of field-measurement is represented slightly later by Siculus Flaccus and Junius Nipsus.

Chapter II

TACITUS

The spice of problems – Facts and inferences concerning Tacitus
– His official career – Tacitus as a speaker – Memory of 'The Ter-
ror' – The three minor works – Speculation on secondary motives
– Aspects of the *Dialogue on Oratory* – Vexed questions – *Agri-
cola* – Its form and purpose – Later style in the making – *Germania* –
Points of interest – Matter and manner – *Histories* – Plan –
Character-drawing – Other dramatic qualities – *Annals* – Great
episodes – Sources – Outlook on human life, history and politics –
Anti-imperial bias – Attitude to Tiberius – Language and style –
Vicissitudes of his fame.

CONCERNING P. Cornelius Tacitus, the greatest historian of
the Silver Age, there is no dearth of problems to awake interest,
though they do not affect his unchallenged mastery of one of the
most wonderful prose styles in literature. His very praenomen is uncertain.[1] We do not know when or where he was born; we do not know
when or where he died; and, while scholars are now nearly unanimous[2]
in ascribing the *Dialogus de Oratoribus* to him, they are not agreed on
its date of composition or on the explanation of its contrast in style with
the other works of Tacitus. Differences of opinion have arisen about
the author's real aim in his monographs on Agricola and on Germany;
rival suggestions have been made about the number of books which the
now mutilated *Histories* once contained; and more serious controversies
have raged over the sources from which Tacitus drew, his method of
using them, his credibility in general and his presentation of Tiberius
in particular.

Approximately his birth-year may be given as A.D. 55. This is an
inference from two facts: first, that, looking back on the year 75, the
dramatic date of his *Dialogus*, Tacitus referred to himself as then 'quite
a young man' (*iuuenis admodum, Dial.* i); and next, that, while the
younger Pliny considered himself and Tacitus 'nearly of an age'

[1] Other writers call him 'Tacitus' or 'Cornelius Tacitus'; *e.g.* Plin. *Epist.*
IX. xxiii. 2. *Codex Med.* I gives his praenomen as 'Publius': Sidonius Apollinaris twice calls him 'Gaius' (*Epist.* IV. xiv. 1, xxii. 2), with which the later
MSS. agree.
[2] R. Novak once more claimed it for Quintilian in his ed. of Tacitus's *opera
minora*, Prague 1889.

447

(*propemodum aequales*), he mentioned efforts of his own as an *adulescentulus* to imitate Tacitus, who had already made a name.[1] We can prove Pliny to have been born in 61 or 62, and from his words we may guess that Tacitus was some half-dozen years his senior. Possibly the historian's father was the *eques* Cornelius Tacitus mentioned by the elder Pliny[2] as a procurator in Belgic Gaul: the surmise at least would accord with Tacitus's standing in public and private life. His official honours under the three Flavians are summarised by himself as 'begun by Vespasian, increased by Titus, and further advanced by Domitian,'[3] the interpretation being that under the first of these emperors he held one of the offices in the vigintivirate and had served in the army as *tribunus militum laticlauius*; that Titus nominated him to the quaestorship in 80, when twenty-five; and that under Domitian he was either aedile or tribune, and afterwards, we know, praetor in 88.[4] In A.D. 77, when still a *iuuenis*, he had been betrothed to the daughter of the Roman general Agricola, who was consul at the time, and married her next year shortly before his father-in-law's appointment to Britain.[5]

The keenness with which Tacitus studied rhetoric under eminent masters appears from his own statement.[6] Following with closest attention the court-pleadings of M. Aper and Julius Secundus, he took lessons from them at their homes on the principles of argument and style. It is not impossible, although unproved, that he was one of Quintilian's pupils: the Ciceronianism of his earliest work rather favours the idea. Certainly the *Dialogus* marks deep interest in the prospects of Roman oratory. A good rhetorical education, turned to practical account, earned him fame as a speaker; and among his noted appearances in public were one in 97,[7] when as *consul suffectus* he delivered a funeral eulogy over Verginius Rufus, and another in 100, when as counsel with Pliny for the African provincials he impeached Marius Priscus their ex-proconsul. Pliny's explicit compliment to his eloquence on both occasions was, we may take it, deserved; and it is significant that, in regard to the second occasion, he singles out as a quality of Tacitus's oratory its impressive dignity.[8]

Duties in an unknown province having kept Tacitus and his wife abroad for the four years from 90 to 93, they returned to Rome too late to attend the death-bed of his illustrious father-in-law.[9] At once he

---

[1] Plin. *Ep.* VII. xx. 3.   [2] *N.H.* VII. 76.
[3] *Hist.* I. i: 'dignitatem nostram a Vespasiano incohatam, a Tito auctam, a Domitiano longius prouectam non abnuerim.'
[4] *Ann.* XI. xi.
[5] *Agr.* ix: 'consul egregiae tum spei filiam iuueni mihi despondit. . . .'
[6] *Dial.* ii.
[7] This date for his consulship is now usually accepted instead of A.D. 98.
[8] Plin. *Ep.* II. i. 6: 'laudator eloquentissimus'; II. xi. 17: 'respondit Cornelius Tacitus eloquentissime et, quod eximium orationi eius inest, σεμνῶς.'
[9] *Agr.* xlv: 'nobis tam longae absentiae condicione ante quadriennium amissus est.'

found himself in the gloom of a reign of terror when senators were
cowed by Domitian into conniving at the emperor's judicial murders.[1]
The atmosphere of calculating espionage and of inexorable repression,
now imposing silence, now inviting adulation, coloured all the after-
life and after-writing of Tacitus. However gratefully he recognised that
the dark clouds had lifted with the accession of Nerva in 96, and that
at the dawn of 'a most blessed age'[2] he was at length free to express his
views, we yet feel that the iron had entered into the soul of this man of
over forty before he ever embarked on his career as historian, and that
his outlook upon events must inevitably reflect the sombre hues of
fifteen years of dumb helplessness which could not be forgotten.[3]
Though after Domitian's death he accepted a consulship and though
an inscription found in Caria shows he was proconsul of Asia about 112–
116, still we may assume that henceforward his extensive plans for
historical composition occupied most of his time. These plans proved
in the event too extensive for the span of life allotted to him. After the
Histories came the *Annals*, completed, as we shall see, between 115 and
117. But for his old age he had, he tells us, set aside the reigns of Nerva
and Trajan; and he had also contemplated a work on the times of Augustus.[4] These latter projects he never carried out, so that it looks as if he
did not long survive the publication of the *Annals* about the end of
Trajan's reign.

The three minor works of Tacitus, the *Dialogus*, *Agricola*, and
Germania, written before his prolonged historical labours, are linked
together in several ways. The text of all three descends from the same
lost archetype (*Hersfeldensis*), usually identified with a codex observed
and recorded at Rome in 1455[5] as containing the *Germania*, *Agricola* and
Dialogus with the extant portions of Suetonius's *De Grammaticis* and

---

[1] *Agr.* xlv: 'mox nostrae duxere Heluidium in carcerem manus . . . nos
innocenti sanguine Senecio perfudit.'

[2] *Agr.* iii: 'nunc demum redit animus; sed quamquam primo statim beatis-
simi saeculi ortu Nerua Caesar res olim dissociabiles miscuerit, principatum ac
libertatem, augeatque cotidie felicitatem temporum Nerua Traianus. . . .'

[3] *Agr.* ii. 3: 'dedimus profecto grande patientiae documentum . . . memoriam
quoque ipsam cum uoce perdidissemus, si tam in nostra potestate esset obliuisci
quam tacere'; iii. 2: 'quid? si per quindecim annos, grande mortalis aeui
spatium . . . pauci . . . nostri superstites sumus, exemptis e media uita tot annis
quibus iuuenes ad senectutem senes prope ad ipsos exactae aetatis terminos per
silentium uenimus.'

[4] *Hist.* I. i: 'quod si uita suppeditet, principatum diui Neruae et imperium
Traiani . . . senectuti seposui'; *Ann.* III. xxiv: 'cetera illius aetatis (*sc.* Augusti)
memorabo, si, effectis in quae tetendi, plures ad curas uitam produxero.'

[5] Sabbadini in 1901 (*R.F.I.C.* xxix. 162–164), intimated Decembrio's note to
that effect. Romance seemed to have entered into palaeography when the announcement was made to the Historical Congress at Rome in 1903 of the discovery at Iesi, near Ancona, of a 15th-century MS. in which is incorporated, it
is claimed, one quaternion of the *Agricola* from the veritable parent codex. *Atti
del Congresso internaz. di scienze storiche*, ii. 227–232. *Cf.* R. Sabbadini, *Storia
e critica di testi latini*, Catania 1914, p. 278; J. G. C. Anderson, Introd. to his
ed. of *Agricola*.

Q

De Rhetoribus. All three works are of importance for the preliminary stages in the evolution of Tacitus's style. Further, all three have been made the subjects of much theorising about secondary purposes which, it has been alleged, they were written to subserve. Certain critics are not content with the motive professed in each case by the author, but have insisted on looking beneath the surface. Thus the *Dialogus*, ostensibly an inquiry into the decadence of oratory, has been declared, in keeping with the more than doubtful hypothesis that it was composed after Domitian's reign, to be the author's farewell to public speaking and an implicit apology for deserting the rhetorical art in favour of history.[1] The *Agricola* has been asserted to be not only a memorial of piety to an honoured relative,[2] but a semi-political monograph meant to explain to Trajan and others the conduct of both Agricola and Tacitus in the troublous times of Domitian; while the *Germania*, the contention runs, is no mere sketch of the homes and habits of northern tribes, but a pamphlet with a definite tendency, either to hold up to luxurious Rome an accusing mirror which should reflect the healthier simplicity of the Germans, or, with far-sighted historic sense, to inculcate on the Romans the need for guarding against danger from the barbarian, or virtually to justify the prolonged absence of the new emperor Trajan on so vital a frontier as the Rhineland. The ingenuity, however, displayed in pressing such secondary motives has tended in some measure to push the real motive into the background and to distract attention from the literary value of the works.

The *Dialogus de Oratoribus*, in the form of a discussion among eminent men of the day, supplies an answer to a question put to Tacitus by Fabius Justus about the reasons for the decline in oratory. The participants are four – Curiatius Maternus, poet and dramatist, at whose house the scene is laid; Marcus Aper, an advocate of Gallic origin; Julius Secundus, a polished historian, and, like Aper, a native of Gaul; and Vipstanus Messalla, a Roman of high birth. It is part of the author's dramatic skill to represent them in debate as speaking in character. Aper, utilitarian and practical, contrasts his own remunerative profession of pleader with the uselessness of poetry: Maternus, as poet and idealist, disdains wealth and influence, preferring the 'privacy of woodland and grove' (*nemora et luci et secretum*)[3] and the 'blest camaraderie' (*felix contubernium*) of the Muses. Secundus is a quiet and refined speaker, while the true Roman Messalla is the admiring champion of the past, with a dislike for the faults of contemporary oratory and education. The earlier part of the *Dialogus* consists of Aper's eulogy on a lawyer's calling

[1] S.H. § 429: 'wir gewinne den Eindruck, als wollte der Verfasser des Dialogs einem Gegenstand alter Liebe das letzte Lebewohl zurufen,' u.s.w.

[2] *Agr.* iii. 4: 'hic interim liber, honori Agricolae soceri mei destinatus, professione pietatis aut laudatus erit aut excusatus.'

[3] It is not impossible that in Pliny, *Ep.* IX. x. 2, addressed to Tacitus (though some think written by Tacitus), there is a direct reference to this.

and Maternus's reply on behalf of poetry. On Messalla's entrance, a preliminary exchange of views leads to Aper's speech in praise of modern oratory at the expense of the 'ancients'; whereupon he is, at Maternus's request, followed by Messalla as a critic of defects in present-day eloquence. Maternus interrupts to recall Messalla to the real subject – the causes of deterioration in oratory – which is handled in the last part (xxviii–xli). A lacuna marked in the MS. has deprived us of the opening of Secundus's historical review of factors in politics and in legal procedure which fostered the oratory of the republican era. In contrast therewith 'the emperor's discipline had tranquillised eloquence as it did everything else.'[1] A second lacuna must be assumed, where we have lost the first part of Maternus's closing speech, which proceeds in the extant portion to argue that unsettled political conditions and party spirit in ancient times had favoured the rise of great speakers. 'Eloquence is the nursling of licence' (*eloquentia alumna licentiae*), so that too well organised a government is fatal to first-rate speaking.

The *Dialogus* is a piquant combination of the fascinating and the provoking; for, while it handles an attractive theme with a charm that justifies its old description as an *aureus libellus*, it yet raises problems that remain unsolved and are, some of them, perhaps insoluble.[2] The Tacitean authorship is now soundly upheld on the basis of manuscript authority, the general agreement of views with those in Tacitus's unquestioned writings, and, despite obvious differences, the presence of significant similarities in style. With this prevalent acceptance, the claims made for Quintilian, the younger Pliny, Suetonius and others (including a hypothetical anonymous author) fall to the ground. The dramatic date of the conversation is widely accepted as A.D. 74–75, on the reasonable interpretation of the phrase *sextam stationem* as the sixth year of Vespasian's reign.[3] The actual time of composition by Tacitus is a much more vexed question; but Gudeman's contention that it must have preceded the reign of Domitian appears still the most satisfactory. In opposition to this a theory[4] is maintained that the *Dialogus*

---

[1] *Dial.* xxxviii. 4: 'principis disciplina ipsam quoque eloquentiam sicut omnia depacauerat.'

[2] They are adequately and convincingly treated by A. Gudeman in 138 pages of prolegomena to his ed. of 1914. See his bibliography. For bibl. on the question of authorship to 1934 see S.H. § 429. More recently E. Paratore (*Tacito*, Milan 1951) argued against the Tacitean authorship, and he was answered by V. Capucci, 'Il Dial. de Orat. op. giov. di T.' (*Annal. Fac. di Lett. e Fil.*, Naples 1952, pp. 79 ff.) and H. Bardon, 'T. et le D. des Or.,' *Latomus* 1953, pp. 186–187). For a classification of opinions on authorship and date, see J. Frot in *R.E.L.* 1955, p. 120 ff.

[3] *Dial.* xvii. 3. The figures given there of succeeding reigns as amounting to the sum of 120 years from Cicero's death in 43 B.C. to the time of the dialogue need slight adjustment, because that total would bring out the date at A.D. 78.

[4] Gudeman (*op. cit.* proleg.) successfully controverts Leo's hypothesis (*Göttinger gel. Anzeigen*, 1898), of a date after *Agric.* and *Germ.*, and refutes the support lent to that hypothesis in the theory of style propounded by Norden (*Kunstprosa*, p. 322), and Wilamowitz (*Hermes* xxxv (1900)). Vogt's pamphlet, *Tac. als Politiker*, Stuttg. 1924, ends with a brief defence of the early date. For

came after the other minor works in Trajan's reign and that the divergence in literary manner presents little difficulty for the reason that in
antiquity style was often not the man himself but a garb which a clever
author could don or doff at will. Yet, when all is weighed, the *Dialogus*
would have been a literary anachronism at the end of the first century.
It is difficult to discern any occasion for Tacitus, so late as A.D. 98 or 99,
when he ranked as one of the foremost speakers of the day, to write a
dialogue on decay in oratory and to connect the subject with circumstances over twenty years earlier. Is it credible that a man of nearly
forty-five, who was of recognised literary power and, according to hypothesis, already the author of both *Agricola* and *Germania*, would profess
himself unable by his own effort to treat the causes of decadence directly
and so feel obliged to employ the device of dialogue-form? And would a
promise to repeat exactly a discussion almost a quarter of a century old
strike readers as a plausible one? Another consideration is that the contrast between the sunny spirit of the *Dialogus* and the oppressive atmosphere of the *Agricola* makes it hard to assign them to the same period
of their author's life. Tacitus's own reference to his silence under
Domitian throws us back on an earlier date, and, if we fix that date as
A.D. 81, a short time before Domitian's accession in September of that
year, it is not unnatural that Tacitus looking back from the age of twenty-
six should have thought himself *iuuenis admodum* at the supposed period
of the dialogue, A.D. 74–75.

For his *Dialogus* Tacitus drew considerable inspiration from works of
Cicero like the *De Oratore* and the lost *Hortensius*. Quintilian's known
Ciceronianism is likely to have influenced Tacitus, whether he studied
under the great professor or not; and those who place the composition
of the *Dialogus* after Domitian's time are entitled, without violating
chronology, to believe that it was written with a bearing on the lost
treatise by Quintilian *De Causis Corruptae Eloquentiae*. Tacitus mentions
as available in libraries the *acta* and *epistulae* collected by Mucianus.
He may have used Varro's *Catus de liberis educandis*, and, like Quintilian in the *Institutio* and the pseudo-Plutarch in Περὶ παίδων ἀγωγῆς,
he probably went back to their common source, a Stoic work by Chrysippus, if we may judge by the array of resemblances set out by Gudeman.[1]

In the *Agricola* Tacitus feels that he has a great man for the subject of
his monograph: sincerity of admiration, therefore, lifts him above the rhetoric with which he was conversant. His epigrams here, as in his later
works, are effective because they show grip of the eternal realities of

---

other works on this point, see S.H. § 428 ('Abfassungszeit des Dialogs') and J.
Frot in *R.E.L.* 1955, p. 120 ff. Recently R. Syme (*Tacitus*, Oxf. 1958, pp. 670–
673) has argued for a date in Trajan's reign, perhaps 101, the year before the
consulship of Fabius Justus to whom the *Dialogus* was dedicated. Syme cites other
cases in which works were dedicated to patrons about the time of their consulates.

[1] Ed. 1914, pp. 92–96.

human nature. So there is no small amount of the universal – of that which is true for all time – in the little book. It has besides the great interest of reflecting truthfully important aspects of the Roman imperial administration.

The introduction (i–iii) gives reasons for issuing a biography in an age when satire enjoyed more vogue. Personal memoirs – a class of writing with ancient traditions – must from their nature contend against prejudice, and in the recent reign of terror had been impossible; 'for every good art had been exiled so that nothing honourable could cross one's path anywhere.' But in the changed times of Nerva and Trajan[1] an enforced silence may at length be broken, though, after past methods of repression, the harm still visible renders it hard to revive literature:

> Nevertheless it will not be an uncongenial task to compose, even in a rugged and unpolished style, the record of previous servitude [under Domitian] and a testimony to present blessings. Meantime I issue this book designed to honour my father-in-law, Agricola, and in virtue of its expression of loyal affection it will be, if not commended, at least excused.[2]

After this preface the author, turning to his theme, relates in six chapters (iv–ix) the life of Agricola up to his appointment as legate of Britain, describing his parentage, education, civil offices, and periods of service in Britain before his consulship. Into this earlier narrative Tacitus skilfully weaves characteristic qualities of a hero whose greatness is to culminate in his British victories. The all-important central portion of the work is therefore preceded by two excursuses, a brief description of Britain with its inhabitants (x–xii), and a sketch of the past conquests of Rome in the island (xiii–xvii). Twenty-one chapters (xviii–xxxviii) are then devoted to the main subject of Agricola's British campaigns during the seven years of his command, from the defeat of the Ordovices and surrender of Mona to the victory over the Caledonians near Mons Graupius and the circumnavigation of the northern coast. Throughout he is depicted as not only a successful commander skilled in strategy, but an able administrator, a discerner of men, and himself fair-minded, loyal and modest. The final portion (xxxix–xlvi), on Agricola's recall and last years of retirement in Rome, begins with the ominous note of Domitian's jealousy (*fronte laetus, pectore anxius*) and indicates that the ex-general by his unostentatious conduct was fulfilling the part of a good citizen in evil times. The shadow of an emperor's enmity falls darkly over the later pages; and suspicions of poison are not absent from the fatal illness of A.D. 93. The work closes in a rhetorical apostrophe to the dead man and an epilogue on immortality:[3]

---

[1] A comparison of the references to the emperors in chaps. iii and xliv indicates that the *Agricola* was published soon after Trajan's accession in A.D. 98. He is called *princeps* in xliv. From *Agr.* i–iii it is plain that the *Agricola* preceded the *Germania.*   [2] *Agr.* iii. 3.   [3] xlv. 3–xlvi.

'Thou wast blest indeed, Agricola, not only in the brilliance of thy life, but also in the timeliness of thy death! They who were present to hear thy last words recount thine unflinching and cheerful welcome of thy fate, as though thou wert doing a man's best to make a gift of "not guilty" to the emperor. But for me and for thy daughter, beyond the bitterness of having a parent torn away, there is an added sorrow. It was not ours to sit by thy sick-bed, to support thine ebbing strength, and take our fill of looks and embraces. Assuredly we should have received instructions and utterances to imprint in the depths of memory. Here lies our grief, our wound. By the circumstance of so long an absence abroad, thou wast lost to us four years before. Doubtless, best of parents, with a most loving wife sitting by thee, everything was done abundantly to show respect. Still it was with too few tears that thou wast lamented; in that last day of life there was something for which thine eyes yearned in vain.

'If there is a land for the spirits of the just, if philosophers are right in holding that great souls are not extinguished with the body, then mayst thou rest in peace! Summon us, thy household, from a paralysing sense of loss and from womanish moanings to the contemplation of thy good qualities. To weep or beat the breast for such were sin. It is by admiration rather than by transient praise, it is by rivalling thine example if nature allows that we must pay thee respect. That is genuine honour. That is the dutiful regard of one's nearest kindred. This too I should enjoin on his daughter and his wife – so to revere the memory of a father and husband, as to meditate inwardly on his every act and word and cherish the mould and fashion of his soul rather than of his body. It is not that I think a veto should be set on images fashioned of marble or bronze; but, as with the face of man, so the likeness of the face is but frail and perishable, while the mould of the mind is everlasting – you can preserve and reproduce it, not through a foreign substance and by art, but in your very character. Whatever we loved, whatever we admired in Agricola, abides and will abide in the memories of men, in the eternity of the ages, through the reputation of his deeds. Many an ancient will oblivion overwhelm, as if inglorious and ignoble: Agricola, whose story is thus recorded for posterity, will survive.'

On the literary form and aim of the *Agricola* a surprising amount has been written.[1] Biography, an established form of literature among the Romans, was akin to the *laudationes funebres* pronounced over the dead. Such encomia went back for their artistic pedigree to Greek models like the *Agesilaus* of Xenophon and the *Evagoras* of Isocrates, while formal rules for their construction were laid down in rhetorical handbooks. It does not, however, follow that Tacitus – though Gudeman[2] would

---

[1] See Bibl. *re* p. 447 for the most important works.
[2] Germ. ed., Berl. 1902; similarly, G. L. Hendrickson, *Proconsulate of Agric. in relation to Hist. and Encomium*, publn. of Univ. Chicago, 1902.

have it so – scrupulously conformed to these regulations; for his was not a genius to imprison itself within mechanical bounds. His growing interest in history was little likely to be content with laudation, but prompted him to introduce narrative freely, even to the extent of an enlivening digression such as the adventurous voyage of the Usipian cohort, or an excursus such as that on the geography and tribes of Britain, where the doubtful relevance from the standpoint of biography may be excused on the ground of irresistible didactic impulse. This very blend of narrative with eulogy has tempted some to regard the central portion of the *Agricola* as one of Tacitus's preliminary studies destined for incorporation in his contemplated account of Domitian's reign. But an examination of the sections dealing with Roman governors in Britain will show that in order to suit them for insertion in the *Histories* radical alterations in the scale of treatment¹ would have been inevitable, especially in recording the services not only of Agricola but of Cerialis and Frontinus. Besides, certain domestic details appropriate in a biographical study would have been out of place in a chapter of imperial history. Both recasting and omissions therefore would have been necessitated. As it stands, the author's illustration of his father-in-law's eminence by the story of concrete achievement constitutes a more effective, if more subtle, form of praise than a direct panegyric like Pliny's upon Trajan. The purely personal element was presumably strong in the lost Republican autobiographies of Scaurus, Rutilius Rufus, Catulus and Sulla, and under the Empire in the *Lives* of Pomponius Secundus by Pliny the Elder and of Julius Asiaticus by Julius Secundus, as well as in the kindred eulogies upon Paetus Thraesea and Helvidius Priscus. It was the example of Sallust's *Jugurtha* and *Catilina* that served to recommend to Tacitus a more impersonal mode of treatment through an increased admixture of history; and the result is a composite work where both structure and style are, throughout the narrative, affected by Sallustian precedent. Livy's influence also operates in the delivery of speeches by the Caledonian chief and by his Roman antagonist, while Cicero's appears particularly in the apostrophe near the close.

As to the purpose of the *Agricola*, some scholars insist that it is no simple tribute of *pietas*, as Tacitus's words suggest, but a political manifesto in favour of moderation under tyranny, and thus a reply to critics of Agricola's and his own past subservience.¹ Now, it is true that Tacitus dislikes extremists and commends moderate men, but he does so in all his writings; and no evidence exists to show that he, any more than contemporaries like Pliny, stood after Domitian's death in special

¹ Among those who see a political aim in the *Agric.* are Hoffmann, *Zeitschr. f. d. österr. Gymn.* 1870; Gantrelle, *Rev. de l'instr. belge*, xxi, p. 217; Furneaux, *Agr.* Intr. pp. 7–15; Boissier, *Tacite*, 1903, pp. 161–166; *cf. L'Opposition sous les Césars*, pp. 317 ff. On the other side, Hirzel, *Ueber d. Tendenz des Agr.*, Tüb. 1871; Anderson, *Agr.* Intr., and others.

danger of virulent attack for years of non-resistance. The sorrowful
admission which he makes[1] of the shame incurred by forced acquiescence in Domitian's outrages is very far from the tone, which Gantrelle
professes to hear in the *Agricola*, of 'an angry advocate defending a
client.' Surely, after all, his attitude had not been different from that
of Nerva and Trajan[2] themselves or the majority of the senatorial
class, so that hostility to Tacitus on the ground alleged would logically
have been an unreasonable position for all but a few irreconcilables,
and even in their case would have logically implied a censure upon
two emperors as well.

The *Agricola* is a book to which one can always return with pleasure.
In a venture through its pages one gets, within marvellously brief compass, a memorable revelation of a period in history and a noble personality. The rapid strokes of its prose, though not yet, as a rule, in Tacitus's
most condensed manner, are still sufficient to mark out the author as a
great stylist and at the same time a student of humanity. No intelligent
reader of the opening three chapters is likely to forget their lurid picture
of the despotic villainy from which Rome was just recovering. In this
setting begins a tale which holds a world of meaning in its pregnant
statements. Take a few as one meets them. With a withering glance at
Caligula, Tacitus says of Agricola's father that 'his very virtues won the
resentment of Gaius Caesar.' A personal touch lends interest to the
reminiscence concerning Agricola himself: 'I recollect he used to say
that in early youth he might have imbibed the tenets of philosophy too
eagerly for a Roman and a senator (*quam concessum Romano ac senatori*,
iv), had not his wise mother curbed his burning and ardent enthusiasm.'
Later, the first stirrings of military ambition felt by the young officer in
Britain are ominously pronounced to be 'unwelcome at an era when
sinister misconstruction encountered eminence and a great name was
as risky as a bad one' (*nec minus periculum ex magna fama quam ex
mala*, v). Deep significance underlies the words 'for his quaestorship
the lot assigned him Asia as province and Salvius Titianus as chief:
neither corrupted him' (*neutro corruptus est*, vi). Success as a subordinate
could not be more pointedly summarised than in the balanced terms:
'so by valour in obeying orders, and modesty in his reports, he avoided
jealousy without avoiding distinction' (*extra inuidian nec extra gloriam
erat*, viii). A pretty irony characterises the reflection on the belief current
about the time of Agricola's consulship that his next appointment would
be the governorship of Britain; 'rumour is not always astray: sometimes it actually picks the man' (*haud semper errat fama, aliquando et
eligit*, ix);[3] and no less ironical is the comment on the British adoption

---

[1] *Agr.* xlv: 'nostrae duxere Heluidium in carcerem manus,' etc.
[2] Pliny, addressing Trajan, *Pan.* xliv. 1, said, 'Vixisti nobiscum, periclitatus
es, timuisti, quae tunc erat innocentium uita.'
[3] These words scan as a senarius. Tacitus may be quoting from drama or
fable.

of Roman dress, baths and banquets: 'with the unsuspecting it all
passed for civilisation, though it was but a piece of their slavery'
humanitas uocabatur, cum pars seruitutis esset, xxi).

We may put his *sententiae* down to rhetoric, but it is a human rhetoric,
based proverb-like on the experience of ages. 'Successes everybody
claims, failures are laid at one man's door' (*prospera omnes sibi uindicant,
aduersa uni imputantur*, xxvii) is an adage that applies to more than
soldiering. 'Everything unknown passes for the marvellous' (*omne
ignotum pro magnifico*, xxx) is a safe declaration for others than
the Caledonian chief to make. 'It is the way with human nature to hate
the man you have wronged' (*proprium humani ingenii est odisse quem
laeseris*, xlii) makes a cynical reminder of man's unfairness to man.
With the *Agricola*, in short, Tacitus has reached his Sallustian period,
but already a greater than Sallust is here: in both *Agricola* and *Germania*
the unique style of the later works can be seen, as it were, in the making.

The *Germania*, naturally of vital importance for early Teutonic history, belongs to the same year as the *Agricola*. The northern tribes of
Europe had been powerful enemies of Rome for 210 years, Tacitus
reckons, from the Cimbrian invasion of 113 B.C. to Trajan's second
consulate[1] in A.D. 98; 'so long has the conquest of Germany been going
on' (*tam diu Germania uincitur*). The title, originally perhaps *De Situ
Germaniae*, has received in the MSS. such expansions as *De origine et
situ Germanorum* or *De origine, situ, moribus ac populis Germanorum*.
There is no parallel in antiquity to this separate study of a people,
viewed first generally (i–xxvii) in respect of geography, climate, warfare, government, religion, divination, meetings, punishments, chieftains,
dwellings, dress, morality, food, drink, tillage, funeral as well as other
customs; and then specially (xxviii–xlvi), in respect of the various tribes.
In this second part Tacitus, starting with western and northern tribes,
passes to the Suebi in central Germany and thereafter from the tribes
along the Danube and on the east to island folk and folk near the Baltic,
ending with Wends (Veneti) and Finns (Fenni) bordering on Sarmatia.
One does not need to be an anthropologist to appreciate the attraction
of a little treatise so neat in its description and sometimes so biting in its
swift comments. All sorts of curiously instructive and diverting details
are given about those tall men with fierce blue eyes and red hair (*truces et
caerulei oculi, rutilae comae*, iv). Was it, Tacitus asks, the kindness or
anger of the gods that denied them silver and gold, so that, though
frontier tribes adopted money, barter remained the trade-custom of the
interior? We learn how German women were held in respect and how
their near presence was felt to be a stimulus by warriors in battle. We
read of the tribesmen's fixed times for meetings at the new or the full
moon, and we recognise the origin of our English 'fortnight' and
obsolete 'sennight' in their non-Roman mode of computing time

[1] *Germ.* xxxvii.

Q*

(*nec dierum numerum, ut nos, sed noctium computant*, xi). Their observance
of the marriage tie, their payment of blood-money to end a feud, their
open hospitality, their primitive love of a gift, and reckless dicing up to
the final stake of personal freedom, all go to fill the picture. Their liquor
fermented from barley or other grain was evidently responsible for
much insobriety. 'To spend a whole day and night in drinking disgraces
no one. Their quarrels, frequent as usual among the intoxicated, are
seldom settled with abusive words, but commonly with wounds and
bloodshed.'[1] One of their curious habits was to take counsel at a feast,
when the true feelings are disclosed amidst the freedom of the carousal,
but to make a decision next day by a sort of appeal from Germans drunk
to Germans sober: 'they deliberate when they are unable to dissemble,
they resolve when they cannot make a mistake' (*deliberant dum fingere
nesciunt, constituunt dum errare non possunt*, xxii).

Too much ink has been wasted on speculations whether the treatise
is fundamentally an ethnographic essay, or a moral lesson for voluptuous Rome, or a political brochure to commend plans of aggression
against the Germans.[2] If we could be sure that the province which
Tacitus once governed was in the north, we might then divine the origin
of his interest in the tribes across the frontier. Though there is nothing
in the treatise that proves personal contact, there is much that might
very well have been conveyed by oral inquiry apart from reading. Supposing that his father was the procurator of Belgica named Cornelius
Tacitus, the author clearly had opportunities for questioning a useful
witness on many points. His own purpose of writing a history of Domitian's reign during which there had been German campaigns, and Trajan's absence for the first year of his reign on the German frontier,
were enough to attract Tacitus to the subject. But it is most unlikely
that these forty-six chapters were designed as part of his future *Histories*:
it is a different thing, however, to view an independent monograph as a
preliminary survey of ground some of which he would one day have to
cover historically. The only previous authority whom he names is
Caesar; but that he drew from more than one source is indicated by his
vague plurals, *quidam affirmant* or *quidam uocant*. Fragments of Sallust
prove that he dealt with German customs; Tacitus may or may not have
used him; and the same possibility holds with regard to Livy (the
periocha of whose hundred and fourth book gives part of its contents as
situm Germaniae moresque), and with regard to Velleius Paterculus, Pomponius Mela, and the twenty books on German wars by the elder Pliny.

The best reason assignable for the genesis of the book is that Tacitus
found the subject interesting. Had he intended to secure a political
effect, such as the advocacy of a forward policy on the frontier, it is

---

[1] *Ibid.* xxiii: 'potui humor ex hordeo aut frumento'; xxii: 'diem noctemque
tinuare potando nulli probrum: crebrae ut inter uinolentos rixae,' etc.
See, *e.g.*, works by Weinberger and Müllenhoff cited in Bibl. *re* p. 447.

unimaginable that he should have left his object a secret to be penetrated by a very few critics with whom all others disagree. His one conceivable thought in representing the Germans as dangerous enemies from the days of the Cimbrian menace must have been approval for the policy of caution such as Trajan favoured.

And if he took up the subject because it interested him, he wrote about it in a way meant to interest the reader. Of course he points out differences between Germans and Romans, and of course he passes caustic remarks, because they are likely to capture the attention. People enjoy them, because they are excellent literature. Even Roman *grauitas* might permit a smile now and again over a clever gibe at obvious national failings. But this is not to say that Tacitus constructed his essay to be either a monitory or a minatory mirror for Rome. The Germans are not idealised in it. Though Tacitus admires their bravery, loyalty, purity, hospitality and simplicity of life, he does not overlook their faults, like idleness, drunkenness, gaming, and unpunctuality in attending popular assemblies. He is entitled, then, with an investigator's impartiality, to redress the balance by implied or express censure on blemishes in Roman civilisation – its absurd deification of women belonging to the imperial family; its demoralising spectacles; its over-costly banquets and funerals; its ineffectual enactments against exorbitant interest. The widespread laxity of social life at Rome is no doubt before his eyes when he writes 'no one in Germany smiles at vice: to corrupt and to be corrupted is not styled up-to-date' (*nec corrumpere et corrumpi saeculum uocatur*, xix). He has in mind Rome's carelessness of her offspring when, after recording that infanticide is an infamy in Germany, he adds, 'good morals have more force there than good laws elsewhere' (*plusque ibi boni mores ualent quam alibi bonae leges*, xix). The social influence of the childless rich is what, like any satirist, he inwardly stigmatises in the remark that among the Germans there are no advantages in childlessness (*nec ulla orbitatis pretia*, xx); and it is of the notorious predominance of freedmen at certain epochs that he is thinking when he points out that they are of no importance in German states except in those ruled by kings: 'elsewhere the inferiority of the freedman is the proof of freedom' (*impares libertini libertatis argumentum sunt*, xxv). Pronouncements so pithily sarcastic illustrate the same general characteristics of style in the *Germania* as those noticeable in its immediate predecessor.

In the *Historiae* Tacitus treated a period of some twenty-eight years (A.D. 69–96) which he had himself lived through.[1] The work, when complete, covered the last days of Galba and the five following principates, those of Otho, Vitellius, Vespasian, Titus and Domitian; in

[1] For historical background, see B. W. Henderson, *Civil War and Rebellion in Rom. Emp.*, Lond. 1908; for literary aspects, E. Courbaud, *Les procédés d'art de T. dans les Hist.*, Par. 1918. More works are cited in the Bibl.

other words, its main theme was the Flavian imperial house with the preceding struggle during which three nominees of different sections of the army fell successively after short-lived tenure of power. Beginning with 1st January, 69, it may have been originally meant to continue a history written by Fabius Rusticus. The title is guaranteed by Pliny's prophecy 'I augur (and in augury I am expert) that your *Histories* are to last,' and by Tertullian's reference to the Jewish wars related to the fifth book.[1] What we have left breaks off before the middle of Book V in the second Medicean MS., the sole authority for the text of the *Histories*, as it is also for that of *Annals* XI–XVI (a run of books which begin and end in a gap). Since that MS. numbers Book I of the *Histories* as the seventeenth of the combined work from the death of Augustus, there is, *prima facie*, a presumption that the *Annals* ended with Book XVI, which, when unmutilated, must have treated about three years and a half (middle of A.D. 65 to end of 68). That, however, was about the length of time covered in Books III and XIV and XV. From Jerome we learn that Tacitus's complete narrative of the Caesars, beginning with Tiberius and ending with Domitian, consisted of thirty volumes.[2] If, then, the *Annals* were in sixteen books, the *Histories* had fourteen. Some assign eighteen to the former and twelve to the latter.[3] This would imply a symmetrical hexadic division, so that six books of the *Annals* would in that case have treated Tiberius, six Caligula and Claudius, and six Nero.

The composition of the *Histories* preceded that of the *Annals*, where Tacitus alludes to having already dealt with Domitian's times.[4] Pliny had portions of the *Histories* sent to him for revision, and occasionally supplied Tacitus with material like the account of the eruption of Vesuvius. References in his letters – we have eleven addressed to Tacitus – enable us to fix the period of publication for the *Histories* as the years from A.D. 104 to 109.[5]

One cannot read the first twenty chapters without recognising that they come from a historian of grasp, who realises the momentous issues involved in the troublous times which formed his theme. His plan is clearly stated, the dark character of the period foreshadowed, the state of the Empire and feeling in Rome sketched, before he brings on his stage most of the leading personages in the sanguinary contests which followed the death of Nero. Vitellius for the moment receives only

[1] Plin. *Ep.* VII. xxxiii: 'auguror . . . historias tuas immortales futuras'; Tert. *Apol.* 16: 'Cornelius Tacitus . . . in quinta historiarum suarum.'
[2] Hieron. *Comm. ad Zach.* III. 14.
[3] F. Ritter, ed. Camb. 1848, I, p. xxii; *cf.* O. Hirschfeld, *Kl. Schr.* 842 ff.; E. Wölfflin, 'Die hexadische Comp. des T.' *Hermes* xxi (1886) p. 157 ff.; P. Fabia, *Les Sources de T.*, Paris 1893, p. 437 ff.; H. Goelzer, ed. of Tac. *Hist.*, Paris 1920, p. xxxvii. ff.
[4] *Ann.* XI. xi.
[5] S.H. § 435. Pliny, *Ep.* VI. xvi. 1, shows that shortly before 106 Tacitus had not completed his collection of material for the year 79.

passing mention; but one cannot fail, even within the earlier chapters, to be interested in the figures of Galba, Piso, Otho, and Mucianus, who is the champion of the two coming Flavians, already, says Tacitus, marked out for imperial power. Much of the interest, when one pauses to analyse it, is awaked by Tacitus's never-failing psychological skill. We have almost at once brought home to us old Galba's obstinate parsimony. 'He was undone by his old-fashioned strictness and an excessive severity to which nowadays we are not equal' (I. xviii). His murder is followed by a fuller estimate, in which his seventy-three years prompt the reflection that, having lived under five emperors, 'he had been luckier in the reign of others than in his own.' The estimate then describes his character as one 'rather free from vices than distinguished by virtues,' and ends in the well-known terms, 'by general consent he would have been declared equal to empire, had he never been emperor' (I. xlix). Piso's behaviour at his adoption by Galba is excellently depicted: 'not the least change did he show in look or manner: it was as if he had the power rather than the wish to rule' (I. xvii). Of Otho we are told that 'he had spent a slack boyhood and unruly youth; Nero liked him for rivalling his own profligacy' (I. xiii). In Mucianus we see one better fitted for emperor-maker than for emperor: 'he was a blend of dissipation and energy, courtesy and arrogance, good and bad qualities. His self-indulgence was excessive in leisure hours: whenever he was on service, he displayed great qualities. . . . He was a man who would find it easier to confer imperial power than to hold it' (I. x).

The summary of the times is impressive in its melancholy force:

> The period I am entering upon was rich in disasters, appalling in its battles, and rent asunder by mutinies – even in peace a cruel time. Four emperors were cut off by the sword. There were three civil wars, still more against the alien, and often wars with both characters combined.

After a review of troubles in the Roman world at large, he concentrates on Rome:

> The city was wasted by conflagrations, its oldest sanctuaries consumed, and the Capitol itself fired by the hands of citizens. Holy rites were profaned; there was immorality in high places; the sea was full of exiles and its rocks dyed with butcheries. The savagery in the city was more outrageous. Nobility, possessions, magistracies declined or filled, invited accusation: merit meant surest destruction. . . . Slaves were bribed to betray masters, freedmen to betray patrons: those without enemies were ruined by friends. Yet the age was not so barren in good qualities as not to exhibit fine examples as well. Mothers accompanied sons in flight: wives followed husbands into exile: there were brave kinsfolk and faithful sons-in-law: the fidelity of slaves bade defiance even to torture: there were distinguished men driven to the last necessity, when compulsory death was faced with

gallantry, and the last scenes of all rivalled the renowned deaths of antiquity. . . . At no time did more terrible disasters to the Roman people or plainer evidence prove that what the gods care for is not our peace of mind but our chastisement (*non esse curae deis securitatem nostram, esse ultionem*, I. iii).

Such was the far from roseate aspect which, on a general survey, the period wore in the eyes of its historian. One tragedy follows another in this historical drama with the inevitability of fate. The prominent characters being as Tacitus depicted them, no other *dénouements* seem possible. Galba's meanness was sure to undo him with the praetorians; Otho's faintheartedness to drive him on suicide; Vitellius's gluttony to prevent a successful stand against the Flavianists. The secret of the imperial system had now, as Tacitus says, been revealed: emperors could be made elsewhere than in Rome, and the Empire, despite the veil drawn by the plausible fictions of Augustus and his successors, was demonstrated to be essentially a military, not a civil, institution. The pretence of hereditary right to the succession vanished before the decrees of contending armies. If only, then, as documentary evidence for a new epoch of vital significance the *Histories* must be of lasting value. Book I leaves Otho momentarily in power. Much skill is shown in the employment of speeches to serve historical purposes; for example, Galba's address to Piso at his adoption is an essay on the duties of an emperor (xv–xvi), and the speech put into Otho's mouth after praetorians and marines have sworn allegiance to him is intended, through an indictment of Galba's rule, to explain the reasons for its collapse (xxxvii–xxxviii). Among many impressive moments in what makes a most readable book is that which immediately precedes the murder of Galba and Piso. Like dramatists ancient and modern, Tacitus divined the power of silence: in the third book it is through the deserted halls of the palace that the doomed Vitellius wanders alone (*terret solitudo et tacentes loci*, III. lxxxiv), and in the fourth book there is a memorable picture of a disgraced legion on its gloomy march like a dumb funeral procession (*silens agmen et uelut longae exsequiae*, IV. lxii). So here, in the opening book, as Galba and his adopted successor reach the forum, the stage is set for tragedy:

> Not an accent came from people or crowd; but looks were those of dismay, and ears turned to meet any sound. There was no uproar, no respose: it was a hush like that of a mighty terror and mighty wrath (I. xl).

Danger to the new ruler declares itself at once from the legionaries in Germany, who proclaim Vitellius emperor. Otho is therefore compelled to face hostile armies pouring into Italy from the north. This struggle is the main subject of Book II, which, owing to the historian's constant dramatic sense, begins by directing attention to Vespasian and his son

Titus, who are on the alert to challenge the victor in the latest duel. The description of the first battle of Bedriacum, which left the Vitellianists in possession of the field, is clearly not the work of an expert military historian; but Otho's speech to his men choosing self-inflicted death as the only honourable course is a fine performance which throws into the light unsuspected traits of nobility in one who had misspent his life. Next comes the turn of the victorious gourmand. Vitellius, in betraying his indecent joy when nearly six weeks after the battle he rode over the field among heaps of putrefying dead, appears with unconscious dramatic irony to be provoking nemesis. Meanwhile that nemesis is drawing near in the shape of the generals who invade Italy on behalf of Vespasian, the nominee of the eastern troops. This fresh struggle for the throne is the subject of the third book – a powerful one, containing such thrilling episodes as the terrible sack of Cremona, the burning of the Capitol at Rome, and the last miserable hours of Vitellius. The fourth book brings the acknowledgement of Vespasian as emperor, and is largely concerned with the bold scheme of the Batavian Civilis to establish a northern empire free from the yoke of Rome. The narrative of his operations continued in part of the next book is, like most of the military history in Tacitus, hard to follow – 'more remarkable,' says Gibbon, 'for its elegance than perspicuity.'[1] But the most interesting portions of the fifth book are those in which Tacitus turns to the war with the Jews at the outset of Vespasian's reign. Unluckily, the account of the siege of Jerusalem is lost, but there is a curious fascination in the ludicrously distorted version of the Israelitish exodus from Egypt and of the mode whereby Moses put an end to the sufferings of his people in the wilderness. In many matters touching Jewish religion Tacitus betrays an amount of Roman prejudice and ignorance more tolerable in a satirist like Juvenal than in an investigator of history. One cannot but think it a pity that, if Josephus was not yet accessible, Tacitus failed to consult the Septuagint.[2]

Concluding his *Histories* with the year A.D. 96, Tacitus turned back to deal with a period of over half a century from the death of Augustus in A.D. 14. The title of this narrative of the Julian dynasty through the reigns of Tiberius, Caligula, Claudius and Nero, is given in the sole MS. authority for Books I–VI (the first Medicean or Laurentian) as *Ab excessu diui Augusti*. Since Tacitus, however, several times[3] refers to his work as *Annales*, we are justified in using the traditional title. It is at least appropriate to his plan of following the yearly succession of events, although Tacitus, being too great an artist to enslave himself to such bare monotony as is found in the *Anglo-Saxon Chronicle*, deviates

[1] *Decline and Fall*, etc., ed. Bury, 1896, vol. i, ch. ix, p. 232 n.
[2] J. Morr, 'Die Landeskunde von Palästina bei Strabon u. Josephos,' *Philol.* lxxxi (1926) p. 256 ff., considers Posidonius a source for Strabo and Josephus as well as for Tacitus's *Hist.* and Justinus.
[3] *Ann.* III. lxv; IV. xxxii; XIII. xxxi.

from chronological order, should his subject appear to demand it.[1] Thus he relates in sequence two summer campaigns as a relief from miseries in Rome, and elsewhere combines the interconnected transactions of several years so that they may be more easily remembered.[2]

A clue to the date of composition is got from a reference to the Persian Gulf as a contemporary limit of the Empire. This held good only between Trajan's conquest of A.D. 115 and Hadrian's order for withdrawal on his accession in 117.[3] That the division into books was the author's own is plain from allusions like 'in prioribus libris.'[4] The conclusion of a book was often arranged to synchronise effectively with some striking event: thus II ends with the death of Arminius (*liberator haud dubie Germaniae*), XI with the fall of the empress Messallina, XII with the poisoning and deification of Claudius, XIV with the cruel fate of Octavia, XV with the crushing of the Pisonian conspiracy. We may guess that the now imperfect Book V culminated in the overthrow of Sejanus. Out of what once amounted to at least sixteen books, there have survived the first four, a fraction of the fifth with more of the sixth, and, although defective at beginning and end, the series from the eleventh to the sixteenth. Interpreted in terms of history, the losses are parts of Tiberius's reign, the whole reign of the imperial madman Caligula, the reign of Claudius up to A.D. 47, and over two years at the close of Nero's reign.

Regrettable though these losses are, we possess in the remainder one of the greatest monuments of historical genius – the ripest work of a penetrating critic of affairs who expressed his thoughts in accents that are absolutely unique. Whatever its gloom or its bias, lack of interest cannot be alleged against the broken story of fifty years. In Tiberius's reign we have placed before us the enigmatic character of the emperor, his varying attitude to Senate and senators, his ultimate withdrawal from Rome, the sinister growth of sycophancy and delation, mutinies theatrically engineered and as theatrically suppressed, the exploits of Germanicus in the North and his untimely death in the East, the fortunes and misfortunes of the elder Agrippina and of the children whom she bore to Germanicus, the ambitious projects of the dangerous minister Sejanus, and the alleged smothering of the third Caesar in his seventy-eighth year. Even so, the record cannot always be thrilling, and we find the historian regretting the necessity for inserting details which may look trivial in spite of their significance and for using matter that may appear monotonous.

[1] *Ann.* IV. lxxi: 'ni mihi destinatum foret suum quaeque in annum referre, auebat animus antire. . . .' On the annalistic principle he defers treating certain events: 'in tempore memorabo,' I. lviii; 'in loco reddemus,' II. iv.

[2] VI. xxxviii: 'duabus aestatibus gesta coniunxi'; XII. xl: 'plures per annos gesta.'

[3] *Ann.* II. lxi . . . 'Romani imperii quod nunc rubrum ad mare patescit'; S.H.A. *Hadr.* v. 1–4.

[4] *Ann.* VI. xxvii. He applies the term *libri* to his previous *Histories* in *Ann.* XI. xi.

This is why he breaks off his depressing tale of judicial murders to relate the legendary account of the marvellous phoenix in view of the rumour that it had reappeared in Egypt, and why he suggests that even Eastern troubles with Parthia – not the most attractive theme in his narrative – might afford a welcome change from affairs in Rome. But in fact the variety of topics touched upon within the compass of this single reign is amazing, and room is found for social and economic phenomena – extravagance in living, scarcity of corn, financial crises, fires in the city, inundations from the river, increase of slave establishments, Oriental worships, the seductions of astrology, relief from taxation for Asiatic cities ruined by earthquake, the questionable right of sanctuary for criminals and so forth.

A break of about a decade after Tiberius's death takes us six years into the reign of Claudius, when Messallina was empress and Suillius conducted his dastardly prosecutions. Interested in completing a magnificent aqueduct from Subiaco to the capital, in adding new letters to the alphabet, and in supporting the claims of leading provincials for admission into the Senate, the emperor, himself a puppet in the hands of his freedmen officials, is the last to realise the public scandal caused by Messallina's misbehaviour. Thanks to energetic steps taken by the *libertus* Narcissus she is despatched, and Claudius marries his niece the younger Agrippina, Germanicus's daughter, who by her first husband was the mother of Nero. Intrigue at court is unabated; Claudius is poisoned and Nero elevated to the throne to the exclusion of Claudius's son Britannicus. Nero's reign begins at Book XIII and is full of incident. His earlier years of high promise are followed by the growth in him of depravity, megalomania and cruelty. At times unpleasant, the chronicle is scarcely ever uninteresting and is often exciting. Among episodes which enchain the attention are Nero's plots against his imperious mother, his callous repudiation of Octavia to marry his mistress Poppaea, heavy fighting in Armenia, a fresh revolt in Britain, the execution of a whole household of slaves for a murder committed by one, a treasure-hunt in North Africa on a false scent, the emperor's roystering in the streets by night, his public display of his musical talents, his conduct after the great conflagration in Rome, the ramifications of the ill-starred Pisonian conspiracy, the dramatic deaths of men so different as Seneca and Petronius, and the fate of the daringly independent Stoic senator Paetus Thrasea. By a coincidence, time has cut short the *Annals* in the midst of the account of Thrasea's enforced death just after he had severed his arteries and let the blood flow with words which virtually repeat those of the dying Seneca and which Tacitus in a freer reign must have rejoiced to write – 'we pour out a libation to Jupiter the Deliverer' (*libamus Ioui liberatori*).[1]

To do full justice to the debated subject of the historical sources of

[1] *Cf. Ann.* XV, lxiv; XVI, xxxv.

Tacitus would require a separate chapter, if not a book. Here it must be lightly touched upon. Let us first note what obligations he specifies, remembering that such acknowledgements were never *de rigueur* in antiquity. In the *Histories* he names three authors, Vipstanus Messalla (twice), C. Plinius and Sisenna.[1] In the *Annals* he mentions more sources: C. Plinius three times, once as a writer on wars with the Germans, Fabius Rusticus also three times, Cluvius twice, Corbulo[2] once, Tiberius's orations, a letter from Tiberius to the Senate (quoted in part, perhaps from a previous historian rather than from the *acta senatus*), the *commentarii Agrippinae filiae*, *acta diurna*, and *commentarii* (or *acta*) *senatus*.[3] But he is often content with vaguer references, implying a plurality, and sometimes a conflict, of authorities: *e.g.*, *inuenio apud quosdam auctores* or *celeberrimos auctores habeo* or *tradunt plerique*.[4] Clearly there was a large amount of potential material – literary works, public or private records, oral tradition, and, for the period of the *Histories*, the author's own observation. It could not all, however, be either equally available or equally valuable for the historian. Among different sorts of records, the *commentarii principales* were probably not accessible to him, the *acta senatus* could not always be trusted, and the *acta diurna* contained too much petty detail. In one passage[5] he mentions the circulation of fictitious speeches and decrees purporting to be genuine *acta senatus*; he was, then, on his guard against forgeries, and we may imagine that in some cases his account of proceedings in the Senate was a combination of the 'Hansard' of the day with oral tradition.[6] In another passage, relating to Nero's amphitheatre, he disdainfully relegates to the 'Daily Register,' or *acta diurna*, all details of foundations and timber-work as beneath the dignity of history.[7] Fortunately, although here he seems to imply that the concern of history is with 'illustrious events,' he at once proceeds to record the strengthening of two colonies by drafts of veterans, a money dole to the people, a payment into the exchequer, and the remission of a 4 per cent tax on slaves for sale – most of these being facts of social or economic import rather than *res illustres*.

Over and above authors whom he actually mentions, we know of several who might have provided material. For the period of the *Histories* there were Cluvius, Vespasian in his memoirs, and Antonius Julianus; and for the *Annals* the elder Seneca, Velleius, Tiberius

---

[1] *Hist.* III. xxv, xxviii, li.

[2] W. Schur in *Klio*, xix (1925) ('Untersuchungen zur Gesch. d. Kriege Corbulos') argued that Tacitus used Corbulo's military reports, while Cluvius was the main authority for A.D. 60–63.

[3] *Ann.* I. lxix, lxxxi; III. iii; IV. liii; VI. vi; XIII. xx; XIV. ii; XV. xvi, liii, lxi, lxxiv (*cf.* II. lxxxviii).

[4] *Hist.* II. xxxvii; III. li; *Ann.* I. xxix.

[5] *Ann.* V. iv. 4.

[6] *E.g. Hist.* IV. xxxix *sqq.*, where *decretae*, *censuit*, etc., are official echoes.

[7] *Ann.* XIII. xxxi. 1,

in his autobiography, Aufidius Bassus, Servilius Nonianus, Suetonius Paulinus, and Claudius. But in all this there are no more than possibilities. Indeed, throughout the whole question of Tacitus's sources, one is always brought back to a baffling uncertainty due to the loss of even such sources as he specifies.[1] One avenue which at first sight promised to lead to something definite was the investigation into the striking coincidences between Tacitus's Latin and Plutarch's Greek in their handling of Galba and Otho.[2] There have been upholders of the theory that in this case Plutarch used Tacitus; but the general conviction is that both used the same authority, and apparently with considerable closeness.[3] Beyond that, in spite of much ingenuity in argument, nothing tangible has been attained. A wide diversity of opinion prevails on the identification of this particular source. No less uncertainty has resulted from the attempts at assessing Tacitus's debt to his authorities in general and his method of employing them. Nissen, and after him Fabia, would have us believe that Tacitus's method was to follow closely the subject-matter of a single author for large tracts of his work, neglecting secondary sources (especially in composing the *Histories*), and devoting his attention to the embellishment of his borrowed material so as to produce a composition highly effective from the standpoint of style. It is as difficult now, as it was when Boissier first criticised Nissen's hypothesis, to accept an attitude which would imply a slavish lack of independence in Tacitus, and a dishonest pretence of consulting several authors at a time. The idea does not agree with Tacitus's known desire to get first-hand knowledge, as proved by the letters in which he secured from the younger Pliny information about the eruption of Vesuvius. In the entire absence of the original sources, there is the utmost difficulty in comprehending how one can comfortably assert that Tacitus drew from a single main source for large tracts of his work, or how one can claim to identify the source as the elder Pliny for the *Histories*, Aufidius Bassus for earlier parts of the *Annals*, and Cluvius Rufus for the reign of Nero.

Modern historical research demands methods of rigorous investigation which it is futile to expect in Tacitus. He will leave a matter of debate unsettled, and the uninitiated might wonder whether this is due to impartiality or natural hesitancy or an academic suspension of

[1] See Bibl. *re* p. 447 and S.H. § 437.

[2] The resemblances are arrayed by E. G. Hardy, Plut. *Galba and Otho* (Introd.), Lond. 1890.

[3] The view that Plutarch used Tac. is supported by O. Clason, *Plut. u. Tac.*, Berlin 1870; C. Nipperdey, ed. *Ann.*, 1874; R. Lange, *De Tacito Plutarchi auctore*, Halle 1880, and others. Most, however, guess at a common source, either the (inadequate) *acta diurna* (Hirzel), or Cluvius (H. Peter and Mommsen), or the elder Pliny (Nissen, Hardy, Fabia): refs. for these in S.H. § 437. Th. Wiedemann, *De Tac. Suet. Plut.* etc., diss. Berl. 1857, conjectured that Tac. used Pliny, and Plutarch both Pliny and Cluvius. C. E. Borenius (*De Plut. et Tac. inter se congruentibus*, diss. Helsing. 1902) argued that Plutarch used both Tacitus and the common source. For other variations, see S.H. § 437.

judgement. His criterion for decision in face of a conflict of evidence was usually what he deemed probable in the circumstances. The subjectivity of such a test, while it removes him from the category of strictly scientific historians, at the same time makes it important to note that personal outlook on the world, on politics and on history, which was certain to colour his interpretation of facts. Broadly his leanings are Stoic, though he wavers between freewill and predestination. At one time his language postulates an overmastering fate; at another it ascribes an event to the combined operation of a transcendental fate and human agency;[1] at yet another it betrays a doubt whether 'mortal affairs proceed by the unchangeable necessity of fate or by chance' (*in incerto iudicium est fatone res mortalium et necessitate immutabili an forte uoluantur, Ann.* VI. xxii). If his views of the world are chaotic,[2] he is not the only great writer who has found its mystery indefinable. He well realised how the misfortunes of the good and the prosperity of the wicked made plausible the Epicurean creed that the gods took no interest in mankind (*non denique homines dis curae,* VI. xxii); for himself, his melancholy observation of life made him not an atheist but a believer in the frequent wrath of heaven.[3] Yet even this was a matter of the prevailing mood, for he was ready to think it a kindly intervention of providence that vouchsafed a brilliant starlit night with the calm of a tranquil sea, as it were to unmask the crime of Nero's attempt to drown his mother.[4] With all this is mixed up a share of superstitious credulity towards prodigies and divination; but the essential point for us is that Tacitus, on the whole, believed in some law or principle which holds good among historical occurrences and so gives meaning to the quest after a cause. Early in the *Histories* he says:

> Before composing my purposed work, I intend to survey the condition of the capital, the temper of the armies, the attitude of the provinces, and what made for strength or weakness anywhere in the world, so that one may recognise not merely the incidents and issues of events, which are mainly affairs of chance, but also their meaning and causes.[5]

[1] *Hist.* I. x: 'occulta fati'; xviii: 'quae fato manent'; *Ann.* V. iv: 'fatali quodam motu . . . seu praua sollertia'; *Ann.* I. lv: 'Varus fato et ui Arminii cecidit.' Contrast *Ann.* III. xviii: 'ludibria rerum mortalium'; IV. xx: 'dubitare cogor fato et sorte nascendi . . . an sit aliquid in nostris consiliis.'

[2] R. von Pöhlmann, *Die Weltanschauung des T.* ed. 2, Mun. 1913, calls his views 'ein Chaos von unabgeklärten u. unausgereiften Meinungen.' Fabia's notice of Pöhlmann appeared in *J. Sav.* 1914, p. 250 ff., in art. entitled 'L'irréligion de Tacite.'

[3] *Hist.* IV. xxvi: 'quod in pace fors seu natura, tunc fatum et ira diuom uocabatur'; *Ann.* IV. i; 'non tam sollertia . . . quam deum ira . . .'; XVI. xvi: 'ira illa numinum in res Romanas'; *Hist.* I. iii: 'adprobatum est non esse curae deis securitatem nostram, esse ultionem.'

[4] *Ann.* XIV. v. i.

[5] *Hist.* I. iv. . . . 'non modo casus euentusque rerum . . . sed ratio etiam causaeque.'

With such expectations Tacitus could feel confidence in the dignity of history¹ and in its power to instruct the future:

> My design is not to set forth all motions made in the Senate, but only those which were remarkable for nobility or by reason of notorious infamy. This I consider the outstanding function of history to save excellence from oblivion and to confront evil words and evil deeds with the menace of reprobation from posterity (*ne uirtutes sileantur utque prauis dictis factisque ex posteritate et infamia metus sit*, *Ann.* III. lxv).

Towards this aim at teaching by example, character is of vital importance; and among the causes of events which most engage Tacitus's attention are human temperament and motives; so that, whatever the defects which made him in Mommsen's eyes the most unmilitary of historians, he is at the same time one of the most psychological.

In theory Tacitus was republican, and in his writings a *laudator temporis acti*, whether he had to contemplate the pre-imperial state or its eloquence, its education, its historians. Yet he admitted that circumstances had rendered inevitable the concentration of power in the hands of a single individual.² The old free republic, to him ideally preferable,³ could never come again.⁴ The duty of the citizen was therefore to pray for good emperors, but put up with such as one had,⁵ and to choose the safe path between brusque insolence and unseemly toadying (*inter abruptam contumaciam et deforme obsequium*, *Ann.* IV. xx). We have noted in the *Agricola* his admiration for moderate aristocrats and his disapproval for intransigent members of the opposition who concluded a defiant parade of independence with a theatrically ostentatious death (*ambitiosa morte*, *Agr.* xlii). Some consolation was obtainable from the fact that emperors like Nerva or Trajan could, he points out, square the principate with freedom. But, after all, the Empire remained for him a *pis aller*. With some emperors he could not but associate despotic cruelty, and with the period which he himself had to treat 'barbarous edicts, perpetual prosecutions, teacherous friendships, the ruin of the innocent, the same causes producing the same consequences while one meets only a surfeit of sameness (*obuia rerum similitudine et satietate*).'⁶ It is nothing short of a triumph of intellect and art that, insisting as he does upon his depressingly sombre theme, Tacitus should still be able to captivate his reader. The reader must, however, be content to be thus held while he is subtly indoctrinated;⁷ for dispassionate history is not to be expected from a hostile judge.

---

¹ *Ann.* XIII. xxxi: 'cum ex dignitate populi Romani repertum sit res inlustres annalibus, talia diurnis urbis actis mandare.'
² *Hist.* I. i: 'omnem potentiam ad unum conferri pacis interfuit.'
³ *Ann.* VI. xlii: 'populi imperium iuxta libertatem. . . .'
⁴ *Hist.* II. xxxvii–xxxviii. ⁵ *Hist.* IV. viii. ⁶ *Ann.* IV. xxxiii.
⁷ *Ibid.* 'plures aliorum euentis docentur: ceterum ut profutura, ita minimum oblectationis adferunt.'

The ineradicable prepossession in Tacitus is his conviction that Rome had fallen on evil days. No less than in the *Histories*, the opening chapters in the *Annals* have a sombie tone as of one looking back upon a long period of national woe. The rapid conspectus, in a sentence or two, of the evolution of Roman history towards one-man-rule closes in a glimpse at a world outworn with civil strife and subject to an emperor. Immediately one breathes an asphyxiating atmosphere of oppression and adulation which Tacitus feels must have impaired history. The deeds of the old Roman people, he remarks with pride, were recorded by famous historians, and even under the newly established Empire the Augustan age produced fine intellects capable of assessing and transmitting its achievements, had not court influence militated against the free utterance of opinion. But with later reigns came a blighting terrorism, so that, for the times of Tiberius, Gaius, Claudius and Nero, contemporary evidence was vitiated by dishonest flattery, and subsequent criticism vitiated by the reaction of loathing. From such extremes of feeling – from partiality as from bitterness – Tacitus at least claims to be exempt.[1] He proceeds to note the concentration of supreme power in the person of Augustus and the acquiescence of the provinces in an imperial control which guaranteed them protection against the worst rapacity of arbitrary officialdom. If this latter fact be viewed as a bright spot in the new system, the dynastic plans of Augustus to support his disguised despotism by recognised heirs are described as clouded by a series of misfortunes. The death of the young Marcellus, the untimely ends of the 'princes of the youth,' Gaius and Lucius Caesar, 'cut off by destiny or by their stepgrandmother Livia's treachery,' and the unfair banishment of the aged emperor's only surviving grandson, Agrippa Postumus, served in turn, through a tragically entangled net work of intrigue, to open for Livia's son Tiberius the path to the succession.

Such is the way in which the stage is cleared for the entrance of the figure around which the battle concerning Tacitus's credibility has been most fiercely fought.[2] It is noticeable that in several points this introduction anticipates the summary in which he takes leave of the life and

---

[1] *Ann.* I. i. . . . 'sine ira et studio, quorum causas procul habeo.'

[2] The question of Tiberius's character is older than the histories of Ihne and Duruy, and goes back to the 17th cent., when a justification of Tiberius was attempted by A. de la Houssaye, *Tibère*, Amst. 1686. For some modern views, see A. Stahr, *Tiberius*, Berl. 1863, ed. 2 1873; L. Freytag, *Tib. und Tac.*, Berl. 1870 (indicates inconsistencies in Tac.); E. S. Beesly, *Catiline, Clodius and Tib.*, Lond. 1878 (a rehabilitation); Furneaux, ed. *Ann.*, vol. i, on 'Char. and Govt. of Tib.' (moderate view); I. Gentile, *L'imp. Tiberio secondo la moderna critica storica*, Mil. 1887 (summarises points at issue); F. Faust, *De Vellei Pat. fide*, Giessen 1891; J. C. Tarver, *Tib. the Tyrant*, Westminster 1902 (a defence of Tib.); T. S. Jerome, *Roman Memories*, Lond. 1914, pp. 220–248 (refutation of 'Orgy in Capri'); J. S. Reid, 'Tac. as a Historian,' *J.R.S.* xi (1921), p. 191 ff. (protest against too high an estimate). Against Reid, Tacitus is defended by L. E. Lord, 'Tac. the Historian,' *C.J.* xxi (1925–26), p. 177 ff. E. Bacha, *Le génie de T.*, la

character of Tiberius at the close of the sixth book. That summary
divides his life into phases, and implies that a signal deterioration took
place in his final years of seclusion on the island of Capri, when, throwing off the habitual mask of hypocrisy, he came out in his true colours
(*remoto pudore et metu suo tantum ingenio utebatur*). During a first perusal
of the *Annals* one is so far overmastered by the accumulated effect attained
by reprobation and innuendo as to take Tiberius for an execrable though
accomplished tyrant. The author's skill whereby he first disarms suspicion with a profession of impartiality, and thereafter loses few opportunities of imputing sinister motives to the emperor, bears its intended
fruit in the reader's willingness to accept the historian's hostility for
independence. By a train of devices one is almost unconsciously en-
rolled as a sympathiser with the aristocratic opposition to empire. But
in time, upon reflection, there arise questionings. On a broad survey of
facts, how came it that the Roman Empire of the first century was on
the whole so well managed and so contented, if it was cursed with such
monsters for its governors as Tiberius, Caligula, Nero and Domitian
were traditionally represented to have been? And as to Tiberius in
particular – whose portrayal is the great test for the veracity of Tacitus –
how came it that his competence as ruler and his advanced years could
stand the strain of the prolonged debauchery which is alleged to have
disgraced his retirement at Capri?

The rehabilitation of an over-maligned Tiberius, however, runs a
risk of going so far as to do injustice to Tacitus in turn. Tacitus can
scarcely be charged with having invented libels upon the emperor:
for everything he most likely had some authority, and he believed in his
own impartiality. What can be pressed against him is the indictment
that his own imperfectly realised prejudice debarred him from weighing
judicially his information, drawn, as much of it was, from authorities
with strong senatorial sympathies. Tacitus had no canon of the credible
and incredible where his partisan passions were concerned. It is not,
therefore, surprising that great inconsistencies can be pointed out in
Books I–VI of the *Annals*. Reports of contemporary comments do not
necessarily make historical evidence; and whether Tacitus did or did
not set them down in malice, it was in malice that many of them were
conceived. The suspicion is not an unreasonable one that he drew from
tainted sources, like the memoirs of the younger Agrippina, which would
be decidedly anti-Tiberian in tone. If we consider the alleged orgy of
sensuality by Tiberius on Capri, the story may have originated in gossip

---

création des annales, Par. 1906, takes the extreme line that the work is a mendacious and poetic romance. Among more recent studies may be mentioned:
F. B. Marsh, *Reign of Tiberius*, Oxf. 1931, pp. 1–15 and index *s.v.* Tacitus;
G. A. Harrer, 'Tac. and Tib.,' *A.J.P.* 1920, p. 57 ff.; D. M. Pippidi, 'Tacite
et Tibère,' *Ephem. Dacoromana* 1938, p. 233 ff.; B. Walker, *The Annals of
Tacitus*, Oxf. 1952 (see index *s.v.* Tiberius); R. Syme, *Tacitus*, Oxf. 1958,
p. 420 ff.

provoked by the ruler's impenetrable seclusion on the island, or, according to another guess, it may have been a legacy from scurrilous writings designed to damage his moral character during his previous retirement in Rhodes, and then, if submitted confidentially to Augustus, possibly retained among state-papers to which a century later both Tacitus and Suetonius had access. Whatever the genesis of such tales, Tacitus's fault lay not in creating slanders but in failing to reject them critically. It is true that Suetonius, in ascribing loathsome profligacy to Tiberius, descends into details which Tacitus would pass over in lofty disdain;[1] but Tacitus ought to have noted the inherent unlikelihood of this particular scandal, which is not substantiated by anything in writers like Philo and Josephus. The view that Tacitus of set purpose draws Tiberius with the conventional qualities of the tyrant in rhetoric (such as cruelty, injustice, suspicion, craft, lust, and anguish of soul) seems too mechanical a conception. What one can admit is that Tacitus is not above visiting upon Tiberius the faults of some of his worst successors, and that just as Velleius, an admiring rhapsodist, overstresses his hero's merits, so Tacitus, although he records examples of the emperor's ability, wisdom, fairness, and even generosity, allows prejudice so to blind him to many commendable traits in Tiberius that he paints him too black. Tacitus had no more unfortunate limitation than the inability to think imperially: he never grasped the stupendous achievement involved in Augustus's reorganisation of the Empire, and he betrays a cardinal weakness when he misjudges Tiberius for his statesman-like adherence to the Augustan policy of consolidation in preference to aggrandisement.

The Latin of Tacitus, considered from the standpoint of vocabulary, grammar and syntax, bears the impress of his age; but no mere analysis of language can estimate the qualities of his style. Words were for him instruments handled with an individual touch of genius which makes his Latin different from that of all other writers. Careful investigators have examined his language and recorded their results in books or pamphlets written in Latin and various modern languages: here a few leading aspects may be noted. It has become almost traditional, and it remains sensible, to approach the subject under Bötticher's headings of brevity, variety, and poetic colour. Brevity is so inseparable from Tacitus that the schoolboy recognises it as a difficulty to be overcome. Verbs and connectives are freely dropped, and puzzlingly elliptical bits of syntax occur.[2] It was a condensation reached by a long process of experiment in thought and expression – an abrupt terseness pushed sometimes to the verge or over the verge of obscurity. The developed manner of the

---

[1] Voltaire's article, 'Pyrrhonisme' in his *Dictionnaire Historique*, stated doubts regarding Suetonius's account of the foulnesses alleged to have disgraced the old age of Tiberius.

[2] *E.g.* of the type met with in later bks. of *Annals*, such as XV. v: 'Vologesi uetus et penitus infixum erat arma Romana uitandi.'

Annals, which is in strong contrast to what some might call the cloying amplitude of Ciceronian prose, indicates that Tacitus has travelled far from the comparative fullness of his own earliest work. Though he can at times employ the period with fine effect, his sentence-structure in general represents a reaction from the Ciceronian. In Tacitus, as in Virgil, thought or feeling is compressed into chosen expressions of a brevity so profoundly significant that they capture the imagination. The soul which he breathed into prose makes his words live: almost unbidden, they revisit the memory, haunting it with their ironic, melancholy, often tragic power. One does not easily forget sayings like 'Heaven's wrongs are heaven's concern' (*deorum iniurias dis curae, Ann.* I. lxxiii), or 'short-lived and ill-starred are the darlings of the Roman people' (*breues et infaustos populi Romani amores, Ann.* II. xli). His terseness is at its most effective pitch in his epigrams and summaries of character. Again and again the finished neatness of the Latin seems to elude rendering. Take the picture of the inscrutability of Tiberius:

> His words were always halting and mysterious, but, now that his aim was the thorough concealment of his feelings, they became more than ever a tangled maze of uncertainty (*suspensa semper et obscura uerba: tunc uero nitenti ut sensus suos penitus abderet, in incertum et ambiguum magis implicabantur, Ann.* I. xi).

A deep glance into a warped nature is conveyed in the thumbnail sketch of a martinet's cruelty – 'an old hand at hard military tasks and the crueller for having suffered' (*uetus operis ac laboris et eo immitior quia tolerauerat, Ann.* I. xx). The policy of taking no notice of personal insults is inimitably expressed – 'calumnies wither up, if ignored: resentment gives them seeming recognition' (*spreta exolescunt: si irascare, agnita uidentur, Ann.* IV. xxxiv).

Variety is a phase of his independence. He gives changed meanings to words,[1] indulges in novel extensions of idiom (*e.g. pudet dictu, Agr.* xxxii); and, with a passion for the irregular, departs from the normal symmetry of expression where there is a balance in thought.[2] It is not surprising that a long list is available of words which occur only, or for the first time, in Tacitus, such as *adcumulator, adulatorius, concertator, eiectamentum, imitamentum, inlacessitus, instigator, instigatrix, peramoenus, regnatrix.* In keeping with this goes a preference for the less usual form of a word, *claritudo* and *firmitudo* rather than *claritas* and *firmitas*;[3] the form in -*men* like *fragmen, medicamen, tegumen*, where the commoner prose forms end in -*mentum*; and conversely, those in -*mentum*,

---

[1] See Dräger, *Syntax u. Stil des T.*, ed. 2, Lpz. 1874.
[2] *Germ.* xlvi: 'uictui herba, uestitui pelles, cubile humus'; *Hist.* I. liii: 'corpore ingens, animi immodicus'; *Ann.* III. lxv: 'insignes per honestum aut notabili dedecore'; XII. xxix: 'subsidio uictis et terrorem aduersus uictores.'
[3] Cicero never uses *claritudo*; Sallust uses *claritudo*, not *claritas*; in Tacitus's *Ann. claritudo* is frequent and *claritas* rare, though they are fairly equal in the *Hist.*

like *cognomentum* and *leuamentum* rather than *cognomen* and *leuamen*. The so-called Graecisms are to be set down to the same pursuit of variety, although linguistically they are mainly not so much direct borrowings from the Greek as inheritances from native Latin idiom developed under Greek influence,[1] or actual imitations of previous Roman writers: thus what is termed the Greek attracted dative (*quibus bellum uolentibus erat, Agr.* xviii) had already appeared in Sallust and Livy, both of whom exerted influence upon Tacitus.

The poetic colouring is ubiquitous. It is noticeable in poetic, and especially Virgilian, words, which he often shares with prose-writers of the Silver Age as a result of the predominance of poetry in academic education. Examples are *adolere, breuia* ('shallows'), *crebrescere, exspes, gestamen, meatus, regnator.*[2] It is noticeable also in turns of phrase which recall Virgil, in frequent metaphors, and in personifications such as the informers' 'eloquence dripping with blood' (*sanguinantis eloquentiae, Dial.* xii); 'nowhere is the sea more widely a queen' (*nusquam latius dominari mare, Agr.* x); 'a night that threatens and will break forth into crime' (*noctem minacem et in scelus erupturam, Ann.* I. xxviii).[3]

Partly poetic association, partly a desire for variety sent Tacitus back sometimes to old-fashioned words, though, in spite of his liking for Sallust, he is more of an innovator than an archaiser. He occasionally employs Plautine words like *mercimonium* or *perduellis* or *dissertare*, and by a kindred impulse substitutes the simple verb for the compound, *e.g.*, *cernere* for *decernere* and *firmare* for *affirmare*. But he does not resort to the antique in the manner of Apuleius and Gellius later in his century. Like one of the interlocutors in his *Dialogus*, he recognised the current demand for novel smartness and poetic turns 'unstained by the rust (*ueternus*) of Accius and Pacuvius, but taken from the sacred treasury of Horace, Virgil or Lucan.'[4] It is an unwarrantable assumption to regard his hexametric opening in the *Annals* (*Vrbem Romam a principio reges habuere*) as a citation from Ennius.[5]

[1] K. Brugmann in *Indogerm. Forsch.* v, p. 100; F. Stolz and J. H. Schmalz, *Latein. Gramm.* (Müller's Hb. II. ii.), ed. 3, Mun. 1900, p. 474.

[2]

	Pre-Silver Poetry	Silver Prose apart from Tacitus
adolere	Lucr., Virg., Ov.	Columella, Plin. Mai.
breuia ('shallows')	Virg.	
crebrescere	Virg.	Quint., Plin. Min.
exspes	Accius, Hor., Ov.	
gestamen	Virg., Ov.	Sen. Phil., Plin. Mai.
meatus	Lucr., Virg.	Sen. Phil., Quint., Plin. Mai. et Min.
regnator	Plaut., Naev., Virg.	

All the above appear in silver poetry also. Many similar words are listed in Dräger, *op. cit.* § 249.

[3] Cf. *Agr.* xxii: 'intrepida hiems'; *Germ.* xxvii: 'sepulcrum caespes erigit'; *Ann.* I. lxxiv: 'uestigia morientis libertatis.'

[4] *Dial.* xx. 5.

[5] In reviewing De Groot's 'Antike Prosarhythmus,' *J.R.S.* xi (1921), pp. 116–117, I pointed out that the identity of the possibly un-Tacitean title *Annales*

Yet to scrutinise his language is only to note the mechanism of his style. What most matters is the use to which he could put his words, and his achievement of imperishable effects through his mastery over vividness, irony and an elevation of style too dignified to tolerate lapses into the petty or the repulsive. Many of his qualities, like his epigrams, sprang from rhetoric: it would be idle to pretend that he is free from affectation, but it is an affectation tempered with sound sense that never allows him to be carried into exuberance. Brilliant in his brevity, Tacitus does not depend for his fame solely on his bright flashes. His style is one of sustained power which does not admit triviality or dullness. 'Le plus grand peintre de l'antiquité,' as Racine called him, showed himself a master of portraiture and description when his theme was a character, a conflict, a mutiny, a disaster, a plot, a trial, a debate. All is rapidity and the interest never flags. His originality is a phase of his intense subjectivity. He leaves his imprint on his writings because, as we have seen, he abandons the normal for a surprising terseness and for daring novelties, and because his vigour of expression reflects his realistic conception of the men and events which made his material.

Strange vicissitudes mark the history of Tacitus's posthumous fame.[1] Notwithstanding Pliny's confidence in his friend's literary immortality, the immediately succeeding generations showed faint interest in his writings. He was not spicy enough in detail for admirers of the Suetonian type of biography, not quaint enough in style for the archaising school later in the century, not appreciative enough of either Christians or Jews to please the Fathers of the Church. Even his monograph on Agricola seems to have been little read, and grammarians do not quote him. In the final quarter of the third century, the emperor Tacitus claimed relationship with the historian, and in alarm lest his works should be lost *lectorum incuria*, issued orders for the multiplication of copies, making it compulsory for libraries to possess them.[2] In the fourth century it was the fond ambition of Ammianus Marcellinus, the last considerable historian in antiquity, to prove himself another Tacitus by continuing his works in thirty-one books (of which the last eighteen survive) on the Empire from the reign of Nerva to that of Valens. We can prove that Tacitus was known to the Aquitanian presbyter Sulpicius Severus, to Augustine's Spanish friend Orosius, and to Sidonius Apollinaris; but when Cassiodorus in the sixth century, on the subject of amber, refers to 'a certain Cornelius' as having mentioned it, we realise how misty his reputation had grown.[3] That the Carolingian period had

---

with that of Ennius's poem makes a shaky foundation for the guess that Tacitus is citing Ennius, and a shakier one for the dogmatic statement (*op. cit.* p. 27), 'die Annalen fängt er aber so gar mit einem ganzen Hexameter des Ennius an.'
[1] F. Ramorino, *Cornelio Tacito nella storia della coltura*, Mil. 1898; F. Haverfield, 'T. during late Roman period and the Middle Ages,' *J.R.S.* vi (1916), p. 196 ff. [2] S.H.A. *Tac.* x.
[3] Cassiod. *Var.* v. 2: 'quodam (*quondam*, Müllenhoff) Cornelio scribente.'

access to the *Germania* and the earlier books of the *Annals* can be demonstrated from the works of Rudolf of Fulda in the second half of the ninth century. Thereafter silence falls for some centuries until we find Boccaccio possessed of a manuscript, perhaps identical with our 'Second Medicean,' containing the later books of the *Annals* with the *Histories*. The facts concerning the arrival at Rome from Germany in 1455 of the sole source for the minor works, and the discovery at Corbey in 1508 of the 'First Medicean,' the sole source for the earlier part of the *Annals*, are thrilling reminders how near the world came to losing Tacitus. All that we possess of him has been available in print since 1515, and has interested generations of politicians, historians, and essayists from Macchiavelli, Guicciardini and Montaigne onwards. When one reads of French revolutionaries relying upon Tacitean doctrine, one is amused to think that Milton had to rebut Salmasius's misreading of him as an upholder of autocratic rule.

His influence upon early English drama should not be forgotten. It may be illustrated by Ben Jonson's *Sejanus His Fall*, first acted in 1603 (when Shakespeare played a part), but not published till 1605. The playwright's address 'To the Readers' acknowledges his debt to Tacitus, Dio and Suetonius among others; and the same three sources were drawn upon some years later for the anonymous play of *Nero*. Abroad, Tacitus's stimulus towards dramatic production is visible under Louis XIV in Corneille's *Otho* and Racine's *Britannicus*; towards the end of the eighteenth century in Alfieri's *Ottavia*; and about the beginning of the nineteenth in Marie-Joseph Chénier's *Tibère* and Arnault's *Germanicus*.

His style militated against popularity with humanists so strictly trained on the norm of Ciceronianism as to be unable to see the merits of a different type of prose; but one most interesting phase of his influence is traceable in Justus Lipsius, whose edition of Tacitus in 1574 was a masterpiece of scholarship. Lipsius's editorial labours transformed his Latin from Ciceronian into Tacitean and, in establishing his claim to breadth of literary taste, at the same time bore witness to the vital power transmitted by the great historian of the early empire.

Chapter III

JUVENAL

Perplexities of biography – Medieval *uitae* – Contradictory and incredible elements – Tradition of Juvenal's exile – Was he in Egypt? – Was he in Britain? – The lost inscription from Aquinum – Martial and Juvenal – Publication of the Satires in books – A few dates obtainable – Survey of the Satires – Motives for writing – Pretence of satirising a previous generation – Men of evil life – A gallery of detestable women – An honest Roman's farewell to Rome – Dramatic elements – Hosts and clients – Prospects of literature – Vanity of human wishes – Plain living and extravagance – Legacy-hunters – Revenge a weakness – Parental example – Egyptian villages at feud – A soldier's advantages – Change of spirit in later Satires – Lucilius, Horace, Juvenal – Power of vivid delineation – Dark colours – Grimness of humour – Control of rhetorical artifice – Familiar quotations – Debt to predecessors – Juvenal's hexameter – Words from the common speech – Influence on later writers.

THE life of D. Junius Juvenalis is full of perplexities which investigation has not disentangled. Outside the scanty data obtainable from his works and certain scholia, there is little on which to rely with absolute security: yet there is a considerable amount of apparent evidence consisting of some thirteen biographies, mostly medieval, attached to many of the interpolated MSS., an inscription of possible relevance from Aquinum, three poems addressed by Martial to a Juvenal whom we can hardly suppose to have been other than the satirist, mention by a few later authors,[1] and an allusion in a hendecasyllabic poem by Sidonius Apollinaris[2] to one who had the misfortune, like Ovid, to be banished and who was the 'exiled victim of an actor's wrath' (*irati fuit histrionis exsul*). Since the banishment of Juvenal is a tradition among the *uitae*, though its alleged time and place vary, this last allusion is not unnaturally taken to apply to him. Juvenal was too much of a contemporary to figure in Suetonius's book *De Viris*

[1] Ioannes Malalas, *Chron.* X, p. 341 (Chilmead), says Juvenal was banished to the Pentapolis in Libya for attacking Domitian's favourite Paris. Suidas has an entry regarding 'Ιουβενάλιος to like effect. Juvenal is coupled with Marius Maximus in Amm. Marcell. XXVIII. iv. 14, and with Turnus in Rut. Namat. *Itin.* I. 604, and in Ioannes Lydus, *De Mag.* I. 41.
[2] IX. 269.

Illustribus,[1] so that even the best written of the *Lives* – namely, that added to the Codex Montepessulanus or Pithoeanus in a later hand – cannot be surmised to rest on so good a foundation as Suetonius, or indeed to be of earlier date than the fourth century. Twelve *uitae* seem to be variations of the earliest one, independent variations being almost certainly attempts to add conjectures based upon passages in the satires. Thus, the prevailing tradition of a banishment to Egypt is varied in two *uitae* to '*contra Scotos*' – a change presumably suggested by Juvenal's references to Britain. How little intelligence might underlie a *uita* can be gauged from the absurd explanation, given by one in a Harleian MS., that Juvenal's last satire, an attack on the unfair advantages of soldiers, was meant to encourage recruiting. This looks as if the innocent fabricator had confined himself to the opening sentence – *Quis numerare queat felicis praemia, Galli, militiae?*

The chief statements in the most highly commended *uita* are that Juvenal was either a son or foster-son of a rich freedman (a closely allied *uita* adds Aquinum as his birthplace); that he practised declamation until middle life more for the sake of amusement (*animi magis causa*) than for academic or forensic use; that he composed lines directed against Domitian's pantomime-actor Paris; that later, when he had become famous, he inserted those lines into what we know as the seventh satire;[2] that there happened then to be at court a favourite actor who took the lines as directed against himself; that Juvenal's supposed allusion was resented in the highest quarters; and that, under pretext of giving him a military command but in reality by way of punishment, the authorities gazetted him at the age of eighty to the prefecture of a cohort in a distant part of Egypt, where he very soon (*intra breuissimum tempus*) died of grief and weariness.

Difficulties arise at once. If Juvenal was either son or foster-son of a rich *libertinus*, how comes it that he is so obviously acquainted with poverty at first hand, and why does he assail the class of freedmen, if he owed it either birth or up-bringing? His tone convinces us that, for at least one part of his life, far from being wealthy, he had experienced the indignities put upon clients, hated the pampered lackeys of arrogant patrons, and felt deep sympathy with the poor.[3] Horace could attack an individual freedman, as he did in the fourth epode, but Juvenal detests the whole category: not only does he despise the purse-proud upstart who had once been his barber, but he writes in general with so Roman a prejudice against the foreigner that one cannot but distrust the allegation of an alien strain in him.[4] The more one examines the *uitae*, the more do they appear to be manufactured: here the suspicion arises

---

[1] Published probably before A.D. 114. Juvenal was alive after A.D. 127.

[2] VII. 90–92.

[3] *E.g.* on the dole, I. 95 *sqq.*; lackeys, III. 188–189; poverty, III. 152–153, 163–165.

[4] I. 24–30; III. 58–125; X. 226.

that Juvenal, being a satirist, has been by some wrong-headed parallel-hunter credited with a *libertinus* for a father simply because Horace had one before him. If it is just conceivable that the lines cited as offensive enough to get him banished might have been twisted against the author in the way alleged, at any rate the appointment of an octogenarian to a military post in an important province appears too incredible a prank for the Roman Empire: and, in any case, this statement in three *Lives* is contradicted by that in another group, which indicates it was Domitian, not Trajan, who punished Juvenal. According to that, the exile would have occurred earlier in Juvenal's career.

Confusion increases as we look through the *uitae*. One declares Juvenal to have come back to Rome from his command, and to have died of melancholy because he did not see his friend Martial (who had left the city for Spain in A.D. 98): another declares he died worn out with old age as late as the reign of Antoninus Pius, having been exiled by Domitian but not recalled by his immediate successors. In this latter *uita* he is said to have 'amplified his satires in exile and made many changes in them,' a statement which bore fruit in part of Ribbeck's theory about two Juvenals. An additional *uita* found by Dürr in a MS. in the Palazzo Barberini at Rome agrees with twelve of the *uitae* that Juvenal belonged to Aquinum: it also provides him with a mother and sister named alike Septumuleia, which betrays medieval ignorance of the classic usage whereby any daughter of Junius Juvenalis would have been called Junia. The inconsistencies in these biographies cannot but throw doubt even on any consistent residuum, unless it be independently supported. Though a majority of the *uitae* mention a military command in Egypt, one has the uncomfortable suspicion that this may have come from an impression that Juvenal's treatment of an Egyptian subject in Satire XV necessarily implied residence near its scene:[1] and, again, though in a majority of the *uitae* he is said to have practised declamation till middle life, this may have been an invention from the rhetorical manner characteristically persisting in satires which were manifestly composed long after he had been an academic pupil.[2]

The all-but-unanimous record of a banishment appears to receive some confirmation in the allusion already cited from Sidonius Apollinaris; but one realises that there is no certainty about the emperor who pronounced the sentence, nor any means of deciding whether the command in Egypt is or is not a confusion with previous military service in Britain. The almost complete consensus about Aquinum as Juvenal's birthplace agrees with, and indeed may be ultimately due to, the passage in the third satire where Umbricius, who is supposed to be saying good-bye to the poet, employs the phrase 'tuo Aquino.'[3] That there was a

[1] 'Quantum ipse notaui,' XV. 45, is not absolutely convincing proof of his having been in Egypt. His topographical mistake about the two villages Ombi and Tentyra does not add to one's confidence.

[2] *E.g. cf.* I. 15–17 with 25.

[3] III. 318–321.

Juvenal at Aquinum is clear from the inscription discovered there and
long since lost.[1] It recorded a dedication to Ceres (the very goddess mentioned towards the close of the third satire) by Junius Juvenalis (the
praenomen had disappeared), who was an officer in a cohort of Dalmatians,
and who, in respect of being a *duumuir quinquennalis* and *flamen* of the
deified Vespasian, was evidently the holder of two local offices of
importance. The reference to Vespasian-worship places the inscription
late in the first century, and, as more than one Dalmatian cohort served,
we know, in Britain about this period, it is tempting to think that here
we have an explanation of the satirist's repeated references to so far-off
an island – his mention of the captured Orkneys and the short night of
the North, the chariot-fighting of Britons, the oysters of Rutupiae
(Richborough in Kent), the British whale, the forts of the Brigantes in
Yorkshire, the spread of Latin eloquence to Thule (a designed exaggeration), and his use of the rather official form *Brittones*.[2] But here again
questions arise. If Juvenal had seen war-service, did it leave him inimical to a military life, as he appears to be in his last satire? And, in
addition to his undoubtedly close acquaintance with Roman city life,
was he long enough resident at Aquinum to hold important magistracies
there?

If Martial's Juvenal is, as seems most likely, our Juvenal, then we
have the evidence of two epigrams in the seventh book belonging to
A.D. 92, and one in the twelfth book issued in 101 or 102, after Martial
had returned to Spain.[3] By 92 Juvenal is regarded by his friend as
facundus, which may refer either to style in writing or to eloquence in
speech. The eloquence has in this case generally been associated with
rhetorical powers, but it may have a forensic reference. Juvenal is
possibly speaking of his own practice at the bar when, after stigmatising
the high fee paid to a nobleman as advocate, he adds 'and yet *we* pleaded
better.'[4] Besides, it is worth noting that Martial applies the epithet
facundus to his lawyer friend Pliny, and that Juvenal too uses it of
lawyers.[5] Granted that banishment ever befell Juvenal, there was time
for it to have occurred between 92 and 101 or 102, when Martial again
addressed Juvenal; and whether Juvenal was an advocate or not, he was
then pictured as a struggling citizen wearing his sweaty gown (*sudatrix
toga*) at receptions in the mansions of the great. Between the two poets
a great sympathy of outlook is discernible.[6] They not only touch often
upon the same subjects and persons, but adopt a very similar attitude
towards literature and patronage; they unveil alike the vices of their

[1] *C.I.L.* X. 5382=Dessau, *I.L.S.* 2926.
[2] II. 159–161; IV. 126, 141; X. 14; XIV. 196; XV. 111–112, 124.
[3] Mart. VII. xxiv and xci; XII. xviii.
[4] Juv. VII. 124–125, 'et melius nos egimus.' See F. J. Merchant, *A.J.P.*
xxii (1901), p. 51 ff.
[5] Mart. X. xx. 3; Juv. VIII. 48; *cf.* VII. 145.
[6] Nettleship, *L. and E.* II, pp. 124–131; Pearson and Strong's ed. pp. 41–43.

day; and they exhibit considerable resemblance in words and expressions.

Fortunately a few unquestioned dates can be extracted from his works. The sixteen satires were issued in five sets or books at different times.[1] Internal evidence as to date discoverable from any one satire has therefore significance for the whole volume to which it belongs. The first book contained satires I–V, and the bitter tone regarding Domitian in the second and fourth satires would alone prove that their composition was later than his assassination in 96.[2] But we do not need to rely on inference; for a definite reference is made in the fourth satire to his murder.[3] The opening satire, which, being prefatory, may have been written last, alludes to the sentence on Marius Priscus for misgovernment in Africa;[4] and, as we can date this trial, in which Pliny held a prosecuting brief, at A.D. 100, we see that Juvenal's earliest published work belongs to the beginning of the second century. It seems natural to think that Domitian's reign was not yet far in the past, and that Juvenal writes with a fierce, because recent, recollection of the repression which had been removed, to the equal relief of writers like Pliny and Tacitus. This spirit makes it difficult to believe that Friedländer is right in dating the first book so late as the years between 112 and 116 in order to bring it nearer in time to the succeeding book.

The long sixth satire formed the second book. The comet and the earthquake[5] there mentioned have been convincingly assigned to the year 115, so that the volume can be dated about A.D. 116.

The third book consisted of satires VII, VIII and IX. The first of these three opens with the declaration that the future of literature depends on the emperor entirely – *et spes et ratio studiorum in Caesare tantum*. Which Caesar? Some have said Trajan; Nettleship argued for Domitian,[6] without winning much support for a theory which would badly break the chronological sequence of the volumes. A more fitting emperor and period can be found in Hadrian, soon after his accession. He had poetic tastes, and Juvenal's words were a not unbecoming compliment to the new ruler who reached Rome from the East in 118. Satire VIII was probably written earlier: its allusion to Marius Priscus suggests a date not long after A.D. 100.[7]

The date of the fourth book, containing X, XI, and XII is undiscoverable. The remaining four satires constituted the fifth book. Two

---

[1] F. Leo, 'Doppelfassungen bei Juv.,' *Herm.* xliv (1909), p. 600 ff., argued for two complete editions, one published by the poet himself, the second (containing alterations) after his death; and attempted to reconstruct double versions in Juvenal (*cf.* the Bodleian fragment). If copies of both editions were known to commentators for centuries, then the posthumous text might in places be interpolated from the earlier.

[2] II. 29–33; IV. 37, 73, 84–88.   [3] IV. 153.
[4] I. 49–50.
[5] VI. 407, 411.
[6] *J.Ph.* xvi, p. 55 ff.   [7] VIII. 120: 'nuper Marius discinxerit Afros.'

R

passages in it give clues to a date, and fix the thirteenth satire to 127 and the fifteenth to 128 A.D.[1]

This brief summary indicates a literary activity of some thirty years. If, as we may infer, Juvenal had reached middle life when the first volume was published, a date about A.D. 60 might be conjectured for his birth. By the time of the eleventh satire he writes as an old man.[2] Unlike Lucilius and Horace, his acknowledged masters in satire, Juvenal reveals little about himself. His rhetorical education was the one customary for Romans of standing.[3] For the philosophy professed by exalted minds he felt a respect proportionate to his contempt for philosophical hypocrites; but the philosophy which appealed to him was not so much that of the Greek schools[4] as that of life:

> Great is Philosophy, whose holy writ
> Ordains commandments and who conquers Chance.
> We deem those happy too whom life hath taught
> To bear life's ills nor fret against the yoke.[5]

He himself had been schooled by hardship, though later in his career we know he owned a small farm at Tibur, and was able to offer hospitality to friends in his own house at Rome.[6]

The sixteen Satires consist of nearly 3,900 hexameters, and range in length from the 661 lines (or, including the Bodleian[7] fragment, 695 lines) of the devastatingly horrible sixth satire to the 60 lines of the incomplete sixteenth. In particular, the first, third and tenth – each making a different appeal – can be read again and again without losing their freshness: they stand the true test of the classical. It is impossible to miss either the nobility of spirit pervading the thirteenth or the terrific, if overdriven, power of the indictment against women in the sixth.

The first satire is a characteristic prelude – the poet's *apologia*, to explain why he should write satire, and what his manner and matter should be. A careful examination of it, therefore, reveals the underlying aim. Deafened with recitations from authors, and, like Martial, sick of hackneyed mythology, must not Juvenal too have his say?

> Shall I just listen always? ne'er repay
> Hoarse Cordus bawling his heroic lay?

[1] XIII. 17; XV. 27: 'nuper consule Iunco.'
[2] XI. 203   [3] I. 15–17.   [4] XIII. 121–123.
[5] XIII. 19–22:

> 'Magna quidem, sacris quae dat praecepta libellis,
> Victrix Fortunae Sapientia: ducimus autem
> Hos quoque felices, qui ferre incommoda uitae,
> Nec iactare iugum, uita didicere magistra.'

[6] XI. 65, 190.
[7] This piece, 34 lines long, was discovered in 1899 by E. O. Winstedt. The sceptical attacks of a few Continental critics only served to establish its authenticity; but Dralle, in a Marburg dissertation, 1922, renewed the ineffectual attempt. See S.H. § 420a (Literatur über die bodleianischen Zusätze).

> Shall one recite his comedies at me,
> Another elegiacs, and go free? ...
> I too learned rhetoric beneath the cane:
> My essays counselled Sulla sleep to gain
> In private life. 'Tis clemency misplaced,
> When everywhere with swarms of bards you're faced,
> To spare the paper someone sure will waste.[1]

So much to justify writing. But why satire? Why should Juvenal follow the career of Lucilius? The answer comes pat: the difficulty is *not* to write satire (*difficile est saturam non scribere*). The prominence of offensive and vicious persons goads one into invective. One loathes the spectacle of the impotent who dares to marry, or the masculine woman aping a man, or the fabulously wealthy ex-slave and ex-barber flaunting his riches. Annoying beyond endurance are the over-smart lawyers, the teacherous informer and the unabashed will-hunter. How one's anger blazes to think of an innocent ward driven to evil courses by the knavery of an unscrupulous guardian, or of a guilty proconsul receiving so light a sentence that he can enjoy exile on his ill-gotten gains! Such abuses need the Venusian lamp of Horace, and, somewhat in Martial's spirit, Juvenal claims that he has no taste for legendary themes, when, from lust of filthy lucre, a cuckold encourages his wife's lover, or when horse-racing spendthrifts expect commissions in the army. In fact, the temptation is rather to compose a whole volume in the open street, when an imposing *lectica* brings along a forger lolling at ease or a wealthy widow who poisoned her husband. If you would cut a figure, dare some black deed that ought to earn transportation or jail: honesty gets praise but is left in the cold (*probitas laudatur et alget*):

> To crime men owe their table, park, estate,
> Goblets in high relief or antique plate.
> Say, who could find the calm repose they need
> When a son's wife is bribed to sin for greed,
> When brides prove frail and boys turn paramours?
> Though nature jibs, yet wrath my verse ensures.
> (*si natura negat, facit indignatio uersum*).[2]

So, like Martial again, but in an angrier tone, Juvenal proclaims his subject to be human life – a gallimaufry of everything from the days of the Flood:

> Whate'er men do, their vows, fears, pleasure, rage,
> Joys, hustle, make the hotchpotch of my page.[3]

And when was there ever a heavier crop of villainy and avarice? Picture

[1] I. 1–4, 15–18.
[2] I. 75–79.
[3] I. 85–86:

> 'Quidquid agunt homines, uotum, timor, ira uoluptas,
> Gaudia, discursus, nostri est farrago libelli.'

the gamester attended by his steward, armed squire-like with a money-chest for the battle of the gaming-table, ready to stake a fortune but refusing raiment to a shivering slave. Think of the many country-seats one rich individual may possess; think of his dining off seven courses in solitary state; think of the miserable dole of the *sportula* given at his door to poor dependants, and the care taken to confer this charity upon as few as possible. The scramble for the dole, and the degrading tricks by which it is sought, are inimitably narrated with all Juvenal's power of realistic detail. 'Wealth,' he remarks bitingly, 'is our most revered divinity: how singular that we Romans have raised no temple to Money – no altars to the coinage to match our worship of Pax, Fides, Victoria, Virtus and Concordia!' The gluttony of the rich, however, brings its penalty in sudden death: and no one feels sorry. Nowadays vice has reached its zenith – 'so then, my satire, hoist sail, crowd on full canvas!' (*utere uelis, totos pande sinus*). Yet one caution must be observed. If, following Lucilius, you attack those in high station, you may be sentenced to a cruel death. Therefore count the cost before the trumpet sounds. It is safer to satirise a past generation – those who lie buried beside the Great North Road (the *Flaminia*), or the South-Eastern Road (the *Latina*). Dead men do not retaliate.

Juvenal's claim here to occupy himself with the past is noteworthy. The profession is less an attempted blind for his own safety than simply another way of disavowing, as Martial explicitly did, the intention of attacking individuals of his own times. Some critics have emphasised the unreality of Juvenal's working himself into a fury against dead men and bygone abuses; but it may be urged that conceivably part of his material was secretly written up (it was certainly noted in the mind) under Domitian, and that anyhow, as society does not radically change within a few years, there obviously remained, even under the better rule of Trajan, abundance of human types inviting satiric attack. Contemporary observation would then reinforce memory. The theory that represents Juvenal's eye as mainly upon the past fails to account for his vigour of style, which is not adequately explained as artificial rhetoric.

Satires II, VI and IX may be considered together. Their plain-spokenness on sexual excess or perversion has excluded them from many editions. Satire II denounces the atrocious profligacy of hypocritical philosophers 'who pose as Puritans, but live in vice' (*qui Curios simulant et Bacchanalia uiuunt*). After a Zolaesque glance at diseases caused by evil living, it is conceded that an open offender is less obnoxious than a counterfeit moralist: 'who'd stand a Gracchus railing at revolt?' (*quis tulerit Gracchos de seditione querentes?*). In contrast with the sixth satire, a woman is here introduced as a critic of the unnatural depravity of some of the male sex. She protests that not women but men deserve the rigours of the law. Yet 'censure acquits the crow but damns the dove' (*dat ueniam coruis uexat censura columbas*). Men begin with effeminate luxury and

end as such monstrosities that the other world would have to be dis-
infected after receiving them! One great lesson is driven home – the
steps in degradation must be jealously watched; 'No man becomes a
blackguard in a trice' (*nemo repente fuit turpissimus*).

Satire VI is a long gallery of women to be avoided. Some are incurably
bad and deserve all they get: others, whom we might call merely objectionable, like the loud-voiced virago or ostentatious she-pedant, incur
equal castigation from the angry author. About his brilliant vehemence
there can be no doubt. One must, however, not expect a strictly logical
summary; for careful planning is not Juvenal's forte. He will not limit
his energy to a fixed programme. Thus in VI he harks back to its opening jeremiad on the disappearance of primitive chastity from a degenerate world; and more than once he introduces the capricious cruelty of
mistresses to slaves, or the passion for public spectacles. It is inevitable,
then, that, in satires like the first, critics should note signs of imperfect
construction. What, however, is lost in methodical arrangement is
often gained in free vigour.

His immediate keynote is the insanity of a man's contemplating marriage so long as ropes are available to hang himself with! With characteristic exaggeration he declares there are few pure women left in
Rome – few that do not behave as dangerous temptresses. Can one
imagine a woman content with one husband? Scarcely could one discover an honest girl in the country. Roman ladies are spectators of
indecent pantomimes, they fall in love with players or gladiators –
they will desert home and children for a pet 'Sergy'[1] – and they prove
exacting in the costliest fancies.

Should you chance on that astounding rarity (*rara auis in terris nigro-
que simillima cygno*) – a good woman – she is likely to exhibit intolerable
pride (*grande supercilium*): and the boastfulness that ruined Niobe
spoils all other feminine merits. Then there is the annoying affectation
of using Greek words (like the wanton ζωή and ψυχή) which turned an
Italian girl into 'a maid of Athens' with Hellenic blandishments. Even
true love for your bride constitutes a danger; you become her thrall and
Madame rules the house, prescribing your affections, settling your will,
sentencing a slave to death, and in the end leaving you if it suits her.
Figure to yourself the wife of eight husbands in five autumns – an
elegant epitaph! (Here again Martial might be speaking.) Besides, there
is your mother-in-law, schooling the young mistress in rapacity and
duplicity. If there is a law-suit, *cherchez la femme* (*nulla fere causa est
in qua non femina litem mouerit*). Another bugbear is the unsexed woman
who takes up fencing, or the guilty consort whose hypocritical tears
conceal her offence, who brazens out the charge if detected in an amour,
and is eloquent where a trained rhetorician would be hard put to it for an
excuse. Riches, drunkenness, foreign ways, strange rituals have all

[1] 'Sergiolus' VI. 105.

contributed to Rome's deterioration. The advice may be offered to set a guard on one's wife – 'but who shall guard the guards themselves?' (*quis custodiet ipsos custodes?*)

The unpleasant series of portraits continues: the housewife whose ruinous extravagance knows no bounds and takes no lesson; she who dotes on eunuchs or musicians; the gossip who retails the latest news with additions; the bad-tempered woman, imperious in demands on her slaves and coolly keeping guests waiting for dinner if she chooses to have a bath. There is also the victim of disgusting intemperance; but Juvenal's grim humour represents as worse still[1] the lady who will talk literature at table – Madam Oracle, beside whom not even another woman (to say nothing of an attorney or town-crier) could get a word in:[2] and, with a suggestive alliteration, he adds:

> The wave of words, you'd swear, that from her wells
> Sounds like so many basins banged with bells.[3]

Therefore do not let the Roman matron go in too much for logic, history, grammar, or rhetoric, for she will then quote verses you don't know, and pedantically correct her friend's slip in grammar. He returns to the maltreatment of slaves – a displaced curl may cost a lashing: he then pillories the devotees of Eastern superstition, and those who avoid motherhood, smuggle supposititious children into a home to delude a husband, and resort to magic charms or philtres or even to poisons. But – and here Juvenal anticipates the criticism that he paints too dark a picture – you will say, this is all tragic rant.[4] No, it is too true: Roman women are guilty of the enormities described. Alcestis died for her husband; the modern woman would have a husband die for a pet dog. There are Clytemnestras everywhere.

It is a lurid ending, all the more effective after the clever protest that he has only been telling the truth. In this satire we seem far away from the respectable society of the satirist's contemporary, Pliny the younger. Yet if the picture is too much overdrawn to be sound history, the genius of the author makes it great literature.

The ninth satire need not occupy us fully. In treating the unpleasant theme of a reprobate's sorrows, Juvenal introduces just enough of the element of dialogue to remind one of the manner of Persius. Answering the interlocutor's request that he should withhold his revelation of

---

[1] VI. 433:
> 'Illa tamen grauior, quae cum discumbere coepit,
> Laudat Vergilium, periturae ignoscit Elissae.'

[2] VI. 438–440.

[3] VI. 440–442:
> 'Verborum tanta cadit uis,
> Tot pariter pelues ac tintinnabula dicas
> Pulsari.'

[4] VI. 634 *sqq.*: 'Fingimus haec . . .'

depravity in high circles, the poet asks in turn whether rich offenders can ever successfully hide their infamy – the very talk of one's slaves should set a check on evil living. The other, mourning over years misused, replies in one of the most notable passages in Juvenal:

> What cure for my lost time and hopes deceived?
> The little span of our poor narrow life
> Hastes like a fading blossom to a close.
> We drink; we call for garlands, perfumes, girls;
> But Age creeps on us ere we understand.[1]

Satire III, paraphrased by Johnson under the title of 'London,' as he paraphrased Satire X under the title of 'The Vanity of Human Wishes,' is deservedly among the most admired of Juvenal's poems. The picture of Rome as a good place to be out of lends itself to so much realistic and even dramatic treatment that it forms an unforgettable social document. The attack is put in the mouth of one of the poet's friends, Umbricius, who unburdens his mind just outside the Porta Capena, as he and a cartful of household belongings are about to quit the city and take the road for Cumae on the Bay of Naples. The capital is no place, he asserts, for honourable men or honest work; he cannot be a useful accomplice in crime; he cannot lie and flatter like smooth-tongued versatile jacks-of-all-work from Greece or yet farther East. Bitter invective is directed against the *Graeculus esuriens* who belongs to a nation of consummate actors, cringing sycophants, and dangerous spies; but there is also much stinging criticism upon the Rome and Romans of the day. Where money, not worth, is the test of character, poverty meets with the unkindest cut of all – it is jeered at.[2] How hard it is to rise in straitened circumstances! Rural simplicity is in sharp contrast to the showiness of the town, where everything has its price, where one must bribe a pampered valet for an interview with his master, where life is threatened by tumble-down tenements or conflagrations or street accidents.

The sudden collapse of a wagon loaded with marble is made the subject of a miniature drama worthy of the ancient traditions of *satura*. Within fourteen lines[3] we have three vivid scenes:

I. A street in Rome; heavy traffic; cart upset; fatal accident to a passer-by.

II. (The scene is changed, *domus interea*.) The victim's home; busy slaves, in unconscious dramatic irony, preparing the bath for their master who will never return alive.

[1] IX. 125–129:
> 'Nunc mihi quid suades post damnum temporis et spes
> Deceptas? festinat enim decurrere, uelox
> Flosculus, angustae miseraeque breuissima uitae
> Portio; dum bibimus, dum serta unguenta puellas
> Poscimus, obrepit non intellecta senectus.'

[2] III. 152–153.

[3] III, 254–267.

III. (Another change of scene.) Hades, whither master has already gone (*at ille iam sedet in ripa*), a shuddering novice waiting for the dread ferryman across the gloomy stream.

Nor are the perils less by night. Make your will before you venture to sup from home! A strikingly picturesque sketch is given of the dark streets where the drunken swashbuckler bullies those he can waylay. Here again (278 *sqq.*) Juvenal shows mastery of his effective semi-dramatic method in a series of brief scenes:

    I. Night: restless *apache* of ancient Rome tossing sleepless on his couch; he has killed nobody that day; hence his insomnia! – murdering is an indispensable soporific.

    II. Dark street; *apache* eluding the patrol.

    III. Moonlight; lonely wayfarer returning from a supper-party; enter *apache* (*stat contra*):
        He calls a halt: and you must needs obey:
        What else? he's wild, and brawn can force its way.

Swift angry dialogue follows, if dialogue it can be called, where the surprised citizen scarcely gets time to reply. 'And where may you come from?' he bawls. 'Whose sour wine and beans have blown you out? Who's the cobbler you've been with gorging chopped leeks or boiled sheep's head? Eh? no answer? Speak or take a sound kicking! Out with it! Where do you hold forth? In what praying-shanty am I to look for you?' It is the poor man's privilege to get mauled and implore leave to go home with just a few teeth left! After a final complaint about shop-breakers, footpads and highwaymen, Umbricius, in Juvenal's hyperbolical manner, affects to fear a shortage of iron owing to the quantity of chains needed for the criminal population.

Satire IV is a half-playful account of an enormous turbot which a fisherman decided must be presented to Domitian, who summons his privy council to deliberate on the proper treatment of the fish. We are made vividly to realise the perilous friendship of an imperial tyrant, his distrust of his counsellors, and their pallid nervousness in his proximity. The brief strokes of portraiture which recreate the figures at court show great power.

The fifth satire is a scathing exposure of the shabby entertainment of clients by mean hosts. 'If,' says the poet to the client, 'you can tamely suffer the indignities put upon you at a rich patron's table, you must be absolutely worthless. Better be a beggar out and out. The height of your aspirations (*uotorum summa*) is to get even the worst place at the great man's board, where one is not allowed to drink the same wine, or eat the same bread or fish as he. A blackamoor rascal attends to you whom you wouldn't like to meet on a dark night (*cui per mediam nolis occurrere noctem*) on the Latin Way, while a handsome slave stands by your patron, who regales himself upon *foie gras*, capon and boar with truffles in season. The best dainties you are permitted to watch without tasting. Don't suppose all this is entirely mean economy on your host's part: he does it maliciously to wound: it is such fun to watch a client's angry disappointment. To endure such insults proves you deserve them (*omnia ferre si potes, et debes*).'

Satire VII anticipates the dawn of better days for literature and learning under the patronage of a new ruler (*et spes et ratio studiorum in Caesare tantum*). In contrast with these brighter prospects, the poem is a growl of discontent over the present condition of literature, which does not pay. Patrons are mean and poverty chills authorship. Only the pantomime actor thrives and wields influence (*quod non dant proceres dabit histrio*): so the most promising thing poets can do is to sell a libretto for a *fabula saltica* on the stage: otherwise a Statius might starve in spite of popular readings from his *Thebaid*. Take the literary professions: they are all miserably rewarded. The historian gets no adequate return for his exacting toil: the advocate is not recompensed in proportion to real skill – a jockey of the red colour can eclipse in fortune a hundred lawyers. Nowadays a Cicero would not be prized unless he wore a fine ring: a poor man has no chance, however eloquent (*rara in tenui facundia panno*), and would do well to retire to Gaul or Africa – a sagacious testimony by Juvenal to the intellectual force of these provinces. The teachers of declamation are no better off: they are killed by the deadly monotony of repeated exercises (*occidit miseros crambe repetita magistros*). They are expected to post students up in useful points without receiving proper fees (*nosse uolunt omnes, mercedem soluere nemo*), and they are blamed for a pupil's want of proficiency. Compute the fees earned by a teacher of singing and music, and you will tear up your manual of rhetoric. If a great professor like Quintilian made a good income, that was an exceptional freak of fortune. And, with a touch of poetry, Juvenal calls for heaven's blessing on former generations who knew how to respect the instructor of the mind:

> Grant that the earth, ye gods, above the shades
> Of our forefathers may lie soft and light:
> Sweet-breathing crocus, spring that never fades,
> Grant to the tombs of those who held it right
> To honour teachers as one would a sire.[1]

In the eighth satire the uselessness of pedigrees is exposed (*stemmata quid faciunt?*) as Juvenal laughs at the claims of long descent on the part of those who live unworthy lives:

[1] VII. 207–210:
> 'Di, maiorum umbris tenuem et sine pondere terram
> Spirantisque crocos et in urna perpetuum uer,
> Qui praeceptorem sancti uoluere parentis
> Esse loco.'

R*

> Though decked with olden busts great halls may be,
> Virtue remains the sole nobility.[1]

Good character is the true patent of high rank:[2] there should be a rapturous welcome for real goodness to match that of votaries greeting Osiris. In breeds of dumb animals we expect the old qualities to be maintained: otherwise, the degenerate is rejected: so a man must be capable of winning distinction by his own conduct instead of relying on his ancestors' renown (*miserum est aliorum incumbere famae*). Juvenal nowhere strikes a loftier ethical note than in his admonitions here that the truth must be spoken were it even at the risk of torture, that a governor of a province must rule his own desires, that the triumphs of peace outnumber those of war (*plures de pace triumphos*), and – in two of his most memorable lines – that death is preferable to disgrace.

> Hold it black sin 'fore honour breath to choose –
> For living's sake the grounds of life to lose.[3]

With the famous tenth satire we encounter Juvenal's later and more reflective manner. In length it comes next to the sixth, though about 300 lines shorter. The main thesis is that a survey of mankind over the globe from the Pillars of Hercules to the Ganges, or, as Johnson has it, 'from China to Peru,' shows the blind foolishness of human desires. Ignorant of what is really beneficial, man everywhere craves for what may prove his ruin. Such a world of idiocy may move equally well a Democritus to laughter or a Heraclitus to tears. The theme is vigorously illustrated by instances exhibiting the perils of political ambition (Sejanus, Crassus, Pompey, Caesar); eloquence (Demosthenes and Cicero); military glory (Hannibal, Alexander the Great); long life (Nestor, Priam, Croesus, Marius, and others who outlived their best days); beauty (Lucretia, Verginia, Hippolytus, and Messallina's ill-starred favourite Silius). More abstract in subject, the satire retains much of Juvenal's old vivid and dramatic manner. In one compact line an admirably complete picture can be conveyed: a traveller, nervous over the risk of robbery on a lonely road (like the Appian), passes through a marshy district (such as the Pomptine), and in the moonlight fancies each stirring of the bulrushes may mean a lurking highwayman.[4] Nothing could exceed the vigour shown in describing the outburst of popular fury against the statues of the fallen idol, Sejanus, and in the dramatic comments by those whom we might introduce as 'first citizen' and 'second citizen.'[5] Much else remains familiar in the satire – the gibe

---

[1] VIII. 19–20.   [2] VIII. 24–28: '. . . Agnosco procerem. . . .'
[3] VIII. 83–84:
> 'Summum crede nefas animam praeferre pudori
> Et propter uitam uiuendi perdere causas.'
[4] X. 21: 'et motae ad lunam trepidabis arundinis umbram.'
[5] X. 56–89.

at Cicero's poetry, the nauseous realism in recounting drawbacks of old age, and the sketch of Hannibal's career leading up to the contemptuous dismissal:

> Go, madman, o'er the cruel Alps make speed
> To please young spouters of a college screed![1]

Juvenal's cynicism is not entirely negative. After denouncing all ordinary human aims, he still leaves something to pray for. The concluding passage owes much of its nobility to the Stoicism which inspires it: and though there is no need to question the author's sincerity, he comes in one flippant line very near spoiling the whole effect. Half ashamed of his own seriousness, he seems unable to resist the temptation to have his jest at one of the religious rituals of the day (*exta et candiduli diuina tomacula porci*):

> Shall men then pray for naught? If 'tis advice
> You crave, then let the deities themselves
> Apportion us our due and helpful lot.
> The gods will grant not joys but all that's meet.
> They love man more than man loves self. Impelled
> By yearning heart, by might of blind desire,
> We seek a bride and offspring; but the gods
> Alone know what the child or wife will be.
> Still, that you may ask something, paying vows
> At shrines with victims' entrails, offering
> Prophetic mincemeat of a piglet white,
> Pray for a sound mind in a body sound.
> Ask for the valiant soul that fears not death,
> But counts long life the least among the gifts
> Of nature, and can suffer any pains,
> Stranger to wrath and lust, preferring all
> The cruel toils and woes of Hercules
> To banquets, love, or cushions from the East.
> Behold – I show what you may give yourself –
> Through goodness lies the only path of peace.
> O Chance, thy power is foiled if men be wise:
> We men make thee a goddess in the skies.[2]

The interest of the eleventh satire, which contrasts plain living with sumptuous junketing, is in part autobiographic; for after its prelude of fifty-five lines on the folly of extravagant gourmands who neglect the heaven-sent and ever-valuable maxim 'Know thyself,' it consists of an invitation from the poet to a simple meal which shall draw produce from his own Tiburtine farm. Only Homer and Virgil are to be read at table, while the roar of the holiday-makers in the circus can be heard afar off. The author's old age is suggested in his declaration that it is for the young to attend the games and shout and bet with a smart damsel

[1] X. 166–167.   [2] X. 346–366.

seated by their side: 'but let my shrivelled skin bask in the spring sun-shine free from the formal gown.'[1]

Though the twelfth is the shortest of the satires except the fragmentary sixteenth, it hardly makes an artistic unity. The safe arrival of Juvenal's friend Catullus at Ostia after imminent danger of shipwreck gives occasion for a pious sacrifice in token of thanksgiving by the poet. His motives however must not be misconstrued. He is no legacy-hunter seeking to curry favour. An awkward transition leads to a gibe at such legacy-hunters as would purchase a place in a will by offering the costliest victims, an elephant (and here the satire becomes doubly elephantine), or a slave, or a child devoted like Iphigeneia. The closing note is the forcible imprecation on a fortune-seeker:

> Long may Pacuvius live, as Nestor old,
> Possess as much as Nero snatched, pile gold
> In mountains, loving none, by none beloved.[2]

The elevated moral teaching of Satire XIII must win our admiration. Calvinus has been cheated of 10,000 sesterces by a fraudulent friend. The solace which the poet has to offer is that genuine punishment is inflicted by a guilty conscience: no wrong-doer can elude that court. After all, we live no longer in the Golden Age, but in corrupt times, when money exerts its lure and perjury is rampant. 'The wrath of gods is great, yet worketh slow' (*ut sit magna tamen certe lenta ira deorum est*). The offender, then, must be left in the hands of heaven; and Juvenal feels for vindictive passions only a biting, and, at the same time, misogynistic contempt:

> Vengeance is the delight of petty minds,
> Paltry and weak. Infer this truth, because
> None like a woman dotes upon revenge.[3]

The influence of parental example is the theme of Satire XIV – the third longest of the collection. There are many faults which children learn from their parents, such as gambling, gluttony, cruelty, intrigue. Therefore all that is unseemly to hear or see must be excluded from the home: the utmost respect is due to the child (*maxima debetur puero reuerentia*). You take pains to make your house clean to receive a guest: should you not, for your son's sake, keep it free from evil? The later part of the poem deals with avarice, a fault which the young practise

---

[1] XI. 203:
> 'Nostra bibat uernum contracta cuticula solem
> Effugiatque togam.'

[2] XII. 128–130.

[3] XIII. 189–192:
> 'quippe minuti
> Semper et infirmi est animi exiguique uoluptas
> Vltio. Continuo sic collige, quod uindicta
> Nemo magis gaudet quam femina.'

reluctantly and which wears a spurious resemblance to virtue. Hence too often a father inculcates the passion for gain upon a son by precept and example; and hence the modern quest for wealth at the cost of crime and risk of death. The final counsel is to get enough for the support of life; and, with a glance at the Stoic ideal of living *secundum naturam*, he declares:

Nature ne'er contradicts Philosophy.[1]

If you need more, adopt the equestrian income as a standard, or even twice that amount; beyond that, the treasures of Croesus are little likely to satisfy your desires.

The fifteenth satire tells of a feud between two Egyptian townships, Ombi and Tentyra. The Tentyrites having attacked their neighbours in the midst of a festival were put to flight. In the retreat one fugitive who slipped was hacked to pieces by the victors and devoured. This revolting cannibalism gives Juvenal occasion for the reflection that tenderness of heart as shown by tears is the noblest attribute of man.[2]

Only partially finished, the last satire complains of unfair advantages possessed by a soldier over a civilian. When it is cited as evidence throwing doubt upon the records of Juvenal's military service, one ought in fairness to remember that not every soldier leaves the army as its panegyrist.

In spirit there are signal differences between the earlier and the later satires. If Satires X and XII–XV be compared with the rest, an increase in prolix bookishness will be noted alongside of a decrease in concrete force. Ribbeck's theory of two Juvenals, a genuine satirist and a spurious declaimer, is long since dead; but it possessed the merit of resting upon a close examination into points of difference in the satires. The hypothesis viewed the traditional Juvenal as a Janus-head (*Janus-kopf*) looking on one side at the full fresh life of Rome and the present, but on the other side at the dead past and the dusk of academic tradition. The contrast was likened to passing from one of Schiller's dramas to a drowsy afternoon sermon (*eine sanft einschläfernde Nachmittagspredigt*). Unfortunately the theory overestimated the differences, failed to see that there was no fundamental incompatibility in style, and interpreted the actual differences with a perverse misconception of the true explanation. Above all its other absurdities, the theory would ask us to believe that the tenth satire was the work of some unknown forger and was merely one of the alleged 'drowsy afternoon sermons.' The solution lies not in positing a duality of authorship, but in recognising that the real Juvenal had grown older, and in his later manner let his satire down from the old level of full-blooded vitality and devil-may-care invective.

---

[1] XIV. 321: 'Nunquam aliud Natura, aliud Sapientia dicit.'
[2] XV. 131–133: 'Mollissima corda' etc., *cf.* 142 *sqq.*: 'Separat hoc nos a grege mutorum' etc.

The figment of the true and the false Juvenal could be maintained only in cheerful oblivion of the evolution, and sometimes deterioration, in style, characteristic of many other authors. There is no greater unlikeness between the early and the late Juvenal than between the Horace of the earliest *Satires* and the Horace of the *Epistles*; or, to cite a prose-writer, between the first and last works of Tacitus. In English literature Carlyle and Browning are apt parallels.

Juvenal, we have seen, proclaims his literary ancestry in his first satire, legitimately affiliating his *genre* to that of both Lucilius and Horace. His insistence on indignation as the mainspring of his censorious utterances definitely connects him with the fierce invective of the former. Though the influence of Horace is manifest in his language, one finds no imitation of Horatian geniality. To turn from Juvenal to the fourth satire in Horace's first book is to breathe an entirely different atmosphere. We are there in the company of an apologist for the satiric attitude who does not wish to be feared or hated or to write dangerously, who guarantees that ill-natured rancour shall be absent from his sketches, and who pleads for an indulgent attitude towards any outspoken jest.[1] Aware of his own faults, Horace can take himself, as well as others, gently to task, with a sort of Chaucerian smile for pardonable human weaknesses. His very habit of jotting things down on paper (*inludo chartis*) is one of those venial peccadilloes (*mediocribus illis ex uitiis unum*). This is the reason why his sportive verses win the reader's heart, as Persius felt – *circum praecordia ludit*. Juvenal's strength lies elsewhere: the genial smile has gone: he cannot laugh at himself as Horace does. There is no self-revelation; for Juvenal takes himself as seriously as he takes the world. If there is humour, it is grim; since the times are out of joint, the lash must be plied to put them right again. Some elements of Persius's earnest spirit, especially some Stoic traits, enter into him, though his method of censure is not so much homily as fiery attack. Both alike, however, are fighters, waging a warfare to improve the diseased society against which they find themselves in reaction.

For Juvenal's purpose he had at his command the gift of extraordinarily vivid and succinct presentation of men and things. This gift renders him the most powerful delineator of Roman society at the beginning of the second century, so that he recreates for his readers the life that was led then and the human figures who moved in the street, house, or palace. This constitutes what, for want of a better term, we call his realism. The secret of it he had learned, not in any rhetorical academy, but in the severe school of life:[2] he had undergone the privations of poverty, and almost certainly of war and exile: he possessed the observant eye, the retentive memory, the faculty of direct expression needed to make an experience live again in literature. A few essential and picturesque details, recorded with the utmost parsimony, place a whole

[1] Hor. *Sat.* I. iv. 33–38, 78–85, 100–106, 129–139.   [2] XIII. 20–22.

scene before us. Thus, we cannot fail to see the scramble for the dole, with such subterfuges as the curtained, though empty, *lectica* supposed to contain a lady caller.[1] Again, we seem to be uncomfortably present among Domitian's counsellors – one, an unwieldy mountain of flesh (*uenter adest abdomine tardus*); another, an informer whose gentle whisper could slit a victim's throat (*tenui iugulos aperire susurro*); yet another, a repulsive blind flatterer, pouring out words of admiration for the emperor's great turbot, and at the same time 'turning to the left, though in fact the fish was lying on his right!' In the same passage[2] the allusion to 'the beggar at the carriage wheels, who throws wheedling kisses as it drives down hill' is as true to Italy today[3] as it ever was. Certain dramatic aspects of this realism have been illustrated in the survey of the Satires. Not unnaturally it is a realism concentrated mainly on what will favour satiric treatment. A satirist never achieves, or even aims at, a universal or impartial view of life. Juvenal's professed subject may be the *farrago* of all mankind's doings during postdiluvian ages; but actually a great proportion of human affairs can offer no challenge to a mordant critic. Goodness, for instance, even at its most humdrum, is little likely to stir the *indignatio* which is Juvenal's driving force. That he should be darkly pessimistic is involved in the nature of the case and in his temperament. He tends to look only at the gloomy side, and therefore to obscure the fact that not everything around him was a cesspool of vice, but that on the contrary much in contemporary Roman and Italian life was sound, healthy, and beautiful. Undeniably, we could have spared some of the coarseness with which he made wickedness revolting.

What humour exists in Juvenal is of a kind to match his serious disposition. It tends to be grim and ironical: and the want of kindly sunshine in it has led some to doubt its existence.[4] His roundabout allusive manner sometimes produces quaintly humorous effects through its smack of flippancy: thus he substitutes 'Ceres' son-in-law' for Pluto; and 'the youth preferred to jealous Iarbas' for Aeneas. But his grim irony is best seen in passages like those in which he treats the unexpected fate of the citizen killed in the street accident of the third satire, or when he sums up the aim of all ambition as nothing but the laudatory inscription on a sepulchre which is itself so far from immortal that even a tree may burst it asunder – 'the very tombs have their allotted span' (*data sunt ipsis quoque fata sepulcris*, X. 146). Here he has taken one impressive step beyond the idea in Gray's line, 'The paths of glory lead but to the grave.'

---

[1] I. 120–126: '. . . "Profer, Galla, caput. noli uexare; quiescet."'
[2] IV. 117–118.   [3] Written in the 1920's.
[4] The laughable at any rate is present. Some of its aspects were made the subject of a 'program' by Neissner, *Ueber das komische Element in d. Sat. des J.*, Dresd. 1876. *Cf.* J. Jessen, 'Witz u. Humor im J.,' *Philol.* xlvii (1889); F. S. Dunn, 'J. as a Humorist,' *Cl. Weekly*, iv (1910), p. 50 ff.; G. Highet, *J. the Satirist*, Oxf. 1954 (see 'humour in Juv.' in his index).

Occasionally there is a feeling for beauty, doubly welcome because not much may be expected in a satirist. A transient gleam of romance illumines the grotto of the inspired Egeria when he prefers nature's loveliness to artificial improvements:

> Down to Egeria's vale we fared, to caves
> From Nature's work transformed. How much more near
> Would be the fountain nymph, if simple grass
> Enclosed the waters with its margent green,
> Nor marble kerb profaned the native stone.[1]

Allusion has already been made to the beauty of idea and language in his prayer that the last resting-place of those who revered the teachers of the young shall be brightened by 'fragrant crocus and unfailing spring' (*spirantisque crocos et in urna perpetuum uer*, VII. 208).

It is not however in the realm of pure poetry but in his free mastery of rhetoric and his skill in adapting it to his literary aims, that Juvenal's true eminence lies. This is not to suggest that he could ever be dismissed as a rhetorician. He is not controlled by, but controls, his instrument. It is very easy to accumulate copious examples of his recourse to rhetorical artifices – interrogation, apostrophe, antithesis and the rest. Scores of *sententiae* could be reckoned up, like

> Travellers with naught sing in the robber's face.[2]

or

> 'There's many a thing which they
> Whose coats are threadbare never dare to say.'[3]

Attention could also be called to his fondness for hyperbole, like 'men at sea outnumber those ashore!' or 'pillars split by the everlasting reciter,' or the jest that, if asked to enumerate the legion ailments of old age, one could more readily tell 'how many patients Dr. Themison killed off in one autumn season.'[4]

Akin to this penchant for overstatement is his diverting use of an anticlimax where a series of objectionable things or persons ends intentionally in a surprise. Thus, nothing worse, he says, could be conceived than to stay in Rome dreading conflagrations, the constant fall of houses, the thousand dangers of a cruel town, and – to cap all – poets giving readings from their works in the hot August days![5] But the truth is

---

[1] III. 17–20:
> 'In uallem Egeriae descendimus et speluncas
> Dissimiles ueris. Quanto praesentius esset
> Numen aquis, uiridi si margine clauderet undas
> Herba, nec ingenuum uiolarent marmora tofum.'

[2] X. 22: 'cantabit uacuus coram latrone uiator.'

[3] V. 130–131:
> 'plurima sunt quae
> non audent homines pertusa dicere laena.'

[4] XIV. 276; I. 13; X. 221.   [5] III. 6–9.

that, tricks notwithstanding, his style in its complexity and individuality is much more than merely rhetorical. The statement of the *uitae* that he practised declamation till middle life has produced a misleading effect on some critics who have impeached his sincerity. His place, however, in literary history is secure: he is one of the great satirists – to some the greatest – and one refuses to believe that greatness of style can be based on rhetorical knack alone. Admittedly declamatory, he yet drew his real strength from a passion for serious morality, which, without, perhaps, very deep religious feeling[1] or convinced attachment to philosophy,[2] still gave him the right to cherish his *saeua indignatio* against abuses constituting social dangers.

Genuine feeling, then, forced him to raise an original voice in utterances which the world has not allowed to die. Lines or phrases that readily recur to the memory (some of them already quoted) are so many reminders of his permanent contribution to literature: *e.g., probitas laudatur et alget; quis tulerit Gracchos de seditione querentes? nemo repente fuit turpissimus; omnia nouit Graeculus esuriens; haud facile emergunt quorum uirtutibus obstat res angusta domi; nemo malus felix; rara auis in terris; hoc uolo, sic iubeo, sit pro ratione uoluntas; sed quis custodiet ipsos custodes? soloecismum liceat fecisse marito; facies dicetur an ulcus? occidit miseros crambe repetita magistros; stemmata quid faciunt? propter uitam uiuendi perdere causas; panem et circenses; mens sana in corpore sano; pictores quis nescit ab Iside pasci? prima est haec ultio, quod se iudice nemo nocens absoluitur; maxima debetur puero reuerentia; lucri bonus est odor ex re qualibet.*

Allusions and verbal reminiscences prove Juvenal's memory for previous literature. His reader is expected to understand an ordinary reference to Greek poetry or history and to recognise now a Horatian, now a Virgilian tag, as, for example, we find *rusticus expectas* and *parcendum est teneris* in the same satire.[3] As regards his versification, he makes a noticeable departure from his fellow-satirists, Horace and Persius, in favour of Virgil. His control, and it is masterly, over the hexameter is in the main Virgilian rather than Ovidian, though it has some Lucretian quality. One finds, then, in him an epic ring, which appears to suggest that at least in his longer passages Juvenal may be represented in English by the traditional blank verse of narrative poetry more appropriately than by what too easily becomes the ding-dong of the rhymed heroic couplet.

In those satires which Dryden selected for rendering, his neat distich is at its best among the terse sententious parts; and the experiment whereby the great English satirist set himself to translate his Roman

---

[1] Nisard was too sweeping when he wrote: 'Quant à la religion, ce qu'il en a dit en se moquant ôte toute autorité aux endroits où il en parle sur le ton sérieux,' *P. lat. déc.* II, p. 59.

[2] XIII. 121–122.

[3] XIV. 25 and 215; *cf.* Hor. *Epist.* I. ii. 42; Virg. *G.* II. 363.

prototype must always remain of extraordinary interest, although one may feel that Gifford's heroic couplets achieve in some respects a more successful version. Briefly, however, Juvenal's variety of line-structure, his freedom in pause and *enjambement*, cannot be conveyed within the rigid limits of the couplet. This ease of movement accounts for his range – occasional beauty, occasional harshness, but prevailing rapidity. Cleverly intertwined alliterations may be made not merely emphatic and decorative as in *dat ueniam coruis, uexat censura columbas*, but realistic in their unmistakable echo of the sense, as in the likening of a woman's torrential talk to the banging of tin basins and tinkling bells – *tot pariter pelues ac tintinnabula dicas pulsari*. Or, again, the excited bustle of a house on fire is suggested by the final and initial dentals which recur, like the rat-tat of a kettle-drum in

> 'iam poscit aquam, iam friuola transfert
> Ucalegon, tabulata tibi iam tertia fumant.'

Totally different effects are produced by the slow melancholy movement at the close of a line to express the fate of a poor wretch who has found favour with the dangerous Messallina:

> 'rapitur miser extinguendus
> Messallinae oculis.'

Like all the satirists, Juvenal draws a modicum of words from the common speech of town and country – *caballus, olla, scrofa, potestas* (like the Italian *podestà*, a magistrate). He delights in such diminutives as the *sermo cotidianus* preserved all through the history of Latin and handed down to modern Italian. One may specify as examples, *candidulus, cuticula, flammeolum, foculus, fraterculus, Graeculus, hortulus, igniculus, improbulus, liuidulus, nutricula, ofella, pallidulus, palliolum, paruulus, pellicula, rancidulus, sarcinula, seruulus, sordidulus, virguncula*.

The influence of the Satires is not traceable before the fourth century, when Ammianus Marcellinus proves they had admirers. Both pagans and Christians felt their spell: they were imitated by Ausonius, Claudian, and Prudentius, and quoted by Lactantius and Servius. Medieval interest in Juvenal's ethical value was well marked – Chaucer apostrophises him; and from Elizabethan times onwards the satirists of England and France have studied his poems. Readers of Boileau, Dryden, Pope, Johnson and Byron know that they all in varying degrees were indebted to the works of the Roman satirist.

PART V

Literature in the Reign of Hadrian

A.D. 117—138

SUETONIUS AND FLORUS

Hadrian's reign a literary diminuendo – The emperor himself – His tastes – Archaism and Greek – Suetonius – An imperial secretary in disgrace – Encyclopaedic fruits of his leisure – Works extant and lost – Date of *De Viris Illustribus* and *De Vita Caesarum* – Sources – *De Grammaticis* – *De Rhetoribus* – *De Poetis* – The doubtful *Life of Virgil* – Characteristics of *Lives of the Caesars* – Suetonius and Tacitus – Suetonius and Pepys – Portraits of emperors – Entertaining realism – Style – Influence.

Three Flori in one – Florus the rhetor – Florus the poet – Doubtful ascription of *Peruigilium Veneris* to him – Florus the historian – The Roman people his hero – Eulogy and rhetoric.

THE REIGN OF HADRIAN

TEMPTING though it is to make a study of the Silver Age culminate crescendo-wise in the unique artistry of Tacitean prose, there are difficulties in leaving out the diminuendo of Hadrian's reign[1] (A.D. 117–138). One must acknowledge that literary history has but a faint interest in the jurists of the period like Salvius Julianus and Pomponius; or in the rhetoricians and philosophers, who mostly wrote in Greek; or again in versifiers, skilful rather than inspired, like Annianus, Septimius Serenus, Alfius Avitus, and the restless emperor himself, although his dying farewell to his soul is at least a perpetual bait for translators.[2] One notes, too, little of significance among the grammarians, except perhaps the commentaries, now in fragments, written by Terentius Scaurus on Plautus, Virgil and Horace, and his linguistically important *De Orthographia*, of which we possess two abstracts. It is also true that the greatness of Tacitus eclipses the work of Suetonius and Florus, the only two Hadrianic historians who are noteworthy, if, as is most likely, the abridgement of Trogus's Macedonian history by Justinus is Antonine rather than Hadrianic.[3] But chronologically there is no

[1] For historical background, F. Gregorovius, *Der Kaiser Hadrian*, ed. 3, Stuttg. 1884; Eng. tr. M. E. Robinson, Lond. 1898; B. W. Henderson, *Life and Principate of H.*, Lond. 1923 ('H.'s Literary Activities,' p. 240 ff.). C.A.H. XI, 1936, ch. viii.

[2] *Translations . . . of Dying Hadrian's Address to his Soul*, collected by D. Johnston, Bath 1876 (in several languages).

[3] This was my view in *L.H.R.* p. 463. Galdi's examination of the style and *clausulae* of Justinus tends to show 'che è assai verosimile ch'egli visse sotto gli Antonini, e propriamente tra il 130–180,' *L'epitome n. lett. lat.*, p. 108.

natural break just before Suetonius, who was one of Pliny's junior friends; nor should the fall-off from Tacitean brilliance blind one either to Suetonius's merits in a different kind of biography from the *Agricola* or to the debt which literary history owes him for preserving, with an almost Varronian interest in the past, much that could not otherwise have been known about the poets and the teachers of Rome.

Before studying Suetonius and Florus, a glance at the reign seems appropriate. Its total literary achievement makes a somewhat ironic comment on Juvenal's hope *et spes et ratio studiorum in Caesare tantum*, and shows that patronage does not of necessity beget literature. Patronage, indeed, while clearly it never can create genius, is not always even good for such genius as may emerge. The prince himself was a lover of learning and architecture. He established a library at his spacious villa whose ruins still impress us under the slopes of Tivoli: he had another at Antium, and a third was attached to his famous academy at Rome, the Athenaeum. 'The little Greek' (*Graeculus*), as some dared to call him, was a student of eloquence and drama. He published some of his speeches: he patronised but also quizzed scholars and philosophers. Pieces of mediocre verse by his Majesty have survived, and we know the ugly title of his lost miscellany, *Catachannae*. Only once did inspiration visit him: as he lay under the shadow of death, there came to him a few simple lines immortal in their suggestion of the mysterious parting between body and soul:

> *Animula, uagula, blandula,*
> *Hospes comesque corporis,*
> *Quae nunc abibis in loca,*
> *Pallidula, rigida, nudula,*
> *Nec ut soles dabis iocos?*

The tender diminutives add to the difficulty of translation, but one more attempt may be made:

> Ah! little fondling soul and fleeting,
> My body's guest and travel-friend,
> To what far land art thou retreating,
> Poor little wan, stark, naked sweeting –
> Thy wonted frolic at an end?[1]

In several ways the example set by imperial taste contributed to give to literature the particular turn which it now took. Hadrian had a preference for the archaic – a feature of Roman criticism accentuated later

---

[1] Or, *Scotice*:

> Wee flutterin' dawtit saul an' bonnie,
> Ma body's verra guest an' crony,
> For whatna land maun ye awa',
> Sae pale, sae cauldrife, stripp'd o' a',
> Wi' fient a joke tae play on ony?

in the century. That he was a pronounced philhellene and a great traveller were both facts which influenced others. Suetonius, we shall find, furnishes a good instance of the extent to which authors were now composing in Greek as well as in Latin; and no long time elapses before a Roman emperor, Marcus Aurelius, chooses Greek as the proper language for his *Meditations*. Apollodorus composed his treatise on siege-operations expressly for Hadrian, and military writing was continued by Aelian in his work on Greek tactics. Many Greek volumes of the time on history have perished; for example those of Crito, a Macedonian who accompanied Hadrian on his journeys, and treated Syracuse, Macedonia, Persia in addition to Trajan's Dacian war. The best work of Arrian, from Bithynia, belongs to Hadrian's time. If he is chiefly remembered as a second Xenophon who produced a new set of *Memorabilia* in handling the Stoic philosophy of his master Epictetus, and a new *Anabasis* in narrating the Asiatic expedition of Alexander, it should likewise be borne in mind that he became a Roman citizen and a consul. Though he was still alive in the days of Marcus Aurelius, it was for Hadrian that Arrian wrote the *Periplus* of the Black Sea. Geography, one feels, ought to have flourished under so indefatigable a traveller: certainly mathematical geography was, thanks to the genius of Ptolemaeus, to make a notable advance under the Antonines.

SUETONIUS

No one in antiquity appears to have thought of writing the biography of one of its most famous biographers, C. Suetonius Tranquillus. For information about him, we are in consequence dependent upon a few allusions of his own,[1] sundry letters of the younger Pliny, and a statement in the *Life of Hadrian* which Spartianus wrote in or after Diocletian's reign. His father, Suetonius Laetus, fought at the first battle of Bedriacum as a *tribunus angusticlauius* of the thirteenth legion in A.D. 69, and about that year Suetonius Tranquillus must have been born.[2] This conclusion hangs largely on the meaning attached to the term *adulescentia*; for he looked back on himself as having been *adulescens* in A.D. 88 (when a pretended Nero appeared twenty years after the real Nero's death), and as still *adulescens* late in Domitian's reign.[3] He may have been born in Rome; but this is no more certain of him than it is of Lucretius or Julius Caesar.

The external evidence about his life consists of references in Pliny's

[1] There are seven: *Aug.* vii; *Cal.* xix; *Nero* lvii; *Otho* x; *Dom.* xii; *De Gramm.* iv (recollection of hearing instances of students going straight from *grammatici* to the bar); *Vita Luc.* (recollection of Lucan being lectured on).
[2] This is Macé's view, *Essai sur Suét.* Paris 1900, p. 35 ff. Mommsen's date, A.D. 77 (*Herm.* iii. 43) seems too late. Shuckburgh (ed. Suet. *Aug.*, p. xxviii) prefers 75, which Teuffel (§ 347. 1) thinks the latest possible year.
[3] *Nero* lvii; *Dom.* xii. 2.

letters within the period from 96 to 112.[1] These references show that he
practised in the law-courts; that he was allowed to transfer to a kinsman a military tribunate for which he had himself been nominated;
that he was appreciated as a writer, but slow to issue works; and that
Pliny valued his advice on such a question as reading verse in public.
Pliny's request submitted on Suetonius's behalf to Trajan for the concession of the *ius trium liberorum* proves that, though he was married,
he had either no children or fewer than the statutory requirement.
The letter is a warm testimony to the integrity and learning of a man
who had been for a time an inmate of Pliny's house, and for whom, he
assures the emperor, he felt a stronger affection the closer his acquaintance became.[2] In the next reign Suetonius held an imperial secretary-
ship,[3] when access to the archives gave him presumably the first
impulse, and certainly considerable material, towards his *Lives of the
Caesars*. Hadrian, however, in A.D. 121 dismissed him along with others,
including Septicius Clarus, prefect of the Praetorian guard, for some
offence against court-etiquette in relation to the empress Sabina.[4]
Never a public man, Suetonius thenceforward devoted his leisure to
what most attracted him – historical, academic and antiquarian studies.
The list of his works proves that his productivity was great; but we
know from Pliny that he produced slowly.[5] It may, therefore, easily
be credited that Suetonius lived till he was an old man under the
emperor Antoninus Pius.

Time has spared only the *Lives of the Caesars*, and from the *De Viris
Illustribus*, on men eminent in literature, the greater part of the sections
De Grammaticis and *De Rhetoribus*, as well as the *Life* of the elder Pliny
among the historians, that of Passienus Crispus among the orators and
the *Lives* of Terence, Horace and Lucan.[6] These last three are all (except such morsels as Jerome preserved in his amplification of Eusebius's
chronicle) that can safely be counted genuine portions of the *De Poetis*,
the loss of which has left lamentable blanks in our knowledge.

A catalogue given in Greek by Suidas under the heading Τράγκυλλος
includes the *De Vita Caesarum* and *De Viris Illustribus* and adds nine
titles: *On Games among the Greeks* (in Greek); *On Spectacles and Games
among the Romans*; *On the Roman Year*; *On [critical] Signs in Writings*;
On Cicero's Republic (a book in answer to six books by the grammarian
Didymus against Cicero); *On Proper Names, Dress and Shoes* (probably

---

[1] *Ep.* I. xviii; III. iii; V. x; IX. xxxiv; X. xciv.
[2] *Ep.* X. xciv; esp. § 1 'in contubernium adsumpsi tantoque magis diligere
coepi quanto hunc (? nunc, ? tunc) propius inspexi.'
[3] 'Ab epistulis'; or, acc. to the later title used in S.H.A. *Hadr.* xi. 'epistu-
larum magister.'
[4] S.H.A. *Hadr.* xi.
[5] *Ep.* V. x. 2: 'Sum et ipse in edendo haesitator: tu tamen meam quoque
cunctationem tarditatemque uicisti.'
[6] The *Lives* of Virgil and Persius have had defenders, but are not usually
accepted as by Suetonius.

a history rather than a philosophy of clothes); *On Abusive Terms and their Origin* (in Greek, and grouped by their application to the vicious, to busybodies, fools, slaves, etc.); *On the Manners and Customs of Rome* (two books which we can imagine to have been full of interest); and the enigmatic Συγγενικόν.[1] Some of these are also vouched for by Latin writers like Aulus Gellius, Tertullian, Censorinus, and Servius; while some may be not independent works but sections of a larger treatise. Traces of yet other books are found in Orosius, Servius, Lydus, Priscian and Isidore: namely, an account of Julius Caesar's campaigns in Gaul;[2] *On Physical Blemishes* (*De Vitiis Corporalibus*, conceivably treated in connexion with his work on dress); *On Eminent Courtesans*; *On Organisation of Public Duties* (*De Institutione Officiorum*); *On Kings* (*De Regibus*); *On Various Matters* (*De Rebus Variis*), possibly identical with the miscellaneous *Pratum* or *Prata*, which, as can be inferred from later references, was divided into books on different subjects, antiquarian and scientific (*e.g.* Rome and Roman customs, the Roman year, the universe, nature of animals, etc.), probably including some of those in Suidas's list.[3] When it is remembered that Suetonius wrote both in Greek and in Latin, and handled a vast range of themes, one can realise his long years of laborious industry and understand his influence upon historians, grammarians, antiquaries and encyclopaedists for several centuries.

If the work whose appearance in whole or part Pliny in one of his letters expected from Suetonius was the *De Viris Illustribus*, then its publication may be put about A.D. 113.[4] One is on fairly sure ground in dating the *De Vita Caesarum* about 121, *i.e.* before the disgrace of Septicius Clarus to whom the imperial biographies were dedicated. There is, however, hardly justification for attempting to give, even with reserve, as Macé does, an approximate date for the *De Institutione Officiorum* and the *De Rebus Variis*.

Much of his antiquarian lore Suetonius drew from Varro; for facts about illustrious men he could lay under contribution Fenestella, Santra, Nepos, Hyginus, Seneca the elder, and Asconius; and for poets the commentators upon them. The citations and references to authorities in the *Life of Terence* indicate that he was well read. His main reliance upon books and documents may be one reason (apart from an instinctively historical interest in Julius and Augustus) why the *Lives* grow shorter as they approach his own period, when oral evidence was more abundant than written histories. But he did not ignore verbal witnesses: on the contrary, much in him was due to popular opinion and

---

[1] Possibly it should be connected with Καισάρων ιβ', 'The Twelve Caesars,' which it immediately precedes in Suidas.

[2] This would make up for their dismissal with one chapter in Suet. *Iul.* xxv.

[3] The theories of Reifferscheid and Schanz are summarised in S.H.K. § 534.

[4] Plin. *Ep.* V. x; Macé, *op. cit.* Roth (*Praef.* to ed. 1904, pp. lxxvi–lxxviii) gives A.D. 106–113.

gossip. Thus, stories about Claudius on the bench are recorded from the recollections of elderly persons (*a maioribus natu audiebam, Cl.* xv). The painstaking inquiries (*quamuis satis curiose inquirerem, Vesp.* i) about Vespasian's ancestors were presumably conducted in districts likely to know the family. Quite definitely he made use of matters which he heard mentioned by his grandfather (*auum meum narrantem puer audiebam, Cal.* xix), by his father (*Otho* x), or by others (*ex nonnullis comperi, Nero* xxix). Similarly, he had several informants (*e pluribus comperi, Tit.* iii) to vouch for Titus's expertness in shorthand and that adroitness in imitating signatures which might in other circumstances have turned the prince into an arch-forger. Yet the bulk of Suetonius's material came from his reading, which could be more exactly estimated, had it been part of his method to name his sources regularly instead of frequently contenting himself with a colourless *quidam . . . nonnulli tradunt* (*Vesp.* i). Though he may characterise authorities as trustworthy (*nec incertis, Nero* xxxiv), this only leaves one curious as to their identity. When Suetonius was in Hadrian's service *ab epistulis*, the archives under charge of the associated department *a studiis* were easily accessible to him; while his intimacy with Pliny's circle had not only given an aristocratic colour to his outlook, but probably directed him by preference to writers of a corresponding hue. At court he had opportunities for examining collections of imperial letters and speeches, state-papers, edicts and ceremonial eulogies, and among public documents, the *acta diurna, senatus consulta* and *senatus acta.*[1] It is interesting to remember that Suetonius mentions his possession of verses by Nero in the emperor's own handwriting;[2] nor is his reading without literary acumen when he remarks of Claudius's autobiography in eight books that it was lacking not so much in style as in common sense (*composuit . . . magis inepte quam ineleganter*).[3] Among historians whom he does name are well-known figures like Nepos, Hirtius, Asinius Pollio, Cremutius Cordus and a few others unfamiliar to us.[4] Diligent though he was, he cannot be called critical of his material: he was too well satisfied with amassing it. A conflict of evidence he prefers to leave undecided (*quod discrepat sit in medio, Vitell.* ii). It is the more surprising that upon occasion he can weigh his authorities. The most memorable instance is the chapter discussing the birthplace of Caligula,[5] where a brief investigation into his sources decides him to follow the official *acta* or *publici instrumenti auctoritas* in preference to the authors Lentulus Gaetulicus

---

[1] Macé, *op. cit.*, has discussed the imperial documents available for consultation by Suetonius.

[2] *Nero* lii.   [3] *Cl.* xli.

[4] Monroe Deutsch contended that the author who recorded the story of Caesar's extravagant gifts to his reputed mistress Queen Eunoe of Mauretania was not (M. Actorius) Naso, but (P. Attius) Varus, one of Pompey's officers, and therefore hostile to Caesar. The argument is that in Suet. *Iul.* lii, the true reading is 'ut Varus scripsit,' *C.J.* xvii (1921) pp. 161–163.

[5] *Cal.* viii.

and the elder Pliny. In another passage he reasons critically about the
variation between complimentary and uncomplimentary accounts of
Vitellius's ancestry: it was not, he observes, simply due to prejudice for
or against the emperor himself, since older accounts presented the same
conflict of evidence; and, in this connexion, he cites as one of his first-
hand authorities a memoir by Q. Elogius in the Augustan period.[1]

The *De Grammaticis* contains in brief space much of interest in the
chronicle of literary teachers at Rome, throwing incidental light on such
points as the demarcation of grammar from rhetoric, the effect of literary
teaching on poetry, the fees earned, and the taste for old-fashioned
writers which lingered in the provinces after it had vanished in Rome.
Here and there we find amusing touches, like the request made by a
pleader for adjournment of a case to enable a litigant to take lessons in
grammar, or Asinius Gallus's epigram on the ex-boxer who had turned
to teaching:

> The don who gives us glosses in a list
> Once learned to dodge his head:
> His mouth's no good – but he has got a fist!
> Why doesn't he box instead?[2]

In the still shorter *De Rhetoribus* we are told incidentally about enactments against professors of rhetoric, dangerous innovations in the
educational system, instances of long-continued practice of declamation
by famous men, varying methods and standard exercises. The work
unfortunately ends in an interrupted list of prominent teachers.

Among the *Lives of the Poets* we face the double misfortune that few
have survived, and that the *Life of Virgil* cannot with confidence be
pronounced Suetonian. It strikes in its very first chapter a note different
from the other literary biographies. There is something appropriately
mysterious in the record of Virgil's lowly birth by the wayside, the mild-
eyed tearless babe, his mother's symbolic dream, and the poplar branch
which was planted where he was born and which grew with miraculous
speed into a tree hallowed by prayers and veneration. All this is indicative of a reverential attitude towards the personality of Virgil already
enshrined in educational tradition and honoured by worshipping poets
like Statius, in preparation, as it were, for the medieval belief in his
wizardry. The tone has led many critics to ascribe it to Donatus; but
it is only right to quote Nettleship's defence of the Suetonian authorship.[3] 'The style,' he says, 'is in the main the peculiar style of Suetonius; the Latin is the quiet, sober, terse and yet distinguished Latin
which characterises him among other writers of his period, and separates
him from the later writers of the *Historia Augusta*.' Of the accepted
Lives the *Terence* has among its verse quotations interesting criticisms
by Cicero and Caesar (*o dimidiate Menander!*) while the *Horace* gives

---

[1] *Vitell.* i. [2] *De Gramm.* xxii.
[3] *Anct. Lives of Virgil*, Oxf. 1879, p. 28 ff.

illuminating glimpses into Horace's affectionate intimacy with Maecenas and Augustus.

On the *Lives of the Caesars* the reputation of Suetonius rests. Yet it is easy to pick faults in the work. A great deal of it partakes of the nature of a *chronique scandaleuse* based upon tittle-tattle about the emperors and compiled by a literary man with the muck-rake, toó keen upon petty and prurient detail to produce a scientific account of his subjects. The author is neglectful of dates and over-rigid in his scheme of biography. A measure of monotony is inevitable in his typical arrangement of ancestry, birth, years before accession to power, then public life and private life grouped under different aspects, portents presaging death, personal appearance and so on.[1] The stiffness of plan is, however, considerably softened by a wealth of illustrative anecdote. But there is no grasp like that of a Tacitus, no deep penetration of motive, no appreciation of historical movements. One reads the biographies of Galba, Otho and Vitellius without getting any connected view of their struggle for sovereignty as presented in the *Histories* of Tacitus. On the other hand, the truth remains that Suetonius is readable and continues to be read. In strong contrast to Tacitus he hardly ever indulges in a general reflection; but he succeeds in drawing attention to significant facts and outward characteristics. The names of Suetonius and of Pepys have been mentioned together;[2] and some analogy indeed exists between their matter-of-fact, concrete, gossiping styles, and their official relationship to the most elevated personages of their day. There, however, the likeness, such as it is, ends; for the English diarist is pre-eminent for naïve honesty in setting down his own personality with his pen. The self-revelation made with his intimacy of detail belongs to a different world from the record of the Caesars which Suetonius compiled from documents and hearsay. Pepys is internal, subjective and autobiographic: Suetonius is external, objective and biographic.

If, again, one thinks of Tacitus's vividness, Suetonius is vivid in a different way. Compared with Tacitus, he is as a photograph to a picture or a finished engraving. He is plain-spoken, and it may at least be urged that, after the lunacy of certain high-flown writers, Suetonius comes like a whiff of plebeian common sense. To him nothing is common or unclean. He descends, if need be, into the coarse without qualms or condemnation. He is a recorder, not a moralist: so, in regard to Tiberius, as Hérédia has it,

> Égratignant la cire impitoyable, il a
> Décrit les noirs loisirs du vieillard de Caprée.[3]

---

[1] *Cf. Iul.* xliv, his mapping out of *forma, habitus, cultus, mores, ciuilia studia, bellica studia,* as themes to precede the omens of death.

[2] Philarète Chasles, *Études sur le seizième siècle,* Par. 1876: 'Brantôme, Pepys et Suétone,' pp. 339–352.

[3] *Les Trophées,* sonnet on 'Tranquillus.'

The great thing is that his personages live. His method is brevity
of fact, story and description. Attracted by details such as Tacitus
would have considered beneath the dignity of history, many may wish
to know what the early emperors looked like. Here are some vignettes
with which Suetonius can oblige them – Julius Caesar, a tall, clear-
complexioned, well-formed man with keen black eyes, close-shaven
and rather sensitive about his baldness; Augustus, handsome though
not tall, with striking eyes, curly yellowish locks, a nose prominent
at the top, and complexion between dark and fair; Tiberius, of robust
build and stature above the average, left-handed, wearing his hair pretty
long at the back, with particularly large eyes capable of seeing even in
the dark, a stern person with hardly anything to say; Caligula, pale-
complexioned, hollow-eyed and ugly; Claudius, not without dignity
while he sat or stood, but shaky on his legs when he walked, and ridiculous by reason of his unseemly guffaw, his stammering utterance, and
his perpetually nodding head; Nero, of about medium height, with
features handsome rather than winning, light hair arranged in tiers of
curls, weak bluish-grey eyes, thick-set neck, projecting paunch and
slender legs; Galba, bald in front, blue-eyed, hook-nosed, his hands
and feet twisted with arthritis.[1] We need not go through the whole
realistic gallery, which suggests the Dutch School of portraiture.

Similar vividness marks the facts and incidents with which Suetonius
entertains us. So full is he of his facts that as a rule he gives them in the
briefest possible compass. Just occasionally does he allow himself to
expand into longer passages which impress the memory. Among such
memorable ones is the narrative of Caesar's arrival at the Rubicon
after missing his way in the darkness, the pause to weigh the question
whether to cross or not to cross, and the strangely gracious figure that
appeared to him piping by the river-side.[2] Here a slight gleam of romance has lit up a prevailingly matter-of-fact style. Other passages
somewhat more sustained than his customary terse strokes are the engrossing description of Caesar's murder, the account of Tiberius at
Rhodes, the graphic chapter on Caligula's mad cruelty, where one almost
seems to hear the eerie laugh of the insane tyrant tickled at the thought
that on a nod from him his two unsuspecting consular guests could
have their throats cut; and the complete tale of the closing days in
Nero's life when he was at bay, a series of ten chapters forming a unity
unusually elaborate for Suetonius and thrilling in its culminating three
chapters.[3]

Much, however, is on a smaller and less connected scale. As with a
diarist like Pepys, one can dip anywhere into Suetonius at haphazard

[1] *Iul.* xlv; *Aug.* lxxix; *Tib.* lxviii; *Cal.* 1; *Cl.* xxx; *Nero* li; *Galba* xxi.
[2] *Iul.* xxxi–xxxii (where the well-known 'iacta alea est' occurs). *Cf.* Lucan's
account, translated p. 242 *supra*.
[3] *Iul.* lxxxii; *Tib.* xi; *Cal.* xxxii; *Nero* xl–xlix.

510 LITERATURE IN THE REIGN OF HADRIAN

and chance upon incidents that may be isolated but are certainly entertaining. It holds one to read about Caligula's megalomaniac jealousy
of great writers like Homer, Virgil and Livy, whose works he wished to
destroy; his lunatic pranks in treating Castor and Pollux as his *concierges*
so that from their temple Romans might enter the imperial palace; his
flirtations with the Moon-goddess and confidential talks with brother
Jove; his scathing disrespect for relatives in characterising his great-
grandmother Livia as 'a Ulysses in petticoats' and in regarding his
uncle Claudius as merely a butt. In the next *Life*, the ridiculous side in
Claudius is illustrated repeatedly from the emperor's feeble jokes, his
silly remarks, and an absentmindedness so supreme as to sanction the
despatch of invitations to the dead. The reader is not expected to honour
an emperor who, while he could declaim marvellously, talked, as Gold-
smith did, like poor Poll.[1] The *Life of Nero* has many good things. It
tells of the way in which his ancestors the Ahenobarbi got their red
beards; and of the young ruler's exclamation over signing his first death-
warrant, 'How I wish I did not know letters!' (*quam uellem litteras
nescire!*) It reveals the system of *claqueurs* whom Nero had trained in
different sorts of applause ('boomings,' 'rain-patter,' 'dish-clash'),[2]
and acquaints us with his touchy conceit, his hooliganism in the streets
at night, his ominous interest in fires, and his childish conduct in exhibiting water-organs after the news of the revolt of Vindex had reached him.

The sketches of the three Flavians contain metal just as attractive.
The *Life of Vespasian* is masterly in its own way, from the entertainingly
superstitious portents heralding the great future of the destined prince
from the East (*e.g.* the sign of the three oak branches, the sign of the
street-mud, and the sign of the dog that brought in a man's hand one
day when Vespasian was at lunch) up to the dying emperor's grim jest
'Alack! I'm growing into a god, I suppose' (*Vae, puto, deus fio*). The
short *Life of Titus* gives a mere glance at his notorious passion (*insignem
amorem*) for Queen Berenice; and a little later what might have been
handled as a romance closes in the curt statement about the parted
sweethearts; *Berenicem statim ab urbe dimisit inuitus inuitam*. Like
Gibbon, Titus presumably sighed as a lover but obeyed as a son. To
Suetonius we owe the record of the prince's deservedly commended
utterance that a day in which he had done good to nobody was a lost
day – '*perdidi diem,*' *memorabilem illam meritoque laudatam uocem*. In
the *Life* of his brother we are doubtless intended to catch the sinister
bearing of Domitian's morbid pleasure in fly-catching at the beginning
of his reign, and his incessant reading of little beyond the memoirs
written at Capri by Tiberius – *son digne émule*, remarks Cucheval.[3]

---

[1] Extract from Augustus's letter, *Claud.* iv: 'Nam qui tam ἀσαφῶς loquatur,
qui possit cum declamat σαφῶς dicere . . . non uideo.'
[2] *Bombi* (deep or hollow sounds); *imbrices* (roof-gutters for catching the
rain); *testae* (earthenware vessels); Suet. *Nero* xx.
[3] *Hist. de l'éloq. rom. . . . mort de Cicéron . . . à . . . Hadrien*, Paris 1893, I. 311.

The free-and-easy style of Suetonius makes a sort of business-like match for his systematic marshalling of material. He is too much absorbed in what he has drawn from his documents to trouble about rhetorical display. His facts are left to speak for themselves, and sometimes they speak badly. Inelegantly used participles or ablatives, jerky and unpolished clauses, and an inartistic structure of sentence are frequent results of this carelessness. One feels as if something has gone wrong with sentences like *sed ea quoque paulatim repleta assidua equi uectatione post cibum* (*Cal.* iii); or, again, one finds an important remark tacked loosely on to a sentence, *e.g.* in telling how the doubtful reputation of Titus as a possible second Nero 'changed into rapturous praise when no fault was discovered in him, but the noblest virtues instead' – *at illi ea fama pro bono cessit conuersaque est in maximas laudes neque uitio ullo reperto et contra uirtutibus summis* (*Tit.* vii). There is something modern in this escape from the conventional order of words and this absence of decoration. Hence it comes that the Elizabethan pomp and quaintness of Philemon Holland's version are too opulently distracting to convey the simple matter-of-fact tone of the greater part of Suetonius, so that there is critical point in the old epigram:

> Philemon with 's Translations doeth so fille us,
> He will not let Suetonius be Tranquillus.

Yet it has been noted that Suetonius is not without a rhythm in his prose. De Groot's statistics for the sentence-endings examined by him suggest that the frequency of the double trochee in Suetonius is much the same as in Quintilian, of cretic followed by trochee less than in Quintilian, and of double cretic much the same as in Quintilian, though less than in the younger Seneca.[1] Macé has considered, on Havet's method, the rhythm of Suetonius's *clausulae* in relation to both quantity and accent.[2]

Preferring a neat simplicity[3] in the statement of facts, Suetonius has yet an individuality of style which, in spite of Silver Age constructions and vocabulary, marks him off from writers like Velleius and Florus as much as from Caesar and Cicero. We owe it to his dislike of affectation that he often quotes documents verbatim without any attempt at rewriting in his own manner. To the same dislike of affectation we owe the comparative infrequency of archaisms and neologisms in his works. It is noticeable that while Suetonius, as a scholar, had literary and antiquarian interests in common with Hadrian, his critical tastes were different. Unlike the emperor, he did not prefer Ennius to Virgil, Cato to Cicero and Caelius to Sallust:[4] on the contrary, he was an admirer

[1] De Groot, *Prosarhythmus*, pp. 108–109.
[2] Macé, *op. cit.* pp. 379–398. Shuckburgh (ed. Suet. *Aug.*, pref. ix) declares 'For rhythmical prose he has either no ear or no patience.'
[3] S.H.A. *Firmus* etc., i: 'Suetonius Tranquillus, emendatissimus et candidissimus scriptor . . . cui familiare fuit amare breuitatem.'
[4] For Hadrian's preference see S.H.A. *Hadr.* xvi.

of Cicero, and, if he found blemishes in Sallust,[1] must have seen more in Caelius. In his vocabulary, as might be expected, there are many words, or meanings of words, not to be found in Caesar or Cicero; but, as in most other Silver Age writers, these are, to a large extent, words taken over in first-century prose from the poetry of Virgil and Horace, or words already occurring in the prose of Livy and post-Augustan authors. Thus the Virgilian *austrinus* ('southern') had been used by Columella and the elder Pliny before Suetonius; and *adapertus* ('open') descended to him from Varro, Livy and Ovid through both prose and poetry of the first century. Occasionally Suetonius harked back to the old-fashioned: *cerritus* ('crazed') is a Plautine word transmitted through Horace, and *aquilus* ('swarthy') is a rare adjective borrowed from Plautus. Sometimes there are comparative novelties. *Extemporalis* ('on the spur of the moment') represents the sort of term which Suetonius naturally shares with writers like Quintilian, Tacitus, the younger Pliny and Martial, who have occasion to mention rhetorical fluency. Much the same holds of the non-Ciceronian, but ultimately most useful, words *prosa* (sc. *oratio*) for 'prose,' and *breuiarium* for 'an abstract.' Suetonius has a remarkable fondness for Latinised Greek words, for diminutives, for words ending in *-arius* or *-orius*, for participles in *-atus* of verbs connected with nouns or adjectives (*e.g. loricatus, albatus*), for adjectives in *-osus* and adverbs in *-im*, and for intensive adjectives beginning with *per* or *prae*.[2]

The Suetonian tradition is traceable in the biographical character of histories for generations. It ousted the Tacitean type until Ammianus Marcellinus (*c.* 330–*c.* 400) modelled his work on Tacitus. Suetonius's formal arrangement was imitated in the lost writings of Marius Maximus (*praefectus urbi* in 217), and it is evidently followed in the *Augustan History*, once ascribed in part to Diocletian's reign.[3] Christian authors also copied his structure, as did Paulinus in his biography of Ambrosius, and after the same pattern Einhard, or Eginhard, composed his life of Charlemagne. As regards language, writers like Eutropius, Aurelius Victor, and Orosius show traces of having read Suetonius. The influence of his *Lives* of literary celebrities upon Jerome is a familiar fact. His Greek writings appealed to some of the Byzantines, while his miscellaneous range secured him notice from many different writers in Latin. Thus, Tertullian used his work on games for the *De Spectaculis*; Censorinus, Solinus and Macrobius found antiquarian lore in him; and other borrowers were the Virgilian commentator Servius, the scholiasts on Horace, on Germanicus, on Lucan and on Juvenal; as well as the encyclopaedist Isidorus of Seville.

[1] *De Gram.* x.
[2] Examples in G. W. Mooney, *op. cit.* in bibl., appendix i.
[3] See footnote on *Historia Augusta*, p. 525 *infra*.

FLORUS

Great probability attaches to the arguments that Florus the historian, Florus the rhetor, and Florus the poet, who all lived at this period, were one and the same person. Accepting this identification, we must take the correct name to have been P. Annius Florus, as the rhetor was called, and explain as confusions the 'Julius Florus' and 'L. Annaeus Florus' in MSS. of the historian. The academic dialogue by the rhetor on the question whether Virgil was more of an orator or a poet (*Vergilius Orator an Poeta*) is lost, but from a Brussels MS., containing an introduction[1] to this lost theme, important details about the author's life have been recovered. He was African. While at Rome in his youth under Domitian, he took part in the Capitoline competition, but was unfairly denied the prize and in chagrin took to wanderings which eventually brought him to Tarraco. Settled in Spain, he was one day in Trajan's reign taxed by a friend with his long absence from the capital, where his verses, the friend reminded him, found appreciative readers. By Hadrian's time he was in Rome again, and intimate enough with the emperor to banter him in miserable trochaics upon his travelling propensities:

> To be Caesar I've no notion,
> Or to roam the British Ocean
> Or in Scythian fog be frozen.

The imperial retort was:

> To be Florus I'd be sorry,
> Round the city inns to hurry,
> Or thro' every cookshop scurry,
> Where the plump mosquitoes worry.[2]

Better verses by Florus[3] have come down in five hexameters on spring-roses and twenty-six, on the whole pleasing, trochaic tetrameters *De Qualitate Vitae*, which include reflections on womankind, bad companionship, and foreign morality. In one quatrain a lover, who has cut his sweetheart's name on the bark of a tree, declares with an agreeable assonance:

[1] Printed in Halm's ed., Lpz. 1854, pp. 106–109.
[2] S.H.A. *Hadr.* xvi; Bährens, *Frag. P.R.* p. 373; W. Morel, *F.P.L.* p. 136.

> Florus: 'Ego nolo Caesar esse,
> Ambulare per Britannos,
> Scythicas pati pruinas.'
> Hadr.: 'Ego nolo Florus esse,
> Ambulare per tabernas,
> Latitare per popinas,
> Culices pati rotundos.'

One of Florus's lines may have dropped out.
[3] Bährens, *P.L.M.*, iv. 279 (uenerunt aliquando rosae' etc.) and 346. Duff, *M.L.P.* pp. 426–430. Other verses, perhaps by Florus, are printed along with the above.

S

As the tree grows, so my zeal glows: passion fills the graven words.
(*Crescit arbor, gliscit ardor: animus implet literas.*)

Another quatrain plays with a fancy concerning the Sun-god and the
Wine-god:

As Apollo, so is Bacchus, bearer of a fiery load:
Both the gods were flame-created: both the gods were born in fire:
Both have heat to give as guerdon in the sunlight or the vine:
One dispels the dark of night-time, one the darkness of the mind.
(*Sic Apollo deinde Liber sic uidetur ignifer:*
Ambo sunt flammis creati prosatique ex ignibus:
Ambo de donis calorem, uite et radio, conferunt:
Noctis hic rumpit tenebras, hic tenebras pectoris.)

His work in trochaics gives colour to the guess that Florus composed
the *Peruigilium Veneris*, nearly one hundred trochaic tetrameters celebrating the eve of a joyous festival devoted to the Lady of the Springtime
and of Love. Though now sadly disarranged, the poem was originally
perhaps in twenty-two quatrains,[1] marked off by the chanted refrain:

Let the lover love to-morrow; let the loveless learn to love.
(*Cras amet qui nunquam amauit, quique amauit cras amet.*)

If one could be confident in the ascription to Florus, the reign of Hadrian
would be credited with one of the sweetest and most romantic poems in
all Latin literature, a hymn of esctasy over the coming of a new season
of brightness and fertility upon the earth:

'Tis the fresh and tuneful Springtide – Spring first brought the
    world to light,
In the Spring fond hearts draw closer: in the Springtime birds unite:
(*Ver nouum, uer iam canorum; uere natus orbis est;*
Vere concordant amores; uere nubunt alites.)

In contrast to the prevailing glee comes the personal note of melancholy at the end:

She is singing: we are silent: when doth Spring for me awake?
When shall I grow like the swallow? When may I my silence break?
I have lost the Muse by silence, and Apollo heeds me not.
(*Illa cantat, nos tacemus; quando uer uenit meum?*
Quando fiam uti chelidon, ut tacere desinam?
Perdidi musam tacendo, nec me Apollo respicit.)

On the whole one must doubt whether the poem is not too good to be
by Florus. In style it might be called Apuleian, and if it is not Hadrianic
there is little to prevent one from believing that it at least belongs to
some part of the second century, unless its almost entire avoidance of

---

[1] Mackail pointed out the quaternary arrangement and printed a reconstruction in *J.Ph.* xvii (1888).

quadrisyllabic endings is considered too suggestive of the manner of Tiberianus in the fourth century.[1]

With Florus as historian, or rather epitomiser, we are on surer ground. The best MS., the *Bambergensis*, gives the title of his work as *Epitoma ... de T. Liuio bellorum omnium annorum DCC* and the correct number of books as two. The *Nazarianus* follows a division into four books. In the title Florus's dependence on Livy is recognised; but, besides this main source, he used Sallust, Caesar, and possibly the elder Seneca's *Histories*. He is no geographer, but he alludes in his preface to geographical charts, and may have consulted Mela and Pliny. The *Natural History* would give him authority for his reference to the richness of Spain in gold, *chrysocolla* and *minium*.[2] Perhaps Lucan also was a source.[3] The work was probably written early in Hadrian's reign.[4]

His preface shows his attitude. It is an attitude of praise rather than of studied narration.[5] The seven hundred years which he counts from Romulus to Augustus had been, he feels, so full of the greatness of the Roman people that one might suppose the history had been longer. To study it is to study the destiny not of one people but of the human race. Valour and Fortune had combined to establish a world-wide dominion. On the analogy of geographers, Florus submits at the outset a kind of plan (*breui quasi tabella*) to illustrate the evolution of the Roman people. For him it was an organism, and had passed through four ages: infancy, 250 years of regal government; youth, 250 years of warfare in Italy; robust maturity, 200 years of world-conquest up to Augustus; old age and decline, 200 years from Augustus until the writer's own day – with, however, he is careful to add, a renewal of youth under Trajan, His figures, it should be noted, need correction; for chronology is not his strong point. A recapitulation (*anacephalaeosis*) is given with each of the first three ages; but the decadence is not treated. There is at the end of Book I an anticipatory review of growing luxury in the third age suggestive of the cause of the decline: the attack, as so often in the Silver Era, is couched in rhetorical terms.[6]

Genuine historical thought is impossible in an author whose criterion of value was the extent to which events redounded to the glory of Rome, and whose criterion of credibility was an entry in the annals (*quae nisi in annalibus forent, hodie fabulae uiderentur*). His mode of treatment

[1] See Appendix to J. A. Fort's trans. of *Peruig. Ven.* (Oxf. 1922).
[2] Flor. II. xxxiii; Plin. *N.H.* XXXIII. 66, 86–91, 118.
[3] His 'plus quam bellum,' II. xi, in reference to civil strife, seems an echo of Lucan's opening line. But see footnote on p. 257 *supra*.
[4] *Prooem.* 8: 'A Caesare Augusto in saeculum nostrum haud multo minus anni ducenti . . . sub Traiano principe mouit (mouet, *Naz.*) lacertos et praeter spem omnium senectus imperii . . . reuiruit (reuirescit, *Naz.*).' I. v. 5, 'hactenus pro libertate . . . Euphrates,' could not have been written before A.D. 115.
[5] Augustine must have had Florus in his mind when he wrote the words 'qui non tam narrare bella Romana quam Romanum imperium laudare instituerunt,' *Civ. Dei* iii. 19.
[6] *E.g.* the anaphora 'unde . . . nisi . . .' three times, I. xlvii.

scarcely admits a touch of romance. Egeria's mysterious prompting of Numa's policy is merely a useful state-figment (*quo magis barbari acciperent*). Occasionally we find a story, but it is in general told with almost grudging curtness, like that of Nevius and the whetstone. Occasionally, too, a great exploit rouses Florus to something approaching enthusiasm, like the recovery of Spain by Scipio; though it is a blemish that the enthusiasm is not always worked into the narrative but confined to parenthetic outbursts. Inevitably, however, much of the fascination of Roman history vanishes in the dry condensation of a summary. Its very neatness becomes tiresome, for the brevity tends to pass into abruptness. But in fairness it must be judged with regard to the author's intention of writing a eulogistic sketch, where the Populus Romanus shall be the single hero throughout.

Because the aim was eulogistic instead of unimpassioned history, there is too frequent indulgence in exclamatory asides—*quae superbia! mira res dictu! quis credat? immane dictu! mirum et incredibile dictu! fidem numinum! o nefas!* Some of his comments have a naïve banality in their search for antithetic point. Of Julius Caesar's assassination he says, 'so he who had drenched the world with citizens' blood at last drenched the senate-house with his own' (*sic ille qui terrarum orbem ciuili sanguine impleuerat tandem ipse sanguine suo curiam impleuit*); and, when the murdered Cicero's head was fixed on the *rostra*, he states, 'there was as great a rush to see him as there usually was to hear him' (*nec aliter ad uidendum eum quam solebat ad audiendum concurreretur*). It is not surprising that the poetic element in him overloads his expression with metaphor, while the rhetorical element tempts him to exaggerate, as when Antony's high turreted ships, 'forts and cities in appearance, sailed not without the groaning of the sea and the toil of the winds' (*castellorum et urbium specie, non sine gemitu maris et labore uentorum ferebantur*). It is unsafe for a prose-writer to expand the idea of Virgil's *urbis opus*. On the other hand, he is happy in certain of his comparisons: there is force in likening the final resistance of Carthage to the dangerous bite of a dying beast; or the diminution in the Gauls' resistance, after a first effort, to the melting of the snow upon their mountains. It may not be entirely fanciful to impute to African Latinity the more bizarre and brusque turns in him.[1] In any case, though some of his rhetoric is absurd, it redeems his work from being a totally dry abstract. His sentences are, as a rule, well written, and not unpleasing in their *clausulae*. His language is characteristic in the use of post-Augustan words like *captiuitas* and *diuersitas*, and in the position of *igitur* at the start of a sentence.[2] *Receptator* seems to be a word of his

---

[1] P. Monceaux, *Les Africains*, Paris 1894, p. 209, thinks that Florus, 'prépare les voies aux grands rhéteurs d'Afrique . . . et s'il tombe fréquemment dans la déclamation, l'afféterie et le mauvais goût, ce seront là justement des défauts familiers à la prose africaine.'

[2] Not, however, invariably: *e.g.* 'reuersus igitur' (I. xlv).

own, outside legal phraseology. The way in which he overworks *quasi*
and *quippe* is ludicrous.[1]

The popularity of Florus was assured in the third and fourth centuries,
when the demand for epitomes rose to its height. It is no longer a current
belief, as it once was, that the Livian *periochae* (which should not
be mistaken for epitomes) were the work of Florus. But Lucius Ampe-
lius borrowed from him for his short manual of general knowledge, the
Liber Memorialis, compiled perhaps early in the third century.[2] Ammianus, Orosius, Festus and Jordanes used him, as did the Byzantine
historian Malalas; and the multiplication of manuscripts of his text
testifies to the favour in which he stood with the Middle Ages.

[1] Teuffel (§ 348. 4) records 125 occurrences of *quasi* and 75 of *quippe* in the 81
chapters. The single chapter cited in the previous note illustrates several inartistic
repetitions of both words.

[2] Ed. by Wölfflin, Lpz. 1854; *cf.* Galdi, *L'Epitome n. lett. lat.*, pp. 80–89.

Conclusion

AN EPILOGUE – THE SECOND CENTURY AND AFTER

The passing of the Silver Age – Factors hampering literary creation – *Elocutio nouella* – Fronto, Gellius, Apuleius – Anarchy of third century – Energy diverted towards law, scholarship, epitomes – Vigour of Christian apologists – Prose of Minucius, Tertullian, Cyprian, Arnobius, Lactantius – Poetry of Commodianus, Ambrose, Prudentius – A Greek renascence – Echoes of Silver Age in Gallic *Panegyrici*, in *Historia Augusta*, and in Ammianus – Poetic revival in fourth century – Nemesianus, Ausonius, Claudian – End of national Roman literature – The European Latin of the Middle Ages – Vitality of literary influence of Rome at Renaissance and later periods.

BEYOND the time of Suetonius the Silver Age does not extend.[1] We are not, therefore, strictly concerned with the Roman literature which followed, or with its phases of decadence, barrenness and revival. Yet it is instructive to consider what took the place of Silver Latin, and why changes set in. Obviously, Latin continued to be written, though for a time not in the same quantity; but such Latin as continued was written with a difference in quality. Several factors, indeed, during the immediately succeeding period militated against the production of what had been the prevalent type of literature. In the first place, there arose that natural desire for change which ensures periodic reaction in all literary history. What one might call the Silver spirit had spent itself. Pointed epigram palled: neither interest nor dexterity in it any longer existed. The chief sign of the altered tendency was the appearance of the archaising school of Cornelius Fronto, which, by turning back to Ennius, Cato and the Gracchi as models of style, implicitly undervalued the Silver Age and revolted against its conventions. Born in Numidia about the beginning of the second century, Fronto had studied at Alexandria, had been a successful pleader at Rome in Hadrian's time, and was, under Antoninus Pius, made tutor to the future emperor Marcus Aurelius, his correspondence with whom has in part survived. Fronto never was in any deep sense a thinker. His

---

[1] Summers in his *Silver Age of Lat. Lit.* omits even Suetonius.

primary concern being eloquence, he manifestly did not sympathise with his imperial pupil's devotion to philosophy. Touching canons of style, no less than the supremacy of wisdom, he was poles asunder from Seneca. A zealous champion of archaism in composition, Fronto maintained that old-fashioned Latin writers were preferable to the Greeks and to the later Romans, and that a virile *elocutio nouella* (the phrase is his own) would spring from a union between the ancient and the spoken Latin. The direct plainness of the older writers and speakers he felt, with some justice, to be more in touch with life; but his fundamental misconception lay in failing to realise that to copy them, as if Roman literature had not run a distinguished course during some centuries since their day, was to fly in the face of evolution, and that to reintroduce obsolete words, however natural they had been at one time, was merely to displace one system of artificiality in favour of another. Yet for a space the movement was novel enough to live. Fronto's unbounded enthusiasm for the antiquated won the admiration of Aulus Gellius, who about the middle of the century began his miscellany of the *Noctes Atticae* during a winter spent at Athens. He used to buy old volumes in order to dig in them for contributions towards those brief essay-like studies of his which constitute an ancient museum of curiosities in literature, learning, language, philosophy and custom. As Gellius occupied himself particularly with the correct use of Latin words and idioms, his illustrations are often of great value. Not only did he transcribe passages from old authors like Ennius, Plautus, Caecilius or Afranius, and discuss points of Virgilian or Ciceronian expression and text, but he recorded critical views held by contemporary rhetoricians like Fronto, Herodes Atticus and Favorinus. In the *Attic Nights* one never knows on what odd piece of information one may chance. When, for instance, he writes about the perversity of Laberius in inventing bits of doubtful Latinity or in borrowing words from the common speech, Gellius tells us that *botulus*, a rare name for a sausage which we associate with the modern medical term *botulism* for certain sorts of food-poisoning, was a vulgar word used instead of the more proper *farcimen* in one of Laberius's mimes. All such philological preoccupation was symptomatic of a period of literary decadence, when critics could not see what a miserable substitute for good Latin style was offered by the obscure, ill-sounding and strained language which they were now manufacturing.

The culmination of the *elocutio nouella* which marked the collapse of the Silver Latin is to be found in the work of the African Platonist and rhetorician Lucius Apuleius, and especially in his *Metamorphoses*, the fantastic tale relating, not without some prurience, the adventures of his namesake Lucius in Thessaly, the home of witchcraft and the supernatural. The main account of the consequences following the hero's magical transformation into an ass came from a Greek source; and so did the incidental tales, such as the charming fairy-story of Cupid and Psyche, which the author dovetailed into his narrative. Based thus as its matter was on Greek, the romance is not unaffected by Hellenisms, but its prevailing exuberance follows the new Latin fashion. The short runs of words in a clause seem partly to recall a primitive, partly to anticipate a modern type of prose. The phrasing is unusual, often bizarre: it is a fantastic blend of elaborate archaism and bold innovation – now poetic, now colloquial. The diminutives of the vulgar tongue jostle far-fetched artifices. Such is the general effect that the reader accustomed to normal Latin feels as if he had adventured into a strange land with a strange speech.

There were other contemporary factors which tended to reduce the output of Latin literature. Tranquillity under the good government of the Antonines appeared to be as unpropitious for letters as was the anarchy of the third century. It is significant that there were no fewer than twenty-five Roman emperors between Commodus (180–192) and Diocletian (284–305). Besides, intellect was being diverted into other than purely literary channels. In law, the reigns of Septimius and Alexander Severus are famous for the eminent jurists Papinian and Ulpian. Attention was also devoted to scholarship and criticism. Authorities on metre like Terentianus Maurus, and grammarians or commentators of the third century, had in the fourth many renowned successors like Donatus, Charisius, Diomedes, Servius and Macrobius. Very symptomatic too was the demand in these centuries for epitomes of the more voluminous writers of the past. There is evidence of a definite distaste – from which emperors were not free – for the trouble of reading older and fuller authors; so that epitomators, on the principle that half a loaf is better than no bread, could at least claim to be ministering to culture by their condensed products. How much the epitomes contributed to the disappearance of their originals is a question easier to raise than to settle. Sometimes both original and epitome have come down together, as holds good of Vitruvius. Two abridgements did not kill Valerius Maximus, nor did epitomators and excerptors cause Pliny's *Natural History* to be lost. Half of the elder Seneca's *Controuersiae* and nearly three and a half decades of Livy survived in spite of being summarised. Sometimes, however, the abridgement alone has descended to posterity. Justinus, for example, remains, while his foundation Trogus has perished. Here, however, we may be content to conclude that the period was not only as a whole uncreative but that it felt itself unequal to the task of digesting the creations of more fertile times.

The truth is that the most virile thought which now found expression in Latin for some generations was the thought connnected with the new faith in Christ, so that henceforth a history of Latin literature must take into account theological and patristic authors. Minucius Felix, a Roman lawyer, about the end of the second century, composed in his dialogue *Octauius*, which opens prettily on the sands at Ostia, a defence of certain aspects, though not the most significant aspects, of the Christian religion. This work was based on older models; but a new manner is coupled unmistakably with new matter in the works which the African Tertullian wrote after his conversion to Christianity. His previous training had been that of an advocate in the law-courts of Carthage; and he now consecrated a fiery eloquence to a fresh cause. The fervid indictment of paganism, in his *Apologeticum* especially, sounds like a break with classical tradition, because he unsparingly denounces the poetry and philosophy of the Greeks and Romans as a perversion of Holy Writ. His uncompromising puritanism could spare no admiration for ancient culture. Yet, in spite of this, the break is not absolute. Even among Christian writers two lines of literary influence are discernible. On the one hand Tertullian's Latin is akin to the African Latinity of Apuleius, and may, with some qualifications, be classed beside the better style of Cyprian, who was bishop of Carthage in the middle of the third century. On the other hand, a more classic tradition is seen not only in the above-mentioned *Octauius* by Minucius who continued the literary preference of Quintilian for Ciceronian standards, but also in *The Institutes of Divinity* (*Diuinae Institutiones*) by Lactantius, who, though a pupil of Arnobius, the author of *Aduersus Nationes*, departed from his master's unpolished style in favour of that elegant diction which he cultivated as a professor of rhetoric at Nicomedia late in the third century, and which won him the title of 'the Christian Cicero.' His Ciceronianism was merely one of many links between him and the past: he was in reality widely read in classical verse as well as prose, and a poem on the *Phoenix* in finished elegiacs may well be his. The poetry which Commodianus wrote after his conversion is a deviation from the classical manner, and in its mixture of quantitative with accentual principles marks a step towards medieval versification; but in general the attempts at Christian verse-writing bore little fruit until, about the end of the fourth century, St. Ambrose and Prudentius composed their hymns.

The contemporary prominence of Greek was another indication and contributory cause of the decadence of Latin. The fashion among Romans of composing in Greek and the genius of the actual Greek writers at this epoch, like Plutarch, Arrian and Lucian, helped to throw Latin into the shade as something outworn. Once more history tended to pass into Hellenic hands. Appian, in the time of Antoninus Pius, set himself to compose a Roman history, of which we possess a considerable portion; and later Dio Cassius, a grandson of the rhetorician Dio Chrysostom esteemed by Trajan, conceived the scheme of relating in eighty books the development of Rome from Aeneas's time to A.D. 229, the year of the author's return to his native Nicaea. The extant parts form an important, though not infallible, historical document. Greek writers in contact with Rome were never more admired than they were from Flavian to Antonine days. Hadrian's reign, we have seen, inaugurated what may be fairly called a Hellenic revival; for little of the highest importance had appeared in secular Greek literature from Strabo and Diodorus in Augustan times to Dio Chrysostom and Plutarch. There was now, however, a sort of sophistic renascence of Greek prose, brilliant enough to dazzle contemporaries, which is transmitted from Dio Chrysostom, Lucian and Aristides, the rhetorician who studied under Herodes Atticus, down to Libanius who was Julian's teacher in the fourth century. It is a movement which had points of contact with Latin writers such as Apuleius; but it laid no firm hold upon the world.

Latin, however, never so lost its vitality as to be wholly supplanted by Greek in the late Silver Age of Hellenism.[1] Though it may be argued that classical Latin in a sense ended with Suetonius, and though the literary ages which followed the Silver might be named after inferior metal, there were various resuscitations, if only spasmodic, of the classical manner. Mention has already been made of Ciceronian elements in Minucius and Lactantius. Although inferior in execution, some writers at least looked to the old exemplars. The rhetorical panegyrists of the Gallic school in the third century had Pliny's *Panegyricus* in their eye; the six authors who composed, professedly under Diocletian and Constantine, the *Historia Augusta*[2] were, however feebly, continuing Suetonius's studies of the Caesars; and the Asiatic Ammianus Marcellinus, though he never attained to mastery over Latin, intended his history of nearly three centuries from the beginning of Nerva's reign until the death of Valens (96–378) to be a sequel to Tacitus. The last eighteen of his thirty-one books survive to enable us to judge of his obscurity and inflation in manner. Among poets under Diocletian and his successors, the revival of style became more evident; for the lethargy which had fallen on the third century was being thrown off. Even then the Virgilian tradition was plainly at work in the *Cynegetica*, a didactic poem on hunting by the Carthaginian Nemesianus, and in his bucolic pieces it combined pleasantly with the influence of Calpurnius Siculus. Still more varied classical influences unite in the works of Ausonius of Bordeaux. Whether one looks at his miscellaneous light verse, often amusingly egotistic, or at his renowned description of the river *Mosella*, written about 370, one finds a great deal that marks him as standing between the two worlds of classicism and romance. Towards the turn of the same century Claudian had come from Alexandria to the imperial court at Milan. In contrast to Ammianus, his use of Greek in early life

[1] Certain aspects of this later Hellenic literature are sketched in Mahaffy's *Silver Age of the Gk. World*, Chicago 1906.
[2] Dessau, *Herm.* xxiv (1889), assigned it to the days of Theodosius the Great, Emperor of the East 379–395. But N. H. Baynes, *Hist. Aug., Its Date and Purpose*, Oxf. 1926, argues for 362–363, under Julian.

did not prevent him from gaining wonderful control over the Latin manner. His historical epics revive the Virgilian tradition dear to the poets of the Silver Age; his *Rape of Proserpine* is reminiscent of Ovid; and his laudatory pieces are under obligations to Statius. Claudian's patriotism, no less than his style, is only one among many recurrent illustrations of Rome's power of attracting and remaking the alien. The beneficence of the Roman Empire is the idea underlying his lines:

> Rome only takes the vanquished to her breast,
> Fostering mankind beneath one common name,
> Like mother, not like mistress: citizens
> She calls them, bound by ties no distance breaks.[1]

With him or with the Gaul Rutilius Namatianus the national poetry might be said to close. Namatianus wrote in half-classical diction and half-classical metre at the time when the Empire was splitting up into new kingdoms; and there is a fitting note in his farewell apostrophe to Rome:

> Thou mad'st a city what was erst a world.
> (*Vrbem fecisti quod prius orbis erat.*)

Yet, in another sense, Latin literature does not end either with Claudian or with Namatianus: nor does it make much difference whether, with some authorities,[2] we take Boethius for the last of the ancients, or, with others,[3] take him for the first medieval Latin writer. Both positions are defensible and instructive. Two events, in particular, may serve to illustrate the continuity of influence, apart from questions of classic quality in style. First, Jerome's translation into Latin of the Scriptures from Genesis to Acts, which came to be known as *The Vulgate*, was published in 405. Its Latinity, very different from the Ciceronian, must be recognised as one of the great formative influences on expression during medieval times. Secondly, the sack of Rome in 410 by a host of Goths and Huns under Alaric stimulated Augustine to undertake his work *De Ciuitate Dei*. No better link between antiquity and the Middle Ages could be discovered. The ideal claim to citizenship in a more abiding state than an earthly one had received a telling confirmation in the barbarians' triumphant challenge to the power of Rome; and Rome herself was now to become 'the Eternal City' rather through the greatness of the universal Church than through that of the Roman Empire.

[1] *De Consulatu Stilichonis*, III. 150:
> 'Haec est in gremium uictos quae sola recepit,
> Humanumque genus communi nomine fouit,
> Matris non dominae ritu: ciuesque uocauit,
> Quos domuit, nexuque pio longinqua reuinxit.'

[2] *E.g.* G. A. Simcox, *A Hist. of Lat. Lit. from Ennius to Boethius*, Lond. 1883. Teuffel extends his *Geschichte* beyond Cassiodorus and Gregory of Tours so as to include some writers of the seventh and eighth centuries.

[3] Manitius begins his *Gesch. der lat. Lit. des Mittelalters*, 1911–1923, with Boethius. Pichon, *Litt. lat.*, p. 933, says 'Sidoine, Boèce, Ennodius et Cassiodore sont tout à fait aux confins du moyen âge.'

Latin literature, then, did not close in the fourth or the fifth century; but thenceforward it was no longer national, no longer Roman. Latin became in the Middle Ages European, whether employed by the Venerable Bede, by Isidore of Seville, or by Carolingian scholars like Alcuin and Einhard. Even the birth of modern languages from their parent did not supplant Latin as an international medium for conveying ecclesiastical, legal, historical and philosophical learning: so, following Dante, it came that Petrarch and Boccaccio made use of Latin and Italian indifferently; and not till after the end of the seventeenth century was Latin really shaken in its supremacy as the general language for philosophy and science. That century had seen issued Bacon's *Nouum Organum* and *De Augmentis Scientiarum* in its first quarter and Newton's *Philosophiae Naturalis Principia Mathematica* in its last quarter.

There can be no more interesting pendant to a literary history of Rome than a glance at later periods when the influence of the best writers acted strongly enough to inspire an artistic use of the Latin language. It must never be forgotten how much the humanism of the Renaissance, vitalised as it was by the rediscovery of Greek culture, included also a revival of Latin studies and of the power to write good Latin. In prose many names rise easily to the mind – among them, Valla and Ficino in Italy, Budaeus and Langolius in France, Erasmus and Grotius in the Low Countries, Sir Thomas More in England and George Buchanan in Scotland. In verse, the various collections of *Deliciae*, drawn from the poets of Italy, France, Holland, Germany, England and Scotland, contain excellent examples of supreme ability to recapture, in fresh circumstances, the manner of the greatest authors of Rome. Other countries may not have had a galaxy of modern Latin poets to compare with the Italians Baptista Mantuanus, Poliziano, Bembo Pontano, Sannazaro, Vida, Fracastoro, Navagero and Flaminio, but there is no mistaking the literary merit of such Latin poems as were written by the Dutch scholars Grotius and Daniel Heinsius or by the Scottish scholars Buchanan and Arthur Johnston. Of England it may be said that, even if Latin poems like those of Milton and Cowley be taken into account, her finest work in Latin verse was yet to come from scholars of the nineteenth century, when in this field she had no equals abroad. While it is true that much of this modern skill consisted in translation or light *jeux d'esprit*, the elegance and taste shown in composition has borne eloquent testimony to the living literary influence of the best poets of the Gold and Silver Ages of Rome.

TABLE OF ABBREVIATIONS

(*The most obvious are omitted*)

A.J.P.   American Journal of Philology, Baltimore, 1880–

Anz. A.W.   Anzeigen für die Altertumswissenschaft, hrsg. von der Oesterreichischen Humanistischen Gesellschaft, Vienna 1948–1955, Innsbruck 1956– (Similar to Burs. J. *infra*.)

Atkins, Lit. J. W. H. Atkins, Literary Criticism in Antiquity, vol. ii,
Crit. Ant.   Graeco-Roman, Cambridge 1934, rp. London 1952

B.L.L.   N. I. Herescu, Bibliographie de la littérature latine, Paris, 1942

Budé   Collection des Univ. de France, publiée sous le patronage de l'Assoc. Guillaume Budé, Paris

Burs. J.   Jahresbericht über die Fortschritte der klassischen Altertumswissenschaft, begrundet von C. Bursian, herausgegeben von A. Thierfelder, Leipzig, 1873–1944. (Contains *inter alia* critical bibliographies for various authors and subjects over certain spans of years.)

Butler,   H. E. Butler, Post-Augustan Poetry (Seneca to Juvenal),
Post-Aug. P. Oxford, 1909

C.   Commentary

C.A.H.   Cambridge Ancient History, 1923–1939

C.I.L.   Corpus Inscriptionum Latinarum, Berlin, 1862–

Cichorius, C. Cichorius, Römische Studien, Leipzig, 1922
Röm. Stud.

C.J.   Classical Journal, Evanston, Illinois, 1905–

c. not. var. Cum notis variorum (or what amounts to same)

Conc.   Concordance

C.P.   Classical Philology, Chicago, 1906–

C.P.L.   *See* Postgate

C.Q.   Classical Quarterly, Oxford, 1907–

C.R.   Classical Review, Oxford, 1887–

C.R.F.   Comicorum Romanorum Fragmenta, being vol. ii of O. Ribbeck, Scaenicae Romanorum Poesis Fragmenta, ed. 3 (Teub.) 1898

C.W.   Classical Weekly, New York, 1907–1957; Classical World, New York, 1957–

De Groot, Prosarhythmus	A. W. de Groot, Der Antike Prosarhythmus, Groningen, 1921
Dessau, I.L.S.	H. Dessau, Inscriptiones Latinae Selectae, 3 vols. Berlin, 1892–1916
D.S.	C. Daremberg and E. Saglio, Dictionnaire des antiquités grecques et romaines, Paris, 1877–1919
Duff, L.H.R.	J. W. Duff, A Literary History of Rome from the Origins to the Close of the Golden Age, ed. 3, London, 1953
Duff, M.L.P.	Minor Latin Poets from Publilius Syrus to Rutilius Namatianus: Text and Trans. by J. W. Duff and A. M. Duff (Loeb) 1934
Duff, Rom. Sat.	J. W. Duff, Roman Satire: Its Outlook on Social life; (Sather Classical Lectures), Berkeley (Calif.) and Cambridge, 1937
Ed. Pr.	Editio Princeps
E.E.	Early Editions
Fleck. Jb.	Neue Jahrbücher für Philologie und Paedagogik, hrsg. von A. Fleckeisen, Leipzig (ended in 1897)
F.P.L.	Fragmenta Poetarum Latinorum epicorum et lyricorum praeter Ennium et Lucilium. Post E. Baehrens ed. W. Morel (Teub.) 1927
F.P.R.	Fragmenta Poetarum Romanorum (=E. Baehrens, Poetae Latini Minores), vol. vi (Teub.) 1886
Galdi, L'Epitome n. lett. lat.	M. Galdi, L'Epitome nella letteratura latina, Naples, 1922
Gesam. Schr.	Gesammelte Schriften
G.I.F.	Giornale italiano di filologia, Naples, 1948–
G.L.	See Keil
Hb.	Handbuch
Herm.	Hermes, Berlin, 1866–
H.R.F. H.R.R.	} See Peter
I.G.	Inscriptiones Graecae, Berlin, 1873–
I.L.S.	See Dessau
Indogerm. Forsch.	Indogermanische Forschungen, Berlin, 1892–
Jb.	Jahrbuch (or Jahrbücher)
J.Ph.	Journal of Philology, New York, 1868–1920
J.R.S.	Journal of Roman Studies, London, 1911–
J.Sav.	Journal des Savants, Paris, Nouv. Sér. 1903–
Kbg.	Königsberg

Keil, G.L.   H. Keil, Grammatici Latini, 7 vols. (w. suppl.), Leipzig,
               1857–1878
Kl. Schr.   Kleine Schriften
L. and E.   *See* Nettleship
L.H.R.   *See* Duff
Litt. Lat.   *See* Pichon
Lm.   Lustrum, Internationale Forschungsberichte aus dem Be-
               reich des klassischen Altertums. H. J. Mette and
               A. Thierfelder, Göttingen, 1956– (A continuation of
               Bursian's Jahresberichte – see Burs. J. above)
Loeb   Loeb Classical Library
Lpz.   Leipzig
Meyer,   H. Meyer, Oratorum Romanorum Fragmenta, ed. 2,
O.R.F.   Zurich, 1842
Mnem.   Mnemosyne, Leyden, 1852–
M.L.P.   *See* Duff
Nettleship,   H. Nettleship, Lectures and Essays, 2 vols. Oxford, 1885
L. and E.   and 1895
Neue Jb.   Neue Jahrbücher für das klassische Altertum, Geschichte
K.A.   und Deutsche Literatur und für Pädagogik, 1898–
Nisard, P.   J. M. N. D. Nisard, Études de moeurs et de critique sur les
lat. déc.   poètes latins de la décadence, ed. 3, Paris, 1867.
Norden,   E. Norden, Die antike Kunstprosa, vom 6 Jahrh. v. Chr.
Kunstprosa   bis in d. Zeit d. Renaissance, 2 vols. Leipzig, 1898 (rp.
               w. supplements, 1909)
O.C.D.   Oxford Classical Dictionary, 1949
O.C.T.   Oxford Classical Texts
O.R.F.   *See* Meyer
O.W.   Other Works
Paravia   Corpus Scriptorum Latinorum Paravianum (Turin)
Peter,   H. Peter, Historicorum Romanorum Fragmenta (Teub.)
H.R.F.   1883
Peter,   H. Peter, Historicorum Romanorum Relliquiae, vol. i,
H.R.R.   ed. 2, Lpz. 1914; vol. ii, ed. 1, Lpz. 1906
Philol.   Philologus, Berlin, 1846–1949
Pichon,   R. Pichon, Histoire de la littérature latine, ed. 5, Paris,
Litt. Lat.   1912
P.L.M.   Poetae Latini Minores, ed. E. Baehrens, 5 vols. (Teub.)
               1879–83; rev. by F. Vollmer (i, ii, v, alone completed)
               (Teub.) 1911–35
P.lat.déc.   *See* Nisard
Post-Aug.   *See* Butler
P.
Postgate,   Corpus Poetarum Latinorum, 2 vols., ed. J. P. Postgate,
C.P.L.   London, 1894 and 1905

Plessis, Poésie lat.	F. Plessis, La poésie latine, Paris, 1909
P.W.	A. Pauly, G. Wissowa, W. Kroll, Real-Encyclopaedie d. klassischen Altertumswissenschaft, Stuttgart, 1893–
R.B.Ph.	Revue belge de philologie et d'histoire, Brussels, 1922–
R.E.A.	Revue des études anciennes, Paris, 1899–
R.E.L.	Revue des études latines, Paris, 1923–
R.F.I.C.	Rivista di filologia e di istruzione classica, Turin, 1873–
Rh.M.	Rheinisches Museum für Philologie, Frankfurt-am-Main, 1827–; Neue Folge, 1842–
R.I.F.D.	Rivista internazionale di filosofia del diritto, Rome, 1921–
R.I.L.	Rendiconti dell' Istituto Lombardo, Classe di lettere, scienze morali e storiche, Milan, 1864
R.Ph.	Revue de philologie de littérature et d'histoire anciennes, Paris, 1877–
S.H.	M. Schanz, Geschichte d. römischen Literatur (I. von Müller's Handbuch der Altertumswissenschaft, Abt. VIII) Teil II, ed. 4, Munich, 1935 by C. Hosius.
S.H.A.	Scriptores Historiae Augustae
S.H.K.	M. Schanz etc. (see S.H. above). Teil III, ed. 3, Munich, 1922 by C. Hosius and G. Krüger
S.I.F.C.	Studi italiani di filologia classica, Florence, 1893–
Sitzb. {Berl. Heid. Mun. Wien}	Sitzungsberichte der Akademie der Wissen-schaften (Philos.-Hist. Klasse) {Berlin Heidelberg Munich Vienna}
Supplbd.	Supplementband.
Symb. Osl.	Symbolae Osloenses, Oslo, 1920–
T.	Text
Teub.	Bibliotheca Scriptorum Graecorum et Romanorum Teubneriana, Lpz. 1849–
Teuffel } Tfl.	W. S. Teuffel, Geschichte d. römischen Literatur, 3 vols., ed. 6 (vol. II, ed. 7) by W. Kroll and F. Skutsch. Lpz. and Berlin, 1913–1920; Eng. Tr. by G. C. Warr of L. Schwabe's revision (=5th Germ. ed.) 2 vols. London, 1900
Tr.	Translation
Tr.Am. Ph.A.	Transactions of the American Philological Association, Univ. of Wisconsin Pr. and Oxford U.P.
T.R.F.	Tragicorum Romanorum Fragmenta, being vol. i of O. Ribbeck, Scaenicae Romanorum Poesis Fragmenta, ed. 3 (Teub.), 1898

Bibliography

(for abbreviations see p. 528)

IN the following bibliography (which does not claim to be exhaustive) I have embodied the bibliographies which my father in the 1927 edition arranged in footnotes to the text where the treatment of an author started. Thus I have avoided the separation of the original bibliographies from a supplementary bibliography, which was an awkward feature of my edition of my father's earlier volume. In the compilation I owe a great deal to the bibliographical footnotes in the first edition of this work; to J. Marouzeau, *Dix années de bibliographie classique* (covering 1914–1924) and *L'Année philologique* (covering 1924 onwards); to Carl Hosius's revision of M. Schanz's *Geschichte der römischen Literatur*, teil ii, Munich 1935; to N. I. Herescu, *Bibliographie de la littérature latine*, Paris 1943; and to J. A. Nairn's *Classical Handlist* (Blackwell, Oxford) edition 3, 1953.

The paginal reference to the left of subject or author indicates the place where the subject or author is introduced in the text. Immediately after each author-heading I have inserted in brackets references to the *Bände* of Bursian's *Jahresberichte*a nd occasionally some other bibliographies. In the longer sections the order of editions, commentaries and translations is (within the various subdivisions) chronological, while that of other works is alphabetical, except that references to Schanz-Hosius, Teuffel, Herescu, and collections of fragments, are usually placed either at the beginning or the end of each section.

GENERAL WORKS (literature)

A. G. Amatucci, La letteratura di Roma imperiale (being vol. xxv of 'Storia di Roma' a cura dell' Istituto di Studi Romani) Bologna 1947

J. W. H. Atkins, Literary Criticism in Antiquity, vol. ii Graeco-Roman, Camb. 1934, rp. London 1952

H. Bardon, La littérature latine inconnue, vol. ii L'époque impériale, Paris 1956

J. Bayet, La littérature latine, ed. 6, Paris 1953

E. Bickel, Lehrbuch der Geschichte der röm. Literatur, Heidbg. 1937

H. E. Butler, Post-Augustan Poetry (Seneca to Juvenal) Oxf. 1909

A. Cartault, La poésie latine, Paris 1921

M. L. Clarke, Rhetoric at Rome, London 1953

M. S. Dimsdale, Hist. of Latin Literature, London 1915

J. Wight Duff, Roman Satire, Berkeley (Calif.) and Cambridge, 1937

M. Grant, Roman Literature, Cambridge 1954; new ed. London 1958

M. Hadas, A History of Latin Literature, New York 1950

A. Klotz, Geschichte d. römischen Literatur, Bielefeld and Leipzig 1930

U. Knoche, Die röm. Satire, ed. 2, Göttingen 1957

W. Kroll, Studien z. Verständnis d. röm. Literatur, Stuttgart 1924

W. A. Laidlaw, Latin Literature, London 1951

M. L. W. Laistner, The Greater Roman Historians, Berkeley (Calif.) 1947

F. Leo, Die griechisch-römische Biographie, Lpz. 1901

J. W. Mackail, Latin Literature, ed. 2, London 1896 (rp. 1927)

H. Nettleship, Lectures and Essays, series i, Oxf. 1885; ii, ib. 1895

J. M. N. D. Nisard, Les poètes latins de la décadence, ed. 3, Paris 1867

E. Norden, Römische Literatur, ed. 5, Lpz. 1954

E. Norden, Antike Kunstprosa, 2 vols. ed. 3, Lpz. 1915–18

E. Paratore, Storia della letteratura latina, Florence 1950

H. Peter, Die geschichtliche Literatur über d. röm. Kaiserzeit, Lpz. 1897

R. Pichon, Histoire de la litt. latine, ed. 5, Paris 1912

F. Plessis, La poésie latine, Paris 1909

O. Ribbeck, Gesch. d. röm. Dichtung, vol. iii, ed. 2, Stuttgart and Berlin 1913

H. J. Rose, Handbook of Latin Literature, ed. 2, London 1949

A. Rostagni, Storia della letteratura latina, vol. ii L'Impero, ed. 2, Turin 1954

M. Schanz, Gesch. d. röm. Literatur (I. von Müller's Handbuch der Altertumswissenschaft Abt. viii) teil ii, ed. 4 by C. Hosius, Berlin 1935; teil iii, ed. 3 by C. Hosius and G. Krüger, Berlin 1922

D. R. Stuart, Epochs of Greek and Roman Biography, Berkeley (Calif.) 1928

W. C. Summers, The Silver Age of Latin Literature, London 1920

N. Terzaghi, Storia della letteratura latina da Tiberio a Giustiniano, Milan 1933

N. Terzaghi, Per la storia della satira, Messina 1944

W. S. Teuffel, Gesch. d. röm. Literatur, revd. by W. Kroll and F. Skutsch, Berlin, vol. ii ed. 7, 1920; vol. iii ed. 6, 1913. Eng. Tr. by G. C. Warr of L. Schwabe's revision (=5th Germ. ed.) vol. ii, London 1900

INTRODUCTION

Chapter I

5. HISTORY OF SILVER AGE (apart from literature)

See Bibl. in C.A.H. vols. X, XI; O.C.D. s.vv. Art, Religion, Rome; relevant sections in J. A. Nairn's Classical Handlist (ed. 3, Oxf. 1953)
The following is a brief selection:

(General)

E. Albertini, L'Empire romain, ed. 3, Paris 1939
Camb. Anc. Hist. X, Camb. 1934. XI, Camb. 1936
H. Dessau, Gesch. d. röm. Kaiserzeit, Berlin 1924–30
L. Homo, Le Haut-Empire (Histoire Ancienne, ed. G. Glotz, III. iii) Paris 1933
E. T. Salmon, Hist. of the Roman World 30 B.C. to A.D. 138 (Methuen's Hist. of Gk. and Rn. World) London 1944, ed. 2, 1950
G. H. Stevenson, The Roman Empire, London 1930
J. Wells and R. H. Barrow, A Short History of the Roman Empire to the Death of M. Aurelius, ed. 5, London 1950

(Provinces)

V. Chapot, The Roman World (Eng. tr.) London 1928
G. H. Stevenson, Roman Provl. Admin. till Age of the Antonines, Oxf. 1939

(Constitutional)

L. Homo, Roman Political Institutions (Eng. tr.) London 1929

(Social and Economic)

J. Carcopino, Daily Life in Anc. Rome (Eng. tr.) London 1940
S. Dill, Roman Society fr. Nero to M. Aurelius, ed. 2, London 1905
T. Frank, Econ. Survey of Ancient Rome, vol. V, Rome and Italy of the Empire, Baltimore 1940

L. Friedländer, Sittengeschichte Roms, ed. 9 and 10, Lpz. 1921–3; Roman Life and Manners, Eng. tr. of ed. 7, London 1908–13
M. Rostovtzeff, Social and Econ. Hist. of Rom. Empire, ed. 2 by P. M. Frazer, Oxf. 1957

(Religion)

F. Altheim, Röm. Religionsgeschichte, ed. 2, Baden-Baden 1951–3; Eng. tr. of ed. 1, 1931–3, by H. Mattingly, London 1938
C. Bailey, Phases in Relig. of Anc. Rome, Oxf. 1932
G. Boissier, La Relig. romaine d'Auguste aux Antonins, Paris 1874
G. Costa, Religione e politica nell' impero romano, Turin 1923
T. R. Glover, Conflict of Religions in early Rom. Emp., ed. 11, London 1927
G. Wissowa, Religion u. Kultus d. Römer (Müller's Handbuch) ed. 2, Munich 1912

(Art)

L. Bruhns, Die Kunst der Stadt Rom, Vienna 1951
A. Hekler, Greek and Roman Portraits, London 1912
D. S. Robertson, Hdbk. of Greek and Roman Architecture, ed. 2, Camb. 1943
E. Strong, Art in Anc. Rome, London 1929
E. Strong, Roman Sculpture fr. Aug. to Constantine, London 1907
H. B. Walters, Art of the Romans, ed. 2, London 1928
F. Wickhoff, Roman Art (tr. by E. Strong), London 1900

20. ROMAN EDUCATION

C. Barbagallo, Lo stato e l'istruzione pubblica nell' imp. rom., Catania 1911
G. Boissier, art. 'Declamatio' in D.S.
G. Boissier, L'Instruction publique dans l'emp. rom., Rev. des deux Mondes 1884
G. Boissier, Les écoles de déclam. à Rome, ib. 1902
S. F. Bonner, Roman Declamation in late Rep. and early Empire, Liverpool 1949
D. L. Clark, Rhetoric in Greco-Roman Education, N.Y. and London 1957
V. Cucheval, Histoire de l'éloquence Rom. depuis la mort de Cicéron jusqu'à l'avènement de l'emp. Hadrien, Paris 1893
N. Deratani, De Rhetorum Romanorum Declamationibus, in R.Ph. 1925, 101 ff. and 1927, 289 ff.
L. Grasberger, Erziehung u. Unterricht im klass. Altertum, 3 vols., Würzburg 1864–81
A Gwynn, Roman Education from Cicero to Quintilian, Oxf. 1926
H. I. Marrou, Hist. de l'éduc. dans. l'antiquité, Paris 1948 (Eng. tr. by G. Lamb, London 1956)
P. Monroe, Sourcebk. of Hist. of Educ. for Gk. and Rom. Period, N.Y. and London 1902
E. P. Parks, Rom. Rhetl. Schools as Preparation for the Courts under the early Empire, Baltimore 1945
R. Pichon, L'éduc. rom. au prem. siècle de notre ère, d'après les Controverses de Sen. le Rhéteur, in Rev. Universitaire 1895, 156 ff.
A. S. Wilkins, Roman Education, Camb. 1905
See also works listed below under Seneca the Elder.

PART I

LITERATURE UNDER TIBERIUS, CALIGULA AND CLAUDIUS

A.D. 14 - 54

Chapter I

37. SENECA THE ELDER (*Burs. J.* 183, 240)

E.E. Before 1587 editions of elder Seneca were combined w. his son's works.
Sep. Edns.:
N. Faber, Paris 1587
J. F. Gronovius, Leiden 1649; c. not. var. ex rec. Gronovii, Amst. 1672
T., C. Bursian, Lpz. 1857
    A. Kiessling (Teub.) 1872
    H. J. Müller, Vienna 1887
T.Tr., H. Bornecque, ed. 2, Paris 1932
T.C.Tr. (*Suas.* only) W. A. Edward, Camb. 1928
O.W., Works listed above under Roman Educ. and
    H. Bornecque, Les déclamations et les déclamateurs d'après Sénèque le père, Lille 1902
    A. Chassang, De corrupta post Ciceronem a declamatoribus eloquentia, Paris 1852
    W. Hoffa, De Seneca patre quaestiones selectae, Gött. 1909
    C. Jullien, Les professeurs de littér. dans l'anc. Rome, Paris 1885
    H. T. Karsten, De elocutione rhetorica qualis invenitur in Ann. Sen. *Suas.* et *Contr.*, Rotterdam 1881
    L. Koerber, Ueber d. Rhetor Sen. u. d. röm. Rhetorik seiner Zeit, Marb. 1864
    O. Rossbach in P.W. (s.v. Annaeus no. 16)
    M. Sander, Der Sprachgebrauch d. Rhet. Ann. Sen., Berlin 1877 and 1880
    T. S. Simonds, Themes treated by elder Sen., Baltimore 1896
    H. Tivier, De arte declamandi et de Rom. declamatoribus, Paris 1868

51. TIBERIUS, CALIGULA AND CLAUDIUS AS ORATORS AND SCHOLARS
Tfl. 275, 286. S.H. 357-9

52. TIBERIAN RHETORS AND ORATORS
Tfl. 259.7, 267, 268, 270, 276. S.H. 336, 450, 480

52. CALIGULAN AND CLAUDIAN RHETORS AND ORATORS
Tfl. 268, 276, 297. S.H. 336, 450

Chapter II

54. VALERIUS MAXIMUS (*Burs. J.* 63, 97, 217, 247)

E.E., Aldus Manutius, Ven. 1534
    S. Pighius, Antw. 1567
    J. Vorst, Berlin 1672 (c. notis perpetuis)
    A. Torrenius, c. not. var. (good index) Leiden 1726
T., C. Kempf, ed. 2 (Teub.) 1888

Tr., S. Speed, London 1678
T.Tr., P. Constant, Paris 1935
O.W., C. Elschner, Quaestiones Valerianae, Berlin 1864
R. Helm in P.W. (s.v. Valerius no. 239)
C. Kempf, Novae Quaestiones Valerianae (textual) Berlin 1866
C. Kempf, Proleg. to his ed. 1854
E. Lundberg, De eloc. V.M. (diss. Upsala) Falun 1906

(Sources)
C. Bosch, Die Quellen des V.M., Stuttg. 1929
R. Helm, V.M., Seneca, u.d. 'Exemplasammlung', Hermes 1939, 130 ff.
A. Klotz, Studien z. Val. Max. u. den Exempla, Sitzb. Mun. 1942, heft 5
B. Krieger, Quibus fontibus V.M. usus sit . . ., Berlin 1888
M. L. Paladini, Rapporti tra Velleio Patercolo e V.M., Latomus 1957 (suggesting a source common to both)
W. Thormeyer, De Valerio Max. et Cicerone quaest. crit., Gött. 1902
F. Zschech, De Cicerone et Livio Val. Max. fontibus, Berlin 1865
S.H. § 424

Chapter III

67. HISTORIANS

Tfl. 277, 291. S.H. 414 (for Gaetulicus), 440

68. VELLEIUS PATERCULUS (Burs. J. 72, 217, 247)

E.E., Ed. Pr. Beatus Rhenanus, Bâle 1520
J. Lipsius, Leiden 1591 (c. animadv.)
D. Ruhnken, Leiden 1779 (c. integr. animadv.) Re-edited C. H. Froscher, Lpz. 1830–9
J. C. Orelli, Lpz. 1835
T., F. Kritz, ed. 2, Lpz. 1848
R. Ellis, ed. 2 (O.C.T.) 1928
E. Bolaffi (Paravia) 1930
C. Halm, ed. 2 by C. Stegmann de Pritzwald (Teub.) 1933
T. C. (Book II, 41–131) F. E. Rockwood, Boston 1893
T.Tr., F. W. Shipley (Loeb) 1924 (w. Res gestae divi Augusti)
P. Hainsselin and H. Watelet, Paris 1932 (w. Florus)

O.W., A. Dihle in P.W. (s.v. Velleius no. 5)
F. A. Schöb, V. u. s. literar.-histor. Abschnitte, Tübingen 1908

(Style)
E. Bolaffi, De Vell. sermone et quibusdam dicendi generis quaestionibus selectis, Pesaro 1925
E. Bolaffi, Alcuni aspetti dell'opera di V.P., Bologna 1935
C. de Oppen, De Vell. Pat., Rostock 1875
Fritsch, Ueber den Sprachgebrauch des V.P., Arnstadt 1876
H. Georges, De elocutione V., Lpz. 1877
O. Lange, Zum Sprachgebr. des V., Putbus 1878, Stettin 1886
F. Milkau, De V.P. genere dicendi quaestiones selectae, Kbg. 1888
N. Oestling, De elocutione V.P., Upsala 1874

(Hist. value)
F. Faust, De V.P. rerum scriptoris fide, Giessen 1891
W. Goeke, De Vell. Tiberii imagine iudicium, Jena 1876
I. Lana, Velleio Patercolo o della propaganda, Turin 1952

C. Morgenstern, De fide historica V.P., imprimis de adulatione ei obiecta, Danzig 1798
A. Pernice, De V. fide historica, Lpz. 1862
W. Schaefer, Tiberius und seine Zeit im Lichte der Tradition des V.P., Halle 1912
L. Speckert, De la sincérité de V.P., Paris 1848
J. Stanger, De V. fide, Munich 1863
C. Windheuser, Quid de V. fide in iis locis qui ad Tiberii mores spectant statuendum sit, Neuss 1867

(Sources)
P. Kaiser, De fontibus V.P., Berlin 1884
M. L. Paladini, Rapporti tra V.P. e Valerio Massimo, *Latomus* 1957, 232 ff. (suggesting a source common to both)
R. Perna, Le fonti storiche di V.P., Bologna 1935
R. Rau, Chronol. und Quellenfrage bei V.P., Tübingen 1922 (unpubld.)
H. Wegner, V.P., eine philol. Quellenuntersuchung zur Gesch. des Kaisers Aug., Berlin 1922 (unpubld.)

81. Q. CURTIUS (*Burs. J.* 22, 217, 247)

E.E., D. Erasmus (cum annot.) Strasb. 1518
J. Freinsheim (cum comm. et suppl.) Strasb. 1648
H. Snakenburg (c. not. var.) Delft 1724
J. Mützell (mit krit. u. exeg. Anm.) Berlin 1841
T., E. Hedicke (Teub.) ed. maior 1908; min. 1931
K. Mueller, Mun. 1954
T.Tr., V. Crépin, Paris 1932
J. C. Rolfe (Loeb) 1946
H. Bardon (Budé) 1947
K. Mueller and H. Schoenfeld, Mun. 1954
Tr., T. Brende, London 1553
R. Codrington, London 1661, 1670, 1673
J. Digby, London 1714
P. Pratt, London 1809, 1821

O.W., S. Dosson, Étude sur Quinte-Curce, Paris 1887
F. Helmreich, Die Reden bei Curtius, Paderborn 1927
W. Kroll, Studien zum Verständnis d. röm. Lit., Stuttgart 1924 (pp. 331 ff.)
E. Schwartz in P.W.

(Sources) S.H. 426 a.

Chapter IV

92. CELSUS (*Burs. J.* 158, 180)

E.E., *Ed. pr.* B. Fontius, 1478
T. J. van Almeloveen (c. not. var.) Amst. 1687
L. Targa (w. lexicon) Padua 1769
E. Milligan, ed. 2, Edinb. 1831
T., C. Daremberg, Lpz. 1859, 1891
F. Marx (*Corp. med. Lat.* vol. i) Lpz. 1915
T.Tr., A. Lee, 2 vols., London 1831-6
A. Védrénes, Paris 1876
W. G. Spencer (Loeb) 1935
C.Tr., E. Scheller, ed. 2 by W. Frieboes, Brunsw. 1906
O.W., J.Ilberg, A. Cornelius Celsus u. d. Medizin in Rom., *Neue Jb. K.A.* xix (1907) 377 ff.

F. Marx, proleg. to ed. of 1915
O. Temkin, Celsus u. d. Begriff d. röm. Medizin, *Janus* 1929, 340 ff.
M. Wellmann in P.W. (s.v. Cornelius no. 82)

(Sources)

F. Marx, proleg. to ed. lxxiv ff.
O. Temkin, Celsus's 'On Medicine' and the Ancient Medical Sects, *Bull. Inst. Hist. Med.* 1935, 249 ff.
M. Wellmann, A. Corn. Celsus, eine Quellenuntg., Berlin 1913 (agst. which J. Ilberg argues *Neue Jb. K.A.* 1913, 693–6)

(Place in medicine)

O. M. Braungart, Zahn- u. Mundkrankheiten bei C., Jena 1922
A. Castiglioni, A. Corn. Celsus as an historian of medicine, *Bull. Hist. Med.* 1940, 857 ff.
E. Geiger, Die Zahnärtzlichen Anschaungen des C., Halle 1921 (unpubld.)
O. Prager, Die chirurgische Behandlung der Mundkrankheiten bei C., Jena 1922 (unpubld.)
E. Silberstein, Die zahnärtzlichen Lehren des C., Berlin 1920
S.H., § 474, sub-section on 'Stellung zur Medizin.'

(Philosophy)

A. Dyroff, Der Philosophische Teil der Encyclopädie des Corn. Celsus, *Rh.M.* 1939, 7 ff.

(Style)

T. T. Jones, De Sermone Celsiano, Harvard 1929

101. POMPONIUS MELA (*Burs. J.* 217, 247)

E.E., J. F. Gronovius, Leiden 1696, (c. not. var.) *ib.* 1722
C. H. Tzschucke, Lpz. 1807
T., G. Parthey, Berlin 1867
C. Frick (Teub.) 1880
T.Tr., D. Nisard (w. Macrobius and Varro), Paris 1883
C.Tr., H. Philipp, Lpz. 1912
O.W., J. Fink, Pomp. Mela u. seine Chorographie, Rosenheim 1881
H. Folmer, Stilistiska studier öfder Pomp. M., Upsala 1920
F. Gisingen in P.W.
L. Havet, La prose de P.M., *R.Ph.* xxviii (1904) 57–9 (for *clausulae*)
A. Klotz, Quaestiones Plinianae Geog., Berlin 1906
H. Oertel, Über den Sprachgebrauch des Pomp. M., Erlangen 1898
H. F. Tozer, Hist. of Anc. Geography, Camb. 1897; ed. 2 by M. Cary, 1935
G. Wissowa, Die Abfassungszeit der Chorographia des Pomp. M., *Hermes* 1916, 89 ff.
H. Zimmermann, De Pomp. M. sermone, Dresden 1895

105. SCRIBONIUS LARGUS (*Burs. J.* 180)

E.E., *Ed. Pr.* J. Ruellius, Paris 1528
J. Rhodius, Padua 1655 (w. comm.)
M. Bernhold, Strasb. 1786
T., G. Helmreich (Teub.) 1887
O.W., P. Jourdan, Notes de critique verbale sur S.L., Neuchâtel 1919
F.E. Kind in P.W.
J. Lottritz, De S.L. genere dicendi, Bonn 1913
S.H. § 499

542

BIBLIOGRAPHY

105. JURISTS

Tfl. 281. S.H. 488. 1 and 489. 1
F. P. Bremer, Jurisprud. Antehadr. (Teub.) 1896–1901

106. GRAMMARIANS

Tfl. 282. 1–3, 283. S.H. 475, 475a, 495, 497 *fin.*
K. Barwick, Remmius Palaemon u. d. röm. Ars Grammatica, Lpz. 1922

106. APICIUS

E.E., *Ed. Pr.* Milan 1498
M. Lister, London 1705
T., T. Schuch, ed. 2, Heidelberg 1874
C. Giarratano and F. Vollmer (Teub.) 1922
C.Tr. (French), B. Guégan, Paris 1933
Tr., B. Flower and E. Rosenbaum, 'The Roman Cookery Book,' London 1958
O.W., E. Brandt, Untersuchn. zum röm. Kochbuch, *Philol.* Suppl. xix. 3 (1927)
F. Vollmer, Studien zu d. röm. Kochbuche von Apicius, *Sitzb. Mun.* 1920
M. Wellmann in P.W. (s.v. Caelius no. 5)

Chapter V

107. PHAEDRUS (*Burs. J.* 39, 43, 55, 59, 68, 84, 101, 126, 143, 183, 204, 240, 265)

E.E., *Ed. Pr.* P. Pithoeus, Autun 1596
P. Burman, Amst. 1698; (c. not. var.) Hague 1718
R. Bentley (w. Terence) Amst. 1727
J. C. Orelli, ed. 2, Zurich 1832
T., L. Müller, Lpz. 1877
U. Robert, Paris 1893 (w. facsim. of *Cod. Pithoeanus*)
L. Havet, Paris 1895 (w. *Disquisitiones criticae*)
J. Gow in *C.P.L.* ii
J. P. Postgate (O.C.T.), 1919
T.C., E. Talbert, Paris 1890 (w. imitns. of La Fontaine and Florian)
G. H. Nall, London and N.Y. 1895
L. Havet, ed. 14, Paris 1923 (w. imitns. of La Fontaine)
F. Cantarella, ed. 7, Rome 1928
T.Tr., A. Brenot (Budé) 1924
O.W., C. Causeret, De P. sermone, Paris 1886
J. W. Duff, Rom. Sat. ch. 6
R. Ellis, The Fables of P. (inaug. lect.) London 1894
J. J. Hartman, De P. fabulis commentatio, Leiden 1890
Hausrath in P.W.
L. Herrmann, Phèdre et ses Fables, Leiden 1950
L. Hervieux, Les fabulistes latins, ed. 2 (vols. i and ii), Paris 1893–99
(vol. i, Ph. et ses anciens imitateurs directs et indirects; vol. ii, texte de Ph. et des imitateurs)
J. Jacobs, The Fables of Aesop, 2 vols., London 1889
L. Müller, De Phaedri et Aviani fabulis, Lpz. 1875
Nisard, P. lat. déc.
C. Pascal, Poeti romani, ed. 4, Turin 1924
W. A. M. Peters, Phaedrus, Nijmegen 1946
N. Terzaghi, Per la storia della satira, Turin 1932 (pp. 59 ff.)
H. Vandaele, Qua mente P. fabellas scripserit, Paris 1897

O. Weinreich, Fabel, Aretalogie, Novelle: Beiträge zu Phädrus, Petron, Martial u. Apuleius, *Sitzb. Heid.* 1931
C. M. Zander, Phaedrus Solutus vel Phaedri fab. novae XXX, Lund 1921

124. GERMANICUS (*Burs. J.* 153, 171, 212; *Lm.* 1).
E.E., *Ed. Pr.* U. Rugerius, Bologna 1474
Aldus Manutius, Venice 1499
H. Grotius, Leiden 1600
J. C. Orelli in his ed. of Phaedrus, Zurich 1832
T., A. Breysig (cum scholiis), Berlin 1867; (sine scholiis) (Teub.) 1899
E. Baehrens, *P.L.M.* i
O.W., J. Frey, De G. Arati interprete, Culm 1861
M. Gelzer and W. Kroll in P.W. (s.v. Iulius no. 138)
A. E. Housman, The Aratea of G., *C.R.* 1900, 26 ff.
J. Maybaum, De Cicerone et G. Arati interpretibus, Rostock 1889
G. Sieg, De Cicerone, G., Avieno, Arati interpretibus, Halle 1886

125. ALBINOVANUS PEDO
T., W. Morel, *F.P.L.* 115
O.W., Tfl. 252. S.H. 315
V. Bongi, Nuova esegesi dei fragm. di A.P., *R.I.L.* 1949, 28 ff.
O. Haube, Beitrag zur Kenntniss des Alb. Pedo, Fraustadt 1880
R. G. Kent, *C.R.* 1903, 311 ff. (for the storm picture)
A. Stein, Alb. Pedo, Vienna 1901

126. COMEDY
S.H. 417

126. TRAGEDY
Mamercus Scaurus. S.H. 357 and 450.1
Pomponius Secundus. S.H. 381; Tfl. 204.7

PART II
LITERATURE OF THE NERONIAN PERIOD
A.D. 54 – 68

Chapter I

131. COLUMELLA (*Burs. J.* 153, 212, 217, 247; *Lm.* 1)
E.E., In *Scriptores Rei Rusticae Veteres Latini*, P. Victorius, Leiden 1541; J. M. Gesner, Lpz. 1735
T. (*De Arb.*; *R.R.* i, ii, vi–xi) V. Lundstrom and A. Josephson, Upsala 1897–1955
(*R.R.* x) J. P. Postgate, *C.P.L.* 1905
T.C., J. G. Schneider (*Script. R.R.* vol. ii) Lpz. 1794
(*R.R.*) J. H. Ress, Flensburg 1795. Only vol. i publd.
T.C.Tr. (*R.R.* x) A. Santoro, Bari 1946
T.Tr., H. B. Ash and E. S. Forster, E. Heffner (Loeb): vol. i (*R.R.* i–iv) by Ash 1941; vol. ii (*R.R.* v–ix) by Forster and Heffner 1954; vol. iii (*R.R.* x–xii and *De Arb.*) by Forster and Heffner 1955

O.W., M. Ahle, Sprachliche u. krit. Untersuchungen zu Col., Mun. 1915
V. Barberet, De Col. vita et scriptis, Nancy 1887
G. Carl, Die Agrarlehre Columellas in soziologischer Betrachtung, Heidelberg 1925
W. E. Heitland, Agricola, Camb. 1921, pp. 250–69
A. Kappelmacher in P.W. (s.v. Iunius no. 104)
W. Koller, Beitrag zur Gesch. der Tierheilkunde... nach... Col., Mun. 1926 (unpubld.)

Chapter II

138. PETRONIUS (*Burs. J.* 139, 175, 204, 235, 260, 282; *Anz. A.W.* IX. i; *C.W.* 50; *Transns. Bibliog. Soc.* 10)
E.E., *Sat.* (without *Cena*) *Ed. Pr.* Milan circa 1482 in *Script. Paneg. Lat.*
    P. Pithoeus, Paris 1577
    (*Cena* only) P. Frambotti, Padua 1664
    (*Sat.* in whole) P. Burman, Utr. 1709; Amst. 1743 (w. comm.)
T., F. Buecheler, ed. maior, Berlin 1862; ed. min. (6th revised) W. Heraeus 1922
T.C. (*Sat.*) E. T. Sage, N.Y. and London 1929
    (*Cena*) A. Maiuri, Naples 1945
    E. V. Marmorale, Flor. 1947
    W. B. Sedgwick (w. Sen. *Apocol.* and some Pompeian inscriptions) ed. 2, Oxf. 1950
T.C.Tr. (*Cena*) L. Friedländer, Lpz. 1891, ed. 2, 1906
    W. D. Lowe, Camb. 1905
    M. J. Ryan, London 1905
    (*Bell. Civile*: i.e. *Sat.* 119–124) F. T. Baldwin, N.Y. 1911
C. (*Sat.*) E. Paratore, Flor. 1933
    (*Cena*) P. Perrochat, ed. 2, Paris 1952
T.Tr., M. Heseltine (w. Sen. *Apocol.* by W. H. D. Rouse) Loeb, 1913
    F. Hoffmann, Munich 1948
    A. Ernout (Budé) ed. 3, 1950
C.Tr., J. M. Mitchell, London 1922
Tr., Burnaby, London 1694
    Wilson, Burnaby and others, London 1708
U. Dettore, Milan 1953

(Poems)
T., E. Baehrens, *P.L.M.* vol. iv
F. Bücheler ed. min. (see above)
T.Tr., M. Heseltine (see above)
A. Ernout (see above)

Lexicon, J. Segebade and E. Lommatzch, Lpz. 1898

O.W., F. F. Abbott, Origin of Realistic Romance, *C.P.* 1911, 257 ff.; rp. in his 'Common People of Anc. Rome,' London 1912, pp. 117–44
F. F. Abbott, P.: a study in Anc. Realism (pp. 115–30 in his 'Society and Politics in Anc. Rome,' London 1914)
Atkins, Lit. Crit. Ant. ii. 159–66
G. Bagnani, Arbiter of Elegance: a study of the Life and Wks. of C. Petr., Toronto and London, 1954
C. Beck, The Age of Petronius, Camb. Mass. 1856
C. Beck, The MSS of the Sat.. . . . described and collated, Camb. Mass. 1863
G. Boissier, Un roman de moeurs sous Néron, ch. V in his 'L'opposition sous les Césars,' ed. 6, Paris 1909
R. Cahen, Le Satiricon et ses origines, Paris and Lyon 1925

V. Ciaffi, La Struttura del Satyricon, Turin 1955
A. Collignon, Étude sur P., Paris 1892; P. au moyen age, etc. Paris 1893
Duff, Rom. Sat. ch. V.
A. Giusti, Motivo Erodoteo nel romanzo di P., *Athenaeum* 1930, 88 ff.
R. Heinze, P. u. d. griech. Roman, *Herm.* 1899, 494 ff.
R. Helm, Der antike Roman (Snell u. Erbse Hb.) Berlin 1948; ed. 2, Gött. 1956
G. Highet, P. the Moralist, *Tr. Am. Ph. A.* 1941, 176–194
U. Knoche, Die röm. Satire, ed. 2, Gött. 1957
W. Kroll in P.W.
E. V. Marmorale, P. nel suo tempo, Naples 1937
E. V. Marmorale, La questione Petroniana, Bari 1948
C. Mendell, P. and the Greek Romance, *C.P.* 1917, 158 ff.
E. Paratore, Il Satiricon di P., vol. i Introd.; vol. ii Commento; Flor. 1933
L. Pepe, Studi Petroniani, Naples 1957
J. E. Pétrequin, Nouvelles recherches hist. et crit. sur P., Paris and Lyon 1869
E. Thomas, P.: L'envers de la société rom. et études diverses, ed. 3, Paris 1912
P. Thomas, L'âge et l'auteur du Sat., Ghent 1905
O. Weinreich, Fabel Aretalogie Novelle: Beitrage zu Phädrus, Petron, Martial u. Apuleius, *Sitzb. Heid.* 1931

(Language)

F. F. Abbott, The Use of Language as a means of Characterisn. in P., *C.P.* 1907, 43 ff.
G. A. Cesareo, De P. sermone, Rome 1887 (esp. on Neapolitan elements)
F. T. Cooper, Word-Formation in Roman sermo plebeius, N.Y. 1895
J. Feix, Wortstellung und Satzbau in Petrons Roman, Breslau 1934
H. von Guericke, De linguae vulgaris reliquiis apud P. et in inscr. parietariis Pomp., Gumbinnen 1875
M. Hadas, Oriental Elements in P., *A.J.P.* 1929, 378 ff.
W. Heraeus, Die Sprache des P. u. den Glossen, Lpz. 1899; rp. in his Kl. Schr. Heid, 1937
E. Ludwig, De P. sermone plebeio, Marb. 1869
A. Marbach, Wortbildung, Wortwahl u. Wortbedeutung als Mittel der Charakterzeichnung bei P., Giessen 1931
H. L. W. Nelson, P. en zijn 'vulgair' Latijn (w. Eng. summary), Aalphen-am-den-Rijn 1947
A. H. Salonius, Die Griechen und das Griechische in Pets. Cena, Helsingfors 1927
H. Schuchardt, Der Vocalismus des Vulgarlateins, 3 vols., Lpz. 1866–8
H. Stubbe, Die Verseinlagen im P., Lpz. 1933
W. Suess, De eo quem dicunt inesse Trim. Cenae vulgari sermone, Dorpat 1926
W. Suess, Petronii imitatio sermonis plebei qua necessitate coniungatur cum grammatica doctrina, Dorpat 1927

Chapter III

159. SENECA THE PHILOSOPHER (*Burs. J.* 79, 96, 108, 192)

E.E., *Ed. Pr.* Naples 1475
D. Erasmus, Bâle 1515, 1529
J. Lipsius, Antw. 1605, 1615
'C. notis J. F. Gronovii,' Leiden 1649; 'C. notis J. F. Gronovii et aliorum,' Amst. 1672
T

E. E. Ruhkopf, Lpz. 1797–1811
F. Haase, Lpz. 1852 ff.
T., E. Hermes and others (Teub.) 1905 ff. (Vol. I. i *Dial.* E. Hermes 1905;
    I. ii *Ben.* and *Clem.* C. Hosius, ed. 2, 1914; II *N.Q.* A. Gercke 1907;
    III *Ep. Mor.* O. Henze, ed. 2, 1914)
(*Ep. Mor.*) A. Beltrami, ed. 2, Rome 1949
U. Boella, Turin 1951
(*Dial.*) M. C. Gertz, Copenhagen 1886.
T.C. (*Dial.* Bks. 10, 11, 12) J. D. Duff, Camb. 1915
    (*De Otio*) R. Waltz, Paris 1909
    (*Ad Marciam de Consol.*) C. Favez, Paris 1928
    (*Ad Helviam de Consol.*) C. Favez, Laus. 1918
    (*Ad Serenum de Const. Sap.*) W. Klei, Utrecht 1950
    (Select Letters) W. C. Summers, London 1910
C. Index omn. verborum (*De Clem.*) P. Faider, C. Favez, P. van de Woestijne,
    Bruges 1950 (being second part to Faider's ed. of text, Ghent 1928)
C.Tr. (*N.Q.*) 'Physical Science in Time of Nero,' by J. Clarke and A. Geikie,
    London 1910
C. (*Const. Sap.*) P. Grimal, Paris 1953
T.C.Tr. (*Br.V.*) H. Dahlmann, Munich, 1949
T.Tr. (*Dial.*) A. Bourgery and R. Waltz, 4 vols. (Budé) 1922 ff.
    (*Dial., Ben., Clem.*) J. W. Basore (Loeb) 3 vols. 1932–5 (entitled 'Moral
    Essays'); vol. ii ed. 2, 1951
    (*Ben.*) F. Préchac, 2 vols. (Budé) 1926–7
    (*Clem.*) F. Préchac (Budé) 1921
    (*N.Q.*) P. Oltramare (Budé) 1929
    (*Ep. Mor.*) R. M. Gummere, 3 vols. (Loeb) 1917–25
    F. Préchac and H. Noblot (Budé) in progress 1945–
Tr. (*Ben.* w. *Clem.* and *Dial.*) A. Stewart, London 1889
    (*Ep. Mor.*) E. P. Barker, Oxf. 1932

O.W., P. Grimal, Sen., sa vie, son oeuvre, avec un exposé de sa philos., Paris
    1948
F. Holland, Seneca, London 1920
I. Lana, Lucio Anneo Seneca, Turin 1955
O. Rossbach in P.W. (s.v. Annaeus no. 17)

(Life)

A. Bailly, La vie de Sénèque, Paris 1929
C. Marchesi, Seneca, Messina 1920; ed. 2, 1934
R. Pichon, Hommes et choses de l'ancienne Rome, Paris 1911, pp. 177–232
R. Waltz, Vie de S., Paris 1909

(Chronology of Works)

E. Albertini, La composition dans les ouvrages philos. de S., Paris 1923
A. Bourgery, Sénèque prosateur, Paris 1922
A. Gercke, Seneca-Studien, Lpz. 1895
F. Giancotti, Cronologia dei dialoghi di S., Turin 1957
L. Herrmann, Chronol. des oeuvres en prose de S., *Latomus* 1937, 94 ff.
F. Jonas, De ordine librorum Sen. philosophi, Berlin 1870
E. Köstermann, Untg. zu d. Dialogschriften Senecas, *Sitzb. Berl.* 1934,
    684 ff.
A. Martens, De L. Ann. S. vita et de temp. quo scripta . . . composita sint,
    Altona 1871
K. Münscher, Ss. Werke. Untg. zur Abfassungszeit und Echtheit, *Philol.*
    Suppl. xvi (1922)

R. Pichon, Les travaux récents sur la chronol. des oeuvres de S., *J. Sav.* 1912, 212 ff.

S.H. § 453–67

(Philosophy)

V. d'Agostino, Studi sul neostoicismo—Seneca, Plinio il giovane, Epitteto, M. Aurelio, Turin 1950
E. V. Arnold, Roman Stoicism, Camb. 1911
A. Bailly, La vie et les pensées de S., Paris 1929
D. Bassi, Seneca morale. Studi e saggi, Flor. 1914
P. Benoît, Les idées de S. sur au-delà, *Rev. d. sciences philos. et théol.* 1948, 38 ff.
S. Blankert, Sen. (*Ep.* 90) over natuur en cultuur en Posidonius als zijn bron, Amst. 1941
A. de Bovis, La sagesse de S., Paris 1948
G. Boissier, La religion rom. d'Auguste aux Antonins, Paris 1874
C. Burnier, La morale de S. et le neostoïcisme, Laus. 1908
C. Corsi, Lo stoicismo romano . . . particolarmente in S., Prato 1884
J. Delhez, Les portraits du sage stoïcien dans les oeuvres en prose de S., *R.B.Ph.* 1949, 421 ff.
W. Gauss, Das Bild des Wesen bei S., Freiburg 1952
A. Guillemin, S. directeur d'âmes, *R.E.L.* 1952, 202 ff. and 1953, 215 ff.
R. M. Gummere, S. the Philosr. and his Modern Message, Boston 1922
T. P. Hardeman, The Philosophy of L. Ann. Sen. (diss. Univ. Illinois) Urbana 1956
F. Husner, Leib u. Seele in der Sprache Senecas, *Philol.* Suppbd. xvii (1924) heft 3
A. D. Leeman, S. and Posidonius, *Mnem.* 1952, 57–79 (Sen. *Ep.* cii, 3–19)
L. Levy-Bruhl, Quid de deo S. senserit, Paris 1884
C. Martha, Les moralistes sous l'emp. rom., ed. 3, Paris 1872
C. Martha, Études morales sur l'antiquité, Paris 1882, pp. 135–89 (Les Consolations dans l'antiquité)
F. Martinazzoli, Seneca: studio sulla morale ellenica nell' esperienza romana, Flor. 1945
M. Pohlenz, Philosophie und Erlebnis in Senecas Dialogen, *Nachrichten v.d. Gesellschaft der Wissenschaft zu Göttingen*, 1941, 55 ff.
S. Rubin, Die Ethik Sen. in ihr. Verhält. z. älter. u. mittler. Stoa, Mun. 1901
O. Weissenfels, De Sen. Epicureo, Berlin 1886
J. H. L. Wetmore, S's Conception of the Stoic Sage as shown in his Prose Works, Edmonton (Alberta) 1936

(Language)

E. Albertini, La composn. dans les ouvrages philos. de S., Paris 1923
B. Axelson, Seneca-Studien, Lund 1933
B. Axelson, Neue Senecastudien, Lund 1939
A. Bourgery, Sénèque prosateur, Paris 1922
A. M. Guillemin, Sénèque second fondateur de la prose latine, *R.E.L.* 1957, 265 ff.
A. Hoppe, Ueber d. Sprache des Philos. S., Lauban 1873
F. J. Merchant, Seneca the Philosr. His Theory of Style, *A.J.P.* 1905, 44 f.
E. Norden, Kunstprosa, ii. 306
U. Nottola, La prosa di S., Bergamo 1904
A. Pittet, Le vocab. philos. de S. (pt. 1 only) Paris 1937
H. Weber, De S. philos. dicendi genere Bioneo, Marburg 1895

548 BIBLIOGRAPHY

188. MISCELLANEOUS LEARNING
(Historians) Tfl. 286.6 and 291. S.H. 360 *sub. fin.*; 442, 1, 2, 3; 443 fin. (also for
Balbillus, J. Schwartz in *Bull. Inst. français d'arch. orientale*, Cairo 1949,
45-55)
(Jurists) Tfl. 298; S.H. 487-9
(Philosophers) Tfl. 299; S.H. 441

189. CAESIUS BASSUS
Tfl. 304, 1-2; S.H. 385

189. ASCONIUS (*Burs. J.* 139, 142, 188, 248, 285)
Ed. Pr. Ven. 1477
T., J. G. Baiter in J. C. Orelli's Cicero, Zürich 1826 ff. (V. ii. 1)
A. Kiessling and R. Schoell, Berlin 1875
A. C. Clark (O.C.T.) 1907
T. Stangl in *Ciceronis Orationum Scholiastae*, Vienna 1912
C. Giarratano, Rome 1920
O.W., J. Humbert, Contribn. à l'étude des sources d'Asconius dans ses relations
des débats judiciaires, Paris 1925
G. Wissowa in P.W.
S.H. 476

189. VALERIUS PROBUS (*Burs. J.* 113, 139, 188, 231)
J. Aistermann, De M. Val. Probo Berytio capita quattuor, accedit reliquiarum
conlectio, Bonn 1910
Tfl. 300-1; S.H. 477-9

189. ORATORS
Tfl. 297; S.H. 441, 450. 4, 5, 6

190. RHETORS.
S.H. 480

Chapter IV

191. APOCOLOCYNTOSIS OF SENECA (*Burs. J.* 192; *C.W.* 50
E.E., *Ed. Pr.* (*In morte Claudii ludus*) Rome 1513
C. E. Schusler, Utrecht 1844
T., F. Buecheler (w. Petronius) ed. 6 by W. Heraeus, Berlin 1922
O. Rossbach, Bonn 1926.
T.C., F. Buecheler, *Symb. Philol. Bonn.*, Lpz. 1864-7
W. B. Sedgwick (w. *Cena Trim.* and some Pompn. inscrns.) ed. 3, Oxf. 1950
T.C.Tr., A. P. Ball, N.Y. 1902
C. F. Russo, Flor. 1948
T.Tr., W. H. D. Rouse (w. Petronius by M. Heseltine) Loeb, 1913
R. Waltz (Budé) 1934
A. Rostagni, Turin 1944
A. Ronconi, Milan 1947
Tr., O. Weinreich, Berlin 1923 (w. Einführung, Analyse, Untersuchungen)
O.W., Introdd. to some of the above, esp. Buecheler, Ball and Weinreich
C. Gallo, L'Apocolocintosi di S.: Saggio critico, Arona 1948
J. J. Hartman, De ludo de morte Claudii, *Mnem.* 1916, 295 ff.
U. Knoche, Die röm. Satire, ed. 2, Gött. 1957

198. SENECA'S SHORT POEMS

T., E. Baehrens, *P.L.M.*, iv (1882) pp. 55 ff.
F. Buecheler and A. Riese, *Anth. Lat.* (Teub.) 1884
T.C., C. Prato, Bari 1955
O.W., K. P. Harrington, Seneca's Epigrams, *Tr. Am. Ph. A.* 1915, 207–15
E. Herfurth, De Senecae Epigrammatis, Jena 1910
A. Riese, Ueber d. Echtheit d. Gedichte d. S., d. Petronius u. anderer,
Fleck.Jb. xcix (1869) 279, and *Anth. Lat.* I. i. 191, 195, 312
G. Stauber, De L. A. Seneca Philosopho epigrammatum auctore, Mun. 1920

199. SENECAN TRAGEDY (*Burs. J.* 93, 134, 158, 171, 192; *Lm.* 2)

E.E., *Ed. Pr.*, Ferrara c. 1481
J. Lipsius, Leiden 1588
J. Gruter, Heidelberg 1604
J. F. Gronov, Leiden 1661
J. Pierrot, Paris 1829–32
T., F. Leo, Berlin 1878–9 (vol. i obs. crit.; ii text)
R. Peiper and G. Richter (Teub.) ed. 2, 1902
U. Moricca, Turin 1947
T.C. (*H.F.*, *Tro.*, *Med.*) H. M. Kingery, N.Y. 1908
(*Phaedra*) R. Giomini, Rome 1955
(*Agam.*) R. Giomini, Rome 1956
T.Tr., F. J. Miller (Loeb) 1916–17
L. Herrmann (Budé) 1924–6
Tr., T. Heywood and others, London 1581
E. Paratore, Rome 1956
(*Oed.*) M. Hadas, N.Y. 1955
(*Med.*) M. Hadas, N.Y. 1956
Index, W. Oldfather, A. S. Pease, H. V. Canter, Univ. of Illinois Studies, Urbana
1918
O.W., E. Cesareo, Le tragedie di S., Palermo 1932
L. Herrmann, Le théâtre de S., Paris 1924 (ample bibliog.).
F. Leo, vol. 1 of his ed. 1878
(Dating of plays). See footnotes 2 and 3 to p. 200
(Models, dramatic art and thought etc.)
J. Charlier, Ovide et Sen., *Mem. de lic. Univ. libre de Bruxelles* 1954–5
F. Egermann, Sen. als Dichterphilosoph, *Neue Jb. für Antike u. deutsche
Bildung* 1940, 18 ff.
P. J. Enk, Roman Tragedy, *Neophilologus* 1957, 282 ff.
W. H. Friedrich, Untersgen. zu Ss. dram. Technik, Lpz. 1933
F. Giancotti, Saggio sulle tragedie di S., Rome 1953
U. Knoche, Senecas Atreus, *Die Antike* 1941, 60 ff.
W. Lesowsky, Götter u. göttliche Wesen in Ss. Trag. im lichte seiner Philo-
sophie, Vienna 1950
B. Marti, Seneca's Tragedies, *Tr. Am. Ph. A.* 1945, 216 ff.
B. Marti, The Prototypes of S.'s Tragedies, *C.P.* 1947, 1 ff.
G. Mueller, Ss. Oedipus als Drama, *Hermes* 1953, 447 f.
Nisard, P. lat. déc. i. pp.65 ff.
E. Paratore, Sulla Phaedra di S., *Dioniso* 1952, 199–234
E. Paratore, La poesia nell' Oedipus de S., *G.I.F.* ix (1956) 97 ff.
E. Paratore, Sulle sigle dei personaggi nelle trag. di S., *S.I.F.C.* xxvii–
xxviii (1956) 324 ff.
N. T. Pratt, Dramatic Suspense in Seneca and in his Gk. Precursors, Prince-
ton 1939.

N. T. Pratt, Stoic Base of Senecan Drama, *Tr. Am. Ph. A.* 1948, 1–11
R. Schreiner, S. als Tragödiendichter in seinen Beziehungen zu den griech. Originalen, Mun. 1909
K. Stackmann, Senecas Agamemnon: Untersuchn. zur Gesch. des Agamemnonstoffes nach Aischylus, *Classica et Mediaevalia*, 1950, 180 ff.
R. B. Steele, Some Roman Elements in the Trag. of S., *A.J.P.* 1922, 1 ff.
K. H. Trabert, Studien zur Darstellung des Pathologische in den Trag. des S., Erlangen 1953

(Language)

H. V. Canter, Rhetl. Elts. in the Trag. of S., Univ. of Illinois Studies, Urbana 1925
F. Kunz, Sentenzen in Sen. Trag., Wiener Neustadt 1897

(Dramatic Influence)

J. Cunliffe, Infl. of S. on Eliz. Trag., London 1893
A. D. Godley, Senecan Tragedy, Oxf. 1912
C. Hastings, Le théâtre français et anglais, ses origines grecques et latines, Paris 1900
E. F. Jourdain, Drama in Europe in Theory and Practice, London 1924
L. E. Kastner and H. B. Charlton, The Poetical Works of Sir Wm. Alexander, vol. 1 (introd. essay on growth of Senecan tradition in Renaissance tragedy) Manchester 1921
A. Krug, Étude, sur la Phèdre de Racine et l'Hippolyte de S., Colmar 1883
F. L. Lucas, Sen. and Eliz. Tragedy, Camb. 1922
E. M. Spearing, Eliz. Translns. of S's Tragedies, Camb. 1912
P. Stachel, S. u. d. deutsche Renaissancedrama, Berlin 1907

220. OCTAVIA (*Burs. J.* 134, 158, 171, 192; *Lm.* 2)

Contained in most edd. of Seneca's tragedies
Separately:
T.C., J. Vürtheim, Leiden 1909
    C. L. Thompson, Boston 1921
    C. Hosius, Bonn 1922
    T. H. Sluiter, Leiden 1949
O.W., E. C. Chickering, An Introd. to Octavia Praetexta, N.Y. 1910
    F. Giancotti, L'Octavia attrib. a Sen., Turin 1954 (on which see B. Walker in *C.Ph.* 1957, 163 ff.)
    R. Helm, Die Praetexta Octavia, *Sitzb. Berl.* 1934, 283–347
    J. Schmidt in P.W.
    S.H. 380 and works there mentioned

223. POMPONIUS SECUNDUS
S.H. 381; Tfl. 284.7

223. CURIATIUS MATERNUS
S.H. 402; Tfl. 318

223. OTHER TRAGEDIANS
S.H. 402; Tfl. 323.3 and 324.5

Chapter V

224. PERSIUS (*Burs. J.* 2, 6, 10, 14, 27, 47, 72, 139, 175, 204, 235, 260, 282; *C.W.* 50; M. H. Morgan, A. Bibliog. of P., ed. 2, Camb. Mass. 1909)

Ancient Biography. See p. 224, note 2

E.E. *Ed.* (?) *Pr.* Paris 1472

  B. Fonte, Venice 1480 (comm.)

  J. Britannicus, Venice 1491 (comm. of editor and of Fonte)

  P. Pithoeus, Paris 1585

  I. Casaubon, Paris 1605 (w. comm.)

  See under Juvenal for early editions of P. and Juv. combined

T., O. Jahn (w. scholia and proleg.) Lpz. 1843; revd. by F. Buecheler, ed. 4 by
    F. Leo, Berlin 1910 (w. Juvenal)

  B. L. Gildersleeve, N.Y. 1875

  W. C. Summers in *C.P.L.* ii

  S. G. Owen, O.C.T. (w. Juvenal) ed. 2, 1908

  Santi Consoli, ed. 3, Rome 1913

  W. V. Clausen, Oxf. 1956

T.C., G. Némethy (Latin Comm.) Buda Pest 1903 (Supplement 1924)

  J. van Wageningen (Latin comm.) Groningen 1911

  F. Villeneuve, Paris 1918

  N. Scivoletto, Flor. 1956

T.C.Tr., J. Conington, ed. 3 by H. Nettleship, Oxf. 1893

  A. Mancini, Flor. 1950

T.Tr., G. G. Ramsay (Loeb) 1918 (w. Juvenal)

  A. Cartault (Budé) ed. 2, 1927

  O. Seel (Germ.) Mun. 1950

Tr., E. Rousse, Paris 1884 (w. étude)

  (Verse) J. Tate, Oxf. 1930

  See under Juvenal for translations of Persius and Juvenal combined

O.W., V. d'Agostino, De A. Persii sermone, *Riv. Indo-Greco-Italica* 1928, 1929,
    1930 (five articles)

  V. d'Agostino, I Diminutivi in Persio, *Atti Acad. d. Sc.* (Turin) 1928, 5 ff.

  Atkins, Lit. Crit. Ant. vol. ii, pp. 137–74

  C. Burnier, Le Rôle des sat. de P. dans le développement du neo-stoïcisme,
    Chaux-de-Fonds 1909

  Duff, Rom. Sat. pp. 114–25

  G. C. Fiske, Lucilius and P., *Tr. Am. Ph. A.* 1909, 121 ff.

  V. Gerard, Le latin vulgaire et le langage familier dans les sat. de P., *Musée Belge* 1897, 81 ff.

  O. Jahn, Proleg. to his ed. 1843

  U. Knoche, Die röm. Satire, ed. 2, Gött. 1957

  W. Kroll in P.W. (supplbd. vii)

  R. C. Kukula, P. und Nero, Graz 1923

  E. V. Marmorale, Persio, ed. 2, Flor. 1956

  C. Martha, Les moralistes etc., Paris 1865 (ch. on Un poète Stoïcien)

  J. M. K. Martin, P., Poet of the Stoics, *Greece and Rome* 1939

  Nisard, P. lat. déc.

  M. Schönbach, De P. in sat. sermone et arte, Lpz. 1910

  J. Sorn, Die Sprache d. Satirikers P., Laibach 1890

  F. Villeneuve, Essai sur Perse, Paris 1918

  T. Werther, De Persio Horatii imitatore, Halle 1883

  H. Wilcke, Quid elocutio Juvenalis a Persiana differat, Stendal 1869

Chapter VI

296. LUCAN (*Burs. J.* 63, 84, 134, 158, 171, 212; *Lm.* 1)
Ancient biographies
(Suet. and Vacca) C. F. Weber, Vitae Lucani collectae i and ii, Marburg 1856–7
A. Reifferscheid, Suetonii . . . reliquiae, Lpz. 1860, p. 50 ff. and p. 76 ff.
Edd. of Lucan by Lejay, Francken and Hosius (see *infra*)
(Minor *Vitae*) Weber, *op. cit.* iii, Marburg 1858
E.E. *Ed. Pr.* Rome 1469
H. Grotius, Antw. 1614, 1639; Leiden 1626
T. Farnaby, London 1618
G. Cortius, Lpz. 1726
F. Oudendorp, Leiden 1728
P. Burman, Leiden 1740
'M. Annaei Lucani Pharsalia cum notis Grotii et Bentleii' etc. [R. Cumberland] Strawberry Hill 1760
C. F. Weber, 3. vols. (c. not. var. in i and ii; scholia in iii) Lpz. 1821–31
C. F. Weber, Editionem morte Cortii interruptam absoluit, Lpz. 1828–9
T., W. E. Heitland in *C.P.L.* ii
C. Hosius (Teub.) ed. 3, 1913
A. E. Housman, Oxf. 1926, 1927 (rp. 1950)
(Fragm.) E. Baehrens, *F.P.R.*, pp. 365–8; W. Morel, *F.P.L.*
T.C., C. E. Haskins, London 1887 (w. introd. by W. E. Heitland)
C. M. Francken (Lat. Comm.) 2 vols., Leiden 1896–7
(Bk. i) P. Lejay, Paris 1894 (w. important introd.)
(Bk. i) R. J. Getty, Camb. 1940 (rp. w. corr. 1955)
(Bk. vii) J. P. Postgate, ed. 2, Camb. 1913
(Bk. viii) J. P. Postgate, Camb. 1917
T.Tr., J. D. Duff (Loeb) 1928
A. Bourgery and M. Ponchont (Budé) 1926–9
Tr. (Verse) Sir A. Gorges, London 1614; T. May, London 1627, 1631; N. Rowe, London 1718; E. Ridley, London 1896, 1905, 1919
(Prose) R. Graves (Penguin) 1956
Index, G. W. Mooney, Dublin 1927
Conc. R. J. Deferrari and others, Washington 1940
(Scholia) H. Usener, Commenta Bernensia (Teub.) 1869
J. Endt, Adnotationes super L. (Teub.) 1909

O.W. (Life and works)
H. Genthe, De L. vita et scriptis, Berlin 1859
G. Girard, Un poète républ. sous Néron, R. *des Deux Mondes* 1875, 423–44
W. E. Heitland, Introd. to Haskins's ed.
P. Lejay, Introd. to his ed. of Bk. I
E. Malcovati, Lucano, ed. 2, Brescia 1947 (1st ed. Milan 1940)
F. Marx in P.W. (s.v. Annaeus no. 9)
Nisard, P. lat. déc.
C. Vitelli, Sulla compos. e pubblic. della Farsaglia, *S.I.F.C.* 1900, 33–72

(Characteristics of *Pharsalia*)

L. Eckardt, Exkurse u. Ekphraseis bei L. (Diss.) Heidelberg 1936
H. Flume, Die Einheit der künstlerischen Persönlichkeit Lucans, Bonn 1951
F. Gro so La Farsaglia di L., Fossano 1901
B. M. Marti, The Meaning of the Phars., *A.J.P.* 1945, 352 ff.

H. C. Nutting, The Hero of the Pharsalia, *A.J.P.* 1932, 41–52
M. Pavan, L'ideale politico di L., *Atti dell' Istituto Veneto* cxiii (1954–5) 209 ff.
A. Thierfelder, Der Dichter Lucan, *Archiv für Kulturgesch.* xxv (1934–5) 1 ff.
M. Wuensch, Lucan-Interpretationen, Lpz. 1930

(Sources—general)

R. Pichon, Les sources de L., Paris 1912

(Historical sources and value)

G. Baier, De Livio Lucani in carm. de bello civ. auctore, Breslau 1874
R. Giani, La Farsaglia ed i commentari della guerra civile, Turin 1888
C. Jullian, Lucain historien, *R.E.A.* 1899, pp. 301 ff.; 1900, pp. 329 ff.
E. Malcovati, Lucano e Cicerone, *Athenaeum* 1953, 288–97
N. Singels, De L. fontibus et fide, Leiden 1884
E. M. Sanford, L. and his Roman Critics, *C.P.* 1931, 233 ff.
V. Ussani, Sul valore storico del poema Lucaneo, *Atti del congresso internaz. di scienze storiche* II. iv, Rome 1903
C. Vitelli, Studi sulle storiche fonti della Fars., *S.I.F.C.* 1902, 359–429
E. Westerburg, Luc., Florus und Pseudo-Victor, *Rh.M.* xxxviii (1882) 34–9
J. Ziehen, L. als Historiker, *Berichte d. freien Hochstiftes*, Frankfurt-am-Main 1890

(Geographical sources)

A. Bourgery, La géographie dans Lucain, *R.Ph.* 1928, 25–40

(Philosophical sources and treatment)

J. E. Millard, Lucani sententia de deis et de fato, Utr. 1891
F. Oettl, Lucans philos. Weltanschauung, Brixen 1888
M. Souriau, De deorum ministeriis in Phars., Paris 1885

(Literary sources)

J. Aymard, Quelques séries de comparaisons chez L., Montpellier 1951
H. Diels, Seneca u. L., *Abhandl. der Berl. Akad.* 1885
E. Fraenkel, L. als Mittler des antiken Pathos, *Vorträge der Bibliothek Warburg* 1924, 229–57
A. Guillemin, L'inspiration virgilienne dans la Phars., *R.E.L.* 1951, 214–27
W. E. Heitland in Introd. to Haskins's ed. (pp. cviii–cxxxi)
C. Hosius, L. u. seine Quellen, *Rh.M.* 1893, 380–97
C. Hosius, De imitatione scriptorum Rom. imprimis Lucani, Greifswald 1907

(Language)

S. H. 391 (under heading 'Komposition')

(Metre)

E. Trampe, De L. arte metrica, Berlin 1884

(Influence)

W. Fischli, Studien zum Fortleben der Phars. des M. Ann. Luc., Hague 1945
E. M. Sanford, Quotations from L. in medieval Lat. authors, *A.J.P.* 1934, 1 ff.
S.H. 392

Chapter VII

264. CALPURNIUS SICULUS (*Burs. J.* 158, 171, 212; *Lm.* 1)

E.E. *Ed. Pr.* [C. Schweynheym and A. Pannartz] (w. Silius Italicus); eleven eclogae under name of C. Calpurnius. Rome 1471
A. Ugoletus, Calpurnii Siculi et Nemesiani Bucolica, Parma c. 1490

T*

P. Burman in *Poet. Lat. Min.* i, Leiden 1731
J. C. Wernsdorf in *P.L.M.* ii, Altenburg 1780
C. E. Glaeser, Gött. 1842
T., E. Baehrens, *P.L.M.* iii (Teub.) 1881
H. Schenkl, Lpz. 1885 and in *C.P.L.* ii
C. Giarratano, ed. 2, Turin 1924 (w. *Carm. Eins.*)
T.C., C. H. Keene, London 1887
T.C.Tr., J. de Sipio, Catania 1935
R. Verdière, Brussels 1953 (without Nemes. but with *Laus Pisonis* and *Carm. Eins.*)
T.Tr., E. J. L. Scott, London 1890 (Calp. Sic. only)
F. Vernaleone, Noicattaro 1927
Duff, *M.L.P.*

with Nemesianus's four eclogues

O.W., E. Cesareo, La poesia di C.S., Palermo 1931
C. Chiavola, Della vita e dell' opera di Tito Calp. Sic., Ragusa 1921
F. Chytil, Der Eklogendichter T. Calp. Sic. u. seine Vorbilder, Znaim 1894
G. Ferrara, C.S. e il Panegirico a Calpurnio Pisone, Paris 1905
M. Haupt, De Carm. bucol. Calpurnii et Nemesiani, Berlin 1854; rp. in his Opuscula i, Lpz. 1875, 358 ff.
L. Herrmann, Les pseudonymes dans les bucol. de C.S., *Latomus* 1952, 27–44
J. Hubaux, Les thèmes bucoliques dans la poésie latine, Brussels 1930
F. Skutsch in P.W. (s.v. Calpurnius no. 119)

268. DE LAVDE PISONIS (*Lm.* 1)

E.E., *Ed. Pr.* in J. Sichard's ed. of Ovid, Bâle 1527, vol. ii, pp. 546–9
J. C. Wernsdorf in *P.L.M.* iv, Altenburg 1785, pp. 236–82
J. Held, Breslau 1831
C. F. Weber, Marburg 1859 (w. proleg.)
T., E. Baehrens, *P.L.M.* i, Lpz. 1879, 221 ff.
B. L. Ullman, *C.P.* 1929, 109 ff. (w. study of text tradn. and authorship)
T.C., G. Martin (diss. Cornell Univ.) Ithaca (N.Y.) 1917
T.C.Tr., R. Verdière (w. Calp. Sic. and *Carm. Eins.*) Brussels 1953
T.Tr., Duff, *M.L.P.*
O.W., Works of Chiavola, Ferrara, Haupt, Hubaux and Skutsch cited under Calp. Sic.
B. L. Ullman, *op. cit. supra*
E. Woelfflin, Zu dem carmen panegyricum in Calp. Pisonem, *Philol.* xvii (1861) 340–4
S.H. 387

270. EINSIEDELN ECLOGUES

T., E. Baehrens in *P.L.M.* iii
C. Giarratano (w. *Bucol.* of Calp. and Nemes.) Turin 1924
T.C.Tr., R. Verdière, Brussels 1953 (w. Calp. Sic. and *Laus Pisonis*)
T.Tr., Duff, *M.L.P.*
O.W. See bibliographies in Duff, *M.L.P.* and in S.H. 388

270. AETNA

E.E. Contained in some early edd. of Virgil
J. Scaliger in Virgilii Appendix, Leiden 1573
J. le Clerc (Gorallus) Aetna c. notis et interp., Amst. 1703, 1715
J. C. Wernsdorf in *P.L.M.*, Altenburg 1780–99
T., R. Ellis in *C.P.L.* ii

M. Lenchantin de Gubernatis, Turin 1911; ed. 2, 1926
F. Vollmer in *P.L.M.* i
T.C., H. A. J. Munro, Camb. 1867
T.C.Tr., S. Sudhaus, Lpz. 1898
R. Ellis, Oxf. 1901
J. Vessereau, Paris 1905
M. R. Russo, Turin 1937
T.Tr., J. Vessereau (Budé) 1923
Duff, *M.L.P.*
O.W., L. Alzinger, Studia in Aetnam collata, Erlangen 1896
K. Buechner in P.W. (s.v. Vergilius 7, cols. 1136–55)
M. Haupt, in his *Opuscula*, Lpz. 1875–6
B. Kruczkiewicz, Poema de Aetna Vergilio potissimum esse tribuendum,
    Cracow 1883
W. Richter, Lucilius, Seneca u. das Aetnagedicht, *Philol.* xcvi (1944) 234–99
A. Rostagni, Virgilio Minore, Turin 1933
S. Sudhaus, Zur Ueberlieferung des Gedichtes Aetna, *Rh.M.* lx (1905)
    574–83
J. H. Waszink, De Aetnae carminis auctore, *Mnem.* 1949, 224 ff.
S.H. 238–9

273. ILIAS LATINA (*Burs. J.* 158, 171; *Lm.* 1)

T., F. Plessis, Paris 1885
F. Vollmer in *P.L.M.* II. iii
O.W., J. Tolkiehn, Homer u. d. röm. poesie, Lpz. 1900, pp. 96 ff.
F. Vollmer in P.W.
S.H. 393–4

276. NERO

Fragm. in W. Morel, *F.P.L.* p. 131
See also C. Morelli, Nerone poeta e i poeti intorno a Nerone, *Athenaeum*
    1914, 117 ff.
S.H. 360; Tfl. 286, 7–11

277. CAESIUS BASSUS etc.

For C.B. see S.H. 385 and Tfl. 304
For others see S.H. 360 and 411 and Tfl. 304

PART III

LITERATURE OF THE FLAVIAN PERIOD

A.D. 69 – 96

Chapter I

281. PLINY THE ELDER (*Burs. J.* 6, 10, 14, 231, 273; *Anz.A.W.* VIII. iv;
    R.E.L. 23)

E.E., H. Barbarus, Rome 1492
J. Dalecampius, Lyon 1587
J. F. Gronov (c. notis) Leiden 1669
J. Harduinus, Paris 1685, 1723

J. G. F. Franz (c. notis Harduini et variorum) Lpz. 1778–91
J. Sillig, Gotha 1851–5
T., L. v. Jan, Lpz. 1854–65, ed. 2 by C. Mayhoff (Teub.) 1892–1909
D. Detlefsen, Berlin 1866–82
T.C., (Selections) K. L. Urlichs, Chrestomathia Pliniana, Berlin 1857
T.C.Tr., (Chemical chapters) K. C. Bailey, London 1929–32
(Chapters on art) K. Jex-Blake and E. Sellers, London 1896
S. Ferri, Storia delle arti antiche, Rome 1946
T.Tr., H. Rackham and W. H. S. Jones (Loeb) in progress 1938–
J. Beaujeu, A. Ernout and others (Budé) in progress 1947–
C. (Bk. ii) D. J. Campbell, Aberdeen 1936
Tr., Philemon Holland, London 1601, 1634
J. Bostock and H. T. Riley, London 1855–7

O.W., H. L. Axtell, Some human traits of the scholar Pliny, *C.J.* 1926, pp. 104–13
M. Baratta, La fatale escursione vesuviana di Plinio, *Athenaeum* 1931, 71–107
F. Dannemann, P. u. seine Naturgesch. in ihrer Bedeutung für die Gegenwart, Jena 1921
F. della Corte, Enciclopedisti latini, Genoa 1946
W. Kroll in P.W. (s.v. Plinius no. 5)
C. Nailis, Studie over de chronologie van het leven en de werken van P. d. Naturalist, *Philol. Studien* 1942–3, 1–23 and 25–77
A. Spellici, I medici e la medicina in Pl. il naturalista, Milan 1936
H. N. Wethered, The Mind of the Anc. World. A considern. of P's Nat. Hist., London 1937

(Sources)

F. Aly, Zur Quellenkritik des ält. Pl., Marburg 1885
H. Brunn, De auctorum indicibus Plinianis disputatio isagogica, Bonn 1856
W. Kroll, Die Kosmologie des ält. Pl., Breslau 1930
F. Münzer, Beiträge zur Quellenkritik des Naturgesch., Berlin 1897
Works mentioned in footnotes pp. 287–293
Much fuller list in S.H. 492 and in H. le Bonniec's bibl. in *R.E.L.* 1945 (also published separately, Paris 1946)

(Style)

J. Müller, Der Stil des ält. Pl., Innsbruck 1883
A. Önnerfors, Pliniana: in Pl. Mai. N.H. studia gramm. semantica critica, Upsala 1956

310. HISTORIANS OF FLAVIAN AGE
Tfl. 314. S.H. 440, 5 and 6; 441, 3; 442, 4

Chapter II

311. QUINTILIAN (*Burs. J.* 6, 18, 51, 109, 148, 192, 212, 222)

E.E., *Ed. Pr.* Campanus, Rome 1470
J. F. Gronov, Leiden 1665 (w. *Declamns.*)
P. Burman, Leiden 1720 (w. *Declamns.*)
C. Capperonnier, Paris 1725;
J. M. Gesner, Gött. 1738
G. L. Spalding, 4 vols. w. notes, Lpz. 1798–1816; vol. v, indices, by C. T. Zumpt 1829; vol. vi, lexicon, by E. Bonnell 1834
T., E. Bonnell (Teub.) 1854

C. Halm, Lpz. 1868–9
F. Meister, Lpz. and Prague 1886–7
L. Radermacher (Teub.) 1907–35
T. Conc., C. E. Little, The I.O. of M.F.Q. w. Eng. Summary and Concordance,
    Nashville 1951. (Eng. summary of and conc. to the whole I.O.; Lat. text
    of Bks. i, ii, x, xii)
T.C. (Bk. i) C. Fierville, Paris 1890
F. H. Colson, Camb. 1924
V. d'Agostino, Turin 1933
(Bk. x) J. A. Hild, Paris 1885
W. Peterson, Oxf. 1891
S. Dosson, Paris 1912
E. Bonnell, ed. 6 by H. Röhl, Berlin 1912
(Bk. xii) A. Beltrami, Rome 1910
R. G. Austin, Oxf. 1948; rp. w. corr. 1954
T.Tr., H. E. Butler (Loeb) 1920–2
H. Bornecque, Paris 1933–4

O.W., Atkins, Lit. Crit. Ant. ii
D. Bassi, Quintiliano, Rome 1929
E. Bolaffi, La critica filosofica e letteraria in Quint., Brussels 1958
F. H. Colson, Introd. to ed. of Bk. i (see supra)
V. Guazzoni-Foa, Quintiliano, Brescia 1947
G. Saintsbury, Hist. of Critm. I, 1900, 289 ff.
L. Schwabe in P.W. (s.v. Fabius no. 137)

(Sources)

J. D. D. Claussen, Quaestiones Quintilianeae, Fleck. Jb. Suppl. vi (1872)
J. Cousin, Études sur Q., Paris 1936 (vol. i, Contribn. à l'étude des sources de
    l'I.O.; vol. ii, Vocab. grec de la terminologie rhétorique)
W. Heydenreich, De Qntli. I.O. libro x, de Dion. Hal. de imitatione libro ii,
    de canone qui dicitur Alexandrino, Erlangen 1900
W. Peterson, Introd. to ed. of Bk. x (see supra)
S.H. 484

(Quintilian and education)

B. Appel, Das Bildungs- und Erziehungsideal Qnts. nach der I.O., Donau-
    wörth 1914
C. Barbagallo, Lo stato e l'istruzione pubblica nell' imp. rom., Catania 1911
D. Bassi, Quintiliano maestro, Flor. 1930
F. H. Colson, Introd. to ed. of Bk. i (see supra)
T. Froment, Quid e Qntli. Orat. Inst. ad liberos ingenue nunc educandos
    excerpi possit, Paris 1874
S. S. Laurie, Hist. Survey of Pre-Christian Educn., London 1895
H. North, Use of Poetry in the Training of the anc. Orator, Traditio (N.Y.)
    1952, 1–33
H. A. Strong, Q. the Roman Schoolmaster, Liverpool 1908

(Style)

Introd. to edns. of Bk. x by Dosson and Peterson and to Bonnell's Lexicon
    (=vol. VI of Spalding's ed. See supra)
G. Assfahl, Vergleich u. Metapher bei Q., Stuttgart 1932
X. Gabler, De elocutione M. F. Quintiliani, Borna-Leipzig 1910
A. Marty, De Quintilianeo usu et copia verborum cum Ciceronianis potis-
    simum comparatis, Glarona 1886
S.H. 484

(Infl. on humanism)

F. H. Colson, Introd. to ed. of Bk. i

A. Messer, Q. als Didaktiker u. s. Einfluss auf die didaktisch-päd. Theorie des Humanismus, *Fleck. Jb.* 1897

S.H. 486

331. DECLAMATIONES QVINTILIANEAE (*Burs. J.* 51, 113, 183, 285)

Both collections are contained in edd. of I.O. by Gronov and Burman (see *supra*)

(Maiores only)

E.E., G. Merula, Ven. 1481

T., G. Lehnert (Teub.) 1905

Tr., J. Warr 'from the Oxf. Theatre ed.' London 1686

(Minores only)

E.E., *Ed. Pr.* T. Ugoletus, Parma 1484

P. Aerodius, Paris 1563

P. Pithoeus, Paris 1580

T., C. Ritter (Teub.) 1884

O.W., N. Deratani, De Rhet. Rom. declam., *R.Ph.* 1925, 101 ff..; 1927, 289 ff.

R. Ellis, The Tenth Declamn. of Ps.-Q.—A lecture, London and Oxf. 1911

Y. Englund, Ad. Qni. quae feruntur Declam. maiores adnotationes, Upsala 1934

G. Fleiter, De minoribus quae sub nomine Qni. feruntur declam., Münster 1890

R. Reitzenstein, Zu Qntls. grossen Deklam., *Hermes* 1908, 104 ff.

R. Reitzenstein, Studien zu Qntls. grösseren Deklam., Strasb. 1909

C. Ritter, Die Quintil. Deklam., Freiburg 1881

A. Trabandt, De minoribus quae sub nomine Qni. feruntur declam., Greifswald 1883

S. Wahlén, Studia critica in declam. min. quae sub nom. Quint. feruntur, Upsala 1930

S.H. 485

336. RHETORICIANS AND ORATORS

Tfl. 315. 2; 326

S.H. 441, 3 and 6; 480

Chapter III

338. FRONTINUS (*Burs. J.* 217, 247)

E.E., P. Scriverius, Leiden 1607 (w. Vegetius etc.)

R. Keuchen. Amst. 1661

Editio Bipontina, 1788

(*Strat.*) *Ed. Pr.* (w. Aelian, Vegetius, Modestus) Rome 1487

F. Modius (w. Vegetius etc.) Cologne 1580

F. Oudendorp, Leiden 1731 (c. not. var.)

(*Aq.*) *Ed. Pr.* (w. Vitruvius) J. Sulpitius, Rome bet. 1484 and 1492

J. Polenus, Padua 1722

T., (*Str.* and *Aq.*) A. Dederich, Lpz. 1855

(*Strat.*) G. Gundermann (Teub.) 1888

(*Aq.*) F. Buecheler, Lpz. 1858

F. Krohn (Teub.) 1922

(Excerpts from Gromatic wk.)
C. Lachmann, *Gromatici Veteres*, Berlin 1848
C. Thulin, *Corp. Agrimensorum Rom.* I. i, Lpz. 1913
T.C.Tr. (*Aq.*) C. Herschel, Boston 1899 and London 1913
T.Tr. (*Str.* and *Aq.*) C. E. Bennett, ed. by M. B. McElwain (Loeb) 1925
(*Aq.*) A. Dederich, Wesel 1841
P. Grimal (Budé) 1944
Index (*Str.*) G. Bendz, Lund 1939
O.W., A. Kappelmacher in P.W. (s.v. Iulius no. 243)

(*Strategemata*)
G. Bendz, Die Echtheitsfrage des vierten Buches der Front. Strat., Lund 1938
H. M. Connor, A Study of the Syntax of the Strat. of Front., Cornell Univ., Ithaca (N.Y.) 1921
P. Esternaux, Die Kompos. v. Frontins Strat., Berlin 1889
E. Fritze, De F. Strat. libro iv, Halle 1888
G. Gundermann, Quaest. de . . . Strat. libris, *Fleck Jb.* supplbd. xvi (1888)
F. Kortz, Quaest. grammat. de F. operibus institutae, Münster 1893
C. Wachsmuth, Über die Unechtheit des vierten Buchs der Frontinschen Strategemata, *Rh.M.* 1860, 574–83.
E. Woelfflin, Frontins Kriegslisten, *Hermes* 1875, 72 ff.

(*De Aquis*)
T. Ashby, Die antiken Wasserleitungen der Stadt Rom, *Neue Jb. K.A.* 1909, 246 ff.
R. Lanciani, Topografia di Roma antica, i commentarii di F. intorno le acque e le acquedotti, *Mem. dei Lincei* 1881, 315 ff.

345. TECHNICAL WRITERS
Tfl. 316 and 328; S.H. 480, 12 and 487–9

Chapter IV

346. VALERIUS FLACCUS (*Burs. J.* 1, 22, 35, 84, 134, 158, 171, 212; *Lm.* 1)

E.E., *Ed. Pr.* Rugerius et Bertochius, Bologna 1474
    Badius, Paris 1517
    Ed. Aldina, Ven. 1523
    L. Carrio, Antw. 1565
    N. Heinsius, Amst. 1680
    P. Burman (c. notis var.) Leiden 1724
    T. C. Harles, Altenburg 1781
    J. A. Wagner, Gött. 1805 (w. comm.)
    N. E. Lemaire, Paris 1825
T., G. Thilo, Halle 1863 (impt. proleg.)
    C. Giarratano, Milan 1904
    J. B. Bury in *C.P.L.* ii
    O. Kramer (Teub.) 1913
T.C., P. Langen, Berlin 1896–7
T.Tr., J. H. Mozley (Loeb) 1934
Index, W. H. Schulte, *Iowa Stud. in Cl. Philol.* iii, Dubuque (Iowa) 1935
O.W., S. S. Brooks, Delin. of Character in the Arg. of V.F., Princeton 1951
    H. Gebbing, De V.F. tropis et figuris, Marb. 1878
    H. Gebbing, De V.F. dicendi genere, Cobl. 1888
    R. J. Getty, Date of Composn. of the Arg. of V.F., *C.P.* 1936, 53 ff.

J. Greiff, De V.F. Argonauticis cum . . . Aeneide comparatis, Trient 1869
R. Harmand, De V.F. Apoll. Rhodii imitatore, Nancy 1898
A. Heeren, De Chorographia a V.F. adhibita, Gött. 1899
A. Kurfess in P.W. (s.v. Valerius no. 170)
E. Marone, Sulla lingua di V.F., Naples 1957
F. Mehmel, Valerius Flaccus, Hamburg 1934
M. N. J. Moltzer, De Ap. Rh. et V.F. Argon., Utr. 1891
J. Peters, De V.F. vita et carmine, Kbg. 1890
J. Samuelsson, Studia in V.F., Upsala 1899
K. Schenkl, Studien zu d. Arg. des V.F., Sitzb. Wien 1871, 271 ff.
H. Stroh, Studien zu V.F. besonders über dessen Verhältnis zu Vergil, Augsb. 1905
J. Stroux, V.F. und Horaz, Philol. 1935, 305 ff.
W. C. Summers, A Study of the Arg. of V.F., Camb. 1894
W. M. Terwogt, Quaestiones Valerianae, Amst. 1898
V. Ussani (jr.) Studio su V.F., Rome 1955

Chapter V

361. SILIUS ITALICUS. (Burs. J. 134, 158, 171, 212; Lm. 1)

E.E. Ed. Pr. [C. Sweynheym and A. Pannartz] Rome 1471
D. Heinsius, Leiden 1600
A. Drakenborch, Utr. 1717 (c. not. var.)
J. C. T. Ernesti, Lpz. 1791–2
G. A. Ruperti, Gött. 1795–8
N. E. Lemaire, Paris 1823 (w. comm.)
T., L. Bauer (Teub.) 1890–2
W. C. Summers in C.P.L. ii
T.Tr., D. Nisard, Paris 1878
J. D. Duff (Loeb) 1934
Tr., F. H. Bothe, Stuttgart 1855–7 (w. notes)
O. Occioni, ed. 2, Turin 1889 (Ital. verse)
Index, N. D. Young, Iowa Stud. in Cl. Philol. x, Dubuque (Iowa) 1939
O.W., A. Klotz in P.W.
O. Occioni, Caio Silio Italico e il suo poema, ed. 2, Flor. 1871
F. G. Casale, Silio Italico, Salerno 1954

(Date)

F. Buchwaldt, Quaest. Silianae, Breslau 1886
A. Cartault, Est-il poss. de fixer exactement la date de la composn. des Puniques de Sil. It.? R.Ph. 1887, 11 ff.
J. Schinkel, Quaest. Silianae, Halle 1883
E. Wistrand, Die Chronologie der Pun. des S.I.: Beiträge zur Interpret. der flavischen Literatur, Göteborg 1956

(Sources and historical value)

Z. Baudnik, Die epische Technik des Sil. It. im Verhältnis zu seinen Vorbildern, Krumau 1906
L. Bauer, Das Verhältnis der Pun. des Sil. It. zur 3ten Dekade des Livius, Erlangen 1884
M. Heynacher, Die Quellen des Sil. It., Jena 1874
M. Heynacher, Die Stellung des Sil. unter d. Quellen zum 2ten pun. Kriege, Ilfeld 1877 (attempts to displace Livy as Sil.'s historical source in favour of some early annalist like Fabius Pictor)

A. Kerer, Ueber d. Abhängigkeit des Sil. It. von Livius, Bozen 1880–1
A. Klotz, Die Stellung des Sil. It. unter den Quellen zur Gesch. des 2ten pun. Kriegs, *Rh.M.* 1933, 1 f.
J. Nicol, The Historical and Geogrl. Sources used by Sil. It., Oxf. 1936
J. Schlichteisen, De fide historica Silii Ital., Kbg. 1881
M. Sechi, Sil. It. e Livio, *Maia* 1951, 280 f.
R. B. Steele, The Method of Silius Ital., *C.P.* 1922, 319 f.
E. Wezel, De Sil. It. cum fontibus tum exemplis, Lpz. 1873

(Language)
S. Blomgren, Siliana: De Sil. Ital. Pun. quaest. crit. et interpret., Upsala 1938
F. E. Brandstäter, De Pun. . . . argumento, stilo, ornatu poetico, Witten 1877
A. T. Lindblom, In Sil. It. Punica Quaestiones, Upsala 1918
O. Occioni, L'arte in Sil. It. etc. in *Scritti di lett. Latina*, Rome 1891
R. Rebischke, De Sil. It. orationibus, Kbg. 1913
A. Zingerle, Zu späteren lat. Dichtern, Innsb. 1879, vol. ii, pp. 12 ff.

Chapter VI

373. STATIUS (*Burs. J.* 1, 22, 35, 84, 134, 158, 171, 212; *Lm.* 1)

E.E. (*Op. Omn.*) *Ed. Pr.* Rome 1475
J. Bernartius, Antw. 1595
F. Lindenbrog (Tiliobroga) Paris 1600
J. F. Gronov, Amst. 1653
K. von Barth (w. comm.) Zwickau (Cygnea) 1664
J. Veenhusen (c. not. var.) Leiden 1671
C. Beraldus (*in usum Delph.*) Paris 1685 (w. index)
(*Silvae*) *Ed. Pr.* Ven. 1472
J. Markland, London 1728
T., A. S. Wilkins, G. A. Davies and J. P. Postgate in *C.P.L.* ii
A. Klotz and R. Jahnke (Teub.) 1898–1926 (i *Silvae* ed. 2; ii.1 *Ach.* ed. 2; ii.2 *Theb.*; iii comm. of Lactantius Placidus)
(*Silvae*) J. S. Phillimore, ed. 2 (O.C.T.) 1920
(*Th.* and *Ach.*) H. W. Garrod (O.C.T.) 1906
T.C. (*Silvae*) F. Vollmer, Lpz. 1898 (Germ. C.)
(*Th.* ii) H. M. Mulder, Groningen 1954 (Lat. C.)
(*Ach.*) M. R. J. Brinkgreve, Rotterdam 1913 (Lat. C.)
S. Jannaccone, Flor. 1950 (Ital. C.)
O. A. W. Dilke, Camb. 1954 (Eng. C.; with bibliography)
T.C.Tr. (*Th.* i) H. Heuvel, Zutphen 1932 (Lat. C., Dutch Tr.).
T.Tr., J. H. Mozley (Loeb) 1928.
(*Silvae*) H. Frère and H. J. Izaac (Budé) 1944
Tr. (*Silvae*) D. A. Slater, Oxf. 1908 (prose)
(*Th.*) W. L. Lewis, ed. 2, London 1773 ⎫
(*Th.* i) Alex. Pope, 1712 (w. Lat. text) ⎪ verse
(*Th.* i–v) T. Stephens, London 1648 ⎬
(*Ach.*) Sir R. Howard, 1660 ⎭
Conc., R. F. Deferrari and M. C. Eagan, Brookland, D.C. 1943

O.W., A. Cartault, Les Silves de Stace, *J. Sav.* 1894
    T. S. Duncan, The Infl. of Art on Description in the Poetry of S., Baltimore 1914
    E. Eissfeldt, Ueber Quellen u. Vorbilder des P. Pap. Statius, Helmstedt 1900
    E. Eissfeldt, Zu den Vorbildern des S., *Philol.* lxiii (1904) 378 ff.
    P. Ercole, S. e Giovenale, *Riv. Indo-Greco-Ital.* 1931, 43 ff.

J. F. Gronov, In Silvas . . . Diatribe, Hague 1637 (also in Veenhusen's ed. 1671)
R. Helm in P.W. (s.v. Papinius no. 8)
R. Helm, De P.P. Statii Thebaide, Berlin 1892
L. Legras, Étude sur la Théb. de S., Paris 1905
L. Legras, Les Puniques et la Théb., *R.E.A.* 1905, 131 ff. and 357 ff.
L. Legras, Les dernières années de S., *R.E.A.* 1908, 34 ff.
L. Lehanneur, De P.P. Statii vita et operibus quaest., Paris 1878
W. Michler, De P.P. Statio M. Ann. Lucani imitatore, Breslau 1914
J. H. Mozley, S. as an imitator of Vergil and Ovid, *C.W.* 1933, 33 ff.
H. Nohl, Quaest. Stat., Berlin 1871
H. Schubert, De P.P. Statii artis gramm. et metr. ratione, Greifswald, 1913
D. Teifel, Gebets- und Kultformen bei S. mit Rücksicht auf sein Verhältnis zur Epik des Vergil u. Lukan, Tübingen 1952
F. Vollmer, Introd. to ed. of *Silvae* 1898

(Statius and Domitian)

J. J. Hartman, De Domit. imp. et de poeta Statio, *Mnem.* 1916, 338 ff.
F. Sauter, Der röm. Kaiserkult bei Martial u. S., Stuttgart 1934
K. Scott, S.'s. Adulation of Domitian, *A.J.P.* 1933, 247 ff.

(Influence) S.H. 411

Chapter VII

397. MARTIAL (*Burs. J.* 2, 4, 6, 10, 14, 27, 47, 72, 212; *Lm.* 1 and 2)
E.E. *Ed. Pr.* [Vindelinus de Spira] Ven. 1470 (without *Spect.*)
J. Gruter, Frankfurt 1602
P. Scriverius, Leiden 1619, 1621 (c. not. var.)
V. Collesso (ed. Delph.) Paris 1660 (w. index verborum)
K. Schrevelius, Amst. 1661, 1670 (w. notes of J. F. Gronov)
T., F. G. Schneidewin, Grimma 1842; Lpz. 1853
W. Gilbert, ed. 2, Lpz. 1896
J. D. Duff in *C.P.L.* ii
W. Heraeus (Teub.) 1925
W. M. Lindsay (O.C.T.) 1903
C. Giarratano, ed. 2 (Paravia) 1951
T.C., L. Friedländer, Lpz. 1886
(Selections)
F. A. Paley and W. H. Stone, London 1868, 1881
W. Y. Sellar and G. G. Ramsay, Edinburgh 1884
H. M. Stephenson, ed. 2, London 1888
R. T. Bridge and E. D. C. Lake, Oxf. 2 vols. 1908 and 1906
L. Valgimigli, ed. 2 by N. Vianello, Turin 1948
(*Spect.*) F. della Corte, Genoa 1947
T.Tr., W. C. A. Ker (Loeb) 1919–20 (2 vols.)
H. J. Izaac (Budé) 1930–3 (2 vols.)
Tr., Bohn ed. 1859 and 1881 (Prose, with verse translns. by various authors)
J. A. Pott and F. A. Wright, London and N.Y. 1924
(Selections) A. L. Francis and H. F. Tatum, Camb. 1924
O.W., Atkins, Lit. Crit. Ant. II. pp. 299–303
G. Bellissima, Marziale: Saggi critici, Turin 1931
G. Boissier, Tacite etc. ed. 6 Paris 1926, Eng. tr. London 1906. (Ch. on *Le Poète Martial*)

Butler, Post-Aug. P. 251–86
J. W. Duff, Rom. Sat. ch. vii
J. W. Duff, Varied Strains in Martial, *Studies in honour of E. K. Rand*, N.Y. 1938
L. Friedländer, Introd. to his ed.
L. Friedländer, Sittengeschichte Roms, ed. 9 and 10, Lpz. 1921–3, vol. iii
C. Giarratano, De M. re metrica, Naples 1908
R. Helm in P.W. (s.v. Valerius no. 233)
H. Huisintveld, De populaire Elementen in de Taal van M. Val. Mart, Nijmegen 1949
L. Illuminati, M. nella vita e nell' arte, Messina 1951
J. Kruuse, L'Originalité artistique de Martial, *Classica et Mediaevalia*, 1941, 248 ff.
G. E. Lessing, Zerstreute Anmerkungen ueber das Epigramm u. einige der vornehmsten Epigrammatisten, pt. iii Marzial (In Lessing's Vermischte Schriften, erster Teil, 1771. Contained in K. Lachmann, Lessings Sämmtliche Schriften, vol. viii, Lpz. 1855.)
W. M. Lindsay, The Ancient Editions of Martial, Oxf. 1903
C. Marchesi, Valerio Marziale, Genoa 1914
Nisard, P. lat. déc.
L. Pepe, Marziale, Naples 1950
A. Pisani, Marziale, Milan 1904
F. Plessis, Poésie lat. 578 ff.
F. Sauter, Der röm. Kaiserkult bei M. u. Statius, Stuttgart 1934
G. Schneider, De M. Val. Mart. sermone observationes, Breslau 1909
A. Serafini, M. Val. Marziale, Treviso 1941
K. Flower Smith, M. the Epigrammatist and other Essays, Baltimore 1920
O. Weinreich, Studien zu M., Stuttgart 1928
O. Weinreich, Fabel Aretalogie Novelle: Beiträge zu Phädrus Petron Martial u. Apuleius, *Sitzb. Heid.* 1931

(Models)

O. Autore, M. e. l'epigramma greco, Palermo 1937
R. Paukstadt, De Martiale Catulli imitatore, Halle 1876
E. Pertsch, De Val. Mart. poet. Graecorum imitatore, Berlin 1911
K. Prinz, M. u. d. griech. Epigrammatik, Vienna 1911 and *Wiener Stud.* 1912, 227 ff.
R. Reitzenstein in P.W. (s.v. Epigramm)
R. Schmook, De M. Val. Martialis epigrammatis sepulcralibus et dedicatoriis, Lpz. 1911
K. P. Schulze, Martials Catullstudien, *Fleck. Jb.* 1887
E. Wagner, De Mart. poet. Augusteae aetatis imitatore, Kbg. 1880
A. Zingerle, Mart. Ovidstudien, Innsb. 1877
A. Zingerle, Zu spät. lat. Dichtern, Innsb. 1879, vol. ii

(Influence)

R. Levy, M. u. d. deutsche Epigrammatik des 17 Jahrh., Heidelberg 1903
P. Nixon, Martial and the modern Epigram, London and N.Y. 1927
T. K. Whipple, M. and the English Epigram fr. Sir Thos. Wyatt to Ben Jonson. *Univ. Calif. Publns. in Mod. Philol.* 1925, 279 ff.
S.H. 557

(*Xenia* and *Apophoreta*)

A. Barbieri, Umorismo antico: introd. a Xenia e Apophoreta, *Aevum* 1953, 385 ff.

421. MINOR FLAVIAN POETRY

Titus and Domitian: Tfl. 312; S.H. 361
Curiatius Maternus: see supra. *re* p. 223
Saleius Bassus: Tfl. 381; S.H. 411
Statius's father: Tfl. 318; S.H. 406
Others: Tfl. 323 and 324; S.H. 402, 411, 416, 416a, 417

PART IV

LITERATURE UNDER NERVA AND TRAJAN

A.D. 96 – A.D. 117

Chapter I

425. Pliny the Younger (*Burs. J.* 6, 35, 63, 84, 109, 117, 153, 221, 242, 282;
Anz. A.W. VIII. i)

Paneg. and *Epistulae*
E.E., A. P. Manutius, *in aed. Aldi*, Ven. 1508, 1518
    J. Gruter, Frankfurt, 1611 (c. not. var.)
    M. Z. Boxhorn, Leiden 1653
    G. H. Schaefer (c. not. var.) Lpz. 1805
    G. E. Gierig, Lpz. 1806
T., H. Keil, Lpz. 1870 (w. index nominum)
    C. F. W. Müller (Teub.) 1903
    R. C. Kukula, ed. 2 (Teub.) 1912
    M. Schuster, ed. 2 (Teub.) 1952
T.Tr., A. M. Guillemin and M. Durry (Budé) 1927–47
Tr., J. Henley, London 1724

Panegyricus
E.E. In *Panegyrici Latini*, Cuspinianus 1513; Beatus Rhenanus, Bâle 1520;
    J. Livineius, Antw. 1599
  (Sep.) *Ed. Pr.* (?) 1476
    J. Lipsius (w. comm.) Antw. 1600, Utr. 1652 and later edd.
    J. Arntzen, Amst. 1738 (c. not. var.)
    G. E. Gierig (w. comm.) Lpz. 1796
    F. Dübner and E. Lefranc, Paris 1843 (w. comm.)
T. In *Paneg. Latini*, E. Baehrens, Lpz. 1874; ed. 2, W. A. Baehrens, Lpz. 1911
T.C., M. Durry, Paris 1938
Tr., Sir R. Stapylton, Oxf. 1644
    G. Smith, London 1702, 1730

Epistulae
E.E. *Ed. Pr.* Ven. 1471 (Bks. i–vii and ix)
    J. Veenhusen, Leiden 1669 (c. not. var.)
    G. Cortius and P. D. Longolius, Amst. 1734 (c. not. var.)
T., E. T. Merrill, Lpz. 1922
T.C. (Selns.)
    C. E. Prichard and E. R. Bernard, ed. 3, Oxf. 1896
    E. T. Merrill, London 1903 (rp. w. corr. 1919)
    G. B. Allen, Oxf. 1915
    R. C. Kukula, ed. 4 Vienna 1925
  (Bks. i, ii) J. Cowan, London 1889

BIBLIOGRAPHY 565

(Bk. iii) J. E. B. Mayor, London 1880
(Bk. vi) J. D. Duff, Camb. 1906
(Bk. x) E. G. Hardy, London 1889
T.Tr., W. L. M. Hutchinson (W. Melmoth's tr. revd.) Loeb, 1915
Tr., W. Melmoth, London 1746 and several later edd.
Earl of Orrery, London 1751
J. D. Lewis, London 1879
O.W., M. Schuster in P.W. (s.v. Plinius 6)

(Life and Character)

H. Bender, Der jüngere P. nach s. Briefen, Tüb. 1873
J. Martha, Pline le jeune, *Rev. des Cours et Conf.* 1898 i and ii. *passim* and 1898–9 i *passim* (see analysis in N. I. Herescu, B.L.L. § 503)
T. Mommsen, Zur Lebensgesch. des jüng. P., *Hermes* 1869, 31 ff. (=Gesam. Schr. iv, Berlin 1906, 366–468)
L. Moy, Qualem apud aetatis suae studiosos personam egerit C. Plin. Sec., Paris 1876
W. Otto, Zur Lebensgesch. d. jüng. P., *Sitzb. Mün.* 1919
J. J. Tanzmann, De C. Plinii Sec. vita ingenio moribus quaestio, Breslau 1865.
G. Unità, Vita, valore letterario e carattere morale di Pl. il. giov., Rome and Milan 1933

(Literary Significance)

V. d'Agostino, Studi sul neo-stoicismo. Seneca, Plinio il giov., Epitteto, M Aurelio, Turin 1950
E. Allain, Pline le jeune et ses héritiers, Paris 1901–2
C. de la Berge, Essai sur le règne de Trajan, Paris 1877 (ch. xvi)
M. Galdi, Il sentimento della natura nelle lettere di P., Padua 1905
A. M. Guillemin, Sociétés de gens de lettres au temps de P., *R.E.L.* 1927, 261 f.
A. M. Guillemin, P. et la vie littéraire de son temps, Paris 1929
J. Held, Ueber d. Werth d. Briefsammlung d. jung. Pl. in Bezug auf Gesch. d. röm. Lit., Breslau 1833
S. Prete, Saggi Pliniani, Bologna 1948
S. Prete, De C. Pl. Caec. Sec. ad Corn. Tac. epistulis, *G.I.F.* 1950, pp. 7–81
H. W. Traub, P.'s Treatment of History in Epistolary Form, *Tr. Am. Ph. A.* 1955, 213–32
G. Unità, op. cit. (*supra*.)

(Style)

S. Consoli, Il neologismo negli scritti di P., Palermo 1900
R. C. Kukula, Introd. to his ed. of sel. letters, ed. 4, Vienna 1925
J. P. Lagergren, De vita et elocutione C. Pl. Sec., Upsala 1872
P. Morillot, De P. minoris eloquentia, Grenoble 1888
C. N. Smiley, Latinitas and 'Ἑλληνισμός, Wisconsin 1906
G. Suster, De Plinio Ciceronis imitatore, *R.F.I.C.* 1889, 74 f.

443. MINOR CONTEMPORARIES.
Tfl. 332 and 341–4

Chapter II

447. TACITUS (*Burs. J.* 18, 38, 55, 59, 72, 121, 167, 224, 247, 282; *C.W.* 48)
E.E. *Ed. Pr.* (*op. omn.* exc. *Agr.* and *Ann.* i–vi) [Vindelinus de Spira], Ven. c. 1470

(*op. omn.* exc. *Ann.* i–vi) F. Puteolanus, Milan 1476
(*op. omn.*) F. Beroaldus, Rome 1515
Beatus Rhenanus, Bâle 1533
J. Lipsius, Antw. 1574; (w. comm.) 1587 and later edd
J. F. Gronov, Amst. 1672, 1685 (w. notes of Lipsius and others)
Jac. Gronov, Utr. 1721 (c. not. var.)
J. A. Ernesti, Lpz. 1752 (c. not. var.)
G. Brotier, ed. 2, Paris 1776 (comm.); later edd. Edinb. 1792, 1796;
   London 1812
G. A. Ruperti, Hanover 1832–9 (w. comm.)
F. Ritter, Bonn 1834–6; re-ed. w. comm. crit. et exeg., Camb. 1848
J. C. Orelli, Zurich 1846–8 (re-ed. *Ann.* J. G. Baiter, Zurich 1859; *Germ.*
   H. Schweitzer-Sidler, Berlin 1877; *Dial.* and *Agr.* G. Andresen, Berlin
   1877–80; *Hist.* C. Meiser, Berlin 1895)
F. Haase, Lpz. 1855
C. Halm, ed. 4, Lpz. 1884–9
(*Dial.*) E. Benzelius, Upsala 1706
(*Agr.*) J. Bosius, Jena 1656 (c. notis)
F. L. Wex, Brunsw. 1852
(*Germ.*) Beatus Rhenanus, Bâle 1519
S. Fabricius, Augsburg 1580 (c. not. var.)
(*Hist.*) G. Kiessling, Lpz. 1840
(*Ann.*) G. A. Ruperti (w. comm.) Gött. 1804
G. Kiessling, Lpz. 1829
T. (*op. omn.*) C. Halm and G. Andresen, ed. 7 by E. Köstermann (Teub.)
   1949–52 (*op. min.* ed. 8, 1957; *Hist.* ed. 8, 1958)
(*Dial. Agr. Germ.*) H. Furneaux, O.C.T. 1899
M. Lenchantin de Gubernatis, 3 vols. (Paravia) 1949
(*Dial.*) A. Michaelis, Lpz. 1868
(*Agr.*) K. L. Urlichs, Würzburg 1875
J. J. Cornelissen, Leiden 1881
(*Germ.*) R. P. Robinson, Middletown (Connecticut) 1935 (elab. crit. ed. w.
   full bibl. to 1934)
(*Hist.*) C. D. Fisher, O.C.T. 1910
M. Lenchantin de Gubernatis, 2 vols. (Paravia) 1918 and 1929
C. Giarratano, Rome 1939
(*Ann.*) G. Némethy, Buda Pest 1893
C. D. Fisher, O.C.T. 1906
H. Fuchs, Frauenfeld, 1946–9
(*Ann.* i–vi) M. Lenchantin de Gubernatis, Rome 1943
T.C. (*Dial.*) L. Valmaggi, Turin 1890
W. Peterson, Oxf. 1893
A. Gudeman, Boston 1894; Germ. ed. Lpz. 1914
C. John, Berlin 1899
H. Goelzer, ed. 5, Paris 1914
(*Agr.*) F. Kritz, ed. 3, Berlin 1874
C. Peter, Jena 1876
H. Furneaux, revd. by J. G. C. Anderson, Oxf. 1923
A. Grimal-Fleury and H. Grimal, Paris 1946
(*Agr.* and *Germ.*) A. J. Church and W. J. Brodribb, London 1869
H. M. Stephenson, Camb. 1894
K. Allen and G. L. Hendrickson, ed. 2, Boston 1913
J. H. Sleeman, Camb. 1914
A. Gudeman, ed. 2, Boston 1928
(*Germ.*) F. Kritz, ed. 4 by W. Hirschfelder, Berlin 1878

A. Baumstark, Lpz. 1876
J. Prammer, ed. 2, Vienna 1889
U. Zernial, ed. 2, Berlin 1897
E. Wolff, ed. 3, Lpz. 1915
H. Schweizer and E. Schwyzer, ed. 8, Halle 1923
J. Schmaus, Bamberg 1924
R. Much, Heidelberg 1937
J. G. C. Anderson, Oxf. 1938
V. Bongi, Flor. 1946
(Hist.) W. H. Simcox, London (i and ii) 1875; (iii–v) 1876
A. D. Godley, London 1887–90
W. A. Spooner, London 1891
E. Wolff, ed. 2, Berlin; vol. i 1914, vol. ii revd. by G. Andresen 1926
H. Goelzer, Paris 1920
C. Heraeus, Lpz., vol. i ed. 6 1929, vol. ii ed. 4 1927; revd. by W. Heraeus
(Annals) P. Frost, London 1872
G. O. Holbrooke, London 1882
H. Furneaux, Oxf., vol. i 1884, 1896; vol. ii 1891, ed. 2 by H. F. Pelham
and C. D. Fisher 1907
E. Jacob, Paris 1885–6
H. Nipperdey, Berlin, vol. i ed. 11 1915, vol. ii ed. 6 1908; revd. by
G. Andresen
T.C.Tr. (Germ.) E. Fehrle, ed. 4, Munich 1944
T.Tr., H. Goelzer, H. Bornecque, E. de St. Denis and J. Perret (Budé) 1921–49
M. Hutton, W. Peterson, C. H. Moore and J. Jackson (Loeb) 1914–37 (later
edd. of various vols.)
Tr., A. J. Church and W. J. Brodribb, London (Dial. Germ. Agr. 1877; Hist.
1864, 1872; Ann. 1884)
G. G. Ramsay, London (Ann. 1904–9; Hist. 1915)
W. H. Fyfe, Oxf. (Dial. Ag. Germ. 1908; Hist. 1912)
H. Mattingly (Agr. and Germ.) 'Tacitus on Britain and Germany' (Pen-
guin) 1948
(Annals) M. Grant, 'Tacitus on Imperial Rome' (Penguin) 1956
Lexica, W. Bötticher, Berlin 1830
P. Fabia, 'Onomasticon Taciteum,' Lyons 1900
A. Gerber and A. Greef, Lpz. 1903

O.W., J. Asbach, Röm. Kaisertum u. Verfass. bis auf Traian; eine hist. Einl. zu
den Schr. des P. Corn. Tac., Cologne 1896
G. Boissier, Tacite, ed. 6, Paris 1926
W. Bötticher, Lexicon Taciteum, Berlin 1830 (proleg.)
W. Bötticher, De vita scriptis ac stilo Taciti, Berlin 1834
E. Ciaceri, Tacito, Turin 1941
H. Drexler, Tacitus: Grundzüge einer politischen Pathologie, Frankfurt-am-
Main 1939
E. P. Dubois-Guchan, Tacite et son siècle ou la société rom. imp., Paris 1861
I. Grews, Tacitus (Germ. tr. fr. Russian by L. Behrsing), Lpz. 1952
C. Hosius z. 70. Geburtstag . . . dargebracht v. H. Hommel u. a., Studien zu
Tacitus, Stuttgart 1936
E. Kornemann, Tacitus, Wiesbaden 1946
M. L. W. Laistner, The Greater Roman Historians, Berkeley (Calif.) 1947
C. Marchesi, Tacito, Messina 1924; ed. 4, Milan 1955
C. W. Mendell, Tacitus, the Man and his Work, New Haven (Connecticut)
and London 1957
J. M. N. D. Nisard, Les quatre grands historiens latins, Paris 1874
E. Paratore, Tacito, Milan 1951

H. Peter, Die gesch. Lit. ueber d. röm. Kaiserzeit, Lpz. 1897 (ii. pp. 42 ff.)
R. Reitzenstein, T. u. s. Werk (*Neue Wege zur Antike* iv) Lpz. 1927
H. Schiller, Gesch. d. röm. Kaiserzeit, Gotha 1883 (vol. ii. pp. 586 ff.)
L. Schwabe in P.W. (s.v. Cornelius no. 395)
R. Syme, Tacitus, Oxf. 1958
J. W. Thompson (w. collab. of B. J. Holm) A Hist. of Historical Writing, vol. 1 from earliest times to end of 17th cent., N.Y. 1942
K. L. Urlichs, De vita et honoribus Taciti, Würzburg 1879
G. Walser, Rom, das Reich u. d. fremden Völker in d. Geschichtsschreibung d. frühen Kaiserzeit; studien zur Glaubwürdigkeit d. T., Baden-Baden 1951
P. Wuilleumier and P. Fabia, Tacite, l'homme et l'oeuvre, Paris 1949

(*Dial. de Orat.*)

K. Barwick, Der Dial. de Or. des T. (Motive u. Zeit seiner Entstehung) Berlin 1954
W. den Boer, Die Gegenseitigen Verhältnisse der Personen in Dial. de Orat. u.d. Anschauung des T., *Mnem.* 1939, 193 ff.
L. Bruno, T. e la poesia (Critica dell' oratoria e difesa della poesia nel Dial. de or.) Salerno 1948
V. Capucci, Il Dial. de orat. opera giovenile di T., *Annali Fac. Lett.* (Naples) 1952, 79–136
K. von Fritz, Aufbau u. Absicht des D. de Or., *Rh.M.* 1932, 275 ff.
J. Frot, Tacite est-il l'auteur du Dial. d. Orat., *R.E.L.* 1955, 120 ff.
A. Gudeman, ed. Lpz. 1914 (prolegomena)
R. Guengerich, Der Dial. des T. u. Quintilians I.O., *C.P.* 1951, 159 ff.
B. Klaiber, Die Beziehungen des Rednerdialogs von T. zu Ciceros rhetorischen Schriften, Bamberg 1914
E. Koestermann, Die taciteische Dial. u. Ciceros Schrift De Rep., *Hermes* 1930, 396 ff.
J. Martha, Tacite, le Dialogue des orateurs, *Rev. des Cours et Conf.* 1895, i. 527 ff.; ii. 10 ff., 73 ff., 146 ff., 210 ff.
P. Smiraglia, Il Dial. de Orat.; Cronologia e rapporti coll' insegnamento di Quintiliano, *Annali Fac. Lettere* (Cagliari) v (1955) 159 ff.
F. Weinkauff, Untersuchn. ueber den D. des T., ed. 2, Cologne 1880

(*Agricola*)

Introdd. to most edns. esp. those of Furneaux (revd. Anderson) and Gudeman
G. Andresen, Entstehung u. Tendenz des Tac. Agricola in *Festschr. d. Gymn. z. grau. Kloster*, Berlin 1874
J. Cousin, Histoire et rhétorique dans l'Agricola, *R. de l'Instr. publique en Belgique* 1879, 309 ff.
K. Hirzel, Ueber d. Tendenz des Agr., Tüb. 1871
F. Leo, Die griech.-röm. Biographie, Lpz. 1901, pp. 224 ff.
J. Martha, Tacite, la vie d'Agricola, *Rev. des Cours et Conf.* 1895, ii. 210 ff., 272 ff.
H. Nesselhauf, T. und Domitian, *Hermes* 1952, 222 ff.
D. R. Stuart, Epochs of Gk. and Roman Biography, Berkeley (Calif.) 1928, 237 ff.
R. Till, Handschriftliche Untersuchn. zu Tacitus Agr. u. Germ., Berlin 1943

(*Germania*)

F. Brunot, Étude sur le De moribus Germanorum, Paris 1883
H. Drexler, Die Germ. des T., *Gymnasium* (Heidelberg) 1952, 52 ff.

F. Frahm, Caesar u. Tac. als Quellen für die altgermanische Verfassung: ein Beitrag zur Kritik ihres Sprachgebrauches, *Hist. Vierteljahressch.* 1928, 145 ff.

J. Martha, Tacite, la Germanie, *R. des Cours et Conf.* 1895, ii. 304 ff., 359 ff., 426 ff.

K. Muellenhoff, Die Germ. des T. erläutert, *Deutsche Altertumskunde* vol. iv. 1920, 15 ff.

E. Norden, Die Germanische Urgesch. in Ts. Germania, ed. 3, Lpz. 1923

H. Philipp, Ts. Germ. Die Entdeckungsgesch. der Germanenländer nach T. u. anderen Quellen, Lpz. 1936

R. Till, *op. cit. supra*

I. Weinberger, Die Frage nach Entstehung u. Tendenz der tacit. Germ., Olmütz 1890 and 1891

For sources S.H. 433

(*Histories*)

A. Briessmann, T. u. d. flavische Geschichtsbild, Wiesbaden 1955

C.A.H. X ch. xxiv

E. Courbaud, Les procédés d'art de T. dans les *Hist.*, Paris 1918

E. G. Hardy, T. as a military Historian in the Hist., *J.P.* 1908, 123 ff.

B. W. Henderson, Civil War and Rebellion in Rom. Emp., London 1908

A. M. A. Hospers-Jensen, T. over de Joden: *Hist.* v. 2–13, Utr. 1949

F. Münzer, Die Entstehung des Hist. des T., *Klio* 1901, 300 ff.

(*Annals*)

E. Bacha, Le génie de T. La création des Annales, Brussels 1906

F. Graf, Untersuchn. ueber die Komposition der Ann. des T. (diss. Univ. Bern) Thun 1929

B. Walker, The Annals of T., A Study in the Writing of History, Manchester 1952

J. Mogenet, Le génie dramatique de T. dans les Ann., *Bull. Cercle Pédag. Univ. de Louvain* Nov. 1948, 5 ff.

(Sources of *Histories* and *Annals*)

S.H. 437

P. Bellezza, Dei fonti letterari di T. nelle Storie e negli Annali, *R.I.L.* 1891, 317 ff.

P. Fabia, Les sources de T. dans les Hist. et les Ann., Paris 1893

E. Groag, Zur Kritik von Ts. Quellen in den Hist., *Fleck. Jb.* supplbd. xxiii (1897) 711 ff.

F. A. Marx, Untersuchn. zur Kompos. u. d. Quellen von T. Ann., *Hermes* 1925, 74 ff.

H. Nissen, Die Historien des Plinius, *Rh.M.* 1871, 487 ff.

G. H. Stevenson, Anc. Historians and their Sources, *J.P.* 1920, 204 ff.

R. Weidemann, Die Quellen der ersten sechs Bücher von T. Ann., Cleve 1868, 1869, 1873. (Emphasising *senatus acta*)

(Political Ideas)

F. Arnaldi, Le idee politiche morali e religiose di T., Rome 1921

W. Jens, Libertas bei Tac., *Hermes* 1956, 331 ff.

F. B. Marsh, T. and the Aristocratic Tradition, *C.P.* 1926, 289 ff.

A. de Massico, L'Idea del diritto in T., Rome 1940

R. v. Pöhlmann, Die Weltanschauung des T., Mun. 1913

K. Scott, T. and the Speculum Principis, *A.J.P.* 1932, 70 ff.

J. Vogt, T. als Politiker, Stuttgart 1924

(Language and Style)

W. Bötticher, Lexicon Taciteum, Berlin 1830
G. Clemm, De Breviloquentiae Taciti quibusdam generibus, Lpz. 1881
L. Constans, Étude sur la langue de T., Paris 1893
J. Cousin, Rhétorique et psychologie chez T., R.E.L. 1951, 228 ff.
A. Dräger, Ueber Syntax u. Stil des T., ed. 3, Lpz. 1882
N. Eriksson, Studien zu den Ann. des T., Lund 1934
H. Furneaux, ed. of Annals, Introd. ch. 5
J. Gantrelle, Grammaire et style de T., ed. 3, Paris 1908
W. Heraeus, T. und Sallust, Archiv für lat. Lexikogr. 1906, 273 ff.
F. Knoke, Bemerkungen zu dem Sprachgebrauch des T., Berlin 1925
W. Lundström, Tacitus's Poetiska Källor, Göteborg 1923
R. H. Martin, Variatio and the Develt. of T.'s Style, Eranos, 1953, 89 ff.
J. Müller, Beiträge zur Kritik und Erklärung des Cornelius Tacitus, Innsbruck 1865–75
G. G. Ramsay, Int. to his trans. of Ann., London 1904
A. Salvatore, Stile e ritmo in Tacito, Naples 1951
G. Sörbom, Variatio Sermonis Tacitei aliaeque apud eundem quaest. sel. Upsala 1935
R. Ullmann, La technique des discours dans Sallust, Live et T., Oslo 1927
L. Valmaggi, L'arcaismo in T., Turin 1891
F. Vianey, Quomodo dici possit T. fuisse summum pingendi artificem, Paris 1896
E. Wölfflin, Tacitus, Philol. xxiv (1866) 115 ff.; xxv (1867) 92 ff.; xxvi (1867) 121 ff.; xxvii (1868) 113 ff.

(Influence)

A. Droetto, Il tacitismo nella storiografia groziana, R.I.F.D. 1950, 481 f.
F. Haverfield, T. during the late Roman period and the middle ages, J.R.S. 1916, 196 ff.
F. Ramorino, Cornelio Tacito nella storia della coltura, ed. 2, Milan 1898
G. Toffanin, Machiavelli e il Tacitismo, Padua 1921
S.H. 439

For Tacitus and Tiberius see p. 470. n. 2

Chapter III

477. JUVENAL (Burs. J. 139, 175, 204, 235, 260, 282; C.W. 50)

E.E., Ed. Pr. [Vindelinus de Spira] Ven. 1470
D. Calderinus, Ven. 1475
G. Valla, Ven. 1486
A. Mancinelli, Lyon 1498 (w. comm.)
In aedibus Aldi, Ven. 1501 (w. Persius)
J. Britannicus, Brescia 1501, Paris 1602
T. Pulmannus, Antw. 1565 (w. Persius)
P. Pithoeus, Paris 1585 (w. Pers. and Sulp.) (w. scholia and Pith.'s notes)
N. Rigaltius, Paris 1613 (w. Sulp.)
L. Prateus (in usum Delph.) Paris 1684 (w. Pers. and w. index verborum)
H. C. Henninius, Utr. 1685; c. comm. eruditorum (with I. Casaubon's Persius) Leyden 1695; (w. Casaubon's Pers.) Glasgow 1750
G. A. Ruperti, Lpz. 1801, 1819
C. F. Heinrich, Bonn 1839 (w. anc. scholia)
C. W. Stocker, ed. 3, London 1845 (w. Persius)

O. Jahn, Berlin 1851 (w. Pers.)
C. F. Hermann, Lpz. 1854 (w. Sulpicia)
O. Ribbeck, Lpz. 1859
T., S. G. Owen (O.C.T.) ed. 2, 1908 (w. Pers.)
A. E. Housman, ed. 2, Camb. 1931 (also in *C.P.L.* ii)
O. Jahn, rev. F. Buecheler, ed. 4 by F. Leo, Berlin 1910 (w. Pers.)
N. Vianello (Paravia) 1935
U. Knoche, Mun. 1950
T.C., E. G. Hardy, London 1883, ed. 2 1891
C. H. Pearson and H. A. Strong, Oxf. 1887, 1892
J. E. B. Mayor, London, 2 vols. ed. 4, 1886 and 1888
} (without ii, vi, ix)
L. Friedländer, Lpz. 1895
J. D. Duff, Camb. 1898 (without ii, ix)
H. P. Wright, Boston and London 1901
H. L. Wilson, Boston 1903
} (without ii, vi, ix)
T.C.Tr., J. D. Lewis, ed. 2, London 1882
T.Tr., G. G. Ramsay (Loeb) 1918 (w. Persius)
P. de Labriolle and F. Villeneuve, ed. 2 (Budé) 1931
G. Vitali, Bologna 1947
Tr. (verse) Sir R. Stapylton, London 1647
J. Dryden and others, London 1693 (w. Persius)
W. Gifford, London 1802, 1805 (w. Persius)
(prose) H. A. Strong and A. Leeper, London 1882, 1892 (without ii, vi, ix)
S. G. Owen, London 1903 (without ii, vi, ix)
U. Knoche, Mun. 1951
Index, L. Kelling and A. Suskin, Univ. N. Carolina Pr. 1951
Scholia, P. Wessner (Teub.) 1931
O.W., G. Highet, Juvenal the Satirist, Oxf. 1954 (useful bibl.)
C. Marchesi, Giovenale, Rome 1921
E. V. Marmorale, Giovenale, ed. 2, Bari 1950
N. Salanitro, Introd. a Giovenale, Naples 1944
F. Vollmer in P.W. (s.v. Iunius no. 87)

(Life)

H. J. de Dompierre de Chauffepié, De titulo IRN 4312 ad Juv. poetam perperam relato, Leiden 1889
J. Dürr, Das Leben Juvenals, Ulm 1888
P. Ercole, Note Giovenaliane, *Riv. Indo-Greco-Italica* 1926, 1–14, 121–41
L. Friedländer, De Juv. vitae temporibus, Kbg. 1875
G. Highet, The Life of J., *Tr. Am. Ph. A.* 1937, 480 ff.
J. A. Hild, Juvénal, notes biographiques, Paris 1884
F. J. Merchant, The Parentage of J., *A.J.P.* 1901, 52 ff.
D. Naguiewski, De J. vita observ., Riga 1883
Nettleship, L. and E. ser. ii, pp. 117 ff.
C. Strack, De Juvenalis exilio, Laubach 1880
Introdd. to various edns.

(Satires)

J. de Decker, J. declamans: étude sur la rhét. déclam. dans les sat. de J., *Rec. Fac. Lett. Gand*, fasc. 41, 1913
Duff, Rom. Sat. (ch. viii)
P. Ercole, La cronologia delle satire di Giov., *R.F.I.C.* 1929, 184 ff. and 346 ff.
F. Gauger, Zeitschilderung und Topik bei J., Greifswald 1937
G. Highet, Juvenal the Satirist, Oxf. 1954

U. Knoche, Handschriftliche Grundlagen des Juvenaltextes, *Philol.* supplbd. xxxiii (1940) heft 1

U. Knoche, Die röm. Satire, ed. 2, Gött. 1957

P. de Labriolle, Les sat. de J., étude et analyse, Paris 1932

C. Martha, Les moralistes etc., ed. 7, Paris 1900, 255 ff.

Nisard, P. lat. déc.

A. Piccoli Genovese, Giovenale, Flor. 1933

F. Plessis, Poésie Lat.

O. Ribbeck, Der echte u.d. unechte Juv., Berlin 1865

R. Schütze, Juvenalis Ethicus, Greifswald 1905

A. Serafini, Studio sulle satire di Giovenale, Flor. 1957

F. Strauch, De personis Juvenalis, Gött. 1869

A. Widal, J. et ses satires, Paris 1869

(Style and models)

R. E. Colton, J. and Martial (Columbia Univ. diss.) 1951.

G. Eskusche, Juvs. Versbau (in Friedländer's ed. p. 57) [On E.'s contention that J. is designedly careless in metre see L. Müller, *Berl. Philol. Wochenschrift* 1896, cols. 1270–3]

G. B. A. Fletcher, Alliteration in Juvenal, *Durham Univ. Jnl.* 1943–4, 59 ff.

J. Gehlen, De Juv. Vergilii imitatore, Erlangen 1886

A. Hartmann, De inventione J. capita tria, Bâle 1908 (on satt. i, iii, v)

A. Hartmann, Aufbau und Erfindung d. 7. Satire Juvenals, Bâle 1912

G. Highet, Juvenal's Bookcase, *A.J.P.* 1951, 369 ff. (J.'s use of previous authors)

A. Kappelmacher, Studia Juvenaliana, Vienna 1903

L. O. Kiaer, Sermonem D. Iun. Iuuenalis certis legibus astrictum demonstrare conatus est, Copenhagen 1875

C. Schneider, Juvenal und Seneca, Würzburg 1930

P. Schwartz, De Juv. Horatii imitatore, Halle 1882

I. G. Scott, The Grand Style in the Satires of J., Northampton (Mass.) 1927

W. Stegemann, De J. dispositione, Lpz. 1913

J. Streifinger, Der Stil des Satirikers J., Ratisbon 1892

E. Strube, De rhetorica Juv. disciplina, Brandenburg 1875

H. Wilcke, Demonstratur . . . quid elocutio Juv. a Persiana differat, Stendal 1869

H. L. Wilson, Lit. Infl. of Martial upon J., *A.J.P.* 1898, 193 ff.

(Influence)

G. Highet, Juvenal the Satirist, Oxf. 1954, pp. 180 ff. and 346 (bibliog.)

S.H. 420a

PART V

LITERATURE IN THE REIGN OF HADRIAN

A.D. 96 – 117

501 MINOR HADRIANIC LITERATURE

Salvius Julianus: Tfl. 350; S.H.K. 613–14

Pomponius: Tfl. 350; S.H.K. 615

Annianus	Tfl. 353; S.H.K. 513. Fragments in
Septimius Serenus	E. Baehrens, *F.P.R.* and W. Morel,
Alfius Avitus	*F.P.L.*

Terentius Scaurus: Tfl. 352; S.H.K. 594–5; Remains in Keil, *G.L.* vii, 11 ff.

502. HADRIAN (*Burs. J.* 217; *Lm.* 2—for poetry)

See L. Cantarelli, Gli scritti latini di Adriano imp., *Studi e docum. di storia e diritto* 1898, 113 ff.
(Hist. fragm.) Peter, *H.R.R.*
(Orat. fragm.) Meyer, *O.R.F.*
T. (*adlocutiones* to army in Africa) H. Dessau, *I.L.S.* 2487 (=*C.I.L.* viii. 2532 and 18042)
  (*laudatio Matidiae*) *C.I.L.* xiv. 3579
  (poetry—Lat.) E. Baehrens *P.L.M.* iv. p. 111 and vi (=*F.P.R.*) p. 373
  W. Morel, *F.P.L.* pp. 136–7
  (poetry—Greek) *Anthol. Palatina* vi. 332; vii. 674; ix. 17, 137, 387, 402
T.Tr. (Lat. poetry) Duff, *M.L.P.*
Tr. (address to his soul) Translations . . . of Dying H.'s Address to his Soul collected by D. Johnston, Bath 1876 (in several languages)
  (*adlocut.*) B .W. Henderson, *op. cit. infra* pp. 96–8
O.W., B. W. Henderson, Life and Principate of the Emp. Hadr., London 1923

503. SUETONIUS (*Burs. J.* 97, 113, 134, 139, 188, 226, 273).

E.E. (*De vita Caesarum*) Ed. Pr. J. A. Campanus, Rome 1470
  J. Andreas, Bishop of Aleria, Rome 1470
  P. Beroaldus, Bologna 1493, 1506 (w. comm.)
  D. Erasmus, Bâle 1518
  I. Casaubon, Geneva 1595; Paris 1610
  S. Pitiscus, Utr. 1690; Leeuwarden 1714 (c. not. var.)
  P. Burman, Amst. 1736 (c. not. var.)
  D. C. G. Baumgarten-Crusius, Lpz. 1816–18 (comm. and indices)
T. (*De vita Caesarum*) C. A. Roth, Lpz. 1858
  L. Preud'homme, Gron. 1906
  M. Ihm, ed. maior Lpz. 1907; ed. minor (Teub.) 1908
  I. Lana, Turin 1952
  (*praeter Caes. libros reliquiae*) A. Reifferscheid, Lpz. 1860
  (*Gramm.* and *Rhet.*) C. L. Roth (Teub.) 1871 and 1924
T.C. (*De vita Caesarum*)
  (*Julius*) H. E. Butler and M. Cary, N.Y. and Oxf. 1927
  (*Jul.* and *Aug.*) H. T. Peck, ed. 2, N.Y. 1893
  J. H. Westcott and E. M. Rankin, Boston 1918
  (*Aug.*) E. S. Shuckburgh, Camb. 1896
  M. A. Levi, Flor. 1951
  (*Tib.* to *Nero*) J. B. Pyke, Boston 1903
  (*Claud.*) H. Smilda, Gron. 1898 (Lat. c.)
  (*Galba* to *Vit.*) C. Hofstee, Gron. 1898 (Lat. c.)
  (*Vesp.*) A. W. Braithwaite, Oxf. 1927
  (*Vesp.* to *Dom.*) G. Garavani, Milan 1929
  (*Titus*) H. Price, Menasha (Wisconsin) 1919
  (*Dom.*) J. Janssen, Gron. 1919 (Lat. c.)
  (*Gr.* and *Rhet.*) R. P. Robinson, Paris 1925 (Lat. c.)
  C. Bione, ed. 2, Palermo 1941 (see therewith B.'s art. in *R.F.I.C.* 1941, 19 ff.)
  F. della Corte, Genoa 1947
  (*Poet.*) A. Rostagni, De Poetis e biogr. minori: restituzione e commento, Turin 1944
T.C.Tr. (*Caesares* fr. Galba to Dom.) G. W. Mooney, London 1930
T.Tr., J. C. Rolfe (Loeb) 1914
  H. Ailloud (Budé) 1931–2
  (*De vita Caesarum*) G. Vitali, Bologna 1951

Tr. (Caesars) Philemon Holland, London 1606 (often re-edited)
R. Graves (Penguin) 1957
(Ext. wks.) A. Thomson, rev. by T.Forester (Bohn) London 1848 and later edd.
Index. A. A. Howard and C. N. Jackson, Index verborum C. Suet. Tranq.
    stilique eius proprietatum nonnullarum, Camb. Mass. 1922
O.W., G. d'Anna, Le idee letterarie di S., Flor. 1954
P. Bagge, De elocutione C.S. Tr., Upsala 1875
J. Couissin, Suétone physiognomoniste dans les vies des xii Césars, *R.E.L.*
    1953, 234 ff.
P. Clason, Tacitus und Sueton, Breslau 1870
L. Dalmasso, Un seguace di Quintiliano al principio del sec. secolo, *Atti
    Acad. Sci. Torino* 1906, 805 ff.
J. W. Freund, De C. S. Tr. usu atque genere dicendi, Breslau 1901
G. Funaioli in P.W.
H. R. Graf, Kaiser Vespasianus: Untersuchn. zu Suetons Vita Divi Vesp.,
    Stuttgart 1927
F. Leo, Die griech-röm. Biographie, Lpz. 1901
A. Macé, Essai sur Suétone, Paris 1900
G. W. Mooney, *op. cit. supra*, appendix i on diction and style of S.
E. Paratore, Una nuova ricostr. del De Poetis di S., Rome 1946
A. Reifferscheid, Introd. to ed. of Suet. praeter Caes. libros rel. (see *supra*)
G. W. Schmidt, De Romanorum imprimis Suetoni arte biographica, Mar-
    burg 1891
W. Steidle, S. u. d. antike Biographie, Mun. 1950
D. R. Stuart, Epochs of Gk. and Rom. Biography (chs. vii and viii) Berk.
    Calif. 1928
H. R. Thimm, De usu atque elocutione C. Suet. Tr., Kbg. 1867

513. FLORUS (*Burs. J.* 72, 97, 121, 231, 173)

(Poet. Fragm.)

L. Mueller, Rutilius Namatianus etc., Lpz. 1870, pp. 26 ff.
E. Baehrens, *P.L.M.* iv, pp. 279 and 346; vi (=*F.P.R.*) p. 373
Text and Trans. in Duff, *M.L.P.*

(Rhet. Fragm.) F. Ritschl, *Rh.M.* 1842, 302 ff. (=*Opuscula* iii, 729 ff.)
Contained also in edd. of Florus's epitome by O. Jahn (xli ff.), C. Halm
    (106 ff.) and O. Rossbach (183 ff.). See *infra*

(*Epitome*)

E.E. *Ed. Pr.* Paris c. 1470
    J. Camers, Bâle 1518
    J. Gruter, Heidlbg. 1597.
    C. Salmasius, Heidlbg. 1609 (c. notis Gruteri)
    J. Freinsheim, Strasb. 1632, 1669 (w. comm.)
    J. G. Graevius, Utr. 1680 (w. comm.)
    C. A. Duker, Leiden 1722 (c. not. var.) ed. 2, 1744
T., O. Jahn, Lpz. 1852; revd. by C. Halm, Lpz. 1854
    O. Rossbach (Teub.) 1896
    E. Malcovati, Flori quae exstant, Rome 1938
T.C., G. Seebode, Lpz. 1821
T.Tr., E. S. Forster (Loeb) 1929 (w. Corn. Nepos by J. C. Rolfe)
    P. Hainsselin and H. Watelet, Paris 1932 (w. Vell. Paterc.)

O.W., F. Eyssenhardt, Hadrian u. Florus, Berlin 1882
    Galdi, L'epitome n. lett. lat., pp. 44 ff.

O. Hirschfeld, Anlage u. Abfassungszeit d. Epit. d. F., *Sitzb. Berl.* 1899, 543 ff. (=Kl. Schr. 868 ff.)
S. Lilliedahl, Florusstudien, Lund 1928
P. Monceaux, Les Africains, Paris 1894 (193 ff.)
O. Rossbach in P.W. (s.v. Florus no. 9)
R. Sabbadini, Del numerus in Floro, *R.F.I.C.* 1897, 600–1
R. Sieger, Der stil des Historikers Florus, *Wien. Stud.* 1933, 94 ff.

514. PERVIGILIVM VENERIS (*Burs. J.* 158, 171; *Lm.* 2)

E.E. *Ed. Pr.* P. Pithoeus, Paris 1577
With notes by J. Lipsius and J. Dousa, Utr. 1680 (w. Catullus, Prop. and Tib.)
E. C. F. Schulze, Gött. 1812 (w. comm.)
T., E. Baehrens, *P.L.M.* iv, p. 292
S. G. Owen, London 1893 (w. Catullus)
C. Pascal, Turin 1918
T.C., C. Brakman, Leiden 1928 (Dutch C.)
T.C.Tr., C. Clementi, ed. 2, Oxf. 1928 (on which see G. B. A. Fletcher 'Notes and Addns. to Clementi's P.V.,' *C.P.* 1933, 209 ff.); ed. 3, Oxf. 1936
T.Tr., J. W. Mackail (Loeb) 1912 (w. Catullus by F. W. Cornish and Tibullus by J. P. Postgate)
R. Schilling (Budé) 1944
A. Tate, Cummington Press (U.S.A.) 1943
Tr., J. A. Fort, Oxf. 1922
F. L. Lucas, Camb. 1948 (w. Hom. Hymn to Aphrodite)
O.W., P. Boyancé, Encore sur le P.V., *R.E.L.* 1950, 212 ff.
C. Clementi, Bibliographical and other Studies on the P.V., Oxf. 1913
C. Clementi, Introd. to his ed. 1936
F. Lenz in P.W.
E. K. Rand, Sur le P.V., *R.E.L.* 1934, 83 ff.
D. S. Robertson, Date and Occasion of the P.V., *C.R.* 1938, 109–12
R. Schilling, Introd. to his Budé ed. 1944

INDEX

The letter *n* after a number means a footnote on the page indicated. For the main subjects treated under the leading authors, readers should consult also the summaries prefixed to the relevant chapters. For reasons of space, almost all modern names (i.e. medieval and later) are omitted from this index: the bibliography corresponding to the pages where authors and subjects are dealt with lists the chief modern writers and editors concerned. † indicates a lost work.